1640: Competing private claims to Acadia embroil the colony in war.

1645: Lady La Tour makes a valiant but unsuccessful attempt to defend the Acadian Fort La Tour (Fort Sainte-Marie).

1653: Cromwell assumes the role of "Lord Protector" after England's civil war and the 1649 execution of Charles I.

1654: Acadia falls to English control.

1657: A royal proclamation prohibits the sale of alcohol to the Natives.

1660: The Battle of the Long Sault saves Montreal from attack.

1659: François Laval arrives to assume control of the Church in New France.

The economic doctrine of mercantilism provides a rationale for colonial development in the seventeenth century.

1661: King Louis XIV, crowned as a child, begins his personal rule.

1663: Under Colbert's direction, New France becomes a royal province.

1665: The energetic Jean Talon arrives as first intendant of New France.

1665: The Carignan-Salières regiment is sent to protect New France.

1666: Governor Courcelle leads a disastrous winter campaign into Iroquois Country.

By 1676, New France's population reaches 7832.

1668: Land under cultivation rises by more than 35 percent over the previous year.

1664: The English seize control of New Netherland.

1670: Britain's Charles II grants a charter creating the Hudson's Bay Company.

1670: Talon commissions La Salle to search for the passage to the China Sea.

In the summer of 1672, Frontenac arrives to take up his post as governor of New France.

1682: La Salle voyages to the mouth of the Mississippi and claims the surrounding territory for France.

1682: The governor, Frontenac, and intendant, Duchesneau, are both recalled to France.

1682: The Compagnie du Nord is created to compete with the Hudson's Bay Company.

1686: The French seize control of Hudson's Bay Company posts.

1689: The War of the League of Augsburg leads to fresh hostilities in North America between the British and French and their allies.

1689: Frontenac returns as governor of New France in October.

1690: Frontenac launches raids against English settlements.

1690: The British seize Acadia.

1690: Governor Frontenac makes a defiant defence of Quebec.

1696: The French devastate Iroquois settlements.

1686–1696: The British and French battle over posts on Hudson Bay and James Bay.

1696: Iberville captures English settlements in Newfoundland.

1697: The Treaty of Ryswick ends the War of the League of Augsburg.

1699: Iberville establishes a new French colony, Louisiana, at the mouth of the Mississippi River.

1701: The Great Peace of Montreal brings peace between the French and the Iroquois.

1710: Acadia is conquered by the British.

1713: The Treaty of Utrecht acknowledges English possession of Newfoundland, Acadia, and Rupert's Land.

1720: Construction begins on the French fortress on Île Royale, Lousibourg.

1731–1739: La Vérendrye establishes a chain of new trading posts in the western interior.

1720: Unable to implement representative government in Nova Scotia, Governor Richard Philipps appoints a council.

1726: A treaty is concluded between the Mi'kmaq and Maliseet and the British.

1729: Acadians agree to take an oath when Governor Philipps promises to exempt them from bearing arms.

1744: French forces capture Canso.

1744: French soldiers mutiny at Louisbourg in December.

1745: Louisbourg falls to the English.

NARRATING A NATION

Canadian History Pre-Confederation

Raymond Blake
University of Regina

Jeffrey Keshen
University of Ottawa

Norman Knowles
St. Mary's University College

Barbara Messamore
University of the Fraser Valley

McGraw-Hill Ryerson
Connect. Learn. Succeed.

Narrating a Nation: Canadian History Pre-Confederation

ISBN-13: 978-0-07-095641-4
ISBN-10: 0-07-095641-3

1 2 3 4 5 6 7 8 9 10   TCP   1 9 8 7 6 5 4 3 2 1

Printed and bound in Canada.

VICE-PRESIDENT AND EDITOR-IN-CHIEF: Joanna Cotton
PUBLISHER: Cara Yarzab
SPONSORING EDITOR: Jeremy Guimond
MARKETING MANAGER: Margaret Janzen
SR. DEVELOPMENTAL EDITOR: My Editor Inc.
EDITORIAL ASSOCIATE: Marina Seguin
SUPERVISING EDITOR: Jessica Barnoski
PHOTO/PERMISSIONS RESEARCH: Megan Jones, My Editor Inc.
COPY EDITOR: Valerie Adams
PROOFREADER: Imogen Brian
PRODUCTION COORDINATOR: Lena Keating
COVER DESIGN: Gordon Robertson
COVER IMAGE: Getty Images/Painting by Benjamin West
INTERIOR DESIGN: Kyle Gell
PAGE LAYOUT: Heather Brunton/ArtPlus Limited
PRINTER: Transcontinental Printing Group

Library and Archives Canada Cataloguing in Publication

Narrating a nation : Canadian history
   pre-Confederation / Raymond Blake ... [et al.].

Includes index.

ISBN 978-0-07-095641-4

   1. Canada—History—To 1763 (New France).
2. Canada—History—1763–1867.   I. Blake, Raymond
B. (Raymond Benjamin)

FC161.N37 2010   971   C2010-905108-4

Brief Contents

Table of Contents

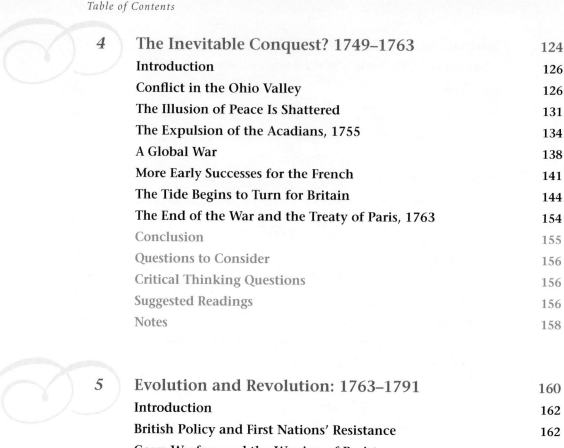
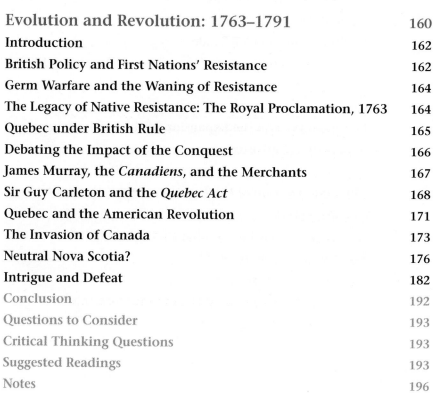

Preface

"Nurture your mind with great thoughts; to believe in the heroic makes heroes." These words, attributed to British Prime Minister Benjamin Disraeli, provide a kind of rationale for the study of history. Of course, this sort of rhetoric may fit better with the credulous Victorian age than it does with the present. We approach historical study today with a kind of detached irony, eager to debunk heroism, "deconstruct" the past, and rescue the marginalized who attracted little notice during their lives.[1] And to a great extent this more analytical approach to history is valuable. It is essential to question received versions of the past. It has long been understood that our interpretation of events can be coloured by our own biases—our faith, our nationality, our gender, our social class, the very age in which we live. Additionally, we have come to recognize that the very selection of *which* events are studied is in itself a subjective decision. The term "historiography," meaning the writing of history, is a useful one; it reminds us to be conscious of the mediation that has necessarily taken place between the past and the present, and reminds us that only *certain* facts have been selected for inclusion. History is no longer only "past politics" as it was once described, but instead encompasses all aspects of life in the past—political, economic, social, and ideological.

But history is also about change; historians, after all, tend to follow the action. Any national history will include enormous gaps where historians have leapt across substantial geographic and chronological divides to focus on the next significant upheaval. Change may be constant but the rate of change is not. Social arrangements—for example, marriage or child-rearing customs—may stay comparatively static for generations. French historian Emmanuel LeRoy Ladurie famously described social history as "history that stands still."[2] This is, of course, an exaggeration, but there is no doubt some correlation between the decline of lively narrative history—the kind of stories of great deeds that inspired Disraeli and his generation—and the wish to write a more inclusive history. The real challenge of today's historical writing is to capture the best of both worlds.

The present text adopts a narrative approach. Events are followed chronologically, focusing on a story developing over time. This is in contrast to the more usual method of today, in which chapters are divided according to theme, region, or perhaps some combination of both—for example, "Industrialization in the Maritimes." The chronological

---

[1] The concept of "deconstructionism"—a notion central to postmodernist literary criticism—involves a close analysis of written texts to discover the implicit assumptions about power relations that underlie them. This concept necessarily implies a skepticism about "metanarratives"—unified stories that ignore the complexity of human experience and alternative methods of arriving at truth.

[2] Emmanuel LeRoy Ladurie, "History That Stands Still," in Emmanuel LeRoy Ladurie, *The Mind and Method of the Historian* (Chicago: University of Chicago Press, 1984).

approach is meant to help events make sense to students, to ground their knowledge of past societies, in all their social, economic and ideological complexity, in a clear political context, with the necessary sense of linkage and causality that is at the bedrock of historical understanding. Timeline marginal icons serve as a reminder of key dates and developments, a pedagogical tool to reinforce understanding of key moments of change. The goal is to help students focus on the events that are significant historical benchmarks or turning points.

Each volume is divided into 12 chapters to correspond to the number of weeks in a typical university academic term. Each chapter revolves around a broad theme. Discussion questions at the end of each chapter are meant to reinforce the reader's understanding of the material and provide an opportunity for reflection.

Where possible, the text addresses issues of historiography—how have historians interpreted an event? How have interpretations changed over time? Such references to more in-depth studies will also signpost works the reader might wish to pursue in order to do further research on an issue. The suggestions for further reading at the end of each chapter are offered in a similar spirit. While they are by no means exhaustive, they suggest a selection of works—primary documents, recent articles, and time-tested standard interpretations—that a student might consult.

Groups that have been at the margins of traditional historical study are woven into this historical narrative in an integrated way rather than treated in addendum "text boxes" or separate chapters. No attempt has been made to achieve chapter-by-chapter balance of any group or region. Inevitably, in following the action, historical inquiry is uneven.

The current volume, which deals with events prior to Confederation, has a special challenge to meet: events before 1867 may seem impossibly remote. What possible relevance can such events have? Historian Ged Martin rejects the usual criteria of "relevance" for historical study as "a blind alley, a present-centred approach that naturally privileges the near past."[3] Students can readily grasp the relevance of Cold War politics, the Vietnam War era, separatist referenda in Quebec, and even perhaps the Second World War, but may struggle to find any meaning in seventeenth- or eighteenth-century events. Indeed, Canadians may believe that the country "began" in 1867, rendering invisible everything before Confederation. Yet relevance is a moving target. The questions that we ask of the past have a great deal to do with what is happening today, and events long forgotten can suddenly be invested with new meaning in the light of changing times. At one time, for example, the Royal Proclamation of 1763 was deemed significant primarily for its blueprint for British rule over the newly acquired French-speaking subjects of Quebec. But the Proclamation is chiefly remembered today for a very different reason: it sets out the principle that has come to be known as Aboriginal title, and the 1982 Charter of Rights and Freedoms makes specific mention of it. The need to appoint one-third of Canada's Supreme Court judges from the province of Quebec can only be understood with reference to the seventeenth-century Custom of Paris, the root of Quebec's distinct civil law.

---

[3]   Ged Martin, *Past Futures: The Impossible Necessity of History* (Toronto: University of Toronto Press, 2004), 191.

The text also seeks to put Canadian events into a larger world context. The 1791 Constitutional Act, for example, set out in statute a model constitution for each of the colonies of Lower and Upper Canada. The essential form, fashioned as it was on the pattern of Britain's constitution, has been carried down to this very day. We see the "bones" of our modern system of government in 1791, political scientist Janet Ajzenstat has argued.[4] Yet it is vital to remember that as British parliamentarians approached their task of constitution writing, just across the Channel France was convulsed by violent revolution. This was a very immediate reminder to the British of what principles they wished to repudiate. Likewise, when the "fathers" of Canada's confederation met at Charlottetown, Prince Edward Island, in 1864, they could hardly have ignored the painful example of the American Civil War on their doorstep. Costing more than a million casualties before it ended, that cataclysmic bloodbath underscored what consequences could flow when a constitution out of balance set a nation at war with itself.

The text attempts to provide some of this context that is so essential to a sound historical understanding. The past is indeed a foreign country, and we must try to learn some of its language, customs, and values. The heroic deeds Disraeli celebrated can only be appreciated if we understand their backdrop and the way in which people can be products of their time. We might perhaps assume that, from the time of contact with European newcomers, native Canadians have always been cast into a subordinate role. Yet a study of such figures as Tecumseh, described by one admirer as "the Wellington of the Indians," may disrupt this paradigm of Aboriginal passivity. Similarly, the story of Marie de l'Incarnation, the dynamic founder of the Ursuline order who came to Quebec in 1639, may challenge the notion that women were relegated to an exclusively domestic sphere. One of the fundamental lessons of history, and the reason, perhaps, why we find historical biography so inspiring, is that those who effect profound change have often fought long odds to do so. Surprisingly often, they are highly flawed individuals, and frequently, too, their prominence was achieved at enormous personal cost. Marie de l'Incarnation, for example, left a 19-year-old single mother by the sudden death of her husband, surrendered her young son to enter the convent. Another historical hero, General James Wolfe, the British commander of the forces at Quebec, did not fit the stereotype of a great leader of men; he was irritable, indecisive, and pessimistic, and disease would probably have finished him if the French had not. Robert Baldwin, who along with Louis-Hippolyte La Fontaine presided over Canada's first responsible government in 1848, loathed the life of a public figure and was frequently mired in depression, especially after he lost his beloved Eliza, the first cousin whom he married over family objections. Conservative Prime Minister John A. Macdonald managed to dominate Canadian politics in the second half of the nineteenth century despite his legendary alcoholism. He was incapacitated by drink at many key junctures in Canada's political life. It is not necessary to attempt to explain away the challenges or flaws that complicated these less-than-perfect historical heroes.

---

4   Janet Ajzenstat, "Celebrating 1791: Two Hundred Years of Representative Government," *Canadian Parliamentary Review* 14, 1 (Spring 1991), 30.

Somehow, their imperfection renders them more, and not less, inspirational; our own inevitable shortcomings do not preclude great aspirations.

In including a strong biographical component, the textbook echoes a traditional approach to history. Yet an attempt has been made to supplement the best aspects of traditional narrative history with analysis and the inclusion of vitally important new social history scholarship. While only the prominent and advantaged—and usually male—may have been in the position to achieve the great acts that made them worthy objects of historical study, the societies from which they arose can only be understood with reference to the lives of ordinary people.

Just as we travel today to experience and learn from differences in countries around the world—after all, if every society were the same we would hardly need to bother—through historical study we enter the foreign territory of the past. We seek after what is good and what is true, the very thing that Plato described as the purpose of education. When we travel however imperfectly into the past, we try to do so without present-centred preconceived ideas that may prevent us from being open to fresh insights. It is all too easy to condemn historical figures or—what is worse—attempt to excuse them by explaining that they lived in a different age, with different values. But it is vital, as English historian E.P. Thompson put it, to rescue those in the past from "the enormous condescension of posterity."[5] The simple explanation that they would have behaved differently were they as wise as we is too pat an answer. Closer examination of the complicated context of some historical actions may offer more nuanced judgments.

Understanding the story of how the Canada of today came to be demands a narrative that encompasses global events, the quiet rhythm of everyday life and work, and—as Disraeli would have it—the occasional heroic figure who drove a quickening pace of change.

---

[5] E.P. Thompson, *The Making of the English Working Class* (Harmondsworth: Penguin Books, 1968), 13.

Comprehensive Learning and Teaching Package

We have developed a variety of high-quality supplements for both teaching and learning to accompany this text.

Online Learning Centre   *(www.mcgrawhill.ca/olc/blake)*

Separated into both Instructor and Student areas, each section holds a variety of material for instructors to develop and use in their course and for students to use and review. Instructors will find an Instructor's Manual, chapter-specific PowerPoint lecture slides, and a Test Bank of multiple-choice, true/false, and essay-type questions for each chapter. The student area offers interactive quizzes and study questions to assist students in preparing for tests and exams.

Superior Service

Service takes on a whole new meaning with McGraw-Hill Ryerson and *Narrating a Nation: Canadian History Post-Confederation*. More than just bringing you the textbook, we have consistently raised the bar in terms of innovation and educational research. These investments in learning and the educational community have helped us to understand the needs of students and educators across the country, and allowed us to foster the growth of truly innovative, integrated learning.

Integrated Learning

Your Integrated Learning Sales Specialist is a McGraw-Hill Ryerson representative who has the experience, product knowledge, training, and support to help you assess and integrate any of our products, technology and services into your course for optimum teaching and learning performance.

Whether it's using our test bank software, helping your students improve their grades, or putting your entire course online, your *i*Learning Sales Specialist is there to help you do it. Contact your *i*Learning Sales Specialist today to learn how to maximize all of McGraw-Hill Ryerson's resources!

*i*Learning Services Program

McGraw-Hill Ryerson offers a unique *i*Services package designed for Canadian faculty. Our mission is to equip providers of higher education with superior tools and resources required for excellence in teaching. For additional information, visit www.mcgrawhill.ca/highereducation/iservices.

McGraw-Hill Ryerson National Teaching and Learning Conference Series

The educational environment has changed tremendously in recent years, and McGraw-Hill Ryerson continues to be committed to helping you acquire the skills you need to succeed in this new milieu. Our innovative Teaching, Technology & Learning Conference Series brings faculty together from across Canada with 3M Teaching Excellence award winners to share teaching and learning best practices in a collaborative and stimulating environment. Pre-conference workshops on general topics, such as teaching large classes and technology integration, are also offered. We will also work with you at your own institution to customize workshops that best suit the needs of your faculty.

CourseSmart

CourseSmart brings together thousands of textbooks across hundreds of courses in an e-textbook format providing unique benefits to students and faculty. By purchasing an e-textbook, students can save up to 50 percent off the cost of a print textbook, reduce their impact on the environment, and gain access to powerful Web tools for learning, including full-text search, notes and highlighting, and e-mail tools for sharing notes between classmates. For faculty, CourseSmart provides instant access to review and compare textbooks and course materials in their discipline area without the time, cost, and environmental impact of mailing print copies. For further details, contact your *i*Learning Sales Specialist or go to www.coursesmart.com.

Create Online

McGraw-Hill's Create Online gives you access to the most abundant resource at your fingertips—literally. With a few mouse clicks, you can create customized learning tools simply and affordably. McGraw-Hill Ryerson has included many of our market-leading textbooks within Create Online for e-book and print customization as well as many licensed readings and cases. For more information, go to www.mcgrawhillcreate.ca.

WebCT and Blackboard

In addition, content cartridges are available for the course management systems WebCT and Blackboard. These platforms provide instructors with user-friendly, flexible teaching tools. Please contact your local McGraw-Hill Ryerson *i*Learning Sales Specialist for details.

Acknowledgments

The two volumes of *Narrating a Nation* have been a collaborative effort from concept to completion, and we owe tremendous gratitude to one another. In accordance with each author's area of expertise, in Volume 1, Norman Knowles wrote the chapters on Furs and Faith: New France, 1632–1663, France in America: 1663–1750, Evolution and Revolution: 1763–1791, and A Contest of Identities: British North America: 1770–1815; and Barbara Messamore wrote the chapters on The Inevitable Conquest? 1749–1763, Development and Diversity: 1815–1836, Rebellion in the Canadas: 1826–1838, The Fate of British North America: 1838–1846, Hinge of the Imperial Relationship: 1846–1849, Colonial Societies in Transition: 1849–1864, and Three Weddings and a Divorce: 1858–1867. They co-wrote the chapter on First Nations and First Contacts. Similarly, in Volume 2, Raymond Blake wrote the chapters on Negotiation, Compromise, and Statehood: 1864–1873, Consolidating Confederation and Managing Diversity: 1874–1896, Uncertainty and Conflict: 1957–1967, Seeking the Just Society: 1968–1984, Seeking a New Consensus: 1984–1993, and Canada's New Century; and Jeffrey Keshen wrote the chapters on Canada's Century: 1896–1914, War and Upheaval: 1914–1919, The Turbulent Twenties, The Great Depression, War and Upheaval, II: 1939–1945, and Consensus and the Cold War: 1945–1957. Great admiration is also extended to all those scholars and teachers of Canadian history who have written books and articles about Canada. We have depended on their scholarship, and much of their hard work is reflected in this book. So, too, is the wisdom and insight of our colleagues across the country who kindly offered criticism and helpful advice on various drafts, and whose suggestions markedly improved the text. For their careful assessment of the manuscripts, we are grateful to

Jean Manore, Bishop's University

Gillian Poulter, Acadia University

Claire Campbell, Dalhousie University

Thor Frohn-Nielsen, Kwantlen Polytechnic University

Todd Webb, Laurentian University

John Zucchi, McGill University

Ken Cruikshank, McMaster University

John Sandlos, Memorial University

Robert Sweeny, Memorial University

Kathleen Lord, Mount Alison University

Steven Maynard, Queen's University

E.J. Errington, Royal Military College of Canada

Ross Fair, Ryerson University

John Reid, St. Mary's University

Gayle Thrift, St. Mary's University College

James Muir, University of Alberta

Sean Kheraj, University of British Columbia

Alan Gordon, University of Guelph

Greg Marquis, University of New Brunswick, Saint John

Karine Bellerose, University of Ottawa

Esyllt Jones, University of Ottawa

Robert Talbot, University of Ottawa

Selena Crosson, University of Saskatchewan

Jan Noel, University of Toronto

Penny Bryden, University of Victoria

Georgia Sitara, University of Victoria

Roger Hall, University of Western Ontario

Michelle A. Hamilton, University of Western Ontario

Robert Wardhaugh, University of Western Ontario

Carolyn Podruchy, York University

Franc Sturino, York University

As well, the authors have accumulated a debt of gratitude to many individuals. Professor Ged Martin (emeritus, University of Edinburgh) provided valuable advice, as did Scott Sheffield (University of the Fraser Valley), Hamish Telford (University of the Fraser Valley), and Kathryn Magee Labelle (Ohio State University). Research assistants Ron Hughes and Everett Messamore did exceptional work. The editors and staff at McGraw-Hill Ryerson have been a pillar of strength and have shepherded this book from just an idea to a finished product. We wish to thank Lisa Rahn, our acquisition editor at McGraw-Hill Ryerson, for her support, patience, and sage advice, and Jennifer DiDomenico for the initial guidance in development. Katherine Goodes, senior developmental editor, became involved at a crucial stage to offer expert advice and leadership as well as the badly needed—but diplomatically delivered—push to get the volumes done, and, along with her assistant Linda Toms, she did a remarkable job in guiding the text through to the completion of the development stage. Megan Jones, permissions editor, did an excellent job in helping to locate and clear the copyright for the reproduction of photographs, paintings, posters, and maps. The authors also wish to express their appreciation for the work done by the copy editor, Valerie Adams; the proofreader, Imogen Brian; the supervising editor, Jessica Barnoski; and the production coordinator, Lena Keating.

Finally, the authors would like to express heartfelt thanks to their families for their support throughout this project that, like most in academe, took somewhat longer to complete than first anticipated. Raymond Blake thanks Wanda, Robert, and Ben, as always, who have listened to the woes about particular sections and offered their advice. More important, they were all there as a family at the end of each day that I was writing this book to show me what really is important in my life. Jeff Keshen extends heartfelt thanks to his wife, Deborah, and to his children, Jacob and Madelaine. Norman Knowles wishes to thank his wife, Margaret Anne, and daughters, Emily and Sarah, who provided constant support and encouragement during the production of this work, which coincided with cancer treatments. Barbara Messamore is grateful to the memory of her late husband, Steve, whose good-humoured encouragement meant so much in the completion of this project, as it did in so many other things in life. The loving support of their children, Keith, Neil, Everett, and Joy, has been a continued blessing.

This book is for our students, who shared our love of Canadian history and asked hard questions that helped us to look at events with fresh eyes.

About the Authors

Raymond B. Blake

Raymond B. Blake completed this book while Craig Dobbin Chair of Canadian Studies at University College Dublin in Dublin, Ireland. Also professor of history at Regina, he has taught Canadian Studies at Mount Allison University and was for several years the director of the Saskatchewan Institute of Public Policy. His research interests include nationalism and identity, social policy, and twentieth-century Canadian politics. He is the author and editor of a dozen books, including *Beyond National Dreams: Essays on Canadian Nationalism, Citizenship, and Identity* (with Andrew Nurse), *Social Fabric or Patchwork Quilt? The Development of Social Welfare in Canada* (with Jeffrey Keshen), *From Rights to Needs: A History of Family Allowances in Canada, 1929–92*, and *Canadians at Last: Canada Integrates Newfoundland as a Province.*

Jeffrey Keshen

Jeffrey Keshen, a professor of history at the University of Ottawa, specializes in post-Confederation Canadian political, social, and military history. Jeff has written or edited a dozen books on modern Canadian history, including *Saints, Sinners, and Soldiers: Canada's Second World War* (translated as *Saints, Salauds et Soldats: Le Canada et la Deuxième Guerre mondiale*) and *Propaganda and Censorship during Canada's Great War.*

Norman Knowles

Norman Knowles is a professor of history at St. Mary's University College and holds an adjunct appointment in the Department of History at the University of Calgary. He has written or edited half a dozen books and more than a dozen articles or book chapters on nineteenth- and early-twentieth-century Canadian social, cultural, and religious history. His works include *Seeds Scattered and Sown: Studies in the History of Canadian Anglicanism* and *Inventing the Loyalists: The Ontario Loyalist Tradition and the Creation of Usable Pasts.* He currently serves on the editorial board of the *Journal of the Canadian Church Historical Society.*

Barbara Messamore

Barbara Messamore teaches Canadian history at University of the Fraser Valley in Abbotsford, British Columbia. She completed her Ph.D. at the University of Edinburgh in 2003 and is the author of *Canada's Governors General, 1847–1878: Biography and Constitutional Evolution.* She has published a number of articles on related topics, edited *Canadian Migration Patterns from Britain and North America*, and is co-founder and editor-in-chief of the *Journal of Historical Biography.*

1

First Nations *and* First Contacts

A Mi'kmaq woman dreamed of a small island floating toward the land of ws-tiqamúk. At first glance, the island appeared to be inhabited by people or animals wearing white rabbit skins; then it became an island of bare trees with black bears on its branches. The woman told her dream to the elders and vision people of the village, but the strange features of the dream could not be understood.[1]

chapter 1

Source: Canadian Museum of Civilization, 2000.129.1.1-10, D2004-11229.

Sky Woman creates the Earth.

Introduction

This chapter examines aspects of Native society prior to the arrival of Europeans, the development of European interest in North America, and the relations that developed between Natives and newcomers. For both Native peoples and Europeans, the story that unfolds is one of change and continuity, cultural persistence and adaptation. It is also a story of conflict and cooperation: for both groups, the encounter contributed to the making of a "new world."

The First Peoples

Like most peoples, Canada's Native nations have their own creation stories that explain how they came to be present in North America. Although these stories differ in detail, most place the Native peoples in North America "when the world began." Creation myths, whether those of Christians or of North American Aboriginal people, reveal a great deal about how a culture understands itself and the world. According to most paleoanthropologists and archeologists, North America was first populated by nomadic peoples from Siberia, hunters who followed game over a land bridge across the Bering Strait into present-day Alaska and the Yukon around the end of the last Ice Age. Whether Natives now living in Canada have always been here, or date their people's occupation back tens of thousands of years, there is little question that they are justified in considering themselves indigenous to the continent.

During the last Ice Age, huge volumes of water were locked up in massive glaciers, lowering sea levels by as much as 100 metres and creating a now-vanished land bridge between Asia and North America that geologists call Beringia. Native oral tradition may support this theory. The Haida people of Haida Gwaii (or Queen Charlotte Islands) in British Columbia tell of a time, long ago, when the islands were much larger. The ocean then rose, and the "flood tide woman" forced them to move to higher ground. The treeless grassland of Beringia seems to have provided an ideal habitat for large grazing mammals such as mammoth, bison, horse, and camel. Archeological evidence suggests that the first ongoing human communities were established in western Beringia around 25 000 years ago. Occupation of the region was apparently only seasonal. A massive ice sheet separated Beringia from the rest of North America, preventing migration further south. With the passing of the Ice Age, the climate began to warm, creating an ice-free corridor along the eastern slopes of the Rockies that evidently allowed both people and game to migrate south. Although there is widespread agreement among scholars that the first peoples of North America originated in northeast Asia, ideas vary about the timing, the routes taken by the early migrants, and the number of migrations.

Traditionally, anthropologists believed that by 12 000 years ago, the Americas were populated, to varying degrees of density, from the Arctic to the tip of South America. More recent estimates place the migration from Asia to the Americas somewhere between 55 000 and 18 600 years ago. Generally, most genetic evidence points to a date approximately 25 000 years ago. As the glaciers retreated, humans returned north into the Great Plains and the boreal woodlands of present-day Canada. At Monte Verde in southern Chile, archeologists have unearthed evidence of tool making, rock painting, and house building that appears to predate the opening of an ice-free interior corridor. This has prompted the theory among some archeologists that migrants did not move overland, but travelled south, "leapfrogging" along the Pacific coast using boats in order to go around the impassable glacial barriers.[2] Further evidence for coastal migration comes from caves and bays along the coast of Alaska and British Columbia that date from the Holocene Period (which began about 10 000 years ago), such as On Your Knees Cave and Ground Hog Bay. Such sites have yielded evidence that suggests earlier occupation along these coastal regions than inland, although it is difficult for archeologists to find older sites, as these would probably have been submerged by rising water levels.[3] It is likely that North America was populated by multiple migrations that used both routes.

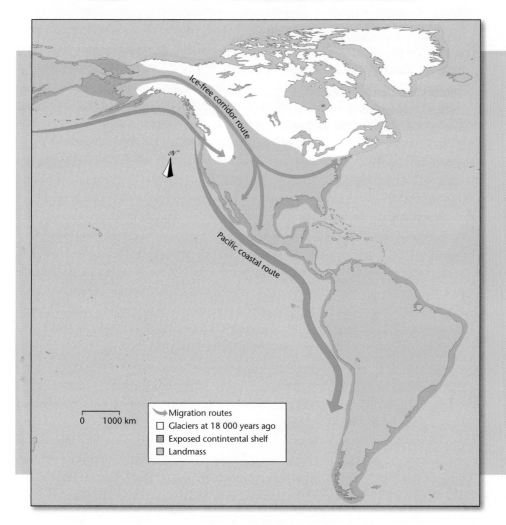

Map 1.1
Possible Migrations at the End of the Last Ice Age.

Linguistic evidence suggests at least two subsequent migrations to North America, although the number of migrations and the divisions of language groups has been the topic of much debate. According to the "three migration theory," most of the known languages of Aboriginal peoples in the Americas are thought to have descended from the first set of migrations. A few anthropologists and historical linguists, following the lead of Joseph Greenberg, consider this group to be a single language family known as the Amerians. However, this view is not widely accepted among linguists, and the Amerian group of languages are typically believed to be unrelated to each other.[4] A second linguistic group, represented by the Na-Dene or Athapaskan family of languages, is believed to have been carried to North America around 7000 B.C.E. (B.C.E., for "Before Common Era," is now widely used in place of the earlier designation B.C., or "Before Christ." In place of the traditional A.D. or "Anno Domini"—in the year of the Lord—C.E., or "Common Era," is now the most widely used term). The Na-Dene settled in what is now Alaska and north-western Canada. Some Athapaskan-speaking people are thought to have later migrated to the American southwest where they became the ancestors of the Navajos and Apaches. There is controversy surrounding whether or not the Haida belong to the Na-Dene family as well.[5] A third migration of Eskaleutian (Eskimo-Aleut) speakers is believed to have begun around 3000 B.C.E. when maritime hunting peoples crossed the Bering Strait in small boats and spread throughout the far north. The three wave migration theory has not been substantiated by subsequent research, however. Recent DNA studies have led many anthropologists to instead believe that there was only a single migration made up of multiple groups, which then spread out across the continent from Beringia, developing their own distinctive languages and cultures.[6] The single migration theory is supported by the observation that the Amerian, Na-Dene, and Eskaleutian groups have more mito-chondrial DNA (mtDNA) similarities to each other than to Asian groups, suggesting that the split occurred after the migration from Asia.[7] Furthermore, in recent mtDNA work, the theoretical linguistic groups were not found to be correlated with genetic relatedness.[8]

Since historians generally draw upon written records, the 25 millennia before encounters between Aboriginal peoples and newcomers may technically be categorized as prehistory. Indeed, most of Europe's past would be as well. Yet by drawing upon the tools and resources of other disciplines, historians are able to gain insight into many aspects of the dynamic past of Native North Americans prior to European contact. Archeology provides evidence of past human behaviour through the careful examination of material remains. Through the study of the nature and structure of language, linguistics enables scholars to reconstruct the linguistic history of the continent. Using the tools of DNA analysis, physical anthro-pologists are able to study the diffusion of biological characteristics over time and inter-relationships between different groups. Scientists who study the human impact on the environment and the effects of environmental changes on human ways of life have revealed a great deal about shifts in settlement and subsistence patterns. Native oral traditions passed on from generation to generation offer insight into the past, and into Native worldviews and values. Ethnohistorians use the evidence generated by scholars of many disciplines, as well as traditional written sources, to reconstruct Native society and culture. The result is a far more complete understanding of Canada's past and its peoples.

Periods in Prehistory

Scholars divide the history of North America's Aboriginal peoples following the initial migration and prior to European contact into distinct periods based on technological developments. The first of these periods, the Palaeo, extends from the time of the first inhabitants to roughly 7000 B.C.E.

The Palaeo period extends to approximately 7000 B.C.E.

During this period, Palaeo peoples spread throughout much of North America, establishing a base from which most regional cultures later developed. These peoples, who are identified by their skilfully crafted stone spearheads, were nomadic hunter-gatherers who subsisted on big game such as mammoth and mastodon and prehistoric caribou and bison. Archeological evidence indicates that Palaeo peoples travelled in small groups of extended family numbering between 20 and 50, and that social and political relations were likely highly egalitarian. Men hunted while women gathered nuts, berries, and other food, and cared for children. Much of the archeological evidence suggests that Palaeo hunting methods involved the mass extermination of prey, and it was once thought that these methods contributed to the mass extinction of many species of large mammals. Many now question this overkill hypothesis, suggesting that changes in climate and vegetation at the end of the last Ice Age were a more likely explanation for the extinction. The discovery of stone spear points and other tools far from the stone's original source suggests that Palaeo peoples travelled over large territories and probably engaged in trading or exchange relationships with other groups.

The climate and environment of North America changed significantly during the Palaeo period. Large lakes fed by melting glaciers formed as the ice retreated, sea levels rose rapidly flooding the Bering land bridge, and vegetation regions shifted north. As the glacial barriers receded, humans spread across much of North America's interior. Because of the distinctive fluted projectile points (sometimes known as a Clovis point) that these Palaeo people left behind, they are known as the Fluted Point people.

By 8000 B.C.E., the climate had stabilized and the Fluted Point people gradually adapted to different environments. This gave rise to distinctive regional cultures: Plano culture in the west, and Archaic culture in the woodlands of the east. Climatic change resulted in the extinction of many species of mega-fauna such as mammoth and mastodon. To compensate for the disappearance of many large mammals, Native peoples developed new survival strategies and learned to hunt smaller game and waterfowl, to fish, and to forage for wild plants. On the western plains, the Plano peoples developed a subsistence technology and way of life that specialized in bison hunting. Plano culture eventually expanded into the northern forests and adopted a new hunting regime that depended upon caribou. There is also evidence that by 4000 B.C.E. Plano culture had penetrated the interior plateau of British Columbia. In the eastern woodlands, Archaic culture developed out of the earlier Fluted Point culture, with Native peoples adopting new means of subsistence and a diversified food base. As Archaic peoples became more efficient in hunting and gathering, their numbers grew and their societies probably became less egalitarian.

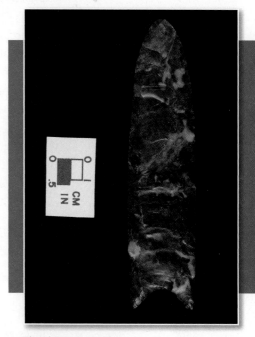

Fluted Point Projectiles.

Source: Courtesy of the Ohio History Central.

Regional Cultural Complexes

As they adapted to particular environments, Plano and Archaic peoples developed special-ized skills and tools to exploit local resources. By classifying these technological innovations, archeologists and anthropologists have identified a number of distinct regional cultures or culture complexes across what is today Canada. The major culture complexes are Maritime, Shield, Plains, Plateau, Pacific Northwest, Arctic, and Great Lakes–St. Lawrence. These cultures are further divided into early (8000–4000 B.C.E.), middle (4000–1000 B.C.E.), and late (1000 B.C.E.–500 C.E.) periods to account for ongoing innovation and adapta-tion. Cultural change occurred through the diffusion of technology, beliefs, and practices, and adaptation to particular local ecological needs. By the time of sustained European contact in the sixteenth century, Canada was occupied by peoples who spoke many dif-ferent languages and belonged to distinct cultures suited to their diverse environments. For ease of geographical identification, modern place names will be used, although of course these came into use much later.

Maritime Culture

In Atlantic Canada, archeologists have unearthed evidence of an early Maritime culture dating from 6000 to 8000 years ago. A maritime and riverine adapted people that drew upon the resources of both land and sea occupied the Atlantic coastal plain. Small in number, they may have moved northward during the spring and summer months in search of particular resources and returned south for the winter. As the climate warmed, people remained within the region and their numbers increased. Small family groups

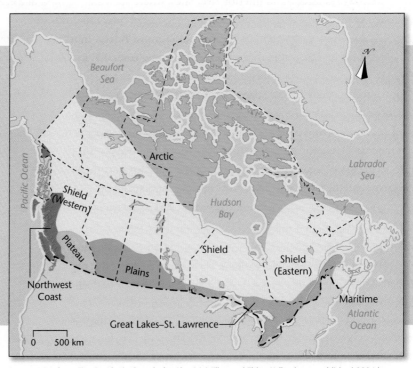

Map 1.2
Aboriginal Cultural Areas.

Source: Map from *First Peoples in Canada*, by Alan McMillan and Eldon Yellowhorn, published 2004 by Douglas and McIntyre LTD. (now D&M Publishers INC.). Reprinted with permission of the publisher.

appear to have converged into larger bands on the coast during the late spring to exploit the resources of the sea, and then divided as they returned to the interior for the winter. Marriages were probably contracted when bands came together to form a broad social network of blood-related families. As the population grew, early Maritime people spread north into Labrador and down the St. Lawrence. The introduction of ritual practice and degrees of social rank is suggested by the distinctive mortuary practices that appeared 5000 to 6000 years ago. Excavations of burial sites have revealed human remains smeared with red ochre, and both functional and ornamental artefacts. Trade with neighbouring peoples is evident in the discovery of copper tools at many coastal sites, and walrus ivory in the Great Lakes–St. Lawrence region. Sometime after 2000 B.C.E., Maritime culture retreated from Labrador, Newfoundland, and the north shore of the St. Lawrence. A number of factors probably contributed to this disappearance. Cooler weather may have made these areas less suitable to the adaptations of Maritime culture. Around the same time, new peoples migrated into the region. Palaeo-Eskimos began to penetrate Labrador, and hunters of the Shield culture began to appear seasonally on the north shore.

Appearance of pottery around 500 B.C.E. marks the beginning of late Maritime culture.

The appearance of pottery vessels around 500 B.C.E. marks the beginning of late Maritime culture. Archeologists and anthropologists also refer to this as the Woodland period in eastern North America. In the past, the introduction of pottery was associated with the advent of a new stage of development characterized by a much more complex society and sophisticated culture. It is now believed that pottery was simply an introduced technology that did not significantly alter Maritime lifeways. Maritime peoples moved between cold weather camps located on tidal estuaries and salt-water lagoons with abundant shellfish and waterfowl resources, and interior river sites, where spawning salmon and eels were harvested in the spring and summer. The appearance of burial mounds similar to those found in the Ohio Valley marked the introduction of Adena mortuary customs into Maritime culture. The origin of these mounds dating from 400 to 300 B.C.E. remains a mystery. Their introduction may have been a product of an expanding network of trade. The presence of such mounds suggests that a priest-shaman class had been introduced into Maritime culture, at least in some localities. At the time of first European contact in the fifteenth century, the Maritime region is estimated to have had a population of between 5000 and 6000 people. This population was divided into two distinct groups: the Mi'kmaq, numbering about 4000 and occupying present-day Nova Scotia, Prince Edward Island, the Gaspé and the northeastern part of New Brunswick; and the Maliseet-Passamaquody, numbering about 1000 and inhabiting western and southern New Brunswick.

Shield Culture

The vast Canadian Shield was occupied slowly between 8000 and 4000 B.C.E. as glacial ice retreated and water levels subsided. Because the population appears to have moved from west to east, many archeologists believe that Shield culture developed out of the Plano culture of the northern plains and parkland. Dependent upon the caribou, small bands of Shield people ranged over a large territory. The Canadian Shield's extensive network of rivers and lakes facilitated this movement, and brought different bands into contact with one another. Inter-band marriages seem to have been common and to have promoted a

Between 8000 and 4000 B.C.E. people begin to occupy the Canadian Shield.

flexible social system with wide-ranging relationships. This interconnectedness promoted a certain cultural sameness among the peoples who lived in this vast region. The location of archeological sites on islands and along waterways suggests that the birch-bark canoe was widely in use at an early date. Shield peoples lived in family-sized semi-subterranean dwellings with hearths and stone-lined pits. Subsistence depended on an annual cycle of hunting, fishing, and plant collecting. Wild rice was especially important in some areas. Some groups along the southern Shield grew corn and squash in their summer camps, but poor soils and short growing seasons meant that they could not rely on these crops. The Algonquian peoples of the Shield traded furs, copper, and stone with the Iroquoian farmers to the south for food. Copper from Lake Superior was in use by 4000 B.C.E., and was being widely traded. Some archeologists speculate that the development of technology to process and store wild rice may have made certain bands in this area wealthy and more sedentary. Pottery and the bow-and-arrow were introduced into southern parts of the Canadian Shield around 1000 B.C.E., but no great cultural break is evident except along the present-day Minnesota–Ontario border, where large burial mounds and multi-family dwellings have been found. The appearance of prominent burial mounds—generally absent in the Shield region—and large band gathering sites suggests a level of authority and social organization not found elsewhere among the Shield peoples. Pictographs of humans, animals, and mythological beings suggest that the peoples of the Shield ascribed spiritual power to all nature. Shield culture was long-lived and provided the basis for the Ojibwe (Ojibwa or Ojibway), Cree, Algonquin, and Montagnais peoples.

Plains Culture

Circa 6000 B.C.E.: Early Plains culture develops in the west.

In the west, Plano Culture gave way to early Plains culture around 6000 B.C.E. This shift corresponded with the advent of a long period of warmer and drier climate (the Altithermal) that resulted in the expansion of prairie grasslands and the retreat of parkland and forest farther north. These conditions supported smaller numbers of bison and humans. Early Plains peoples developed new hunting technologies such as the spear thrower (or *atlatl*) to exploit the bison, and diversified their food resources to include smaller game, fish, and wild berries. With the end of the Altithermal dry period around 3000 B.C.E., moister conditions returned to the plains and the population of bison and humans apparently grew considerably.

The bison dominated life on the Plains. Bison meat was consumed fresh, and dried for winter consumption and trade. Hides were made into clothing and shelters, bone into tools, and sinew into bowstrings and thread. Dried buffalo dung was burned as fuel, and bladders used as containers for storing and boiling water. The Plains people produced pemmican by pounding dried bison meat, mixing it with fat rendered from bones and marrow, and packing it into large bladder sacks. Not surprisingly, bison came to be viewed as the provider and a link between the Creator and humans, and the bison hunt came to be surrounded by ritual. A bison skull was often placed on a large rock at the centre of medicine wheels, circular patterns of rocks laid out on prominent hill tops, to communicate with the spirits who brought rain, good forage, and large herds of bison. The hilltops were also burial sites for the Plains people. In early Plains culture, the bison were stalked by small groups of hunters. The introduction of the buffalo jump and the buffalo pound required greater communal cooperation and solidarity in order to coordinate the efforts of the many people needed to stage a successful hunt. The result was a more complex social and political structure, with bands coming together for the spring hunt. The Sun Dance, an important cultural ritual, which varied in content between nations, followed a successful hunt, and took place before bands dispersed for the winter.

Mobility was essential to life on the plains, and dogs were used as draft animals. Both the bow-and-arrow and pottery entered into the tool kit of Plains culture around 500 B.C.E. Contact with peoples to the south and east resulted in the introduction of burial mounds in what is today southern Manitoba. New peoples also migrated onto the plains. The Athapaskan-speaking Beaver, Sekani, and Sarcee appear to have migrated into northern Alberta and adopted a Plains way of life after 500 C.E. The Siouan-speaking Assiniboine migrated to the eastern Canadian Plains from what would later be central Minnesota early in the seventeenth century. Horses were brought to the Canadian plains early in the eighteenth century through the extensive network of trade that linked Aboriginal peoples across the continent and preceded any significant European penetration of the region.

In the early 1700s, horses begin to appear on the Canadian plains.

Within a short period, the peoples of the Plains became skilled equestrians. The horse transformed the buffalo hunt. It also enabled peoples to range over wider areas, bringing them in contact with other groups and often sparking conflict. Since horses could transport more personal goods than dogs, the accumulation of wealth became more possible and a more stratified society resulted. The northwestern plains were sparsely populated. It is estimated that at the time of European contact there was only one person for every 26 square kilometres.

Plateau Culture

The origins of the Plateau culture of the British Columbia interior are debated among scholars. Some archeologists believe the region was penetrated by elements of Coastal culture 9000 years ago. Others find evidence of early Plains culture, especially in the southeastern part of the interior plateau. Still others suggest Plateau culture resulted when elements of an as yet ill-defined Northwest Interior culture moved south. It is likely that multiple migrations occurred and account for what is one of the most culturally and linguistically complex regions of Native Canada.

By 4000 B.C.E. a seasonal subsistence-settlement pattern based upon salmon had emerged on the southern Plateau. People lived and worked in small mobile bands from spring to fall, and came together in larger villages for the winter months. By 2500 B.C.E. there is evidence of large pit-house villages in the river valleys that indicate more settled village life. Salmon provided the major food source for most peoples of the interior Plateau, and large quantities were dried and stored for winter consumption. The most sedentary and culturally complex of the Plateau peoples were found along the Fraser River, where large salmon runs sustained villages of perhaps a thousand people. The peoples of the Plateau participated in an extensive trade network, exchanging dried salmon and desirable carving stone for copper, obsidian, and turquoise. These materials were used to produce ornamental items that probably conveyed status, suggesting that social distinction was an important element of Plateau society. Rank may also be indicated by variations in house size. While the average pit house was 7 metres in diameter, others were as large as

By 4000 B.C.E., a seasonal pattern of settlement emerges on the southern Plateau.

20 metres. Such large homes may have belonged to chiefs or have been used for ceremonial functions. Rock art depicting humans, animals, supernatural creatures, and abstract symbols indicate that the peoples of the interior possessed a rich cosmology. The rock paintings may record dreams adolescent males received during their vision quests. Cut off by the Rocky Mountains to the east and the Coast Mountains to the west, the Plateau peoples of the interior were among the last to make contact with Europeans. It was not until 1793 that Northwest Company explorer Alexander Mackenzie passed through Chilcotin territory on his way to the Pacific.

Pacific Northwest Culture

On the Pacific coast, mobile hunting and fishing bands exploited both maritime and terrestrial resources. Sea-level fluctuations and tectonic forces appear to have delayed the development of the more sedentary lifestyle that later developed on the west coast. Evidence that these peoples hunted large sea mammals suggests that they must have possessed sea-worthy watercraft. Archeologists and anthropologists distinguish between Southwestern and Northwestern Coastal cultures. It is now believed that the peoples of the Southwestern Coast evolved from Palaeo peoples of the Columbia plateau to the south who migrated northward. Northwestern Coastal culture is thought to have been of Palaeo-Arctic origin. The two cultures eventually met and merged along the central coast. By 4000 B.C.E., the stabilization of sea levels supported the development of an increasingly complex culture that exploited the rich resources of the coastal and riverine ecosystems.

By 4000 B.C.E., more stable sea levels allow for the development of Pacific Northwest coastal communities.

Two resources, salmon and red cedar, were vital to the development of Pacific Northwest culture. Salmon were not only abundant, they appeared at the same places at the same time each year, and were easy to catch and easily preserved. Lightweight, strong, and rot resistant, red cedar was an ideal building and carving material. Red cedar was used to construct the large plank homes, dugout canoes, monumental carvings, and decorated storage boxes that are emblematic of Northwest Coast culture. Red cedar bark was used to weave baskets, hats, and clothing. The abundant resources of the west coast sustained the densest human population and the most complex cultures in Aboriginal Canada. The peoples of the west coast lived in permanent waterfront villages during the winter months, some exceeding 1000 persons. During the summer, smaller groups dispersed to summer camps to exploit seasonal resources.

The plentiful resources of the Pacific Northwest supported a complex of social ranks, customs, and artistic expression not found elsewhere in Aboriginal Canada. Archeological evidence indicates that highly ranked societies had developed on the Northwest coast by 1000 B.C.E. Large quantities of status items such as beads, copper, and shell ornaments have been found in some gravesites. Status differences appear to have been inherited. Skeletal remains reveal that the skulls of some infants were flattened, probably as a sign of noble birth. Social position was sustained and validated through the ritual of giving away large quantities of food and goods at potlatches, elaborate festivals that could last for weeks. Besides asserting status, potlatches contributed to social unity and welfare through the distribution of wealth. The peoples of the Pacific Northwest possessed a rich spiritual life. Success in fishing, hunting, warfare, and potlatching required supernatural

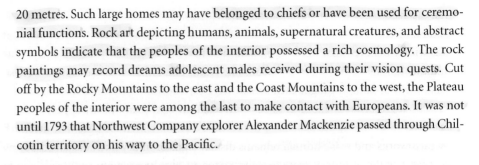

aid. Cleansing rituals were common, and individuals with special ability to control super-natural forces became shamans, and were believed to possess special healing powers. It was widely believed that humans and animals had once been part of the same people and that animals could transform from one realm to another. Because salmon were so vital, the first salmon caught each season were ceremonially welcomed and honoured, their bones returned to the river to be resurrected the next year. Warfare appears to have been common among the peoples of the Pacific Northwest. Many villages were defended by earthworks and some human remains display signs of injury likely sustained during combat. Conflict probably arose to assert status, to acquire property and slaves, and to control access to resources and trade. The peoples of the Pacific Northwest traded exten-sively among themselves and with peoples to the east. At the time of European contact, almost half of Canada's Native people lived in the Pacific Northwest, and some 30 different languages were spoken there.

Arctic Culture

The Arctic was the last part of Canada to be settled by Aboriginal peoples. Palaeo-Eskimo culture spread rapidly across the Arctic from Alaska to Greenland around 2000 B.C.E. While the origins of these peoples are obscure, it is widely believed that they were origi-nally of Siberian origin. Although this was a period of warmer climate and expanded open water, conditions were still harsh. Palaeo-Eskimo culture was adapted to the challenges presented by severe cold, the seasonal migration of game, the lack of plant foods, and the scarcity of fuel and other raw materials. Circular clearings surrounded by rings of stone suggest that the earliest inhabitants of the Arctic were a highly mobile people who lived year-round in tents. The Palaeo-Eskimos survived by hunting caribou and muskoxen with spears and bows and arrows, and seals with harpoons. Life in the Arctic was precarious, and the archeological evidence indicates that changes in climate or scarcity of game caused some areas to be abandoned, or those living there to die out.

Circa 2000 B.C.E.: Aboriginal peoples are believed to have settled in Canada's north.

Significant innovations, such as stone lamps used to burn oil from the blubber of sea mammals, large bone knives used to cut snow blocks for constructing igloos, and ivory sled shoes, were introduced into the Arctic around 1000 B.C.E. These mark the begin-nings of what archeologists term Dorset culture. Dorset culture spread beyond the Arctic down the Labrador coast and onto Newfoundland. Little is known about the spiritual world of the Dorset culture, although sculptures fashioned from bone, antler, ivory, and soapstone depicting humans and animals, as well as masks, suggests shamanic activity.

Around 900 C.E. new peoples appeared in the Canadian Arctic. Norse explorers from Greenland ventured to Baffin Island and northern Labrador but do not appear to have settled or to have had a significant impact on Dorset culture. However, the Dorset may have traded ivory from walrus tusks in return for metal and other goods from the Norse explorers. Depictions of men with European faces and beards on Dorset antler wands provide evidence for interactions with the Norse. Much more momentous was the arrival of the Thule in the twelfth and thirteenth centuries. The Thule migrated eastwards from Alaska and quickly established a presence throughout the region, displacing the Dorset, possibly drawn by the allure of Norse goods.[9]

Circa 1100 C.E.: Thule culture displaces Dorset culture in the Arctic.

The fate of the Dorset people is a matter of considerable speculation. Some scholars believe they were largely exterminated by the Thule. Others maintain that they were simply absorbed into a culture that possessed a superior technology. It has also been questioned whether or not contact even occurred between the two cultures and whether assimilation of Dorset technology by the Thule was merely the result of the Thule finding artefacts that had been left behind.[10] However, the descendants of the Thule, the Inuit, recall in their oral histories encountering a people who, despite their larger stature and strength, were unskilled at fighting and whose weapons were no match for the recurved bows of the invaders. Unable to withstand the encroachment of the Thule, the Dorset people either perished or scattered.[11] Whatever the reasons, the Dorset subsequently disappeared from the Canadian Arctic, except for a few isolated pockets on the eastern shore of Hudson Bay in northern Quebec, where they survived for a few more centuries. Ancestors of the historic Inuit, the Thule lived in semi-subterranean stone and sod houses with whalebone supports for roofs, and erected stone cairns to channel caribou to prime hunting locations. Innovations introduced by the Thule included the kayak, used to hunt whales in summer, and the dog sled, used to travel across the ice in winter. For a time, the Thule manufactured pottery oil lamps, but abandoned the practice because clay was difficult to find and of poor quality. The discovery of smelted iron, bronze, and copper artefacts suggests that the Thule traded with the Norse of Greenland.

Great Lakes–St. Lawrence Culture

The Great Lakes–St. Lawrence lowlands were initially occupied shortly after the glaciers retreated around 11 000 years ago. Although the development of early Archaic culture in this region is poorly defined, by 5000 B.C.E. a distinctive Laurentian Archaic culture is evident. By this time, climatic conditions had stabilized and the hardwood forests of the region sustained a mixed economy based on deer and elk, a wide variety of small game, fish, nuts, and berries. Laurentian Archaic people gathered together in summer camps located on the shorelines of lakes and rivers and dispersed into smaller family groups during the winter months. They manufactured spear throwers, chipped stone dart heads, knives and scrapers, polished stone axes and adzes for wood working, and fish hooks, awls, pendants, and beads made from native copper. The use of native copper and the discovery of exotic shells among burial goods indicate that the people of the Great Lakes–St. Lawrence participated in an extensive trading network with the peoples to their north and south. Burial sites provide a glimpse into Laurentian beliefs and religious practices. The placement of personal goods in graves and the sprinkling of red ochre on bodies suggest that the people of the Laurentian Archaic engaged in some form of ceremonial burial based on a belief in an afterlife. Over time, burial goods became more extensive, indicating both rising levels of prosperity and increased notions of social hierarchy. The discovery of human remains with projectile points lodged in the bone, fractured skulls, and even decapitated remains, testifies that violence and warfare were part of Laurentian Archaic society.

The introduction of pottery cooking vessels, the bow and arrow, and the construction of burial mounds around 1000 B.C.E. mark the beginning of the Woodland period in the Great Lakes–St. Lawrence lowlands. These developments entered the region from the south and reflected the influence of the Adena and Hopewell cultures of the Ohio Valley. The increased number of archeological sites from this period suggests a significant increase in population, although Woodland peoples continued to live as hunter-gatherers who moved between seasonal camps.

Circa 500 C.E.: Agriculture develops in the Great Lakes–St. Lawrence lowlands.

More sedentary lifeways developed following the introduction of agriculture to the Great Lakes–St. Lawrence lowlands around 500 C.E. Maize was the first plant to be cultivated by the Native peoples in the region. Maize was first domesticated in Meso-America sometime between 4000 and 3000 B.C.E., and was vital to the emergence of the Mayan, Toltec, and Aztec civilizations. In the Great Lakes–St. Lawrence lowlands, the introduction of maize marked the beginnings of Iroquoian culture. Other crops followed, with sunflowers in evidence by 1100 C.E. and beans by 1300 C.E. The addition of cultivated crops to an earlier hunting and gathering society resulted in a significant increase in the population, changed settlement patterns, and altered social organization and belief. By the eighth century, the peoples of the Great Lakes–St. Lawrence lowlands lived in multi-family longhouses in small, palisaded villages. By the fifteenth century, these villages had grown to an average of more than three hectares in size and were occupied by as many as 2000 people. Villages were palisaded for defence, indicating that warfare was common. The increase in warfare may have reflected changing gender roles. Women appear to have become the main food producers. The depletion of local game due to population increase and the ability to store food may have deprived men of their traditional role as hunters, leaving warfare as the principal means for men to acquire and assert status. Remains of broken and charred human bones, and ornaments and tools made from bone, further suggest that warfare and possibly ritual cannibalism were not uncommon. By the time of European contact in the sixteenth century, Iroquoian culture had spread up the St. Lawrence as far as Quebec.

Linguistic Categorization

The Aboriginal peoples of the St. Lawrence–Great Lakes lowlands would prove to play a pivotal role in the earliest sustained encounters between Natives and newcomers. Yet the story of the interactions between Europeans and these first peoples of Canada quickly reveals the limitations of the method we have used thus far of categorizing Native groups according to broad cultural complexes. The broad groupings for Native societies—Maritime, Shield, Plains, Plateau, Pacific Northwest, Arctic, and Great Lakes–St. Lawrence—are logical ones: many aspects of human societies tend to be shaped by the physical environment, and groups living in similar settings develop traits in common. But these broad groupings are often insufficient for the purpose of historical explanation. After all, to simply categorize both the Iroquois (Haudenosaunee) Confederacy and their rivals, the Huron (Wendat), as people living in the "Great Lakes–St. Lawrence lowlands" is just as meaningless as it would be to simply call all newcomers "Europeans." Such broad categorizations alone cannot offer a perspective that makes sense of complex events.

Another alternative is to categorize Native societies by linguistic family, although this method also has its limitations. Any such broad categorization is inherently artificial. Natives in Canada may be said to belong to one of eight linguistic families, with further categories for Inuit and Métis. (Some linguists identify 12 separate groups.) The eight families are the Algonquian, Iroquoian, Siouan, Ktunaxa (Kutenai), Salish, Wakashan,

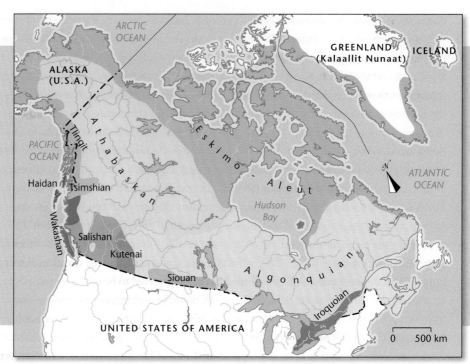

Source: Courtesy of the Canadian Encyclopedia.

Map 1.3
Linguistic Grouping of Aboriginal Peoples.

Tsimshian, and Na-Dene. These linguistic families should not be confused with languages; indeed each encompasses a variety of languages and distinct nations. For example, the Na-Dene linguistic family encompasses more than 40 Athapaskan or Dene languages. The Algonquian (sometimes spelled Algonkian) family is subdivided by region into the Eastern Woodland, Subarctic, and Plains groups, encompassing such diverse peoples as the Mi'kmaq, Maliseet, Beothuk, Montagnais, Ojibwe/Chippewa, Algonquin (or Algonkin), Cree, and Nippissing. The Iroquoian family includes the Iroquois (or Haudenosaunee) Confederacy (consisting of the five nations of Mohawk, Oneida, Onondaga, Cayuga, and Seneca, and later taking in the Tuscarora to become the Six Nations) and also includes the Huron (Wendat) confederacy and the Neutral.[12] It would be wrong to assume that Native nations belonging to the same linguistic family would be necessarily allied to one another. Indeed, the opposite is more logical: those whose economies are similar would be more likely to form alliances with those who could supply other resources. The endemic rivalry between the Iroquois and Huron, though not simply economic in nature, is a case in point. The need to take a more "textured" look at Native societies will become apparent as we explore the history of Native–newcomer encounters.

Newcomers to North America

Earliest Known Contacts: The Norse

The first Europeans to arrive in North America were probably the Norse. Around 800 C.E., the Norse of Scandinavia began to island hop westward across the North Atlantic, establishing a colony on Iceland around 870. In 985, Eric the Red established a Norse colony on

Greenland. Shortly after the establishment of the Greenland settlement, a trading ship blown off course sighted land further to the west, and, around the year 1000, Eric the Red's son, Leif, launched an exploratory expedition. Leif Ericsson explored the coasts of Helluland, Markland, and Vinland, thought to be present-day Baffin Island, Labrador, and Newfoundland, respectively. After camping at Vinland for the winter, he returned to Greenland in the spring with a shipload of timber and stories of a warm and fruitful land. Several attempts to colonize Vinland followed, but conflict with the Native population, isolation from other Norse settlements, and the impracticability of pursuing a pastoral way of life in a heavily forested landscape may have eventually convinced the Norse to abandon their efforts.

The twelfth-century Norse chronicle *Historia Norvegiae* describes encounters in the far north with a "people of small stature who are called Skraelings." "When they are struck with a weapon," the story told, "their wounds turn white and … do not bleed, but if they are killed they bleed almost endlessly." The "Skraelings" did not "know the use of iron," instead arming themselves with "walrus tusks as missiles and sharpened stones in place of knives." This description of the "Skraelings" has been observed to be consistent with what archeologists know about the Dorset people. A possible explanation for the outlandish claim that the Dorset did not bleed is that the animal skin clothing of the Dorset culture was much thicker and not as easily saturated as the cloth that the Norse wore.[13]

In 1960, archeologists made an exciting find on the tip of Newfoundland's Great Northern Peninsula: at L'Anse aux Meadows, they unearthed the remains of a Norse settlement dating from approximately 1000 C.E. The excavation revealed three large Norse dwellings, a kiln, a forge, and a bathhouse. While Newfoundland may not seem like the lush, abundant paradise Norse legends describe, the archeological find lent credence to theories that this had in fact been Vinland.

Although no further attempts at colonization seem to have been made, the Norse continued to voyage to North America for several centuries to trade and to acquire resources.

985: Eric the Red establishes a Norse colony on Greenland.

Remains of Norse sod houses at L'Anse aux Meadows.

Source: Parks Canada H01-11-01-04 (26), J. Steeves, 1983.

Markland provided Greenland with timber, and Helluland supplied the white falcons and polar bears prized in the courts of medieval European monarchs. The discovery of metal Norse artefacts throughout the eastern Arctic testifies to ongoing trade with the Native peoples of the area. By the twelfth century, a dozen parish churches, a monastery, and a convent had been established on Greenland, but the Norse do not appear to have attempted to introduce Christianity to the Aboriginal people with whom they traded. A prolonged period of climactic cooling, the Little Ice Age, began in the middle of the twelfth century and continued for at least the next three centuries. As the climate deteriorated, the Greenland settlements declined, disappearing by around 1500.

The Age of Exploration

Intermittent voyages to North America's Atlantic coast by fishers and others probably continued, but sustained European contact was not renewed until late in the fifteenth century. A number of forces combined at that time to propel Europe into a great age of expansion and discovery. Improvements in navigation and shipbuilding allowed Europeans to travel further from their shores. Carracks were vessels that combined the square sails common in northern Europe with the triangular, or lateen, sails favoured in the Mediterranean. With this design, the lateen sail became the steering sail, and the square sails made the ship speedy, seaworthy, better able to ride out storms, and able to be crewed by fewer men. By the end of the fifteenth century, ships were four times larger than they had been at the century's beginning, permitting more cargo and supplies to be carried. Vessels also began to carry gunpowder ordnance for protection. In fact, after the fifteenth century, new galleons, bigger purpose-built warships, revolutionized naval warfare, something that would add an important dimension to European competition in the new world in the years to come.[14] Instrumentation also improved. The magnetic compass, invented in China, seems to have reached the Mediterranean by means of the Arab world as early as the thirteenth century. The astrolabe had been developed by the ancient Greeks, but had been further refined by the fifteenth century. It was used to measure the height of the sun or stars above the horizon to determine latitude, one's north–south position. Only in the eighteenth century would the chronometer be developed, enabling navigators to determine their longitudinal, or east–west, position. The inability to reliably determine east–west position in earlier ages accounts for some gross geographical misjudgments. Improvements in the science of cartography, or map-making, had also been made by the fifteenth century. It should be noted, however, that improvements in life at sea were only relative. An account of Ferdinand Magellan's Spanish-sponsored 1521 voyage around the world offers a glimpse into shipboard conditions in the age of exploration:

> We were three months and twenty days without taking on any food or water. We ate biscuit, which was no longer biscuit but fistfuls of powder swarming with worms, for they had eaten the better part (it stank strongly of rat urine); and we drank yellow water that had been putrid for many days.

Sawdust, rats, and oxhide soaked in seawater were other items of diet described in this account.[15]

Other factors besides technological innovations also played a role in launching the age of exploration. Historians usually date the "modern" age from approximately 1500, to mark a transition from the Middle Ages (c. 500–1500). A number of important changes account for this label: the rigidly hierarchical social structures and localized agricultural economies that characterized medieval society were giving way to a new order in which expanded trade was becoming more significant. Although a land-owning aristocracy continued to dominate society, in cities and towns new leaders emerged whose wealth derived from commerce. Economic and population growth spurred higher demands for new sources of raw materials and foodstuffs. The rise of commerce slowly eroded the medieval feudal system with its interlocking rights and obligations between lords, vassals, and serfs. As towns grew and trade accelerated, a new class of individualistic and profit-seeking merchants and bankers appeared; money was increasingly substituted for payments in goods and services.

The emerging middle class was increasingly dissatisfied with the limitations of local feudal control and began to support strong leaders who could exercise control over larger areas. In time, Europe's small feudal states gave way to larger nation states. The displacement of medieval feudal structures by centralized monarchies supported by competent bureaucracies and well-equipped armies provided the means needed to support overseas exploration. By the second half of the fifteenth century, European monarchs had increased both their power and authority and were in a position to turn their energies beyond their borders. Spain would initially be the most successful of the European colonizing powers in the western hemisphere, having achieved the internal consolidation of power necessary to have a stable state capable of organizing and financing voyages of exploration. In 1479 the crowns of Castile and Aragon were united, and by 1492 Spain had expelled the Muslims who had controlled Granada in the south. This consolidation of power also dictated the brutal expulsion of Spain's Sephardic Jews, seen by the Inquisition as a threat to the ideal of Christian unity.

Added to these factors spurring overseas expansion was the rising power of the Turks of the Ottoman Empire. The most dramatic and visible symbol of Ottoman expansion was the 1453 capture of Constantinople, the strategic Byzantine city on the Bosporus that commands the approaches to the Mediterranean. The Mediterranean was the great conduit of crucial European trade with Asia, the source of many good things upon which Europe increasingly relied. Spices (used for the preparation and preservation of food and for ritual purposes), silks, rugs, jewels, porcelain, precious metals, and other luxury goods came by way of the Mediterranean, with camel trains providing transport for the overland portions of the route. The vital conquest of Constantinople by the Ottoman Sultan Mehmed was only part of an ambitious campaign that brought the Muslims to the very gates of Vienna in later years. In the immediate aftermath, however, this strategic gain enabled Ottoman pirates to menace their European enemies' Mediterranean shipping. Alternative routes to Asia that bypassed the Mediterranean would thus become especially attractive.

Also underlying Europe's outward thrust was a new curiosity and confidence born of the Renaissance's faith in human intellect and a human capacity to control nature. The discovery of new worlds and contact with different peoples and cultures affirmed Europe's sense of being at the heroic frontier of civilized history. Religious conviction was also key to this impetus to explore and conquer new worlds. Convinced that theirs was a

1453: The fall of Constantinople to the Ottoman Turks lends urgency to the Europeans' quest for alternative routes to Asia.

universal religion, Europeans sought to spread the blessings of Christianity around the globe. Yet the modern age, besides being characterized by more centralized nation states and technological innovation, was also the age of the Protestant Reformation. Martin Luther's famous challenge to Roman Catholic hegemonic Christianity came in 1517 when he nailed his "95 Theses" to a church door in Wittenberg, in what is now Germany. The spread of Reformation ideas was facilitated by the recent invention of the printing press by Johannes Gutenberg of the German city Mainz in the 1450s. Gutenberg's movable type made it possible to mass-produce books and other reading materials at much lower cost. While the Protestant Reformation would rapidly gain ground in Europe, the Roman Catholic Church took the lead in winning converts elsewhere around the globe. New Roman Catholic religious orders in the early modern period, such as the Jesuits, were at the forefront of these efforts. The quest for souls outside of Europe might seem to be a cynical ploy to gain advantage in the crucial struggle against the Protestant challenge, yet it is important to remember that Christian teachings carried the unmistakeable message that those beyond the reach of Christ's message would be denied the chance of everlasting life. The project to convert others was therefore one of considerable urgency.

1492: Christopher Columbus explores the coasts of Cuba and Haiti.

The most famous exploratory voyage to the new world was Christopher Columbus's 1492 sailing to America. Born in Genoa, in what is now Italy, Columbus was sponsored in his voyage by the kingdom of Spain. The Portuguese navigator Bartholomew Dias had rounded the Cape of Good Hope at Africa's southern tip in 1487, and the Spanish feared that Portugal was poised to gain control over direct trade with Asia. Columbus believed that he could reach Asia by sailing westward, and in 1492 crossed the Atlantic to explore the coasts of what is today Cuba and Haiti. He returned to Spain certain that he had reached the Indies—the name that was often applied collectively to India, China, Japan, Indonesia, and other parts of Asia.

His reports of the lands and peoples he encountered captured the imagination of Europeans. The term "Indian" as a general designation for the inhabitants of the Americas stems from Columbus's erroneous geography. He described "los Indios" as a primitive people—naked, immoral, idolatrous, and ignorant. Although he characterized one group as ferocious and cannibalistic savages, he found most of the people to be generous, content, easily pleased, attractive, and well-proportioned. Yet according to the criteria of Christian civilization, they were deemed deficient in a number of respects: letters, laws, government, clothing, arts, trade, agriculture, marriage, morals and—above all—religion. Native beliefs were dismissed as irrational and superstitious. Failing to see any form of government or social organization that Europeans would recognize as equivalent to their own, the Spanish assumed that the Natives were devoid of any culture. The Native peoples were simply part of the American environment, an environment that the Spanish believed they had a God-given mandate to civilize and make productive. Wild America, according to this view, needed to be tamed and domesticated.

Staking Claims

Fearing that rivals would encroach upon their discoveries, the Spanish appealed to the Vatican to recognize their sovereignty over the new territories. The Pope claimed the right to grant sovereignty over any lands not possessed by a Christian ruler, and had already

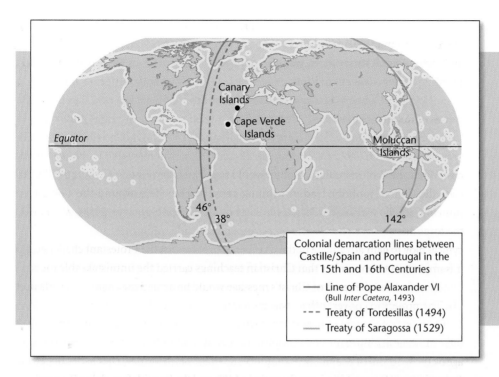

Map 1.4
Treaty of Tordesillas, 1494.

granted the Portuguese title over the lands they had explored along the coast of Africa. In 1493 Pope Alexander VI defined a dividing line through the North Atlantic 100 leagues west of the Azores, running south to the Cape Verde Islands. All lands west of this line he granted to Spain; all lands east were conferred on Portugal. The Pope's blessing of legitimacy on overseas explorations carried with it the requirement to bring the inhabitants of these territories into the embrace of the Catholic faith. The Pope's dividing line was moved 270 leagues further west in 1494 under the Treaty of Tordesillas, giving Portugal a claim to Brazil and a foothold in the Americas.

Henry VII of England ignored the exclusive claims of Spain and Portugal, yet concentrated exploration efforts in more northerly areas. English hopes were high that a northwest passage to Asia might be found: "the shortest route, the northern, has been reserved by Divine Providence for England," an early sixteenth century English geographer speculated.[16] England commissioned the Venetian navigator Giovanni Caboto, whom they called John Cabot, to find it. With financial backing from the wealthy merchants of Bristol, Cabot explored the Atlantic coast of Canada in 1497 and claimed Newfoundland and Nova Scotia for England. He led a second expedition of five vessels the following year, but Cabot himself is believed to have perished on the voyage and never returned.

Although Cabot's explorations did not yield a passage to China, the reports of abundant cod stocks in the Grand Banks fired imaginations. Cabot's reports told of seas so thick with fish that one could walk across their backs. There was a huge demand for cod in Catholic Europe; Portuguese, Spanish, French, Basque, and English fishers were soon making annual trips to the Grand Banks. The fishery grew rapidly and by 1570 there were as many as 400 ships travelling to Newfoundland each spring to harvest the sea.

1497: Giovanni Caboto (John Cabot) claims Newfoundland and Nova Scotia for England.

By the 1530s, whaling operations are underway off Labrador.

In addition to these cod fishers were others who came to harvest whales. Whale oil was a valuable commodity, used for the manufacture of soap and pharmaceuticals, and for fabric treatments. It was also a superior lamp oil. Between the 1530s and 1600, whalers from the Basque country bordering Spain and France, facing depletion of whale stocks in the Bay of Biscay, turned to a new source in the Strait of Belle Isle. Red Bay, Labrador, became the centre of whaling operations, with whalers capturing right and bowhead whales migrating through the strait between the island of Newfoundland and the Labrador coast. The whales were harpooned, their flippers and tails removed to make the carcass more manoeuvrable, and the blubber taken to onshore "tryworks" where the fat could be rendered in copper cauldrons. The oil was then transported in barrels. It is estimated that some 20 000 whales were taken within a 50-year period before the industry declined, owing perhaps to over-harvesting and shifting whale migration patterns.

While on shore to dry their catch of cod or to process whale blubber, Europeans established contact with the local Natives and began to trade. Trade provided the Natives with durable goods, but this contact also introduced European diseases against which they had no immunity. The result was a significant weakening of Aboriginal populations long before the establishment of permanent European settlements. Frequently displaced from their summer fishing camps by European fishers, and desirous of European trade goods, the Native peoples of the Atlantic coast became increasingly preoccupied with trapping furs and dependent on the resources of the interior. As the local supply of furs became depleted, Native groups expanded beyond their traditional territories, and conflict between Native peoples appears to have intensified significantly. Important changes in Aboriginal ways of life were already evident decades before the arrival of settlers and missionaries.

Although Cabot had laid claim to this "newe founde lande" in 1497, the English did little to exercise their dominion beyond the fishery, and Portugal soon launched a more direct challenge. In 1500 Gaspar Corte-Real was commissioned by King Manuel of Portugal to discover and claim lands in the new world and to search for the Northwest Passage. He left that summer and appears to have journeyed around Newfoundland. A second expedition the following year with three ships returned to Portugal with 60 captive Natives, but without the ship bearing Corte-Real himself. Gaspar's brother Miguel attempted to find him in 1502 but he too was lost. A Portuguese attempt to establish a settlement on Cape Breton Island around 1520 also proved to be an ill-fated venture.

Early French Explorations

Preoccupied by European conflicts, the French did not send out an expedition to North America until 1524. That year the French king, Francis I, hired an Italian navigator, Giovanni da Verrazano, to explore the eastern coast of North America for a passage to Asia and to search out gold and silver. War with the Habsburgs prevented the French from launching a second voyage until 1534.

This expedition was led by Jacques Cartier, an experienced seaman from Saint-Malo, Brittany. Setting out on April 20, 1534, Cartier's two ships, crewed by 61 men and guided by favourable winds, crossed the Atlantic in only 20 days and entered the Strait of Belle Isle at the northern tip of Newfoundland. Cartier was not impressed by the land he encountered

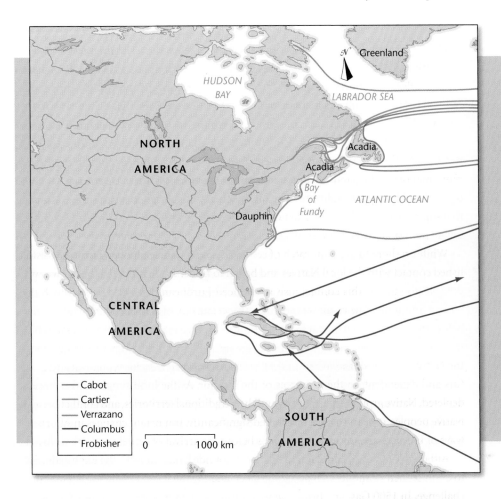

Map 1.5
Early European Explorations of North America.

on the coast of Labrador, noting in his journal that he "did not see one cartload of earth" in any of the places he landed, but only rock. This territory, he suggested, "should not be called the New Land" but, rather, "the land God gave to Cain." But this bleak initial impression gave way to enthusiasm when Cartier journeyed south into the Gulf of St. Lawrence, where one island won his particular favour: it was "covered with fine trees and meadows, fields of wild oats, and of pease in flower, as thick and fine as ever I saw in Brittany."[17]

1534: Jacques Cartier explores the Gulf of St. Lawrence.

Regarding the people that he met, however, little such praise is to be found in Cartier's journal entries. The following is typical:

> This people may well be called savage; for they are the sorriest folk there can be in the world, and the whole lot of them had not anything above the value of five sous, their canoes and fishing-nets excepted. They go quite naked, except for a small skin, with which they cover their privy parts.... They have no other dwelling but their canoes, which they turn upside down and sleep on the ground underneath.[18]

Despite this dismissive assessment, Cartier was cautious when he made his first contact with an Aboriginal people, the Mi'kmaq, at Chaleur Bay. In early July 1534, he and his men saw a flotilla of perhaps 50 "savage canoes" crossing the bay. From these "there sprang out

Portrait of Jacques Cartier.

Source: © McCord Museum, M930.50.3.168.

and landed a large number of people, who set up a great clamour and made frequent signs to us to come on shore, holding up to us some skins on sticks." Travelling in a single longboat, the wary Frenchmen began to row away, but they were soon surrounded by seven canoes full of Mi'kmaq "dancing and showing many signs of joy, and of their desire to be friends." Not willing to risk a close encounter, Cartier ordered cannon fire to scare them off. Undaunted, the Mi'kmaq returned the next day, and Cartier felt confident enough to dispatch two of his men with knives, kettles, and a red cap for the Mi'kmaq "captain." "They showed a marvellously great pleasure in possessing and obtaining these iron wares and other commodities, dancing and going through many ceremonies.... They bartered all they had to such an extent that all went back naked" and made signs that they would return. Trade resumed three days later with the exchange of more gifts and much singing and dancing. "We perceived," Cartier concluded, "that they are people who would be easy to convert."[19] Yet Cartier's dream that his hosts would embrace the ways of Europeans was born of his unreflecting overconfidence, and relations would quickly be poisoned by mutual mistrust, trickery, treachery, and tragedy.

Cartier's experiences with the indigenous people of the St. Lawrence region provide an excellent example of the challenges that commonly confront historians as they seek to provide balanced and accurate information about events long past. The eminent nineteenth-century German historian Leopold von Ranke famously aspired to elevate history to a "science," to definitively determine "*wie es eigentlich gewesen*"—how it really was.[20] In a more relativistic age, we have come to view the discipline of history as an art, and a rather inexact one at that. Historical certainty, elusive in the best of circumstances, can probably never be achieved with respect to Cartier's relationship with the Iroquoians he first encountered in the summer of 1534. Almost five centuries later, historians have yet to unearth more than one side of this story, and almost all of this comes from a single witness, Cartier himself—presumably at least.

The story is told in *The Voyages of Jacques Cartier*, a collection of centuries-old documents first compiled, translated, and edited by Canadian historian Henry Percival Biggar in 1924. Biggar relied upon earlier documents translated into several languages; since no original manuscripts have ever been found, questions have been raised about both the authenticity and authorship of the account. Whether it was Cartier himself, or perhaps a shipmate, who actually wrote the story, Biggar and other credible historians have concluded that it was based on a ship's log kept by Cartier. Yet even if we assume that *The Voyages* represents a firsthand account of the events, a legitimate example of what historians call a "primary source,"[21] we must remember to approach such sources critically, to ask questions about the context in which such material was produced. (A secondary source, by contrast, is an after-the-fact account by one who was not an eyewitness. This textbook, for example, is a secondary source.) No doubt Cartier wished to portray his own actions in a favourable light, either for the sake of posterity, or to preserve his reputation with contemporaries. Tales of potential riches to be found in these new territories might also convince the French Crown to sponsor further explorations. Perhaps ironically, Cartier's own frank and frequent admissions in *The Voyages* of his own deceitfulness in his dealings with the Iroquoians lend a certain credibility to the account. And as we shall see, there seems to have been a degree of duplicity on both sides.

In late July 1534, at Gaspé Harbour where, just a few weeks earlier, he had first encountered Iroquoians from Stadacona (present-day Quebec City) up the St. Lawrence River on their annual fishing expedition, Cartier had a nine-metre cross erected, complete with a shield and a sign that proclaimed in large letters, "VIVE LE ROI DE FRANCE." This was done, Cartier reported, "in the presence of a number of savages," who certainly could not understand the French words but evidently got the message, that by this act Cartier and the French had laid claim to the territory.

After the French had returned to their ships, the Iroquoian chief Donnacona arrived in a canoe with four companions, including three of his sons. It was apparent at once that the French action had aroused their suspicions, as they "did not come so close to the ships as they had usually done." Instead, from a safe distance, the chief, Cartier related, "made us a long harangue, making the sign of the cross with two of his fingers, and then he pointed to the land all about, as if he wished to say that all this region belonged to him, and that we ought not to have set up this cross without his permission." At this point, Cartier employed his undeniable talent for trickery: when Donnacona finished speaking, "we held up an axe to him, pretending that we would barter it" for the old black bearskin he wore. The ruse succeeded, and when the Iroquoians were enticed to come closer, the French seized them and forced them aboard the ship. "Every sign of affection was shown to them, and they were made to eat and drink and to be of good cheer." Cartier's account explains that they made signs to indicate that the cross had been set up merely as a landmark, and that they would come back to bring them iron wares and other goods. The French also said that they wished to take two of Donnacona's sons away with them, and would bring them back again to that harbour. Cartier plied the Iroquoians with gifts, "at which they showed great pleasure," and when the chief and others returned to shore, the two sons, Domagaya and Taignoagny, were "detained" aboard the ship. Later that day, about 30 men came in six canoes to say their goodbyes. "These," related Cartier, "made signs to us that they would not pull down the cross" while, perhaps crucially for students of history, "delivering at the same time several harangues which we did not understand." Might these incomprehensible parting speeches be an indication that the Iroquoians were not as pleased with the proceedings as Cartier's account implies? Indeed, Cartier's account of his second voyage includes a reference to "the two savages whom we had captured on our first voyage."[22]

Historian Ramsay Cook observes that "Cartier made the final departure seem amicable, and perhaps it seemed that way to Donnacona's people who, if they understood what was taking place, probably recognized that resistance was hopeless."[23] Marcel Trudel, on the other hand, seems to accept Cartier's account more or less at face value, explaining that "Cartier had brought off a masterly coup by means of a very simple trick, arousing Donnacona's greed with the offer of an axe. With skill and cunning, he had carried off two of Chief Donnacona's sons, and yet had succeeded in preserving friendship between the French and the Iroquois."[24] If this was so, it was not the last example of Cartier's "skill and cunning" that the Iroquoians were to see.

It would seem, however, that Donnacona and his people had a few tricks of their own. The two sons stayed only nine months in France, and were almost unique among early new world captives in surviving the experience. Had they remained longer, it is probable that they would have fallen victim to European diseases to which they had no immunity. Their speedy return may well have been the result of French greed: Domagaya and Taignoagny told Cartier fabulous stories of mythical kingdoms and precious metals, stories which, over time, grew ever more fantastic. Samples of some of the later stories include tales of men with wings on their arms who flew like bats, and reports of a race of wild men who had no anuses.[25] Having been instructed in French so that they could act as interpreters, in September 1535 Domagaya and Taignoagny guided Cartier's three ships and 110-man crew up the St. Lawrence to their home village of Stadacona, where they were reunited with their father.

Cartier was eager to travel farther upriver to explore the riches of the "kingdom of the Saguenay" and to discover a route to Asia. Donnacona did his best to dissuade Cartier from making the trip, for reasons that are not explained in *The Voyages*, although some historians speculate that the chief was motivated by a desire to maintain control over access to the interior and French trade goods. Undeterred, Cartier proceeded upriver to Hochelaga (present-day Montreal), where the village's thousand residents turned out to greet him enthusiastically. While at Hochelaga, Cartier ascended Mont Royal, where he erected another cross and viewed the rapids that blocked any further progress into the interior and prevented him from reaching the riches of the kingdom of the Saguenay.

Disappointed, Cartier returned to the harbour near Stadacona. Here, he found that the sailors who had stayed behind had built a fort "with artillery pointing every way, and in a good state to defend us against the whole countryside." The next day, Donnacona and his sons arrived to welcome him back, but Cartier suspected that their pleasant greeting was insincere. Within weeks, the relationship became strained. Much to his annoyance, Domagaya and Taignoagny were telling their people "they could as easily get hatchets as knives" for the goods they offered the French. The chief of another village reinforced his growing doubts, warning him that Donnacona and his sons were "traitors and rogues." Acknowledging in his reports that "there was a certain coldness between us," Cartier ordered his men to strengthen the fort.[26]

Things soon got even colder with the onset of a severe winter. Twenty-five of Cartier's men succumbed to scurvy, yet Cartier was loath to reveal the toll the disease was taking, lest the people of Stadacona attack them in their weakness. At last Domagaya provided both the remedy—a curative infusion made from the white cedar tree—as well as the assistance of two women to gather the leaves and bark needed. Cartier's account reveals gratitude to God, but none, apparently, to his Stadaconan benefactors. Indeed, shortly thereafter, convinced of their "treason" and "knavishness," Cartier began to plot another kidnapping.[27]

When spring returned, relations between Cartier and Donnacona remained tense. When Taignoagny asked Cartier's help in removing a rival headman, Agona, Cartier saw an opportunity to break Donnacona's powers and to eliminate opposition to French plans. Feigning cooperation with the plot against Agona, Cartier invited Donnacona and his supporters to a celebration of the feast of the Holy Cross. At the feast, Cartier ordered his men to seize

1535–1536: Cartier makes a second voyage to Canada.

Donnacona, his two sons, and two other headmen. Cartier promised Donnacona's people that he would return in 12 months with their chief and gifts from the French king.

On May 6, 1536, Cartier sailed for France with his captives. When they arrived in France, Donnacona and the others were paraded through the streets as exotic novelties from the new world. The chief appeared before a notary for questioning and met with Francis I, to whom he related tales of the kingdom of the Saguenay and its marvellous riches. None of the captives ever returned to Canada.

Although Francis I was impressed by Donnacona's stories of the kingdom of the Saguenay, war between France and Spain delayed Ca[...] This time, Cartier served under Jean-François de la R[...] not nobleman, mandated by the Crown to establish a[...] kingdom of the Saguenay. Cartier sailed from France [...] tative. For his part, Roberval was to join Cartier in C[...] to defend the new colony.

In August 1541, Cartier returned to Stadacona, [...] Agona. Cartier explained that Donnacona had died a[...] lords in France and did not wish to return to Canada. [...] Agona, he soon feared that he might suffer a similar [...] the Stadaconans once again began to sour. Cartier th[...] defensible position close by at the mouth of the Cap[...] tiny settlement of Charlesbourg-Royal. In September, [...] but, lacking interpreters, he gained little new knowled[...] French boys to the Hochelagans in the hope that they [...] gather intelligence about the kingdom of the Saguena[...]

at the outpost at Charlesbourg-Royal suffered through a miserable winter. Many appear to have died of scurvy, or to have been killed by Natives. Cartier abandoned the settlement in the spring, but drew comfort from one consolation: he had a load of what he believed to be gold and diamonds to bring back to France.

Cartier's wish to hasten back to France was checked, however, by Roberval's arrival. The departing and arriving vessels hailed one another near St. John's, Newfoundland. But Cartier refused to be detained, and, disobeying Roberval's orders to sail back with him to Charlesbourg-Royal, absconded under cover of darkness, returning to France with his cargo of "Canadian diamonds." Despite Cartier's desertion, Roberval and his small company of men and women carried on to Charlesbourg-Royal. Roberval journeyed upriver and unsuccessfully attempted to navigate the Lachine rapids. (The name the French gave to these waters reflected their optimism that China lay just beyond.) An expedition up the Saguenay in search of gold and precious stones proved no more successful. During the winter, the ill-fated company endured cold, famine, and sickness. A strict Calvinist, Roberval was a demanding taskmaster whose severity prompted some of the colonists to rise up to challenge his authority. Determined to maintain order, Roberval had six of the dissidents hanged. Other measures to deal with disciplinary infractions were also harsh: Roberval abandoned a young female relative, Marguerite de La Rocque, on an isolated island with her lover. A petty thief was left alone on another island wearing leg irons. By

[Handwritten note on attached paper:]
Cartier
↳ Tricks Donnacona + others into comming to France where they die after they cured most of their men from scurvy.
↳ Agona (enemy of Donnacona) felt like he may be next, + so Cartier moveed the settlement

[handwritten note: Roberval Tried to set up a collony just as Cartier was leaving + failed his strickt religious views also made him very dictatorial]

... was forced to dispatch a ship to France to plead ..., Roberval and his entire company abandoned ...ce.

...Canada had proven to be a miserable failure. A ...nperament, accompanied by a strange mixture ...criminals, did not make up the most promising ...Moreover, the excitement surrounding Cartier's ...the haul was discovered to be iron pyrites and ...successes of the Spanish conquistadors of the ...d subdued Mexico's powerful Aztec civilization ...l of the Incan empire in Peru. Gold and silver ...new world colonies. But wracked by internal ...erval and Cartier's failure, France lost interest in North America.

England's First Colony

As French interest in Canada waned, English interest revived. England, Protestant since Henry VIII's confrontation with Roman Catholic authority, was determined to meet and challenge the growing power and wealth of Catholic Spain. When Elizabeth I became queen in 1558, England was a relatively minor power. With the defeat of the Spanish Armada in 1588, England emerged as a major force in the world. English supremacy on the seas cleared the way for English colonization in North America. Under Elizabeth I, England sought to find an alternative route to the riches of the Orient and to establish overseas colonies of her own. But England's main tactic was a more predatory one: the Crown issued Letters of Marque to privateers, authorizing piracy against England's enemies. Seafaring English adventurers, many from the southernmost counties of Devon and Cornwall, preyed on Spanish treasure ships and raided coastal colonies, sharing the plunder with the Crown.

In 1578, Sir Humphrey Gilbert, a confidant of Elizabeth I, received a royal patent to claim for the English Crown "heathen and barbarous landes, countries and territories not actually possessed of any Christian prince or people."[28] After several false starts, Gilbert set out in 1583, arriving at St. John's, Newfoundland on August 3. John Cabot had claimed Newfoundland for England in 1497, but fishers from many countries flocked there during the fishing season. The harbour was filled with English, Portuguese, Basque, and French ships. Some of these mariners had been victims of piracy carried out by one of Gilbert's captains the previous year, and Gilbert was denied entry. Gilbert flourished his royal commission and the English ships at least made way. Gilbert went ashore and, with the fishers of different nations assembled before him, read his commission, formally taking possession of Newfoundland for the English Crown. To assert English sovereignty, he issued fishing licences to each of the ships in the harbour, and collected a levy in kind to resupply his poorly provisioned fleet. Gilbert further assigned drying stages or racks in perpetuity on designated areas of the shore to certain fishers, outlawed the public exercise of any religion but that of the Church of England, and erected a wooden pillar bearing the royal coat of arms. Having established England's first overseas colony, Gilbert sailed

1583: Sir Humphrey Gilbert claims Newfoundland for England.

south to claim more territory for the Crown. But it was late in the season and when one of his ships foundered on a sand bar off Sable Island, Gilbert decided to make for home. Gilbert chose to remain onboard the small frigate *Squirrel*, rather than the larger *Golden Hind*. When the two vessels came within hailing distance in the stormy North Atlantic on September 9, he gamely called out, "We are as near to Heaven by sea as by land." These were Gilbert's last recorded words; around midnight, the lights went out and all hands on the *Squirrel* were lost as the sea swallowed up the ship.[29]

Gilbert's proclamation of English sovereignty over Newfoundland had little meaning without the establishment of a permanent settlement. This did not happen until 1610 when a company of Bristol and London merchants received a charter to colonize the whole of the island, especially the Avalon Peninsula. John Guy was named governor of the colony and set out with a group of 39 colonists. The colonists settled at Cuper's Cove on Conception Bay, where they erected dwellings and fortifications, cleared the land, and put in crops. Although they experienced a mild first winter and suffered few losses, the spring brought harassment from pirates and hostility from the seasonal fishers accustomed to coming ashore to dry their catch and repair their gear. Appeals to London for help fell on deaf ears.

Despite these setbacks, Guy was eager to scout out the area for future settlement sites and to make contact with the local people, the Beothuk. Although the Beothuk tended to avoid the Europeans who occupied many of their summer fishing camps, Guy convinced them that he came in friendship. At Bull's Arm, Guy and the Beothuk exchanged gifts, feasted, and traded. But these friendly relations did not last. Unable to use many of their traditional coastal fishing camps, the Beothuk had come to rely on salmon, which they harvested upstream away from the European interlopers. When the English planters, as the colonists were called, began to string nets across the mouths of the salmon rivers, the Beothuk cut the nets and began to plunder the settlers' supplies. Historian and archeologist Ralph Pastore has questioned sensationalist stories that assert that the Beothuk were systematically exterminated by European newcomers, who shot them on sight and paid a bounty for Beothuk heads. The Beothuk did indeed become an extinct people by early in the nineteenth century, and retaliations for thefts were not uncommon, but Pastore maintained that loss of traditional access to resources was a more likely cause.[30]

The colony at Cuper's Cove struggled: the weather was harsh and the soil poor. Nonetheless, additional settlers, including sixteen women, arrived in 1612. Although Guy was named governor of Newfoundland, his attempts to regulate the fishery failed. Relations with the company of merchants financing the colony soured when the venture failed to turn a quick profit. Frustrated, Guy returned to England in 1615. Although he

1610: A permanent English settlement is established at Cuper's Cove, Newfoundland.

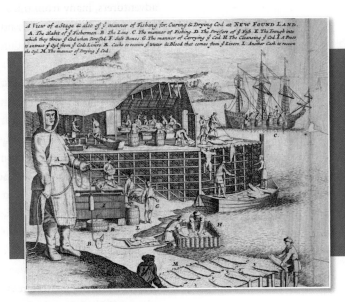

On-shore drying station.

Source: Library and Archives Canada, C-003686.

never came back to Newfoundland, Guy continued to champion the interests of its settlers. Determined to ensure that the colonists had access to the rich resources of the sea, Guy opposed a bill introduced into the British Parliament in 1622 allowing British-based fishers virtually unrestricted access to the Newfoundland fishery. His protests failed, and so began a long history of outsiders reaping most of the benefits of Newfoundland's resources, while its residents struggled for subsistence.

The English Search for the Northwest Passage

In 1576, a few years before Sir Humphrey Gilbert's voyage to Newfoundland, a group of London merchants commissioned Martin Frobisher, a sometime mariner, privateer, and explorer, to lead an expedition to find the Northwest Passage. Frobisher had been captivated by Humphrey Gilbert's *Discourse of a Discoverie for a New Passage to Cataia*, which argued for the existence of a passage to Asia across the top of North America. Besides offering the advantage of a more direct route to Asia, Gilbert believed that new territory discovered could be settled by "such needie people of our Countrie which now trouble the common welth."[31]

Frobisher sailed from London with a tiny armada of three ships that June. During the hazardous North Atlantic crossing, one of Frobisher's ships sank and another turned back. The lone vessel carried on, sighting land on July 28, 1576. This was probably Resolution Island, which he named Queen Elizabeth's foreland. Continuing westward, Frobisher entered what he believed to be a great strait leading to Asia, and named it after himself. The strait was in fact Baffin Island's Frobisher Bay. There he met Inuit who came out to his ship to trade. Frobisher persuaded one of the Inuit to pilot his ship into the "west sea," and sent five of his sailors ashore to accompany the party. None of the men were seen again. Attempts to summon the lost sailors by firing cannon and blowing trumpets did not avail. His crew having dwindled to a mere 13, many of them ill, Frobisher desperately decided to lure an Inuit hostage on to his ship to ransom him for his own men. He rang a bell and pretended to make a gift of this prize to a hunter who came alongside the ship to investigate. In a frantic bid to escape capture, the hunter bit his own tongue in two. The plan to barter prisoners did not succeed, however; when Frobisher returned with the captive hunter to the spot where his men had disappeared, he found the place deserted. The weather was worsening, and a dispirited Frobisher set sail for England, his Inuit captive offering proof that he had indeed reached a far and strange land. London was captivated by the strange man and his boat, but the exotic novelty from the new world was dead within two weeks of reaching England.[32]

Frobisher had also carried some black rock back to England with him as a token of "Christian possession" of the land. When a London assayer declared that the rock contained gold, gold fever swept England. Investors in Frobisher's first voyage joined with others to form the Cathay Company to finance a second voyage. This time, the goal was not discovery of the Northwest Passage, but to search for gold. In July 1577, Frobisher returned to the small island where he had landed the previous summer. There he erected a cross on a high hill and claimed the land in the name of God and the English Crown. Witnessing the arrival and ritual, Inuit came to trade. But Frobisher's capture of an Inuit man to use as an interpreter strained relations, and Frobisher himself was wounded by an arrow during

1576: Martin Frobisher launches his first expedition in search of a Northwest Passage to Asia.

a skirmish. Matters worsened when Frobisher's crew discovered a few items of European clothing among the Inuit. These had presumably belonged to the sailors lost the previous summer. Determined to find the men, Frobisher launched a raid against a nearby village. Five or six Inuit were killed, and a man, woman, and child were captured. Frobisher returned to England with his Inuit prisoners and almost 200 tonnes of black rock. The three captives were a great attraction when they landed at Bristol, but all three died within a few weeks of their arrival. The real attraction, however, was the black rock. Thrilled by the haul, Elizabeth I named the new land Meta Incognita, or the unknown limits. Although assayers gave widely differing estimates of the value of the ore Frobisher had brought back, investors chose to believe the most hopeful reports. A third, more ambitious, expedition was organized.

The expedition was launched in the spring of 1578—a fleet of 15 ships carrying some 400 men—but was plagued with problems from the beginning. Poor weather delayed the passage, one ship was crushed in the ice, and another forced to return to England. Inuit hunters, who had provided fresh meat in the past, now avoided the English and spurned efforts to trade. Spoilage of provisions, and the loss of the timber that was to be used to construct barracks for the men who were to winter at the mine, convinced Frobisher to abandon plans for a settlement. Despite these difficulties, Frobisher returned to England with over 1000 tonnes of what he believed to be gold-bearing ore. Although efforts to refine the ore continued for several years, it was ultimately proven worthless.

With of the passing of the Arctic gold rush, the search for a northern route to the Indies free of Spanish and Portuguese interference resumed. John Davis, who enjoyed the patronage of the Queen's secretary, Sir Francis Walsingham, and the financial support of wealthy merchants in London and Devon, conducted three expeditions in search of the Northwest Passage between 1585 and 1587. Davis charted much of the coasts of Greenland, Labrador, and Baffin Island but did not succeed in finding any northern passage to China.

The English navigator, Henry Hudson, resumed the search in 1610. Hudson passed through the treacherous straits between Labrador and Baffin Island and entered into the bay that would bear his name.

Convinced that he had reached the Pacific, Hudson sailed south before reaching a dead end at the southern tip of James Bay. It was late in the season and Hudson's ship, the *Discovery*, became locked in the ice. Ill-prepared to spend the winter, Hudson ordered his crew to erect a shelter. Surviving on short rations and afflicted with scurvy, the men became increasingly discontented. Hudson's hopes of obtaining fresh meat from the Natives were dashed when they refused contact and set a forest fire to keep the English intruders at a distance from their village. Despite the lack of provisions, the bull-headed Hudson insisted that explorations resume when the ice broke up in the late spring. The crew mutinied, casting Hudson, his son Jack, and few remaining supporters and ill crew members adrift in a small boat. They were never seen again. The mutineers headed back north and landed at Digges Island, where they hoped to acquire food from Inuit hunters. No doubt recalling the treachery of earlier English interlopers, the Inuit attacked the shore party and killed Thomas Greene and William Wilson. When the remaining crew finally returned to England, Greene and Wilson were conveniently identified as the leaders of the mutiny, and none of Hudson's men were ever punished for their mutinous acts.

1577 and 1578: Frobisher's second and third voyages to North America are launched.

1610: English navigator Henry Hudson explores Hudson Bay.

Acadia and the Beginnings of New France

Shortly after the English proclaimed their first North American colony in Newfoundland, the French developed a renewed interest in Canada. The proclamation of the Edict of Nantes in 1598 ended France's long civil war between Protestants and Catholics. With peace, France could once again look beyond its own borders. Anxious not to be shut out of the Americas, the French monarch, Henri IV, sought to promote colonization by granting wealthy merchants an exclusive right to trade with the Natives in return for establishing French settlements there. Although Canada lacked the gold and silver of New Spain, its furs promised to supply the French fashion industry with the beaver felt used to make hats.

After several other ventures failed, the Crown granted a trading monopoly in 1603 to Pierre du Gua de Monts, a Protestant soldier and administrator. The terms of his commission required that de Monts settle 60 colonists a year and that he "lead the natives to the profession of the Christian faith, to civilization of manners, an ordered life, practice and intercourse with the French for the gain of their commerce; and finally their recognition and submission to the authority of the Crown of France."[33] Rather than establish a colony along the St. Lawrence, de Monts searched out a location with a more temperate climate along the Atlantic coast. The French called the region surrounding the Bay of Fundy "Acadia," the name first used by the explorer Verrazano the century before, perhaps in homage to the area's Arcadian beauty. The name may also derive from the Mi'kmaq word "quoddy" (cady, cadie), meaning a piece of land. De Monts named the first land he sighted Cap de la Hève, after the last point seen in France, symbolically linking the old world and the new.[34]

1604: Pierre du Gua de Monts establishes French outpost on Ile St. Croix.

Included among the 80 colonists were assorted artisans, tradesmen, soldiers, vagabonds, noblemen, and both Catholic and Protestant clergy. An interpreter who could speak the Mi'kmaq language, Mathieu d'Acosta, was an African who had earlier travelled to the area with Portuguese traders. Also among the party was the man who would become known as the "father of New France," an experienced soldier, accomplished navigator and mapmaker, Samuel de Champlain. Arriving in May 1604, the party met a group of Mi'kmaq, led by Messamouet, a courteous and experienced trader who spoke French and who had once travelled to France in a Basque fishing boat and been a guest of the governor of Bayonne. This reassuring encounter enabled the newcomers to begin trade and provided valuable knowledge of the area.

After scouting the area, de Monts established his fledgling settlement on a small island in the middle of the Sainte-Croix River, a position that he believed would be defensible against attack. This was just beyond the borders of Míkmáki, in the territory of the Maliseet. The Maliseet nation is also sometime referred to as the Wolastoqiyik, a name that reflects their geographical and spiritual bond with the River Wolastoq (the Saint John River). The interpreter Mathieu d'Acosta was able to assure the local people that they had come in peace, that they wanted to farm but not to take away Maliseet land. Diplomatically, no mention was made of the goal of religious conversion, although Champlain recorded that rosaries were given out as gifts. Most of the expedition did not winter at the settlement. Instead, they returned to France with a load of furs, fish, and a caribou as a special gift to the king. When a customs official hesitated over the bales of imported furs, he was evidently given royal instructions to treat New France as French territory, an extension of the old world.[35]

The unlucky colonists who remained behind spent a miserable winter. By the first week of October, the snow was already waist-deep. Wood for fuel was scarce, most of the island's trees having been used for building. The water spring froze, and even cider rations were frozen solid. Dangerous ice floes, tossed by gigantic tides, made retreat to the mainland or hunting expeditions impossible. Confined to an island with little to do, with little fresh food, most became afflicted with scurvy, and nearly half died. The local Maliseet—whose presence had dictated de Monts's defensive strategy of locating on an island—came to the rescue in the spring when they arrived with fresh meat to trade. The spring also brought supply ships from France and 40 new men to augment the colony. The new arrivals brought news that de Monts's trading monopoly was in jeopardy, and he resolved to return to France to protect his interests. Before leaving, de Monts ordered the structures erected the previous year dismantled and relocated to a new site, Port-Royal, across the Bay of Fundy.

Port-Royal was Mi'kmaq territory. The chief, Membertou, was a tall and aged man with a white beard. In fact, he told the French that he had witnessed the arrival of Cartier. It was Membertou's grandmother who had had the prophetic dream of newcomers wearing white rabbit skins that had presaged the coming of the Europeans. Relations between the Natives and newcomers were good, but Membertou waved off any mention of an alliance. Instead, he linked together his index fingers to symbolize the relationship, and gave them to understand that they were his guests, under his protection. He also required the ceremonial firing of the cannon in salute when he approached the French settlement.[36] These friendly overtures caused Champlain to conclude optimistically that the Natives "would be speedily brought to be good Christians, if their country were colonised, which most of them would like."[37]

De Monts remained in France the following year to defend his business concerns but dispatched supplies and additional men to Port-Royal. During the summer of 1605, Champlain journeyed south as far as Cape Cod, exploring settlement potential. He also oversaw construction of a "habitation," a group of buildings clustered around a central courtyard. This was the earliest substantial European construction settlement in what would later be Canadian territory. While the winter proved less severe than the last, 12 settlers were still lost to scurvy. With the coming of spring, Champlain again resumed explorations, travelling south to map much of the northern Atlantic coast, searching for mineral deposits, and scouting out places to plant a colony. Determined to confront squarely the prospect of another bleak winter, Champlain launched a scheme for a social club, the Order of Good Cheer, to lift the spirits of the men. They organized theatrical productions and took turns supplying the company with game, fish, and fowl for banquets, to which Membertou and other chiefs were invited. The assembled company enjoyed such delicacies as mussels cooked under pine needles, quenelles of cod with lobster sauce, cranberry marmalade, and venison pie. Yet just as the colony seemed poised on the brink of success, de Monts's monopoly was revoked. The colonists returned to France in the fall of 1607, entrusting Port-Royal to Membertou.

De Monts persuaded French authorities to renew his monopoly for a year, and a close associate, Jean de Biencourt de Poutrincourt, returned to Port-Royal in 1610. A devout Catholic, Biencourt was accompanied by a priest, Jessé Fléché, who baptized Membertou and his family. Membertou took the Christian name Henri, after the French king, his wife becoming Marie, after the queen regent. News of the Native baptisms piqued the interest of the Jesuits, who dispatched two priests, Pierre Biard and Enemond Massé, to Acadia the following year. Madame de Geurcheville, the devout wife of the governor of Paris, became their patron, supplying funds in support of the mission. She was the first of several wealthy French women to sponsor religious activities in New France. The Jesuits were shocked to learn that Fléché did not speak Mi'kmaq and had not provided instruction to Membertou and his family. Determined not to repeat Fléché's errors, Massé went to live among the Mi'kmaq to learn their language and their ways.

1613: Samuel Argall of Virginia captures Port-Royal.

Yet this new promising beginning again collapsed in failure. In 1613, Samuel Argall, a pirate adventurer of the English colony of Virginia, led a raiding party who sacked and burned Port-Royal. In 1621, Queen Elizabeth's successor, James I—who was also James VI of Scotland—granted Acadia to Sir William Alexander, who renamed it Nova Scotia ("new Scotland"). A small band of Scots settled at Port-Royal, which they renamed Charlesfort, in 1629. But the Scots, too, were forced to abandon the site after Acadia was returned to France by treaty in 1632.

1608: Samuel de Champlain founds a French settlement at Quebec.

In the meantime, with French interest more acute in the St. Lawrence area, de Monts had dispatched Champlain to locate a suitable site for a trading post and settlement there. In 1608, Champlain sailed up the St. Lawrence and built a new habitation at Quebec. Situated at the point where the river narrowed, Quebec was strategically placed to control access to the interior and to prevent competition from clandestine traders. This vital spot had been the village of Stadacona that Jacques Cartier had visited in 1535. Yet the St. Lawrence Iroquois, Donnacona's people, had vanished from the site by the time of Champlain's arrival.

There is no certain explanation as to why, but various theories have been proposed. It may be that European diseases diminished the population. Others have suggested that crop failure could be to blame: the area is at the northern limit for crops such as corn and beans. The site may have been abandoned in favour of more promising agricultural land. Perhaps the St. Lawrence Iroquois succumbed to the powerful military force created by the formation of the Iroquois League of Five Nations. Perhaps nations further inland, such as the Huron, resented the efforts of the Stadaconans to control access to French trade goods. The presence of Iroquoian-style pottery among the Huron suggests the possibility that Iroquoian women were taken as "captive brides" during raids, since the women were the ones who crafted such pots. Distinctive Iroquoian ceramic pipes found in what is now upstate New York indicate that Iroquoian men were present in this region. Could they have been involved in diplomatic talks with the Iroquois League, perhaps being assimilated in the process?[38] Such explanations are only speculative, of course, and there is no definitive answer.

De Monts and Champlain struggled to keep their colony on the St. Lawrence alive. The fur trade monopoly they had received from the French Crown expired, and the death in 1610 of King Henri IV, whose favour de Monts had enjoyed, meant that the trade was now thrown open to all French competitors. Champlain, therefore, felt that he had little choice when a party of Montagnais, Algonquin, and Huron sought his support for a raid against their Iroquoian enemies to the southwest. A firm military alliance would, he believed, ensure a plentiful supply of high-quality furs for Quebec. On July 30, 1609, the war party confronted a band of Mohawk at Ticonderoga on Lake Champlain. A few shots from French arquebuses easily scattered the enemy war party, who had never seen guns before.

About the time that Champlain joined in the raid on the Iroquois at Ticonderoga, Henry Hudson had been sailing up the Hudson River just to the south. Hudson had been commissioned by the Dutch East India Company to find a route to Asia. Although that endeavour had failed, the voyage alerted the Dutch to the opportunities the region offered for trade and agriculture. Anxious to establish their own foothold in North America, the Dutch quickly formed an alliance with the Iroquois, setting in play the prolonged conflict that pitted rival European powers and their Native allies against one another.

Champlain continued to build on his alliance with his Aboriginal allies. He took part in another raid on the Iroquois in 1610, and demonstrated his personal courage by canoeing down the treacherous Lachine Rapids with a group of Algonquin warriors. As an expression of trust and goodwill, the allies agreed to send representatives to live with their trade and military partners. Champlain entrusted 17-year-old Étienne Brûlé into the care of Iroquet, an Algonquin chief, and in turn received a Huron youth, Savignon. Brûlé spent more than 20 years among the Huron, learning their language and customs, and exploring territory never before seen by Europeans. Champlain himself spent considerable time in the wilderness to consolidate diplomatic relations. On a journey in 1613, while making a portage near Green Lake to avoid rapids on the Ottawa River, Champlain lost his astrolabe. It lay undisturbed until 1867 when a 14-year-old boy helping his father clear trees discovered it. It is now housed at the Canadian Museum of Civilization.

Champlain's success at establishing alliances with the Natives and expanding the fur trade was rewarded in 1612 when he was given vice-regal powers to administer justice, uphold the Crown's laws, and oversee relations with the Natives. He has thus sometimes been viewed as Canada's first "governor general." In the meantime, on a visit home to France, Champlain also married. Already over 40, Champlain wed Hélène Boullé, who was not yet 12 years old. The couple did not spend much time together: Madame Champlain was reluctant to come to Canada, and only lived there between 1620 and 1624.

After 1612, Champlain sought to make New France more than a fur trade colony and increasingly devoted himself to colonization and economic diversification. This shift in priorities had a significant impact on Champlain's relations with the Natives. Champlain was determined to convince them to abandon their traditional ways, take up farming, accept French culture, and embrace Christianity. Influenced by the atmosphere of piety and religious enthusiasm of the Catholic Reformation, Champlain was confident that "in the course of time and through association with others" the Natives would "acquire a French heart and spirit."[39] Ultimately, he hoped the French and Christian Natives would intermarry and form a single people.

1609: The Dutch begin imperial activities in what would later be New York.

Champlain's astrolabe.

Source: Canadian Museum of Civilization.

Champlain took the first tangible steps toward conversion and acculturation in 1614 when he enlisted the services of four Récollet missionaries to convince the Natives to abandon "their filthy habits, loose morals, and uncivilized ways" and "to render them sedentary and to bring them up in our manner and laws."[40] A reformed Franciscan order founded in Paris at the end of the sixteenth century and active in social work among the poor, the Récollets appeared to Champlain to be well suited to work among the Aboriginal people of New France. The Récollets were convinced that the Natives must first be Europeanized if they were to become Christians. At first, the Récollets focused their efforts on the Montagnais, who lived a nomadic hunting life north of Quebec but came to the French to trade. The Montagnais—"Mountain people" to the French—are now known as Innu. Rather than live among the Montagnais, the Récollets established a number of agricultural mission stations around Quebec. The Récollets believed the Natives would benefit from contact with French settlers and exposure to French manners and customs.

The Montagnais proved unwilling to abandon their way of life and the Récollets decided to redirect their efforts to the Huron, an agricultural people inhabiting the lands between Lake Simcoe and Georgian Bay, a strategic location between the Algonquian nomadic hunter-gatherers to the north and the Iroquoian farmers to the south. The Récollets were attracted by the more settled and sedentary life of the Huron, and established a mission among them at the village of Carhagouha in 1616. The Récollets were impressed by the hospitality and generosity of the Huron people, but repelled by the relative power of women, the permissive upbringing of children, and the sexual freedom among youth. The Récollet mission to the Huron was not a great success. The missionaries had difficulty learning the Huron language and were thus hindered in their ability to communicate the Christian message. Unlike the French traders, the Récollets refused to live among the unconverted Natives, and thus did not really get to know them or acquire their trust. The Huron tolerated the Récollets among them, apparently seeing them as a means of cementing their alliance with the French, but did not embrace Christianity. One of the missionaries, Gabriel Sagard, complained that the Huron "leave everyone to his own belief."[41]

The year before the Récollet missionaries came to live among the Huron, Champlain joined a Huron war party in a raid on the Iroquois. But his participation in this 1615 raid differed significantly from that of 1609 and 1610: as he was now the colonial representative of the French Crown, Champlain assumed that the Huron had invited him to command the expedition. The Huron viewed Champlain as an ally, who, like any other, had the right to be consulted and to express an opinion. Champlain's concept of European command had no meaning among the Huron, who were moved by one's powers of persuasion and example, not by any abstract notion of authority. Not only did Champlain misjudge the role he was to play in the raid, he misconstrued the purpose of the raid itself. The objective was not the total destruction of the Iroquois village, as Champlain assumed, but simply to force the Iroquois warriors to engage in traditional hand-to-hand combat. Champlain was frustrated by what he saw as the lack of concerted action during the battle, and the Iroquois victory strained relations between the Huron and the French. Champlain himself had to be carried from the scene of battle with two arrow wounds in his knee.[42]

Appalled by his arrogant behaviour, the Huron compelled Champlain to spend the winter of 1616 at Huronia in the hope that he might better understand their society and culture. This did not happen. Champlain's conviction that Native society was innately inferior and in desperate need of civilization was only reinforced. From 1616 until his death in 1635, chronic misunderstanding plagued Champlain's relations with France's Native allies. In 1616 and again in 1629, Champlain refused gifts offered by the Montagnais as compensation for the murder of two French traders and insisted that the Montagnais turn the perpetrators of the crime over to him for trial. Champlain relented only when the significance of the blood feud in Montagnais society was impressed upon him. When Miristou sought Champlain's support to become headman of his band in 1622, Champlain assumed that this was recognition of his own authority over the Montagnais. In fact, Miristou was simply following a traditional courtesy. Champlain later insisted that a council of headmen of his own choosing be established to regulate relations between the Montagnais and the French. To the disapproval of all, Champlain appointed Chomina to the council, a man who had close ties with the French, but whose trustworthiness was suspect among the Natives. Such callous behaviour threatened to destroy the alliances Champlain had successfully built over the years.

In 1626, Champlain's quest to establish a viable colony took him back to France, where he met with Cardinal Richelieu, Louis XIII's chief minister. Richelieu, convinced by Champlain of New France's vast potential and of the necessity of colonization, obligingly chartered the Company of One Hundred Associates (Compagnie des Cent-Associés), also known as the Company of New France, the following year. In return for a monopoly in the fur trade, the company was required to provide New France with several hundred settlers a year. The charter stipulated that only Catholics were to be settled in New France and that a suitable number of priests were to accompany the colonists; Richelieu did not wish to see France's religious tensions carried over to the new world. With the formation of the Company of One Hundred Associates, it seemed as if Champlain's vision of colonization was about to be realized.

1627: Company of One Hundred Associates is granted a fur trade monopoly in New France.

But that very same year, France's position in North America became precarious when war broke out with England. Determined to profit from the conflict, a company of London merchants sought to establish a trading post on the St. Lawrence and to reassert the British claim to Canada laid by John Cabot in 1497. A fleet of three ships was dispatched to the area in 1628 under the command of privateer David Kirke. Kirke had been born in Dieppe, and his family, which appears to have been Huguenot, had business ties on both sides of the English Channel. His brothers, Lewis, Thomas, John, and James, accompanied him on his expedition. The Kirke brothers easily captured Tadoussac in 1628, and found a warm reception from the Montagnais who, dissatisfied with the French, saw an opportunity to exploit French–English rivalry to gain advantages in trade. Kirke next turned his attention to Quebec, and sent a dispatch to Champlain demanding its surrender. Expecting relief to arrive shortly from France, Champlain rejected the demand. Kirke decided not to press on to Quebec that season, but as the returning fleet reached the open water off the coast of Gaspé, another opportunity presented itself. Champlain's eagerly awaited supply fleet was just arriving, and Kirke captured the four vessels as prizes of war. On board the

French vessels were the first 400 settlers sent by the Company of One Hundred Associates, and these hapless victims of the war found themselves carried to England as prisoners.

Inspired by the Kirke brothers' impressive victory, a group of English and Scottish merchants commissioned a second, larger expedition the following year to take Quebec itself. A French traitor, the Huguenot fur trader Jacques Michel, aided the English cause by piloting the invading fleet down the St. Lawrence to Quebec. His reinforcements having never arrived, Champlain had little choice but to surrender Quebec to the Kirke brothers on July 19, 1629.

1629: Quebec is captured by the English.

Michel was not the only traitor. Étienne Brûlé, sent as a boy to live among the Huron, also converted to the English side during the war and commenced trade with the Iroquois, England's allies. Brûlé little knew that English possession of Canada would not last. When fortunes changed and the French were again in control, their Huron allies tortured Brûlé to death.

The fall of Quebec to the Kirke brothers was a telling sign of New France's weakness and vulnerability. The colony of New France was inhabited by fewer than 100 French traders, fishers, artisans, and missionaries, and could claim only one settled farm family: The apothecary and farmer Louis Hébert and his wife Marie Rollet had arrived with their three children in 1617. By the time of the English attack, Louis was dead, having slipped on the ice in 1627. Madame Hébert opted to stay on in Quebec with her two surviving grown children and her grandchildren, she herself having remarried.

In contrast to the struggling New France, the Dutch and English colonies to the south were beginning to thrive. The Dutch West India Company established a fur trading operation at Fort Orange on the Hudson River in 1624, which quickly became a serious rival to the French. Although the Dutch colony of New Netherland grew slowly, by 1629 its population was three times that of New France. Concerns about Dutch competition prompted Champlain to negotiate a peace treaty with the Iroquois in 1624. But the peace provided by the treaty was only temporary, and came at the cost of increasingly strained relations with France's existing allies, the Montagnais and the Huron. Further south, the English colonies at Jamestown (in the state of Virginia today) and Plymouth (Massachusetts) were growing in prosperity. Founded in 1607 as a commercial venture, the Jamestown colony struggled for several years to overcome disease—the area was a swampy tidal flat and prone to malaria—and hostility from the local Natives. Unsurprisingly, a colony founded for agricultural purposes would have less need for friendship with Natives than would a fur trading post, and in the decades that followed, warfare between Natives and newcomers was endemic. Nevertheless, by the time of Quebec's capture by the English, there was a string of profitable tobacco plantations along the waterways of the Chesapeake. The colony of Plymouth, founded just nine years earlier by Pilgrim separatists who broke from the Church of England, already boasted more than 300 farmers and artisans.

Yet, despite the slower growth of its own North American colonies, France was eager to regain control of the St. Lawrence and Acadia. Profits were to be made in the fur trade, and France was not willing to concede the North American continent to its English and Dutch rivals. France stuck to this goal in treaty negotiations at the war's end, and the 1632 Treaty of St-Germain-en-Laye restored French possession of Canada and Acadia. The cash-strapped Charles I of England, unable to raise funds through his recalcitrant Parliament, had opted to relinquish New France in exchange for a one-million-*livre* payment. Champlain returned to Quebec in 1633, picking through the ruins of a once promising colonial settlement that had been razed to the ground by the departing Kirke brothers. Undaunted, he set about to rebuild New France.

Conclusion

The hundred years since Cartier's explorations had brought permanent change to what would later be Canada. On the face of it, the impact seemed small: only tiny numbers of newcomers occupied New France and the English fishing settlements in Newfoundland. Yet the impact on Aboriginal societies was profound. New trade goods brought irreversible changes to Native economies and ways of life. The introduction of European diseases had already begun to take its grim toll, a devastating process that would recur in cataclysmic waves right up to the early twentieth century and which would all but annihilate some communities. Religious conversions were still modest in scope, but the European project of evangelizing the new world had already begun, with some prominent Native leaders embracing Christianity. European rivalries over interests in North America intersected with complicated traditional alliances and rivalries among Aboriginal nations. In appearance, the imperial impact was superficial; in reality, it reached deep.

Questions to Consider

1. Discuss the different theories about how North America was first populated.

2. Review the emergence of distinct regional indigenous cultures. What factors contributed to the development of different cultural complexes?

3. What developments contributed to European interest in overseas exploration?

4. What were the objectives of French colonization in Acadia and New France? To what degree were these objectives achieved prior to 1629?

Critical Thinking Questions

1. How are historians able to make use of insights gained from other disciplines?

2. How did European explorers describe Aboriginal peoples and their societies?

3. Cite some examples of misunderstandings between Natives and newcomers. What factors lay at the root of these misunderstandings?

4. What is the difference between a primary source and a secondary source? Discuss some of the questions a historian might bear in mind in approaching these sources.

Suggested Readings
Pre-contact Native Society

Dickason, Olive. Canada's *First Peoples: A History of the Founding Peoples from Earliest Years.* Toronto: McClelland & Stewart, 2002.

Fagan, Brian. *The Great Journey: The Peopling of Ancient America.* London: Thames and Hudson, 1987.

Fladmark, K.R. *Prehistory of British Columbia.* Ottawa: National Museum of Man, 1986.

Haynes, Gary. *The Early Settlement of North America: The Clovis Era.* Cambridge: Cambridge University Press, 2002.

Kehoe, Alice. *America Before the European Invasions.* London: Pearson, 2002.

Krech, Shepard. *The Ecological Indian: Myth and History.* New York: W. W. Norton & Company, 2000.

Magocsi, Paul Robert, ed. *Aboriginal Peoples of Canada: A Short Introduction.* Toronto: University of Toronto Press, 2002.

McGee, Robert. *Canadian Arctic Prehistory.* Toronto: Van Nostrand Reinhold, 1978.

McMillan, Alan D., and Eldon Yellowhorn. *First Peoples in Canada.* Vancouver: Douglas and McIntyre, 2004.

Ray, Arthur J. *I Have Lived Here Since the World Began: An Illustrated History of Canada's Native People.* Toronto: Key Porter, 1996.

Rogers, E.S., and Donald B. Smith, eds. *Aboriginal Ontario.* Toronto: Dundurn Press, 1994.

Sioui, George E. *Huron-Wendat: Heritage of the Circle.* Vancouver: University of British Columbia Press, 2000.

Trigger, Bruce. *The Children of Aataenstic: A History of the Huron People to 1600.* Montreal and Kingston: McGill-Queen's University Press, 1987.

Tuck, James A. *Newfoundland and Labrador Prehistory.* Ottawa: National Museum of Man, 1976.

Tuck, James A. *Maritime Provinces Prehistory.* Ottawa: National Museum of Man, 1984.

Wright, J.V. *A History of the Native Peoples of Canada, Volume 1: 10,000–1,000 BC.* Hull: Canadian Museum of Civilization, 1995.

Wright, J.V. *A History of the Native Peoples of Canada, Volume 2: 1000 BC–AD 500.* Hull: Canadian Museum of Civilization, 1999.

Wright, J.V. *Quebec Prehistory.* Toronto: Van Nostrand Reinhold, 1979.

Norse Settlement

Chapman, Paul H. *The Norse Discovery of America.* Atlanta: One Candle Press, 1981.

Oleson, Tryggvi J. *Early Voyages and Northern Approaches.* Toronto: McClelland & Stewart, 1963.

Wallace, Birgitta, "The Norse in Newfoundland: L'Anse aux Meadows and Vinland," *Newfoundland Studies* 19 (Spring 2003): 5–43.

"Where Is Vinland?" Great Unsolved Mysteries in Canadian History. http://www.canadianmysteries.ca/sites/vinland/home/indexen.html.

European Expansion and Exploration

Brebner, J.B. *The Explorers of North America.* London: A. & C. Black, 1933.

Cook, Ramsay. *The Voyages of Jacques Cartier.* Toronto: University of Toronto Press, 1993.

Cooke, Alan, and Clive Holland. *The Exploration of Northern Canada.* Toronto: Arctic History Press, 1978.

Gordon, Alan. *The Hero and the Historians: Historiography and the Uses of Jacques Cartier.* Vancouver: University of British Columbia Press, 2010.

Morison, Samuel E. *The European Discovery of America: The Northern Voyages, A.D. 500–1600.* New York: Oxford University Press, 1971.

Pope, Peter Edward. *The Many Landfalls of John Cabot.* Toronto: University of Toronto Press, 1997.

Rouse, Alfred L. *The Expansion of Elizabethan England.* London: Macmillan, 1955.

The Cod Fishery

Cell, Gillian T. *English Enterprise in Newfoundland, 1577–1660.* Toronto: University of Toronto Press, 1969.

Cell, Gillian T. *Newfoundland Discovered.* London: Hakluyt Society, 1982.

Innis, Harold A. *The Cod Fisheries: The History of an International Economy.* Toronto: University of Toronto Press, 1954.

Marcus, G.J. *The Conquest of the North Atlantic.* Woodbridge, Suffolk: Boydell Press, 1980.

Pope, Peter Edward. *Fish into Wine: the Newfoundland Plantation in the seventeenth century.* Chapel Hill: University of North Carolina Press, 2004.

Early Colonization

Axtell, James. *Natives and Newcomers: The Cultural Origins of North America.* New York: Oxford University Press, 2000.

Crosby, Alfred W. *Ecological Imperialism: The Biological Expansion of Europe, 900–1900.* Cambridge: Cambridge University Press, 2004.

Eccles, W.J. *The Canadian Frontier, 1534–1760.* Toronto: Holt, Rinehart and Winston, 1969.

Eccles, W.J. *France in America.* Markham, ON: Fitzhenry and Whiteside, 1990.

Fischer, David Hackett. *Champlain's Dream.* Toronto: Alfred A. Knopf, 2008.

Grant, John Webster. *Moon of Wintertime: Missionaries and the Indians of Canada in Encounter since 1534.* Toronto: University of Toronto Press, 1984.

Harris, Cole. *The Reluctant Land: Society, Space and Environment in Canada Before Confederation.* Vancouver: University of British Columbia Press, 2008.

Heidenreich, Conrad. *Explorations and Mapping of Samuel de Champlain, 1603–1632.* Toronto: B.G. Gutsel, 1976.

Jaenen, Cornelius. *Friend and Foe: Aspects of French–Amerindian Cultural Contact in the Sixteenth and Seventeenth Centuries*. New York: Columbia University Press, 1976.

Jaenen, Cornelius. *The French Relationship with the Native People of New France and Acadia*. Ottawa: Indian and Northern Affairs Canada, 1984.

Litalien, Raymonde, Denis Vaugeois, and Käthe Roth, eds. *Champlain: The Birth of French America*. Montreal and Kingston: McGill-Queen's University Press, 2004.

Richter, Daniel K. *Facing East from Indian country: A Native History of Early America*. Cambridge, MA: Harvard University Press, 2001.

Trigger, Bruce. *Natives and Newcomers: Canada's "Heroic Age" Reconsidered*. Montreal and Kingston: McGill-Queen's University Press, 1986.

Trudel, Marcel. *The Beginnings of New France, 1524–1663*. Toronto: McClelland & Stewart, 1973.

Detailed, authoritative information on key figures may be found in the *Dictionary of Canadian Biography*. Available online at http://www.biographi.ca.

Notes

[1] Traditional Mi'kmaq story of foreknowledge of European contact. Marie Battiste, "Nilanikinútmaqn," in James (Sákéj)Youngblood Henderson, *The Mi'kmaw Concordat* (Halifax: Fernwood Publishing, 1997), 18.

[2] Herbert S. Klein and Daniel C. Schiffner, "The Current Debate about the Origins of the Paleoindians of America," *Journal of Social History* 37, no. 2 (Winter 2003), 486–488.

[3] Michael R. Bever, "Too Little, Too Late? The Radiocarbon Chronology of Alaska and the Peopling of the New World," *American Antiquity 71*, no. 4 (October 2006), 605.

[4] Alexis Manaster Ramer, "Tonkawa and Zuni: Two Test Cases for the Greenberg Classification," *International Journal of American Linguistics* 62, no. 3 (July 1996), 264–265; Klein and Schiffner, 488.

[5] Alexis Manaster Ramer, "Sapir's Classifications: Haida and Other Na-Dene Languages," *Anthropological Linguistics* 38, no. 2 (Summer 1996), 179.

[6] Klein and Schiffner, "The Current Debate," 486; Sandro L. Bonatto and Francisco M. Salzano, "A Single and Early Migration for the Peopling of the Americas Supported by Mitochondrial DNA Sequence Data," *Proceedings of the National Academy of Sciences of the United States of America* 94, no. 5 (March 1997), 1869–1871.

[7] Bonatto and Salzano, "A Single and Early Migration," 1867–1878.

[8] Keith Hunley, Jeffrey C. Long, and Francisco Mauro Salzano, "Gene Flow across Linguistic Boundaries in Native North American Populations," *Proceedings of the National Academy of Sciences of the United States of America* 102, no. 5 (February 2005), 1315–17.

[9] Robert McGhee, *The Last Imaginary Place: A Human History of the Arctic World* (Toronto: Key Porter Books, 2004), 53.

[10] Robert W. Park, "The Dorset-Thule Succession in Arctic North America: Assessing Claims for Culture Contact," *American Antiquity* 58, no. 2 (April 1993), 225.

[11] Robert McGhee, *The Last Imaginary Place*, 54.

[12] J.R. Miller, "Introduction," *Aboriginal Peoples of Canada: A Short Introduction*. Paul Robert Magocsi, ed. (Toronto: University of Toronto Press, 2002), 8–9.

[13] Historia Norvegiae as quoted by Robert McGhee, *The Last Imaginary Place*, 93.

[14] Leo Block, *To Harness the Wind: a Short History of the Development of Sails* (Annapolis: Naval Institute Press, 2003), 30–35; John F. Guilmartin, Jr. "The Earliest Shipboard Gunpowder Ordnance: An Analysis of Its Technical Parameters and Tactical Capabilities," *Journal of Military History* 71 (July 2007), 649–669.

15 Antonio Pigafetta, Theodore J. Cachey, *The First Voyage around the World, 1519–1522: An Account of Magellan's Expedition* (Toronto: University of Toronto Press, 2007), 24.

16 As quoted in Peter Whitfield, *New Found Lands: Maps in the History of Exploration* (Abingdon: Routledge, 1998), 49.

17 Ramsay Cook, ed., *The Voyages of Jacques Cartier* (Toronto: University of Toronto Press, 1993), 10–14.

18 Ibid., 24.

19 Ibid., 20–22.

20 As quoted in E. H. Carr, *What Is History?* (Harmondsworth: Penguin, 1964), 8.

21 Documents and other materials that historians use to piece together an account of the past are also primary sources. Census data, letters, photographs, journals, statutes, and records of parliamentary debates, are just a few examples are primary sources.

22 Cook, *The Voyages*, 26–27, 43.

23 Ramsay Cook, "Donnacona Discovers Europe," Introduction to *The Voyages*, xxvi.

24 Marcel Trudel, *The Beginnings of New France 1524–1663*, translated by Patricia Claxton (Toronto: McClelland & Stewart Limited, 1973), 17.

25 "Letter From Lagarto To John The Third, King of Portugal (22 January 1539?)" Documents Relating to Cartier and Roberval, in Cook, *The Voyages*, 131; Cook, *The Voyages*, 82.

26 Cook, *The Voyages*, 67–71.

27 Cook, *The Voyages*, 76–83.

28 "The Letters Patent Graunted by her Majestie to Sir Humfrey Gilbert knight, for the inhabiting and planting of our people in America" in Richard Hakluyt, *The Principal Navigations, Voyages, Traffiques and Discoveries of the English Nation*, vol. 3 (London: Hakluyt Society, 1847–1852) 1691–1692.

29 David B. Quinn, "Sir Humphrey Gilbert," *Dictionary of Canadian Biography*, http://www.biographi.ca.

30 More information about the Beothuk may be found at the Memorial University of Newfoundland's Newfoundland Heritage website, http://www.heritage.nf.ca/aboriginal/beothuk.html.

31 Humphrey Gilbert, *Discourse of a Discoverie for a New Passage to Cataia* (Menston: Scholar Press, 1972; rpr of 1st ed. London: W. Middleton, 1576) 3.

32 Alden T. Vaughan, *Transatlantic Encounters: American Indians in Britain, 1500–1776* (Cambridge: Cambridge University Press, 2006), 1–5.

33 Quoted in Cornelius Jaenen, "Problems of Assimilation in New France, 1604–1645," *French Historical Review*, 4:3 (Spring 1966), 267.

34 *The Mi'kmaw Concordat*, 77.

35 Ibid., 78.

36 Ibid., 79.

37 H.P. Biggar, ed. *The Works of Samuel de Champlain*, vol. 1 (Toronto: The Champlain Society, 1922–36), 117.

38 Anthony Wonderley, "Effigy Pipes, Diplomacy, and Myth: Exploring Interaction St. Lawrence Iroquians and Eastern Iroquois in New York State," *American Antiquity* 70, no. 2 (April 2005), 214–217.

39 W.L. Grant, ed., *The Voyages of Samuel de Champlain, 1604–1618*, vol. 1 (New York: C. Scribner, 1917), 264, 323.

40 H.P. Biggar, ed., *The Works of Samuel de Champlain*, vol. 4, 321.

41 Gabriel Sagard, *The Long Journey to the Country of the Hurons*, ed. George M. Wrong (Toronto: The Champlain Society, 1939), 133.

42 Bruce Trigger, *The Children of Aataenstic: A History of the Huron People to 1600* (Montreal and Kingston: McGill-Queen's University Press, 1987), 312–313.

Furs *and* Faith: New France, *1632–1663*

Jesuit Father Paul Le Jeune was at work in Dieppe when he learned that France had regained its North American colony. He had not asked to be assigned to the distant wilderness of New France, but greeted the call of duty with joy, and left the following day. Along with another priest, Anne De Noüe, who had already spent time in New France, and a lay brother named Gilbert, Le Jeune sailed from the port of Le Havre on April 18, 1632, to re-establish the Jesuit mission. Le Jeune and his companions were wretchedly seasick during the two-month journey on heavy seas. The salted food and lack of fresh water kept them in constant thirst, and Le Jeune was unable to stand, kneel, or sit in his cramped cabin, with cold rain leaking in upon his face. When the ship at last dropped anchor at Tadoussac, Le Jeune first saw those he had been sent to evangelize: a party of 10 or 12 Natives entered the ship's cabin. They seemed to him like masqueraders at Carnival; their cheeks were painted black, their noses blue, and the rest of their faces red. Arriving on shore, Le Jeune saw the spectacle of wooden stakes erected in preparation for the torture of some Iroquois prisoners. But such acts of barbarism did not exceed those of pre-Christian Europe, he reflected. He even mused that the Jesuits could meet the same fate if they fell into the hands of the Iroquois. Continuing the journey upriver to Quebec, Le Jeune went to the home of Marie Hébert's family, New France's only remaining farm settlers. "They were seeking some way of returning to France," Le Jeune recalled, "but having learned

Source: Library and Archives Canada, C-005183.

François de Laval, First Bishop of New France.

that the French were coming back to Québec, they began to regain courage. When they saw our ships coming in with their white flags upon the masts, they knew not how to express their joy. But when they saw us in their home, to celebrate the holy Mass which they had not heard for three years, good God, what joy! Tears fell from the eyes of nearly all, so great was their happiness."[1]

Introduction

The seizure of Canada and Acadia by English privateers in 1629 broke the back of France's fragile colonization experiment, and much work had to be done to regain lost ground with the colony's restoration. Father Le Jeune spent a miserable and discouraging winter at Quebec, unable to speak the local language, and facing hostility from French traders who might have been able to assist him, but who saw the Jesuits as a threat. Le Jeune embraced his trials, convinced that he was but an instrument in the hands of God to be used, broken, and thrown aside if providence so dictated. "I sometimes say to the little crosses which come to me, 'And this also, and as many as you wish, O my God,'" he confided to his superior at Paris.[2] Le Jeune's spirits rebounded the following May when in 1633 Samuel de Champlain returned to Quebec bringing with him four more Jesuits. The Jesuits' vision of a settled Catholic colony in which the French and the Natives would become one people encountered indifference and opposition from both the Aboriginal nations and many French traders. This chapter examines the tensions that developed between those dedicated to the fur trade and those committed to winning Christian converts and creating an agrarian Catholic colony. It also considers other difficulties that plagued New France before 1663: trade competition from the Dutch and the English, an increasing Iroquois threat, metropolitan indifference, and the inability to recruit and settle colonists.

Fur Trade Colony

1632: France regains colonial possessions in North America.

With the restoration of New France in 1632, the Company of One Hundred Associates resumed trading activities. At first, the company's prospects appeared extremely promising. The Algonquians and Hurons continued to travel to Quebec to trade during the English occupation, but, not enjoying the same good relations they had with the French, held back large quantities of fur. When trade with the French recommenced, they brought this great bounty to Quebec, rewarding their old allies with windfall profits, but this bold beginning concealed ominous developments that threatened the company's future prospects. The company was still mired in debt, and the English interregnum had impressed upon the Algonquians and the Hurons that the French were not alone in desiring to trade. With the exhaustion of furs south of the St. Lawrence, the Dutch and their Iroquois allies launched a dangerous challenge to New France's supply of furs and sought to redirect trade south to the Dutch Fort Orange. It was clear that the company could not simply rely on the Hurons and Algonquians to bring the furs they had collected to the French settlements—some way had to be found to extend its reach further west up the St. Lawrence and beyond.

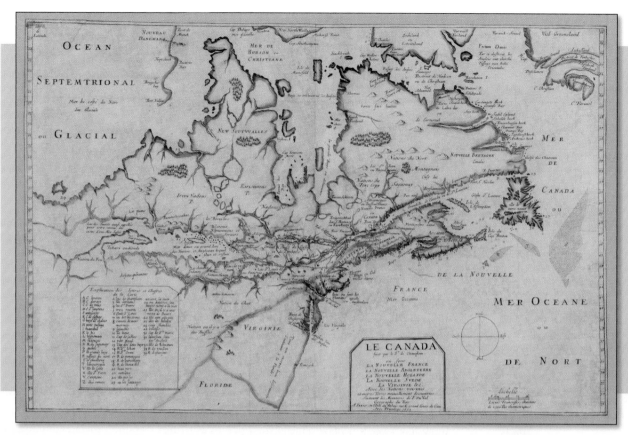

Map 2.1
Canada, 1653.

Source: Library and Archives
Canada, NMC 6333.

*1634: Trois Rivières is
established.*

To Champlain, the solution lay in eliminating the Iroquois threat once and for all and forcing the Dutch and the English to abandon the fur trade. Champlain ordered the construction of new habitations downriver from Quebec at Trois Rivières and on a small island upriver to command the river and protect the town. Determined that the Iroquois should be "brought to reason," Champlain renounced the peace of 1624 and appealed to the Crown to send a militia force out to New France to subdue the Iroquois. Unfortunately for New France, no force was forthcoming, and Champlain's repudiation of the peace treaty simply encouraged Iroquois aggression. Lacking the manpower to launch a direct attack against the Iroquois, Champlain turned to the Church and the missionary efforts of the Jesuits to strengthen the relationship between the French and their Huron and Algonquian allies. If they were Christianized, Champlain reasoned, they would be bound to the French by ties of both faith and commerce and would not succumb to the temptation to trade with the Dutch and English and their Iroquois allies.

Antagonisms and Alliances in Aboriginal Societies

The "beaver wars" between New France and the Iroquois have often been interpreted as a product of competing economic interests. In the nineteenth century, American historian Francis Parkman posited what today we would consider an ethnocentric, if not blatantly racist, explanation of Iroquois hostility: "These crafty savages" were driven both by "homicidal fury" and the hope of "commercial advantage. All five tribes of the [Iroquois] league had become dependent on the English and Dutch of Albany for guns, powder, lead, brandy and many other things that they had learned to regard as necessities. Beaver skins alone could buy them; but to the Iroquois the supply of beaver was limited." To Charles McIlwain, writing in 1915, the stakes were even higher: "The very existence of the Five Nations depended" on their "great role" as "middlemen" of the fur trade.[3] In an influential 1940 study, George T. Hunt asserted that "old institutions and economies had profoundly altered or disappeared completely at the electrifying touch of the white man's trade." This trade divided the tribes of the region "immediately into groups—those who had fur and those who had none," and the ensuing conflict, according to Hunt, could be adequately explained as simply a brutal struggle for control of this lucrative resource.[4]

More recently, historian José Brandao has challenged this view as "monocausal." Questions of historical causation are notoriously difficult to answer with certainty, and many historians are understandably loath to accept simple explanations of complex historical phenomena. Brandao asserts that the Beaver Wars interpretation rests on a number of "unproven assumptions," among these the belief that the Iroquois had run out of furs in their own territory. In addition, far from seeing the warfare as a product of the Iroquois's adoption of European ways, Brandao maintains that "had the Iroquois adopted European materialist values … they might have gained enough economic clout to withstand the pressures put on them by their European neighbours. Instead, they sought to preserve their values and way of life."

Status in Iroquois society did not depend on the accumulation of wealth in the form of material goods. For the Iroquois, warfare was one of the principal means of gaining honour and glory. The blood feud was a defining feature of Iroquois society, and warfare provided a means to avenge an injury or wrong through the taking of captives. Captives might be tortured, a public spectacle meant to strike fear into enemies that appears also to have had a religious significance; alternatively, they might be adopted into families who had lost relatives in war. The latter practice seems to have become increasingly common as, along with warfare, European diseases continued to deplete the Iroquois population. In the mid-1700s, the English naturalist John Bartram observed: "This custom is as antient as our knowledge of them, but when their number of warriors was more than twice as many as now, the relations would more frequently refuse to adopt the prisoners but rather chuse to gratify their thirst for revenge.[sic]"

The French allied themselves with the longstanding enemies of the Iroquois, and were unavoidably drawn into the Iroquois system of honour and blood feuding. "Iroquois efforts to make peace with the French early in the century did not fit with the ambitions the French had for controlling the fur trade and fur-bearing regions," Brandao argues. As the French expanded into lands that the Iroquois considered their own, they "went from being a threat by association and incidental target ... to a direct threat and thus the focus of Iroquois hostilities." The fur trade was important to the Iroquois, but, while Brandao acknowledges this, he makes a subtle but important distinction: "The Iroquois did not want to control the fur trade; they sought only to use it."[5] In other words, it was primarily a means rather than an end of Iroquois military policy—in particular, a means of acquiring weapons needed to defeat their enemies old and new.

The Iroquois (alternatively known as the Haudenosaunee, Haudenoshaunee, or Houde-nosaunee) were a formidable foe. Sometime before the arrival of Europeans, five warring nations—the Seneca, Mohawk, Cayuga, Oneida, and Onondaga—had been brought together in a sophisticated confederacy, the Great League of Peace, by Dekanawidah and Hiawatha. The chronology of this event is disputed: it may have been as early as the twelfth century, or as late as the sixteenth. According to Iroquois tradition, Dekanawidah, a Huron, was a supernaturally gifted individual who received the Great Law of Peace in a vision. With the assistance of Hiawatha, an Onondaga, Dekanawidah convinced the warriors of all five nations to bury their weapons under a great white pine, the Tree of Peace. The Iroquois visualized the League as a longhouse, with the Mohawk the guardians of the eastern door, and the Seneca the guardians of the western door. The centrally located Onondaga were keepers of the fire who called council meetings. The council consisted of 50 chiefs chosen by the female clan elders. Decision making was by persuasion and consensus, with wampum belts made of clam shells used as tangible chronicles of significant events and agreements. Although each nation reserved the right to pursue its own interests and to act independently whenever debate failed to produce a common agreement, the Great League of Peace ensured security. For the French, however, the presence of this powerful confederacy to the south of their fledgling colony produced a constant sense of menace.

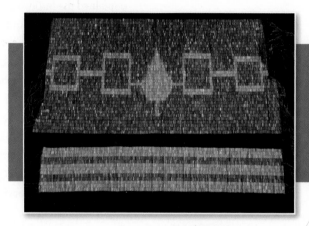

Haudenosaunee wampum belt.

Source: Courtesy of Haudenosaunee.

New France under the Company of One Hundred Associates

As the fortunes of the fur trade faltered, so too did the prospects for the colonization of Canada. In return for its monopoly from the French Crown, the Company of One Hundred Associates had promised to settle 300 Catholic colonists per year in New France. Settling colonists was an expensive business and cut into company profits. Every new colonist also represented a potential free trader and competition to the company. New arrivals frequently found the prospects of a free and adventurous life in the fur trade—shooting rapids in a canoe, and travelling into the backwoods—more appealing than the back-breaking work of clearing land and eking out an existence tilling the soil. The fur trade also offered the possibility of real wealth.

The Company of One Hundred Associates adopted an amended version of the old world's land tenure system, the seigneurial system of medieval France. Large tracts of land called *seigneuries* were granted to individuals and religious orders. Those occupying the individual holdings that made up the seigneurie were called *habitants* or *censitaires*. Because responsibility for settling colonists now rested with the recipients of these land grants, the *seigneurs*, the system also enabled the company to offload the costs of colonization.

Robert Giffard, Quebec's first physician, was one of the earliest seigneurs, receiving a land grant in 1634. Giffard energetically recruited *engagés*, or indentured servants, in France, and set them to work constructing a manor house and clearing the land. Engagés typically laboured for a seigneur for three to five years, receiving a token wage, as well as food and lodging. At the end of their terms of service, engagés could choose either to return to France or to remain in the colony as habitants. The 43 engagés recruited by Giffard represented a significant addition to Canada's population. Father Paul Le Jeune was impressed by the progress made by Giffard, "who has been clearing the land for only two years, and still leaving a great many stumps, hopes to harvest enough this year, if his wheat … yields in proportion to present indications, to maintain twenty persons. The last year's harvest was eight puncheons [barrels] of wheat, two puncheons of peas, three puncheons of Indian corn."[6]

Despite his success, Giffard had few imitators. New France suffered from an acute labour shortage and it was difficult to keep habitants fixed to the land. Why commit oneself to the backbreaking work of clearing the land and eking out an existence tilling the soil when one could easily find work as a tradesmen or labourer or in the fur trade? Such conditions limited seigneurial revenues and discouraged most seigneurs from putting much effort into recruiting colonists. While lords of the manor lived in grand style in France, seigneurs in the colony found that revenues were slim and did not allow them to maintain so elevated a social position. As a result, many held their seigneuries for speculative purposes, the land remaining devoid of settlers for many years. Thus, growth of an agricultural population in New France continued to be very slow.

Religious Establishment in New France

While the fur trade dominated the economic life of New France, religion played an equally important role in the colony's development. New France was founded at a juncture in European history when a revitalized Catholicism was emerging to meet the challenge of the Protestant Reformation. The Roman Catholic Church sought to reform itself by clarifying its teaching and doctrine, educating the clergy, restoring discipline, and eliminating abuses. The Council of Trent (1545–1563), called by Pope Paul III after numerous obstacles, reinvigorated Catholicism: charitable works increased, new religious orders of men and women were formed and older ones expanded, devotional literature flourished, lay devotional societies were founded, and missionary efforts intensified. Historians disagree about what term best captures this phenomenon of renewal. The term "Counter Reformation," which is sometimes used, is problematic, as it implies that all the measures the Roman Catholic Church took in the early modern period were merely reactions to Protestantism. Other terms, such as "Catholic Reform," "Tridentine Reformation," and "Confessional Catholicism," have been championed as replacements. Historian John O'Malley prefers the umbrella term "Early Modern Catholicism," with the other terms used in specific contexts when they are applicable.[7]

The fervency of this reformed Catholicism was carried from France to New France by the Society of Jesus. Founded in 1540 by Basque nobleman Ignatius Loyola, the Jesuits were ideally suited to conditions in New France. Loyola had been a military officer who once dreamed of winning glory through warfare, but in 1521 while Spanish troops tried in vain to defend the fortress of Pamplona against attack by the French, Loyola, fighting for the Spanish, was struck by a shattering cannon blast that broke his legs. While convalescing, a bored Loyola turned to religious tracts and was soon gripped by a profound spiritual crisis. Resolving to turn his back on his past life, he vowed to devote himself to serving Christ and his Church: if he could not be a real soldier, he would become a soldier of God. With a group of like-minded young men, he organized the Society of Jesus, using his military training as a guide to the organization of the Society. Recruiting from among the most elevated ranks of society, the order emphasized utter obedience to the authority of the Pope, along with requiring the traditional vows of poverty and chastity. In his *Spiritual Exercises*, Loyola developed a systematic program for "the conquest of self and the regulation of one's life."[8] He vowed that what his eyes told him to be white, he would believe to be black, if so instructed by church authorities.

With their effective organization, strong discipline, and great sense of purpose, the Jesuits proved to be a formidable instrument of Early Modern Catholicism in Europe, and effective missionaries overseas. The Jesuits had already established an admirable record of winning converts in the Far East. The Jesuit missionary St. Francis Xavier converted Christians in India from 1541 and in Japan from 1549; he was reportedly so successful that he suffered repetitive strain injury from performing so many baptisms. Their cross-cultural experience convinced the Jesuits that attempting to transform the Natives into Europeans like themselves was not the best approach; instead, they should seek to fit into the local milieu, learning local languages and using local customs to spread the Gospel. They played up the similarities between Christian doctrines and existing beliefs, discouraging only what they considered the most jarring elements of the latter. When Canada was restored to France in 1632, it was natural that the Jesuits, with their impressive record and missionary experience, should be granted a monopoly by the Crown to the Canadian mission field.

1634: The Jesuits establish their first missions in New France.

In 1634, the Jesuits joined the fur traders at Champlain's new post at Trois Rivières. Convinced that semi-nomadic peoples could not be fully converted until they were rendered sedentary, the Jesuits hoped to persuade the Montagnais and the Algonquians to settle down and take up farming close to the habitation. It soon became apparent to the Jesuits, however, that the French traders and settlers corrupted the Natives by introducing them to European vices. To the Jesuits, the Natives were seen not only as human beings capable of salvation, but as "*les bons sauvages*" unspoiled by the sins of Europe. Convinced that New France and its Native inhabitants offered the promise of a return to a pristine, unspoiled Christianity, the Jesuits redirected their missionary efforts to the Huron (Wendat), a prosperous agricultural people firmly allied to the French as intermediaries in the fur trade and removed from the corrupting influences of the French trading posts and settlements.

The Jesuits at Huronia

Later in 1634, the Jesuits established their first mission among the Hurons at the village of Ihonatiria (Saint-Joseph) in Huronia (Wendake) near Georgian Bay. Father Le Jeune entrusted this project to Father Jean de Brébeuf, who had spent some time trying to evangelize the Algonquians in the years before New France had fallen under English occupation. The Hurons were so named by the French because the hairstyle of the men reminded the French newcomers of the bristles of wild boar (*hure* in French). They lived in what is now central Ontario between Lake Simcoe and Georgian Bay. The Huron creation story tells of a woman who fell from the sky, Aataentsic ("ancient one"), and was

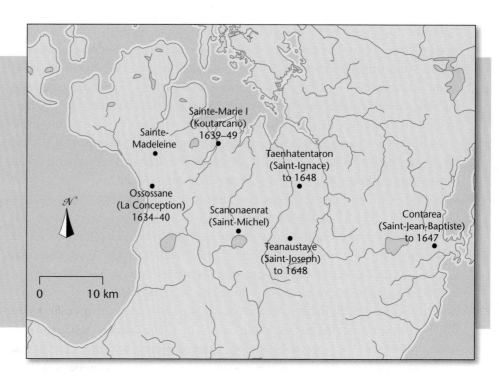

Map 2.2
Huronia.

given refuge on the back of a great turtle. This floating island became the world on which people lived and cultivated their crops. Like the Five Nations Iroquois, the Hurons were a confederacy, with the Bear and Cord nations the original members by about 1400 C.E., and the Deer and Rock nations joining by around 1570. Each nation's population was spread throughout numerous villages, with some villages reaching several thousand people in size. One site occupied by the Wendat was called Taranton, meaning "the place of the fish weirs" (a fish weir is a kind of fence set up in a river to trap fish). This word is probably the origin of the name of the city of Toronto.

Huron farmers grew corn, and *sagamité*, a kind of paste or soup made from crushed corn, sometimes flavoured with fish or meat, was the staple of their diet. Corn was also a vital item of trade with other Aboriginal groups, and Huronia was known as the granary of the Algonquians. Pumpkins and squash, beans, dried fruit and berries, nuts and maple syrup, and sunflowers grown for oil supplemented the Huron diet, as did deer meat and fish. Most farming was done by the women, and village sites were abandoned in favour of new ones when soil productivity lagged. The men hunted in the spring and fall; deer was a common choice of game as it was valued for meat as well as for hides. Deer were often caught in enclosures and shot with bows and arrows, or driven over bluffs. Beaver were taken with snares, arrows, or clubs. Domesticated dogs were used to track bears, but were also eaten in times of scarcity.

The Hurons had been at first reluctant to take Father Brébeuf and the other Jesuits to live among them, and after being pressured to do so, abandoned two of the priests on the canoe journey. The Jesuits refused to give up and at last made their way, starving and exhausted, to their new home in the wilderness. The guests struggled to adapt to life in Huronia, and Le Jeune wryly remarked that those hungry for suffering would find plenty of satisfaction. The smokiness of the longhouses—dwellings that accommodated a half-dozen families or so—was in itself a martyrdom, he remarked. Cold weather and roaming dogs also tested their patience. A drought in 1635, for which a Wendat medicine man blamed the priests, added further strain. This inauspicious beginning was only the start of a period of much greater trials.

Even as the missionary project struggled to gain ground in the *pays-d'en-haut*, or the "upper country" north and west of the St. Lawrence settlements, New France lost its greatest promoter. Champlain's determination to rebuild the colony after the English occupation took a heavy toll on his health; he developed paralysis in October 1635. No longer able to apply himself to colonial affairs, Champlain focused on his own spiritual welfare. The Jesuits encouraged him in prayer and self-examination, and read aloud passages from the lives of the saints. He died on Christmas day that year. Father Paul Le Jeune presided over Champlain's funeral and delivered the eulogy. "I did not lack material," he recalled.

1635: Champlain, "The Father of New France," dies at Quebec.

Although Champlain was widely revered as the father of New France, his wife and relatives back in France were less impressed and successfully contested his will. During his illness, Champlain had amended his will, making the Virgin Mary his heir: all his possessions and shares in the Company of One Hundred Associates were bequeathed to the church of Notre Dame de la Recouvrance, a church he had erected in Quebec in 1633 to celebrate the colony's restoration. His final wishes demonstrate the centrality in his life of his faith, and of New France.

Even though much of Champlain's life had been devoted to the colony, he did not live to see it flourish. In fact, developments during the year of his death again threatened to crush his hard-won gains. With the spread of the Thirty Years' War to France in 1635, France became preoccupied with affairs closer to home. The war, fought between 1618 and 1648, embroiled most of Europe in religious and territorial struggles. With this more pressing concern, French authorities paid little attention to North American developments, or to the failure of the company to live up to the terms of its charter. By 1642, the non-Aboriginal population of Canada was merely 200. As relations with the Iroquois worsened and the prospects of the fur trade deteriorated, the chances of attracting additional settlers dwindled considerably.

1635: The Thirty Years' War (1618–1648) spreads to France.

The Jesuits continued their work in Huronia, but were frustrated by the disinclination of the Hurons to abandon their own beliefs. "When we preach to them of one God, Creator of Heaven and Earth, and of all things, and even when we talk to them of Hell and Paradise and of our other mysteries," Father Jean de Brébeuf complained, "the headstrong reply [is] that this is good for our Country and not for theirs; that every Country has its own fashion."[9] Despite opposition, the Jesuits persisted. One cited the advice of the apostle: "To become all things to all men, in order to win all to Jesus Christ." He noted that "one must be very careful before condemning a thousand things among their customs, which greatly offend minds brought up and nourished in another world." He then counselled others on the best way to abolish Aboriginal customs that were "silly, but not criminal." In such cases, the Natives themselves should be induced gradually "to find out their absurdity, to laugh at them, and to abandon them."[10]

In the spring of 1636, Father Brébeuf witnessed a remarkable Huron ceremony and left a vivid anthropological account of it, an account that suggests he found it far from ridiculous. This was the Feast of the Dead, a highly ritualized event, held every 12 years or so by common consent of the elders and notables in the various villages of Huronia. It was the Wendat custom to inter the dead temporarily on scaffolds, wrapping their bodies in beaver robes. When the feast was to take place, the bodies were taken down from the scaffolds and borne away by family members to a central burial place. The Huron village of Ossossane (now Midland, Ontario) was the site of this mass grave. The bodies, regardless of their stage of decomposition, were carefully prepared, all flesh removed and burned. Family members lovingly tended to the corpses, cleaning the bones, and adorning the body with beads and other artefacts before rewrapping them in handsome new beaver skins. The event was also marked by gift giving and feasting—with guests invited to take food away—competitive games, and singing. From far away, the cries of those bearing the dead through the woods could be heard; they sang a song with a high keening sound—*haée, haé.*

Brébeuf, who had steadily resisted the argument that Huron beliefs were as valid as Christian ones, found much to admire in this custom. He approved of the way that a confrontation with death sharpened awareness of our eventual fate: "The flesh of some is quite gone, and there is only a sort of parchment on their bones; other bodies look as if they had been dried and smoked … and still others are swarming with worms." He was moved by the way that a daughter brushed the hair of her long-dead father, and by the people's unflinching handling of the bloated and putrefying corpses of those more recently deceased. "Is that not a noble example to inspire Christians, who ought to have much more elevated thoughts, to undertake acts of charity and works of mercy toward others? I do not think one could see in the world a more vivid picture or more perfect representation of what man is,… [and] the vanity of the things of this world," he reflected.[11] Brébeuf marked the site of the mass burial with a wooden cross. In 1948, archeologists excavated the remains of several hundred people from the grave and placed them on display in the Royal Ontario Museum. In 1999, owing to the efforts of some Wendat descendants, Michel Gros Louis and Annette Vincent, the remains were recovered and reburied with great ceremony in a sacred site; Wendat elders stood by to welcome home their dead.

Despite Brébeuf's admiration for the Feast of the Dead, the cultural gulf between the Jesuits and Hurons was profound. The priests were shocked by Huron sexual mores; premarital sexual intercourse, and the casualness of marriage and divorce offended French Catholic sensibilities. For their part, the Hurons were baffled by the Jesuits' celibacy. The freedom and indulgence granted to children offended the "black robes." The Jesuits believed that the children had been deliberately encouraged to annoy them in a bid to drive them away. The Hurons in turn condemned what seemed like the greed of the French, their cruelty toward others, and especially the corporal punishment of children. The fact that the Huron language lacked words for such fundamental Christian concepts as sin, Hell, grace, and faith made the missionaries' task even more difficult. Whenever possible, the Jesuits attempted to use Huron images and rituals, reinterpreting them in accordance with Christian belief and practice. The Jesuits attempted to impress the Hurons with clocks and other pieces of European technology and the rich and colourful ceremonial of Catholic liturgy; they often made presents of rosaries and religious medallions. Recognizing the esteem in which elders were held, the Jesuits redirected their efforts from children to adult men. The Jesuits were sustained in their work by the conviction that they had been called by God to save a people who were otherwise doomed to damnation, and by the belief that suffering and self-sacrifice were necessary to secure oneself a place in Paradise after death. "Truly," Father Brébeuf observed, "to come here, much faith and patience are needed; and he who thinks of coming here for any other than God, will have made a sad mistake."[12]

1636–1637: Disease devastates the Hurons and threatens the Jesuit mission.

These problems of cultural accommodation were minor compared to the devastating effects of disease in Huronia. Deadly epidemics of smallpox or perhaps measles in 1634, and influenza in the winter of 1636 and 1637, ravaged the Huron people. Huronia's population—estimated to have been as high as 35 000—fell by more than half. Traditional Huron medicine proved powerless against these scourges, and Native shamans began to suspect witchcraft. The Jesuits' celibacy, their own sound health, and their ability to predict eclipses led many Hurons to believe they possessed supernatural powers. Even more alarming, the Jesuits were apt to baptize those on the brink of death—an apparent cause-and-effect relationship that seemed to confirm Huron suspicions. Opinion turned sharply against the priests. Doors were shut against them, children pelted them with stones, and, at last, a Huron council met to contemplate putting them to death. Brébeuf, now stationed at the village of Ossossane, met with the council to respond to the charges. By late October 1637, he and the other missionaries prepared what they believed would be their final letter to Le Jeune. They insisted that God should be thanked for giving them the gift of martyrdom. They also called their Huron hosts to a farewell feast, warning them that they would have to answer for all eternity for their treatment of Christ's messengers. Whether the message struck a chord with the Hurons, or whether the more prosaic need to avoid alienating French trading partners prevailed, the effect was that the Jesuits were spared from death.

This difficult period past, Jesuit persistence appeared to bear fruit. With the outbreak of influenza that year, some Hurons sought out Christian baptism in the hope that this would cure them or protect them from disease. Undoubtedly, some devout Catholic Hurons were sincere in their conversion. Others converted to Christianity for practical reasons, perhaps to gain trade advantages. By 1648, an estimated one-fifth of Huronia's population had converted to Christianity.[13] These conversions, genuine or not, deeply divided Huron society between Christians and traditionalists. Threatened by the divisions among the Hurons and the growing hostility towards them, the Jesuits decided to consolidate their mission and built a fortified central mission headquarters at Sainte-Marie in 1639. The new superior of the mission, Jérôme Lalemant, hoped Sainte-Marie would lessen the Jesuits' dependence upon the Hurons and serve as a refuge where Christian Hurons could come to worship. With livestock imported from Quebec, and a growing community of priests, lay brothers, engagés, and donnés (laymen who took limited-term vows to work with the Jesuits), Sainte-Marie among the Hurons soon became a self-sufficient community.

1639: The Jesuits establish Sainte-Marie among the Hurons.

Religious Women in New France

During its early years, New France was predominantly a colony of male traders, administrators, and missionaries. While the number of women who crossed the Atlantic to serve

God in the Canadian wilderness was small, their efforts proved far-reaching. Women appear to have been especially moved by the spirit of Early Modern Catholicism. Many joined orders and performed acts of charity; others donated their wealth and used their influence to support religious causes.

Marie Guyart, better known as Marie de l'Incarnation, was the first of many dedicated religious women to immigrate to New France. Born at Tours in 1599, Guyart began to have visions at a young age and felt a deep calling to religious life. Her desire to enter a convent, however, was thwarted by her parents' insistence that she take a husband. Marie acceded to her family's wishes and married. Her husband died two years later after his business failed. Now a destitute 19-year-old single mother, Marie went to live with her sister and assumed an active role in her brother-in-law's cartage business. Despite these worldly concerns, her life continued to be one of prayer and mystical experiences. She wore hair shirts (a garment of rough cloth made from goats' hair and worn in the form of a shirt or as a girdle around the loins) and engaged in self-flagellation to purge herself of sin and prove her worthiness to serve God. In 1626, resolved to resist the call no longer, she became a novice in the Ursuline order, leaving her eight-year-old son in her sister's charge. Guyart's burning sense of mission outweighed the crushing grief of separation from her son, something she likened to a living death, to having her soul torn out of her body. Young Claude, a sensitive and timid boy, ran away and stormed the gates of the convent, crying that they should give him back his mother.

Shortly after she made her life profession in 1633, Guyart dreamed that God called her to go to Canada to spread the gospel. The idea of sending religious women to the wilds of New France met with many objections from the male church hierarchy, but with financial backing from two wealthy noblewomen, a small group of Ursulines and Augustinian Hospitalières were finally permitted to set sail for Canada in 1639. Under Marie de l'Incarnation's direction, the Ursulines built a convent and opened a school for Aboriginal girls at Quebec. Marie embarked on her work among these children with tremendous zeal and hope. "These girls love us more than they love their parents, showing no desire to accompany them," she enthusiastically wrote to her son. "They model themselves upon us as much as their age and condition can permit."[14] This initial optimism proved short lived. Many of their young pupils, separated from their families and culture, and thrown into an alien environment, fell into despair and depression. Some became ill and died. Others tried to escape the regimented life and strict discipline of the school and returned to their families. "It is a very difficult thing, not to say impossible, to make the little Savages French or civilized," a discouraged Marie later wrote. "We have observed that of a hundred that have passed through our hands we have scarcely civilized one. We find docility and intelligence in these girls but, when we are least expecting it, they clamber over our wall and go off to run with their kinsmen in the woods."[15]

Frustrated by their lack of success among the Natives, the Ursulines redirected their efforts toward educating the daughters of the colony's official and commercial classes. Marie de l'Incarnation's talents as a businesswoman and fundraiser proved indispensable in her religious endeavours. She successfully cultivated wealthy patrons in France who lent support to her mission and oversaw the creation of a vibrant community of women.

Source: Library and Archives Canada, C-073422.

Marie de l'Incarnation teaching Native children.

The Founding of Montreal

Women also played a vital role in the founding of Montreal. The idea for a new settlement on the island of Montreal originated in France with the *Compagnie du Saint-Sacrament*, a secret devotional society devoted to evangelization, good works, and the defence of public morality. The company created an auxiliary, the *Societé de Notre Dame de Montréal pour la Conversion des Sauvages de la Nouvelle-France*, to raise subscriptions for the founding of a new religious settlement on the island of Montreal. Ville Marie, as the settlement was then known, was founded on May 17, 1642. It was to be "a Jerusalem blessed by God and composed of citizens destined for Heaven."[16]

Residents of Ville Marie lived by a strict religious code and were subject to severe punishment or ostracism if they violated its terms. Among its first residents was a 35-year-old nurse, Jeanne Mance. Although not a member of a religious order, Mance was a woman of intense personal piety and energy who had devoted her life to religious and charitable

1642: Montreal founded.

work. Upon her arrival at Ville Marie, Mance immediately established a medical dispensary. This would later become the colony's first hospital, the Hôtel-Dieu. An outstanding administrator and entrepreneur, Mance returned to France on three occasions to raise funds and to search out an order of nuns to staff her medical mission. In 1657, Mance convinced several Hospitalières of St. Joseph, a nursing order, to come to Ville Marie. Mance also arranged for the immigration of over 100 soldiers and settlers.

The governor of the new settlement at Montreal, Paul de Chomedey de Maisonneuve, arrived shortly after Jeanne Mance. Like Mance, Maisonneuve had strong religious convictions. An experienced military officer, Maisonneuve resolved to serve in New France after reading some of the published accounts of the Jesuits' ordeals in North America. When colonial authorities at Quebec attempted to dissuade Maisonneuve from establishing a settlement on the island of Montreal, so near the hostile Iroquois, he responded: "My honour is at stake, and you will agree that I must go up there to start a colony, even if all the trees on that island were to change to so many Iroquois."[17] The defence of the vulnerable settlement occupied most of Maisonneuve's energies during the 25 years he spent at Montreal. As governor, he formed the Militia of the Holy Family, and instituted a system of flying camps, or temporary outposts, to keep enemy Iroquois at a distance.

Maisonneuve's sister, Louise de Chomedey de Sainte-Marie, was the mother superior of the Congregation de Notre Dame at Troyes in the French province of Champagne. She shared her brother's stories of New France with other women within her order, and one of these, Marguerite Bourgeoys, resolved to dedicate her life to the service of God in New France. Born into a prosperous commercial family in 1620, at the age of 20 Bourgeoys was inspired by a mystical vision of the Virgin Mary to join a teaching community associated with the Congregation de Notre Dame. After meeting Bourgeoys in 1652, Maisonneuve invited her to come to New France to establish a school.

Bourgeoys arrived at Ville Marie the following year but found no school-age children. A high rate of infant mortality, disease, and attack from the Iroquois all contributed to the settlement's lack of children. Unperturbed, she carried out social work among the settlers and oversaw the construction of the chapel of Notre Dame de Bon Secours, Ville Marie's first stone church. In 1657, she finally opened a school in a donated stable. She later acted as a chaperone for single female immigrants to New France, instructing them in domestic arts and helping them select suitable husbands. To further her educational and social work, Bourgeoys founded the *Soeurs de la Congregation de Notre Dame* in 1671. Unlike most other female religious communities, Bourgeoys's congregation of sisters was not cloistered and did not wear the traditional nun's habit. This was an innovative, and even radical, action that caused some consternation among the colony's male religious authorities. Bourgeoys invoked the example of the Blessed Virgin Mary to justify her extraordinary actions. "The Holy Virgin," she insisted, "was not cloistered, but she everywhere preserved an internal solitude, and she never refused to be where charity or necessity required."[18] Bourgeoys died in 1700, having spent the last two years of her life in prayer and meditation. Like Marie Guyart and Jeanne Mance, Marguerite Bourgeoys embodied the religious fervour and piety characteristic of Early Modern Catholicism. Theirs was a deeply mystical faith of dreams and visions that idealized suffering and demanded a life of strict discipline, their religious zeal directed to the service of others and to the problems that afflicted society. Each of these formidable women had a gift for leadership and demonstrated a talent for administration and business. As the founders and managers of hospitals, schools, poorhouses, and orphanages, these religious women played a central role in the life of New France.

Church and State in New France

Problems of Defence

After Champlain's death in 1635, his place as governor was filled by Charles Jacques Huault de Montmagny, a Knight of Malta who had considerable military experience fighting the Turks and chasing pirates in the Mediterranean. His appointment suggests that the French had realized the necessity of giving more consideration to colonial defence: Montmagny quickly set to work strengthening New France militarily. The Dutch, desperate for furs, had begun trading firearms with the Iroquois, who stepped up their raids on the flotillas of fur-laden Huron and Algonquian canoes bound for Quebec and Trois Rivières. Holding fast to Champlain's policy, Montmagny prohibited the sale of guns to the Aboriginal allies, putting the Huron and Algonquian traders at a serious military disadvantage. Attempts in 1641 to negotiate a new peace treaty failed, and Iroquois raids on the St. Lawrence and Ottawa intensified. Montmagny appealed for military support from France, organized a naval patrol of the St. Lawrence, and built a fort at the mouth of the Richelieu River in an attempt to blockade the routes the Iroquois used to intercept Huron and Algonquian trading parties. These efforts proved futile. The Iroquois destroyed Fort Richelieu in a daring raid, and attacks continued.

Changes in Governance

By 1645, the number of furs had dwindled and the Company of One Hundred Associates faced bankruptcy. Determined to cut their losses, French investors in the company decided to turn the fur trade over to a subsidiary made up of traders who resided in Canada, the *Communauté* (or *Compagnie*) *des Habitants*. Under the terms of its charter from the Crown, the Company of One Hundred Associates had been given title to all of Canada and was alone empowered to choose a governor, grant seigneuries, and dispense justice.

1645: The Compagnie of Habitants takes over the duties of the Company of One Hundred Associates.

With the transfer of the fur trade monopoly to the Compagnie des Habitants, that company assumed responsibility for the costs associated with administering the colony. These obligations included annual payments to the governor and military officers, and the maintenance of the colony's defences. When peace was negotiated with the Mohawks in 1645, trade resumed, and the new Compagnie des Habitants enjoyed a healthy profit. The company's early success aroused resentment among many in New France. Despite its name, the Compagnie des Habitants was made up of 15 prominent traders and merchants, most of whom were related to one another. Grumblings grew about the privileges enjoyed by the small clique that controlled the company.

1645: Peace is negotiated with the Mohawks.

In an attempt to contain the mounting dissatisfaction, French authorities implemented a new form of governance in 1647: an administrative council consisting of the Governor of Quebec, the Governor of Montreal, and the Superior of the Jesuits. Each of Canada's principal centres—Quebec, Trois Rivières, and Ville Marie—was to be represented through "syndics,"

1647: An administrative council is implemented, and changes are made to it the following year.

persons who were elected to advise on the business interests of each town. Although these syndics were elected, only a few leading men held the franchise—that is, had the right to vote. The council was responsible for appointing the officials of the Compagnie des Habitants to three-year terms, regulating the fur trade, spending public funds, regulating local police forces, appointing captains to the volunteer militia, and overseeing the general well-being of the colony.[19] When the council dutifully confirmed the existing officers of the Compagnie des Habitants in their positions, it did not take long for grievances to be heard once more.

The habitants of Trois Rivières complained that they were not represented on the council. Others charged that little had been done to improve the colony's defences. The governor of Trois Rivières and two habitants were added to the council in 1648 to quell the discord. To ensure that the squabbles afflicting the colony would not imperil the conduct of the fur trade, the council assumed responsibility for hearing all legal disputes involving the Compagnie des Habitants. One of the first acts of the new council was to repeal earlier regulations that restricted commerce not related to the fur trade. For the first time, merchants could now import, distribute, and sell goods without involving the fur trade monopoly.

Rival Notions of the Church–State Relationship

To modern readers, the notion that church authorities should be entitled to a voice on the governing council may seem surprising, yet, the appointment of the superior of the Jesuits to a seat on the first council of New France was entirely in keeping with seventeenth-century views. The Roman Catholic Church was the national church of France and her colonies. The Church assumed many responsibilities that would today be managed by the state: maintaining schools, hospitals, orphanages, and charitable institutions, and sustaining the social order by preaching obedience and submission. Moreover, Catholic missionaries cemented vitally important Aboriginal alliances through their work. In return for these services, the Church received land grants and financial support from both the commercial companies that controlled the fur trade and the Crown.

Nonetheless, opinions differed about the precise relationship that should exist between Church and state. In both old world and new, the rival theories of Gallicanism and ultra-montanism vied for dominance. The Gallican view put the monarch, who ruled by divine right, in a position of authority over the Church; the Church was subject to his will and pleasure. The king, not the pope, nominated all church officials in France and controlled the rules and memberships of all religious communities. The French Crown jealously guarded its traditional rights and privileges against what was seen as the overweening power and influence of the papacy in Rome, especially so in an era of bureaucratic state consolidation, which also saw the Catholic Church undergoing renewal and reform.

The ultramontane view, by contrast, held that the pope in Rome was the final authority in all matters, religious and secular. The word *ultramontane* itself—the Latin meaning is "beyond the mountains"—suggests a looking beyond France's borders to an ultimate source of authority in Italy. The early years of New France may have favoured the flowering of an ultramontane tendency: while there was not exactly a political vacuum, France did not exert direct control over the colony. The Jesuit order, known for absolute obedience to the Pope, played a strong role in the colony's development and fortunes.

This affinity between church and government was evident in many aspects of society in New France. Failure to attend mass, ploughing on Sundays, and uttering blasphemous remarks could result in fines or placement in the public stocks. The intense religious atmosphere that characterized New France was evident in the large cross that adorned Mont Royal, the frequent religious processions that made their way through the streets, and the fireworks and bonfires that marked the feast days of Canada's patron saints, Joseph and Jean-Baptiste (John the Baptist). As the custodian of morals, the Church regulated the style of clothing, censored books, and banned theatrical productions. The Church also played an important role in conferring social status. Where one sat in church, stood in a religious procession, and was buried, were all dramatic statements of one's position in the social hierarchy. Religion and morality were seen as the foundation of all civic life so it was natural that Catholicism should permeate all aspects of society and that the institutional church—its hierarchy, religious orders, parish organization, seminaries, educational and charitable foundations—should be a dominant force in society.

War with the Iroquois

Renewed conflict with the Iroquois undercut the potential benefits of the new administrative council introduced in 1647. The western Iroquois nations, who were not part of the 1645 peace treaty, continued to harass the Hurons. The Mohawks believed that the 1645 treaty would ensure them a portion of the Hurons' furs and felt betrayed when the Hurons carried all of their furs to Quebec and Trois Rivières the following year.

As a sign of good faith, Governor Montmagny had arranged for a Jesuit missionary, Father Isaac Jogues, to visit the Mohawks as an ambassador of peace in the spring of 1646. Jogues, once a mild-mannered teacher of literature at Rouen, had already endured much in Canada. Shortly after his arrival in 1636, he had been sent to live in Huronia. In 1641, he travelled with the Hurons deeper into the interior than any Europeans were known to have gone, reaching present-day Sault-Ste-Marie at the junction between Lakes Huron, Michigan, and Superior. While returning to Quebec in 1642, he and his companions were ambushed by Iroquois warriors, who carried them off as captives to Mohawk country. There he was tortured—his flesh burned, his thumb hacked off, his fingers mutilated—and was forced to witness the burning alive of fellow prisoners. After a year of brutal captivity and slavery, Jogues escaped with the assistance of Dutch traders who spirited him back to France. A battered and emaciated Jogues made his way to the Jesuit residence at Rennes in January 1644, gaining access to the rector by claiming that a poor man from Canada wished to see him. When the rector asked if he knew anything of the fate of poor Father Jogues, he was astonished to learn of his visitor's true identity. Even more astonishing was Jogues's wish: he sought to return to New France.

Once back in North America, Jogues accepted the task of acting as an emissary to the same people among whom he had endured such torment. His knowledge of Mohawk ways made him valuable, and he summoned his courage to return to them in May 1646. The visit was not a long one, though, and he returned to Quebec in early July. As the relations between the Mohawks and the French continued to deteriorate over the summer, fresh overtures to keep the peace became necessary. The strain in the fragile truce made such a diplomatic mission riskier than ever, but Jogues was again called into service. He confessed to a fellow Jesuit that he went willingly, but felt in his heart he would never return. He welcomed the prospect of sacrifice in carrying out God's work.

Not only were the Mohawks aggrieved about being denied a share of the furs brought by the Hurons, but they also targeted Jogues as the source of the disease and drought that plagued them that summer. As Jogues neared the village of Ossemenon, the site of his earlier torment, most of his companions fled, but he continued on to meet the fate he had foreseen. In October 1647, Jogues walked into a Mohawk ambush. They stripped him naked and fell upon him with tomahawks. His head was spit upon a spike of the village palisade in a grisly display.

Jogues's death marked the beginning of an all-out Iroquois offensive against the French and their allies in 1647. Earlier wars had been more limited in scale, often driven by the brutal *quid pro quo* of the blood feud. Casualties tended to be few, but armed with Dutch firearms, the Iroquois now became a more deadly force. The Hurons, for their part, were vulnerable. Their population had been halved by the ravages of disease, and Christianity had introduced division, undercutting traditional sources of internal authority. In the tense summer of 1647, no Huron canoes dared bring furs to Quebec or Trois Rivières, and it was unsafe to venture forth beyond the barricades anywhere in Canada. The worst was yet to come.

At Saint-Joseph (Teanaustayé or Teanaostaiae), a substantial palisaded Huron village of about 2000, Father Antoine Daniel had finished saying mass on the morning of July 4, 1648, when some 700 Iroquois warriors descended upon the town.[20] Daniel waded into the panicked throng, and immersing a handkerchief in a bowl of holy water, shook it over the people to hurriedly baptize them. With death closing in, Huron converts clamoured forward to be touched by the falling droplets. "Brothers, today we shall be in heaven," the priest assured them before falling to a volley of arrows and musket fire. His killers bathed their faces in his blood, so as to partake of his brave spirit.[21] Some Hurons managed to escape to Sillery, a reserve for Christian Natives outside Quebec, while hundreds were taken as prisoner. Others in the besieged town had long resented the presence of the black robes and spurned the message of Christianity. Some of these opted to join forces with the attackers. The Iroquois set the town afire, and the bulwark of Huronia was razed to the ground.

In the following spring, news spread that a second, even larger, Iroquois force was about to fall upon Huronia. Before daybreak on the morning of March 16, 1649, 1200 Iroquois, mostly Seneca and Mohawk, struck the nearby village of Saint-Ignace. A deep ravine on three sides, with palisades built all around, protected the settlement, where 400 women, children, and old men awaited the return of the men from hunting and scouting parties. Startled from sleep, the Hurons tried to flee the slaughter, but the Iroquois had entered the village at the weakest point and the strong defences of the other three sides hemmed the Hurons in all around. In a few horror-filled moments, only three escaped.

The alarm was raised at the neighbouring village of Saint-Louis, where most of the 700 Huron residents took to the woods in panic. Only 80 warriors remained behind to mount a defence, and to protect those who were too weak to flee. Two Jesuit priests, Jean de Brébeuf and Gabriel Lalemant, though urged to join their Christian converts in flight, stubbornly remained behind. At last the besieging Iroquois broke through the defences, putting the town to the torch. Those too helpless to escape were consumed in the flames.

1647: The short-lived truce between the French and Mohawks is broken.

1648: The Iroquois destroy Saint-Joseph, the principal village in Huronia.

1648–1649: The Iroquois destroy the remaining villages of Huronia.

As smoke from the blazing village of Saint-Louis billowed above the forest, the Iroquois carried the two captive priests back to Saint-Ignace. They would suffer unspeakable agonies for the sake of their faith.

At Saint-Ignace, the priests were stripped naked and tied to posts. The Iroquois tore out their fingernails and rained showers of blows upon them. In a cruel parody of baptism, they doused the Jesuits in boiling water, and then stripped the burned skin from their bodies. Brébeuf continued to pray throughout his torment, urging his captors to turn to Christ. The Iroquois cut out his tongue, hacked off both lips, and thrust a red-hot iron down his throat to silence him. To the Iroquois chief fell the honour of devouring Brébeuf's still-beating heart, which was torn from his chest. Lalemant's death came later that day. Although his eyes had been burned out by flaming coals, it is hard to believe that he did not bear witness to the suffering of his companion and endure the additional torment of knowing what lay before him. In 1930, these two martyrs were canonized as saints.

Desperate and dispirited, the Hurons abandoned Ossossane, and the Jesuit mission at Sainte-Marie was burned to the ground to prevent it from desecration. Many of the remaining Hurons sought refuge with other nations, such as the Petun, Ottawa, Neutral, Tobacco, and Erie. The Iroquois continued their campaign and subdued the Hurons'

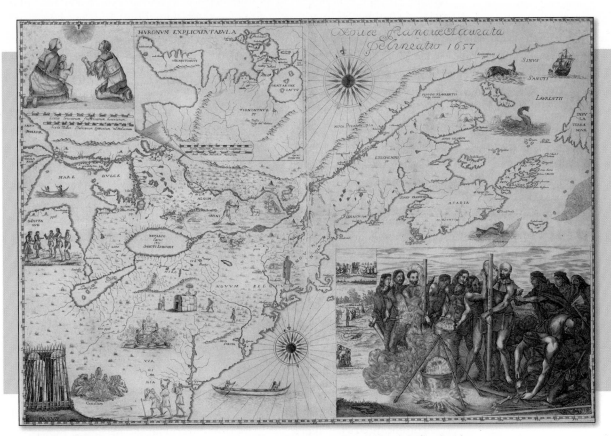

Map 2.3 *Map of New France with Engraved Depiction of the Martyrdom of Jean de Brébeuf and Gabriel Lalemant by the Iroquois in 1649.*

Source: Library and Archives Canada Mikan Number 3805607.

neighbours and allies to the south, the Tobacco and Neutral in 1650 and the Nipissing to the north in 1651. Some of the Hurons displaced in 1649 settled on Christian Island in Georgian Bay. After enduring a winter fraught with disease and starvation, they dispersed, some to Manitoulin Island, others to the western shore of Lake Huron. For many, their dispersal by the Iroquois was only the beginning in a long history of migration that would see them moving south into what is now the United States—to the future Wisconsin, to the Green Bay area, and south to the shores of the Ohio and Mississippi Rivers. In the United States, they are usually called the Wyandot. Others would later establish a community of Christian converts in Lorette, near Quebec.

In the early 1650s, the fur trade seems doomed in New France.

For the French, the gruesome deaths of Brébeuf and Lalemant marked the end of the dream of establishing an enclave of Christian allies in the wilderness. More than that, the destruction of Huronia cut off the supply of furs from the interior and put the very life of New France at risk. No furs came down to Quebec at all in 1653. A Jesuit missionary observed that "the Beavers are left in peace and in the place of their repose; the Huron fleets no longer come down to trade; the Algonquins are depopulated; and the more distant Nations are withdrawing still farther, fearing the fire of the Iroquois." The Montreal warehouse had not bought a single beaver skin for a year, and at Trois Rivières, the little revenue earned had been used to improve defences against an expected attack. "In the Quebec warehouse, there is nothing but poverty."[22]

Canada found itself in a state of siege, with Montreal, Trois Rivières, and even Quebec vulnerable to Iroquois attack. With little support from France, Canada had to rely on its own small population and meagre resources to defend itself. It would take a new commitment from metropolitan France to ensure the survival of the colony. In the meantime, others were labouring to lay the groundwork of a new and distinct French society in the new world.

The Acadian Civil War

Acadia fared little better than Canada during the decades of the mid-seventeenth century. The 1632 Treaty of St-Germain-en-Laye that had restored Quebec to France also put an end to the claims of William Alexander and the British Crown to Nova Scotia. In 1634, the Company of One Hundred Associates appointed Isaac de Razilly governor of Acadia and Charles de Menou d'Aulnay his lieutenant. Acadia, however, did not produce the quantity or quality of furs needed by the company to recover from the years lost to the English between 1628 and 1632. Determined to reduce its costs, the company sold trading licences and granted seigneuries to Razilly, Charles de la Tour, and Nicolas Denys. Razilly's own company, the Razilly-Condonnier Company, operated alongside the Company of One Hundred Associates, and advanced some of the funds necessary to carry out the work of colonization. Denys profited from lumbering and fishing, de La Tour dominated the fur trade, and Razilly successfully recruited 200 colonists to settle in Acadia. Six Capuchin friars accompanied the mission and established a chapel and boarding school.

When Razilly died suddenly in December 1635, his brother, Claude de Launay-Rasilly (each brother used a different spelling) took over the colony's leadership. D'Aulnay, continuing in his earlier capacity, relocated settlers from La Hève to the more fertile area of Port Royal. The construction of dykes was undertaken, and salt-makers arrived to gather sea salt for the local fisheries. These workers, whose craft is commemorated in family names like Saulnier and Saunier, used salt pans set out to take advantage of natural evaporation.[23] It was d'Aulnay's hope that Acadia could become agriculturally self-sufficient.

But d'Aulnay would soon clash with Charles de La Tour over the precise boundaries and trading rights granted to each. When La Tour attempted to exercise his right to inspect the furs and supplies in the Port Royal warehouse in 1640, he was denied. Blasts of cannon fired from the vessels of each claimant signalled that the breach was now an open one. The conflict between the two would embroil all of Acadia and derail the fragile colonization experiment.

1640: Competing private claims to Acadia embroil the colony in war.

D'Aulnay's complaints to the French court culminated in a decree that he should take control of La Tour's forts—Fort Sable, on the southwestern tip of the peninsula, and Fort La Tour, also known as Fort Sainte-Marie—at the mouth of the Saint John River, across the Bay of Fundy from Port Royal. Now emboldened with the support of the French Crown, d'Aulnay launched an attack on Fort Sable and destroyed it. Without trade goods to barter for furs, La Tour was compelled to purchase fresh stock in Boston. This collusion with the English gave d'Aulnay further ammunition, and he claimed that the Huguenot La Tour was a traitor to French interests in Acadia. La Tour was ordered to appear before the king to answer charges against him and was convinced that d'Aulnay had deceived French authorities to gain his own ends. He knew all too well that abandoning his interests to defend his reputation in France would play into the hands of his enemy. Instead, La Tour's wife, Françoise Marie Jacquelin, who had come to Acadia as a teenaged bride two years before, travelled back to France to make her husband's case. She was evidently persuasive, and won consent for the Company of One Hundred Associates to send soldiers and a supply ship to Fort La Tour. When the ship entered the Bay of Fundy in April 1643, they saw that they would be thwarted: D'Aulnay's forces blockaded the mouth of the Saint John River, barring access to the fort. La Tour was compelled to hire additional ships and men in Boston to fight.

This fateful decision to seek further English support seems to have definitively tipped the scales in d'Aulnay's favour, and aroused official suspicions about La Tour's loyalty and motives. When Lady La Tour once more sought support in France, she was refused permission even to leave the country, and had to flee in disguise to England. From there, she contracted to have a vessel take her and some supplies back to the fort. When the ship was waylaid by d'Aulnay's forces off Cap de Sable, Lady La Tour hid among the cargo to avoid detection. After an unplanned diversion to Boston, she at last arrived back at Fort La Tour by the end of 1644.

In April 1645, with her husband temporarily absent in Boston, Lady La Tour faced her greatest challenge yet. D'Aulnay learned that his rival was away, and chose the opportunity to launch an assault on Fort La Tour with a force of 200 and vessels mounting 16 cannons. The redoubtable Lady La Tour, who now had an infant son, led a valiant defence of the fort, with a garrison reduced by desertion to a mere 45 soldiers. On Easter Sunday, after the fort had withstood bombardment for three days and more than half the defenders had fallen, a traitor opened the gates to d'Aulnay's invaders. Lady La Tour surrendered, securing a promise that her soldiers would be spared. Instead, they were

1645: Lady La Tour makes
a valiant but unsuccessful
attempt to defend the
Acadian Fort La Tour
(Fort Sainte-Marie).

hanged for treason; Lady La Tour was forced to watch, all the while with a rope around her own neck. When she was caught in an attempt to smuggle a note to her husband through a Native trader, Lady La Tour herself was thrown into prison. She died a few days later at the age of 24.[24]

La Tour, it seemed, was completely vanquished and learned the sad news as he prepared to launch a relief expedition from Boston. He moved to Quebec to start over. The dream of a thriving colony in Acadia had been consumed in the fires of personal ambition, but by the spring of 1650, the victorious d'Aulnay was dead, having drowned in a canoeing accident. La Tour took the opportunity to reassert his case in France, and after an inquiry, was restored to royal favour, his property and commission as governor returned to him. He set out once again for Port Royal in the summer of 1653, bringing several families of colonists with him. D'Aulnay's widow, Jeanne Motin, had been struggling with the financial aftermath of the protracted conflict. Willing to put past acrimony behind her "for the peace and tranquility of the country and concord and union between the two families," she accepted La Tour's offer of marriage.[25] The couple would go on to have five children.

This surprising end to the enmity between the two rival claimants did not, unfortunately, usher in an era of peaceful security for Acadia. One of d'Aulnay's French creditors, Emmanuel Le Borgne, laid claim to d'Aulnay's rights and assets in Acadia. Leading a large force, Le Borgne arrived in Acadia in 1654 to assert his rights. Determined to take control of the colony, Le Borgne's men seized property belonging to La Tour and captured forts throughout the region.

Internal feuding among French claimants to Acadian territory and trading rights had embroiled the colony for two decades. Yet Le Borgne's military campaign was interrupted by a threat from outside. In July 1654, a fleet from New England arrived led by Robert Sedgwick, who was acting on orders from England's Lord Protector, Oliver Cromwell. While the struggle between La Tour and d'Aulnay had been raging, and while Canada had been at war with the Iroquois, a bigger cataclysm had shaken England. The long and bitter conflict between King Charles I (1625–1649) and his Parliament over the respective rights and privileges of each, and over Charles's disinclination to vigorously oppose Roman Catholicism, had culminated in a civil war by 1642. Charles was beheaded on January 30, 1649, and the Puritan Oliver Cromwell, who had led the parliamentarians to victory over the royalists, assumed the role of Lord Protector in December 1653.

1653: Cromwell assumes
the role of "Lord Protector"
after England's civil war
and the 1649 execution
of Charles I.

When the First Anglo-Dutch War broke out between England and the Netherlands in 1652, largely over maritime trade, Robert Sedgwick was commissioned by Cromwell to lead a campaign to subdue the Dutch in New Netherland. Cromwell added that Sedgwick should feel free to look for other chances to expand English power in North America as well: "If tyme permitt and opertunitye be presented, you are to proseed to the gaineing in any other places from the Enemie who upon advise with a counsel of warr may be judged feizable and conduceing to the settlement of the peace and saiftye of the English plantations."[26] Acadia offered such an opportunity.

Although England and France were not at war, the actions of French privateers had plagued English merchants in North America, and New England had long coveted access to the rich fishery off Acadia's coasts. A devout Puritan, Sedgwick no doubt relished the opportunity to strike a blow against "popery" in the name of "true religion." Weakened by internal dissension, Acadia fell quickly. La Tour surrendered after a three-day battle at Saint John, and Le Borgne followed suit after a brief resistance at Port Royal.

A victorious Sedgwick returned to England, taking La Tour with him, and Major John Leverett was appointed military governor of Acadia. Always the opportunist, La Tour convinced the English to recognize a barony granted his father by William Alexander in 1630, and entered into a partnership with Thomas Temple and William Crowne, close allies of Cromwell. Little changed in the colony, even though Acadia was again under English control. Acadia's French residents were allowed to remain on their land and Catholic missionaries continued to minister to the local population. Temple and Crowne succeeded in attracting only a handful of new colonists from England and New England. Intent on eking out a living and having witnessed Acadia change hands twice in their lifetimes, Acadians were becoming indifferent to questions of loyalty, and readily diverted the produce of the fur trade and fisheries to New England. The Treaty of Breda restored Acadia to France in 1667. Perhaps fortunately, La Tour would not have to explain away this further cooperation with the English: he died at Cap de Sable in 1666. Thomas Temple and William Crowne protested the transfer and petitioned the English Crown for compensation, effectively delaying the transfer back to France until 1670.

1654: Acadia falls to English control.

Coureurs de Bois and the Impact of the Fur Trade on Aboriginal Societies

In Canada, the 1649 defeat and dispersal of the Hurons disrupted old fur-trading patterns. An uneasy truce was reached with the Iroquois in 1654. Embroiled in conflict with nations to the west and south, the Iroquois sought peace with the French, allowing the fur trade to resume. The Jesuits established a mission among the western Iroquois, convinced that Christianity would provide the basis for a permanent peace. Instead of flotillas of Native canoes laden with furs making their way down to Quebec and Trois Rivières each year, fleets of *coureurs de bois* (literally, "runners of the woods") travelled far into the interior carrying trade goods. To ensure that the season's pelts were not lost to the Dutch or the English, French traders wintered among their Aboriginal suppliers and carried the furs back from the *pays-d'en-haut* themselves.

These changes required a liberalization of trading regulations. In the past, only the clerks employed by the authorized trading company could procure furs. With the relaxation of the rules, trading fever swept the colony. "All our young Frenchmen," a Jesuit missionary observed in 1653, "are planning to go on a trading expedition, to find the Nations who are scattered here and there; and they hope to come back laden with the Beaver-skins of several years' accumulation."[27] The rush of young men to the upper country concerned Jean de Lauson, the governor of New France. In 1654 he decreed that no one could go trading "with the Hurons or other Nations without our previous written consent, under penalty of a fine." The governor explained that he simply wanted to know "the number and quality of the individuals who wish to embark on these voyages."[28]

Coureurs de bois.

Source: Library and Archives Canada, C-005746.

The introduction of trading permits provided the governor with a powerful tool of patronage and aroused considerable resentment. As competition with the Dutch and the English increased, firearms and alcohol were increasingly used to secure fur supplies. Although Champlain had outlawed the use of brandy as an item of trade in 1633, traders now insisted that it was essential if the French were to remain competitive. Alcohol was initially valued by the Natives for its hallucinogenic properties and was considered a means of communicating with the supernatural. The fact that alcohol could be consumed on site and did not have to be transported back home added to its appeal for migratory Aboriginal traders who did not accumulate many material possessions. Missionaries and visitors to New France frequently commented on the negative impact of alcohol. "Liquors," observed Marie de l'Incarnation, "destroys all these poor people—the men, the women, the boys and even the girls."[29] In 1657, a royal proclamation prohibited the brandy trade, and the Sulpician superior at Montreal declared the sale of brandy to the Natives a mortal sin.

1657: A royal proclamation prohibits the sale of alcohol to the Natives.

The destructive effect of alcohol has sometimes been interpreted as part of a larger pattern of exploitation, growing Native dependence, and cultural degeneration. For a very long time, the stereotypical historical view has been one of credulous Natives cheated by wily Europeans, sacrificing valuable furs for worthless trinkets. More recently, historians such as Arthur Ray have challenged this idea, pointing out that Aboriginal traders actively sought to trade, and "became good comparison shoppers" who quickly learned to discern quality goods. They rejected, for example, inferior metal goods that would not stand up to the rigours of the Canadian winter.[30] The presence of English and Dutch traders offered an alternative market for pelts, and competition worked to the advantage of Native traders. Moreover, iron goods had a high value to those who traditionally had access only to copper, a metal too malleable for many purposes. An iron kettle, knife, or needle had real utility, and was thus prized. By contrast, the simple task of heating water would be an onerous process if it had to be done by dropping heated stones into a bowl fashioned of birch bark. It is revealing that the Huron word for the French, *Agnonha*, translates as "iron people."[31] Furs, on the other hand, were abundant. "The Beaver does everything perfectly well, it makes kettles, hatchets, swords, knives, bread," a Montagnais man remarked. "The English have no sense; they give us twenty knives like this for one Beaver skin."[32]

While European goods, valued for their utility and beauty, were readily incorporated into Aboriginal economies, the collective self-sufficiency of Native society was not replaced by a helpless dependence on imported trade goods. Aboriginal nations tenaciously held on to their cultures and lifestyles, but their traditionalism was neither blind nor passive, and they readily accepted innovations that would make life easier. Certainly, acculturation could go both ways: French fur traders adopted items of Native dress and swiftly accustomed themselves to the use of canoes and snowshoes.

There was much in Aboriginal society that appealed to French traders. Many abandoned European ideas about sexual relations, taking Native women as companions or wives "*à la façon du pays*"—according to the custom of the country. These alliances, both casual and long lasting, bound the French more closely to their Aboriginal hosts and enabled them, on an individual basis, to understand a new society and culture. The ease with which French traders adapted to Native life could perhaps also have been a product of the elevated status they came to enjoy in North America. Most traders did not come from the elite class—many were former soldiers—yet they were received as honoured guests in Native society. Their prospects were greater under these conditions.

As more *coureurs de bois* travelled inland, the ability of the Compagnie des Habitants to control their activities became strained. The journey west was a long and costly one and traders began to seek out a less arduous way to access the rich beaver country surrounding Lake Superior. Jean Bourdon unsuccessfully attempted to reach the northwest via Hudson Bay in 1657. The need to find an alternative trade route became more urgent with the resumption of Iroquois hostilities in 1658. Despite the rising level of violence, officials and merchants based at Quebec opposed efforts to access the interior via Hudson Bay—and for good reason: a maritime-based fur trade would divert activity away from the St. Lawrence and effectively destroy their ability to control and profit from the fur trade. Frustrated by favouritism, regulation, and taxation, many *coureurs de bois* began to trade illegally with the Iroquois, the Dutch, and the English.

Intermittent French–Iroquois warfare ensured that a constant sense of menace hung over the colony on the St. Lawrence. In 1660, a small party consisting of 17 Frenchmen, along with 44 Huron and Algonquian allies, led by a young French soldier and trader, Adam Dollard des Ormeaux, set out from Montreal in an attempt to ambush what they apparently thought was a small band of Iroquois. They were dismayed to discover that these were only advance scouts at the head of 200 or 300 warriors. Dollard and his men took shelter in an abandoned palisade in a desperate attempt to defend themselves, surviving for a hellish week with limited water and provisions. Any faint hope of repelling the enemy surely evaporated with the arrival of 500 more Iroquois warriors. When a keg of gunpowder behind the walls accidentally exploded, destroying the makeshift fort, the Iroquois warriors swarmed over the crumbled defences and slaughtered or captured those within. According to one report, a French defender used his hatchet to kill some of the wounded, lest they suffer worse in the hands of the Iroquois. Nineteenth-century Québécois historiography saw Dollard elevated to a saviour, a "martyr of the faith" who bravely went out from Montreal to deflect an anticipated attack upon the settlement. Abbé Jean-Baptiste Ferland and Abbé Étienne-Michel Faillon likened Dollard and his companions to the heroes of Greek and Roman legend, asserting that they received the sacrament, made their wills, and vowed to fight to the death. The more prosaic version of events is that Dollard simply wished to seize the furs of a small trading party in an unequal ambush, and was himself caught by surprise.[33] Regardless of his intention, the effect was indeed to engage the enemy and preserve Montreal from attack.

1660: The Battle of the Long Sault saves Montreal from attack.

Internal Conflict in the Church in New France

Renewed conflict with the Iroquois and sagging commerce were not the only challenges New France faced in this era. On the face of it, the colony seemed immune from the religious factionalism of the old world, yet the outward uniformity of homogeneous Roman Catholicism masked a struggle for control. To avoid an open confrontation between the rival notions of church authority, the conflicting principles of Gallicanism and ultramontanism, no diocese had yet been established in New France. The Archbishop of Rouen, from whose diocese many of the colony's settlers originated, claimed jurisdiction over New France and its clergy, but his claims were subject to dispute. The Sulpicians, established in Montreal in 1642, recognized the jurisdiction of Rouen and embraced Gallicanism. The Jesuits, on the other hand, took an ultramontane position that emphasized that authority of Rome and the papacy, and which sought to limit state control of the Church. Both orders sought the appointment of a bishop who shared their views and supported their cause. The Archbishop of Rouen and the Sulpicians championed Thubières de Levy de Queylus, while the Jesuits favoured François de Laval, a talented secular priest—that is, not a member of any religious order—who was of noble birth and a graduate of two of France's finest Jesuit colleges. Unable to break this impasse, in 1658 Rome defiantly appointed Laval vicar apostolic to New France. While not technically a bishop, a vicar apostolic is empowered to administer the diocese under the authority of the pope. The controversy increased when it was learned that Laval was secretly consecrated a bishop, but of Petraea, a dormant Middle Eastern diocese.

1659: François Laval arrives to assume control of the Church in New France.

Upon his arrival in New France in 1659, Laval immediately asserted his authority over religious matters in the colony. His iron will and inflexibility quickly made him enemies, although no one could doubt his piety. He blithely risked infection by visiting the hospital when epidemics raged, and lived a life of poverty and deprivation. Laval's reforms included the establishment of an ecclesiastical court to deal with all disputes involving secular clergy and to judge all matters falling under the jurisdiction of the bishop, a move the governor interpreted as a direct challenge to his civil authority and the prerogatives of the Crown. The clergy and religious orders, who administered the colony's schools, hospitals, and social services, resisted Laval's attempts to manage their affairs. To further his control, Laval attempted to impose a parish system on the colony, and established a seminary to train priests. He also introduced the tithe to lessen the church's dependence on the state. Today, a tithe is a voluntary contribution to one's church—traditionally one-tenth of income. In this era, both in the old world and the new, it was an obligatory payment. Not surprisingly, Laval's ultramontanism encountered stiff resistance. The Sulpicians questioned the authority of the Bishop of Petraea in New France, and established their own seminary in Montreal. When Laval attempted to direct the actions of the female religious orders, they too resisted his efforts. The governor denied the bishop a voice in civil appointments and discouraged his attendance at meetings of the council. Laval's attempts to outlaw the liquor trade with the Natives alienated the colony's traders and brought him into conflict with the civil authorities. Repeatedly frustrated, Laval appealed to Rome to establish a diocese at Quebec so that he could effectively confront "the perpetual and scornful rivals of the ecclesiastical authority" in New France.[34] However, it was not until 1674 that the French Crown agreed to permit the establishment of a diocese.

"Disasters and Portents": New France in 1663

If the Company of One Hundred Associates had fulfilled its obligations, the population of New France should have numbered more than 30 000 by 1663. As it was, New France could claim only 3035 inhabitants. This compared poorly to the English and Dutch colonies to the south; the New England colonies had a population of more than 40 000. The population of the Dutch colony of New Netherland along the Hudson and Delaware rivers numbered 10 000. Further south, the population of the English colony of Virginia had grown to more than 30 000. Not only were these colonies more populous than New France, they had developed prosperous and more diversified economies. Agriculture flourished, especially in Virginia, where tobacco and indigo (used for dye) had become profitable cash crops and supported the emergence of a wealthy and powerful planter class. Artisanal production expanded in New England largely due to the nature of settlement: by locating house lots near the town centre and by granting families no more land than they needed to support themselves, the founders of New England were able to maintain social order and control by keeping families clustered close to one another. The concentration of settlement and limited land grants also encouraged economic diversification and the emergence of a wide range of commercial pursuits and cottage industries.

Economic growth was also encouraged by the British policy of mercantilism. Mercantilism, which was quickly becoming the new European economic orthodoxy in the seventeenth century, refers to a set of policies designed to promote the economic self-sufficiency of a nation by eliminating dependence on foreign suppliers. It was based on the conviction that there was a finite supply of wealth—specifically gold and silver—and that a nation could only enrich itself at the expense of another. The goal was to achieve a favourable balance of trade, to reduce the outflow of currency to a rival state. Under this system, colonies were desirable as a source of raw materials unavailable at home and as markets for the products of domestic industry. Britain's mercantilist policies found expression in a series of Navigation Acts, the first of which was enacted by Parliament in 1651. Under the terms of the Navigation Acts, colonial trade was restricted to British and British colonial vessels, and colonial merchants were prohibited from importing goods directly from any other nation or its dependencies. The Navigation Acts contributed to New England's economic development by ensuring certain colonial goods preferential access to the British market and by limiting competition from foreign goods in colonial markets. The cod, mackerel, halibut, and whales that abounded in New England waters supported a productive fishery that encouraged the development of shipbuilding and a profitable trade with the West Indies, where New England fish fed the growing population of African slaves.

The compact settlements and economic diversification of New England contrasted sharply with conditions in New France. New France was primarily a rural society, with nearly two-thirds of the population residing in the countryside. By 1663, 104 seigneuries had been laid out in rectangular plots along both sides of the St. Lawrence. Only a tiny fraction of land, however, had been distributed among habitants and brought under cultivation. Such a thinly dispersed population was vulnerable to attack, and by the 1650s a significant number of farms had been abandoned due to the ongoing Iroquois threat. Land policies in New England had ensured that land was widely, and more or less equitably, distributed among the population. New France's abundant seigneurial lands were controlled by just 62 individual seigneurs and seven religious foundations. Of the 62 individual seigneurs, 13 had been born in Canada and 51 were resident in the colony. Most seigneurs were of noble birth and related to one another by either blood or marriage. Although seigneurs dominated the affairs of Canada, few seigneurs became wealthy from

The economic doctrine of mercantilism provides a rationale for colonial development in the seventeenth century.

the meagre revenues generated from their extensive land holdings. Even those seigneurs committed to settling their land had little success attracting colonists.

Canada's harsh climate, rugged wilderness, and the Iroquois threat discouraged all but the most adventurous and the devout religious hoping to find a place in Paradise through service, suffering, and even a martyr's death. Of the few hundred colonists who did venture to New France, most were young men from the maritime provinces of Normandy and Aunis. Population growth was further inhibited by the severe imbalance in the numbers of men and women resident in the colony: in 1663, there were six men for every woman. Adding to the difficulty was the fact that a significant number of single women belonged to one of the religious orders.

While the English and Dutch colonies had emerged as economic assets to their mother countries, New France was not even self-supporting: The absence of significant local markets discouraged mixed farming and food often had to be imported from France to prevent starvation. Although Quebec boasted several mills, a bakery, and brewery, there was no industry to speak of anywhere in the colony beyond the fur trade and the fishery. Even Canadian lumber was deemed of inferior quality and did not find a ready market in France.

The fur trade remained the economic lifeblood of New France, but the trade had become anemic and was in desperate need of a lifesaving transfusion. As the supply of furs dwindled, and profits disappeared and debts mounted, traders and merchants began quarrelling among themselves. Disturbed by the rising level of tensions, the Company of One Hundred Associates asserted its rights and convened an inquiry into the Compagnie des Habitants. The inquiry, led by a Paris lawyer, Jean Peronne Dumesnil, only made matters worse. When he returned to France in 1663 to file his report, Dumesnil charged that the Compagnie des Habitants had misappropriated more than 3 million *livres*. Dumesnil spared no one in his report and blamed everyone from the governor to the Jesuits for the mismanagement of the company's, and the colony's, affairs. French authorities were more lenient and concluded that the directors of the Compagnie des Habitants may have been incompetent but were not guilty of fraud. It is hard to imagine how any one could have managed the fur trade more effectively under the circumstances. Not only was the supply of furs unreliable, the market for furs in France was depressed and creditors proved increasingly reluctant to advance the trade goods needed to barter with the Natives.

Whereas the English and Dutch colonies to the south enjoyed relatively stable government, New France suffered from administrative confusion. With the creation of a council in 1647, an attempt had been made to provide the colony with an effective administration, but ongoing rivalries and competing interests limited its effectiveness. Even the Church, which had provided one of the few examples of efficient organization, found itself afflicted with dissension. Determined to assert the Church's supremacy over all aspects of life in New France, François de Laval, the strong-willed vicar apostolic, frequently found himself in conflict with the governor, the religious orders, and the fur traders. Squabbles even erupted over the symbolic issue of who should take precedence in religious ceremonies and public events—the governor or the bishop. While such disputes may seem petty, they assumed great significance in a hierarchical society preoccupied by honours, and proved a distraction from more important matters.

Even more problematic was Laval's attitude to the fur trade. Convinced by the clergy of New France of the destructive impact of the brandy trade upon the Aboriginal peoples and the Church's missionary efforts, in 1660 Laval threatened to excommunicate anyone found to be trading spirits to the Natives. Laval lifted the excommunication edict in 1661 when the liquor traffic appeared to have ceased, but fur traders appealed to the newly appointed governor Pierre Dubois, baron D'Avaugour to reinstate the trade. Unhappy with Laval's increasing interference in civil affairs and sympathetic to the plight of his friends in the fur trade, D'Avaugour permitted the traffic in spirits to resume. Infuriated by the governor's actions, Laval travelled to France to seek King Louis XIV's support in suppressing the brandy trade and D'Avaugour's removal as governor. In July 1663, the governor learned that he was to be recalled. Without waiting for a successor, D'Avaugour took ship from Quebec, disgusted that "base spirits" should attack his honour after more than 40 years of service to the Crown.[35] D'Avaugour returned to military service and was killed the following year defending Croatia from the invading Turks.

Conclusion

The petty struggle between Bishop Laval and Governor D'Avaugour was symptomatic of the larger problems afflicting France's North American possessions. With the constant threat of Iroquois attack, a small population, and precarious economy, and beset by internal tensions and rivalries, the future of New France appeared bleak. Portents of impending disaster seemed everywhere. In a September 1661 letter to her son, Marie de l'Incarnation reported strange signs in the sky that "terrified many people" and that an unborn child was heard to cry in her mother's womb. Charges of sorcery were levelled against several persons said to have cast evil spells and to have conjured up phantoms. Many attributed the appearance of a new and deadly malady that swept through the colony to witchcraft. To Marie de l'Incarnation, these occurrences were signs of God's wrath and impending judgment.[36] Such fears seemed to be confirmed when a massive earthquake shook New France in February 1663. Beset by dark omens, the residents of New France desperately appealed to the mother country for help. Remarkably, after years of neglect and indifference, French authorities began to pay attention to the pleas issuing forth from her beleaguered North American colony. Although few could have believed it at the time, New France stood on the threshold of a new era.

Questions to Consider

1. How did the character and conduct of the fur trade change between 1632 and 1663?

2. What roles did the Church and religion play in the development of New France?

3. How significant a role did women play in the early life of New France?

Critical Thinking Questions

1. To what degree were the interests of the fur trade and the Church compatible?

2. Why did the development of New France lag so far behind that of the English and Dutch colonies to the south?

3. Champlain has often been portrayed as the "father of New France." To what degree does he merit this distinction?

4. How useful as a historical source is *The Jesuit Relations*?

Suggested Readings
General

Eccles, W.J. *The Canadian Frontier: 1534–1760*. New York: Holt, Rinehart, Winston, 1969.

Greer, Alan. *The People of New France*. Toronto: University of Toronto Press, 1997.

Moogk, Peter. *La Nouvelle France: The Making of New France-a Cultural History*. East Lansing: Michigan State University Press, 2000.

Trigger, Bruce. *Natives and Newcomers: Canada's Heroic Age Reconsidered*. Montreal: McGill-Queen's University Press, 1985.

Trudel, Marcel. *The Beginnings of New France, 1524–1663*. Toronto: McClelland & Stewart, 1973.

Native Peoples and the Fur Trade

Axtell, James. *The Invasion Within: The Contest of Cultures in Colonial North America*. New York: Oxford University Press, 1985.

Brandao, Jose Antonio. *Your Fyre Shall Burn No More: Iroquois Policy toward New France and Its Native Allies to 1701*. Lincoln: University of Nebraska Press, 1997.

Delage, Denys. *Bitter Feast: Amerindians and Europeans in the American Northeast, 1600–1664*. Vancouver: University of British Columbia Press, 1993.

Dickason, Olive P. *The Myth of the Savage and the Beginnings of French Colonialism in the Americas*. Edmonton: University of Alberta Press, 1984.

Gilman, Carolyn. *Where Two Worlds Meet: The Great Lakes Fur Trade*. St. Paul: Minnesota Historical Society, 1982.

Heidenreich, Conrad and Ray, Arthur J. *The Early Fur Trades: A Study in Cultural Interaction*. Toronto: McClelland & Stewart, 1976.

Heidenreich, Conrad. Huronia: A History and Geography of the Huron Indians, 1600–1650. Toronto: McClelland & Stewart, 1971.

Innis, Harold Adams. *The Fur Trade in Canada: An Introduction to Canadian Economic History*. Toronto: University of Toronto Press, 1970.

Jaenen, Cornelius. *Friend and Foe: Aspects of French-Amerindian Cultural Contact in the Sixteenth and Seventeenth Centuries*. Toronto: McClelland & Stewart, 1976.

Richter, Daniel K. *The Ordeal of the Longhouse: The Peoples of the Iroquois League in the Era of European Colonization*. Chapel Hill: University of North Carolina Press, 1992.

Trigger, Bruce. *Children of Aataentsic: A History of the Huron People to 1660*. Montreal and Kingston: McGill-Queen's University Press, 1976.

Early Settlement in Acadia and New France

Charbonneau, Hubert et.al. *The First French Canadians: Pioneers in the St. Lawrence Valley.* Newark: University of Delaware Press, 1993.

Clark, Andrew Hill. *Acadia: The Geography of Early Nova Scotia to 1760.* Madison: University of Wisconsin Press, 1968.

Dechene, Louise. *Habitants and Merchants in Seventeenth Century Montreal.* Montreal and Kingston: McGill-Queen's University Press, 1992.

Griffiths, Naomi E.S. *From Migrant to Acadian: A North American Border People, 1604–1755.* Montreal and Kingston: McGill-Queen's University Press, 2005.

Harris, Richard Colebrook. *The Seigneurial System in Early Canada: A Geographical Study.* Montreal and Kingston: McGill-Queen's University Press, 1984.

Reid, John G. *Acadia, Maine and New Scotland: Marginal Colonies in the Seventeenth Century.* Toronto: University of Toronto Press, 1981.

Missions and Missionaries

Blackburn, Carol. *Harvest of Souls: The Jesuit Mission and Colonialism in North America, 1632–1650.* Montreal and Kingston: McGill-Queen's University Press, 2000.

Fay, Terence. *A History of Canadian Catholics: Gallicanism, Romanism, and Canadianism.* Montreal and Kingston: McGill-Queen's University Press, 2002.

Grant, John Webster. *Moon of Wintertime: Missionaries and the Indians of Canada in Encounter since 1534.* Toronto: University of Toronto Press, 1984.

Greer, Allan, ed. *The Jesuit Relations: Natives and Missionaries in Seventeenth Century North America* [an abridged version]. New York: Bedford/ St. Martins, 2000.

Jaenen, Cornelius. *The Role of the Church in New France.* Toronto: McGraw-Hill Ryerson, 1976.

Marshall, Joyce, ed. *Word from New France: The Selected Letters of Marie de l'Incarnation.* Toronto: Oxford University Press, 1967.

Simpson, Patricia. *Marguerite Bourgeoys and the Congregation of Notre Dame, 1665–1700.* Montreal and Kingston: McGill-Queen's University Press, 2005.

Thwaites, Reuben Gold, ed. *The Jesuit Relations and Allied Documents: Travels and Explorations of the Jesuit Missionaries in New France, 1610–1791,* 73 vols. Cleveland: Burrows, 1896–1901. Available at Early Canadiana Online: http://www.canadiana.org.

Notes

1   Father Paul Le Jeune, "Brief Relation of the Journey to New France," *The Jesuit Relations and Allied Documents: Travels and Explorations of the Jesuit Missionaries in New France, 1610–1791*. Reuben Gold Thwaites, ed. (Cleveland: Burrows, 1896–1901), vol. 5, 11–43.

2   "Letter from Father Paul Le Jeune to the Reverend Father Provincial of France, at Paris" in *The Jesuit Relations*, vol. 6, 61.

3   As quoted in José Antonio Brandao, *Your Fyre Shall Burn No More* (Lincoln: University of Nebraska Press, 1997), 8–11.

4   George T. Hunt, *The Wars of the Iroquois: A Study in Intertribal Trade Relations* (Madison: University of Wisconsin Press, 1940), 4–5.

5   José Antonio Brandao, *Your Fyre*, 128, 130, 131. Quotation from John Bartram is on page 41.

6   The Jesuit Relations, vol. 9, 153.

7   John W. O'Malley, *Trent and All That: Renaming Catholicism in the Early Modern Era* (Cambridge: Harvard University Press, 2000), 140.

8   http://www.iveignatianexercises.org/.

9   Jean de Brébeuf, "Relation of What Occurred among the Hurons in the Year 1635" in *The Jesuit Relations*, vol. 8, 119.

10 *The Jesuit Relations*, vol. 33, 143.

11 Jean de Brébeuf "On the Solemn Feast of the Dead" in *The Jesuit relations*, vol. 10, 278–303.

12 Jean de Brébeuf, "Relation of What Occurred among the Hurons in the Year 1635" in *The Jesuit Relations*, vol. 8, 99.

13 Bruce Trigger, *Natives and Newcomers: Canada's Heroic Age Reconsidered* (Montreal: McGill-Queen's University Press, 1985), 266.

14 Marie de l'Incarnation to a Lady of Rank, Quebec, 3 September 1640, in *Word from New France: The Selected Letters of Marie de l'Incarnation*. Joyce Marshall, ed. (Toronto: Oxford University Press, 1967), 74.

15 Marie de l'Incarnation to her son, Quebec, 1 September 1668, in *Word from New France*, 341.

16 Paul Le Jeune, "Relation of What Occurred in New France in the Year 1635," in *The Jesuit Relations*, vol. 7, 273.

17 Marie-Claire Daveluy, "Paul de Chomedey de Maisonneuve" *Dictionary of Canadian Biography*, http://www.biographi.ca.

18 As quoted in Hélène Bernier, "Marguerite Bourgeoys" *Dictionary of Canadian Biography*, http://www.biographi.ca.

19 Raymond Du Bois Cahall, *The Sovereign Council of New France* (New York: Columbia University, 1915), 13–18, http://www.archive.org/details/sovereigncouncil00cahaiala.

20 St. Joseph had earlier been moved from its original site at Ihonatiria.

21 As quoted in Francis Parkman and David Levin, *England and France in North America*. Vol. 2 (New York: Library of America, 1983), 662.

22 The Jesuit Relations, vol. 40, 211.

23 J. Sherman Bleakney, *Sods, Soil, and Spades: The Acadians at Grand Pré and Their Dykeland Legacy* (Montreal and Kingston: McGill-Queen's University Press, 2004), 38–39.

24 Susan Poizner, "The Lioness of Acadia" The Beaver: Canada's History Magazine (February /March 2007); Derek Hayes, *Canada: An Illustrated History* (Vancouver: Douglas and McIntyre, 2008), 28–29; George MacBeath, "Charles de Saint-Étienne de la Tour" Dictionary of Canadian Biography, http://www.biographi.ca; René Baudry, "Charles de Menou d'Aulnay" Dictionary of Canadian Biography, http://www.biographi.ca.

25 From the marriage contract cited in Marcel Trudel, *The Beginnings of New France, 1524–1663* (Toronto: McClelland & Stewart, 1973), 204.

26 As quoted by Naomi Griffiths, *From Migrant to Acadian: A North American Border People, 1604–1755* (Montreal and Kingston: McGill-Queen's University Press, 2005), 76–78.

27 *The Jesuit Relations*, vol. 40, 215.

28 Order of 28 April 1654, cited in Marcel Trudel, *The Beginnings of New France, 1524–1663* (Toronto: McClelland & Stewart, 1973), 225.

29 Marie de l'Incarnation to her son, 10 August 1662, *Word from New France*, 273.

30 Arthur Ray, "Fur Trade History as an Aspect of Native History," in Ian A.L. Getty and Donald B. Smith, eds., *One Century Later: Western Canadian Reserve Indians since Treaty 7* (Vancouver: University of British Columbia Press, 1978), 12.

31 Bruce Trigger, *The Children of Aataenstic: A History of the Huron People to 1600* (Montreal and Kingston: McGill-Queen's University Press, 1987), 360.

32 As quoted in Arthur Ray, "Fur Trade History," 9.

33 André Vachon, "Adam Dollard des Ormeaux," *Dictionary of Canadian Biography*.

34 As quoted in André Vachon, "François de Laval," *Dictionary of Canadian Biography*.

35 As quoted in W.J. Eccles, "Pierre Dubois Davaugour," *Dictionary of Canadian Biography*.

36 Marie de l'Incarnation to her son, September 1661 and 20 August 1663, *Word from New France*, 260–265, 287–295.

France in America: 1663–1750

$\mathcal{A}$t the end of August 1668, Marie Major, a 31-year-old woman from Normandy, arrived in Quebec. She was unmarried, one of several dozen filles du roi ("daughters of the king") who had been recruited that year in France to help increase the population of the fledgling North American colony. Many of these young women were encouraged to come to the colony by their parish priests, and it may have been the hope of building a better future that encouraged Major to undertake the adventure. The bourgeois daughter of a tax collector, Marie had lost both her parents and seems to have faced a life of reduced circumstances. She was past prime marrying age, but had possessions valued at 300 livres—a sum equivalent to several years' wages for most workers. Colonial life offered her a second chance.

On September 11, days after her arrival, Marie Major married Antoine Roy dit Desjardins, who had come to New France a few years earlier as a soldier with the Carignan-Salières regiment. The couple embarked for Batiscan, where Antoine had been granted some land. Their only child, Pierre, was born the following summer. The story of Marie's brave risk in starting over in Canada did not, unfortunately, have a happy ending.

Her new husband, 33 at the time of their marriage, was a cooper (barrel maker), as well as a soldier and a farmer, but he was mired in financial troubles. More worrisome was that he may have left a family behind in France. Archival records from Antoine Roy's hometown of Joigny in Bourgogne (Burgundy) are incomplete, but reveal that a cooper by the same name, born in the same year, was the father of two sons. It is possible, of course, that Antoine's earlier family had died, but the record of Canadian marriage does not list him as a widower. Roy was not a successful farmer in New France, and was only able to clear a few acres and raise a few cattle, evidently not even producing enough for the family's own needs. Their finances were precarious

Louis XIV, the Sun King.

and he was forced to mortgage his property. He owed a total of several hundred livres to a number of creditors, including a debt of 82 livres to Michel Lecourt, a Montreal merchant, for some wheat and green peas. Unable to collect on his loan, Lecourt began legal proceedings against Roy, who left his wife and child to manage the farm in Batiscan on their own.

The law finally caught up with Roy in 1684 and he was sentenced to put up a bond or to work for Lecourt to pay off his debts. During this time, he boarded with Julien Talua-Vendamont, and true to form, fell behind in rent payments. But this was not his worst failing. On the morning of July 10, 1684, Talua-Vendamont arrived home to find Roy in bed with his wife. The enraged husband shot Roy dead. The adulterous wife, Anne Godeby, who had also come to New France as a fille de roi 15 years before, was punished with banishment. While Talua-Vendamont was sentenced to be executed, it does not appear that the sentence was carried out, and it is possible that he escaped. With Roy's death, creditors prosecuted his wife Marie, seizing whatever property had been acquired during her marriage to Antoine. She died penniless on December 8, 1689, at age 52.[1]

After reading this chapter you will be able to:

1. Identify the changes that followed New France's 1663 transition to a royal province.
2. Assess efforts to recreate French society and culture in New France.
3. Understand the sources of conflict within New France and their consequences for the colony's development.
4. Consider the impact of fur trade rivalry after the 1670 founding of the Hudson's Bay Company.
5. Explain the impact of the following successive imperial wars on New France:
    *   War of the League of Augsburg, 1689–1697
    *   War of the Spanish Succession, 1701–1713
    *   War of the Austrian Succession, 1740–1748

Introduction

The tumultuous story of Marie Major and Antoine Roy has many parallels to that of New France itself. Marie and Antoine's life together began with much hope and promise. This period in the history of New France began with a renewed commitment by France to its colonies, and grand plans to re-create the French social order in the North American wilderness. In 1663, the monopoly of the Company of One Hundred Associates was revoked, and New France was made a royal province under the direct control of the Crown. After decades of neglect and indifference, French authorities began to invest in the defence, administration, settlement, and economic diversification of New France. Metropolitan authorities in France aimed to create a highly ordered and hierarchical society under France's firm administrative control. The pillars of this ordered society would include a noble class of office holders modelled on the French aristocracy, government regulation of the economy, the observance of seigneurial rights and obligations, the enforcement of the French legal code—the *coutume de Paris* (Custom of Paris)—and the established Church.

This ambitious plan for New France proved as difficult and unrealistic as the hopes of Marie Major and Antoine Roy to make a new life in Canada. Like these hopeful expatriates, France's colony would fall victim to a whirlwind of external events that it could not control. The distinctive French society built in Canada over the course of a hundred difficult years would ultimately take root and flourish. Pierre, the Roys' only son, left alone in the world at age 20, would go on to father 19 children by three successive wives. He has countless descendants in Canada today. This chapter considers the degree to which the type of society envisioned by French authorities actually came into being in New France. It examines the political administration of the colony, the working of the seigneurial system, and the role of the Church. It also assesses the impact of the fur trade, western expansion, and the effect of imperial rivalries and transplanted European conflicts on the character and evolution of New France.

Colbert's Vision and the Administration of New France

Why did French authorities assume control over the affairs of New France in 1663? There is no doubt that the sorry state of New France demanded action. With the colony vulnerable to Iroquois attack, suffering from a divided administration, underpopulated, economically weak, and dependent on a single industry, its survival required intervention from the mother country. The Crown's renewed interest in the fate of the colony, however, owed as much to developments at home as to the precarious state of its North American possessions.

With the death of Louis XIII in 1643, France found itself beset by internal dynastic struggles and the threat posed by external rivals. Ruled by an infant king and female regent, Anne of Austria, members of the nobility rose to challenge the authority of the Crown. The contest between the Crown and the nobility had weakened France in its struggle with the Habsburgs during the Thirty Years' War. Preoccupied by domestic concerns and foreign threats, France could devote little attention and few resources to New France. France's prospects improved with the signing of the Peace of Westphalia that ended the Thirty Years' War in 1648. Yet the need to recoup the cost of the war through taxation was a factor in a series of uprisings, "the Fronde," sparked by the nobility at the immediate close of the war. This civil war over the respective powers of the Crown and the aristocracy was suppressed in 1653 with the Crown emerging as undeniably victorious. France was able to stand fast against its rivals and become a dominant European power. The child king Louis XIV had been scarred by the brutal memory of the Fronde; even his own bedchamber had been invaded by an enraged mob. With the death of his first minister, Cardinal Mazarin, in 1661, the 23-year-old king began his personal rule. These deep and distasteful impressions sharpened Louis XIV's determination that his power would be beyond challenge.

1661: King Louis XIV, crowned as a child, begins his personal rule.

As France's "Sun King," Louis XIV sat confidently upon the throne, ushering in a new era of royal absolutism. During his 72-year reign (1643–1715)—the longest in European history— Louis XIV centralized the power of the state as never before; he became the personification of the state's power: "*L'état c'est moi*," he declared. The idea of an absolute monarch, reigning by Divine Right—the will of God—seems like an old-fashioned political notion, but this idea represented a modern shift away from the decentralized feudal authority of the medieval past. The visible symbol of centralized power was Louis XIV's grand palace at Versailles. Its construction began in 1669 and would continue for more than 100 years, employing tens of thousands of workers. The awe-inspiring elaborate painted frescoes, sculptured marble, silken draperies, and blazing chandeliers sparkling with crystal pendants set off a flurry of imitation among Europe's lesser monarchs. France's nobility were "domesticated" by the king, and flocked to Versailles to compete for nominal roles at court, vying, for example, to be entrusted with the task of holding the right sleeve of Louis's garment when he dressed upon arising. Increasingly by the mid-seventeenth century, prominent state officials were men who achieved their rank and position by virtue of administrative roles—*noblesse de robe*—as opposed to those whose rank was hereditary, the *noblesse d'épée*, or nobility of the sword.

Louis XIV surrounded himself with capable advisors and lieutenants who created a competent bureaucracy to administer state affairs. Chief among these was Jean-Baptiste Colbert. Colbert reformed the taxation and budget systems and placed France upon a sound financial foundation. These reforms provided France with the means to manage and support its overseas colonies. A dedicated follower of

This late-seventeenth-century painting of Jean-Baptiste Colbert by Jean Marc Nattier is on display at Versailles.

Source: Réunion des Musées Nationaux/Art Resource, NY.

1663: Under Colbert's direction, New France becomes a royal province.

mercantilism, the theory of national economy that held that commerce should be regulated to secure a favourable balance of trade, Colbert strove to replicate the success of the English and Dutch, and transform France's colonies into secure sources of raw materials and ready markets for French manufactured goods. Long overlooked, New France now became a vital part of Colbert's grand imperial plan.

To protect France's commercial interests and to further her imperial ambitions, Colbert built up the navy and reformed the army so that it emerged as one of the best trained in Europe. The arrival in New France of experienced troops of the Carignan-Salières regiment represented a serious commitment to the colony's defence and development. New forts were built at Sorel, Chambly, and the northern end of Lake Champlain to block Iroquois attack. Real security, however, required sound administrative institutions, a substantial increase in the size of the population, and a diversified economy.

The Sovereign Council

In 1663, a sovereign council for New France replaced the unwieldy governing structures of the past. The sovereign council promulgated royal edicts, legislated for the needs of the colony, and sat as a court of first instance and as a court of appeal for matters going beyond local seigneurial courts. This meant that there was no distinction between the legislative (or law-making) and judicial functions, although this distinction would later evolve, with the sovereign council ultimately becoming more akin to a supreme court. "The form of the Sovereign Council reflected the absolutist notions of the young King," historian Raymond Du Bois Cahall explained. It was to be appointed by the two highest officials in the colony: the governor general and bishop. Unlike the council of 1647, in which syndics representing the towns would help to elect councillors, "these men looked to those above, rather than those below.... The King was drawing the reins of government into his own hands." Five councillors were appointed, along with an attorney general and a clerk.[2]

Historian W.J. Eccles offered an alternative perspective on this change from a system of elected syndics, explaining that Colbert wished to have more direct input from the subjects of New France, to have the people speak for themselves. Colbert directed the governor and intendant to call popular assemblies to canvass the views of the people before enacting laws that affected the general interest. Seventeen such assemblies were held between 1672 and 1700, before the practice was made an annual one in 1706.[3]

The governor, as the senior official in the colony, represented the power of the throne, and had responsibility for military matters. The governor was also responsible for diplomatic affairs—relations with Native nations and foreign powers, notably the British colonies to the south. Most governors of New France were members of the nobility and professional soldiers. Deputy governors were appointed for Montreal and Trois Rivières; they reported directly to the governor general and their responsibilities were primarily military.

The day-to-day affairs of the colony were managed by the intendant. Well-educated and trained in the law, the intendant symbolized the rise of a modern bureaucracy. He was responsible for the maintenance of law and order, the provision of justice, the management of the colony's finances, the construction and maintenance of wharves, roads, and fortifications, and the advancement of settlement and economic development. In times of war, the intendant ensured that troops were paid, fed, clothed, and supplied with arms and munitions. The burden of such responsibilities proved too great for one individual, and deputy intendants were later appointed for Montreal, Trois Rivières, and Detroit.

The Bishop and the Church

The final member of this ruling triumvirate was the bishop. The bishop represented the interests of the established Church and the desire to maintain spiritual order and moral stability within New France. Through its control of education, the Church disseminated an ethic calculated to remind each person of his or her allotted place in the social order. According to the rulebook of the Petit Seminaire de Québec, all persons were expected to demonstrate "humility, obedience, purity, meekness, modesty, simplicity, chastity, charity and an ardent love of Jesus and his holy Mother."[4] Catholicism occupied an important place in people's lives. Swedish naturalist Peter Kalm observed in 1749 that "the French in their colonies, spend much more time in prayer and external worship than the English, and Dutch settlers in the British Colonies."[5]

Canadiens—as the settlers along the St. Lawrence came to be known—attached great importance to pilgrimages, relics, and novenas, but they also believed in witchcraft, faith healers, soothsayers, and a variety of folk superstitions. No doubt some, like the common people of the mother country, practised their religion more out of social convention and habit than out of any zealous conviction. Most performed their Easter duties (penance and communion) and took part in midnight mass at Christmas. Fewer people, though, attended mass faithfully every Sunday. Even those who did attend regularly did not always show the respect and attention that one might expect of them. Priests often complained about the poor behaviour of their parishioners during services, their neglect of church obligations, and their love of gambling, dancing, and horse racing. The increasing numbers

This mid-nineteenth century painting by Cornelius Krieghoff, *Habitants Playing at Cards*, presents a nostalgic view of French Canadian life.

Source: © McCord Museum, 13538.

of illegitimate and abandoned children in the colony suggests that the Church's influence was not absolute. The habitants of New France often proved themselves to be independent, self-assertive, and outspoken individuals who did not shy away from challenging the authority of their priest.

The Legal System

Like the French provincial *parlements* upon which it was modelled, the sovereign council included an attorney general, who prepared and presented legal cases. According to French law, anyone charged with an offence was assumed guilty until proven innocent. The panel of judges interrogated the accused and then interviewed any witnesses. Defendants could question witnesses but were not entitled to representation by a lawyer. Because confessions were highly desirable, judges did not hesitate to use torture to secure admissions of guilt. Simple questioning of the accused—the *question ordinaire*—could give way to the *question extraordinaire*, in which a suspect would be encouraged to be more forthcoming with the supposed truth. While court proceedings were secretive, punishment was very public. Depending on the severity of the crime, the convicted could be executed, banished, branded with a red hot iron, flogged, humiliated by being publicly displayed in the stocks, or sent to a harsh life aboard France's galley ships plying the Mediterranean. Offences that resulted in capital punishment included treason, desertion, murder, duelling, theft, arson, abortion, rape, sodomy, and bestiality. Such swift and public justice was seen as an essential tool for maintaining social order.

Conflicting Authorities

Overlapping responsibilities among the governor general, intendant, and bishop, and the personalities of each of these, guaranteed that tensions frequently developed. The Bishop of Quebec, François de Laval, clashed almost immediately with the first governor general appointed under New France's new regime, Augustine de Saffray de Mézy. Although the governor represented the king, he had been appointed to only a three-year term and could be recalled at any time. The bishop, on the other hand, served for life and embodied the authority of the Church. The two men soon found themselves involved in a noisy quarrel over the governor's salary and allowances, appointments to the sovereign council, the implementation of the tithe, and the election of a syndic for Quebec. In September 1664, Laval directed the clergy to read a letter from the pulpit denouncing the governor. Saffray de Mézy responded by having notices posted throughout the colony condemning the bishop. The residents of New France were spared the spectacle of a protracted public feud between the colony's temporal and spiritual leaders by the governor's early death in May 1665, and by Colbert's determination to curb Laval's power.

Colbert deprived the bishop of the right to appoint members of the sovereign council. The tensions between Laval and Saffray de Mézy might have been mitigated by the presence of an intendant, but the first appointee to this office, Louis Robert de Fortel, never made it to Canada.

The office of intendant was not taken up until the arrival of Jean Talon in 1665. An experienced civil servant who enjoyed the confidence of Colbert, Talon soon became the dominant figure on the sovereign council, presiding over its meetings and dispensing

1665: The energetic Jean Talon arrives as first intendant of New France.

justice. Talon's power and influence resulted in conflict with the new governor, Daniel de Rémy de Courcelle. Talon was determined to implement Colbert's "grand plan" for New France. The establishment of a sound justice system was essential to New France's development, and Talon set out to rationalize the colony's courts. The authority of seigneurial courts was reasserted, and lower courts, the Prévôtés, were established in the towns of Quebec, Montreal, and Trois Rivières. The sovereign council reviewed all serious cases heard in the lower courts and served as a court of appeal. Talon resolved to put an end to the costly and time-consuming civil cases in the fractious colony and prohibited lawyers from practising. Despite the governor's opposition, Talon assumed the right to hear all cases where less than 100 livres was involved. In more serious civil cases, Talon encouraged out-of-court settlements and served as arbitrator. The end result was a highly paternalistic legal system, but one that ensured that justice was both expeditious and inexpensive.

Talon also came into conflict with Bishop Laval. Colbert had directed Talon to be assertive with the imperious bishop and to restore a proper balance between the temporal and spiritual authorities. Laval and the Jesuits, Colbert warned, "have acquired an authority that goes beyond the limits of their true profession, which must be concerned only with consciences."[6] To Laval's consternation, Talon reduced the tithe to one twenty-sixth of all cereal production and exempted new colonists from the church tax for five years. As a result, the Church was forced to rely on the state for a considerable part of its revenue. Talon further alienated Laval when he expropriated part of one of the Church's seigneuries, Notre-Dames-des-Anges. For Talon, the Church's vast and largely undeveloped landholdings impeded economic progress by depriving settlers of some of the best land in the colony, and compromised New France's security by leaving large unpopulated gaps on the landscape that facilitated Iroquois attack. Even more vexing to Laval was Talon's decision to repeal the edict that outlawed the trade in alcohol with the Natives. The trade in alcohol, Talon concluded, was essential to combat Dutch and English competition for furs, to maintain influence among New France's Aboriginal allies, and to revive an economy that still depended on the fur trade. Laval responded by declaring it a sin to get Natives drunk and to supply them with alcohol to take back to their villages. Talon accused the bishop of interfering in temporal affairs and "tormenting people's consciences."[7] To counterbalance the power of Laval and the Jesuits, Talon invited the Récollets to return to New France and supported the work of another order, the Sulpicians.

Improved Colonial Defence

Talon also systematically set out to improve the beleaguered colony's defences. In 1665, the same year that Talon arrived in New France, more than 1200 soldiers of the Carignan-Salières regiment took up positions to defend the colony against the Iroquois. The regiment was warmly received by colonists, who craved peace and security, but the presence of such a large number of troops in the colony brought on social problems such as drunkenness, prostitution, rape, and other crimes that strained relations between the regiment and the civilian population. Responsibility for provisioning the troops fell to Talon, who directed his considerable energy and talent to procuring shelter, food, and clothing for the winter months, and to making preparations for an attack on the Iroquois.

1665: The Carignan-Salières regiment is sent to protect New France.

1666: Governor Courcelle leads a disastrous winter campaign into Iroquois Country.

In January 1666, some 300 soldiers of the regiment, along with 200 *Canadiens*, set out on foot for Iroquois territory under the command of Governor Courcelle. This campaign, launched in the dead of winter, proved disastrous. Poorly guided, Courcelle found himself in the Dutch settlement of Schenectady and confronted by a British delegation incensed by the French incursion into lands recently acquired by the English Crown. After a few skirmishes with the Mohawk, the French forces returned to Quebec, exhausted and close to starvation.

Having learned some important lessons during this first failed expedition, the French undertook another campaign during the summer and fall, razing villages, burning crops, and destroying stores of food throughout Iroquois country. The desired effect was achieved, and the Iroquois opted for peace the following year. Although he did not accompany the expedition, its success owed a great deal to Talon's organizational abilities.

With the Iroquois threat momentarily contained, Talon convinced several officers and nearly 450 men of the Carignan-Salières regiment to remain in the colony and to settle along the Richelieu River, providing an important defence against future Iroquois attacks. Some 30 officers were granted seigneuries, and discharged soldiers received both land and livestock. Although this constituted a significant addition to the colony's population, many of the soldiers were not suited to farming, and left their farms to pursue the freer life offered by the fur trade.

With the demobilization of the Carignan-Salières regiment, a colonial militia was created in 1669. Militiamen are citizen soldiers, rather than professional troops, and every able-bodied man in New France between the ages of 16 and 60 was required to take part in regular training drills. The militia was organized by parish, in companies of 50, with each company commanded by a local captain of militia appointed by the governor. The position was unpaid, but it offered prestige, and was accorded to those of demonstrable bravery and leadership. Although in practice the local seigneur was often appointed, a habitant who distinguished himself militarily might win this valued distinction. Such an honour entitled the incumbent to wear a sword like a nobleman, to sit in a prominent place in church, and to a position of precedence in processions, following the seigneur. Moreover, the militia captains would enforce the requirement of habitants to perform a designated number of days' labour on public works projects such as roads and bridges, an obligation known as the *corvée*.

Settlement and the Seigneurial System

New France enjoyed the peace that was essential for settlement. The seigneurial system was well established, but had developed haphazardly. Many seigneuries were underpopulated and underdeveloped, and there remained large stretches of wilderness along the St. Lawrence. Talon began a major reorganization of the entire system, registering all land holdings in the colony; all seigneurs were required to declare the extent of their property, the amount of land that had been cleared, and the number of tenants that had been settled. After gathering this information, Talon withdrew the rights of seigneurs who had neglected their obligations, and granted new seigneuries to those committed to settling and developing their land. Talon required seigneurs and settlers to take up residence within a year, and to clear and cultivate at least two acres (about 0.8 hectare) of land, or forfeit their property. He also sought to create a more compact colony that would enable settlers to better assist each other, support the development of industry and commerce, and provide protection against attacks. Three model villages—Bourg-Royal, Bourg-la-Reine, and Bourg-Talon—were laid out on lands expropriated from the Jesuits near Quebec. Triangular land grants radiated out from a central village where all dwellings and services were located. Despite its merits, the experiment did not continue after Talon's term as intendant ended.

Land grants varied widely in size, and depended on the rank, merit, wealth, and connections of the seigneur. The average seigneurie was 16 kilometres deep and eight kilometres across; the largest grants were up to 100 kilometres deep and 30 to 40 kilometres across. Convinced that such large grants were less likely to be developed, Talon favoured more modest grants. Seigneurs were required to settle their seigneuries, conceding parcels of land (censives) to individuals (censitaires) who requested it. The typical censive was between 40 and 200 *arpents* (13.6 to 68.3 hectares) and consisted of a narrow rectangular strip 179 metres wide that ran 1.6 kilometres back from the river. River frontage provided censitaires with access to the main transportation corridors within New France and to good fishing areas; fish was an important food staple. This pattern of land distribution was easily and cheaply surveyed, allowed censitaires to live close to their neighbours, and often provided access to a variety of soil and vegetation. Long daily treks were required to feed livestock and milk the cows that were kept on the poorer-quality soils far back from the river.

Censitaires were not merely tenants in the modern sense. Initially, they received a temporary deed, a *billet de concession*. Once a censitaire had fulfilled his settlement duties by occupying his concession, clearing the land, and planting crops, he received a final deed of possession entitling him to enjoy the use of his land in perpetuity and enabling him to sell or bequeath his property. French inheritance law required that widows retain half

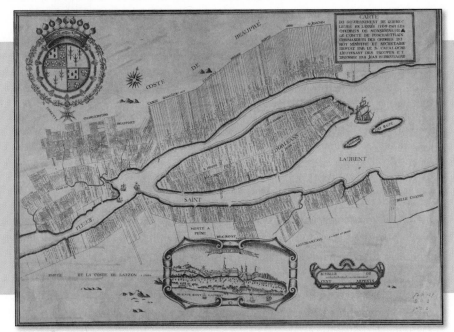

Map 3.1
Seigneurial Landscape, Ile d'Orléans and the North and South Shore of the St. Lawrence, 1709.

Source: Library and Archives Canada, NMC 0048248.

of their husband's estate and that the other half be divided equally among his children. Such fragmentation threatened the viability of farms, and means were found to keep estates intact. In some cases, parents granted land to a single child in return for a promise to maintain them in their old age and to make payments to their siblings. In other cases, additional censives were acquired to maintain a viable operation.

Much like the French feudal system, the seigneurial system sought to create an authoritarian and hierarchical society that rested on a series of mutual obligations. The Crown granted lands to seigneurs in return for obligations of settlement and service. Seigneurs were required to render homage and fealty to the king and his representatives, acknowledge the Crown's claim to all mineral rights, build a manor house, cede land to settlers, render justice to tenants, and maintain a mill, bake oven, and chapel for the use of censitaires.

The censitaires who received land owed rents and services to their seigneur. These obligations included the *cens*, nominal dues that symbolized the censitaires' dependence on the seigneur, and the *rentes*, a more substantial fee paid each year in money or in kind. Censitaires were also obliged to perform three days of unpaid labour, the *corvée*, each year, to provide the seigneur with a share of any fish caught or wood cut on the seigneurie, and to take their grain to the seigneur's mill, paying him one-fourteenth of the flour milled. These monopoly rights and obligations were known as the *banalités*.

Censitaires could sell their land concession, but seigneurs were entitled to a transfer tax, the *lods et ventes*, that amounted to one-twelfth of the value of the sale. In France, this system of mutual obligations could be oppressive. Such was not the case in New France where seigneurial dues were governed by contract and could not be arbitrarily changed. As a result, the burdens of seigneurial dues were significantly less onerous than those that fell upon the French peasantry. Seigneurial power was weakened in New France by the concessions needed to attract censitaires in a society in which land was widely available, labour scarce, and the lure of the fur trade ever present.

Conditions in New France precluded the development of the rigid social structure that defined French feudalism. Most seigneuries did not generate large revenues; many seigneurs were scarcely better off than their tenants. Perhaps for this reason, some seigneurs clung all the more tightly to the trappings of rank, insisting on their claims to distinction. The maypole celebration was a case in point. Historian Allan Greer describes it as a secular event that "symbolized habitant deference towards the seigneur father-figure. Each year on the first of May a tall phallic tree trunk would be planted in front of the manor house." The ceremony included dancing, rejoicing, and the discharge of firearms, and the exact terms of the celebration were spelled out by contract, which even specified the height of the pole. "One insecure seigneur, for example, insisted that his pole thrust at least fifty feet into the air."[8]

The additional income available through fishing, the fur trade, or skilled labour allowed a significant number of censitaires to acquire the wealth and status to become seigneurs themselves. In 1685, a royal edict allowing nobles in Canada to take part in trade opened the door to prosperous North American traders seeking ennoblement, something that would have been impossible in the old world, where the distinction between the aristocracy and the bourgeoisie was firm. Even those who remained censitaires enjoyed a higher standard of living and longer life expectancy than their French counterparts. The options available to the *Canadien* censitaire inculcated a degree of independence, and undermined official efforts to create a highly ordered and hierarchical society. Historian W.J. Eccles suggests that the people of New France were imbued with an "aristocratic ethos"—that they internalized the values of the nobility. "It was not the actual number of nobles that was important," he explains. Rather, it was "the tone that was set, and the influence it had on the way of life of the Canadian people."[9] Aware of the differences between Canada and the mother country, the French-Canadian farmer preferred to be known as a *habitant* rather than by the legal feudal title of *censitaire*. French-Canadian habitants frequently challenged the actions of government officials and their seigneurs. "There is no doubt," one official complained, that "the people of this country, neither docile nor easy to govern, are very difficult to constrain, for they like freedom and no domination at all."[10]

Women in New France and the Formation of Families

Jean Talon actively recruited colonists for New France, promising land, farm animals, seeds, and implements, and some 1500 settlers and indentured servants arrived during his tenure as intendant. Opposition from the French court, however, limited the number of colonists sent to Canada. "His Majesty cannot agree," Colbert admonished Talon, "with the arguments you make on the means of making of Canada a great and mighty state…. It would not be prudent to depopulate his Realm, which would be required in order to have Canada populated."[11] Nevertheless, Talon and Colbert cooperated in addressing another issue critical to the growth of the colony: the shortage of women.

Colbert and Talon worked together to recruit some 1200 marriageable young women known as *filles du roi,* or "daughters of the king." Filles du roi were to be in no way "disgraced by nature" or have anything "repulsive about their exterior person." They were to be "healthy and strong," and to have some "inclination to work with their hands."[12] As an incentive, the Crown provided substantial dowries to suitable women, and paid for their transportation to New France.

Most filles du roi were between the ages of 12 and 25 and came from Paris or other large urban centres. Many were recruited from the *Hôpital General* in Paris, an institution that looked after the disadvantaged, including abandoned children, orphans, unwed mothers, tramps, prostitutes, and the insane. Other filles du roi were young women whose parents could not afford to arrange good marriages for their daughters. Taking advantage of the scarcity of single women, filles du roi often entered into several marriage contracts before finally settling upon a spouse and marrying in the church.

Determined to further family formation, Talon threatened to deprive bachelors of hunting, fishing, and trading privileges if they did not select a wife from among the newly arrived filles du roi, and fines were imposed upon fathers whose sons and daughters had not married by a suitable age. Bonuses were given to young men who married by the age of 20, and to fathers with 10 or more children. By the census of 1676, the population of New France had reached 7832.

By 1676, New France's population reaches 7832.

This figure was disappointing to French authorities who were expending some 25 000 livres per year subsidizing emigrants to boost the colonial population. Traditionally, historians have emphasized the degree to which conditions in New France were an improvement

Arrival of the filles du roi.

Source: Library and Archives Canada, C-029486.

over the old world. W.J. Eccles exemplifies this approach. He contrasted the Canadian habitant with "the peasant in France who spent his life sweating, scrimping, cheating, and saving, … and who had to keep his little hoard well hidden, wearing rags, living in a hovel, giving every appearance of near starvation to prevent the tax collectors from seizing his savings."[13] Those in New France enjoyed the right to hunt and fish, and had plenty of firewood for fuel, along with luxuries like maple sugar. Yet, historian Peter N. Moogk has found that most who came to the colony were "reluctant expatriates" who "left France unwillingly and with no intention of staying abroad."[14]

Of the approximately 27 000 migrants who are estimated to have come to New France before 1760, an astonishing two-thirds opted not to remain. The actual number of migrants who came and stayed during the French regime seems to be approximately 10 500. Some of these migrants were engagés, indentured workers contracted to labour for three years. Moogk estimates the number of these who came and stayed at about 1200 in the period up to 1760, and says that they are better regarded as migrant workers than colonists. Others, perhaps 200, were exiled petty criminals. Approximately 1000 slaves were brought to the colony, perhaps a third of these black slaves carried from the French Caribbean or from the British colonies, and the remainder Amerindian. There were also British captives taken by French and Native raiding parties or seized from ships by privateers, although many of these were later repatriated. Moogk regards the female migrants as "true immigrants—that is, people who intended to settle abroad and establish a new home," in contrast to the majority who saw life in New France as "banishment."[15]

The formation of families was threatened by the constant lure of the fur trade. Growing numbers of men abandoned their homes, farms, and trades to take up the life of a *coureur de bois.* They valued the independence offered by the fur trade and many readily adopted the lifestyle of the Aboriginal peoples. Marie de l'Incarnation complained that "a Frenchman becomes an Indian more readily than an Indian becomes a Frenchman."[16]

Such behaviour violated the moral, social, and religious norms that French authorities wished to impose upon the colony, and the coureurs de bois were condemned for their idleness, libertinage, and degeneracy. Determined to put an end to the loss of young men to the fur trade, Talon forbade anyone from taking to the woods without a licence. His efforts proved futile as a steady stream of men continued to leave for the *pays-d'en-haut.* Despite the constant temptation of the fur trade, the family gradually became the basic social unit of New France.

Family life in New France was governed by the *Coutume de Paris,* the French legal code of the period. According to the law, married women had a status inferior to that of their husbands. As heads of the household, husbands acted as overlords of all family property and had the right to exercise "reasonable correction" over their wives and children, including corporal punishment so long as it did not cause permanent injury or endanger life. Although the law upheld the authority of husbands and fathers, it also contained some important protections for women and children: wives could seek legal separation from a brutal, insane, or profligate husband; husbands and fathers were obligated to provide support for wives and children; husbands could not alienate the property brought into the marriage by wives without permission; and widows were entitled to one half of the family estate. Many noble women sought to protect themselves by insisting on written contracts before marriage.

Most women's lives revolved around the demands of family reproduction. The typical woman in New France gave birth to nine children, six of whom survived to adulthood, a higher ratio of survival than in the mother country. Children remained legally dependent on their parents until reaching the age of majority, 25, and could not leave their father's house without his consent. Fathers had the right to approve the choice of a child's marriage partner before the age of majority and could exercise considerable control over their daughters beyond that age by threatening to withhold a dowry. Children owed their parents honour and respect whatever their age, and were bound to care for them if they should be in want or become infirm. Viewed as an economic asset, children were put to work at an early age. Older children cared for younger children; girls helped in the household and the fields, and sons assisted their fathers. To help with family finances, children were often bound out to others as domestic servants, labourers, or apprentices.

Women spent much of their time with the production of food—butchering, curing, and drying meat; caring for dairy cattle, swine, and poultry; tending vegetable gardens and orchards; and preserving food for the long winter months. Women frequently kept the household accounts, and would often take charge of the household entirely when husbands left to participate in the fur trade or to serve in the militia. The vital contribution that women made to the family economy tempered the patriarchal order entrenched in the law. On a visit to New France in 1749, Peter Kalm observed that men did not undertake "matters of importance without their women's advice and approval."[17]

While most women's lives focused on their children and households, some women became merchants and entrepreneurs. One such woman was Marie-Anne Barbel. After her husband died, Barbel took over his business, founded a successful pottery, and invested her profits in real estate. Louise de Ramezay, the daughter of the governor of Montreal, chose to pursue a highly successful career in business rather than to marry. Over the years, Ramezay profitably managed a sawmill and a brick and tile factory, invested in a tannery and a flour mill, and acquired her own seigneurie.

Diversifying the Economy

The formation of families was an important step in the creation of a stable colonial society, but the long-term success of New France demanded a more diversified economy. "Our neighbours, the English," Pierre Boucher observed in 1664, "build numbers of ships, of all sorts and sizes; they work iron mines; they have beautiful cities; they have stage-coaches and mails from one to the other; they have carriages like those in France; those who laid out money there, are now getting good returns from it."[18] Jean Talon believed that the economic progress made in New England was possible in New France. As a first step, he sought to broaden the economy of New France from its dependence on furs and make the colony less reliant on imports from France. The encouragement of settlement and the development of farms was a key element of Talon's plan and signs of success were already evident. Following Talon's reforms of the seigneurial system, the number of acres under cultivation increased from 11 488 to 15 649 (4650 to 6333 hectares) between 1667 and 1668 and the wheat harvest rose to 130 978 bushels.

1668: Land under cultivation rises by more than 35 percent over the previous year.

While wheat was the staple crop, Talon recognized the dangers of a one-crop economy and encouraged farmers to diversify their production by planting peas, beans, and crops such as hemp, flax, and hops that could be exported or used by new domestic industries to produce rope, cloth, and beer. Talon also encouraged the importation of livestock, and within a few years the colony had become self-sufficient in pork and leather. To provide a market for agricultural produce, Talon supported the establishment of a brewery, two tanneries, and a hat factory, encouraged the importation of looms for spinning, and secured the purchase of flax and hemp harvests to prove their commercial potential. "I now have the means," Talon enthusiastically wrote to the King in 1671, "to clothe myself from head to toe."[19] Unfortunately, mercantilist-minded French authorities showed little enthusiasm for Talon's efforts to produce crops and products that replaced French imports and which might someday compete with French producers in their own market. As a result, most of these commercial ventures disbanded following Talon's departure, and New France reverted back to a subsistence agriculture based almost entirely on wheat.

Colbert, though, was more supportive of Talon's efforts to develop a lumber industry. Timber from New France was essential to Colbert's plans to construct a French navy and merchant marine that could compete with the formidable English and Dutch fleets. Canadian timber was also in demand in the French plantation colonies of the West Indies, where it was used to produce barrels and casks to carry molasses and rum. Rather than simply export raw timber, Talon sought to create value-added industries such as saw milling and shipbuilding, and to produce important industrial products such as potash and tar. Despite Talon's enthusiasm, none of these industries took root. The lack of skilled labour and expertise, the shortage of capital, the small population, the distance from larger markets, and the isolation of the colony during the long winter months when the St. Lawrence froze, precluded significant industrial development in the colony for many decades.

Undeterred, Talon strove to rationalize the fishery and to develop New France's mineral resources. Convinced that a ready market for fish existed in the West Indies and Europe, Talon sought to create a profitable fishery by creating permanent fishing communities on the Gaspé, Bay of Fundy, and Labrador coasts and establishing a commercial company to oversee the harvest and export of fish. Fearing the imposition of the same type of restrictions that regulated the fur trade, independent-minded fishers resisted Talon's efforts. Talon's attempts to exploit the colony's mineral resources suffered a similar fate. Although he encouraged the search for mineral deposits and shipped samples of ore to France for analysis, the lack of experienced prospectors and skilled miners, and the great distance that ore had to be shipped, made mining in New France impractical.

Talon hoped to emulate the highly successful triangular trade that England had developed between her American colonies on the Atlantic seaboard and the West Indies. In a report to the King in 1673, Talon confidently predicted that Canada could export a host of goods, including dried cod, wheat, peas, salted beef and pork, lumber, beer, and even cloth to the West Indies. Each fall, a few ships filled with fish, seal oil, timber, and produce left for the West Indies where they were loaded with sugar, rum, cotton, and tobacco destined for markets in France. The ships returned to New France each summer loaded with manufactured goods. Although a modest trade developed, it did not live up to Talon's high hopes.

His attempts to diversify New France's economic base alienated many of the colony's merchants who accused the intendant of competing with their own commercial interests and using his office to manage the economy for his own benefit. Merchants complained that part of Talon's salary was paid in merchandise imported into the colony duty-free, which the intendant then profitably sold at prices that undercut merchants who bore the full burden of carrying charges and customs fees. While merchants protested, ordinary colonists benefited from the competition and Talon reinvested his earnings in new ventures that broadened New France's economy. Talon believed that the merchant's criticisms were misguided. The real problem for commerce in New France, as he saw it, was the trading and shipping monopoly granted by the Crown to the West Indies Company. Talon set out to persuade French officials that the colony's economic progress depended upon freedom of trade and shipping. His impetuous actions to undermine the company annoyed Colbert, but Talon's indefatigable efforts eventually paid off. Freedom of commerce was granted in 1669 and the West Indies Company dissolved in 1674.

While New France did not develop the self-supporting, diversified economic base Talon envisioned, the colony was undoubtedly stronger because of his efforts. "Since he has been here as intendant," Marie de l'Incarnation observed, "the country has developed and business has progressed more than they have done since the French have been here."[20]

Expanding the Fur Trade

External affairs preoccupied Talon when he returned to New France in 1670 to serve his second term as intendant. Several factors contributed to this reorientation in Talon's thinking. Although Talon had dedicated considerable energy to creating a strong, cohesive, and self-supporting colony centred on the St. Lawrence, the future of New France remained inextricably tied to the fortunes of the fur trade. As fur supplies dwindled, the trade was forced to extend its reach further and further west. It was essential that steps be taken to recognize and to exercise control over New France's natural frontiers, frontiers that were already being contested.

1664: The English seize control of New Netherland.

In 1664, the English seized control of the Dutch colony of New Netherland, which was soon renamed New York, took up trade with the Iroquois, and began to venture westward.

Recognizing the threat that English control of the Hudson Valley represented to New France, Talon advised Colbert that the French must either launch an attack to take control of the English colony of New York, or invest in new fortifications on Lake Ontario and the Richelieu River to protect the fur trade and New France's southern frontier. Failure to act, Talon warned, would allow the English and their Iroquois allies to harass French traders travelling to and from the west, and divert trade away from the colony—it would also leave the colony vulnerable to a two-pronged English attack: overland from the south and by sea up the St. Lawrence. French authorities ignored Talon's advice, a decision that would later prove costly.

Matters became even worse when English expansion of the fur trade directly challenged French Canadian ambitions on the continent. Ironically, two French traders, Médard Chouart Des Groseilliers, and his brother-in-law, Pierre Radisson, would play a leading role in bringing this about. French fur traders had begun to travel west, accessing the rich beaver country surrounding Lake Superior. Previous efforts by French traders to access the interior via Hudson Bay were thwarted by officials at Quebec who knew that a maritime-based fur trade would divert activity away from the St. Lawrence and effectively destroy their ability to control and profit from the fur trade.

Both Radisson and Des Groseilliers were men who had been hardened by years on the frontier. Des Groseilliers served as a soldier and lay assistant with the Jesuits in Huronia. Radisson's apprenticeship was harsher still. Captured by the Mohawks in his youth, he lived among them for years, accompanying war parties on raids against their enemies. On a hunting trip, Radisson and an Algonquin prisoner made a desperate bid for escape by crushing the heads of their Mohawk captors while they slept. The escape attempt failed and the Algonquin prisoner was put to death while Radisson was brutally tortured. But his adoptive Mohawk family came to the rescue and Radisson's life was spared. He endured two more years of captivity before at last managing to flee.

In the summer of 1660, Radisson and Des Groseilliers returned to Trois-Rivières from Lake Superior with a brigade of 50 canoes full of particularly lustrous high quality pelts. The quality and quantity of the furs set the colony abuzz with excitement. Marie de l'Incarnation predicted that this could be their economic salvation. Yet their entrepreneurial spirit was not rewarded: they were fined for unlicensed trading, their cargo of furs was confiscated, and Des Groseilliers was thrown into prison.

Infuriated by such treatment, Des Groseilliers travelled to France the following year and secured financing for a ship that would carry him to Hudson Bay, bypassing officials at Quebec. When the ship failed to appear the following spring, Des Groseilliers and Radisson journeyed to Boston to seek English support for such a voyage. England's interregnum under Cromwell and his successor had ended in 1660 with the restoration of the monarchy, and while Radisson and Des Groseilliers were deep in the Canadian wilderness, King Charles II returned to England from exile in the Netherlands to assume the throne. The King's commissioner in Boston, Sir George Cartwright, was intrigued by the French traders' plans and eager to secure colonial support for the new monarchical regime. He persuaded Radisson and Des Groseilliers to travel to England to meet with London financiers and members of court in 1665. En route, their ship was beset by Dutch pirates, and the pair were set ashore in Spain. Radisson and Des Groseilliers at last reached London, but their arrival there could hardly have been at a less propitious moment: the bubonic plague was raging throughout England, killing as many as 100 000 people in a single year. Only a further cataclysm could check the ravages of the disease: the 1666 Great Fire of London laid waste to more than 13 000 homes. While Radisson and Des Groseilliers witnessed these chilling scenes, something positive emerged from the journey. The English were intrigued by the potential wealth promised by the two men they called "Radishes and Gooseberries." Charles II granted a charter to the Company of Adventurers trading into Hudson Bay (or Hudson's Bay Company) in 1670, giving the company monopoly rights over all the territory drained by Hudson Bay. This enormous area was named Rupert's Land in honour of one of the principals of the new company, the King's cousin, Prince Rupert of Bavaria.

1670: Britain's Charles II grants a charter creating the Hudson's Bay Company.

Disturbed by these developments and determined to thwart the English, Talon sent out explorers to search for the elusive passage to the "China Sea," to assert French claims to the interior of the continent, and to form alliances with the First Nations. Talon commissioned René-Robert Cavelier de La Salle in the fall of 1670 to travel south in search of a passage to the China Sea. In June of the following year, one of Talon's agents, Simon Daumont de Saint-Lusson, summoned Native leaders to a gathering at the Jesuit mission of Sault Ste. Marie. There he proclaimed French sovereignty over all the territory, rivers, and lakes, discovered or otherwise, stretching from Hudson Bay to the north, the Gulf of Mexico to the south, and the Pacific to the west.

1670: Talon commissions La Salle to search for the passage to the China Sea.

Troubled by reports of English ships in Hudson Bay, Talon sent Father Charles Albanel, a chaplain with the Carignan-Salières regiment, on a scouting party to report in 1671. Talon's ventures in exploration and diplomatic initiatives annoyed Governor Courcelle who, quite correctly, claimed jurisdiction over such matters. The achievement of peace with the Iroquois and the good relations New France enjoyed with its traditional Aboriginal allies were largely due to Courcelle's efforts, and Talon's expansionism potentially threatened these hard-won accomplishments.

Relations between the intendant and governor deteriorated a great deal, and Talon let it be known that he would rather be recalled to France than continue to serve under Courcelle. Talon departed New France in November 1672 and Courcelle left shortly afterwards, suffering from ill health. With their departures, an important era in the life of New France ended. Talon and Courcelle left behind a colony that was certainly more secure, better populated, and much larger than the one they had inherited, but many of their accomplishments proved short lived. Few of Talon's enterprises and initiatives survived him, and within a few years New France was again at war with the Iroquois and confronted by a new English threat.

Frontenac and the Fur Trade

In the summer of 1672, Frontenac arrives to take up his post as governor of New France.

The king delayed naming Talon's successor, but replaced Courcelle as governor with Louis de Buade, the Comte de Frontenac. Frontenac was of old noble stock, had served with the French army during the Thirty Years' War and risen to the rank of colonel. After being wounded, Frontenac took up residence at the royal court. He relished the extravagant lifestyle at court, lived and entertained lavishly, and soon ran up debts in excess of 350 000 livres. Marriage to the beautiful and wealthy Anne de La Grange offered Frontenac the appealing prospect of repairing his damaged fortunes, but when her father learned that the two had been secretly wed, he cut off her inheritance. To avoid his creditors, Frontenac secured an appointment as governor of New France.

In the absence of an intendant, and accustomed from his military experience to exercising unquestioned authority, Frontenac assumed total control over the colony, alienating other members of the sovereign council and the governors of Montreal and Trois Rivières. Determined to profit from his position, Frontenac took an immediate interest in the fur trade. Impressed by the opportunities offered by the western fur trade, Frontenac ordered the construction of a fort at the confluence of the Cataraqui River, St. Lawrence River, and Lake Ontario. He placed the new trading post under the command of Robert Cavelier de La Salle, a like-minded opportunist with an interest in making profits. To protect his own interests and to limit competition, Frontenac published a decree directing that coureurs de bois be publicly whipped for trading without a licence. Those who bought goods from unlicensed coureurs de bois would be fined and have their trade goods confiscated. These decrees, along with the construction of Fort Frontenac, infuriated the fur trade merchants of Montreal, who accused the governor of attempting to take control of the western fur trade for his own gain. The establishment of the fort also alienated many habitants who were required to work on its construction without pay when Frontenac invoked the corvée.

Frontenac's critics included the governor of Montreal, François-Marie Perrot, and a Sulpician priest, Abbé Fénelon. A few years earlier, Perrot himself had established a fur trading post upstream from Montreal, illegally deployed coureurs de bois to the west, and quelled opposition from the merchants of Montreal with threats of force. Outflanked by the audacious Frontenac, Perrot now united with the Montreal merchants to oppose the governor. To silence his critics, Frontenac had Perrot arrested for his defiance, and ordered that he be tried by the sovereign council. Abbé Fénelon, who in his Easter Mass homily had already suggested that Frontenac had abused his office by imposing the corvée, offended him further by circulating a petition calling for Perrot's immediate release. Frontenac demanded that Fénelon be dismissed from his order and that he, too, be brought before the sovereign council for trial. Fénelon protested that the governor had no jurisdiction over ecclesiastical affairs and that he himself was accountable to the King alone, and not subject to trial by the council. Familiar with Perrot's ruthless reputation and hesitant to interfere in the affairs of the Church, the council referred Fénelon's and Perrot's cases to the King.

Determined to remove these irritants, Frontenac ordered Fénelon and Perrot to travel to France to defend themselves. After considering the matter, Louis XIV and Colbert found all parties at fault. Perrot was briefly imprisoned at the Bastille before being reinstated as governor of Montreal. Fénelon was prohibited from returning to Canada and was denounced by his order, and Frontenac was privately rebuked for his behaviour and ordered to treat Perrot with the respect his office deserved. Recognizing a man of similar temperament and determination, Frontenac put aside his differences with Perrot, and the two men collaborated in pursuing their illicit interests, intimidating anyone who opposed them.

Resolved to keep Frontenac in check, Colbert finally filled the vacant position of intendant in 1675 with Jacques Duchesneau, an experienced civil servant. When he arrived in New France, Duchesneau bore orders from Colbert to reorganize the sovereign council. The council was now to be chaired by the intendant, and its members appointed by the King rather than the governor. These measures ensured the council's independence and curbed the governor's power. Frontenac was outraged by this perceived assault upon the dignity of his office. Accustomed to acting as he pleased, Frontenac found himself at odds with the intendant and sovereign council, and did not hesitate to resort to bully tactics, including arbitrarily arresting those who stood in his way. Once again, Frontenac was censured by Colbert, and it was only through the influence of his wife, who remained in France, and other friends at court that he was not recalled.

Despite the ongoing wrangling with intendant Duchesneau and the sovereign council, Frontenac continued to pursue his interests in the fur trade and secured permission for his loyal ally La Salle to establish new trading posts at Niagara and Michilimackinac. With Frontenac's support, La Salle launched the first ship on the upper Great Lakes, *The Griffon*, to carry furs and trading goods between the newly established forts.

La Salle also sought to extend France's wilderness empire further south. In this goal, he built upon the foundations laid by Jolliet and Marquette a few years earlier. In the spring of 1673, Louis Jolliet and Jesuit priest Jacques Marquette had set out to explore the Mississippi River in hopes of finding a route to the Pacific, demonstrating French possession of the interior of the continent, and securing the friendship of the First Nations. Jolliet and Marquette travelled as far south as the confluence with the Arkansas River before Native hostility and fear of capture by the Spanish compelled them to turn back. Taking up the challenge anew in 1682, La Salle voyaged to the mouth of the Mississippi on the Gulf of Mexico and claimed for France the surrounding territory, which he named Louisiana in honour of the King.

1682: La Salle voyages to the mouth of the Mississippi and claims the surrounding territory for France.

Although Frontenac, La Salle, and their supporters profited from the extension of the fur trade, the expansion aggravated relations with the Iroquois, who resented the growing French influence among the tribes south of the Great Lakes, especially the Miamis and the Illinois. Committed to regaining control of the fur trade for themselves and their English allies, the Iroquois began harassing French traders and attacking tribes allied to the French. Rather than come to the assistance of France's Aboriginal allies, Frontenac attempted to conciliate the Iroquois. Interpreting this diplomacy as a sign of weakness, the Iroquois stepped up their campaign against tribes trading with the French. To secure trade, Frontenac relaxed restrictions on the sale of brandy to the Natives, much to the consternation of church leaders.

Preoccupied with extending France's inland empire, Frontenac ignored the growing English presence to the north. In 1673, the Hudson's Bay Company established Moose Factory at the southern end of James Bay, and Forts Albany and Severn a few years later. With the establishment of these trading posts, the Hudson's Bay Company began to lure away some of France's traditional Aboriginal trading partners. Despite demands from many traders that something be done to confront the growing English presence on New France's northern frontier, Frontenac had no interest in initiating a confrontation that might interfere with his plans to extend the fur trade to the west and to the south.

Deadlock

Frontenac's single-minded focus upon the extension of the fur trade increasingly frustrated the intendant, Duchesneau, and the sovereign council. In a colony with fewer than 10 000 residents, Duchesneau complained there were as many as 800 coureurs de bois who participated in the fur trade, men who were neglecting their farms and families, and living, he was convinced, licentious and disorderly lives. Determined to reduce the number of coureurs de bois and to entice them back to a more settled life, Duchesneau issued a general amnesty pardoning illegal traders and promulgated new regulations governing the fur trade in 1681. The number of annual trading leaves was limited to 25. These were to be given to noble families in need, deserving officers, and religious communities for free, but could be sold to a third party. To ensure fairness, no one was granted a trading leave for more than two years in a row. Anyone caught trading illegally was flogged for a first offence, branded with *the fleur de lys* for a second, and sentenced to the galleys for a third.

Duchesneau's decrees did not succeed. The number of coureurs de bois remained high, despite his efforts. The granting of licences became a means to curry favour and advantage, ensuring that relations between the governor, intendant, and sovereign council remained strained. Frontenac ordered the arrest of Mathieu Damours de Chauffours, a member of the sovereign council granted one of the new licenses, on charges that he had brought back more furs than his licence permitted. Although he had the support of the intendant and other members of the council, Damours was incarcerated in the governor's residence, the Chateau St. Louis, for more than two months. In a fit of rage, Frontenac had the intendant's son arrested after an exchange of insults took place between the young man and some of the governor's men. Flooded with complaints about this unseemly quarrel between Frontenac and Duchesneau, Louis XIV relieved the ill-tempered governor and ineffective intendant of their duties and recalled them to France in 1682. They left their successors a far-flung, thinly populated colony deeply divided between rival fur trading interests, threatened by the resumption of Iroquois hostilities, and increasingly vulnerable to growing English competition on Hudson Bay and James Bay.

1682: The governor, Frontenac, and intendant, Duchesneau, are both recalled to France.

Regulating the Fur Trade

Frontenac was succeeded by Joseph-Antoine Le Febvre de La Barre, an experienced naval officer who had served in the French West Indies, and Duchesneau was replaced by Jacques

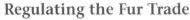

de Meulles, who was related to Colbert through marriage. Before departing for New France, both men were instructed to work together cooperatively for the general welfare of the colony and warned not to repeat the destructive wrangling of their predecessors. Disturbed by the depth of division within the colony and the extent of the Iroquois threat, the new governor and intendant called an assembly of leading men shortly after their arrival in October. They hoped that such an assembly would restore unity and provide concrete solutions to the many problems that faced New France. Persuaded by the assembly that a more aggressive response was needed to the Iroquois threat and the growing English presence to the north, La Barre and de Meulles appealed to the King for additional troops, and established the *Compagnie du Nord* to compete with the Hudson's Bay Company.

1682: *The* Compagnie du Nord *is created to compete with the Hudson's Bay Company.*

Montreal merchants were well represented at the assembly, and convinced La Barre that action needed to be taken against the unlawful traders who had been aligned with Frontenac. They were especially determined to rein in La Salle, who controlled the trading concessions at Fort Frontenac, or Fort Cataraqui (the site of present-day Kingston), and Fort St. Louis on the Illinois River. Both these sites effectively intercepted furs before they arrived at Montreal. La Barre dispatched a fact-finding mission to the interior to survey trading activities in the region and the state of relations with the Natives. La Barre's envoys reported that clandestine trade was widespread and that the unrest among the Iroquois was largely a result of La Salle's unscrupulous activities. This report provided La Barre with the pretext to launch a concerted campaign against La Salle, much to the satisfaction of the Montreal merchants. La Barre wrote the Minister of Marine that La Salle's accounts of his much-vaunted voyages were filled with lies and exaggerations, and he ordered the seizure of Fort Cataraqui, Fort St. Louis, and all La Salle's trade goods, on the grounds that the terms of these concessions had not been fulfilled. When the Iroquois attacked Fort St. Louis in the spring of 1684, La Barre resolved to launch a military operation against their own territory.

La Barre's determination to attack the Iroquois exposed a growing rift with the intendant, de Meulles, who favoured a more cautious, diplomatic approach to the Iroquois threat, at least until additional troops arrived from France. De Meulles accused the governor of having allowed himself to become a pawn of a small clique of Montreal merchants eager to take control of the interior fur trade; he sought out allies of his own among New France's religious establishment, many of whom feared that an all-out war with the Iroquois would imperil their interior missions. Nevertheless, La Barre pushed ahead, vowing that he would destroy them, and assembled a force of 150 regular troops, 700 militia and 400 Aboriginal allies. The expedition began the march towards Iroquois country on July 30, 1684, and a month later neared Fort Frontenac. They encamped on marshy ground, and soon fell victim to fever, with provisions running low. La Barre was not in an advantageous position when he began his discussions with the Iroquois—they, not he, could dictate the terms, and a chastened La Barre returned to Quebec. De Meulles enjoyed the irony: La Barre "goes at the head of a small army corps to make war on the Iroquois, and far from doing that, he grants them all they ask," he wrote home to Colbert. Louis XIV was disgusted by the "shameful peace" that La Barre had negotiated, and ordered the governor's recall, much to de Meulles's delight.[21]

De Meulles's happiness proved short-lived. The fever that ravaged La Barre's army soon spread throughout the colony, and the arrival of additional troops from France that summer added to de Meulles's burdens. Unable to pay or to board the ill-supplied soldiers, de Meulles released them to work for wages. With the treasury drained of resources, the intendant introduced paper money, using decks of playing cards that could be redeemed when the funds were replenished with the arrival of the spring fleet from France. De Meulles's playing card money was a popular and effective means of dealing with New France's chronic shortage of currency.

Denonville's Reforms

La Barre's successor as governor, Jacques-René de Brisay de Denonville, Marquis de Denonville, landed at Quebec in August of 1685 with his pregnant wife and two daughters. An experienced officer with a distinguished record of military service, Denonville seemed to be the sort of man who could suppress the Iroquois menace and restore order to fractious New France. Repeating a familiar pattern, the no-nonsense governor soon found himself at odds with the intendant, whom he accused of mismanaging the King's stores and selling fur trade licences at exorbitant prices for personal gain. When de Meulles failed to change his ways, Denonville arranged for his quick recall to France and his replacement by an old and trusted friend, Jean Bochart de Champigny.

To familiarize himself with conditions in New France, Denonville toured the colony, travelling as far as Fort Frontenac. Appalled by the extent of drunkenness and debauchery, he implemented strict regulations governing the sale of alcohol, and ordered that anyone convicted of drunk and disorderly behaviour be placed in the public stocks. Unsettled by the poverty in which he found many individuals of noble estate, Denonville set out to restore the proper social order, as he saw it, and secured pensions for persons of noble lineage whose fortunes had suffered in New France. Disturbed by the lack of discipline and respect exhibited by the sons of seigneurs, Denonville arranged for a number of them be sent to France to receive military training and to be given commissions upon their return to the colony.

But it was the conduct of the fur trade that Denonville found most troubling. The fur trade, he concluded, was rife with corruption, and was the source of the destructive rivalries that had divided the population and infected the colonial administration. The expansion of the trade westward had seriously weakened New France by drawing too many of its men away from their farms and families, draining limited funds to supply and defend distant trading posts, and entangling the colony in intertribal conflicts. Denonville tried to restore order by limiting the number of voyageurs permitted to journey west, registering the departures and returns, and requiring all traders to obtain letters from missionaries or officers stationed in the west testifying to their good behaviour. Threatened by the English on two fronts, and by Iroquois interests in the western fur trade, the future of New France demanded immediate action. As a first step, Denonville dispatched an expedition of 105 men under the command of Pierre de Troyes, an experienced officer in the regular forces, to evict the English from Hudson Bay. After a long and difficult journey from Montreal, in the summer of 1686, de Troyes seized Moose Factory, Fort Rupert, and Fort Albany, along with

1686: The French seize control of Hudson's Bay Company posts.

50 000 prime beaver pelts. With the conquered Hudson's Bay Company posts in the hands of the Compagnie du Nord, New France's northern frontier was secure for the time being.

The situation was less promising to the south. In a bid to control the western fur trade, the governor of the English colony of New York, Thomas Dongan, commissioned a group of Albany traders to journey to the upper Great Lakes to Michilimackinac to trade with the Ottawa, the main suppliers of furs to the French. Guided by Canadian coureurs de bois disaffected by Denonville's regulations, the Albany traders were directed to lure the Ottawa away from the French by offering trade goods at greatly reduced prices. At the same time, the Iroquois ignored the terms of the treaty they negotiated with La Barre, and resumed ransacking French trading parties.

Convinced that the same decisive action taken on Hudson Bay was required against the Iroquois and the English at Albany, Denonville appealed to France for reinforcements. When additional troops failed to arrive, and with the loyalty of the Ottawa and other traditional allies faltering in the face of English enticements and Iroquois intimidation, Denonville began preparations for a pre-emptive assault. A force of more than 800 regular troops, 900 Canadian militia, and 400 Natives left Montreal in June 1687 for Fort Frontenac under Denonville's command. The force fought several skirmishes, destroyed some Iroquois villages, and took a number of prisoners, including three dozen Iroquois who were sent to France to servitude in the royal galleys. But the campaign was far from the decisive victory Denonville knew was necessary to remove the Iroquois threat. Denonville renewed his pleas to the French authorities, insisting that a force of 4000 with two years' supplies would be necessary to secure New France. He also drew up plans for the naval conquest of New York. In the meantime, New France continued to suffer from Iroquois raids and from outbreaks of disease that killed an estimated 1400 people of the total population of about 11 000.

Denonville's attempts to buy time by negotiating peace with the Five Nations were thwarted by the English colonies. Sir Edmund Andros, who replaced Dongan as governor, claimed that the Iroquois were subjects of the British Crown, and that any peace must be negotiated by him. The Iroquois countered that they were a sovereign people who possessed the right to negotiate on their own behalf, a claim the French supported. But as the peace talks were delayed, tumultuous changes in Europe put a different complexion on North American relations. In 1689, England and France were once again at war.

New France and the War of the League of Augsburg, 1689–1697

England's Glorious Revolution of 1688 deposed the Catholic James II and put William of Orange and his wife Mary on the throne. As *stadtholder* of the Netherlands, William of Orange, a devout Protestant, had fought a running conflict against the expansionist ambitions of the Catholic King of France, Louis XIV. England, which had enjoyed friendly relations with France under James II, now took the lead in forming the League of Augsburg with Spain, the Netherlands, and the German Protestant princes against Louis XIV. Fighting at first broke out in the German states in the autumn of 1688, and the formation of this Grand Alliance brought England and her allies to war with France in 1689. The War of the League of Augsburg soon spread to North America, where it was also known as King William's War.

For New France, the first inkling that war had broken out came on the early morning of August 5, 1689. Some 1500 Iroquois warriors, with the encouragement of their English allies, launched a devastating surprise assault on the French settlement at Lachine, burning most of the houses, killing 24 habitants, and taking at least 70 more prisoner—most of whom never returned. Denonville, who did not yet know that war had been declared and was unaware of the size of the Iroquois force, dispatched a small band of Canadian militia to the area. The *Canadiens* enjoyed a small measure of revenge a few days later when they ambushed an Iroquois war party at Lac des Deux Montagnes, killing 18 and taking three prisoners without suffering any casualties. The Iroquois prisoners were burned alive when news reached Montreal that some of the captives taken at Lachine had succumbed to such a fate.

Denonville was all too aware of New France's vulnerability and ordered that Fort Frontenac be abandoned. Without reinforcements, Denonville could do little except to encourage France's Aboriginal allies to embark on the same kind of guerrilla campaign against English settlements that the Iroquois used to terrorize New France. While tribes to the west were too preoccupied with the Iroquois to respond, the Abenaki to the east did begin to torment frontier settlements in northern New England. It was not until October that the ships arrived from France with news that Denonville had been recalled to France, and carrying his replacement, the irascible Comte de Frontenac.

Historians have sometimes attributed Denonville's recall to the calamitous events of the previous months, but the decision to replace Denonville with Frontenac was made in April, well before the attack on Lachine and the abandonment of Fort Frontenac. Highly regarded at court as a military commander with a long record of distinguished service, Denonville was seen as too valuable a man to be left in New France while war raged in Europe. Given his familiarity with conditions in New France, Frontenac, who had worked tirelessly to restore his reputation, and who had lost much of his estate, was in desperate need of a new appointment, and seemed, under the circumstances, a logical choice as governor.

Although North American events during the War of the League of Augsburg were very much a sideshow to greater battles in Europe, the war did have significant consequences for New France. When Frontenac returned to New France, he found a colony that was virtually defenceless and a population demoralized by the Iroquois' relentless raids. Convinced that something needed to be done to revive morale, restore the confidence of New France's Aboriginal allies, and deter the English from inciting the Iroquois, Frontenac mustered raiding parties of Canadian militia and Natives to attack the English border settlements of Schenectady, in the colony of New York, and Salmon Falls and Fort Loyal in Maine. Adopting the tactics of the Iroquois, the raiding parties descended upon the unsuspecting settlements in February 1690, ruthlessly killing settlers, destroying homes, and taking prisoners. Inspired by the success of the raids and compelled by the shortage of regular forces, Frontenac carried on a guerrilla war against the English and the Iroquois throughout the remainder of the conflict.

This campaign of terror succeeded in uniting the English colonies in their determination to strike a decisive blow against New France. A two-pronged attack was planned for later that year, with a large land force of English colonial militia and Iroquois striking

Montreal, and a naval force taking Quebec. But the English were forced to abandon the assault on Montreal, not least because of a smallpox epidemic that swept through the ranks of the colonial militia. Frontenac was able instead to concentrate his forces at Quebec and to reinforce its defences. Preparations for the English naval assault upon Quebec were entrusted to Bostonian Sir William Phips, a former ship's carpenter who had risen to prominence after hauling in £207 600 worth of loot from a sunken Spanish treasure ship. In May of 1690, Phips had led a force of 450 in seven vessels to capture the Acadian capital of Port Royal. With only 70 defenders and no guns, Port Royal's governor, Louis-Alexandre des Friches de Meneval, surrendered without a fight and was taken into captivity while the Puritan Phips raided the church, desecrating the altar and breaking religious images.

1690: The British seize Acadia.

Later that summer, Phips sailed from Boston with a fleet of 32 small vessels and a force of 2000 Massachusetts militiamen. Progress up the St. Lawrence was slow, and the force did not reach Quebec until October 16. Phips immediately sent word to Frontenac that he had an hour to surrender. Frontenac famously replied that he would make no answer but "from the mouths of my cannon and muskets."[22]

Phips attempted a landing at the mouth of the St. Charles River, but the English forces were easily repulsed. True to his word, Frontenac's cannons bombarded Phips's fleet, inflicting serious damage. Fearing that with winter approaching his ships might get caught in the ice, Phips retreated after an eight-day siege. The huge debt incurred by the expedition, the discontent that emerged among unpaid soldiers and sailors, and the loss of life to smallpox among the invading force, ensured that no further attempts were made by the English colonists to launch a full-fledged invasion of Canada for the duration of the war.

1690: Governor Frontenac makes a defiant defence of Quebec.

In the aftermath of the siege, Frontenac ordered better defences constructed for Quebec. New fortifications and shore batteries were built, as was a handsome new two-storey, slate-roofed residence for the governor, the Château Saint-Louis. Frontenac, true to his profligate form, hosted lavish banquets at the chateau, as well as amateur theatricals and other entertainment.

Having successfully defended Quebec from Phips's attack, Frontenac resumed the guerrilla campaign against the English colonists and directed the establishment of new forts in the west. Frontenac's ongoing operations on the frontier relied mostly upon Canadian militia, more experienced with wilderness warfare than regular troops. This concerned the intendant, Jean Bochart de Champigny, who worried about the consequences of taking men away from their farms, trades, and families for long periods of time, as well as the losses they would likely endure. Convinced that the new forts on the frontier were of little military value, Champigny accused Frontenac of diverting men and money west simply to advance his own financial interests. Emboldened by the appointment of a relative, Louis Phélypeaux de Pontchartrain, as minister of Marine, Frontenac disregarded the intendant's concerns and proceeded with his policy of western expansion. This provoked the Ottawa nation who saw their long-standing position as middlemen in the fur trade threatened, and who were also angered by French commerce with their traditional enemies, the Sioux, especially since firearms were being brokered.

The Ottawa responded by entering into peace negotiations with the Iroquois, a development that threatened the future of New France's fur trade. Unable to mount a major offensive, and needing to play for time, Frontenac undertook peace talks with the Iroquois, disregarding the warnings of the intendant and of Louis-Hector de Callière, the governor

1696: The French devastate Iroquois settlements.

of Montreal, who suspected the Iroquois of trickery. These dire warnings came to fruition when, as soon as the alliance with the Ottawa was struck, the Iroquois broke off negotiations and resumed attacks on New France. With the survival of New France in the balance, Frontenac assembled an army of more than 2000 regular troops, militia, and Native allies in July 1696 to strike directly at the heart of Iroquois country. Weakened by disease and years of warfare, the Iroquois retreated as the French forces advanced, leaving Frontenac's army with little to do but burn crops and villages.

Determined not to miss out on the campaign, even though he was in his mid-70s, Frontenac was carried through the forest in an armchair. The only Iroquois killed was an old Onondaga chief who was too feeble to flee. Frontenac allowed his Aboriginal allies to burn him slowly to death, a torment the captive endured in silence. When the Ottawa learned of the overwhelming French offensive, they, too, turned against the Iroquois, abandoning their treaty. The tables had turned: now it was the Iroquois who petitioned Frontenac for peace.

Iberville's War

1686–1696: The British and French battle over posts on Hudson Bay and James Bay.

The war in North America was not limited to the Great Lakes–St. Lawrence region; significant battles also took place to the north on Hudson Bay and in Newfoundland. The leading figure in these events was Pierre Le Moyne d'Iberville. Born in Montreal, Iberville was the son of a wealthy seigneur and a partner in the *Compagnie du Nord*. Iberville and two of his brothers had already distinguished themselves in a 1686 expedition in which they seized three Hudson's Bay Company posts on James Bay—Moose Factory, Fort Rupert, and Fort Albany. They and a hundred or so others, under the command of the Chevalier de Troyes, had travelled 1300 kilometres over 85 days through unbroken bush and river routes to reach James Bay, setting out by sled, dragging canoes to use when the ice broke up. After taking part in the 1690 raid on Schenectady, Iberville sailed to Hudson Bay, determined to capture the Hudson's Bay Company's headquarters at York Factory. With only three ships and limited men and arms, Iberville was not able to overtake the well-defended post, but did succeed in taking possession of another outpost, Fort Severn. When Iberville returned to Quebec the following spring, Frontenac commissioned him to harass English ships and settlements along the New England coast. These raids only served to increase English determination to maintain control over Acadia, seized by William Phips in the spring of 1690. In 1693, the English succeeded in recapturing their posts on Hudson Bay and James Bay, driving out the French. The following year, Iberville again sailed north with instructions to expel the English and restore the French posts. As an incentive, Iberville was granted a three-year trading monopoly and promised a share of all the spoils.

The governor of York Factory, Thomas Walsh, surrendered to Iberville on October 13. Both sides spent a miserable winter at the fort, suffering from scurvy. Iberville's younger brother, Louis, was among those who died. Hoping to intercept the annual English supply ships, Iberville remained at York Factory for the summer. When the ships failed to appear by September 1695, Iberville left for France with the furs that the Aboriginal traders had brought to York Factory that season. His triumph proved temporary. In his absence, the English retook York Fort in 1696, captured furs valued at 136 000 livres, and again expelled the French from Hudson Bay.

That same year, Iberville took Fort William Henry on the Maine Coast and launched a concerted campaign to dislodge the English from Newfoundland and take control of the lucrative cod fishery. After burning St. John's, Iberville's men pillaged the surrounding communities. Some 36 settlements were destroyed, 200 people killed, another 700 taken prisoner, and 9 million kilograms of dried cod taken in the raids. Isolated coastal communities were no match for Iberville's systematic campaign of destruction and conquest.

1696: Iberville captures English settlements in Newfoundland.

Before the English were routed completely, however, Iberville was ordered to return to Hudson Bay. His flagship, the 44-gun *Pélican,* became separated on the journey from the rest of his fleet in the fog, and on September 4, 1697, off the coast of York Factory, encountered a Royal Navy frigate, the *Hampshire,* and two Hudson's Bay Company vessels, the *Dering* and the *Royal Hudson's Bay.* With 124 guns, the firepower of the English ships was almost three times that of the *Pélican.* Scurvy among the ranks of Iberville's crew, and the absence of some of the crew who had gone ashore, tipped the balance even further. Iberville gamely engaged the enemy in a four-hour battle in stormy seas, outmanoeuvring the *Hampshire,* which was driven into the rocks with the loss of all hands. The captured *Royal Hudson's Bay* foundered and sank in the squall, and the *Pélican* was grounded on a sandbar. Many drowned in the icy waters while making for shore, but after the survivors endured nine cold and hungry days, the rest of the delayed French fleet arrived, and York Factory was captured.

Iberville's victories in Newfoundland and Hudson Bay proved to be in vain. Shortly after Iberville's departure for Hudson Bay, an English flotilla under the command of Sir John Gibsone and Sir John Norris sailed into St. John's harbour, landed 2000 troops and persuaded the fishers, terrorized by the French, to return and rebuild their villages. A week after Iberville departed Hudson Bay in 1697, the Treaty of Ryswick ended the war. What had been won in battle was lost at the treaty table: York Factory was returned to the English. The treaty restored the status quo, with France regaining possession of Acadia, and Newfoundland being restored to the English.

1697: The Treaty of Ryswick ends the War of the League of Augsburg.

Undeterred by this reversal, Iberville sailed for France where he convinced the minister of Marine to place him in charge of an expedition to establish a French colony at the mouth of the Mississippi. "If France does not seize this most beautiful part of America and set up a colony," he argued, the English "will be strong enough to take over all of America and chase away all other nations."[23] His argument found a receptive audience in the court of Louis XIV. An expansionist policy in North America would confine the English to the Atlantic seaboard, east of the Appalachian Mountains. Travelling by sea, Iberville landed on Biloxi Bay, erected a garrison, and proclaimed the new colony of Louisiana in 1699. France's inland empire now stretched from the St. Lawrence to the Gulf of Mexico.

1699: Iberville establishes a new French colony, Louisiana, at the mouth of the Mississippi River.

The Art of Frontier Warfare and the Great Peace of Montreal

While the Treaty of Ryswick restored imperial possessions in North America to their pre-war state, the war had a number of long-term effects. The French had mastered a new style of warfare. Traditional European methods, which relied on the deployment of large numbers of infantry, cavalry and field artillery, were impractical in the North American wilderness. Inspired by Aboriginal tactics, French commanders successfully adopted *petite*

Canadian militiaman on snowshoes going to war.

Source: Library and Archives Canada, C-113193.

1701: The Great Peace of Montreal brings peace between the French and the Iroquois.

guerre—or guerrilla—warfare methods, moving forces quickly in small groups, approaching the enemy without being seen, mounting surprise attacks, and then disappearing immediately. Such methods enabled the French to maintain a vast North American empire, despite having a much smaller population and fewer resources than the English colonies.

Growing French strength and military prowess, and a weakening of their own position, also led the Iroquois to re-evaluate their strategy and diplomatic goals. Prolonged conflict and disease had taken a toll on the Iroquois, who were largely forsaken by their English allies as soon as the war with France had ended. They began peace negotiations with New France and its Aboriginal allies. At the invitation of the new governor of New France, Louis-Hector de Callière, 1300 representatives from the Iroquois and 39 other First Nations from the Great Lakes, Acadia, and the Mississippi assembled at Montreal in August 1701.

After prolonged discussions that adhered closely to Native customs and traditions, all parties agreed to a landmark treaty that ended nearly a century of conflict. According to the terms of the treaty, all prisoners taken captive in previous conflicts were to be returned, and the peace and security of all signatories protected. For their part, the Iroquois promised to remain neutral in any future conflict between the French and the English, and New France agreed to recognize Native sovereignty and to act as a mediator whenever disputes erupted between Native signatories. The Great Peace of Montreal, as it became known, enabled New France to expand its commercial and military presence in the interior and to establish new posts such as Detroit, founded in 1701 by Antoine de la Mothe Cadillac, at the strait (*détroit*) connecting Lake Erie and Lake St. Clair.

The terms of the peace also benefited the Iroquois, whose neutrality and strategic position allowed them to pursue their own interests in the fur trade and profit from the competition between European rivals. By both design and necessity, the French developed a very different relationship with their Aboriginal neighbours than did the English. New France's small population and reliance upon the fur trade required the French to maintain strong, lasting, and mutual alliances that recognized Native independence and possession of the land. The English, on the other hand, tended to view Native peoples as subjects of the Crown rather than allies and, with much greater settler populations and extensive agriculture, English goals required Aboriginal lands, rather than Aboriginal economic partners. New France's vast network of Native alliances proved an invaluable asset during the series of wars with England that followed.

The War of the Spanish Succession, 1701–1713

It was not long before the Great Peace of Montreal was tested. Dynastic struggles once again led to war in Europe. In 1700, the last of the Spanish Habsburgs, Charles II, died without heirs. Both mentally and physically feeble, Charles was the culmination of generations of Habsburg inbreeding. Spain's crown passed to Philip of Anjou, the grandson of France's Louis XIV. A Bourbon power bloc uniting France and Spain raised the spectre of a profound upheaval in Europe's balance of power. "The Pyrenees no longer exist," one alarmed diplomat feared.[24] Further provocations were added when Britain's exiled king, James II, who had been deposed in the "Glorious Revolution" of 1688, died in 1701. Louis XIV recognized his son, the "Old Pretender" James Edward, as Britain's legitimate monarch, challenging the Protestant succession. Britain's William III organized a new coalition to oppose French ambitions. This alliance included the Holy Roman Empire, the Netherlands, Portugal, and other powers. When William died early in 1702, his sister-in-law and successor, Queen Anne, continued the fight, which is sometimes called "Queen Anne's War" in North America.

The war proved a costly one for France, and few resources could be spared for the colonies. Fortunately for New France, New Yorkers were weary of war and the Great Peace of Montreal kept the Iroquois neutral throughout most of the war. With the St. Lawrence heartland secure, most of the fighting took place in the Atlantic colonies. The governor of New France, Philippe de Rigaud de Vaudreuil, invited the Iroquois and Abenakis—whose homelands range over what is today New Brunswick, Quebec, Maine, and Vermont—to join the militia in a series of border raids against New England. This "little war" was not of much strategic value, but it enabled Vaudreuil to keep the Abenakis and the Iroquois engaged against the English. Fur prices were low because of the oversupply brought about by the opening of new posts in the interior, and Vaudreuil feared that both nations might be tempted to take their trade to English posts where they could be persuaded to turn against the French.

English colonists had long been impatient with privateer raids launched from French Port Royal, and new episodes of violence fed a growing conviction that New France must be destroyed if New England were to survive. Throughout the course of the war, settlement communities throughout Maine and Massachusetts fell victim to brutal raids by the French colonists and their Aboriginal allies. On leap year day, February 29, 1704, the French, along with Abenakis, Mohawks, and Hurons—some 250 to 300 in total—swept down upon the small Massachusetts community of Deerfield, burning homes, massacring 50 men, women, and children, and taking some 112 prisoners—the largest number ever taken in a raid on the New England frontier. Many of the captives were ultimately ransomed, and the stories of their terrifying ordeal fed longstanding enmity.[25]

The Conquest of Acadia

Later that spring, a retaliatory offensive sailed north from Boston, burning the small settlement of Grand Pré on the Minas Basin, and taking prisoners, but failing to take the key objective of Port Royal. A second attempt on Port Royal in 1707 by a larger force was also repulsed, thanks to the quick thinking and deceptive tactics of Acadia's governor, Daniel D'Auger de Subercase. Subercase, who had led a successful reconquest of Newfoundland a couple of years earlier, skilfully deployed the few settlers and Aboriginal allies at hand to harass the English colonists as they attempted to land advance parties. Convinced that they faced a large number of settlers, and fearful of being taken prisoner by the Natives, the New Englanders retreated, but not before doing substantial damage—burning homes, and killing livestock.

1710: Acadia is conquered by the British.

With two failed attempts behind them, the New England governors appealed to England for reinforcements to launch a full-scale invasion. English preoccupation with the war on the continent delayed assistance until 1710. In that year, Colonel Francis Nicholson led a naval force of almost 2000 and succeeded in capturing Port Royal. Historian Geoffrey Plank attributes the absence of brutal "collateral damage"—that is, civilian deaths and property destruction—to the fact that this was not a New England operation, but rather one under the firm hand of imperial authorities.[26] The English renamed Port Royal "Annapolis Royal," in honour of the queen.

An Attempt on Quebec and War on the Frontier

The next objective was Quebec itself. On July 30, 1711, an armada of 69 ships carrying 7500 soldiers and 4500 sailors sailed north from Boston under the command of Sir Hovenden Walker. At the same time, Nicholson proceeded to Albany to take charge of a colonial militia force of nearly 2300 men that was to invade Canada from the south, thus diverting French forces from Quebec. Unfavourable winds and heavy fog threw the convoy into confusion, and on August 22, eight transport vessels carrying hundreds of soldiers struck a reef off Anticosti Island in the Gulf of St. Lawrence. Two hundred were swept into the cold sea, while others in the fleet heard their anguished cries but were helpless to save them. Walker abandoned the mission, and sailed back to England. Nicholson was preparing to move up Lake Champlain towards Montreal when he received news of the British fleet's misfortune. With his men already suffering from fatigue, disease, and shortages of supplies, he had little choice but to disband his army and send the men home. Spared once more, New France erupted in jubilation.

The celebrations were tempered in 1712 by news that some Iroquois had resumed their campaign against New France, and that warfare had broken out among the nations of the west. Trouble had been brewing in the west for some time. With an oversupply of furs flooding into French markets, metropolitan authorities insisted that stringent measures be taken to restrict the fur trade. As a result, some trading licences were not renewed, the sale of brandy to the Natives was prohibited, and the military was withdrawn from Niagara and Detroit—forts that had been established to intercept cargoes that would otherwise go to Albany. These measures effectively undercut the fur trade in the west and threatened to destroy New France's alliances with the region's Aboriginal peoples. The demilitarization of both posts emboldened the Iroquois who, with English prodding, wavered in their commitment to the Great Peace of Montreal. To make matters worse, tensions were developing among the Hurons, Ottawas, and Miamis, who had been encouraged to settle close to Detroit. In the absence of a garrison and with little trading taking place, there was not much to prevent these traditional rivals from falling into open warfare. When war finally broke out around Detroit in 1712 with the Fox, Vaudreuil dispatched troops to restore order and to reoccupy French positions. Matters settled down when news arrived in 1713 that the war in Europe was over.

An Armed Peace

Although the scale and scope of combat in North America had been significantly smaller than in the previous war, the peace brought major consequences for France's American empire. With Louis XIV's vision of continental mastery soundly defeated in Europe, France had to accept some hard peace terms. By the 1713 Treaty of Utrecht, England's possession of Newfoundland, Acadia, and all of the lands that drained into Hudson Bay was

1713: The Treaty of Utrecht acknowledges English possession of Newfoundland, Acadia, and Rupert's Land.

confirmed. France retained Île Royale (Cape Breton), Île St. Jean (Prince Edward Island), the St. Lawrence heartland, and much of the interior of the continent stretching from the Great Lakes to Louisiana on the Gulf of Mexico. Because the frontiers between French and English territories were imprecise, the treaty established a joint commission to set boundaries. Another clause in the treaty acknowledged English sovereignty over the Iroquois and permitted Natives to trade with either the French or the British. These terms threatened to embroil the interior region south of the Great Lakes in imperial wrangling for control.

Although all was not lost, Governor Vaudreuil recognized that strong measures needed to be taken if France was to keep what remained of its North American empire. In a report to the minister of Marine, Vaudreuil advised French authorities that the only way to deter future aggression was to increase the population and the number of regular troops permanently stationed in New France. To maintain the allegiance of the Natives and to keep them from trading with the English, Vaudreuil urged officials to reinstate the licensing system, permit the brandy trade, and establish new posts in the west. With the loss of Acadia, Vaudreuil warned that it was essential to protect both land and sea approaches to the St. Lawrence by fostering the continued friendship of the Abenakis and establishing a major fortification on Île Royale to guard the entry to the Gulf of St. Lawrence and ensure French access to the lucrative fishery.

Vaudreuil's program set the direction for French policy until the outbreak of the next major conflict in Europe, the War of the Austrian Succession in 1740. Additional forces were stationed in New France. Despite the efforts of New Englanders to lure them away, good relations were maintained with the Abenakis. New forts were built on Lake Ontario to intercept trade before it reached the English traders at Albany and to assert French control over the region. And in 1720, construction began on a massive fortress, Louisbourg, on Île Royale.

1720: Construction begins on the French fortress on Île Royale, Louisbourg.

Louisbourg's strategic location commanded access to the rich fishing grounds off Nova Scotia and Newfoundland, and posed a real threat to New England's valuable maritime trade. The "bulwark of Canada," it guarded the navigable approaches to the St. Lawrence, and hence Quebec. Louisbourg would grow into an administrative and commercial centre, with a permanent French garrison, and a population of about 2000 by 1740. With an excellent natural harbour capable of sheltering over a hundred ships, Louisbourg could shield France's naval squadrons and its commercial fleets. Unlike the St. Lawrence ports, it did not freeze over in winter, although ice drifts and heavy fogs interfered with navigation. The design for the 4 million-livre construction project of the fortress was inspired by the work of the famous French military engineer Sébastien le Prestre de Vauban (1633–1707). Vauban's designs applied geometric principles, setting out projecting bastions to reduce the target area offered to the enemy, while providing an opportunity to cover a wider range with enfilading fire. The core of a Vauban-style fortress was designed like a pentagon, with successive lines of outer defences that compelled an attacker to commence siege operations from a great distance. Vauban's engineering ideas were also copied in the orderly and symmetrical layout of Louisbourg's urban spaces.

Montreal and Quebec were also fortified during the lull between the War of the Spanish Succession and the War of the Austrian Succession, but the initial construction of these defences was more modest, taking advantage of local enforced labour by the habitants—the corvée.[27]

La Vérendrye and the Expansion of the Fur Trade

Since the Treaty of Utrecht had recognized the claims of the Hudson's Bay Company, the French fur trade had to find a way to deal with the problem of British competition. Attracted by the range, quality, and price of trade goods that the Hudson's Bay Company was able to bring in each season by sea, increasing numbers of Aboriginal traders were diverting their furs away from the French to the English posts on Hudson Bay. Convinced that the only way to reverse this development was to reach the Natives first, the French traders began to push for a major advance of the fur trade beyond the Upper Great Lakes. Vaudreuil resisted the pressure, fearing that New France's resources were already stretched too thin. Vaudreuil's successor, Charles de Beauharnois, relented and permitted Pierre Gaultier de La Vérendrye to set out for the west on an exploratory expedition in 1731.

Born in Trois-Rivières, La Vérendrye was the youngest of 13 children. His father had been a seigneur, and governor of Trois-Rivières, but left the family destitute when he died four years after Pierre was born. La Vérendrye enlisted in the army as a young man and served in Europe during the War of the Spanish Succession, where he suffered both gunshot and sabre wounds. He returned to New France in 1712, married the daughter of a large landowner, and began farming. After a few years of trying to support his growing family by working the land, La Vérendrye entered the fur trade. His brother commanded the *poste du Nord*, headquartered at what is now Thunder Bay, which oversaw a large area north of Lake Superior, and La Vérendrye made up his mind to join him there. While he was stationed in the west, La Vérendrye became convinced that exploration of the region would lead to the discovery of the western sea flowing into the Pacific Ocean—a supposed gulf in the western part of the continent, like the Gulf of Mexico in the south, or Hudson Bay in the north. To discover such a western sea would enable the French to outflank the English on Hudson Bay.

La Vérendrye was already 45 years of age when he set out in the summer of 1731 to pursue the dream of discovering a western sea. He was accompanied by three of his sons: Jean-Baptiste, 17, Pierre, 16, and François, 15, and a nephew, Christophe Dufrost de La Jemerais. The youngest son, Louis-Joseph, later joined the family enterprise when he reached 17, after being schooled in the art of mapmaking. Travelling beyond Lake Superior, La Vérendrye established Fort Saint-Charles on Lake of the Woods, and set up a chain of new posts—west to Lake Winnipeg and to Portage La Prairie, locations ideally located to intercept Aboriginal traders on their way to trade with the English on Hudson Bay. In 1735, the far western posts produced half of all the furs delivered to Montreal that year. The minister of Marine, Maurepas, was not impressed, however, and accused La Vérendrye of seeking not the western sea, but the "beaver sea." Determined to restore his reputation, La Vérendrye continued the search. Unfortunately, the conviction that the Missouri River was the most likely route to the west consumed eight years of explorations by two of La Vérendrye's sons—in fact, it flows southeast to the Mississippi and the Gulf of Mexico. In the course of this exploration, the two sons, Louis-Joseph and François, in 1743 reached what was probably the Big Horn Mountains in what is today Wyoming.

La Vérendrye paid a high price for his quest: his nephew fell ill and died at one of the western posts, and Jean-Baptiste was killed by the Sioux. When he died in 1749 at 64, La Vérendrye was still making plans for another journey west.

1731–1739: La Vérendrye establishes a chain of new trading posts in the western interior.

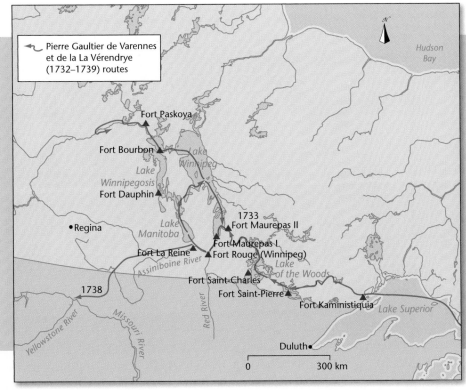

Map 3.2
The Explorations of the La Vérendryes.

Source: Canadian Museum of Civilization.

Acadia under British Rule

With the signing of the 1713 Treaty of Utrecht, England controlled Acadia, which was once more known as Nova Scotia. Isolated from Quebec and long ignored by Versailles, the Acadians were an independent people. They had perfected agricultural techniques that converted thousands of hectares of salt-soaked tidal meadow into rich fertile farmland protected by dykes. The giant tides on the Bay of Fundy rise an astonishing 12 to 15 metres daily in some areas. Whole families of Acadians worked together to build dykes to reclaim the marshland and hold back the sea, using sharp-edged spades to cut bricks of sod. The dykes were laid upon a base of hardwood brush, interlaid with marsh mud and sod, built high and wide enough to have footpaths along the top. Sluice boxes, or "*aboiteaus*," allowed fresh rainwater to drain from the dyked marshland, gradually washing the salt from the soil to render it useable, but did not allow seawater to flow in from the other direction. Fishing techniques were also adapted to the area, with the Acadians using farm wagons, not fishing vessels, to gather fish from nets set out at low tide.[28] The Acadians traded with the local Natives, and carried on active trade with "*nos amis les ennemis*"—our friends the enemy—as they referred to their neighbours in New England.[29]

While Acadia technically became the British colony of Nova Scotia in 1713, it remained, as historian Barry Moody puts it, "precariously positioned at the very edge of the British empire in North America."[30] No great flood of British Protestant settlers arrived to instantly transform the nature of the colony. Despite the urging of French officials and missionaries to

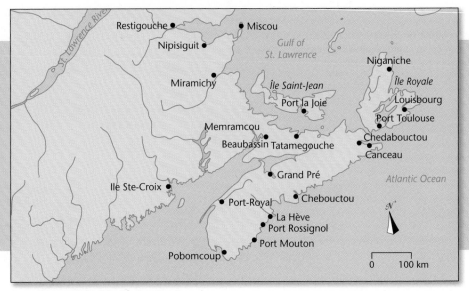

Map 3.3
Acadia.

Source: Courtesy of the Canadian Encyclopedia.

relocate to Île Royale, most Acadians chose to remain in Nova Scotia. They were permitted to keep their property and exercise their religion so long as they pledged their allegiance to the British Crown. None of the early administrators of Nova Scotia convinced the Acadians to take the oath. Each time an attempt was made to administer the oath, Acadians objected; they had not been required to do so the last time England occupied the region.

Acadia had long been a pawn in the struggle between England and France, and the present situation might well prove temporary. Few Acadians were willing to forsake their French Catholic heritage by swearing their loyalty to a Protestant English king. Then, too, even if the Acadians had sworn the oath, under English law their Roman Catholicism would have made them ineligible to hold public office or sit on juries. This fundamental difficulty stood in the way of state formation in British Nova Scotia. Historian Elizabeth Mancke sums up the difficulty: "How was Nova Scotia to be governed when, by law, the majority of the European population could not participate in government?" With only a small garrison at their disposal, the early administrators of Nova Scotia did not dare to press the matter. The problem went deeper than mere security—it was the fact that the Acadians were "snakes in [our] bosom," as one governor later put it. The more fundamental problem, as Mancke explains, was that day-to-day civil government could not be carried on in the British tradition. "Land could not be granted or deeded. Taxes could not be assessed, except for minimal charges. The Navigation Acts made Acadian trade illegal."[31]

Oath or no oath, the British Crown's agents in Nova Scotia recognized the Acadians' value. Not only did the Acadians supply food and labour for the garrison at Annapolis Royal, they provided an important buffer from the Mi'kmaq, who at this time were hostile to the British. For the Acadians, their reluctance to take an oath was reinforced by worries about how such a gesture might be viewed by their Mi'kmaq allies.

Britain showed little interest in the affairs of Nova Scotia until the appointment of Richard Philipps as governor in 1717. Concerns about the growth of the French settlement on Île

Royale and the mismanagement of the small garrison at Annapolis Royal prompted the British government to reconsider its neglect of Nova Scotia. When Philipps arrived in the colony in 1720, he appointed a council. The nature of the population made any form of representative government impossible, but his critics condemned his solution as rule by military government.

When Philipps made it clear he was determined to administer the oath of allegiance, a delegation of 150 Acadians, led by Father Justinien Durand, presented a protest. Standing his ground, Philipps ordered that anyone who had not taken the oath within the next four months would have to leave the colony. Such bravado did not impress the Acadians, who knew that Philipps had few resources at his disposal to enforce his edict. The deadline passed, and all Philipps could do was appeal to Britain for more troops to enforce his authority. When Philipps informed the home government that the Acadians would neither swear the oath nor leave, he was advised that, as they "will never become good subjects of His Majesty," they should be "removed" as soon as circumstances permitted.[32]

Another, more pressing, problem stemmed from increased tensions with the Mi'kmaq. Because the Mi'kmaq had been allied with the French, British authorities assumed that they too were a defeated people and required to swear an oath of loyalty as subjects of the Crown. The Mi'kmaq refused, insisting that the British were unwelcome intruders. In August 1720, Mi'kmaq warriors began harassing New England fishers on the disputed waters that separated mainland Nova Scotia from Île Royale. The Mi'kmaq resented this trespass upon their traditional fishing grounds, and were supported in this action by the French at Louisbourg, who feared the presence of English ships so close to their remaining colony on the Atlantic. Determined to protect the New England fishing fleet, defend Nova Scotia's frontiers, and keep watch on French activities on Île Royale, Philipps dispatched Major Lawrence Armstrong to build a fort at Canso and to begin negotiations with the Mi'kmaq. When diplomacy failed to put a stop to the attacks, Philipps sent orders to eradicate the Mi'kmaq from the area. Although the campaign succeeded in removing the immediate threat, it intensified Mi'kmaq enmity toward the English. Philipps departed for England in the fall of 1722, leaving Armstrong and the council to manage Nova Scotia's affairs as best they could.

Between 1722 and 1725, the Abenaki were at war over land encroachment with the colony of Massachusetts, and the Mi'kmaq were drawn into this war "as much because of their alliance with the Abenaki as because of their own concerns regarding the Massachusetts fishery," historian William Wicken argues. He emphasizes that in this war, the Wabanaki (as the Mi'kmaq and the other allied nations are collectively known) fought the British for reasons that were unconnected to any European war, at a time when Britain and France were at peace. A peace treaty was concluded in 1726 between imperial representatives of the British colonies of Massachusetts, New Hampshire, and Nova Scotia, and the Abenaki, Passamaquoddy, Maliseet, and Mi'kmaq people. The Treaty of Utrecht had transferred Acadia to British rule, but had not discussed Britain's relations with the Aboriginal peoples in the area. Negotiations for the 1726 treaty had to take into account the existence of an Aboriginal political order. In later years, a more forceful British military presence in the area would encourage a different reading of this agreement.[33]

In 1725, Armstrong attempted to administer the oath to the Acadians once again, and summoned those who resided close to Annapolis Royal to the fort. The Acadians insisted that any oath exempt them from bearing arms. Armstrong responded that no such provision was necessary, since British law prohibited Roman Catholics from serving in the army anyway. The Acadians persisted and, after much discussion, Armstrong agreed to write a note in the margin of the oath. The note had no official standing, but left the Acadians with the impression that they were entitled to remain neutral during times of war. Convinced that they had won an important concession, the Acadians rebuffed Armstrong's subsequent attempts to administer a more unqualified oath. Armstrong attributed the Acadians' obstinacy to the intrigue of Catholic priests and missionaries. Some priests and missionaries were agents of the governor of Louisbourg, Joseph de Monbeton de Brouillan, sent out to foster the loyalty of the Acadians and the Mi'kmaq to the French and to encourage distrust and hostility towards the English. Meanwhile, back in England, Philipps tried to persuade authorities of the impossibility of holding on to Nova Scotia without additional troops, new fortifications, and a large numbers of Protestant settlers. News of dissatisfaction among the Acadians with Armstrong's administration, rather than any renewed commitment to the province, induced the British to send Philipps back to Nova Scotia in 1729.

Philipps found that the Acadian population had almost doubled since his last visit and that English settlement remained negligible. Without any significant immigration, the Acadian population continued to double about every 20 years between 1713 and the early 1750s. "They constitute a powerful group," Philipps reported, "which like Noah's offspring are spreading across the face of the province."[34] Despite the unsettled political status of the Acadians during this era, historian Naomi Griffiths describes the period between 1713 and 1748 as a kind of a "golden age." Acadian life expectancy exceeded that in France; families were large; crops grown on the fertile marshland soil were varied and plentiful—visitors reported on the quality of orchard crops, especially apples. Many families kept poultry and livestock, milk was abundant, and pork in particular was a favoured item of their diet. "The ravages of the Four Horsemen of the Apocalypse were remarkably absent, for famine, disease, and war barely touched the Acadians during these years," Griffiths remarks.[35]

1729: Acadians agree to take an oath when Governor Philipps promises to exempt them from bearing arms.

After touring the province to "mend fences," Philipps attempted to administer the oath. The governor verbally promised the Acadians that they would be exempt from having to bear arms against the French or the Natives, and appended a note to this effect to the document signed by each individual. The exemption, however, was not included in the oath itself, which read: "I promise and swear by my Faith as a Christian that I will be entirely faithful and will truly obey His Majesty King George II, whom I acknowledge as the sovereign lord of Acadia or Nova Scotia, so help me God."[36]

Philipps reported triumphantly to the British government that over 4000 Acadians had taken the oath. He neglected to mention his verbal assurance that the Acadians would never be called upon to take up arms. The consequences of this oversight became apparent when Britain and France found themselves on opposite sides in another dynastic war in Europe.

The War of the Austrian Succession, 1740–1748

This new European war was, again, on the face of it, a controversy over succession: the Habsburg Holy Roman Emperor and Archduke of Austria, Charles VI, had no sons, and had tried to implement the "Pragmatic Sanction" to guarantee the right of his daughter,

Maria Theresa, to succeed him. Soon after Charles's death and the succession of the 23-year-old Maria Theresa in 1740, Prussia, under the rule of the militaristic Emperor Frederick the Great, attempted to seize Austrian territory, using the supposed illegitimacy of the monarchy as a pretext. Other European powers likewise disavowed the Pragmatic Sanction, notably other Germanic states of the Holy Roman Empire, which hoped to gain territory at the expense of Austria. The plucky young Maria Theresa took her newborn son to Hungary and, holding the infant in her arms, convinced the Hungarian parliament to pledge their support for her defence.

Spain opposed Austria and attempted to regain Italian territory lost in the War of the Spanish Succession. Bourbon France, now under the reign of the Sun King's great-grandson, Louis XV, supported Spain against Austria, and saw the war as an opportunity to gain Habsburg territory in Belgium. In supporting German princes against the Habsburgs, France sought to keep the Holy Roman Empire divided, lest these unified powers threaten Bourbon ambitions in Europe. Britain supported the claims of Maria Theresa, partly in a bid to contain the French, but also had independent grievances with the Spanish, stemming from conflict in the empire and on the seas. Robert Jenkins, a British sea captain, complained of indignities suffered by the British in the Spanish Caribbean. He testified in an impassioned plea to the British House of Commons, displaying a box holding his withered ear which he claimed had been cut off by the Spanish. In Britain, the war was also known as the War of Jenkins's Ear.

Britain and France were not formally at war until 1744, but, just as in earlier wars, the War of the Austrian Succession soon spread to North America. Here, the war is sometimes referred to as King George's War—the Hanoverian George II was now Britain's king. Most of the action took place in the Atlantic region. In May 1744, the governor of Louisbourg, Jean-Baptiste-Louis le Prévost Duquesnel, directed French privateers to harass New England shipping and ordered an attack on the English fort at Canso. The fort fell easily and Duquesnel decided to strike at the provincial capital, Annapolis Royal.

1744: French forces capture Canso.

Duquesnel directed an advance party of Mi'kmaq, led by the missionary priest Jean-Louis Le Loutre, to lay siege to the garrison until the arrival of a force of regular soldiers from Louisbourg and a squadron of ships from France. When the promised ships did not appear, the disgruntled Mi'kmaq departed from the scene. Undeterred, Duquesnel dispatched a small force of troops from Louisbourg under the command of François du Pont Duvivier, a native Acadian and the great-grandson of Charles de La Tour. Duvivier expected to be greeted as a liberator by his fellow Acadians, but, despite urgent emotional appeals and repeated threats that they would be punished for their refusal to stand against the English, very few joined his march on Annapolis Royal. Disappointed by this indifferent response, and by the reluctance of the Mi'kmaq to rejoin the campaign, Duvivier pressed ahead and attacked Annapolis Royal early in September. After a four-week siege, Duvivier abandoned the fight and returned to Louisbourg. In the absence of reinforcements and with winter fast approaching, he had little choice. Duvivier's failure to take the lightly armed British garrison exposed serious problems within the French forces at Louisbourg. Like many other officers, Duvivier owed his position to the patronage of the governor and the influence of his family, rather than his military experience and capacity to command. He also suffered from a sense of self-importance and entitlement that

1744: French soldiers mutiny at Louisbourg in December.

1745: Louisbourg falls to the English.

1745: Britain is preoccupied by the Jacobite threat.

clouded his judgment and alienated many around him. Discontent with the quality and behaviour of their officers was a major factor in the full-scale mutiny that broke among the soldiers stationed at Louisbourg in December 1744.

The attacks of French privateers, the fall of Canso, and the siege of Annapolis Royal re-ignited old animosities in New England, where anxiety about the construction of the formidable fortress at Louisbourg had reached a fever pitch. Convinced that the future of New England was at stake, Governor William Shirley of Massachusetts commissioned prominent fish and lumber merchant William Pepperrell to organize a massive assault against Louisbourg. In late March 1745, British warships under the command of Commodore Peter Warren blockaded the harbour. A few weeks later, colonial transports landed the forces unopposed—an army of nearly 4300 New England militia and 800 marines from the Royal Navy—eight kilometres to the west of the fortress. Pepperrell proceeded overland and set up siege batteries on a low range of hills overlooking Louisbourg. Despite its reputation as the Gibraltar of North America, and its formidable seaward defences, the fortress was vulnerable to a land attack from the rear. To make matters worse, Governor Duquesnel died suddenly, leaving command of the fortress in the hands of Louis Du Pont Duchambon de Vergor, a career officer with little battle experience, who inspired no confidence among the already discontented and demoralized men of the garrison. After seven weeks of bombardment, the French forces capitulated. All the bells in Boston rang out to celebrate the news.

The humiliating loss of Louisbourg constituted a major blow to French fortunes in North America, and preparations were immediately begun to assemble a large naval force to recapture the fortress. Buoyed by their success at Louisbourg, New Englanders began to devise plans of their own to capture Quebec, to seal France's fate in North America once and for all. Both sets of plans went awry.

The loss of Louisbourg disrupted French shipping, adding to the ability of British vessels to harass and capture French commercial trade, both with Canada and the West Indies. The governor of New France, the Marquis de Beauharnois, warned that a serious shortage of trade goods threatened to destroy the entire western fur trade and the system of Aboriginal alliances upon which it rested. "There is reason to fear," he wrote, "that the little merchandise which has been sent this year, be it to Niagara or the other posts, will disgust the Indians and encourage them to pass over to the English in order to satisfy their needs."[37]

Britain, too, had pressing problems. In 1745, the Jacobite rebellion at home threatened to topple the monarchy. The Jacobites were supporters of the Stuart kings, exiled in 1688. The 1745 rising, supported by the French, sought to depose the Hanoverian king, George II, and place Charles Edward Stuart, "Bonnie Prince Charlie," on the throne. A 1745 invasion launched from Scotland did not, in the event, draw the degree of Roman Catholic assistance that Stuart supporters had banked on, nor did the French supply all the aid promised.

The April 1746 Battle of Culloden in Scotland crushed the hopes of the Jacobites, and led to punitive English measures against Scottish Highlanders—the confiscation of land and the banning of traditional Highland symbols such as the kilt and the bagpipes. As for North America, the demands of warfare at home meant that England could not spare ships or troops for the planned conquest of Quebec, and the New Englanders' aspirations to follow up the success at Louisbourg could not be fulfilled.

France's bid to regain Louisbourg and Acadia was entrusted to the Duc d'Anville, who was provided with a squadron of 56 ships and 7000 men. The armada sailed in June 1746, but made poor progress because of unfavourable winds. They were within sight of Acadia on September 13 when a sudden violent gale scattered the ships. The Duc d'Anville's second-in-command, Constantin-Louis d'Estourmel, reached Chebucto Harbour two weeks later, only to learn that the commander had been seized by a sudden attack of apoplexy and died a couple of days before. D'Estourmel assumed command, but was tormented by inner demons; he was convinced that he was surrounded by enemies, and attempted suicide. The third in command, the Marquis de La Jonquière, took control of the battered fleet, and, with hundreds dead and the crew suffering the effects of an epidemic, abandoned the planned assault.

1746: A French bid to retake Louisbourg and Acadia goes awry.

Meanwhile, although the governor of New France, the Marquis de Beauharnois, had concerns about a rumoured invasion of Quebec itself, he dispatched a force of 680 Canadian militia and more than 1000 Aboriginal warriors to Acadia to join the planned offensive under the Duc d'Anville. When the ill-fated fleet departed, the Canadians remained in Acadia under the command of Jean-Baptiste de Ramezay. After an unsuccessful siege of Annapolis Royal, Ramezay withdrew to Beaubassin on the strategic Chignecto isthmus. The presence of this large force nearby alarmed Governor Shirley of Massachusetts, who feared that Ramezay might rouse the Acadians and the Mi'kmaq against the English. When London failed to strengthen the British garrison in Nova Scotia, Shirley took the initiative and, in December 1746, dispatched Lieutenant-Colonel Arthur Noble and a regiment of 500 New England militiamen to occupy Grand-Pré, and defeat Ramezay. Shirley also hoped that the presence of the New England troops would deter the Acadians from supporting Ramezay's Canadians. Unable to construct a garrison, Noble's forces billeted among the local population. Only a few skirmishes disturbed the peace until events took a dramatic turn on February 12, 1747. Around three in the morning, amidst a raging snowstorm, the Canadians fell upon Noble's unsuspecting forces at Grand-Pré. The New England militia were forced to surrender.

Outraged New Englanders portrayed the attack as a massacre and claimed that the traitorous Acadians were complicit. The Acadians had warned Noble that an assault was imminent, but he had refused to believe the Canadians would attempt such a raid at the height of winter. Far from being massacred in their beds, most of the New Englanders were permitted to withdraw to Annapolis Royal. The events at Grand Pré confirmed the conviction in New England that the "neutral French" were a treacherous menace that must be removed.

1747: Canadian militia defeat New England force at Grand Pré.

As the war continued, Governor Beauharnois's fears that the war would imperil the fur trade and France's Aboriginal alliances were coming true. Insufficient trade goods were reaching Quebec and in the west, English traders exploited the discontent among Natives to siphon off trade. The effectiveness of such tactics was evident in the spring of 1747 when disaffected Hurons, Ottawas, and Ojibwes laid siege to Detroit and burned surrounding farms. In the face of French weakness and English provocation, the Mohawk broke with their fellow Iroquois, abandoned the Great Peace of Montreal, and resumed their attacks on the French settlements along the St. Lawrence for the first time in nearly half a century. Although he was short of men and munitions, Governor Beauharnois realized that some show of strength was needed to maintain the confidence of the western

Natives, deter the Mohawks, and restrain English mischief-making. The French launched a series of border raids against the English colonists, who, having now mastered the art of frontier warfare, retaliated with their own strikes against outlying French posts and settlements. In the east, in 1747, the French failed to recapture Louisbourg for a second time when the British intercepted and defeated the French fleet at sea.

The War of the Austrian Succession formally ended with the Treaty of Aix-la-Chapelle in 1748. With no party victorious, gains made during the war were reversed by the treaty. France regained Louisbourg, much to the dismay of New England. Both in Europe and North America, tensions continued, and unfulfilled territorial ambitions ensured that new conflict was on the horizon.

1748: The Treaty of Aix-la-Chapelle restores Louisbourg to the French.

The Militarization of the Maritimes and the Mi'kmaq War

Determined to counter the power of Louisbourg, the British established a fortified town and naval base of their own. On June 21, 1749, some 2500 settlers and disbanded soldiers, led by Edward Cornwallis, landed on Chebucto Bay to found Halifax. Halifax soon replaced Annapolis Royal as the capital of Nova Scotia. With its protected harbour, Halifax was favourably located to defend New England shipping, and, far removed from the main areas of Acadian settlement, was not dependent on "the neutral French" for supplies.

1749: The British establish a fortress at Halifax.

The founding of Halifax and the appointment of Cornwallis as governor marked an end to England's long neglect of Nova Scotia. Resolved to increase the loyal population within the colony, Cornwallis recruited over 2500 additional settlers—English and German Protestant colonists.

The establishment of Halifax alarmed the acting governor of New France, Roland-Michel La Galissonière. The growing English presence in Nova Scotia further complicated the uneasy relationship between the Acadians and their imperial masters. In an attempt to consolidate French strength, La Galissonière appealed to the Acadians to relocate to Île Royale. When few left their farms, La Galissonière dispatched missionaries such as Jean-Louis le Loutre to the disputed territory north of the Bay of Fundy to remind the Acadians of their French heritage and Catholic religion, and to incite the Mi'kmaq against the English. The Mi'kmaq needed little encouragement. After the founding of Halifax, a Mi'kmaq chief protested:

> The ground where you stand, where you build your houses, where you build a fort, where you wish to enthrone yourself, this land of which you wish to make yourselves absolute masters, this same land belongs to me. I have grown up on it like the grass, and it is the very place of my birth and my residence. It is my land…. But at the present time you force me to speak out because of the considerable theft you inflict upon me.[38]

Encroachments upon their traditional homelands sparked new Mi'kmaq frontier warfare against the English. Cornwallis responded by issuing a bounty of 10 guineas for every Mi'kmaq scalp and offering a reward of £50 for the capture, dead or alive, of that "good for nothing scoundrel" Abbé le Loutre.[39] Both the French and British raised the stakes in the Atlantic region. In 1750, the British constructed Fort Armstrong on the south bank of the Missaguash River (a few kilometres from what is now Amherst, Nova Scotia). The French responded the following spring by constructing Fort Beauséjour nearby on the Chignecto isthmus. As much as the Acadians sought to avoid becoming embroiled in war between European rivals, the pressure of this military build-up was threatening to overtake them.

1750–1751: The British establish Fort Lawrence and the French build Fort Beauséjour.

Conclusion

The New France of the mid-eighteenth century was different from the beleaguered company colony taken under Crown control in 1663. By 1750, the population had grown to more than 50 000. Most of the inhabitants lived in the countryside, farmed the land, and enjoyed comfortable lives. Despite official intentions to reproduce the rigid social hierarchy of France, *Canadiens* enjoyed a degree of social mobility and independence unheard of in the mother country. Although the fur trade continued to dominate the economy, agriculture had grown in importance and New France now produced enough food to supply its needs and to export surplus crops to the French colonies in the West Indies. Nearly a quarter of the population lived in the principal towns—Quebec, Montreal, and Trois Rivières. With a population of over 5000, Quebec had emerged as a vibrant administrative, commercial, religious, and military centre.

Street scene in Quebec c. 1750.

Source: Library and Archives Canada, C-000043.

As the centre of the fur trade, Montreal had become a town of shops and warehouses, merchants and voyageurs. New France's first highway, the King's Road, linked Montreal and Quebec and a string of forts and trading posts stretched from the St. Lawrence to the Gulf of Mexico. Peter Kalm was impressed by the piety and character of the people, and found the *Canadiens* polite, cheerful, and industrious. "Anyone who considers how alive, joyous, courageous, inured to fatigue the *Canadiens* are," Kalm concluded, "must equally foresee that Canada, will in the near future, become a very powerful country and the Rome of the English provinces."[40] Kalm's glowing description attests to the great progress that had been achieved since New France became a royal colony in 1663.

Impressive as these developments seemed, New France was not to enjoy the future Peter Kalm predicted. With over a million people, the English colonies to the south needed room to expand. The conflicts of the previous half century had begun to unite the English colonists and steeled their resolve to force a final showdown with the French for control of the continent. New France had been successful in expanding and defending its domain, but for how long could this continue, given the colony's thin defences, dependence on Aboriginal allies, reliance on a civilian militia, and vulnerable supply routes? Would the tactics of frontier guerrilla warfare and the network of alliances that had effectively contained the English in the past stand up to a well-planned and concerted assault? It would not be long before New France would have to confront these questions.

Questions to Consider

1. To what degree were efforts to replicate the French social order in New France successful?

2. Was New France well served by its administrative structures and administrators?

3. What were the advantages and disadvantages of western expansion for New France?

4. How did the Acadians respond to the conquest by the British in 1710? Why?

5. What role did Native peoples play in the imperial struggle for North America?

Critical Thinking Questions

1. How does an appreciation of Native cultures and interests change our understanding of the fur trade and colonial rivalries?

2. Some histories of New France during this period focus on dominant personalities such as Talon and Frontenac. Other studies concentrate on the significance of broader social, political, and economic forces. How might one reconcile these two different approaches to the study of New France?

3. How does an appreciation of gender roles and the process of family formation contribute to our understanding of New France's development?

4. To what degree was the society, culture, politics, and economy of New France shaped by war?

Suggested Readings

General

Eccles, W.J. *Canada under Louis XIV, 1663–1701.* Toronto: McClelland & Stewart, 1964.

Miquelon, Dale. *New France: a Supplement to Europe, 1701–1744.* Toronto: McClelland & Stewart, 1987.

Moogk, Peter N. *La Nouvelle France: The Making of French Canada—A Cultural History.* East Lansing: Michigan State University Press, 2000.

Stanley, George F. *New France: The Last Phase, 1744–1760.* Toronto: McClelland & Stewart, 1968.

Society and Culture

Bosher, John F. *Business and Religion in the Age of New France.* Toronto: Canadian Scholars Press, 1994.

Coates, Colin M. *The Metamorphoses of Landscape and Community in Early Quebec.* Montreal and Kingston: McGill-Queen's University Press, 2000.

Crowley, Terrence. "Thunder Gusts: Popular Disturbances in Early French Canada," *Historical Papers/Communications Historique.* Ottawa: Canadian Historical Association, 1979.

Dechene, Louis. *Habitants and Merchants in Seventeenth Century Montreal.* Montreal and Kingston: McGill-Queen's University Press, 1992.

Dumont, Micheline, Michele Jean, Marie Lavigne, and Jennifer Stoddart. *Quebec Women: A History.* Toronto: Women's Press, 1987.

Greer, Allan. *The People of New France.* Toronto: University of Toronto Press, 1997.

Greer, Allan. *Mohawk Saint: Catherine Tekakwitha and the Jesuits.* New York: Oxford University Press, 2004.

Harris, Richard Colebrook. *The Early Seigneurial System in Early Canada: A Geographical Study.* Montreal and Kingston: McGill-Queen's University Press, 1984.

Jaenen, Cornelius J. *The Role of the Church in New France.* Toronto: McGraw-Hill Ryerson, 1986.

Johnston, A.J.B. *Religion and Life at Colonial Louisbourg, 1713–1758.* Montreal and Kingston: McGill-Queen's University Press, 1984.

Johnston, A.J.B. *Control and Order in French Colonial Louisbourg, 1713–1758.* East Lansing: Michigan State University Press, 2001.

Moogk, Peter N. "Les Petits Sauvages" in *Childhood and Family in Canadian History.* Joy Parr, ed. Toronto: McClelland & Stewart, 1982.

Moogk, Peter N. "Reluctant Exiles: Emigrants from France in Canada Before 1760." *William and Mary Quarterly* 46 (July 1989), 463–450.

Noel, Jan. "Les Femmes Favorisées in New France," *Atlantis,* 6 (1981), 80–98.

Noel, Jan. *Women in New France.* Ottawa: Canadian Historical Association, 1998.

Zoltvany, Yves. *The French Tradition in America.* Toronto: Fitzhenry and Whiteside, 1969.

Acadia and the Acadians

Arsenault, B. *History of the Acadians.* Quebec: Lemac, 1966.

Bleakney, J. Sherman. *Sods, Soil, and Spades: The Acadians at Grand Pré and Their Dykeland Legacy.* Montreal and Kingston: McGill-Queen's University Press, 2004.

Brebner, J.B. *New England's Outpost: Acadia before the Conquest of Canada.* New York: Columbia University Press, 1927.

Crowley, Terry. *Louisbourg: Atlantic Fortress and Seaport.* Ottawa: Canadian Historical Association, 1990.

Griffiths, Naomi. *The Contexts of Acadian History, 1686–1784.* Montreal and Kingston: McGill-Queen's University Press, 1992.

Griffiths, Naomi E.S. *From Migrant to Acadian: A North American Border People, 1604–1755.* Montreal and Kingston: McGill-Queen's University Press, 2005.

Plank, G. *An Unsettled Conquest: The British Campaign Against the Peoples of Acadia.* Philadelphia: University of Pennsylvania Press, 2001.

Reid, John G., Maurice Basque, Elizabeth Mancke, Barry Moody, Geoffrey Plank and William Wicken. *The Conquest of Acadia, 1710: Imperial, Colonial and Aboriginal Constructions.* Toronto: University of Toronto Press, 2004.

Native Relations and Imperial Conflict

Eccles, W.J. *The Canadian Frontier, 1534–1760.* Toronto: Holt, Rinehart and Winston, 1969.

Francis, Daniel and Toby Morantz. *Partners in Furs: A History of the Fur Trade in Eastern James Bay, 1600–1870.* Montreal and Kingston: McGill-Queen's University Press, 1983.

Jaenan, Cornelius J. "French Sovereignty and Native Nationhood during the French Regime," *Native Studies Review,* 2.1 (1986).

Pritchard, James. *The Anatomy of a Naval Disaster: The 1746 French Expedition to North America.* Montreal and Kingston: McGill-Queen's University Press, 1995.

Rawlyk, George. *Nova Scotia's Massachusetts: A Study of Massachusetts–Nova Scotia Relations, 1630–1784.* Montreal and Kingston: McGill-Queen's University Press, 1973.

Reid, Jennifer. *Myth, Symbol and Colonial Encounter: British and Mi'kmaq in Acadia.* Ottawa: University of Ottawa Press, 1996.

Steele, I.K. *Guerrillas and Grenadiers: The Struggle for Canada, 1689–1760.* Toronto: Ryerson Press, 1969.

Steele, I.K. *Warpaths: Invasions of North America.* New York: Oxford University Press, 1994.

Upton, L.F.S. *Micmacs and Colonists: Indian–White Relations in the Maritimes, 1713–1867.* Vancouver: University of British Columbia Press, 1979.

White, Richard. *The Middle Ground: Indians, Empires, and Republics in the Great Lakes Region, 1650–1815.* Cambridge: Cambridge University Press, 1991.

Wicken, William. *Mi'kmaq Treaties on Trial: History, Land, and Donald Marshall Junior.* Toronto: University of Toronto Press, 2002.

Notes

[1] Aurore Dionne Eaton, "The Story of Antoine Roy-Desjardins," http://pellgene.tripod.com/roy-desjardins.htm.

[2] Raymond Du Bois Cahall, *The Sovereign Council of New France* (New York: Columbia University, 1915), 22. Available online at http://www.archive.org/details/sovereigncouncil00cahaiala.

[3] W.J. Eccles, *The Government of New France.* Canadian Historical Association Booklet number 18. (Ottawa: Canadian Historical Association, 1971), 13. Available online at http://www.collectionscanada. gc.ca/obj/008004/f2/H-18_en.pdf.

[4] Archives du Séminaire de Québec, MS-179, *Rulebook for Boarders of the Petit Séminaire,* 1.

[5] A.B. Benson, ed., *Peter Kalm's Travels in North America,* vol. 2 (New York, 1927).

[6] Colbert, Instructions to Talon, 25 March 1665, LAC, MG 1, Series C11A, vol. 1, pp. 50–51.

[7] Talon, as quoted by André Vahon, "Jean Talon," *Dictionary of Canadian Biography,* http://www.biographi.ca.

[8] Allan Greer, *Peasant, Lord, and Merchant: Rural Society in Three Quebec Parishes, 1740–1840.* (Toronto: University of Toronto Press, 1985), 100.

[9] W.J. Eccles, *The Canadian Frontier, 1534–1760* (Albuquerque: University of New Mexico Press, 1983), 101.

[10] As quoted by Richard Colebrook Harris, *The Seigneurial System in Early Canada: A Geographical Survey* (Montreal and Kingston: McGill-Queen's University Press, 1984), 181.

[11] Colbert to Talon, 5 January 1666 in *Rapport de l'Archiviste de la Province de Québec, 1922–1923* (Quebec: L.-Amable Proulx, 1923), 41.

[12] Talon quoted in *Canadian Women: a History,* 2nd. ed. (Toronto: Harcourt Brace, 1996), 36.

[13] W. J. Eccles, *The Canadian Frontier,* 95–96.

14 Peter Moogk, *La Nouvelle France: The Making of French Canada—A Cultural History* (East Lansing: Michigan State University Press, 2000), 119.

15 Peter N. Moogk, "Reluctant Exiles: Emigrants from France in Canada before 1760," *The William and Mary Quarterly* 46 (July 1989): 463–505.

16 Marie de l'Incarnation as quoted by André Vachon, "Jean Talon," *Dictionary of Canadian Biography*.

17 A.B. Benson, ed., *Peter Kalm's Travels in North America*, vol. 2 (New York: 1927).

18 Pierre Boucher, *True and Genuine Description of New France Commonly Called Canada* (Paris: Florentine Lambert, 1664) trans. E.L. Montizambert (Montreal, 1883), 73–74.

19 As quoted by André Vachon, "Jean Talon," *Dictionary of Canadian Biography*.

20 Marie de l'Incarnation to her son, 1668, *Word from New France: The Selected Letters of Marie de l'Incarnation,* Joyce Marshall, ed. and trans. (Toronto: Oxford University Press, 1967), 345.

21 As quoted by R. LaRoque de Roquebrune, "Joseph-Antoine Le Febvre de La Barre," *Dictionary of Canadian Biography,* http://www.biographi.ca.

22 As quoted by W.J. Eccles, "Louis de Buade de Frontenac et Palluau," *Dictionary of Canadian Biography,* http://www.biographi.ca.

23 As quoted in "The Explorers," Virtual Museum of New France, Canadian Museum of Civilization, http://www.civilization.ca.

24 As quoted by Manus I. Midlarsky, *The Onset of World War* (Winchester, MA: Unwin Hyman, 1988), 99.

25 Evan Haefeli and Kevin Sweeney, eds. *Captive Histories: English, French and Native Narratives of the 1704 Deerfield Raid* (Amherst and Boston: University of Massachusetts Press, 2006), 1.

26 Geoffrey Plank, "New England and the Conquest" in *The Conquest of Acadia, 1710: Imperial, Colonial, and Aboriginal Constructions* (Toronto: University of Toronto Press, 2004), 74.

27 Terry Crowley, *Louisbourg: Atlantic Fortress and Seaport.* Ottawa: Canadian Historical Association booklet, 1990, http://www.collectionscanada.gc.ca/obj/008004/f2/H-48_en.pdf. See also A.J.B. Johnston, "Sébastien le Prestre de Vauban: Reflections on his Fame, his Fortifications, and his Influence," *French Colonial History* 3 (2003) 175–188.

28 J. Sherman Bleakney, *Sods, Soils, and Spades: The Acadians at Grand Pré and Their Dykeland Legacy* (Montreal and Kingston: McGill-Queen's University Press, 2004), 5–7, 44–50.

29 As quoted by Maurice Basque, "Family and Political Culture in Pre-Conquest Acadia" in *The Conquest of Acadia, 1710: Imperial, Colonial, and Aboriginal Constructions* (Toronto: University of Toronto Press, 2004), 50.

30 Barry Moody, "Making a British Nova Scotia," in *The Conquest of Acadia, 1710,* 128.

31 Elizabeth Mancke, "Imperial Transitions" in *The Conquest of Acadia, 1710,* 180, 190–191.

32 Thomas Beamish Akins, *Selections from the Public Documents of the Province of Nova Scotia* (Halifax: Charles Annands, 1869).

33 William Wicken, *Mi'kmaq Treaties on Trial: History, Land, and Donald Marshall Junior* (Toronto: University of Toronto Press, 2002), 71–74.

34 Thomas Beamish Akins, *Selections from the Public Documents of the Province of Nova Scotia* (Halifax: Charles Annands, 1869).

35 N.E.S. Griffiths, "The Golden Age: Acadian Life, 1713–1748," *Histoire Sociale/ Social History* 17 (May 1984): 21–34.

36 Thomas Beamish Akins, *Selections from the Public Documents of the Province of Nova Scotia* (Halifax: Charles Annands, 1869).

37 As quoted by S. Dale Standen, "Charles de Beauharnois de La Boische, Marquis de Beauharnois," *Dictionary of Canadian Biography,* http://www.biographi.ca.

38 As quoted by Abbé Maillard to Abbé Du Fau, 18 October 1749, Letter P, No. 66, Archives du Séminarie de Québec.

39 As quoted by J. Murray Beck, "Edward Cornwallis" *Dictionary of Canadian Biography,* http://www.biographi.ca.

40 A.B. Benson, ed., *Peter Kalm's Travels in North America*, vol. 2 (New York, 1927).

*T*he Inevitable Conquest?
1749–1763

*I*n early June 1758, British forces launched the greatest-ever invasion by sea of North American territory. Some 157 vessels transported 27 000 troops to launch an assault on the French fortress at Louisbourg on Île Royale, the formidable guardian of the Gulf of St. Lawrence. The 7000 defenders, sheltering within a fort that had never been fully repaired since the last assault during the War of the Austrian Succession, had already withstood a long naval blockade throughout the winter that had reduced them to the point of starvation, and they were doubtful if they had enough ammunition to sustain a prolonged siege. Only six French vessels in the harbour could offer naval support; several more had been deliberately scuttled to bar entry to the British. Yet, the French commander at Louisbourg, the Chevalier de Drucour, knew that every day he could hold out would better the chances that Quebec itself would not be attacked that season. The British commander of the assault, General Jeffery Amherst, made a show of courtesy, even sending a pineapple to Madame Drucour with his compliments. But he was determined to accept nothing less than unconditional surrender.

Under Amherst's command, James Wolfe led an advance landing party, and soon the British occupied the island in force, bringing ashore cannon and mortars. The invaders, skilled in the art of siege warfare, built a network of trenches to bring their cannon ever closer to the fort. By July, their shells were falling behind the walls. Cast iron mortar shells weighing 90 kilograms and filled with exploding charges wreaked devastation on the city. On July 6, a bomb crashed through the roof of Louisbourg's

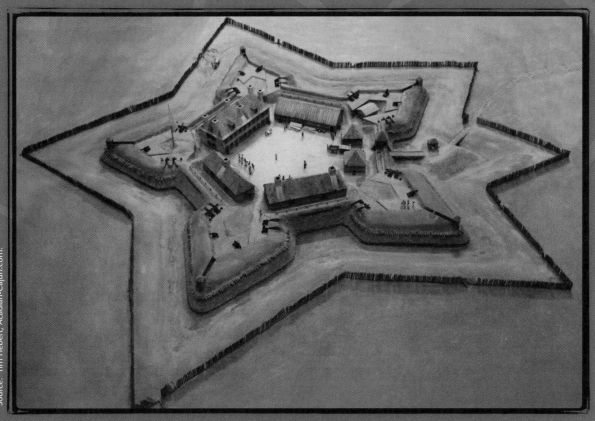

Fort Beauséjour, built by the French in 1751 on the disputed territory of the Isthmus of Chignecto, employed a star-shaped design.

Source: Tim Hebert, Acadian-Cajun.com.

hospital, killing several, including the attending surgeon. On July 21, one of the French ships in the harbour, struck by a British cannonball, began to burn, the fire igniting cannon cartridges on deck. Flames leapt to two nearby vessels, and dense smoke filled the harbour, spreading choking fumes through the fort. Cannons aboard a burning French ship discharged, raining more artillery fire onto Louisbourg. Fire engulfed the powder magazine of another vessel, touching off a huge explosion; still, the defenders hung on. At the height of the siege, British firepower ranged against the town surged to more than 300 mortar shells a day, with incendiary devices spreading fire throughout Louisbourg's devastated buildings. On July 25, the British timed a massive bombardment to coincide with their capture of the remaining French warships. The last shred of naval protection for the fort disappeared, and British naval artillery could now move within range of the devastated defences. At last, Drucour surrendered the fort. The way for an all-out assault on Quebec was clear.

> **After reading this chapter you will be able to:**
>
> 1. Understand the sources of French and British competition in the Ohio Valley.
> 2. Explain the context and historiographical treatment of the expulsion of the Acadians.
> 3. Situate the Seven Years War in North America in a larger global context.
> 4. Assess the role of Aboriginal alliances in the war.
> 5. Identify the most significant battles of the Seven Years War in North America.

Introduction

The mid-eighteenth century would witness the most profound event shaping North America since colonization itself. By 1763, France would be all but driven from the continent as a colonial power, left with only some sugar producing islands in the Caribbean, and a tiny toehold in the Gulf of St. Lawrence. The conquest of New France would leave tens of thousands of French Roman Catholic subjects under the rule of an alien British Protestant power. The protracted war for empire, described by some historians as the first truly *world* war, had far-reaching historical implications. The American Revolution, ignited in 1775, and the French Revolution, which followed in 1789, were in a very real way linked to the Seven Years War—the enormous costs of the war for both the victors and the vanquished necessitated unprecedented taxation measures, measures that would play a role in touching off these conflicts. A consolidation of Britain's power in India also flowed from its success in driving out the French imperial rival.

In Canada, the conquest is often seen as a great wound in the history of the country, a symbol of English hegemony over the French. Generations of English Protestant historians trumpeted the British victory as a symbol of Anglo-Saxon superiority over Gallic backwardness, and rationalized attempts at cultural assimilation with references to Britain's historic victory at the Plains of Abraham. Such a view, however, ignores much relevant history surrounding the Seven Years War, or—as it is sometimes called in North America—the French and Indian War. Historian Allan Greer has posited that it might be more appropriate to see New France as a "ceded colony" rather than a "conquered nation."[1] Britain's much larger colonial presence in North America gave added impetus to their war effort, and contributed to a determination to make warfare in the colonies a priority. France was more ambivalent about the colonial experiment in general, and the settlement on the St. Lawrence in particular. More urgent European struggles, and Britain's growing mastery of the seas, made it impossible for France to marshal enough forces to ensure that New France could be held. The implications for the population of that colony would be enormous.

Conflict in the Ohio Valley

On the map, France's colonial possessions in North America on the eve of this war covered an enormous swathe of territory. French claims stretched from the Arctic to the Gulf of Mexico, including all of modern-day Labrador, the entire St. Lawrence and Great Lakes region, and extending south through what is now the United States to take in the Ohio River Valley and Mississippi River delta. Actual occupation, though, was modest: there were perhaps 55 000 colonists living in New France, most of them clustered along the banks of the St. Lawrence River. By contrast, the number of English settlers in North America had multiplied significantly since a colonial presence was first established there in the seventeenth century. Approximately 1.5 million settlers occupied the 13 English colonies that stretched along the Atlantic seaboard from Massachusetts south to Georgia, north of Spanish-controlled Florida. Beyond this populous colonial region in the future United States, British possessions on the continent included Newfoundland, the vast interior territory of Rupert's Land controlled by the Hudson's Bay Company, and the colony of Nova Scotia that had been in British hands since the 1713 Treaty of Utrecht. It would be in the American continental interior, the Ohio River Valley, where the first significant clash of arms would happen, signalling the outbreak of what would become a worldwide conflict. The burgeoning population of the English colonies along the Atlantic coast was a critical factor in much of the trouble. In 1749, the English colony of Virginia granted a charter to the Ohio Company to expand Virginia's settlement west of the mountains into the Ohio River Valley. The entrepreneurial speculators of the Ohio Company hoped to take advantage of the land hunger of settlers hemmed in east of the Allegheny Mountains (part of the Appalachian range). While this interior territory was claimed by the French, the English believed that their own nominal sovereignty over the Iroquois, which the French had recognized in the Treaty of Utrecht, ought to also give them control over the land that the Iroquois occupied. To the Natives living in the Ohio Valley, settler incursions were a threat, yet, in the short term, the growing English presence was not seen as altogether bad: increased trade competition offered an alternative to the French traders who plied the Ohio River route. One chief of the Wea tribe, in present-day Indiana, explained to the French commandant in the region that it was impossible to prevent young Aboriginal traders from dealing with the English, "who give them every thing very cheap."[2]

1749: The Ohio Company aims to expand English settlement west.

The marquis de La Galissonière, a French naval officer, had been hastily appointed governor of New France in 1747 when the original appointee, the marquis de La Jonquière, had been captured by the British as he sailed to North America during the War of the Austrian Succession. La Galissonière was determined that the British should be driven from the Ohio Valley, that a chain of French posts be constructed to join Canada securely to Louisiana, and that the wavering loyalties of the Natives in the interior be cemented. In the summer of 1749, La Galissonière sent Pierre-Joseph Céloron de Blainville, an experienced Canadian-born officer, on a mission south to consolidate the French claims. Travelling with a party of 213 men in 23 canoes, and accompanied by a Catholic chaplain, Céloron ceremoniously buried lead plates proclaiming the sovereignty of the French king at the Allegheny River, and at the junction of the Ohio and Miami Rivers. He sternly warned interloping British traders and the Natives friendly to them that unauthorized trade would not be tolerated. But this blustering visit could not disguise the fact that the British presence west of the Alleghenies was growing, and Céloron confessed to his superiors that he found the Natives very badly disposed toward the French and entirely devoted to the English.

The presence of French forts to assert control over disputed territory was also part of La Galissonière's plan. Construction of Fort de La Présentation (at present-day Ogdensburg, New York) began in the summer of 1749 at the junction of the St. Lawrence and Oswegatchie Rivers. Fort Detroit had been established earlier on the western frontier, and La Galissonière, mindful of Detroit's importance in communications with the Mississippi Valley, reinforced France's position there. An older French fort at Fort Niagara was meant to control Lake Ontario. A rival English fort further east on Lake Ontario's southern shore, Fort Oswego, was a special concern to La Galissonière, and he urged French authorities that "nothing must be spared to destroy this dangerous post."[3] For La Galissonière, the overriding concern was that the English would use control of the Ohio Valley to launch an attack on the St. Lawrence colony. The loss of the valley as a buffer zone could augur the loss of all of New France.

At the end of 1749, La Galissonière returned to France, and the marquis de La Jonquière, now freed, took up the governor's post. Although the War of the Austrian Succession was ended by 1748 with the Treaty of Aix-la-Chapelle, the growing evidence of tensions over colonial possessions, particularly in North America, made some diplomatic action on the part of the respective mother countries necessary. British and French authorities organized a joint commission in 1750 to settle differences and La Galissonière acted as commissioner for France. The role was a challenging one. Not only did Louis XV's advisors downplay the significance of France's possessions in North America, but the British seemed entirely uncompromising. Governor William Shirley of Massachusetts advised the British government on conditions in North America, but confessed that his goal was to keep the French talking until the time "when it shall be thought proper to reduce 'em."[4]

That time seemed to be drawing ever nearer. Even while Britain and France were technically at peace, episodes of violence in the Ohio Valley were claiming lives. When La Jonquière died in his post, La Galissonière recommended that the marquis Duquesne be named as governor, and Duquesne's declared goals of ousting the English from Fort Oswego and driving them from the Ohio Valley bore the stamp of La Galissonière's ideas. On his arrival in Quebec in July 1752, Duquesne was pleased to learn that a punitive expedition of Canadian militia and Native allies of the Ottawa tribe had already been sent to the Ohio country. On June 21, the French and Ottawa descended upon the village of Pickawillany and launched a devastating attack on the Miami tribe headed by "Old Briton," a chief who had boldly ignored French warnings to stop trade with the British. Fourteen Miami were killed, including Old Briton himself.

Duquesne, delighted with his victory, authorized another, larger expedition the following spring. This force of 2000, led by Paul Marin de La Malgue, erected fortifications as they travelled south: Fort Presque Isle on the south shore of Lake Erie, and Fort Le Boeuf on a tributary of the Allegheny. This spring 1753 expedition attracted the attention of Natives friendly with the British. Tanaghrisson, a Seneca chief known as the Half-King, confronted the French, warning that he would strike at any invaders.

By the autumn of 1753, Virginia Governor Robert Dinwiddie was prepared to challenge the French presence in the Ohio Valley. He commissioned a 22-year-old militia officer, George Washington, to deliver a letter warning the French to vacate Virginia's territory. While Tanaghrisson was skeptical about how intimidating Washington and his half dozen companions were likely to be to the determined French, he and three other warriors agreed to accompany the party. When he reached Fort Le Boeuf, Washington was treated with courtesy: in fact, the French commander invited him to dine with him. But he was instructed to convey to Dinwiddie the message that France's claim to the Ohio Valley was absolute and would be defended.

1750: French and British diplomats attempt to settle disputes.

Clash on the Monongahela Sets "the World on Fire"

Even before this dismissive message was conveyed to him, Governor Dinwiddie had authorized a further step. Winter had not yet left the region when in early 1754 a small force from Virginia began building a crude stockade at the strategic spot where the Allegheny and Monongahela Rivers meet to form the Ohio River. Confronted in mid-April by a French force of several hundred, the ill-equipped English colonials vacated the site, agreeing to leave their carpentry tools behind in exchange for rations.

1754: The French construct Fort Duquesne in disputed territory in the Ohio Valley.

The French finished construction of a proper fort, named Fort Duquesne in honour of their governor, on the site. Virginia's governor had already sent George Washington on a fresh expedition to reinforce the English position there. Only by promising substantial land grants in the Ohio Valley could Washington recruit 132 inexperienced fighters to join him. The spring 1754 expedition soon learned the disheartening news that the fort was in French hands, yet Washington, in part encouraged by a pledge of assistance from Tanaghrisson, the Half King, decided to carry on. Washington's strategy of building a substantial road as his force advanced made progress slow, and they were forced to halt at Great Meadows, 80 kilometres from Fort Duquesne. Hasty defensive arrangements were made at the site, which Washington aptly named "Fort Necessity." The Virginia militia were exhausted, and many had deserted, alarmed by reports of a sizeable French force and disillusioned over late pay.

Washington's arrival in the area did not escape the notice of the French. A party of 30 men, under the command of Ensign Joseph Coulon de Villiers de Jumonville, was dispatched from Fort Duquesne. The French considered this party not spies or scouts, but emissaries; Jumonville bore a letter to be given to the English. When the group made camp in an enclosed glen on the night of May 27, 1754, they failed to post any sentries. Tanaghrisson warned Washington of the nearing presence of the French, and Washington, fearful that an attack was imminent, decided to seize the initiative. Washington, Tanaghrisson, and a blended force of 40 set out through the rainy night, blundering through the unmarked forest. Hours later, at daybreak, they reached the French encampment. Jumonville's men were just beginning to awake when the English and their allies opened fire upon them. Tanaghrisson's warriors prevented escape from the hollow, and, within minutes, 14 French soldiers had fallen. Among the wounded was Jumonville, who struggled to identify himself as the commander and to have a translation read of the message that he bore. As Washington stepped away to bring the document to his own translator, Tanaghrisson came forward and addressed the fallen Frenchman: "*Tu n'es pas encore mort, mon père,*" he proclaimed—you are not yet dead, my father.

Raising his tomahawk, Tanaghrisson drove the hatchet into Jumonville's skull, killing him instantly. Tanaghrisson then reached among the broken bone fragments to wash his hands in the brains. Others set upon and killed the remaining French wounded, scalping them, stripping the bodies, and, in a final indignity, driving a stake through the severed head of one of the victims to make a grisly display. Washington managed to escort 21 French prisoners to safety at Fort Necessity, but his position was not a tenable one. Predictably, the French, incensed at the attack on Jumonville by a nation with whom they were ostensibly at peace, launched a much larger retaliatory force with Jumonville's brother in command.

1754: French forces triumph over George Washington's Virginia militia in the Ohio Valley.

After confronting Washington in a short skirmish near Fort Necessity on July 3, 1754, the French obtained a complete surrender. Washington obediently signed a document that described the disputed area of his fort as French territory and the killing of Jumonville as an assassination. His blundering raid had, in the words of the British writer Horace Walpole, "set the world on fire."[5]

Preparations for War in the Colonies

The crisis of open hostility between the French and English in the Ohio Valley made some sort of united defence strategy imperative in the Thirteen Colonies. In the summer of 1754, the British government convened a conference at Albany, New York, and representatives of seven colonies agreed to meet. Representatives of the Six Nations Iroquois were also invited to take part in the Albany Conference, and British and colonial officials were especially eager to secure the uncertain loyalties of their traditional allies. The British government authorized the purchase of presents in order to try to buy Iroquois friendship, but, just as the English colonies were divided, so too were the members of the Iroquois League. Mohawk Chief Hendrick (Theyanoguin), a staunch British ally who had twice travelled to England to meet reigning monarchs, had earlier been angered by the unwillingness of New York Governor George Clinton to strike against the French. He harangued the delegates of Albany, urging them to act like men. But not all of the Aboriginal representatives supported an aggressive position, and most attempted to steer a neutral course.

1754: Albany Conference contemplates a union of the "American" colonies.

One of the great, unrealized goals of the conference was to encourage a union of the American colonies. Benjamin Franklin of Pennsylvania had drawn up a plan to have each colonial legislature elect representatives to send to an American continental assembly which would be administered by a royal governor. Some of Franklin's ideas would later be put into practice after the American Revolution, but for the moment, the individual colonies were loath to surrender any authority to a central body—nor were they united in their resolve to finance large-scale military operations against the French.

Virginia did not send a delegate to the Albany Conference, perhaps reluctant to be restrained from pursuing its expansionist policy: Virginia's Governor Dinwiddie was a personal shareholder in the Ohio Company. Colonial critics would later complain that military action in the Ohio Valley had been launched "to serve the interest of a private company at the expense of the welfare of the public."[6] Similar accusations of corruption and vested interests were being made on the French side. The intendant of New France, François Bigot, was notorious for lavish spending and rewarding cronies with fat government contracts for military supplies. He hosted magnificent banquets and wracked up staggering gambling debts. Under his administration, expenditures surged from 6 million livres in 1755 to over 30 million livres in 1759. The French commander Montcalm later condemned Bigot's corruption, noting that he and a few associates were engaged in the "business of plundering." The "criminal acts" of such speculators, driven by their "own selfish interests, provided the English with the pretext their ambitious schemes required in order to light the blaze," he charged. After the war, 55 official and commercial men of New France were called before a commission of inquiry in Paris. Bigot was punished with forfeiture of property and was imprisoned in the Bastille.[7]

The Illusion of Peace Is Shattered

When news of Washington's surrender at Great Meadows reached London in August of 1754, plans were put into place for an infusion of armed forces into North America. Major General Edward Braddock, a seasoned but inflexible military commander who had been serving as governor of Gibraltar, was given overall command. Braddock lost no time: shrugging off the danger of a stormy Atlantic passage in winter, he reached Virginia in February 1755. The French, he knew, would be unable to reach their own winter-locked colonial ports until the ice broke up, and he was eager to make what preparations he could in the English colonies in the meantime.

In Europe, each side hastened to prepare in secrecy, while still maintaining the pretense that the two nations were at peace. By late spring 1755, French and British fleets were en route to North America. A British plan to intercept the French fleet south of Newfoundland failed when most of the French ships eluded them, but three vessels lost in the fog came within hailing distance of the British *Dunkirk*. "Are we at peace, or war?" the French captain of the *Alcide* called out. "La paix, la paix," came the reassuring reply, followed by a devastating volley from the *Dunkirk*'s guns.[8] The illusion of peace was shattered. Yet this brash and provocative act—much like Washington's 1754 attack on the Jumonville party—had not offered much real military advantage to the British. Only two ships of the large French convoy had been intercepted, and most of the 3000 French reinforcements were able to land safely at Louisbourg or Quebec. When news reached London, Lord Hardwicke, the Lord Chancellor, lamented, "We have done too much or too little."[9]

Britain's Early North American Offensive

Braddock's plan called for a four-pronged offensive against the French; he himself would lead the assault on strategic Fort Duquesne. Once successful, he would march north to join Massachusetts governor William Shirley's attack on Fort Niagara. From there, his forces would swing east to assist Colonel William Johnson who, along with Mohawk allies, was to take Fort Saint-Frédéric at Crown Point on Lake Champlain. Lieutenant Colonel Robert Monckton, the acting governor of Nova Scotia, was to take the Maritime Fort Beauséjour, located at the head of the Bay of Fundy. Unlike Fort Duquesne and Fort Beausejour, where imperial possession was in dispute, Fort Saint-Frédéric and Fort Niagara had long been in French hands. A British assault on these positions would be an open act of war.

Braddock predicted that he would have more success expelling the French than George Washington had: "These Savages may indeed be a formidable Enemy to your raw American Militia; but, upon the King's regular and disciplined Troops ... it is impossible they should make any impression."[10] Braddock's force of 3000 made its way slowly west from Alexandria, Virginia, led by 300 axemen, who cleared a road through the dense forest for a line of packhorses, wagons, cannon, and regular and colonial troops that sometimes stretched back over six kilometres. Fodder for the horses was scarce, and cutting roads passable by heavy artillery and lumbering wagons proved difficult in slippery mountainous terrain with deep ravines and rushing waters. At times, progress slowed to less than five kilometres per day. An Oneida chief, Scarouady, had allied himself with the advancing British, but grew disenchanted as the weeks dragged on. Braddock, he complained, "looked upon us

1755: British launch a four-pronged attack on French positions.

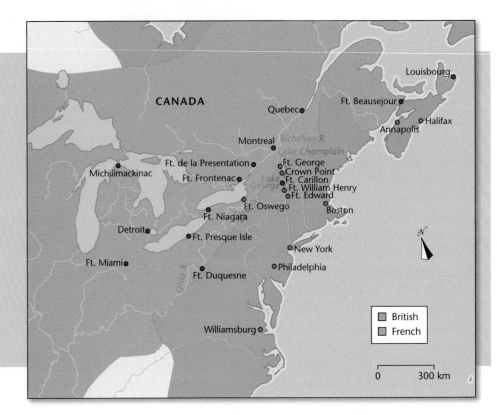

Map 4.1
Map of Fortifications.

as dogs and would never hear any thing that was said to him." Dozens of Aboriginal war-riors deserted, leaving only six to support Braddock's increasingly demoralized mission.[11] French scouts and their Aboriginal allies skirted the British force at a distance, launching occasional raids to pick off stragglers, and the sense of constant menace from the shadowy forest strained the nerves of Braddock's men. Sudden alarms, real or imaginary, would set off a hair-trigger response. Chief Scarouady's own son fell to friendly fire. When Brad-dock learned the discouraging news that hundreds of reinforcements were on their way to relieve the French at Fort Duquesne, he resolved to tarry no longer. Leaving the main force, he set out on July 9, 1755, with an advance party of 1200 men.

Those hoping to defend Fort Duquesne against him were not themselves optimistic. The commander, a Canadian-born seigneur and long-serving military officer, Claude-Pierre Pécaudy de Contrecoeur, had been dismayed to discover that the force sent from Montreal to relieve him consisted of only 200 men and no cannon. He doubted that he could hold the fort against Braddock's larger force and superior artillery. Desperate to slow Braddock's advance, he dispatched Captain Daniel-Hyacinthe-Marie Liénard de Beaujeu, along with 250 colonial militia and regulars, to try to ambush them. Experienced in the guerrilla warfare of the frontier, Beaujeu knew that European tactics of open confrontation were no match for techniques of deception and stealth in the rugged interior terrain. He also knew that without the aid of Aboriginal warriors, he would have no chance against Braddock. Eight or nine hundred Natives had camped near the fort: some from the Ohio Valley—Ottawa and Delaware natives—along with Huron, Caughnawaga, and Abenaki from the St. Lawrence valley. Beaujeu dressed himself in a fringed buckskin jacket and went among them to beseech them to join him. The Natives, however, recognized that the contest was too unequal, and shrank from taking part in the doomed defence. Beaujeu defiantly announced, "I am determined to go and meet the enemy. Will you let your Father go alone?" At that moment, word reached the assembly that Braddock's force had forded the Monongahela River and were approaching the fort. The electric atmosphere, and Beaujeu's own inspiring resolve, won his wavering allies over.[12]

As Braddock's scarlet-clad men, marching in steady formation to the music of fife and drum, neared Fort Duquesne on July 9, 1755, the trap was sprung. Sharpshooters hidden in ravines and shielded by the dark forest opened fire upon them as they stood in bewilderment. Some of Braddock's men, Virginia militia who knew the ways of frontier warfare, emulated their enemies by attempting to take cover, but were ordered to withstand fire in the open, and were shot down. Bodies of dead and wounded soldiers littered the ground, and in the confusion, amid the smoke, the terrifying war whoops of the Native warriors, and the panicked plunging of wounded horses, the ambushed men fired blindly, sometimes shooting down their own comrades. Braddock frantically tried to master the situation, but was himself the target of snipers, who shot four successive horses out from under him. British officers fell all around. Governor Shirley's son, who had acted as Braddock's secretary, was shot through the head. The French and their allies suffered the loss of only a couple dozen men, although among them was the commander, Beaujeu, who was felled by a British volley as he waved his hat in signal to his troops.

With his clothes torn by bullets, Braddock gamely mounted a fifth horse, but was forced to order a retreat. Having withstood three hours of fire, his men abandoned all pretext of order and fled in panic towards the ford, plunging through the water to escape, leaving the wounded to be scalped and mutilated. But for Braddock it was too late. A bullet, possibly fired from his own side, entered his lung. He collapsed into the bush, gasping for breath. Despite his orders that he should be left where he fell, Braddock's junior officers took him away on a stretcher improvised from the general's own sash.

More than 900 of the fallen were left behind—along with detailed plans of the four-pronged invasion. The flight of the survivors became a rout. Stores, ammunition, and wagons were set alight in a frantic retreat spurred on by the threat of Native attacks. Those caught at the bank of the Monongahela were butchered by their pursuers, and the river ran with blood. When his bearers reached Great Meadows a few days later, Braddock succumbed to his wounds. "Who would have thought it?" he murmured as he neared death.[13]

Another component of Braddock's grand plan had also foundered. Governor Shirley's objective of marching on Fort Niagara was doomed by logistical difficulties: the untamed wilderness between Albany, New York, and Fort Oswego proved impossible to traverse within the few weeks allotted, and Shirley had to give up any plan of an attack on Fort Niagara that summer.

Colonel William Johnson, whose objective, according to Braddock's planned offensive, was to take Fort Saint-Frédéric on Lake Champlain, had the advantage of a firm alliance with the Mohawk. The Irish-born Johnson was a long-time friend of key Mohawk leaders and had been named superintendent of Indian Affairs for the colony of New York.

1755: Braddock's British forces are soundly defeated by a combined French and Native force at Fort Duquesne.

Johnson hosted a huge assembly for more than 1000 members of the Six Nations at his estate where, after feasting, drinking, smoking, dancing, and discussing, he urged the warriors to take up the hatchet with him against the French. Events took a dismal turn when news reached them of the debacle of Braddock's defeat on the Monongahela, but Johnson's ally, his "brother" Chief Hendrick (Theyanoguin), stood by him, and rallied others to the cause. Johnson was able to marshal a force of about 3000 colonial militia and a couple hundred Mohawk to capture Fort Saint-Frédéric.

The French commander, Baron Dieskau, knew of the plan from Braddock's captured papers, and moved to intercept the attack with a force of 4000. Among this force were Native warriors, including 300 so-called "French Mohawk" from Caughnawaga, some of whom were ambivalent about taking up arms against their Mohawk cousins allied with the British. The two sides met in early September 1755 at the southern end of Lake George. While the British claimed victory, and captured the wounded Baron Dieskau, Johnson did not achieve his objective of capturing Fort Saint-Frédéric. Each side suffered comparable casualties—around 300—and Chief Hendrick was among those killed.

Johnson quickly adapted to the situation, and, having failed to take Fort Saint-Frédéric, opted to consolidate Britain's presence with the construction of Fort William Henry nearby. The French began new fortifications at the outlet of Lake George. The name, Fort Carillon, was suggested by the bell-like sound of the rushing waters.

1755: Construction of the British Fort William Henry and French Fort Carillon marks conflicting claims in the area south of Lake Champlain.

The only unqualified success for the British in these earliest engagements of the Seven Years War was at Fort Beauséjour. The French had begun to build Fort Beauséjour (near what is Sackville, New Brunswick today) in 1751, in response to the British construction of Fort Lawrence nearby. Beauséjour, built with a star-shaped layout, was protected by 24 cannons.

Both fortresses were symbolic of the growing militarization of the area, a development that threatened the traditional neutrality of the Acadian people living close by. In June 1755, a few weeks before Braddock's disaster at Fort Duquesne, Colonel Robert Monckton and a force of 2200 New England militia and 250 British regulars laid siege to Beauséjour. The French commander there, Louis Du Pont Duchambon de Vergor, a dull leader who owed his appointment to his friendship with the corrupt Intendant Bigot, had capitulated at Louisbourg during the last war, and now quickly surrendered Fort Beauséjour. The activities of the spy Thomas Pichon, commissary of stores at Beauséjour, also did much to undermine the fort's defence. Born in France to an English mother, Pichon fed secrets to the British at Fort Lawrence. Acadians and Mi'kmaq allies played a part in attacking the British outside the fort, but to no avail. On June 16, 1755, the British seized Fort Beauséjour, renaming it Fort Cumberland. The capitulation of the fort would have disastrous consequences for the French Acadian population in the area.

1755: The British capture of Fort Beauséjour is a threat to continued Acadian neutrality.

The Expulsion of the Acadians, 1755

The speedy and successful resolution of what he had feared would be a long campaign meant that the British governor of Nova Scotia, Charles Lawrence, had an opportunity. He saw a chance to deal with the threat of a potentially hostile population at the outset of what promised to be a brutal period of war. He had almost 2500 paid and provisioned troops at the ready, and was encouraged by the quick collapse of Fort Beauséjour. The

Acadians had lived peacefully under British rule for more than a generation—Britain's possession of Nova Scotia dated from the 1713 Treaty of Utrecht, but recent events had raised concerns about the loyalty of that population. Adding to the sense of urgency was news that the large French fleet en route to North America, with a force of 3000, had managed to elude British warships off the coast. At Halifax, Charles Lawrence grew increasingly skittish about the possibility of a French counterattack.

In the spring of 1755, before the capture of Beauséjour, the Acadian population had been asked for an oath of allegiance as British subjects; only a small number complied. Since most had lived their entire lives under British rule, successfully negotiating neutrality even during the previous war, it is probable that they failed to recognize the degree to which circumstances had changed. They wavered between the wholehearted loyalty demanded by their British rulers and the loyalty to France that the imperial policy of that nation sought to encourage. The Roman Catholic missionary Jean-Louis Le Loutre was a link between the authorities in New France and the Acadians, whom the French hoped might help them fight the coming war. Earlier Protestant historians, perhaps wishing to rationalize the brutal treatment of the Acadians at the hands of their British colonial masters, have emphasized Le Loutre's incendiary role in stirring up agitation among the Acadians and Mi'kmaq. Francis Parkman charged the French with heartless behaviour toward the Acadians, who were, he claimed, "treated as mere tools of policy, to be used, broken, and flung away."[14] Yet, neither side could be sure of the Acadians' allegiance. Thomas Pichon, the spy, claimed to have heard some declare that they would be "on the side of the strongest."[15] With the fall of Fort Beauséjour, Le Loutre fled, reportedly dressed in women's clothing, but was captured by the British a few months later when sailing from Louisbourg. He languished in an English prison until the end of the war.

Another traitor to British rule—or, in the eyes of others, heroic freedom fighter—was the Acadian resistance leader Joseph "Beausoleil" Brossard (the name is sometimes spelled "Broussard"). Brossard had run afoul of the English during the War of the Austrian Succession for giving aid and supplies to the French troops. The British also believed that Brossard was responsible for leading a group of some 60 Natives in a brutal attack in 1751 on the English colony of Dartmouth, Nova Scotia, in which eight were killed and 14 taken prisoner. The attackers scalped some of the victims, among whom were women and children. Brossard led an attack against the British camp on the day that Fort Beauséjour was captured. With the French defence collapsed, Brossard approached Monckton with an offer to mediate with the Mi'kmaq, subject to a grant of personal amnesty. British authorities in Nova Scotia, resolved upon a merciless course of action, were in no mood to be conciliatory. Brossard fled to the woods and when the opportunity presented itself, rejoined the resistance.

If the presence of the "neutral French" in Acadia conflicted with Britain's broader goals for consolidation of empire, it conflicted even more with the interests of land speculators in New England. The growing population of the English colonies to the south of Nova Scotia had looked longingly on the fertile farmland carefully dyked by generations of Acadians along the Bay of Fundy and Minas Basin. Governor Shirley of Massachusetts and Governor Lawrence of Nova Scotia had begun to make plans for the expulsion of the Acadians as early as 1754, encouraged by a rash letter from British Secretary of State

Thomas Robinson, who later disavowed the plan. Settlers from New England would be ideal candidates to occupy the vacated agricultural land.

The appointed council of Nova Scotia had already decided on expulsion when in July 1755 they received a small delegation of Acadians from Grand Pré on the Minas Basin. The Acadians had come to present a petition calling for the return of some boats and arms that had been confiscated. Governor Lawrence seized the opportunity to demand an unqualified oath of allegiance. He scoffed at the explanation offered by some that they had been compelled to take part in the defence of Fort Beauséjour against their will. When the delegates hesitated in the face of the governor's demand, claiming that they needed to consult the rest of the population, Lawrence ordered them imprisoned. More Acadian representatives were summoned from the Minas area and from Annapolis, and warned that they must immediately take the oath "without any Reserve or else quit their lands."[16] Determined not to take any oath that would bind them to take up arms against the French, they refused. They, too, were thrown into prison as French prisoners of war. Parish priests, suspected of sowing disaffection, were rounded up and arrested.

1755–1758: Some 10 000 Acadians are banished from their homes.

In the summer and autumn of 1755, the British began a brutal "scorched earth" policy against the Acadians that would continue for the next three years. Acadian communities were obliterated, village by village, and an estimated 10 000 sent into exile. Crops were burned, and homes and churches put to the torch to prevent the Acadians from returning to re-occupy them. All livestock was to be forfeited to the king: nearly 20 000 head of cattle, 30 000 sheep, 1600 horses, and an untold number of pigs. Monckton oversaw the expulsion of Acadians from the Chignecto isthmus, Captain Alexander Murray those from Pigiguit, and Major John Handfield those from Annapolis Royal. Colonel John Winslow, who had what he described as the "disagreeable" task of expelling the Acadians from the Minas Basin, summoned them to the church at Grand Pré for the reading of a proclamation. Many present expected another call to take the oath and hoped that they could bide their time as before, but they were shocked to see the church surrounded by soldiers. Nearly 2000 unarmed settlers were given an hour to gather their belongings before being herded onto transport ships.

While most historical accounts have Nova Scotia governor Charles Lawrence as the villain of the story, historian John Mack Faragher emphasizes the degree to which the "*Grand Dérangement*" was carried out by American colonists. The Acadians were forced from their homes by New England troops and officers, transported in vessels organized by Boston trading houses, and displaced by settlers from New England. "It was a thoroughly Yankee operation," he explains. The *Pennsylvania Gazette* rhapsodized about the benefits that would flow from the "great and noble Scheme of sending the neutral French out of this Province, who have always been secret Enemies, and have encouraged our Savages to cut our throats. If we effect their Expulsion, it will be one of the greatest Things that ever the English did in America.... In case therefore we could get some good English Farmers in their Room, this Province would abound with all Kinds of Provisions."[17]

Nearly a third of the exiled Acadians died from diseases such as typhoid and yellow fever that resulted from the squalid conditions on board the crowded ships. Most were taken to Britain's other American colonies and dispersed among a hostile and alien population. Ironically, the New England settlers who displaced them in the fertile lands around the Bay of Fundy found that Acadian expertise was needed to maintain and repair the dykes. In 1760, Lawrence had 2000 refugee Acadians brought back to their homeland to serve as labourers for the new proprietors. This was to be his last contribution to the Acadian problem: in October 1760 the previously strong and healthy governor died suddenly from complications following a cold.

Some of the most troublesome Acadians were interned in England and eventually sent to France, truly a foreign country to them. Others, like Brossard, who was forced to surrender to British authorities late in 1761, were held prisoner in Nova Scotia. At the war's end, most of the exiles opted to leave the English colonies along the Atlantic seaboard to settle anew in a more congenial place. Several hundred Acadians travelled to the French Caribbean colony of Saint Domingue (Haiti). Brossard led a party there soon afterward, but they remained only a short time before moving on to Louisiana. France had secretly ceded the colony of Louisiana to Spain in 1762 in exchange for Spanish aid in the war against Britain, but France continued to administer the colony until 1766. Brossard's party was soon joined by hundreds more Acadian arrivals. The French governor at New Orleans welcomed Brossard as a hero and, in 1765, named him Captain of Militia and Commandant of the Acadians. Brossard, like a leaf buffeted about by the churning currents of history, had reached a new home where generations of Acadians, now called "Cajuns," would follow. His own future there was limited, though: in 1765 he died in an epidemic.

The deportation of the Acadians is among the most tragic episodes in Canadian history. One of the best-known iconic images of the tragedy is "Evangeline," a fictional character created by the American poet Henry Wadsworth Longfellow in 1847. Longfellow's poem, which has done much to shape popular historical memory, is a deeply emotional indictment of the brutal expulsion. The fictional heroine, torn away from her lover Gabriel on their wedding day by the sudden deportation, spends the remainder of her life searching for him, only to be reunited with him in old age as he lay dying.

Some historians have explained the expulsion as a consequence of the Acadians' own persistent refusal to take an unqualified oath, the ongoing tensions between the colonies, and the context of war. In some respects, the controversy resembles that surrounding the internment of Canada's Japanese population, forced to leave British Columbia coastal areas during World War II. Other historians have argued that the deportation was both cruel and unnecessary: most Acadians had lived peacefully under British rule for more than 40 years. When peace was restored, the British governor of Quebec, James Murray, issued a proclamation welcoming Acadians willing to take an oath of allegiance. By 1770, at least 6000 Acadians were living along the St. Lawrence, and in Maritime areas such as Miramichi, Baie des Chaleurs, and other communities.

Fictional Evangeline, engraving, copied 1863, William Notman (1826–1891) 1863.

Source: © McCord Museum, I-12071.1.

A Global War

Just as the French and English had been waging war in North America without an open declaration, so, too, was this the case in India. The French East India Company dated as far back as 1664—about the time that New France became a royal province in North America. French influence in India was greatest on the east coast of the subcontinent; Pondichéry (Puducherry) was at the centre of French power. Through elaborate intrigues with Indian princes, the two rival imperial powers jockeyed for influence, and India was a theatre of war when the French and English fought throughout the late seventeenth and eighteenth centuries. In the years leading up to the Seven Years War, French governor Joseph François Dupleix so vigorously matched the machinations of his British counterpart, Robert Clive, that the French government recalled him in 1754, lest he embroil them in an expansionist policy beyond their ability to control.

The undeclared war was also being waged at sea, and Britain resolved to capture any vessel flying the French flag anywhere in the world. The goal was to break French commercial power. French ministers protested impotently against these acts of piracy "in defiance of the law of nations, the faith of treaties, [and] established custom among civilized people." But the British strategy seemed to be working. By the end of 1756, numerous French merchant houses had collapsed in bankruptcy, and the French press reported that 250 merchant ships had been lost: "The English gain this considerable advantage over us every day, and if this went on we should finally be ruined."[18] Nevertheless, the French navy remained a threat despite these attacks on French merchant shipping, and neutral powers continued a thriving trade in French ports—as did some British vessels that violated the laws. The British navy was more powerful still: in 1755, Britain possessed some 148 first-rate ships of the line carrying 50 to 100 guns each, 103 frigates, and 80 smaller vessels, manned by a total of 42 000 sailors. The French navy consisted of fewer than half this number, and an intensive British naval building campaign on the eve of the war threatened to tip the balance still further. The spectre of a French alliance with Spain, which possessed some 50 battleships, made the British less sanguine. Moreover, the French were busy drawing up plans for the invasion of the British Isles and France's land forces were far superior. On the north coast of France, 118 infantry battalions massed, a force that exceeded, and almost doubled, the entire British army.[19]

The European dimensions of the Seven Years War are often treated as secondary to the colonial sphere where events proved most decisive. The provocations that drew Britain and France into war did indeed come primarily from the imperial periphery—from continental North America and the Caribbean and from India. In Europe itself, antagonisms between the two nations were part of a centuries-old struggle for supremacy. Despite an uneasy status quo after the War of the Austrian Succession, old antagonisms and jealousies remained. "It is in the blood of Englishmen to hate Frenchmen and to wish them ill," an anonymous French memoirist theorized. "Enamoured as they are of their so-called liberty, they consider us the only nation powerful enough to cause them to lose it…. They are constantly preoccupied with the need to undermine our power."[20] It took little to fan these smouldering resentments into open flame: in May 1756 war was declared.

Some alliances among world powers had shifted since the War of the Austrian Succession. During the Seven Years War, France was allied with Saxony and Sweden as before, and would eventually also have the aid of Spain, but was now also allied with Austria and Russia.

May 1756: The British and French are now openly at war.

Perhaps more significantly, Britain was allied with Prussia, a nation that had emerged from the last war with new territorial gains and a reputation for military might. Frederick II of Prussia, known as Frederick the Great, implemented new systematic training for his armies with an emphasis on precision manoeuvres that made them an enviable model to the ill-disciplined troops of other European powers. It was said that he sought to make his forces more afraid of their own officers than of the enemy.

Prussia's forces almost tripled under Frederick's intense program: the nation of 2.5 million was able to raise an army that grew from 30 000 to 80 000 strong. These formidable troops would prove to be of enormous value to British interests in North America by keeping the French engaged with continental European warfare. British Prime Minister William Pitt later boasted that America had been conquered in Germany. The annual drain on the British treasury of £600 000 would have to be reckoned with later.[21] Britain also had an alliance with Hanover, an inevitable consequence of the British King George II's position as Elector of Hanover.

Montcalm in New France

Days before the formal declaration of war, the new commander of France's forces in North America, Louis Joseph de Montcalm, the Marquis de Montcalm, arrived in Quebec to take up his new post as replacement for the captured baron de Dieskau. Montcalm was a career soldier, born of a noble family distinguished for military service. He had been commissioned as an ensign at the age of nine, began active service at age 20, and had been wounded three times. Montcalm was both a soldierly and scholarly man, whose education included a good grounding in Latin, Greek, and history. At home in peacetime at his estate in the south of France, Montcalm supervised his children's education. When duty took him overseas, he remained a devoted family man, assuring those at home that "there is not an hour in the day when I do not think of you."[22] Yet Montcalm may have exhibited some of the same failings as his late British counterpart, General Braddock, and critics have described him as high-handed and contemptuous of colonial ways.

1756: Montcalm arrives in North America to command the French forces.

Montcalm's position was subordinate to that of the governor of New France, Pierre de Rigaud de Vaudreuil de Cavagnial, the marquis de Vaudreuil, who had taken up his position the previous year after a stint as governor of Louisiana. Vaudreuil was Canadian born—his father had himself been governor of New France—and was temperamentally at odds with the aristocratic military commander over whom he now had authority. Montcalm kept up a private channel of correspondence with the French minister of war, the comte d'Argenson, through which he could be as frank as he liked about Vaudreuil's shortcomings, Canadian conditions, and his increasingly pessimistic view of their prospects in the war. Montcalm and Vaudreuil quickly came to dislike one another, and their fundamental differences about how France's military resources could best be deployed complicated questions of military strategy.

The Marquis de Montcalm.

Source: Library and Archives Canada, C-027665.

The French forces varied in type. In theory, the most numerous were the Canadian militia, citizen soldiers, all able-bodied men in the colony between 16 and 60 years of age—perhaps 12 000 in total. Of course, important competing duties like farming and other civil tasks impeded the effectiveness of this force. Although these men knew the ways of the frontier, they were not fully trained as disciplined soldiers. A further colonial force, the *troupes de la marine,* consisted of colonial regulars—professional soldiers under the administration of the department of Marine. They numbered some 2000. The main fighting force, the *troupes de la terre,* were regulars from France. In 1755, four battalions were sent to New France; in 1756, two more, and in 1757 another two. With these battalions numbering 500 men on average, the total strength of regular soldiers sent to New France would have reached about 4000. Seamen were also used as combatants ashore, although their effective numbers were limited to perhaps 1500 men. Added to this, of course, was the formidable strength of France's Aboriginal allies.

Aboriginal Allies in the Seven Years War

The number of Aboriginal warriors who fought on the side of the French seldom exceeded a couple of thousand at any one time. Some of these Native warriors came from among the Canadian Iroquois who lived in seven main communities in the St. Lawrence Valley, a group distinct from the Six Nations Iroquois Confederacy. The French also drew support from a number of other Native nations: the Abenaki, Algonquin, Huron, and Nipissing; in the west the Ojibwe, Ottawa, Menomiee, Mississauga, Potawatomi, and Wyandot; in the Maritimes the Mi'kmaq and Maliseet; and to the south the Delaware, Fox, Iowa, Miami, Oneida, Sauk, and Winnebago nations.

D. Peter MacLeod has suggested that Aboriginal fighters pursued "parallel warfare." They fought at the request of the French, but "in so doing they surrendered neither their independence nor their freedom to wage war in their own way."[23] Their guerrilla methods did not always accord with European ideas of engagement, but were often effective in the wilderness. The Natives were particularly loath to adopt European tactics that squandered their warriors' lives needlessly, and would often refuse to attack fortified positions or face artillery fire. MacLeod has also shown that the usual reasons historians have posited for fluctuations in Aboriginal support for the French cause may not tell the whole story. France claimed victory in most of the earliest battles of the Seven Years War, something that undoubtedly would have made a favourable impression on their allies. The French custom of gift diplomacy— the giving of annual presents to the Native communities—also helped to secure alliances. But MacLeod also points to a strong correlation between outbreaks of smallpox and sharp reductions in the number of Aboriginal volunteers—they would opt not to fight when the risk of contagion was high.[24] Alliances of individual nations could and did waver, throughout the course of the war, in response to shifts in circumstances, diplomatic overtures by one European party or the other, and the Natives' simple calculation of the policy best suited to their own interests. An observer noted that Aboriginal nations would exploit divisions among their own ranks to "play off" one European power against another:

The policy of those people is so shrewd that it is difficult to penetrate its secrets. When they undertake any enterprise of importance against a nation whom they fear, especially the French, they seem to form two parties—one conspiring for and the other opposing it; if the former succeed in their projects, the latter approve and sustain what has been done; if their designs are thwarted they retire to the other side. Accordingly, they always attain their objects.[25]

The calculation of mere numbers does not complete the picture. Aboriginal warriors were a vital psychological weapon to the French, and even the prospect of confronting them could be enough to deter colonial militia from the Thirteen Colonies. Vaudreuil admitted that atrocities were a sure way "to sicken the people of the English colonies of war."[26] Critics condemned the brutality of Natives in battle, their refusal to respect European conventions of the rules of war, and the treatment of non-combatants.

More Early Successes for the French

When Montcalm arrived in the spring of 1756, he found that Vaudreuil had already launched operations against strategically important Fort Oswego. This site, on the southern shore of Lake Ontario at the mouth of the Oswego River, had long been vital to British interests in the area. New Yorkers carried out a flourishing trade with Natives who travelled to this location, which was conveniently located by water traffic. The advance operations Vaudreuil had launched against Oswego relied upon a few hundred Canadian militia, French regulars, and Aboriginal allies to harass Oswego's supply lines. Months of privation had left the British garrison suffering from the effects of hunger, scurvy, and dysentery, and feeling the strain of constant menace from guerrilla fighters in the area.

By the early summer, Montcalm, at Vaudreuil's urging, was ready to launch the main offensive. He carefully cultivated alliances, hosting a gathering of ambassadors from the Oneida and Onondaga at Fort de la Présentation, at which the Iroquois representatives sang a war song and lined up in battle formation. Montcalm's force of some 1300 regulars, with an equal number of militia, and 250 Native allies, armed with 80 pieces of field artillery was the largest European army to date to march into the North American wilderness.

Siege operations against Fort Oswego were begun on August 13, and the British commander, Lieutenant-Colonel James Mercer, was quickly forced to adapt. He abandoned nearby Fort Ontario, which was indefensible, but in so doing left an ideal offensive position for Montcalm's forces to occupy, one from which the French could train their guns upon the main fort. Under the pounding of French artillery, Mercer's garrison of 1800 men frantically tried to reposition their guns, none of which faced Fort Ontario. Mercer himself was beheaded by a cannon ball. At last, the British were forced to surrender.

To Montcalm's horror, his Native allies swarmed into the fort and butchered some of the sick and wounded, carrying others away as prisoners, including women and children. Montcalm was especially appalled that even some Natives who were Roman Catholic converts took part in the atrocities, and arranged to ransom some of the captives from his own allies. But Vaudreuil was delighted by what he referred to as "my victory": the British had surrendered the position, 1700 prisoners had been taken, and several armed

1756: The French win an important victory at Fort Oswego.

vessels had been seized, along with cannon, munitions, and supplies, and currency valued at 18 000 livres. From Fort Oswego, which they called Fort Chouaguen, the French could exert control over Lake Ontario. The British colony of New York was exposed to attack from the northwest, and the interior waterways that linked the Great Lakes to Louisiana were secured for the French. Far from boasting about victory, Montcalm, who had expressed reservations before the operation began, wrote an apologetic report home in the aftermath, explaining that his tactics had been very much at variance with accepted European rules.[27] Canadian observers, meanwhile, speculated sourly that if it had been left to Montcalm, the fort would still be in English hands.

The loss of Fort Oswego was one in a series of British disasters around the globe in the early years of the war. Several weeks before, a French naval force, under the command of the former governor of New France, the marquis de La Galissonière, had succeeded in taking the strategic British possession of Minorca in the Mediterranean. So bungled was the British attempt to relieve the garrison at Minorca that the British commander of the operation, Admiral John Byng, was later executed for his failure. News of disaster in India soon followed. In June of 1756, Fort William in Calcutta, built to protect Britain's trade interests against the French, was captured by the Nawab of Bengal, Siraj ud-daula, who had earlier ordered the British to cease the build up of fortifications. A reported 146 prisoners were cast overnight into the infamous "Black Hole of Calcutta," an unventilated cell measuring 4.3 by 5.5 metres. Only 23 of the captives were said to have emerged alive the following morning, the rest having succumbed to heat exhaustion, thirst, and suffocation, or having been trampled to death during the hellish night. Modern commentators have challenged details of this horrific story, but the inflammatory account that reached England in the wake of the event whipped the press, public, and policymakers into an outraged frenzy. Combined with the news of North American defeats and the loss of Minorca, the blow to British prestige around the world was profound.

As disaster piled on disaster, the British ministry led by the Duke of Newcastle was forced to resign, and in December 1756 George II appointed a new government. The nominal head was William Cavendish, the Duke of Devonshire, but the real leader was William Pitt. George II despised Pitt and found an excuse to dismiss him a few months later, but by July 1757 was compelled to recall him to office in a new Newcastle-Pitt ministry. The King's personal loathing for Pitt would no longer be enough to keep from office a man who many were convinced held the keys to British victory. "Ministers are Kings in this country," George II grumbled resignedly.[28] Frederick the Great in Prussia cheered the news: "England has been a long time in labour but she has at last brought forth a man."[29]

Pitt himself was no less grandiose in his own estimation: he proclaimed himself the only man who could save the nation. Impatient, sarcastic, arrogant, and vain, unable to accept any authority but his own, Pitt cannot be faulted for lack of commitment to the cause of Britain's greatness. He drove himself mercilessly, damaging his physical health and being torn by swings in mood so violent as to be labelled madness. Despite all of this, Pitt's vision of the pursuit of the war was clear: he believed that the war must be fought primarily overseas, in the colonial prizes themselves, not in Europe. The navy was key, both to Britain's imperial possessions around the globe and to the protection and extension of British trade. Global trade funnelled wealth into the tiny island nation.

1756: The appointment of a ministry dominated by William Pitt marks a new British commitment to war in the empire.

Even though there was a fresh infusion of forces into North America, 1757 did not augur instant victory for the British. The Duke of Cumberland suffered defeat at Hastenbeck in Hanover; a naval operation against the French port of Rochefort failed; and confidence was steadily eroding in the British commander in North America, Lord Loudoun. John Campbell, the fourth Earl of Loudoun, was a Highland clan chief who had fought as a committed royalist during the abortive 1745 Jacobite uprising of Charles Stuart, "Bonnie Prince Charlie." Loudoun, however, had no actual victories to his credit and, when he arrived to chaotic conditions in New York in the summer of 1756, he quickly alienated colonial governors and militia leaders. Residents recoiled at being required to quarter— feed and house—hardened soldiers, some of whom were paroled prisoners.

1757: British plan for an attack on Louisbourg fails to come to fruition.

Loudoun's prodigious energies seemed to be expended in all the wrong directions: he personally toiled over the most minute correspondence, and his secretary complained of being worked 15 hours a day. Worse still, in the summer of 1757 Loudoun squandered a golden opportunity. With more than 10 000 troops, 16 ships of the line, and several frigates at his disposal, Loudoun planned an attack on Louisbourg. If this fortress fell, the way could be laid open for an assault on Quebec, but constant delays, worrisome intelligence about an even stronger French force, and unfavourable winds all spelled disaster for the attack, and Loudoun sailed back to New York without having struck a blow. Only in India was the news good for Britain that year. In June, Robert Clive, the British governor of Bengal, won a decisive victory at Plassey, avenging the Black Hole of Calcutta and preparing the way for the collapse of French power in India. This encouraging news would be very much needed as things took an even blacker turn in North America later that summer.

The French had been reinvigorated with fresh supplies in July, and Aboriginal support was at its highest peak to date, prompting the cautious Montcalm to action. He marched a force of 6000 to Fort Carillon, an equal mix of regular troops and militia, which was supplemented by a further 2000 Native allies. The objective was an assault on Fort William Henry, at the southern tip of Lake George. With 500 British soldiers in the fort, and a further 3300 in the vicinity, Montcalm could confidently confront the enemy with double that number. The aborted plan to attack Louisbourg had drained British manpower from the area, and an early clash with a reconnaissance party had enabled the French to learn the strength of the garrison.

As the French besieged Fort William Henry early in August 1757, a desperate Lieutenant-Colonel George Monro appealed for help from General Daniel Webb at nearby Fort Edward. Webb's discouraging reply instructed Monro to try to arrange favourable terms for surrender. Native scouts captured the messenger and Montcalm passed Webb's message on to Monro with his compliments. By August 9, having withstood several days of siege and a virulent outbreak of smallpox within the fort, Monro sought terms. Montcalm gallantly agreed to grant the defeated honours of war: they could carry out their regimental flag in procession and the captured force would be escorted to nearby Fort Edward to be paroled, meaning these forces could not be used for 18 months. Montcalm called a council of chiefs to explain these terms to his Aboriginal allies, and the chiefs assented.

1757: The slaughter of the sick and wounded after the British defeat at Fort William Henry sparks outrage.

As the evacuation procession began, Native warriors descended upon the fort in search of the spoils of war. They set upon the 70 sick and wounded who had been left behind.

French soldiers and missionaries intervened to save some, but were too late to prevent others from being massacred by tomahawk and scalped. Many of the thwarted warriors had spent the night consuming rum found in the fort, and feelings boiled over as the defeated British marched away. At the sound of blood-chilling war whoops, the Native warriors swarmed the retreating column of soldiers and camp followers, including women and children. The French proved unable to effectively intervene: while many of the defeated British were safely escorted to Fort Edward, as many as 185 were killed and some 300 to 500 taken prisoner. By sunset, all but 300 of Montcalm's Native allies were already paddling north with their plunder and captives.[30]

Outrage in the British colonies knew no bounds. The promise of parole was repudiated, and many vowed that no quarter would be given to any captured French. Some reflected with satisfaction that the smallpox epidemic had been carried back to the Natives' own villages. The classic American story by James Fenimore Cooper, *The Last of the Mohicans* (1826) would later keep the bitter memory of Fort William Henry alive. In the immediate aftermath, indignation was mixed with apprehension. Fears grew in the Thirteen Colonies, where grisly tales of butchery by Natives in war paint had long been traded. Montcalm might well have capitalized on his victory by capturing Fort Edward, and then Albany, and perhaps even New York, but, to Vaudreuil's disgust, Montcalm refused to advance further, citing the poor condition of the road, the probability of substantial British reinforcements at Fort Edward, and the need of his militia to return home for the harvest.

The Tide Begins to Turn for Britain

1757: Despite a string of French victories, the French commander Montcalm grows increasingly pessimistic.

Historians such as W.J. Eccles have condemned Montcalm's defeatism in the face of what should have been encouraging early successes. Montcalm's private letters to the minister of war radiated gloom. He was sharply critical of Vaudreuil and Bigot, and complained about runaway inflation and a growing shortage of supplies, some of which he attributed to Bigot's corruption. Lacking beef, his troops were reduced to eating horsemeat. Gifts to the Natives, so essential in keeping alliances intact, began to dry up, the flow of such goods hampered by Britain's mastery of the seas. Threats to French fishing vessels had also sharply curtailed the supply of cod for the colony. The string of victories notwithstanding, Montcalm's sombre message was that New France would inevitably fall to the British.[31] Even as success followed success for the French, Montcalm may have presciently foreseen that the tide was turning. Whether the French had the will to send adequate resources to North America was debatable, but the growing menace of the British navy was not, and the effects were being felt in New France.

At home in England, William Pitt was exasperated with Loudoun's inept command of the resources put at his disposal in North America. Loudoun had done nothing, Pitt raged. At the end of 1757, with a series of defeats as his legacy, Loudoun was recalled home in disgrace, and his second-in-command, Major General James Abercromby, was elevated to commander-in-chief. Beyond this, Pitt also offered specific details about how new offensives should be launched in the upcoming season. A three-pronged assault in the summer of 1758 would call for attacks on French positions at Louisbourg, Fort Carillon, and Fort Duquesne.

While the commander of the planned assault at Louisbourg, General Jeffery Amherst, was technically subordinate to Abercromby, in reality he was answering directly to Pitt.

The prime minister was determined that there would not be a repeat of Loudoun's wasted opportunity. Throughout the winter, the British navy enforced a punishing blockade on the fortress at Louisbourg. Reinforcements from France could not be sent, and supplies of food dwindled. While Louisbourg offered excellent natural defences and a commanding strategic position, it was dangerously dependent on imports. Only in the spring were six French vessels able to elude their enemies and bring some much-needed relief. But with the supplies came the sobering intelligence that Britain was marshalling forces for an all out offensive against the fortress. By the beginning of June 1758, the blow was struck. Naval commander Admiral Edward Boscawen's massive fleet anchored in Gabarus Bay to the west of Louisbourg, while Amherst's brigadier, James Wolfe, braved the pounding surf, treacherous rocks, and bombardment from the French battery, to lead landing parties ashore. Wolfe later confessed that the operation had been rash and ill advised, succeeding only by "the greatest good fortune." The hero of Louisbourg would adopt a similarly rash strategy at Quebec the following year.[32]

For more than a month, British forces laid siege to the fort. Louisbourg's commander, Augustin de Boschenry de Drucour, Chevalier de Drucour, and the force of 7000 behind the walls, knew that every day that they could hold out would buy more time for Quebec; if they held out long enough, the onset of the winter freeze would send the British navy home. But an unremitting bombardment of the fortress, and the loss of the few French naval ships that had protected the harbour, doomed the defence. On July 26, Drucour ordered that a white flag of surrender be raised from the crumbling Dauphin's Bastion.

1758: The British capture the strategically important fortress at Louisbourg.

While Amherst carried out the successful operation against Louisbourg in 1758, Major-General James Abercromby himself prepared to move against Fort Carillon (Ticonderoga) that same summer. William Johnson had been less successful than before at convincing the Six Nations warriors to support the British assault: only some 400 joined the force. Yet, manpower was not in short supply. The British were able to marshal forces of some 6000 regulars and 9000 militia who travelled by boat up Lake George toward Fort Carillon. One of Abercromby's most effective brigadiers was the popular and charismatic George Howe, Viscount Howe, who came from a distinguished family—his two brothers, Richard and William, would later serve with distinction during the American Revolution—and who was described by James Wolfe as the best officer in the British army. Howe attempted to adapt this formidable British force to frontier conditions, and his innovations in adopting guerrilla tactics boosted morale. Things did not go as planned: Howe was lost in an early skirmish, a deadly accurate musket ball tearing through his lungs and heart, and shattering his backbone. With his death, the spirit seemed to go out of the British force.

1758: A British defeat at Fort Carillon (Ticonderoga) staves off an immediate assault on Quebec.

Two days later, on July 8, 1758, Abercromby's army prepared to launch an assault on Carillon. Fearing that the French position would be reinforced, Abercromby abruptly announced to his officers that "we must attack any way, and not be losing time in talking or consulting how." It would take too long to bring the heavy artillery to the site, he decided.[33] Montcalm's defending force numbered a little over 3500, less than a quarter of the strength of those that opposed them. Fort Carillon was surrounded by water on three sides, and along the only viable invasion route the French hastily threw up a crude barricade of fallen trees, logs, and rough branches. This defensive "abatis" served the same function as a modern barbwire barrier. French marksmen picked off the surging British troops that ineffectually stormed the barrier. Among Abercromby's forces were the legendary Highland regiment, the Forty-second Black Watch, to whom the Native allies extended the compliment of considering them a kind of Indian. Some of the Highlanders succeeded in leaping atop the tangled mass of timber and branches, only to be bayoneted when they cleared it. At last, British casualties having mounted to some 1945, Abercromby recalled his forces to Fort George.

The corpses of the brave dead remained suspended on the jagged branches, a reproachful reminder of the ill-conceived tactics that had reduced the British to humiliation. While his forces still grossly outnumbered the French present in the area, the dispirited Abercromby took no further action. That autumn, he would be recalled home, and Amherst elevated to the top rank in his place. The Native allies, who had reluctantly come to fight, and who shrank from following Abercromby's plan of assault, came away less devoted than ever to the British alliance.

The victorious French defenders at Fort Carillon lost 377 men, but carried away a fresh infusion of abandoned British supplies. More significantly, this vital chokepoint on the Richelieu River route to the main St. Lawrence settlements remained in French hands: despite the British success at Louisbourg, an attack in the heart of New France was impossible for the moment. When Governor Vaudreuil next met with Montcalm, however, he criticized him for failing to pursue Abercromby to destroy his army. Even Madame Vaudreuil chimed in to offer her own analysis. Montcalm respectfully suggested that ladies should not speak of war; his own wife would no doubt have remained silent, were she present, he averred. This fresh victory did not render Montcalm any more optimistic about France's long-term prospects in North America. The defence of Fort Carillon had

1758: The French surrender Fort Frontenac (Cataraqui).

weakened the French position at Fort Frontenac (Cataraqui) and, on August 27, 1758, a British force of 3600 led by Lieutenant Colonel John Bradstreet began an artillery barrage. The small French garrison of 100, commanded by the 63-year-old Pierre-Jacques Payen de Noyan et de Chavoy, had little option but to surrender.

The British burned the fort, carried off a large quantity of supplies—some of which were intended for France's Native allies—and destroyed whatever cannon they did not take. Bradstreet's bold stroke deprived the French of their route to Lake Ontario, and hence access to the other Great Lakes. The loss of supplies hampered France's ability to reward its allies. This, and the growing evidence that France would be defeated, prompted some of the Ohio Valley Natives to conclude a separate peace with Britain.

1758: The French abandon Fort Duquesne.

The loss of Fort Frontenac also doomed Fort Duquesne. According to Pitt's plan for a three-pronged invasion, Brigadier-General John Forbes had begun to march to Fort Duquesne in June of 1758 with a force of almost 7000. While the French succeeded in beating back an assault made by an advance British party in September, it was becoming increasingly apparent that the French would have to relinquish the position. The slow progress of the main British force brought them at last by late November to within a day's march of Fort Duquesne, steady cold rain and mist beginning to give way to snow. Forbes himself was tortured by the pain of "bloody flux," which left him in a weakened state. Near midnight on November 24, 1758, the British camp heard a distant dull explosion carried through the wintry woods: when they reached the fort the next morning, passing the decomposing bodies of those who had fought for it, they found a smouldering ruin. The evacuating French were determined to deny their enemies the position.

The British success in gaining Louisbourg, Fort Frontenac, and Fort Duquesne (which they renamed Pittsburgh in honour of the prime minister) came too late in 1758 to be followed by an assault the same year on the main French position at Quebec. Amherst nevertheless sent detachments to destroy French communities surrounding the Bay of Fundy and up the Saint John River, and to attack settlements and fisheries along the Gulf of St. Lawrence near Gaspé and around the Baie des Chaleurs. James Wolfe took command of the latter operations, ordering the systematic burning of farms and the destruction of any communities that might lend aid to a French defence against the British navy when it moved up the St. Lawrence to assault Quebec. It had been Wolfe who urged Amherst to order these preparatory raids, even threatening to leave the army should Amherst refuse. More than that, Wolfe favoured an immediate attack on Quebec, a rash plan that stood in marked contrast to the caution shown by British commanders in North America. Amherst did not follow the latter suggestion.

The winter of 1758 and 1759 saw both British and French policymakers in Europe discussing strategies with those who fought in North America. Montcalm dispatched a subordinate officer, Louis-Antoine de Bougainville to make a case for more support for the war in New France. Bougainville was an intelligent and articulate young man—he would later gain renown as the author of calculus books—but he had had no actual combat experience before coming to North America, and his message to the French court at Versailles was tainted by Montcalm's gloomy pessimism. He described the best policy in metaphorical terms, suggesting that Canada should be treated like a sick patient being kept alive by stimulants, and that France should only send what was absolutely necessary for its defence. Bougainville speculated that, in any event, any reinforcements sent would be unlikely to pass through Britain's naval blockade. He also sought advice about capitulation terms. Such a message was unlikely to inspire an all-out fight for France's possessions in North America. The French colonial minister responded with his own metaphor, explaining that when the house is on fire, one does not bother about the stables. All French hopes lay in a plan to invade England itself.

The court of Versailles was liberal with promotions and decorations for their officers in North America, but offered little in the way of concrete aid. Montcalm's promotion to lieutenant-general, the second highest rank in the French army, meant that Governor Vaudreuil was now subordinate to him. When Bougainville returned to Canada, he also reported that he had fulfilled a personal commission on Montcalm's behalf, arranging for the marriage of his eldest son and daughter to suitable partners. Before setting sail, though, Bougainville had heard reports that one of Montcalm's daughters had died; he did not know which one. To this grave news was added another troubling message: Bougainville had learned that a massive British fleet was en route to attack Quebec. Montcalm's letters home to his wife hinted at his growing despair. He longed to be with her and lamented the price he had to pay for his occasional mentions in the military gazette. He would, he vowed, renounce every honour if he could see her again: "Adieu, my heart! I believe that I love you more than ever."[34]

As the 1759 season begins, France's commitment to North America's defence is minimal.

James Wolfe also had the opportunity to consult with superiors in England over the winter. He came away with a commission as major-general and commander-in-chief of the land forces for the expedition against Quebec. He would officially be under Amherst's authority, but far from any effective control. Wolfe's sterling reputation at Louisbourg and offensive zeal appealed to Pitt. A closer acquaintance, however, made the prime minister uneasy: when they dined together on the eve of Wolfe's departure, Wolfe horrified Pitt by boasting of what he would accomplish and waving his sword theatrically above his head. Pitt cringed to think that he had entrusted Britain's fortunes in Quebec to such a posturing braggart. Wolfe explained, in a letter to his uncle, that he had been given a larger role than he had wished, but attributed the promotion to the backwardness displayed by so many older officers. He himself had just turned 32.

Tall and scrawny, with a pale, freckled complexion, red hair, a prominent nose, and a weak chin, Wolfe was not an inspiring physical specimen. Moreover, he had been plagued by ill health for years. He suffered from rheumatism and kidney stones that produced agonizing attacks and caused him to urinate blood. He described his own physique as consumptive, but it is not certain that he suffered from tuberculosis. His irritable disposition—a known symptom of tuberculosis—does lend credence to the theory. Eighteenth-century medicine offered a variety of ineffectual treatments for Wolfe's ailments. Drinking liquid soap had not availed, and a friend urged him to try mercury instead, the usual remedy for syphilis. Hearing that his landlady's brother had died from similar symptoms, he grimly joked that at least some distant relief was at hand. Unremitting illness might have made Wolfe a poor candidate for marriage, but while taking the restorative waters at Bath before returning to North America, he met and fell in love with a young woman named Katherine Lowther. No engagement was announced before Wolfe set sail, but their letters suggest that they planned to marry. Wolfe's will specified that, in the event of his death, the miniature of Miss Lowther that he carried with him should be set in jewels valued at 500 guineas and returned to her. Besides the portrait, she had also given him a copy of Thomas Gray's famous poem "Elegy Written in a Country Churchyard." This melancholy verse seemed to strike a chord with Wolfe as he undertook his daunting commission: he underlined the prophetic line "The paths of glory lead but to the grave."[35]

When Wolfe reached Halifax late in April 1759, he was dismayed to see that the squadron that preceded him had not yet entered the Gulf of St. Lawrence. The ice that supposedly prevented this had not been enough to stop a French supply fleet, some 26 ships, from eluding the British warships and bringing much-needed reinforcements to Quebec. The 300 or 400 troops, several dozen engineers and sappers, and quantity of arms, ammunition, and provisions represented France's minimal response to Montcalm's plea for support: "A little is precious to those who have nothing," the French commander reflected philosophically.[36] Montcalm's total strength amounted to some 3500 French regular troops, another 1500 *troupes de la marine* (colonial regulars), and perhaps 13 000 colonial militia in Canada, besides the small number of militia

James Wolfe.
Source: Joseph Highmore.

in various outposts and Acadia, and the uncertain number of Native allies, whose effective strength might be 1000 to 2000. This 18 000 to 20 000 men would seem to give him a numerical advantage over the British force that would be sent against him, but the bulk of Montcalm's force were militia, and not professional soldiers. Montcalm's conviction was that the French could not hold Quebec, and with this idea in mind, he arranged to have the bulk of his supplies stored at Batiscan, 80 kilometres upriver. If the fortress should fall, France's honour could be preserved, he believed, with a strategic retreat to Louisiana via a fleet of canoes.

The British government was battling a budgetary crisis of massive deficits racked up by the outflow of precious currency to Germany and America, but nonetheless threw enormous support behind the conquest of North America. Pitt's decision to do so was made all the more difficult by growing rumours of a cross-channel invasion of England itself. Admiral Charles Saunders was given overall command of a powerful fleet of 50 armed warships and 150 transport and other vessels, nearly a quarter of the strength of the British Royal Navy, a surprisingly formidable force at a time when the British Isles lay under threat. The commitment of troops was also unequivocal: Wolfe was entrusted with 8500 to capture Quebec. Amherst had an army of 11 000 to secure the Champlain-Richelieu River corridor, and Brigadier-General John Prideaux was allotted 5500 to capture Niagara, thus securing the Great Lakes route.

Spring 1759: Despite a budgetary crisis and fears of imminent invasion, Britain makes a strong commitment to the North American campaign.

Jeffery Amherst knew that, while the overall plan was to "lay the axe to the root"—to attack the heart of New France at Quebec—possession of the Champlain-Richelieu River route was essential.[37] Once he had secured this, he was to advance north. On the first day of summer, June 21, 1759, Amherst arrived at the head of Lake George, just at Lake Champlain's southern tip. As his forces advanced on Fort Carillon, the badly outnumbered French opted to abandon the position and destroy the fort. Having taken possession of the remains of Fort Carillon (Ticonderoga) in late July, the British pursued the retreating French to nearby Fort Saint-Frédéric. This, too, was evacuated by the French and blown up before the British reached it on August 4. The new French line of defence had moved north to Fort Île aux Noix on the Richelieu River. Amherst opted to end his campaign for the season and ordered the construction of elaborate fortifications at Crown Point, the former French fort of Saint-Frédéric. Aid to Wolfe's assault on Quebec would have to wait.

Summer 1759: The French are forced to abandon both Fort Carillon and Fort Saint-Frédéric.

The British offensive against Fort Niagara, led by Prideaux, also commenced in June 1759. Sir William Johnson's appeals to the Six Nations yielded almost 1000 allies to the British side at Niagara to supplement the main force of more than 5000. The French defenders, numbering only about 500, were no match, but held out as the artillery barrage began in mid-July, hopeful that a relieving party of French militia from Fort Detroit and the surrounding area, along with allied Natives, some 1400 strong, might reach them in time. Unfortunately for the British, Prideaux himself was an early casualty of the artillery bombardment, falling to friendly fire while inspecting the defences. William Johnson assumed command in his place. Within a few days, Johnson devised a strategy to confront the relieving French force in a surprise ambush. He achieved a complete victory at La Belle Famille. Not only did the French sustain heavy casualties, but the message to the defenders at Fort Niagara was clear: on July 25, 1759, the French garrison there surrendered.

July 1759: The British and their Iroquois allies take Fort Niagara.

The Battle of Quebec

Meanwhile, the toughest nut of all to crack would be the fortified heart of New France, Quebec itself. Despite Montcalm's overall doubts about French prospects in the war, in many respects he held the better position in Quebec. It was true that the formidable British naval fleet that entered the St. Lawrence early in June 1759 stretched some 80 kilometres in length: it took 12 hours to pass any one point. British command of the critical St. Lawrence was unequivocal. Despite earlier French plans to install batteries that could devastate a naval invasion fleet from key strategic narrows on the river's banks, nothing had been done. Both Montcalm and Vaudreuil believed that the channels so far upriver would be too difficult for a foreign fleet to negotiate, and expected an attack to come from the south from Lake Champlain. As the British drew near, using captured Canadian pilots to guide the fleet, the French took hasty measures to fortify the northern shoreline between the St. Charles River and the Montmorency. More alarmingly, on June 27, 1759, Wolfe was able to land most of his soldiers on Île d'Orléans. Soon afterward, more were placed on the south shore of the St. Lawrence, at Beaumont, and 3000 more, under the command of Brigadier-General Robert Monckton, were situated at Point Lévis across from Quebec. For all that, though, Montcalm held a critical advantage: time was not on Wolfe's side. He had only the summer to act. The fleet would have to depart early in autumn, before the freeze. If Montcalm could hold out for three months, he would have a victory without engaging the enemy. As W.J. Eccles explains, "he did not have to defeat them in a set battle, merely make sure that they did not defeat him."[38]

The evening after Wolfe's landing on the Île d'Orléans, the French made a bold move to attempt to destroy the British fleet. Fire was the deadliest enemy of a wooden sailing fleet, and the French sacrificed some aging vessels to send against the British as fireships. Loaded with pitch, tar, and all kinds of other combustible material, along with old artillery and a range of explosives—bombs, fireworks, and grenades—seven ships were moved

June 1759: British forces under Wolfe land within view of the fortified city of Quebec.

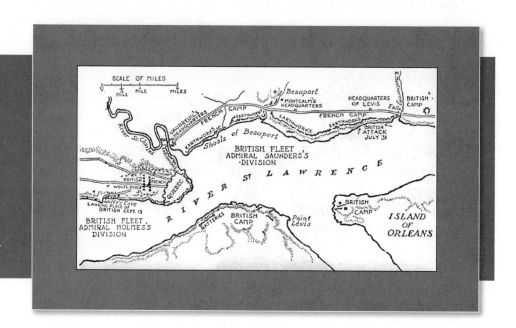

Siege of Quebec, 1759.

quietly into range of the British fleet on a moonless night. But this daring manoeuvre utterly failed—the ships were set alight too soon, and British sentries on the Île d'Orléans took warning. The air was suddenly filled with a spectacular cacophony as sheets of flame engulfed the masts of the fireships and explosions sent missiles flying through the dense black smoke and glare. One French captain and several crew members failed to escape in time and were burned alive in the conflagration. British sailors stood aboard their own vessels with long pikes ready to fend off the menacing craft. Those ships with no time to weigh anchor frantically cut the anchor cables to escape being rammed; other sailors bravely grappled the burning hulks and towed them harmlessly to safety. The British fleet remained intact, sheltering just out of range of the guns of Quebec.

Montcalm was sure that the shores at Beauport would be the likeliest target for invasion, and having fortified this position, situated the bulk of his army there, more than 12 000 men. On July 8, Wolfe succeeded in landing a force on the north shore of the St. Lawrence, on the far bank of the Montmorency River, a position separated from Beauport by raging falls that plunged 83 metres. The British landing at Montmorency met no opposition: Montcalm was convinced that it was a feint. A French raid against the British force at Point Lévis that followed failed miserably, and on July 12, the British used their position there to begin a massive artillery bombardment of Quebec. Within the first week, 240 of the city's houses were destroyed. Over the course of the two-month siege, more than 36 000 cannonballs and 6000 bombs rained down on the city. The lower town had to be evacuated and was soon half consumed by fire.

Wolfe recognized the inherent difficulty of his position, and grew increasingly frustrated by the defensive tactics of the "wary old fellow" who opposed him.[39] Wolfe made and abandoned a succession of plans for attack, much to the annoyance of his brigadiers. In late July, he ordered a raid against Pointe-aux-Trembles, a good deal up the river, in anticipation of Amherst's northern thrust toward Montreal. This operation may have helped to plant the seed of future victory: some 200 women and children, briefly taken prisoner in the attack, were released the following day and Wolfe may have noted their ability to clamour up the river's steep bank.

July 1759: The French repel an abortive British raid on Beauport.

On July 31, Wolfe launched a frontal assault against Montcalm's most heavily fortified lines at Beauport, a desperate but doomed enterprise that cost the British some 400 lives. The French strength was greatest there, and as a sweltering humid day gave way to a sudden soaking downpour, they were able to easily repel the attack. Vaudreuil crowed that the ineptitude of the assault relieved any anxieties he had about Quebec.

Wolfe's health, which had never been strong, began to falter still more, and he started to despair that success was out of reach. Where he had once trumpeted his superiority over a succession of old men—earlier commanders who had failed in North America and been recalled in disgrace—he now dreaded similar failure. He feared coming home, he wrote to his mother, only to be ridiculed by people ignorant of the difficulties he faced. Admiral Saunders had warned Wolfe that the fleet must set sail back to England by September 20 at the latest. If Quebec could not be taken, Wolfe was determined to wreak as much havoc as possible. He ordered Brigadier James Murray to torch farms and villages along the south shore of the St. Lawrence. *Canadiens* who had already faced the privation

Late summer 1759: British forces carry out a punitive campaign of destruction against Canadian farms and villages.

of war, and the forced confiscation of food and livestock, now saw their homes destroyed. Murray returned from this distasteful duty with some heartening news for Wolfe: he had intercepted a French dispatch intended for Montcalm that reported on Fort Niagara's fall to the British. The campaign of destruction intensified. In early September, Captain George Scott was ordered on a further mission to ruin the harvest and buildings, and carried out his commission so successfully, laying waste to almost 1000 buildings, that hardened soldiers burdened with the task began to sicken at the spectacle.

Wolfe's brigadiers roundly protested an ill-conceived plan to launch another wasteful raid on Beauport, and urged instead that the attack be made upriver from Quebec to cut Montcalm's access to his supply base at Batiscan and sever communications with Montreal. Such a move would force the French into the open, they believed. Instead, on September 10, Wolfe announced that the site for attack would be Anse-au-Foulon, close to Quebec itself, a cove with a narrow beach leading up to a bank so steep that the French had left it lightly defended. Brigadiers Monckton, Townshend, and Murray attempted to dissuade their commander about the plan, and to share their misgivings about their many unanswered questions, but Wolfe was adamant: he would attack the French, and if his plan was mistaken, he was sorry for it. There was little time to lose.

On the night of September 12, 1759, Wolfe's troops commenced operations for one of Canada's most fateful battles. The plan was a desperate one: everything depended on surprise, and no retreat would be possible once the British forces scaled the 53-metre cliffs to reach the Plains of Abraham outside the walled fortress of Quebec. British warships at Beauport created a diversion, and British forces in landing boats drifted in the dark from where they had been moved upriver, fortuitously mistaken by the French sentries for an expected supply fleet. Challenged by a sentry on the cliffs above—"Qui vive?"—a francophone Scottish officer gave the reply. "France" was the only answer he offered, followed by an imperious demand that the sentry lower his voice to avoid being heard. Remarkably, the sentry was cowed by this display of overbearing authority. Brigadier James Murray brought the first invaders ashore and, as they gained the heights, managed to deceive the officer in command of the French guard post, Louis Du Pont Duchambon de Vergor, the same man who surrendered Fort Beauséjour in 1755. Murray signalled the capture of the French guard post, and British troops began to swarm up the cliffs to take up a position on the plains outside the city.

September 13, 1759: The famous Battle of the Plains of Abraham is fought for Quebec.

As dawn broke on the rainy morning of September 13, the French took alarm: they were shocked to find that the enemy was on the heights. With reports of the landing at first discounted, it would be almost seven o'clock before Montcalm would begin to march troops from Beauport. He hoped that Bougainville, upriver at Cap Rouge with 3000 men, would have received word of the landing and be hastening to the scene. Montcalm knew that Wolfe's forces had managed to bring two artillery pieces up the embankment and feared that delay would enable them to dig in. By ten o'clock in the morning, Bougainville not having arrived, the French commander resolved to wait no longer. He met the enemy at the time and place of their choosing, with roughly equal numbers—each side fielding some 4500 troops. Historical observers have noted that Wolfe's position was a vulnerable one, and time alone might have handed Montcalm a victory. "Wolfe had dug a grave for his army, but Montcalm marched his own army into it," is one summation.[40]

Wolfe's combat lines, commanded by Brigadiers Murray, Townshend, and Monckton, showed admirable discipline as they faced fire from the flanks by Canadian militia and their aboriginal allies. At last, Montcalm, astride a black horse and holding high his sword, led his troops into battle. His lines were ragged, surging forward unevenly, some firing out of effective range, but the disciplined British regulars held fast, awaiting orders to fire, as they endured successive French volleys. When the coordinated British curtain of lead and smoke thundered back in answer, the wavering French lines broke. In less than half an hour, it was all over. Wolfe, on the right flank, felt a lead ball tear into his wrist. He bound up the wound, but the enemy's fire soon found him again. Hit in the stomach and the chest, he fell. As his life ebbed away, Wolfe was conscious of a nearby officer's voice: "They run, see how they run!" "Who runs?" Wolfe murmured. "The enemy, Sir," the officer cried. "Egad! They give way everywhere!"

Wolfe brushed aside offers to fetch a surgeon: "It is needless; it is all over with me." He ordered a force to the Charles River to cut off the French retreat. "Now, God be praised, I will die in peace."[41] Montcalm followed his retreating troops into the city on horseback, and was just about to enter the Saint-Louis gate, when he, too, received fatal wounds. He lived until the following day, long enough to take the sacrament and to dictate a letter of farewell to his beloved family, but not so long as to have to witness the entry of the British army into Quebec.

1759: The Battle of Quebec claims the lives of both Wolfe and Montcalm.

The French Strike Back

These dramatic events have become synonymous in many minds with the final defeat of French power in North America. But, in fact, it is only in retrospect that this battle seemed to be decisive. In the immediate aftermath of the Battle of the Plains of Abraham, Vaudreuil was obliged to surrender Quebec. The British entered the ruined city, marching past smouldering rubble and empty storehouses. James Murray was entrusted with command, becoming military governor of Quebec. General François-Gaston de Lévis took command of the French forces, still hopeful that he could reverse the effects of Montcalm's precipitant action—an action which Lévis congratulated himself for having no part in. With the British holding the fortified city of Quebec, and the French on the outside, positions had changed, but hostilities had not ended. The looming onset of winter meant that the British fleet had to depart, and Lévis was able to slip a small number of French vessels out to sea late in the season to carry with them his pleas for help from the royal court of Versailles. He assured them that fresh troops, artillery, and supplies could enable them to retake Quebec.

Lévis knew that the spring would bring succour to his enemies; British policymakers had shown themselves to be uncompromising in their support for an all-out bid for control of North America. In late April 1760, the St. Lawrence still locked with ice, Lévis made a bold move against British-controlled Quebec. Murray's garrison had endured a hungry winter, the victors of the Plains of Abraham reduced by death from wounds and by scurvy. Lévis was able to collect almost 7000 men to oppose an enemy force now reduced to approximately 3800. On April 28, 1760, Murray rose to the challenge and marched his force to nearby Ste. Foy to engage the enemy. In his journal, he noted how very determined he was to confront the French before they could establish themselves, an inexplicable rationale that is striking in its parallel to Montcalm's idea of the previous autumn. In the end, he was forced to retreat back behind the city walls, having lost some 20 pieces of field artillery and 1104 casualties, 259 of them fatal. Lévis's losses amounted to 833, of which 193 were killed. The 1760 Battle of Ste. Foy, all but forgotten in the shadow of the very famous 1759 battle, was a far bloodier one than the one fought over much the same ground the year before. Losses in the 1759 battle have been estimated at 658 on the British side, with 58 dead, and approximately 650 on the side of the French.[42]

Naval Defeat Dooms New France

Lévis's victory at Ste. Foy could not preserve French power in North America. Unknown to him, a distant naval battle late the previous autumn had already doomed their hopes. On storm-tossed seas on November 20, 1759, the British Royal Navy foiled France's long-cherished dream of an invasion of the British Isles. A French squadron of 21 ships of the line was intercepted off France's Biscay coast at Quiberon Bay. The British fleet, under the command of Sir Edward Hawke, boldly chased their quarry under full sail into dangerous waters, causing a large part of the French fleet to be sunk, captured, or run aground. The bells of London rang out in a prolonged celebration of victory. While historian Fred Anderson identifies the Ohio Valley as the "crucible" of the Seven Years War, he points to these far distant events as the critical determinant of the outcome. "The Battle of Quiberon Bay, and not the more celebrated Battle of Quebec, was the decisive military event of 1759," he notes.[43]

On May 15, 1760, the French in North America learned that their fate was sealed. That evening, the first relieving ships of the season sailed into the port of Quebec: three British vessels. Murray's garrison in Quebec, seeing the flags flying from the masts, cheered joyously. A dejected Lévis was forced to confront the truth that he had feared: France had abandoned its North American colony.

Montreal remained in French hands, and in the summer of 1760 the British commenced a three-pronged assault to capture it. With James Murray moving upriver from Quebec, Brigadier-General William Haviland moving north from Crown Point on Lake Champlain up the Richelieu River corridor, and General Jeffery Amherst moving his 10 000 forces down the St. Lawrence from Lake Ontario, a massive force was converging upon the last French stronghold. Bougainville's bid to defend the Île aux Noix sector on the Richelieu was doomed, not least by the defection of his Aboriginal allies who could no longer be rewarded for their aid, and who no doubt could foresee the probable outcome. He was compelled to evacuate the area. By early September, the three British armies converged upon Montreal. With much of the militia having deserted, Vaudreuil and Lévis were left with a mere 2000 men. Surrounded by a force of 17 000, they surrendered the city on September 8, 1760. Denied the honours of war on the orders of the vindictive General Amherst, who held the French responsible for the acts of their Aboriginal allies, the defeated French regiments burned their colours rather than relinquishing them to the British.

The End of the War and the Treaty of Paris, 1763

For New France, the war had ended, yet complex world events kept the great powers at war for some time to come, and indeed by January 1762 Spain and Britain were also at war. The British navy struck at Spain's colonial possessions around the globe, capturing

Havana late that summer, and Manila in the Philippines a few weeks later. The French Caribbean colonies of Martinique and Guadeloupe also fell into British hands. The British used their commanding control of the oceans to take millions of pounds in prizes of war throughout 1762, helping to redress the financial drain of several years of war. The French succeeded in embarrassing General Amherst by capturing St. John's, Newfoundland, in June 1762 while Amherst was preoccupied with these other offensive measures. Amherst dispatched his brother William to recover it, and, in the September 1762 Battle of Signal Hill, the British regained possession of St. John's.

September 1762: In the Battle of Signal Hill, the British recapture St. John's from the French.

The capture of lucrative Caribbean possessions late in the war proved to be an important strategy for Britain. Far more value was attached to the tiny sugar-producing islands than to the vast expanse of the cold Canadian wilderness. The belligerent nations began to talk of peace late in 1762, and in February 1763, the Treaty of Paris ended the war. Around the treaty table, Spain regained Cuba and Manila, and France bargained for Guadeloupe, Martinique, St. Lucia, and the island of Gorée off the coast of Senegal, which was vital to the African slave trade upon which Caribbean colonialism depended. France was also determined to retain a base for the Grand Banks fisheries, and won continued rights to the "French shore," an area of the Newfoundland coast west from Cape Bonavista to Notre Dame Bay, and around the northern tip of the island to Point Riche. This concession did not include rights to colonization, but was essential to the preservation of France's Newfoundland fisheries, also guaranteeing that the area would continue to be a nursery for French sailors, and a means to preserve the power of the French navy.

1763: Territories are traded in the Treaty of Paris ending the war.

The treaty also recognized France's claim to the islands of St. Pierre and Miquelon in the Gulf of St. Lawrence. Spain was compelled to surrender Florida to the British, but was rewarded by their French allies with possession of Louisiana. While some of the French in Canada were dismayed that the treaty did not restore them to the protection of the French Crown, all the European belligerents seemed to realize that the steady growth of Britain's American colonies doomed any attempt by a rival nation to gain a foothold on the continent. The duc de Choiseul, negotiating for the French, was philosophical about surrendering Canada, foreseeing that Britain was poised to lose still more: the powerful American colonies would soon be in a position to throw off British rule, and France might just be able to help them in their efforts.

Conclusion

The transfer of Canada from French control to British was part of a much larger picture. The same forces of global competition and hard-headed calculation that had originally prompted the rival nations to colonize North America forced France to withdraw from the contest, abandoning its colonial experiment on the St. Lawrence. In the meantime, the war wrought great changes to other people living on the North American continent. Aboriginal nations calculated the risks and opportunities inherent in alliances with the warring powers. The Acadians, having successfully lived for decades under a foreign power, could no longer be beyond the reach of conflict, and suffered upheaval. Canadians would have to adapt to a new form of European governance, and found, with relief, that practice of their Roman Catholic faith was afforded some protection under the treaty. The years that followed the conquest proved that Canada could never be immune from the effects of outside currents of change. The Seven Years War had set in motion a great many forces whose impact would become clear in the coming years.

Questions to Consider

1. Why did the British expel the Acadians from Nova Scotia?

2. The French commander Montcalm has sometimes been characterized as a defeatist. Is that a fair assessment? Explain.

3. Was the British victory in the Seven Years War inevitable? What factors contributed to it?

4. How important were the Native allies to the warring European powers? What factors influenced Native decisions in choosing alliances?

Critical Thinking Questions

1. Do you agree with historian Allan Greer that New France was a "ceded colony," rather than a "conquered nation"? Explain.

2. Do the events of the Seven Years War offer any examples of differing European and Native conceptions of warfare? Explain.

3. In what ways did the outcome of the Seven Years War raise problems for the future?

Suggested Readings
General

Anderson, Fred. *Crucible of War: The Seven Years' War and the Fate of Empire in British North America, 1754–1766.* New York: Vintage, 2001.

Dale, Ronald J. *The Fall of New France: How the French Lost a North American Empire, 1754–1763.* Toronto: James Lorimer, 2004.

Deschênes, Gaston. *L'Année des Anglais: La Côte-du-Sud à l'heure de la Conquête.* Sillery: Septenrion, 1998.

Dull, Jonathan R. *The French Navy and the Seven Years' War.* Lincoln: University of Nebraska Press, 2005.

Eccles, W.J. *The Canadian Frontier, 1534–1760.* Toronto: Holt, Rinehart and Winston, 1969.

Fowler, William M., Jr. *Empires at War: The Seven Years' War and the Struggle for North America, 1754–1763.* Vancouver: Douglas & McIntyre, 2005.

Frégault, Guy. *Canada: The War of the Conquest.* Toronto: Oxford University Press, 1969.

Grenier, John. *The First Way of War: American War Making on the Frontier, 1607–1814.* Cambridge: Cambridge University Press, 2005.

Herman, Arthur. *To Rule the Waves: How the British Navy Shaped the Modern World.* New York: HarperCollins, 2004.

Jennings, Francis. *Empire of Fortune: Crowns, Colonies and Tribes in the Seven Years War in America.* New York: Norton, 1988.

Johnston, A.J.B. *Endgame 1758: The Promise the Glory, and the Despair of Louisbourg's Last Decade.* Lincoln and London: University of Nebraska Press 2007.

MacLeod, D. Peter. *Northern Armageddon: The Battle of the Plains of Abraham.* Vancouver: Douglas & McIntyre, 2008.

Marston, Daniel. *The Seven Years' War.* Oxford: Osprey Publishing, 2001.

Stacey, C.P. *Quebec, 1759: The Siege and the Battle.* Toronto: Macmillan, 1959.

Steele, Ian K. *Warpaths: Invasions of North America.* Toronto: Oxford University Press, 1994.

Detailed, authoritative information on key figures may be found in the *Dictionary of Canadian Biography.* Available online at http://www.biographi.ca.

Generals Wolfe and Montcalm

Brumwell, Stephen. *Paths of Glory: The Life and Death of General James Wolfe.* Montreal and Kingston: McGill-Queen's University Press, 2006.

Hibbert, Christopher. *Wolfe at Quebec.* London: Longmans, Green and Co, 1959.

Parkman, Francis. *Montcalm and Wolfe.* Markham: Viking, 1984

Native Peoples

Dowd, Gregory Evans. *War under Heaven: Pontiac, the Indian Nations and the British Empire.* Baltimore: Johns Hopkins University Press, 2002.

Dowd, Gregory Evans. "The French King Wakes up in Detroit: 'Pontiac's War' in Rumor and History," *Ethnohistory* 37: 3 (Summer 1990): 254–278.

MacLeod, D. Peter. *The Canadian Iroquois and the Seven Years' War.* Toronto: Dundurn, 1996.

Parmenter, Jon William. "Pontiac's War: Forging New Links in the Anglo-Iroquois Covenant Chain, 1758–1766," *Ethnohistory* 44: 4 (Autumn 1997): 617–654.

Richter, Daniel K. and James H. Merrell, eds. *Beyond the Covenant Chain: The Iroquois and Their Neighbours in Indian North America, 1600–1800.* University Park, Pennsylvania: Penn State Press, 2003.

White, Richard. *The Middle Ground: Indians, Empires, and Republics in the Great Lakes Region, 1650–1815.* Cambridge: Cambridge University Press, 1991.

The Acadian Expulsion

Faragher, John Mack. *A Great and Noble Scheme: The Tragic Story of the Expulsion of the French Acadians from Their American Homeland.* New York: Norton, 2005.

Notes

1   Allan Greer, *The People of New France* (Toronto: University of Toronto Press, 1997), 115.

2   As quoted in William M. Fowler, Jr. *Empires at War: The Seven Years' War and the Struggle for North America, 1754–1763* (Toronto: Douglas & McIntyre, 2005), 10.

3   As quoted in Étienne Taillemite, "Barrin de La Galissonière, Roland-Michel, Marquis de La Galissonière," *Dictionary of Canadian Biography*, http://www.biographi.ca.

4   Governor Shirley to the Duke of Bedford, 24 April 1749, as quoted in William M. Fowler, Jr, *Empires at War*, 15.

5   As quoted in W. J. Eccles, "Joseph Coulon de Villiers de Jumonville" *Dictionary of Canadian Biography*. The account of the death of Jumonville is from Fred Anderson, *Crucible of War: The Seven Years' War and the Fate of Empire in British North America, 1754–1766* (New York: Vintage Books, 2001), 5–7.

6   The New York Mercury, January 1756 as quoted in Guy Frégault, *Canada: The War of the Conquest* (Toronto: Oxford University Press, 1969), 32.

7   Guy Frégault, *Canada: The War of the Conquest*, 32–33.

8   As quoted in Francis Parkman, *Montcalm and Wolfe* (New York: Viking, 1984), 108–109.

9   As quoted in William Fowler, *Empires at War*, 75.

10 As quoted in John Grenier, *The First Way of War: American War Making on the Frontier* (Cambridge: Cambridge University Press, 2005), 119.

11 As quoted in William Fowler, *Empires at War*, 60.

12 Ibid, 68.

13 As quoted in Francis Parkman, *Montcalm and Wolfe*, 132.

14 Francis Parkman, *Montcalm and Wolfe*, 143.

15 As quoted in John Mack Faragher, *A Great and Noble Scheme: The Tragic Story of the Expulsion of the French Acadians from their American Homeland* (New York: Norton, 2005), 302.

16 Lt. Col. John Winslow, Journal, 5 Sept. 1755 in Public Archives of Canada, Report, vol. 2 (Ottawa: King's Printer, 1905).

17 John Mack Faragher, *A Great and Noble Scheme*, 333.

18 As quoted by Guy Frégault, *Canada: the War of the Conquest* (Toronto: Oxford University Press, 1969), 112–113.

19 A battalion typically numbers from several hundred to 1000 men. Arthur Herman, *To Rule the Waves: How the British Navy Shaped the Modern World* (New York: Harper Collins, 2004), 265. Details of French naval strength may be found in Appendix A through Appendix C in Jonathan Dull, *The French Navy and the Seven Years' War* (Lincoln: University of Nebraska Press, 2005).

20 As quoted in Guy Frégault, *Canada: the War of the Conquest* (Toronto: Oxford University Press, 1969), 3.

21 William Fowler, *Empires at War*, 21–22, 134.

22 As quoted in Francis Parkman, *Montcalm and Wolfe*, 264.

23 D. Peter MacLeod, *The Canadian Iroquois and the Seven Years' War* (Toronto: Dundurn, 1996), 21.

24 D. Peter MacLeod, "Microbes and Muskets: Smallpox and the Participation of the Amerindian Allies of New France in the Seven Years' War," *Ethnohistory* 39:1 (Winter 1992): 42–64. A list of the most significant aboriginal nations allied with the French appears in footnote 4, page 57.

25 Claude Charles Le Roy, dit Bacqueville de La Potherie, "History of the Savage People who are Allies of New France (1753) as quoted in Jon William Parmenter, "Pontiac's War: Forging New Links in the Anglo-Iroquois Covenant Chain, 1758–1766," *Ethnohistory* 44: 4 (Autumn 1997), 621.

26 As quoted in Guy Frégault, *Canada: the War of the Conquest*, 120.

27 W.J. Eccles, "Louis Joseph de Montcalm, Marquis de Montcalm" *Dictionary of Canadian Biography*, http://www.biographi.ca.

28 As quoted in Richard Middleton, *The Bells of Victory: The Pitt-Newcastle Ministry and Conduct of the Seven Years' War 1757–1762* (Cambridge: Cambridge University Press, 2002), 19.

29 As quoted in Charles Clive Bigham Mersey, *The Prime Ministers of Britain, 1721–1921* (London: Ayer, 1969), 79.

30 Fred Anderson, *Crucible of War*, 197–198.

31 W.J. Eccles, "Montcalm," *Dictionary of Canadian Biography*, http://www.biographi.ca.

32 Ronald J. Dale, The Fall of New France: How the French Lost a North American Empire (Toronto: James Lorimer, 2004), 46.

33 As quoted in William Fowler, *Empires at War*, 149.

34 As quoted in Francis Parkman, *Montcalm and Wolfe*, 409.

35 As quoted in Stephen Brumwell, *Paths of Glory: The Life and Death of General James Wolfe* (Montreal and Kingston: McGill-Queen's University Press, 2006), 186. See also 185, 69, 88.

36 As quoted in Francis Parkman, *Montcalm and Wolfe*, 407.

37 As quoted in C.P. Stacey, "Jeffery Amherst, First Baron Amherst" *Dictionary of Canadian Biography*, http://www.biographi.ca.

38 W.J. Eccles, "Montcalm" *Dictionary of Canadian Biography*, http://www.biographi.ca.

39 He used the phrase in a letter to his mother. As quoted in C.P. Stacey, "James Wolfe," *Dictionary of Canadian Biography*, http://www.biographi.ca.

40 As quoted in William Fowler, *Empires at War*, 198.

41 As quoted in C. P. Stacey, *Quebec, 1759: The Siege and the Battle* (Toronto: Macmillan, 1959), 150.

42 Ibid., 164, 152.

43 Fred Anderson, *Crucible of War*, 383.

5

*E*volution *and* Revolution: *1763–1791*

*O*n the morning of April 19, 1775, American colonists clashed with British troops at Lexington, Massachusetts, not far from Boston. Edward Winslow Junior, the son of an old and respectable Boston family, immediately rushed to the scene to assist in putting down the "rebellious mob." When the British army evacuated Boston in 1776, Winslow made the difficult decision to leave his family, and journeyed with the troops to Halifax, where he was commissioned Muster Master General of Britain's American provincial regiments. Winslow was confident that that the American rebels would be subdued quickly, and that his service would further his social aspirations. Events did not unfold as he predicted.

By 1778, Winslow was troubled by grave doubts about the conduct of the war and the morale of Britain's forces, complaining about "a damnable series of treating, retreating, piddling, conciliating &commissioning" that had taken the place of fighting.[1] When the rebel forces emerged victorious and the 1783 Treaty of Paris ended the American War of Independence, he found himself in a world turned upside down. Winslow's aged parents, sisters, wife, and children had been harassed by their rebel neighbours, and were forced to flee their homes for the British stronghold of New York, where thousands of other refugees were gathering. "Our fate seems now decreed," Winslow's sister Sarah wrote, "and we are left to mourn out our days in wretchedness. No other resource for millions but to submit to the tyranny of exulting enemys or settle a new country."[2]

Winslow's dreams of returning to Massachusetts and rising in the ranks of Boston society shattered, he acquired a farm at Granville in Nova Scotia's Annapolis Valley.

Cover of Letter to the Inhabitants of Canada *from the First Continental Congress, 1774.*

"We are monstrous poor," he wrote a friend. "I have not a spade, hoe, axe, or any article of any kind.... Blankets are so dear that I can't think of purchasing and we are badly off."[3] He made frequent trips to meet with the governor at Halifax, seeking compensation for discharged soldiers and some type of appointment for himself worthy of his service and station. Disillusioned by the "Council of Republicans" that governed Nova Scotia, Winslow approached British authorities with the idea of partitioning the colony and creating a new Loyalist province that would become "the envy of the American states."[4] Rightly counted one of New Brunswick's founders, Winslow never regained the power and prosperity his family had enjoyed before the war. His story of defeat, exile, poverty, and new beginnings is a vivid reminder of the tumultuous changes that transformed North America in the eighteenth century.

After reading this chapter you will be able to:
1. Explain the context and impact of the 1763 Royal Proclamation.
2. Identify the key challenges Britain faced in governing post-conquest Quebec.
3. Understand the purpose of, and reactions to, the 1774 Quebec Act.
4. Assess the impact of the American Revolution on Nova Scotia and Quebec.
5. Assess the role of the Loyalists in the American Revolution, their experience as refugees, and their impact on the development of British North America.

1763: The end of the Seven Years War leaves the British treasury mired in debt.

Introduction

With the end of the Seven Years War in 1763, Britain acquired the new colony of Quebec, once the heart of New France. But British mastery of the North American continent was not as complete as it seemed. Britain confronted the challenge of governing an alien French Roman Catholic population in Quebec. Even more pressing, immediately on the heels of the Treaty of Paris, a strong Native resistance in the continent's interior revealed the fragile nature of British control. Then, too, there was the question of costs: the all-out commitment Britain had made to winning the war had almost doubled the mother country's national debt, which now stood at a staggering £133 million. Since the war had been fought to guarantee the security of Britain's American colonies, it seemed only fitting to British policymakers that those colonists should bear some of the costs. The colonists vigorously resisted attempts by Britain's remote Parliament to tax them.

This chapter considers British colonial policy from the 1763 Treaty of Paris and the Royal Proclamation of that same year, through the *Quebec Act* of 1774, the invasion of Canada during the Revolutionary War (1775–1783), the 1776 American Declaration of Independence, to the migration of Loyalists from the United States at the war's end and the migration of a larger number of uncertain politics in subsequent years. This era was a crises-filled one, and Britain's responses played a determinative role in shaping the course of history. British policy to address Aboriginal grievances, in the form of the 1763 Royal Proclamation, laid the groundwork for Native–newcomer relations for subsequent centuries. The compromise of the 1774 *Quebec Act* contributed to both the persistence of a distinct *Canadien* culture and society in Quebec and the outbreak of the Revolutionary War. The British colonies of Quebec and Nova Scotia opted not to join their rebellious neighbours, and in the aftermath of the war received a flood of refugee Loyalists. These much-mythologized newcomers swelled the populations of Quebec and Nova Scotia, and led to the creation of new British colonies in North America.

British Policy and First Nations' Resistance

The long negotiations that followed the capitulation of New France ended with the ratification of the Treaty of Paris on February 10, 1763. Important parties, however, had been excluded from the peace talks that reshaped North America—the First Nations. Most tribes of the Great Lakes and Ohio country had allied themselves with the French during the Seven Years War and were confused and angered by its outcome. Undefeated in the interior, and hopeful that the French would return to reclaim their lost empire, the Natives of the northwest continued to harass the British who now occupied the former French forts of the region and the American settlers who began to sweep into the Ohio country. As traders and soldiers, the French had used the lands of the interior on a seasonal and nomadic basis, much like the Natives themselves. The settlers from the seaboard colonies attempted to divide, clear, and cultivate traditional Aboriginal territory. Whereas the French maintained an extensive system of Native alliances through gift giving, the British, who viewed the Natives as a conquered people, soon abandoned the practice as an unnecessary expense.

Sir William Johnson, whose long friendship with the Mohawk people gave him valuable insights, had already warned that the Natives would interpret the sudden withdrawal of presents as a clear sign of "contempt, dislike, and an inclination to reduce them so low as to facilitate designs of extirpating them."[5] The Ojibwe war chief Minweweh spoke for many when he warned Alexander Henry, one of the first English traders to venture into the interior:

> Englishman, although you have conquered the French you have not yet conquered us! We are not your slaves. These lakes, these woods, and mountains were left us by our ancestors. They are our inheritance; and we will part with them to none…. Englishman, your king has not sent us any presents, nor entered into any treaty with us, therefore he and we are still at war.[6]

In 1762, an Ottawa war chief, Pontiac, began to meet with the leaders of other First Nations, encouraging them to join together in a confederacy to resist British domination. His cause was strengthened by the visions of Neolin, a charismatic Delaware prophet, who preached a return to traditional ways and the annihilation of the English intruders. "Wherefore do you suffer the whites to dwell in your lands?" Neolin asked. "Drive them away; wage war against them."[7] His words were echoed by Pontiac: "And as for the English—these dogs dressed in red, who have come to rob you of your hunting grounds, and drive away the game—you must lift the hatchet against them. Wipe them from the face of the earth…. The children of your great father, the King of France, are not like the English."[8]

In May 1763, Pontiac and a diverse group of warriors laid siege to Fort Detroit. The conflict then spread rapidly throughout the Ohio country and Great Lakes region, with eight British-held forts destroyed and hundreds of settlers killed or captured. Uprisings erupted spontaneously as news of Pontiac's actions was carried through the ranks of alienated Natives elsewhere in the northwest. Native military tactics added to the sense of British outrage. On the morning of June 2, at Fort Michilimackinac, Ojibwe warriors staged a game of lacrosse outside the walls of the fort. British soldiers stood by watching the competition, and allowed the players behind the walls of the palisade to retrieve an errant ball. Once inside, the Natives sprung the trap, and with weapons concealed beneath their garments, took possession of the fort. Twenty-two British soldiers and traders were killed, and a number were taken prisoner. Significantly, some French-Canadian traders within the fort were left unharmed.

The events of that deadly summer have sometimes been labelled "Pontiac's Rebellion," or "the Conspiracy of Pontiac." Both of these historical labels are problematic in some respects. To brand a conflict a "rebellion" implies the legitimacy of the authority being resisted. Although the French had surrendered their own interests in North America, the Natives of the interior did not regard themselves as a defeated people subject to the British.

1763: Throughout the summer, Native warriors seize British posts in the North American interior.

"Pontiac's War" is thus a more suitable way to describe the conflict. Historian Gregory Evans Dowd, reflecting on the motives for warfare, observes that "war is never reducible to reason alone; powerful sentiments—senses of loyalty, honour, hatred, jealousy, vengeance, and fear—must be involved to bring men and women to kill and risk death." While certainly seeing in Pontiac's War a "worldly, material, reasonable dimension," Dowd argues that these "might have been negotiated had it not become clear that other issues, pressing matters of the heart, were beyond discussion. British officials clearly conveyed their intention to dominate ... a conquered continent.... Indians demanded recognition, honour, and respect."[9]

Germ Warfare and the Waning of Resistance

The siege at Detroit dragged on throughout the summer, at great cost to both sides. At Fort Pitt in the Ohio country, beleaguered British officers grew desperate enough to resort to biological warfare. Pontiac was not alone in his resolve to wipe his enemies from the face of the earth. British officials at Fort Pitt infected blankets with smallpox and distributed them in medicine boxes during a parlay with a Native delegation. Historians are divided over the effectiveness of this desperate action.

1763: British officials deliberately spread smallpox in a bid to break Aboriginal resistance.

According to Francis Jennings, the British attempt at germ warfare was "unquestionably effective" and greatly weakened the Aboriginal cause. Others have argued that smallpox was already widespread throughout the region, and that the outbreak in 1763 cannot be definitively traced to contaminated British blankets.[10] By the fall of 1763, there were signs that support for the uprisings was beginning to wane. At Detroit, nearby French-Canadian settlers failed to join the siege and some of Pontiac's own warriors began to abandon the field to return to their hunting grounds. Elsewhere, the shortage of critical supplies of powder and guns, or the arrival of British reinforcements, forced a Native retreat. Furthermore, Pontiac's confederacy suffered from an inherent weakness—traditional Native rivalries resurfaced and eroded what was an essentially artificial unity.

The Legacy of Native Resistance: The Royal Proclamation, 1763

1763: The Royal Proclamation sets out a pattern for treaty negotiation.

The uprisings of 1763 failed to force a British withdrawal from Native territory, or to produce a lasting First Nations confederacy. Native resistance did, however, compel British authorities to recognize "the great dissatisfaction" among the Aboriginal nations resulting from "great frauds and abuses" perpetuated against them by unscrupulous land speculators, settlers, and traders. Conceding that frontier stability could only be achieved through negotiation and accommodation, the Crown issued a Royal Proclamation on October 7, 1763, that drew a boundary line along the crest of the Appalachians. Lands to the west of the line were declared "Indian Territory," not to be settled or purchased unless acquired by treaty between the Crown and the Aboriginal nation affected; no private person could buy or take possession of Native land. The Royal Proclamation further relieved colonial officials of all authority over the Native peoples and placed them under the protection of the Crown.

The Royal Proclamation set out in writing what became the constitutional basis for all future treaty negotiations, and, most significantly, recognized what would later come to be known as "Aboriginal title"—the idea that Native nations had an inherent claim to lands they

Map 5.1
North America after the Treaty of Paris and the Royal Proclamation of 1763.

Source: *Historical Atlas of Canada*, vol. 1. University of Toronto Press, 1993. Reprinted with permission of the University of Toronto Press.

continuously occupied.[11] Taking a page from French policy, the British also attempted to restore good diplomatic relations by resuming the practice of annual gift-giving to Aboriginal nations.

Although these changes in British policy succeeded in restoring a greater peace and security among Aboriginal nations, at least temporarily, they resulted in considerable indignation in other quarters. American colonists were determined to avenge their losses, and land hungry speculators coveted the interior for themselves. In time, the Proclamation line proved ineffective against the tide of American settlers that spilled over the Appalachians. The ultimate loss of control over this territory, however, does not undercut the importance that the legal principle expressed in the proclamation would have in Canada's future.

Quebec under British Rule

The Royal Proclamation of 1763 also had significant consequences for French Canada, prescribing boundaries, government, and law for the new British colony of Quebec. Deprived of "Indian Territory," Quebec was now confined to the old seigneurial heartland that lay on either side of the St. Lawrence. The Royal Proclamation anticipated that Quebec's French Catholic population would soon be overwhelmed by an influx of English-speaking and Protestant settlers from the American colonies, and would be quickly assimilated. In light of this expectation, it seemed reasonable to set out a plan to govern Quebec like the

1763: The Royal Proclamation proposes to govern Quebec like Britain's other North American colonies.

other British colonies. The Royal Proclamation directed that the governor should call a general assembly "in such Manner and Form as is used and directed in those Colonies and Provinces in America which are under our immediate Government."

The new subjects would be subject to English law. "All Persons Inhabiting in or resorting to our Said Colonies may confide in our Royal Protection for the Enjoyment of the Benefit of the Laws of our Realm of England," the Proclamation stated. Difficulties loomed: Roman Catholics in England did not enjoy political rights—not the right to vote, seek election, or hold public office. How could any representative system of government be introduced into a population of Roman Catholic British subjects? This was the same difficulty that had stymied British authorities after Acadia was acquired in 1713. Nor did English law have provisions to deal with the seigneurial system, which had been retained in Quebec. The vision for Quebec outlined in the Royal Proclamation proved unworkable, and within a few years British authorities were forced to recognize the social and institutional realities of French Canada. The impact of the conquest and the consequences of British rule, however, have been among the most hotly contested issues in Canadian history.

Debating the Impact of the Conquest

The views of nineteenth-century American historian Francis Parkman influenced many generations of English Canadians. Parkman described the conquest as an act of liberation from French despotism and praised the blessings British rule brought to a backward and priest-ridden people. "A happier calamity never befell a people than the conquest of Canada by the British arms."[12] Early nationalist historians such as François-Xavier Garneau viewed the conquest as a humiliating defeat that threatened the survival of French Canadian identity. Some Catholic historians disagreed, instead praising the stability of British institutions and crediting the conquest with saving French Canadians from the horrors of the French Revolution. As nationalist and separatist sentiment increased in Quebec during the 1960s, historians such as Maurice Séguin and Michel Brunet argued that the conquest and British rule brought about a social revolution that transformed the class structure of French Canada.

According to Séguin and Brunet, the change in imperial control "decapitated" *Canadien* society, depriving it of its dynamic middle class. The restriction of trade within the British Empire, the British monopoly on shipping, and the difficulty establishing connections with unknown suppliers and creditors, combined to destroy the profitable external trade that the *Canadiens* had engaged in before the conquest. Unable to carry on, the wealthiest and most successful elements of the colony's commercial class departed. Those who remained were small entrepreneurs with modest incomes and ambitions who were quickly pushed aside by merchants and traders from Britain and the American colonies, who benefited from British imperial connection. With the loss of its bourgeoisie, Brunet and Séguin maintained, French Canada became a predominantly agrarian society dominated by an Anglophone commercial and governing class. In order to control the *Canadien* majority, they argued, Quebec's new rulers forged an alliance with the Roman Catholic clergy and the remaining seigneurs, giving both groups far more power than they had exercised during the French regime.

This "decapitation thesis" has been challenged by Jean Hamelin, José Igartua, and Fernand Ouellet. Hamelin questioned the very existence of a dynamic *Canadien* commercial class prior to the conquest, arguing that the intendants' correspondence, tax records, and estate inventories all attest to the general poverty of *Canadien* merchants and traders. The whole-sale and retail trades were dominated by the opportunistic agents of French companies who only stayed in New France for a few years and had little interest in developing the colony's economy and limited influence on *Canadien* culture.

José Igartua pointed out that the economy had been tightly regulated during the French regime. After the conquest, *Canadien* traders and merchants found themselves thrown into a new competitive business environment that caused them to seek out partnerships with the British and American newcomers. The *Canadien* bourgeoisie was, therefore, not decapitated, but rather integrated into a new economic system. Acknowledging that it was certainly the initial intention of British authorities to assimilate the *Canadiens* and to create a British-dominated mercantile state in Quebec, Fernand Ouellet insisted that no such social revolution occurred. With few settlers arriving from the American colonies and a high birth rate among the habitants, Quebec remained an overwhelmingly *Canadien* society. The Church, which owned a quarter of all seigneurial lands and controlled schools and hospitals before the conquest, continued to do so afterwards. Owing to their experience and connections with the Aboriginal nations, *Canadiens* maintained an important place in the fur trade, Quebec's principal economic activity, for many years to come. Ouellet argued, however, that the *Canadien* bourgeoisie lacked entrepreneurial spirit and preferred to channel any profits from the fur trade into acquiring seigneuries and living aristocratic lifestyles. This mentality impeded economic growth and innovation before the conquest, and contrasted with the free enterprise spirit brought to Quebec by British and American merchants, who diversified their interests and invested in new enterprises such as the timber and grain trades. It was this difference in outlook, more than anything else, Ouellet concluded, that contributed to the gradual economic ascendancy of the British community.

James Murray, the *Canadiens*, and the Merchants

Responsibility for implementing the terms of the Royal Proclamation fell to James Murray, a veteran of the Seven Years War who had served as Quebec's military governor since the capitulation. In the absence of a large English-speaking population, James Murray proceeded slowly, introducing English criminal law and appointing justices of the peace and bailiffs, but maintaining French property and civil law. Murray's procrastination displeased the small British merchant community that demanded the full and immediate introduction of English law and the establishment of a legislative assembly to protect their rights. Francis Maseres, Murray's attorney general, warned that any assembly would be "representative of only the 600 new English settlers, and an instrument in their hands of domineering over the 90 000 French." "Can such an assembly be thought to be just or expedient, or likely to produce harmony and friendship between the two nations?" Maseres asked rhetorically.[13] The answer was obvious to Murray. While an assembly might please the English minority, it was sure to offend the *Canadien* majority who, as Roman Catholics, would be ineligible to participate under English law. An aristocratic soldier, Murray had little patience for the noisy demands of merchants interested only in profits, and refused to call an assembly.

1763: British Governor James Murray avoids implementing British-style political institutions in Quebec.

Like many English Protestants, Murray was suspicious of Roman Catholics in general and of the Jesuits in particular, who had a reputation for political intrigue. British authorities instructed Murray not to re-establish "the Popish hierarchy," to work towards the establishment of the Church of England "in both principle and practice," and to take measures to induce *Canadiens* "to embrace the Protestant religion and to raise their children in it." Despite his prejudices, Murray recognized that, with few Protestants in the colony, there was little hope of converting the *Canadien* majority. Consequently, he adopted a pragmatic approach to the Roman Catholic Church. Although this was counter to his instructions, Murray advised London that the appointment of "a superintendent of the Romish religion" would provide his administration with a valuable ally capable of keeping French Canadians loyal to their new government. Murray regularly used the new bishop, Jean-Olivier Briand, to circulate pastoral messages in support of the state, and in return for his cooperation and "good behaviour" rewarded Briand with an annuity.[14] For his part, Briand adopted a pragmatic "render unto Caesar" attitude, and directed that prayers should be offered to the British royal family at mass: "They are our masters, and we owe them what we owed the French when they were our masters. Does the Church now forbid his subjects to pray for their prince?"[15]

Murray favoured a hierarchical social order and also looked to seigneurs and the seigneurial system to maintain peace, order, and loyalty among the habitants. The governor's aristocratic background may have given him something more in common with the old elite of Quebec than with the striving new middle class merchants, despite the fact that the latter were generally British and Protestant. Class trumped ethnicity.[16] Murray's attempt to conciliate the *Canadien* majority antagonized the English merchant community, and they accused him of governing as a despot. "The Governor," the merchants complained in a petition to the King, "instead of acting agreeable to that confidence reposed in him by your Majesty, in giving a favourable reception to those of your Majesty's subjects … doth frequently treat them with rage and rudeness of language, as dishonourable to the trust he holds of your Majesty as painful to those who suffer from it." Murray dismissed the petitioners as "licentious fanatics" who would be content with nothing less than the expulsion of the French Canadians, "perhaps the bravest and best race upon the globe." He urged the extension to Canadian Roman Catholics of privileges which "the laws of England deny" to them at home, confident that this would make them faithful and useful subjects.[17] But amid angry petitions from the Anglophone merchant class of Quebec, Murray was recalled to London in 1766.

1766: James Murray is recalled and Sir Guy Carleton is appointed governor of Quebec.

Sir Guy Carleton and the *Quebec Act*

Sir Guy Carleton, one of Murray's lieutenants, replaced him as military governor. An ambitious career soldier with a fiery temper, Carleton was convinced that Murray's "favouritism" towards the *Canadiens* had been a mistake. He cultivated good relations with the British merchants and promised to abolish French civil law and call an assembly. But Carleton, like Murray before him, soon came to distrust the clamouring of the Anglophone commercial class, which he likened to the increasing restlessness within the 13 older British colonies to the south. Carleton also grew to admire the national spirit of the *Canadiens*, and recognized the utility of both the seigneurial system and the Roman Catholic Church. As a result, he began to reconsider British policy in Quebec.

Given the lack of English-speaking immigrants and the high birth rate of the *Canadiens*, Carleton concluded that "barring catastrophe shocking to think of, this country must, to the end of time, be peopled by the Canadian race, who already have taken such firm root, and got to so great a height, that any new stock transplanted will be totally hid."[18] Quebec, Carleton advised British authorities, was a province unlike any other and its distinctive circumstances needed to be acknowledged, including the French civil law and seigneurial system of land holding. As well, he contended, the rights and privileges of the Catholic Church should be confirmed. Quebec's boundaries should be redrawn to include its natural hinterland around the Great Lakes. Because the *Canadiens* lacked a tradition of representative government, Carleton felt there was no need for an elected assembly. French Catholics should, however, be permitted to serve in an appointed legislative council and other official posts. If such concessions were granted, Carleton concluded, the *Canadiens* would become loyal British subjects and Quebec would remain a bastion of imperial strength.

Carleton returned to London in 1770 and spent the next four years trying to persuade British officials to abandon the assimilationist agenda of the Royal Proclamation of 1763, and to restructure Quebec's laws and institutions to better reflect the French reality of the province. Carleton was joined in London in 1773 by François Baby, a prominent Francophone Montreal merchant. Baby carried with him a petition, signed by most of Quebec's prominent French-Canadian families, appealing for Catholic civil rights and the restoration of French law. "Then our fears will be removed," Baby promised, "and we shall pass our lives in tranquility and happiness, and shall be always ready to sacrifice them for the glory of our prince and the good of our country."[19]

1773: François Baby petitions the British government for the rights of Canadiens.

As tensions increased in the American colonies, such professions of loyalty began to sway opinion in England towards Carleton's position. Still, many objected in Parliament to any change in policy towards Quebec and the *Canadiens*. Edmund Burke complained that the establishment of French law would make the monarchy despotic. Lord Chatham warned against the establishment of "popery" and arbitrary power. Lord Cavendish cautioned that the recognition of Quebec's customary laws would forever make them a distinct people. Conversely, Alexander Wedderburn insisted "experience demonstrates that the public safety has been often endangered by restraints [on religious freedoms], and there is no instance of any state that has been overturned by toleration."[20] Carleton's recommendations were at last incorporated into the *Quebec Act* of 1774.

1774: With the Quebec Act, *British authorities retreat from the original goal of assimilating French Canadians.*

"For the more perfect security and ease of the minds of the inhabitants" of the province, the *Quebec Act* protected the practice of the Roman Catholic faith, providing a revised oath of allegiance that would not require pledging one's faith to the Church of England. While English criminal law would continue to prevail, as it had since the conquest, for property and civil matters the "Laws of Canada" would be in force. This restored the familiar French civil code, which had provisions for questions arising out of the seigneurial system, which was also to be retained. This retention of a distinct civil law in Quebec has persisted down to the present day, and explains why it is necessary to appoint three of Canada's nine Supreme Court judges from the province of Quebec.

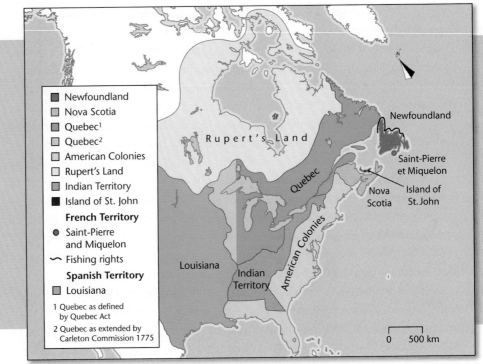

Map 5.2
British North America after the **Quebec Act, 1774.**

Legend:
- Newfoundland
- Nova Scotia
- Quebec[1]
- Quebec[2]
- American Colonies
- Rupert's Land
- Indian Territory
- Island of St. John

French Territory
- Saint-Pierre and Miquelon
- Fishing rights

Spanish Territory
- Louisiana

1 Quebec as defined by Quebec Act
2 Quebec as extended by Carleton Commission 1775

Source: *Historical Atlas of Canada*, vol. 1. University of Toronto Press, 1993. Reprinted with the permission of the University of Toronto Press.

The 1774 *Quebec Act* also extended the colony's boundaries to include the Great Lakes and the Ohio country. One of the most striking aspects of the Act was its retreat from the 1763 plan to establish representative government. The Act declared that it was "at present inexpedient to call an Assembly"—undoubtedly because it would have been dominated by the tiny Anglophone minority. Instead, the governor was to appoint a legislative council to make laws. The revised oath meant that Roman Catholics would be eligible for such appointments.[21] Some observers today view the *Quebec Act* as a milestone in French-Canadian national identity. While the Act made no specific mention of the French language, it did contain, in essence, statutory recognition of the distinctiveness of the *Canadiens* as a people.

Responses to the *Quebec Act*

On the surface, the *Quebec Act* signalled an abandonment of the assimilationist agenda of earlier British policy. Accompanying the Act, however, were a set of secret instructions directing Carleton to introduce English common law gradually, to subject the Roman Catholic Church to state supervision, and to discourage the growth of religious orders, especially the Jesuits. These instructions suggest that British authorities viewed the concessions of the *Quebec Act* as temporary responses to the immediate challenges posed by the growing unrest in its other North American colonies. Carleton, for the most part, ignored the instructions, not wanting to undermine the relationship he had cultivated with church authorities and the seigneurs.

Reaction to the *Quebec Act* was mixed. Although Roman Catholic Church leaders and French Canadian seigneurs embraced the terms of the *Quebec Act*, ordinary French-Canadian habitants were far less enthusiastic about the reintroduction of tithes and the legal recognition given to seigneurial dues. Montreal's Anglophone merchants welcomed the incorporation of the old fur trade heartland back into the province, but complained bitterly about the concessions to the French majority and the absence of any provision for an assembly. The strongest reaction to the *Quebec Act* came from the American colonies.

Quebec and the American Revolution

To American colonists, the *Quebec Act* was a betrayal, and the latest in a series of provocations passed by the British Parliament. Discontent had been building in the colonies since the end of the Seven Years War; the war itself had taken a heavy toll. Rising prices, disruption of trade, and high levels of colonial debt caused serious economic hardship in the colonies for many years to come. The cost of empire also weighed heavily upon the debt-laden British government, which was determined to restore its finances by shifting some of the cost of empire to the colonists through taxation and a more tightly regulated colonial trade.

For example, in 1764, in the immediate aftermath of the war, Britain's Parliament passed the *Sugar Act*, which was aimed at capturing more revenue from the sale of sugar and molasses that flowed into the American colonies from the West Indies for rum production. Perhaps surprisingly, the new legislation reduced the tariff by half, but was accompanied by new measures to enforce payment of the tax and crack down on smuggling. The previous tariff—or tax on imports—had been largely regulatory in nature; that is, it had aimed to make sugar products coming from the French or Spanish Caribbean islands prohibitively expensive, and thus prop up Britain's sugar-producing colonies. The new measure signalled the shift to a revenue-generating tariff.

1764–1765: Britain's Parliament imposes new taxation measures on the American colonies.

In addition, Britain introduced the *Stamp Act* in 1765: revenue stamps had to be affixed to all types of commercial and legal documents that circulated in the North American colonies, including reading material such as newspapers and almanacs, and even playing cards. During the debates on the measure, the British Chancellor of the Exchequer (finance minister) Charles Townshend eloquently and rhetorically asked if "these Americans, children planted by our care, nourished up by our Indulgence until they are grown to a degree of strength and opulence, and protected by our arms, will ... grudge to contribute their mite to relieve us from heavy weight of the burden which we lie under."[22] The American colonists saw things differently.

Indeed, disillusioned colonists began to question the very authority of Britain's Parliament to tax the colonies. Spokespersons for the discontented began to give voice to a coherent set of political ideas that were rooted in the Whig ideology that had emerged during Britain's Glorious Revolution of 1688. American Whigs argued that the power of the Crown over the colonies had to be restrained, and the freedom of colonial assemblies strengthened. They looked back to John Locke's famous 1690 *Second Treatise on Civil Government*, which sanctioned the revolution of 1688, and found support in his conviction that when a government was tyrannical, subjects had not only a right, but a duty, to overthrow it. Throughout the colonies, popular discontent increasingly found expression in petitions to the king, the burning of effigies, the erection of liberty poles, boycotts on British goods, the wearing of homespun fabric (not subject to import taxes), and even rioting.

While the unifying phrase "American colonists" has been used for convenience, in truth there were 13 separate older British colonies along the Atlantic seaboard—Massachusetts, New Hampshire, New York, New Jersey, Connecticut, Rhode Island, Pennsylvania, Delaware, Maryland, Virginia, North Carolina, South Carolina, and Georgia. These colonies did not have an inherent unity, but the shared sense of grievance against British policy promoted a closer tie over time. Massachusetts was the centre of protest, and many of the iconic events of the American Revolution took place there. On March 5, 1770, British soldiers on duty in Boston clashed with a group of civilians who had turned out to harass them and pelt them with snowballs and oyster shells. When the large crowd jostled a soldier, knocking him to the ground, he discharged his musket. The melee ended with five colonists shot dead. The historical label "Boston Massacre" may seem hyperbolic, given the modest toll in lives, but it reflects the outrage of the American colonists and the role of the clash in galvanizing public opinion. The same might be said of an event almost exactly 200 years later that has striking parallels—the May 4, 1970 shooting by Ohio National Guardsmen of four Kent State University students protesting the war in Vietnam and the invasion of Cambodia. History can turn on such pivots.

Coordinated colonial action against the hated *Stamp Act* forced Britain to retreat from that measure, and smuggling and boycotts had produced disappointing yields from other revenue taxes. While the British Parliament relented on some of these measures, they retained a tax on tea, in part to assert the principle of Parliament's right to tax the colonies. Further, in 1773 they granted special privileges to the struggling East India Company, which hoped to dispose of a glut of tea accumulating in their London warehouses due in part to the American boycott. Other taxes on tea were rolled back, with the effect that legitimately shipped British tea could now be purchased more cheaply in the colonies than tea illegally smuggled in from other nations. American agitators worried that colonists might be tempted to abandon their principles for the sake of cheap tea. The radical "Sons of Liberty," first established in Massachusetts, took revenge on anyone who defied the non-importation tactic. Soon, "Sons of Liberty" groups sprang up in the other colonies too. Late in 1773, when three vessels reached Boston with a cargo of tea, protestors—unconvincingly disguised as Mohawks—boarded the ships and, cheered on by a large crowd, pitched 342 chests of tea into the harbour.

In the aftermath of the blatant civil disobedience of the "Boston Tea Party," Britain responded with a series of measures designed to punish Massachusetts and restore order. These 1774 "Coercive Acts" or, as the Americans called them, "Intolerable Acts," among other provisions, closed the port of Boston to shipping until restitution was made for the lost tea. Perhaps more ominously, the constitution of Massachusetts was suspended, with no assembly to be summoned, meetings forbidden, and government placed under the firm hand of the British-appointed governor. The *Quebec Act*, passed the same year as the "Intolerable Acts," seemed all the more provocative in light of these conditions. One New England pamphleteer described the form of government set out in the *Quebec Act* as a blueprint for slavery, and worried that this new despotic design would be carried forward to

1773: The Boston Tea Party was an open act of colonial defiance against British taxation.

extinguish liberty in all the other colonies. Residents of the older British colonies along the Atlantic seaboard also chafed at the extension of Quebec's borders under the *Quebec Act*, which interfered with their own inevitable expansion. New England Puritans resented the *Quebec Act*'s concessions to "popery." Why was Parliament rewarding Britain's traditional enemy in North America, but punishing those who had helped to defeat them?

In September 1774, representatives from 12 of the 13 American colonies gathered to meet in the First Continental Congress at Philadelphia. George Washington, hastening to attend as a delegate from Virginia, wrote to a friend with unintentional irony: "The Crisis is arriv'd when we must assert our Rights, or Submit to every Imposition that can be heap'd upon us; till custom and use, will make us as tame, & abject Slaves, as the Blacks we Rule over with such arbitrary Sway."[23] Although far from united, delegates issued a Declaration of Rights and Freedoms that outlined colonial grievances, demanded that Parliament repeal the "Intolerable Acts," and justified colonial defiance by appealing to the "immutable laws of nature and the principles of the English constitution."

The First Continental Congress also issued an appeal to "friends and fellow subjects" in Quebec. "Your province is the only link wanting to complete the bright and strong chain of union," the delegates urged. "Take a noble chance for emerging from a humiliating subjection under Governors, Intendants, and Military Tyrants. You are a small people, compared to those who with open arms invite you into a fellowship," the manifesto warned, and "a moment's reflection should convince you which will be most for your interest and happiness, to have all the rest of North America your unalterable friends, or your inveterate enemies."[24]

1774: The "Intolerable Acts" spark a continental congress of American colonies.

The Invasion of Canada

Most *Canadiens* were unmoved by the manifesto's combination of enticement and intimidation, and remained on the sidelines as the American colonies moved towards rebellion. Plans were already in place for a second Continental Congress in May 1775. In the meantime, on the morning of April 19, 1775, a small, but crucially important, battle at Lexington Green, Massachusetts, between local militiamen and British forces signalled the beginning of the American Revolutionary War, or War of Independence. The night before, silversmith Paul Revere had ridden from house to house to alert his compatriots that the British forces were moving to arrest the rebel leaders and seize their armaments; the forewarned colonists were ready to defy them. Ralph Waldo Emerson's evocative words in the poem "Concord Hymn" written in 1836, lends an air of dignity and righteousness to their struggle:

April 19, 1775: American colonial minutemen clash with British soldiers at Lexington Green, Massachusetts.

> By the rude bridge that arched the flood,
> Their flag to April's breeze unfurled,
> Here once the embattled farmers stood,
> And fired the shot heard round the world.[25]

The "Congressionalist" army raised by the second Continental Congress authorized an invasion of Quebec in the hope of rallying support from French Canadians and preventing the British from using the province as a base from which to suppress the rebellious colonies. In the summer of 1775, two American armies marched north to take Canada.

One force, under Richard Montgomery, advanced by way of Lake Champlain toward Montreal; another, under Benedict Arnold, struggled through the dense wilderness of Maine to strike directly at Quebec. The Americans were confident that French Canadians would welcome the American invaders and join the revolt against Britain. Carleton was equally confident that the Canadiens, grateful for the concessions of the *Quebec Act*, would rally to the defence of the province. Both sides were disappointed. When Carleton called up the militia, few answered the call, despite the admonitions of their seigneurs "to defend your country and your king with all your power" and the threat of church leaders to excommunicate anyone who aided the Americans.

As Montgomery's army entered the province of Quebec, he was surprised to discover that few *Canadiens* came forward to welcome and to support their American "liberators." Thomas Walker, a merchant who had moved to Montreal from Boston in 1763, had assured the Americans that "the bulk of the people both English and Canadian wish well to your cause … which alone will free us from those fears and apprehensions that rob us of our peace."[26] Walker—who was among the most vocal critics of British policy in Quebec—worked tirelessly to recruit French Canadians. He promised money and arms to anyone who joined the American cause. Most *Canadiens*, however, had little interest in supporting either their new British overlords or their traditional American rivals, and opted to remain neutral. And although there were some notable exceptions, such as Walker, only a small number of the English-speaking merchant community were American sympathizers. Most of the British merchants recognized that their economic stake in the imperial system outweighed their political dissatisfaction with the *Quebec Act*.

In September, Montgomery's army of 1500 volunteer militiamen reached Fort St. Jean on the outskirts of Montreal. A small of force of 200 British regulars and a handful of *Canadien* militia held off the Americans for eight weeks. With supplies running short, casualties mounting, and winter approaching, Major Charles Preston finally surrendered on November 3, 1775. When he received news that Fort St. Jean had fallen, Carleton retreated to Quebec, and Montgomery marched into Montreal unopposed. Five days later, Arnold's army reached Quebec, having endured a gruelling overland journey that claimed nearly half of its 1200 men. On November 15, Arnold marched to the citadel gates and demanded the immediate surrender of the town.

November 3, 1775: The Congressionalist army takes Montreal.

Carleton ignored Arnold's ultimatum, although he was unsure of the loyalty of the town's residents. Even when Montgomery and 300 reinforcements joined Arnold, Carleton continued to stand fast. Montgomery and Carleton had once been friends, and together had served the British cause during the Seven Years War. Some years after the war, Montgomery had sold his commission and settled down to farm in the colony of New York. Now, the two men fought on opposite sides.

The siege of Quebec lasted through December, but the Americans were unable to breach the defences. As winter set in, smallpox ravaged American ranks, and morale deteriorated. With nearly half of the American troops due to be discharged at the end of the year, Montgomery and Arnold launched a desperate and unsuccessful attack on Quebec's lower town during a blinding snowstorm on New Year's Eve. Montgomery was killed in the struggle, Arnold wounded, and nearly 400 Americans taken prisoner.

ARNOLD'S MARCH through the WILDERNESS
The Americans under Gen. Arnold, penetrated though an unexplored Wilderness to Quebec, in the Fall of 1775, after severe difficulties and privation

Source: Library and Archives Canada, C-008724.

American rebels advancing on Quebec.

The next morning, the frozen bodies of Montgomery and several others were recovered from a snow bank. Carleton personally paid the expenses of a decent funeral for his late "deluded friend."[27]

In Montreal, the conduct of the American invaders had squandered whatever support existed among the local population. Betraying an intense anti-Catholic prejudice, the American commander left in charge of the city, Brigadier-General David Wooster, prohibited the celebration of Christmas mass and permitted his troops to use churches as stables for their horses. When supplies began to run short, the American occupiers further alienated the local population by paying for goods with worthless Congressionalist paper money, and by seizing crops from habitant farms.

In April 1776 the Second Continental Congress sent a commission to Montreal to "convince" the *Canadiens* "of the Uprightness of our Intentions towards them."[28] But Wooster's heavy-handedness and the behaviour of his troops spoke louder than the soothing reassurances offered by Benjamin Franklin and the other commissioners.

The commissioners found the *Canadiens* openly hostile and their own troops diseased and dispirited. When a British fleet with 10 000 soldiers arrived at Quebec on May 5, 1776, what remained of Arnold's exhausted army immediately fled. Hoping that the rebels might

1776: Benjamin Franklin comes to Montreal in April in a vain attempt to convince French Canadians to join the Patriot cause.

yet be reconciled to the empire, Carleton did not unleash British forces upon the retreating Americans, and ordered them to proceed toward Montreal slowly. On June 15, 1776, the Americans withdrew from Montreal, and the invasion of Canada was over.

Neutral Nova Scotia?

On July 4, 1776, the Second Continental Congress issued its Declaration of Independence. Any hope that the differences between Britain and the American colonies might be settled peacefully through negotiation and compromise was now past. The Declaration of Independence attracted the attention of Nova Scotians, many of whom were disaffected with Britain's colonial policies and the administration of the governing elite in Halifax. Much of this discontent focused on the governor, Francis Legge. Legge, a career soldier, owed his position to the patronage of the secretary of state for the American Colonies, the Earl of Dartmouth, a distant relative. Shortly after his arrival in 1773, Legge found himself caught in a struggle between the assembly and the executive council for control of the government's finances. The colony of Nova Scotia, a British possession since 1713, had enjoyed representative government since 1758. This had not been implemented by any imperial legislation, but rather simply by instructions issued to its colonial governor. The first assembly was tiny, consisting only of 19 Protestant male white owners of substantial property. While on the one hand this assembly was hardly democratic in the modern sense, it did signal the first representative government in what would later be Canada.

The Binney Affair

The dispute between Governor Legge and the colony of Nova Scotia in the 1770s centred on Jonathan Binney, a Boston merchant who moved to Halifax in 1753. Binney became a close associate of the Halifax merchant elite that dominated the appointed executive council. Through his connections, Binney secured an appointment as the magistrate and collector of provincial duties at Canso. Many within the elected assembly were critical of such absentee patronage appointments and refused to vote to provide Binney an allowance. The council routinely overrode the assembly's wishes, and its members appealed to the new governor. Finding Binney a "serviceable and necessary officeholder," Legge cavalierly dismissed the assembly's protest and turned his attention to Nova Scotia's large debt. Determined to restore the public finances, Legge ordered an audit of the province's books in 1774. During the audit, it was discovered that Binney routinely drew upon the fines and duties he collected and used the stolen money for his personal use. Legge issued a warrant for Binney's arrest, and Binney was tried and convicted before the governor by a far-from-impartial jury.

When Binney protested the proceedings and refused to pay back the funds for which he was found liable, Legge ordered that Binney be imprisoned, along with his wife and children. Legge's conduct not only outraged Binney's supporters within the executive council and Halifax's merchant elite, but his critics within the assembly as well. In the spring of 1775, just as the American colonies were erupting in revolution, the assembly decided they had had enough of Legge's authoritarian behaviour. They petitioned the British government "on the subject of the Grievances the People of this Province labour under," and demanded Legge's immediate recall.[29]

The Nova Scotia Uprisings

To many Nova Scotians, Binney was a victim of British persecution. Such sentiments were especially strong among the large community of New England planters who had settled the fertile lands vacated by the Acadians. One of these planters, Jonathan Eddy, represented Chignecto (an isthmus connecting Nova Scotia with New Brunswick) in the assembly during the Binney affair. Disgusted by the proceedings, Eddy appealed to George Washington and the Continental Congress to send "an army of liberation" to Nova Scotia. The failure of the Canadian campaign, the powerful British garrison at Halifax and the lack of an American navy dissuaded Congress from committing any resources to Nova Scotia. Undeterred, Eddy approached the government of Massachusetts, which promised to arm and supply any volunteers he might enlist to free Nova Scotia. Through a combination of persuasion, deception, and intimidation, Eddy eventually gathered a force of 180 planters and Natives. He promised that a large American army was on its way to assist their cause, and, for good measure, threatened to attack the property of any who would not join them. On November 12, 1776, Eddy's army attacked Fort Cumberland on the Chignecto isthmus. The small British garrison easily held at bay a rebel force that quickly dispersed as soon as reinforcements arrived.

November 12, 1776: Jonathan Eddy leads an attack on Fort Cumberland.

Another American sympathizer, John Allan, attempted an assault on the small garrison at the mouth of the Saint John River in June 1777. Allan was the son of Scottish immigrants, had held a number of public positions, and served in the assembly as the representative for Cumberland. Although not of New England stock, Allan shared American aspirations and disillusionment with imperial governance. Allan did not participate in Eddy's ill-fated expedition against Fort Cumberland, and fled to Machias, Maine, with a price on his head after failing to convince Eddy to abandon the poorly supported scheme. During the rebellion, Allan's wife was imprisoned, his farm burned, crops destroyed, and livestock confiscated.

June 1777: John Allan organizes an abortive uprising at the mouth of the Saint John River.

The complete failure of Eddy's uprising did not dissuade Allan from his goal of liberating Nova Scotia, and he began to rouse the Maliseet and Mi'kmaq, many of whom were already disaffected with the British administration and hoped that the overthrow of the British might lead to the return of their traditional allies, the French. Ambroise Saint-Aubin, a leading Maliseet chief, joined Allan's forces, which were assembling upriver at Pointe-Sainte-Anne (present-day Fredericton) for the campaign against the small fort and settlement at the mouth of the Saint John River.

Almost at once, Allan's plan began to unravel. Both supplies and recruits were scarce. Much to Allan's disappointment, few among the Maliseet followed Saint-Aubin's lead, Acadians seemed indifferent to the cause, and most of the other settlers were either staunch Loyalists or preferred to remain aloof from the conflict. Before he could even launch an attack, a British naval squadron arrived, forcing Allan's small army to retreat to Machias. Although Eddy's and Allan's invasion plans failed to amount to much, many Nova Scotians did identify with American grievances. Why did Nova Scotia not join with the other American colonies in their revolt against British rule?

Certainly, the presence of a large British garrison at the naval base at Halifax allowed the British to respond quickly and forcefully to any attempt to invade the province or incite the locals. Despite their disillusionment with the colonial administration, the close commercial ties with England and dependence upon government contracts kept Halifax's merchant elite from joining with their Boston counterparts and declaring independence.

Geography and the make-up of the population also played a role. The distribution of settlements along Nova Scotia's long and rugged coastline impeded communication and the organization of a coordinated resistance to British rule. Although nearly half of Nova Scotia's 19 000 residents were New England planters, significant numbers of Ulster Irish Protestants, Yorkshiremen, Scots, and returning Acadians had arrived in the province in the early 1770s. The cultural diversity and recent arrival of so many settlers precluded the development of a unified political identity and collective sense of grievance. Whatever sympathy existed for the rebels was undermined by the activities of American privateers who routinely pillaged Nova Scotia's coastal settlements in the name of liberty. The unwillingness of Nova Scotians to support the rebellion owed a great deal as well to a religious awakening that swept through rural planter communities in the 1770s and '80s.

Henry Alline and the "New Light" Movement

The "New Light stir," as it was called, was led by a charismatic itinerant preacher, Henry Alline. Born in Newport, Rhode Island, to a family who traced its origins to the *Mayflower* pilgrims, Alline came to Nova Scotia at the age of 12 with his parents in 1760. The family settled in the remote farming community of Falmouth on the Minas Basin. Like many New Englanders, Alline was raised in a Congregational home—that is, his family believed in the complete autonomy of local churches, rather than any overarching ecclesiastical authority. Even before the family arrived in Nova Scotia, Alline felt he had been "moved upon by the spirit of God." There was no church in Falmouth, so he studied the Bible on his own, read popular devotional works, and discussed religious matters with his parents. As he grew older, Alline feared that his salvation was endangered by "frolicking and carnal mirth," and wrestled constantly with his soul "groaning under a load of guilt and darkness, praying and crying continually for mercy." After an intense conversion experience in which Christ's "redeeming love broke into [his]… soul," Alline resolved to "labour in the ministry and ... preach the gospel." In 1776, he began an itinerant ministry and launched his New Light movement. Alline's emotional extemporaneous preaching and effective use of music drew large crowds and resulted in great spiritual awakening wherever he went. He attracted a large following in the poor and isolated communities of rural Nova Scotia. Economically deprived and cut off from the centres of power, these farmers and fishers found empowerment in Alline's message that true worth rested on personal intimacy with God rather than status, wealth, or influence. Alline had little interest in the external trappings of religion—creeds, hierarchy, doctrine, and liturgy—and called upon individuals to break free of tradition and become "new and spiritual men."[30] In the midst of the political turmoil sweeping the American colonies, Alline offered Nova Scotians a spiritual assurance that rejected and transcended the tribulations of the secular world; he insisted that God, not the rebels or the British, commanded the allegiance of Nova Scotians. Until his death in 1784, Alline preached throughout the area and caused a revival of faith that eventually laid the foundation of the Baptist movement in the Maritimes.

1776: Henry Alline launches the "New Light" movement in Nova Scotia.

America's First "Civil" War

The American Revolution divided families, communities, and regions, and is rightly considered America's first "civil" war. It is estimated that about one-third of Americans actively supported independence; another third remained loyal to Britain and the empire; and the remaining third preferred neutrality. Many Loyalists tended to be recent arrivals to the colonies and members of ethnic and religious minorities who had not yet fully assimilated to American ways, and who believed their rights and interests would be better protected within the empire. Backcountry farmers who feared the domination of the powerful mercantile elites who resided in the towns and cities along the Atlantic seaboard also figured prominently in Loyalist ranks. Loyalist leaders, disparagingly referred to as "Tories" by the American rebels, were typically drawn from those classes whose position and livelihood depended on maintaining the British connection.

It has been argued that Loyalist leaders possessed an ideology distinct from the republican ideology of the American rebels, or "patriots," as they called themselves. From the Loyalist perspective, the movement towards independence was driven by factions of self-interested power seekers, demagogues who sought to direct public anxiety against public authorities and institutions for their own gain. This diagnosis was rooted in a worldview that emphasized humanity's tendency to act on the basis of passion and self-interest rather than reason and the common good. To Loyalists, the state was a necessary and positive force that controlled the passions, thereby ensuring everyone the quiet enjoyment of their rights and liberty. Loyalists warned that the self-interested actions of the rebels only served to undermine authority and order, and thus posed a far greater threat to liberty than the actions of a government 5000 kilometres away. Loyalist and patriot did not differ in their love of liberty, but in their perceptions of where the threat to liberty originated, and in their prescriptions for its safekeeping. Loyalist leaders acknowledged problems in the imperial relationship, but insisted that the empire could be reformed in ways that both protected colonial rights and strengthened the Anglo-American community. Independence, Loyalists predicted, would expose divisions between and within the colonies, and lead to a state of economic and political chaos.

The Burdens of Loyalty

With the outbreak of hostilities in 1775, Loyalists were condemned as "enemies of American liberty," and subjected to various forms of persecution. Loyalist newspapers were shut down and presses destroyed; Loyalist property was confiscated and sold without compensation; and individual Loyalists were tarred and feathered, beaten, lynched, and imprisoned. The burden of loyalty was especially heavy for Loyalist women. War compelled many Loyalist women to assume roles beyond their normal experience. Many took charge of the family farm or business while their husbands and sons enlisted in Loyalist regiments. A significant number of women played an important role in the war by passing on useful information to the British and providing safe houses for Loyalist fugitives. It was often Loyalist women who were brought before Patriot Committees to plead for their families' safety and the security of their property. As the war ran its course, growing numbers of Loyalist women and children were forced to flee their homes and seek refuge behind

British lines. Displaced from their homes and support networks, refugee women found life in the makeshift refugee camps established in New York and Quebec physically, emotionally, and psychologically challenging. Far from appreciating their service and sacrifice, British authorities often viewed these women and their children as unwelcome burdens.

The experience of the Bowman family was typical of many. Jacob Bowman was the son of German immigrants. He joined the British army during the Seven Years War and was awarded 600 hectares of land on the Susquehanna River in New York for his services. Suspected of being a Loyalist, Bowman was apprehended by patriots in November 1775. "He was surprised at night while his wife was sick by a party of rebels," his granddaughter Elizabeth later recalled, "and with his eldest son, a lad of sixteen years of age, was taken prisoner; his house was pillaged of every article except the bed on which his sick wife lay and that they stripped of all but one blanket. Half an hour after my grandfather was marched off, his youngest child was born." With their cattle and grain all taken away by the rebels, the family only survived with the assistance of "some friendly Indians."[31] The family struggled to get by for a year before joining other Loyalist women and children in an overcrowded refugee camp at Machiche near Trois Rivières. When he was 13, Elizabeth Bowman's father, Peter, joined Butler's Rangers, one of several companies of Loyalist refugees organized during the American Revolution. The company, formed by John Butler, a wealthy landowner from New York's Mohawk Valley and a veteran of the frontier warfare of the 1750s, wreaked revenge throughout the Susquehanna, Wyoming, and Schoharie valleys. These raids proved effective in spreading terror and keeping the patriots on the defensive. The success of the campaign owed much to the Iroquois warriors who fought alongside Butler's Rangers.

Britain's Aboriginal Allies

With the exception of the Tuscaroras and some Oneida, most of the Six Nations Iroquois supported the British during the American Revolution. Three people—Sir William Johnson, and Joseph and Molly Brant—worked to maintain the Iroquois alliance with the British. Johnson settled near Schenectady, New York, in 1738 where he traded with the local Natives, mastered the Mohawk language, and became thoroughly familiar with Iroquois customs and beliefs. Having earned their confidence and respect, Johnson was adopted into the Mohawk nation and named a sachem (chief). From 1744 until his death in 1774, Johnson was superintendent of Indian affairs for New York. He was greatly assisted in his business and diplomatic dealings with the Iroquois by Molly Brant with whom he established a relationship in 1759. Brant came from a distinguished Mohawk family and exercised great influence among her people. She managed Johnson's household, and together they raised seven children.

Although Johnson did not always enjoy the support of his superiors, he pursued a policy of diplomacy and consultation that accommodated Iroquois needs and aspirations, and respected Native ownership of the land. Johnson strove to uphold the terms of the Royal Proclamation of 1763, which restricted settlement west of the Appalachians until treaties had been negotiated and Native lands purchased. By the 1770s, however, increasing numbers of settlers defied the Royal Proclamation and encroached upon Iroquois lands. Despite these pressures, Johnson did his best to maintain good relations with the Iroquois, a tradition that was carried on by his son Guy after his death in 1774. When hostilities broke out in 1775, Guy Johnson sought an Iroquois pledge of support against the rebels. The Iroquois agreed to protect British supply routes in the interior should they be attacked, but refused to participate in an active campaign to put down the rebellion.

The Iroquois decision to enter the conflict came only after Molly Brant's brother Joseph (or Thayendanegea) travelled to England as an emissary for the Six Nations to meet with British authorities in 1775. During the Seven Years War, a young Joseph Brant had been among the warriors who accompanied Sir William Johnson in the attack on Fort Niagara. Impressed by Brant's abilities, Johnson arranged for him to be educated at the school for Aboriginal boys run by the Reverend Eleazar Wheelock. Brant excelled in his studies and embraced Christianity. Following his education, he served alongside British forces in maintaining order among the western tribes and lived for a time with the Anglican missionary John Stuart, with whom he prepared a Mohawk translation of the Gospel of Mark and the Book of Common Prayer.

Shortly before his death, Sir William Johnson granted Brant an appointment as an interpreter, and used his influence among the Mohawk to secure his selection as a war chief. In the spring of 1776, while in England, Brant met with the secretary of state for the colonies, Lord George Germain, and expressed Iroquois frustration with the intrusion upon their land by settlers breaching the Royal Proclamation line: "We are tired out in making complaints and getting no redress." Germain assured Brant "of every support England could render them" in addressing their grievances once the rebellion in the colonies had been suppressed.[32] Brant returned to North America convinced that the future of the Iroquois would be better protected by standing with Britain against the colonial rebels, who he feared would finally "ruin us" if their cause succeeded.

1776: Mohawk chief Joseph Brant makes a pledge of mutual support with the British.

Joseph and Molly Brant rallied most of the Iroquois to Britain's side. Molly fed and sheltered Loyalist families driven from their homes, and Joseph led an effective campaign, winning decisive victories at Oriskany in August 1777 and Cherry Valley in November 1778. Determined to put a stop to the heavy toll, George Washington ordered Major General John Sullivan to crush the Iroquois. With an army of 3500 soldiers, Sullivan stormed through Iroquois country in September 1779, destroying villages, burning crops, and taking many prisoners. In the wake of the devastation, some 2600 Iroquois took refuge at Fort Niagara, straining British resources. Far from neutralizing the Iroquois, Sullivan's campaign stiffened their resolve. For the remainder of the war, Iroquois warriors and Loyalist rangers attacked American frontier settlements as far away as Kentucky. The Iroquois who sided with the British did so as allies and not as subjects of the Crown. They fought largely to preserve the integrity of their tribal lands against the rising tide of American settlers.

Portrait of Joseph Brant painted by George Romney during Brant's visit to Britain, 1776.

Source: Courtesy of the National Gallery of Canada.

Intrigue and Defeat

The guerrilla war fought by the companies of Loyalists and Iroquois on the frontier succeeded in keeping the Americans from attempting another invasion of Canada. The efforts
of Britain's regular forces to use Canada as a base from which to regain control of the rebellious colonies proved less successful. In the spring of 1777, General John Burgoyne launched
an invasion of New York from Quebec via the Lake Champlain corridor. At first, Burgoyne's
army of 7500 British regulars succeeded in forcing the Americans to retreat. Delays at Ticonderoga, however, enabled the American General Horatio Gates to gather reinforcements to
the south. On September 17, 1777, the two armies confronted each other at Freeman's Farm
near Saratoga on the Hudson River. Burgoyne dug in, but his expected reinforcements never
arrived. By October, Gates had virtually surrounded Burgoyne and on October 12, the
British were forced to surrender, giving the Americans their first major victory in the war.

*October 1777: British
forces suffer a defeat
at Saratoga.*

France and the American Revolution

With the British defeat at Saratoga, France saw an opportunity to avenge its losses in
the Seven Years War and to reassert its position on the world stage. France had covertly
encouraged and assisted the American rebels almost from the beginning of the conflict.
Now that the Americans had demonstrated that they could best the British, the French
recognized American independence and entered into a formal alliance with the United
States. Having modernized its army and rebuilt its navy, France's entry into the war constituted a serious threat to Britain's efforts to keep its American empire. To prevent the
French from establishing a naval base in the Gulf of St. Lawrence, the British launched
an expedition against the small French islands of St. Pierre and Miquelon, and reinforced
the garrison in Newfoundland. Quebec's governor, Sir Frederick Haldimand, worried
about the effect of France's participation in the war on the *Canadiens*. French agents were
known to be circulating a proclamation from Louis XVI in the province urging *Canadiens*
to remember their heritage. "I see myself surrounded by enemies," Haldimand fretted,
"since France has allied herself with the rebels."[33]

   Haldimand's fears proved unfounded. Although the French and the Americans drafted
invasion plans for Canada, nothing came of them. Determined to first free American soil of
British forces, George Washington had little interest in invading Canada again. In its treaty
with the United States, France had forsaken any ambitions to regain Canada. With the
exception of a daring naval raid against Fort Prince of Wales on Hudson Bay, French forces
did not attack Canada. France's real contribution to the American War of Independence
took place in 1781, when the French navy inflicted heavy casualties upon the British fleet
on Chesapeake Bay, Virginia, on September 5, and 8000 French troops joined with an
equal number of Americans to defeat the British at Yorktown that same autumn.

*1781: The French aid
the American cause
at Chesapeake Bay
and Yorktown.*

Exile and New Beginnings

With their defeat at Yorktown, British hopes for victory in America evaporated. On February 27, 1782, the House of Commons voted against continuing the war, and on March 5
passed a bill directing the Crown to negotiate peace with the Americans. The negotiations
concluded on September 3, 1783, with the signing of the Treaty of Paris. According to the

*September 3, 1783:
Treaty of Paris recognizes
American Independence.*

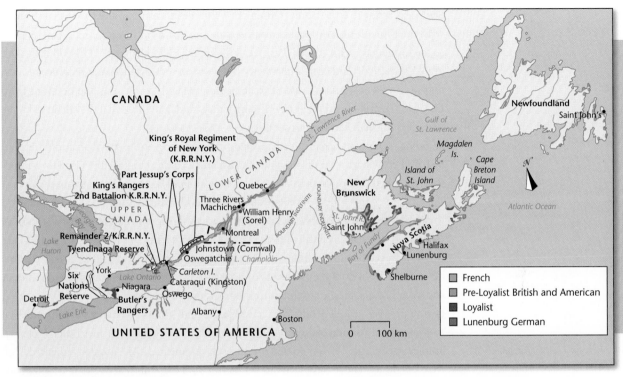

Map 5.3 *Loyalist Settlements.*

terms of the treaty, Britain recognized American independence, accepted a new northern boundary between the United States and what remained of British North America, and granted the Americans access to the important Newfoundland fishery.

The Treaty of Paris also urged Congress to "earnestly recommend" to the states the return of all property confiscated from the Loyalists. Congress had little power to enforce this term, and state legislatures were not really interested in compensating anyone who had opposed independence. Not only were the Loyalists' claims ignored, victorious patriots continued to persecute their Loyalist neighbours and to seize their property. Under such conditions, some 80 000 "loyal Americans" decided to flee the new republic and seek refuge under the Crown in Nova Scotia, Quebec, and the British colonies of the West Indies.

Nova Scarcity

Beginning in 1783, shiploads of Loyalists left New York City, the last bastion of British strength in the American colonies, bound for Nova Scotia. Tent communities arose at Shelburne on Nova Scotia's south-eastern tip, and at Parr Town and Carleton at the mouth of the Saint John River on the Bay of Fundy. By 1784, more than 35 000 Loyalists had arrived in Nova Scotia, more than doubling the province's population and stretching its resources to the limit. Responsibility for the deluge of refugees fell to Nova Scotia's new governor, John Parr. After a long and distinguished military career, Parr came to Nova

Scotia expecting to enjoy a quiet retirement. With the influx of Loyalists he was confronted with the difficult task of feeding and housing thousands of destitute refugees. As soon as the immediate crisis passed, Parr faced the even greater challenge of distributing land grants, provisions, and farm implements. Delays in surveys, disputes over the size of grants, and shortages of supplies caused Parr to be flooded with complaints and petitions from Loyalists frustrated with their new circumstances and convinced that they deserved to be rewarded for their service and sacrifice.

Some prominent Loyalist leaders, determined to recover the social position they had lost, and convinced that only a landed aristocracy could maintain the Crown's authority, demanded that more than 100 000 hectares of land be set aside for themselves. Such extravagant claims offended the Loyalist rank and file who insisted that "an enquiry into their respective losses, services, situations and sufferings" would demonstrate that all "shall be found equally entitled to the favour and protection of the Government."[34] Parr was not swayed by those claiming social privilege, and strictly adhered to the instructions he received from London. All heads of households received 40 hectares of land and an additional 20 hectares for each family member; only discharged officers who had served during the War of Independence received larger land grants according to their rank.

Many Loyalists soon became disillusioned with "Nova Scarcity," as they bitterly referred to their new home. "All our golden promises have vanished," one Loyalist lamented. "We were taught to believe this place was not barren and foggy, as had been represented, but we find it ten times worse…. It is the most inhospitable climate that ever mortal set foot on. The winter is of insupportable length and coldness, only a few spots fit to cultivate, and the land is covered with a cold, spongy moss instead of grass, and the entire country is wrapt in the gloom of perpetual fog."[35] The plight of the Shelburne Loyalists was especially miserable. Governor Parr confidently predicted that Shelburne would soon surpass Halifax in importance. Although Shelburne boasted an excellent harbour, the rocky countryside was ill-suited to farming, and within a few years the town was all but abandoned. Many of the Shelburne Loyalists returned to their former homes in the new republic; others sold their land and attempted to start over yet again elsewhere in the province.

The Envy of the American States

The nearly 15 000 Loyalists who settled along the Saint John River valley and on the north shore of the Bay of Fundy fared better. Here at least the soils were fertile, but bitterness and dissension set in nonetheless as Loyalists bickered among themselves over the distribution of land and supplies, and jockeyed for political power and social prominence. The one thing that united these Loyalists was a general disaffection with the authorities in Halifax and the desire to create a separate Loyalist province. "Take the general map of this province," Edward Winslow wrote to Ward Chipman in July 1783, and "observe how detached this part is from the rest—how vastly extensive it is…. Consider the numberless inconveniences that must arise from its remoteness from the Metropolis [Halifax] & the difficulty of communication. Think what multitudes have & will come here—and then judge whether it must not from the nature of things immediately become a separate government, and if it does it shall be the most Gentlemanlike one on earth."[36] Anxious to quell Loyalist discontent and to create positions for former officeholders displaced by the American Revolution, the British government agreed to the partition of Nova Scotia and created the new colony of New Brunswick on June 18, 1784. To members of the Loyalist elite, such as Edward Winslow and Ward Chipman, New Brunswick was soon to become a model of order and hierarchy and the "envy" of the rebellious American states, proving to all that the Loyalists' sacrifice had not been in vain.

Few concessions were made to the Aboriginal peoples and Acadians already living in the area when the Loyalists arrived. Many years earlier, in 1760, as the British neared victory in the Seven Years War, Britain had concluded a treaty of peace and friendship at Halifax with the Mi'kmaq. It was clear that no further help from the French could be anticipated, and it would be easy to conclude that the Mi'kmaq concluded this agreement as defeated allies.

June 18, 1784: Nova Scotia is divided and the Loyalist province of New Brunswick is created.

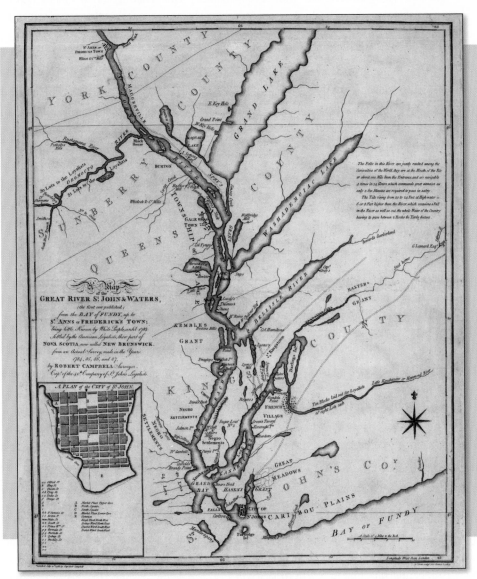

Map 5.4
A Map of the Saint John River from the Bay of Fundy to Frederick's Town, circa 1787.

Source: Library and Archives Canada, NMC-254.

Yet historian William Wicken emphasizes the essential continuity between this treaty and that negotiated between the British and Mi'kmaq in 1726 (see Chapter 3). There had been a number of earlier renewals of the 1726 treaty. Wicken describes Britain's control of North America in the spring of 1760 as still tenuous, and asserts that "the British were unable to impose their law on the Mi'kmaq, or to make them live as if they were the king's subjects."[37]

These eighteenth-century treaties underwent close scrutiny in 1999 when Canada's Supreme Court considered the case of Donald Marshall, Jr., who had been charged with catching eels out of season and selling them without a licence. The court ruled that Marshall, a Mi'kmaq, had a treaty right to catch and sell fish. As a teenager, Marshall had already been wrongfully convicted of murder and had spent 11 years in prison. The high profile of that dramatic case is eclipsed, however, by the longer-term significance of the 1999 Supreme Court ruling. The court's recognition of the Mi'kmaq right to fish for a moderate livelihood—that is, beyond mere subsistence—opens the door to other court challenges. Yet the salient point is that the integrity of the treaties was upheld by the court. Justice Binnie explained: "I accept as inherent in these treaties that the British recognized and accepted the existing Mi'kmaq way of life."[38]

With the influx of Loyalists to the Maritimes, British authorities did not uniformly recognize Aboriginal title to the land. Rather than purchase the land or negotiate land cessions through treaty (the practice defined by the Royal Proclamation of 1763), British authorities simply issued "licenses of occupation" to the Natives with respect to sites they inhabited. These licences had little legal weight and failed to stop the Loyalists from occupying the fertile valley of the Saint John River and forcing the Natives off their traditional lands. Nor did the Loyalists recognize the claims of Acadians who had returned from exile and settled along the lower Saint John. The region's Acadians were compelled to relocate far upriver to Madawaska, or joined others along the northeast coast, far removed from the main centres of Loyalist settlement.

African-American Loyalists

Nearly 3500 African Americans were among the 35 000 Loyalists who settled in Nova Scotia. During the War of Independence, the commander-in-chief of the British forces, Sir Henry Clinton, promised freedom and security to any slaves who deserted their rebel masters and joined with the British. Such a policy, it was hoped, would provide the British with additional soldiers and labourers, and upset the rebel cause by disrupting the economy and provoking a slave rebellion. Although a widespread slave uprising never occurred, thousands of slaves did seek refuge behind British lines and fought their own "war of independence" for freedom, justice, and equality as members of black regiments.

Military considerations, rather than opposition to slavery, lay behind Clinton's policy, and little thought seems to have been given to what would happen to freed slaves when the war ended. After the British defeat at Yorktown, freed slaves flocked to New York where they joined thousands of other Loyalists seeking refuge and safe passage. During the peace talks, American negotiators insisted that all confiscated property, including slaves, be returned. Responsibility for overseeing the evacuation of British troops and Loyalist refugees from New York fell to Sir Guy Carleton, who succeeded Clinton as British commander-in-chief in North America in 1782. Carleton reasoned that slaves who had

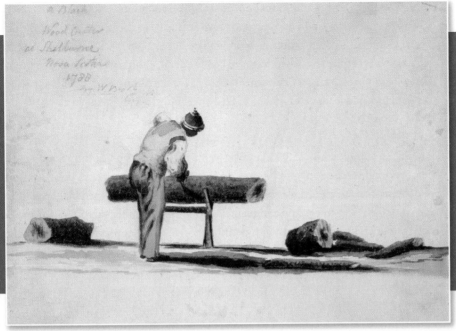

A black labourer at
Shelburne, 1788.

Source: Library and Archives Canada, C-040162.

abandoned their masters and supported the British could not rightly be considered confiscated property. He insisted that Britain honour its promises and evacuate the slaves as free men to Nova Scotia or Britain's colonies in the Caribbean. This decision outraged George Washington and not a few white Loyalists who had slaves of their own.

The largest contingent of black Loyalists settled at Birchtown, across the harbour from Shelburne. For a time, Birchtown was the largest settlement of free blacks anywhere in North America. Freedom, however, did not mean equality. Black Loyalists received fewer provisions and less land than other Loyalists, and became the targets of white hostility. "Great Riot Today," deputy surveyor Benjamin Marston recorded in his diary on July 26, 1784. "The disbanded soldiers have risen against the Free negroes to drive them out of Town, because they labour cheaper than they—the soldiers." Marston's diary for the following day noted: "The soldiers force the free negroes to quit the town—pulled down about 20 of their houses."[39]

1784: Workers in Nova Scotia seek to drive out black competitors in a July 26 riot.

After enduring years of deprivation and discrimination, and after repeated petitions to local authorities for fair treatment, the black Loyalist community dispatched Thomas Peters to London in 1790 to present their grievances directly to the British government. Peters had served as a sergeant with the Black Pioneers during the Revolutionary War and oversaw the settlement of 200 fellow veterans near Digby. In his meetings with British officials, Peters let it be known that black Loyalists were dissatisfied with their lives in Nova Scotia and New Brunswick, and that many were "ready and willing to go wherever the Wisdom of Government may think proper to provide them as free Subjects of the British empire."[40] Secretary of State Henry Dundas sent instructions to Governor Parr to investigate the black Loyalists' complaints, but he also arranged for Peters to meet with directors of the Sierra

1792: Black Loyalists depart Nova Scotia for Sierra Leone.

Leone Company, an organization founded by British abolitionists to establish a colony of free blacks in Africa. Upon his return to Nova Scotia, Peters began to promote the Sierra Leone Company's colonization plan. In January 1792, 1196 black Loyalists sailed from Halifax to begin their lives anew in Sierra Leone. Many of those who left were community leaders—ministers, teachers, craftsmen—leaving the remaining black population without the guidance and leadership needed to challenge injustice and inequality.

Loyalist Discontent and Disappointment in Quebec

Another group of nearly 12 000 Loyalists came to Quebec, significantly increasing that colony's English-speaking population. As in Nova Scotia, discontent, disappointment, and division characterized the settlement process. Loyalists encamped in Quebec during the winter of 1783 constantly complained about their primitive accommodations, and besieged government officials with petitions for supplies and assistance. Exasperated by their "extravagant" demands, the governor of Quebec, Frederick Haldimand, curtly advised the Loyalist refugees that he would find passage for them at the earliest date for Nova Scotia. Disenchanted with conditions, many left the camps, not for Nova Scotia, but to return to their former homes in the new republic to salvage what they could.

Haldimand faced the difficult decision of where to settle those who remained. Fearing undue influence from Americans nearby, Haldimand rejected the area that stretched south of Montreal to the new international boundary. This decision irked the many Loyalists who had travelled overland from New England and upstate New York and were already encamped in the area at Sorel. Sensitive to relations with French Canadians, Haldimand also rejected the largely unsettled seigneuries that stretched immediately west of Montreal along the St. Lawrence. Having eliminated these two areas as options, Haldimand was forced to look further afield to more remote parts of the province. A few Loyalists were directed to the Gaspé, but most were settled in new townships laid out in the wilderness along the upper St. Lawrence from Lake St. Francis to Lake Ontario, around the Bay of Quinte on Lake Ontario, and along the Niagara River.

1784: The Mississauga cede 1.2 million hectares of land to make way for Loyalist settlement.

Before settlement could begin, however, title to the land had to be acquired from the Native population, in keeping with the terms of the Royal Proclamation of 1763. In 1784, the Mississauga ceded 1.2 million hectares of land along the Niagara Peninsula for less than £1200 worth of gifts. Similar agreements followed, extinguishing Native title to most of what is now southern Ontario. In many cases, the exact terms of the agreements were vague and subject to different interpretations—British notions of private property were foreign to Natives who held land communally. While Natives were willing to share their land with the newcomers, they evidently did not intend to give it away forever, nor did they expect the massive influx of settlers that followed.

Relocating thousands of Loyalists to new homes in the wilderness proved difficult. Incomplete surveys, inadequate supplies, and disputes over location tickets, produced widespread bitterness and resentment. Civilian settlers charged that regimental Loyalists received favourable treatment and were allotted the best land. A deliberate policy of settling officers and soldiers of the same regiment together, in order to carry over into civilian life the cohesion and organizational discipline of the military, produced considerable

Encampment of the Loyalists at Johnstown a New Settlement, on the Banks of the River St. Lawrence in Canada...

Source: Library and Archives Canada, C-002001.

Encampment of Loyalists at Johnstown, a new settlement on the banks of the St. Lawrence River in Canada, June 6, 1784.

resentment among the ranks of discharged soldiers. Such were the divisions among the Loyalists that, in the Royal Townships laid out along the St. Lawrence, settlers were divided, at their own request, according to their ethnicity and religion. Many Loyalists arrived on their lots too late in the season to put in crops, and remained dependent on government assistance. Desperate for provisions, some Loyalists sold their location tickets to speculators, ensuring that large tracts of land remained undeveloped for many years to come.

The Six Nations Loyalists

The Loyalists who settled in Quebec included some 2000 Six Nations Iroquois. The majority of Iroquois had sided with the British during the American Revolutionary War. Despite their vital service to the British cause, Iroquois interests were completely ignored during the peace negotiations. The Treaty of Paris did not recognize Iroquois property rights or provide any protection for Britain's Native allies. Joseph Brant felt betrayed. The British had "sold the Indians to Congress," he exclaimed.[41] "We could not believe it possible," Brant complained to the British Home Office, "[that] such firm friends and allies could be so neglected by a nation remarkable for its honor and glory whom we had served with so much zeal and fidelity."[42] Concerned that they might rise up to avenge their poor treatment, Haldimand appealed to the British government to secure a land grant to compensate the Iroquois for their losses. In 1784, Joseph Brant and his followers received a tract of 273 000 hectares along the Grand River purchased from the Mississauga nation. A smaller group of Mohawks who did not wish to submit themselves to Brant's leadership settled on another tract on the Bay of Quinte.

1784: Joseph Brant and Six Nations Loyalists take up a land grant along the Grand River.

Not content to simply start over on the Grand River, Brant attempted immediately after the war's end to organize an alliance between the Iroquois and the western tribes to oppose American expansion. Following the War of Independence, the British continued to occupy western forts on what was now American soil from Oswego to Michilimackinac on the pretext that Americans had not adhered to the terms of the Treaty of Paris and compensated the Loyalists for their losses. More important, the western posts allowed the British to defend Quebec's frontiers, to restore relations with the Native peoples, and to exercise control over the fur trade. For these reasons, the British encouraged Brant's efforts. But Brant had his own reasons: such an alliance, he believed, would strengthen the Iroquois' ability to limit American encroachment on their traditional lands, and increase Iroquois influence with the British.

Brant persisted with his unity plans for a number of years, but the Americans exploited divisions within the confederacy to negotiate treaties with some aboriginal nations and used force to intimidate others into submission. He also experienced difficulties with British authorities. Determined to exercise Iroquois sovereignty and profit from incoming settlers, Brant maintained that the Six Nations could sell or lease their lands to whomever they chose. British officials insisted that the Six Nations were subjects of the Crown and that the government must approve all transactions involving the Grand River lands. Although he was thoroughly committed to maintaining Iroquois independence, Brant was convinced that his people must adapt to British ways if they were to survive. He encouraged the Grand River Iroquois to embrace Christianity, to seek an education, and to become farmers. Brant himself lived a genteel lifestyle in a grand manor and owned several slaves.

Division and Duality: The Creation of Upper and Lower Canada

Having fought and suffered to uphold the British constitution and to preserve the British Empire, the Loyalists who settled in Quebec were unwilling to now be subject to French civil law and the seigneurial system. Insisting that they were entitled to live under British institutions, and not the plan set out under the 1774 *Quebec Act*, the Loyalists petitioned the British Parliament in 1785 to demand the establishment of English law and a representative assembly. "The inhabitants of this territory," the petitioners protested, "were born British subjects, and have ever been accustomed to the government and laws of England. It was to restore that government, and to be restored to those laws, for which from husbandmen they became soldiers, animated with the hope … that should they fail in their attempts to recover

Portrait of Sir Guy Carleton, Lord Dorchester.
Source: © McCord Museum, M2459.

their former habitations by a restoration of Your Majesty's government, they would still find a resource in some parts of the British dominions, where they might enjoy the blessings of British laws and of British government."[43] Convinced that the Loyalists would never amount to a large part of the population, Frederick Haldimand opposed the repeal of the *Quebec Act* and the establishment of an elected assembly. These views were shared by Sir Guy Carleton (who was now Lord Dorchester), who returned to Quebec in 1786 to take up the office of governor once more.

Dorchester found himself caught between Loyalist demands for change and the commitments made to the French-Canadian majority in the *Quebec Act*. Suspicious of representative government, Dorchester advised British authorities against establishing an elected assembly. He did recommend, however, the creation of four administrative districts, each with its own courts, in the western part of the province, which was beginning to attract many settlers from the United States. Drawn more by land than by any attachment to the empire, these "late Loyalists" greatly increased the population of the western districts. Historian James J. Talman pronounced the frequently used term "late Loyalist" absurd. "If a man was 'late' he was not a Loyalist," he argued.[44] Soon, these newcomers began petitioning for the division of Quebec into two provinces, each with its own assembly. Nova Scotia, Quebec Loyalists pointed out, had already been divided. Dorchester remained resolute and counselled London that partition was not advisable.

Loyalist Myth and Reality

The Loyalists have traditionally been portrayed as a highly principled and well-educated elite who chose to sacrifice comfortable lives and endure the hardships of a northern wilderness rather than submit to the tyranny of democratic republicanism. United by their ideology and suffering, it was claimed that the Loyalists formed a close-knit community characterized by an unwavering fidelity to the British Empire and an intense hatred of all things American. The traditional portrait of the Loyalists as aristocratic imperialists and anti-American anglophiles bears little relationship to the historical reality. The Loyalists were not members of a noble class representing gentle birth, wealth, and learning. Some Loyalists did come from urban centres such as New York, Boston, and Charleston, where they were part of the governing Anglican establishment, but many more were farmers, artisans, labourers, and merchants of modest means. In a report to the Loyalist Claims Commission in 1786, the administrator of Quebec, Henry Hope, observed that the Loyalists were "chiefly landholders, farmers and others from the inland part of the continent" and that there were few "persons of great property or consequence" among them.[45]

The Loyalists came from a wide range of ethnic and religious backgrounds. Their ranks included Dutch Calvinists, German Lutherans, French Huguenots, Swiss Mennonites, Scottish Catholics, and Quaker pacifists. Loyalty, moreover, was often a product of mixed motives. While some Loyalists were undoubtedly motivated by a sincere commitment to the idea of the Empire and the principles of the British constitution, the motives of many were decidedly mixed. Loyalty was often a product of patronage and commercial ties; many Loyalists were officeholders or employees or suppliers of the British military or the Indian Department. Others were merely opportunists who pledged allegiance to whichever side happened to be in ascendance locally. Still others were reluctant Loyalists who only took sides when forced out of a preferred state of neutrality by Rebel harassment or Tory intimidation. The motives of the Loyalist refugees did not impress Frederick Haldimand's secretary, Robert Mathews. Most of the refugees, Mathews asserted, were "in fact only Mechanics [manual workers] ... removed from one situation to practice their Trades in another."[46]

The Loyalists did not comprise the united and cooperative community dedicated to the collective good idealized by later generations. Discontent, disappointment, and division dominated the settlement process. Nor is it true that the Loyalists venerated all things British and detested all things American. A rather cantankerous lot, the Loyalists were quick to criticize the policies of the British government and demanded the creation of the same type of public institutions they had experienced in the American colonies. As for the Loyalists' supposed anti-Americanism, contemporary observers noted that hostility quickly subsided as personal ties were renewed and new commercial relationships forged.

Where then did the myths and traditions surrounding the Loyalists originate? Historians have played a large part in perpetuating the Loyalist tradition. During the tumultuous 1960s, for example, historian S.F. Wise argued that the arrival of the Loyalists set the foundation for a distinctive identity that differentiated Canada from the United States. According to Wise, the Loyalists were determined to establish and maintain "a counterrevolutionary society on the borders of a revolutionary one. The sheer hatred of those who lost property, suffered indignities, lost members of their families, lost their homeland, lost the war," Wise contended, "congealed into permanence" and accounts for the development of English Canada in a conservative direction. The Loyalists' conservatism "did not simply mean adherence to Crown and Empire"; it "meant as well adherence to those beliefs and institutions the conservative considered essential in the preservation of a form of life different from, and superior to, the manners, politics, and social arrangements of the United States."[47]

Such sweeping conclusions about the Loyalists' state of mind and the continuing impact of their ideas are fraught with difficulties. To suggest that the Loyalists are responsible for a Canadian preference for "peace, order, and good government" and evolutionary change, over an American emphasis on "life, liberty, and the pursuit of happiness" and revolution, ignores the fact that remarkably little is known about the ideological convictions of the Loyalists, and the few fragments of evidence that do exist can be used to come to quite different conclusions. To ascribe the views of an articulate few to the Loyalist rank and file risks creating a coherent pattern of thought that would have been unrecognizable at the time. There is little doubt that the Loyalist migration, as the first large scale influx of English-speaking settlers, changed the direction of Canada's development, but to credit the Loyalists with establishing a distinct English-Canadian identity overstates the case.

Historian Norman Knowles argues that the Loyalist tradition was invented in the century following the Loyalists' arrival by a variety of different groups who sought to construct usable pasts to further particular interests and causes. These groups included Loyalist settlers themselves intent on furthering claims to compensation and maintaining their social status and political influence, filiopietistic descendants seeking to honour their ancestors and to share in their accomplishments, nationalists and educators determined to produce an inspiring and unifying official history, and imperialists promoting closer ties between Canada and the British Empire. The Loyalist tradition peaked in the aftermath of the 1884 Loyalist centennial celebrations, when the changes accompanying urbanization and industrialization created both a sense of anxiety about the present and nostalgia for a simpler, more stable past. The influence of the Loyalist tradition declined in the years following the First World War, as ties to the Empire weakened, anti-American sentiment waned, and the middle class embraced an ethic of progress and development.

Conclusion

In 1791, British North America consisted of seven colonies: Newfoundland, Nova Scotia, New Brunswick, Prince Edward Island, Cape Breton, Lower Canada, and Upper Canada, and a vast western domain under the control of the Hudson's Bay Company. Each of these colonies was populated by a diverse collection of peoples and had its own distinct character and history. Newly established colonies such as Upper Canada and New Brunswick were peopled largely by Loyalist newcomers, who were only beginning to establish themselves. Others, such as Lower Canada and Newfoundland, already had long histories and well-defined cultures.

Everywhere different cultures and races, languages and lifestyles coexisted, resulting in remarkably complex societies. The colonies shared little in common beyond their ties to Britain, manifest locally through the authority of Crown-appointed governors. In the absence of any central body to encourage unity, each of the colonies developed more or less independently of the others. Economically, British North America developed within a mercantilist framework that valued colonies as markets for the manufactured goods of the mother country and suppliers of needed raw materials. The result was the emergence of societies of primary producers subject to a high degree of external ownership and control, and extremely vulnerable to vagaries of the market. While the American Revolution had bonded disparate colonies into one nation, British North America developed as a collection of distinct societies that, for the most part, remained politically and economically isolated from each other.

Questions to Consider

1. How do you account for the changes in British policy towards the Native peoples and the Canadiens from the 1763 Treaty of Paris to the outbreak of the American Revolution?

2. Identify some key historiographical interpretations of the impact of the conquest.

3. In what ways was the American Revolution a civil war?

4. Compare the motivations and objectives of Six Nations, African, and other American Loyalists.

Critical Thinking Questions

1. Why might a resurgent nationalism in Quebec in the 1960s and 1970s produce new historical interpretations of the impact of the conquest?

2. Why did Nova Scotia and Quebec not join in the American Revolution?

3. What were the immediate and long-term consequences of the arrival of the Loyalists on the development of British North America?

Suggested Readings

British Rule and Native Resistance

Cave, Alfred A. "The Delaware Prophet Neolin: A Reappraisal." *Ethnohistory* 46 (Spring 1999): 265–290.

Dixon, David. *Never Come to Peace Again: Pontiac's Uprising and the Fate of the British Empire in North America.* Norman: University of Oklahoma Press, 2005.

Dowd, Gregory Evans. "The French King Wakes Up in Detroit: 'Pontiac's War' in Rumor and History." *Ethnohistory* 37 (Summer 1990): 254–278.

Dowd, Gregory Evans. *War under Heaven: Pontiac, the Indian Nations and the British Empire.* Baltimore: Johns Hopkins University Press, 2002.

Fenn, Elizabeth, A. "Biological Warfare in Eighteenth-Century North America: Beyond Jeffery Amherst." *The Journal of American History* 86 (March 2000): 1552–1580.

Jennings, Francis. *Empire of Fortune: Crowns, Colonies and Tribes in the Seven Years War in America.* New York: Norton, 1988.

White, Richard. *The Middle Ground: Indians, Empires and Republics in the Great Lakes Region, 1650–1815.* Cambridge: Cambridge University Press, 1991.

British Policy and Quebec

Brunet, Michel. *Les Canadiens après la conquête 1759–1775: De la revolution américaine.* Montreal: Fides, 1969.

Burt, A.L. *The Old Province of Quebec.* Toronto: McClelland & Stewart, 1968.

Creighton, Donald. *The Empire of the St. Lawrence: A Study in Commerce and Politics.* Toronto: Macmillan, 1956.

Greer, Allan. *Peasant, Lord and Merchant: Rural Society in Three Quebec Parishes, 1740–1840.* Toronto: University of Toronto Press, 1985.

Hamelin, Jean. *Economie et Société en Nouvelle-France.* Quebec: University of Laval Press, 1960.

Igartua, José. "A Change in Climate: The Conquest and the Marchands of Montreal," Canadian Historical Association, *Historical Papers* (1974), 115–134.

Lawson, Philip. "'Sapped by Corruption': British Governance of Quebec and the Breakdown of Anglo-American Relations on the Eve of the Revolution," *Canadian Review of American Studies* 22, 3 (Winter 1991): 301–324.

Mann, Susan. *The Dream of Nation. A Social and Intellectual History of Quebec.* Second edition. Montreal and Kingston: McGill-Queen's University Press, 2002.

Neatby, Hilda. *Quebec: The Revolutionary Age, 1760–1791* Toronto: McClelland & Stewart, 1966.

Ouellet, Fernand. *Economic and Social History of Quebec, 1760–1850.* Toronto: Macmillan, 1980.

Quebec and the American Revolution

Hatch, Robert McConnell. *Thrust for Canada: The American Attempt on Quebec, 1775–1776.* Boston: Houghton Mifflin, 1979.

Lawson, Philip. *The Imperial Challenge: Quebec and Britain in the Age of the American Revolution.* Montreal and Kingston: McGill-Queen's University Press, 1989.

Stanley, George F.G. *Canada Invaded: 1775–1776.* Toronto: Hackert, 1973.

Nova Scotia and the American Revolution

Brebner, J.B. *The Neutral Yankees of Nova Scotia.* Toronto: McClelland & Stewart, 1969 [1937].

Clark, Ernest. *The Siege of Fort Cumberland, 1776: An Episode in the American Revolution.* Montreal and Kingston: McGill-Queen's University Press, 1995.

Conrad, Margaret. *They Planted Well: New England Planters in Maritime Canada.* Fredericton: Acadiensis Press, 1988.

Mancke, Elizabeth. *The Fault Lines of Empire: Political Differentiation in Massachusetts and Nova Scotia, 1760–1830.* New York: Routledge, 2005.

McNutt, W.S. *The Atlantic Provinces: The Emergence of Colonial Society, 1712–1857.* Toronto: McClelland & Stewart, 1965.

Rawlyk, G.A. *Nova Scotia's Massachusetts: A Study of Nova Scotia-Massachusetts Relations, 1630 to 1784.* Montreal and Kingston: McGill-Queen's University Press, 1973.

Rawlyk, G.A. *Ravished by the Spirit: Religious Revivals, Baptists and Henry Alline.* Montreal and Kingston: McGill-Queen's University Press, 1984.

Stewart, G., and G.A. Rawlyk. *A People Highly Favoured of God: The Nova Scotia Yankees and the American Revolution.* Toronto: Macmillan, 1972.

The Iroquois and the American Revolution

Calloway, Colin. *The American Revolution in Indian Country: Crisis and Diversity in Native American's Communities.* Cambridge: Cambridge University Press, 1995.

Graymont, Barbara. *The Iroquois in the American Revolution.* Syracuse: Syracuse University Press, 1972.

Kelsay, Isabel Thompson. *Joseph Brant, 1743–1807: Man of Two Worlds.* Syracuse: Syracuse University Press, 1984.

Taylor, Alan. *The Divided Ground: Indians, Settlers and the Northern Borderland of the American Revolution.* New York: Vintage, 2007.

White, Richard. *The Middle Ground: Indians, Empires and Republics in the Great Lakes Region. 1650–1815.* Cambridge: Cambridge University Press, 1991.

The Loyalists

Allan, Robert, ed. *The Loyal Americans: The Military Role of the Loyalist Provincial Corps and Their Settlement in British North America.* Ottawa: National Museum of Man, 1983.

Bell, D.G. *Early Loyalist Saint John: The Origin of New Brunswick Politics, 1783–1786.* Fredericton: New Ireland Press, 1983.

Brown, Wallace. *The King's Friends: The Composition and Motives of the American Loyalist Claimants.* Providence: Brown University Press, 1965.

Brown, Wallace, and Hereward Senior. *Victorious in Defeat: The Loyalists in Canada.* Toronto: Methuen, 1984.

Condon, Ann Gorman. *The Envy of the American States: The Loyalist Dream for New Brunswick.* Fredericton: New Ireland Press, 1984.

Knowles, Norman. *Inventing the Loyalists: The Ontario Loyalist Tradition and the Creation of Usable Pasts.* Toronto: University of Toronto Press, 1997.

MacKinnon, Neil. *This Unfriendly Soil: The Loyalist Experience in Nova Scotia, 1783–1791.* Montreal and Kingston: McGill-Queen's University Press, 1986.

Marshall, Peter. "Americans in Upper Canada, 1791–1812: 'Late Loyalists' or Early Immigrants?" *Canadian Migration Patterns from Britain and North America.* Barbara J. Messamore, ed. Ottawa: University of Ottawa Press, 2004.

Moore, Christopher. *The Loyalists: Revolution, Exile, Settlement.* Toronto: Macmillan, 1984.

Potter, Janice. *The Liberty We Seek: Loyalist Ideology in Colonial New York and Massachusetts.* Cambridge: Harvard University Press, 1983.

Potter-MacKinnon, Janice. *While the Women Only Wept: Loyalist Refugee Women in Eastern Ontario.* Montreal and Kingston: McGill-Queen's University Press, 1993.

Walker, James W. St. G. *The Black Loyalists: The Search for a Promised Land in Nova Scotia and Sierra Leone, 1783–1870.* Toronto: University of Toronto Press, 1992.

Notes

[1] W.O. Raymond, ed., *Winslow Papers* (New Brunswick Historical Society: 1901), 65.

[2] Sarah Winslow to Benjamin Marston, 10 April 1763, *Winslow Family Papers*, vol. 2, 67.

[3] *Winslow Papers*, 82–83.

[4] Winslow to Ward Chipman, 7 July 1783, *Winslow Family Papers*, vol. 2, 104

[5] As quoted by Gregory Evans Dowd, *War Under Heaven: Pontiac, the Indian Nations, & the British Empire* (Baltimore: Johns Hopkins University Press, 2002), 71.

[6] Alexander Henry, *Travels and Adventures in Canada and the Indian Territories between the Years 1760 and 1766* (New York: I. Riley, 1809), 44.

[7] Anthony F.C. Wallace, *The Death and Rebirth of the Seneca* (New York: Alfred A. Knopf, 1970), 118.

[8] As quoted by J.R. Miller, *Skyscrapers Hide the Heavens: A History of Indian–White Relations in Canada* (Toronto: University of Toronto Press, 1989), 74.

[9] Gregory Evans Dowd, *War Under Heaven,* 89.

[10] Francis Jennings, *Empire of Fortune: Crowns, Colonies and Tribes in the Seven Years War in America* (New York: W.W. Norton, 1988), 447–448; David Dixon, Never Come to Peace Again: Pontiac's Uprising and the Fate of the British Empire in British North America, 1754–1766 (Norman: University of Oklahoma Press, 2005), 154; Michael N. McConnell, *A Country Between: The Upper Ohio and its Peoples, 1724–1774* (Lincoln: University of Nebraska Press, 1992), 195.

[11] The Royal Proclamation of 1763 may be read at http://www.canadiana.org/view/42695/0030.

[12] Francis Parkman, *The Old Régime in Canada,* Vol. 2 (Toronto: George Morang, 1899), 204–205.

[13] Francis Maseres, Report, in J.H. Stewart Reid, Kenneth McNaught and Harry S. Crowe, *A Source-book of Canadian History: Selected Documents and Personal Papers* (Toronto: Longmans, Green and Company, 1959), 52.

[14] Instructions to Governor James Murray, 1763 in Reid, *Source-book of Canadian History,* 50.

[15] As quoted by André Vachon, "Jean-Olivier Briand" Dictionary of Canadian Biography. Online at http://www.biographi.ca. The biblical passage to which Briand referred is from Paul's Epistles to the Romans, 13: 1–7.

[16] For a broader discussion of class and race in the British Empire, see David Cannadine, *Ornamentalism: How the British Saw their Empire* (Oxford: Oxford University Press 2001), 3–10.

[17] Merchant's Petition and James Murray's response, 1764, in Reid, *Source-book of Canadian History,* 51–52

[18] Sir Guy Carleton, in Reid, *Source-book of Canadian History,* 54.

[19] *Quebec during the American Revolution: The Journals of François Baby, Gabriel Taschereau and Jenkin Williams.* Michael P. Gabriel, ed. Translated by S. Pascale Vergereau-Dewey (Ann Arbor: Michigan State University Press, 2005).

[20] As quoted in Philip Lawson, "'Sapped by Corruption': British Governance of Quebec and the Breakdown of Anglo-American Relations on the Eve of the Revolution," *Canadian Review of American Studies* 22, 3 (Winter 1991): 301–324.

21 The *Quebec Act*, 1774, may be read at http://www.canadiana.org/view/48786/5.

22 As quoted by Edmund S. Morgan and Helen M. Morgan, *The Stamp Act crisis: Prologue to Revolution* (Chapel Hill: University of North Carolina Press, 1995), 69.

23 George Washington to Bryan Fairfax, 24 August 1774, Papers of George Washington, http://gwpapers. virginia.edu/documents/revolution/letters/bfairfax3.html.

24 *Manifesto to the People of the Province of Quebec* in Reid, *Source-book of Canadian History*, 59–60.

25 Ralph Waldo Emerson, "Concord Hymn," *Poems*, Vol. 9 (Boston: Houghton-Mifflin, 1854). The poem was composed to commemorate the Concord battle site on July 4, 1837.

26 Quoted in G.F.G. Stanley, *Canada Invaded, 1775–1776* (Toronto: Hackert, 1973).

27 As quoted by Stuart R. J. Sutherland, "Richard Montgomery" *Dictionary of Canadian Biography*, http://www.biographi.ca.

28 Instructions and Commission from Congress to Benjamin Franklin, Charles Carroll and Samuel Chase for the Canadian Mission, Congress, 20 March 1776, Franklin papers.

29 As quoted by J.M. Bumsted, "Francis Legge," *Dictionary of Canadian Biography,* http://www.biographi.ca.

30 Henry Alline, *Life and Journal* (Boston: 1806), 34–35.

31 A letter from Elizabeth Bowman Spohn to Egerton Ryerson, 23 July 1861, in J.J. Talman, *Loyalist Narratives from Upper Canada* (Toronto: Champlain Society, 1946), 316–317.

32 As quoted by Barbara Graymont, "Thayendanegea (Joseph Brant)," *Dictionary of Canadian Biography*, http://www.biographi.ca.

33 As quoted by Stuart R.J. Sutherland, Pierre Tousignant and Madeleine Dionne-Tousignant in "Sir Frederick Haldimand," *Dictionary of Canadian Biography*, http://www.biographi.ca.

34 "Vindication of Governor Parr and his Council against the Complaints of certain Persons who sought to Engross 275,000 Acres of Land in Nova Scotia, at the Expense of the Government, and to the great Prejudice of the Province and Loyalists in General," in L.F.S. Upton, *The United Empire Loyalists: Men and Myths* (Toronto: Copp Clark, 1967), 69.

35 Quoted in Neil Mackinnon, *This Unfriendly Soil: The Loyalist Experience in Nova Scotia, 1783–1791* (Montreal and Kingston: McGill-Queen's University Press, 1986), 69.

36 Edward Winslow to Ward Chipman, 7 July 1783, *Winslow Family Papers*, vol. 2, 104.

37 William Wicken, *Mi'kmaq Treaties on Trial: History, Land, and Donald Marshall Junior* (Toronto: University of Toronto Press, 2002), 191.

38 As quoted in Ken Coates, *The Marshall Decision and Native Rights: The Marshall Decision and Mi'kmaq Rights in the Maritimes* (Montreal and Kingston: McGill-Queen's University Press, 2000), 10.

39 As quoted by James W. St. G. Walker, *The Black Loyalists: The Search for a Promised Land in Nova Scotia and Sierra Leone, 1783–1870* (Toronto: University of Toronto Press, 1992), 48.

40 As quoted by James W. St. G. Walker, "Thomas Peters," *Dictionary of Canadian Biography*, http://www.biographi.ca.

41 As quoted by Barbara Graymont, "Thayendanegea (Joseph Brant)" in *Dictionary of Canadian Biography*, http://www.biographi.ca.

42 As quoted by William L. Stone, *Life of Joseph Brant-Thayendanegea* (New York: A.V. Blake, 1838), 253–254.

43 "Petition of Sir John Johnson, Bart. and others in Behalf of the Loyalists settled in Canada, 11 April 1785," in A. Shortt and A.G Doughty, eds. *Documents Relating to the Constitutional History of Canada, 1759–1791*, Vol. 2 (Ottawa: J. de L Tache, 1918), 775, http://www.canadiana.org/view/9_03425/0003.

44 As quoted by Peter Marshall, "Americans in Upper Canada, 1791–1812: 'Late Loyalist' or Early Immigrants? *Canadian Migration Patterns from Britain and North America*, Barbara J. Messamore, ed. (Ottawa: University of Ottawa Press, 2004), 33.

45 Quoted in A.L. Burt, *The Old Province of Quebec*, vol. II, (Toronto: McClelland & Stewart, 1868), 79.

46 Major Robert Mathews to Stephan Delancey, 15 April 1784 in Ernest Cruikshank, ed., *The Settlement of the United Empire Loyalists on the Upper St. Lawrence and the Bay of Quinte in 1784: A Documentary History* (Toronto, 1934), 67.

47 S.F. Wise, "The Origins of Anti-Americanism in Canada," *Fourth Seminar on Canadian–American Relations* (*Windsor*, 1962), 300–301 and "Upper Canada and the Conservative Tradition," Edith Frith, ed., *Profiles of a Province: Studies in the History of Ontario* (Toronto, 1968), 20, 31.

6

A Contest *of* Identities: British North America: *1770–1815*

*I*n 1799, 21-year-old Daniel Harmon left home to seek a life of adventure in the fur trade. His Vermont family were Congregational puritans, and as Harmon travelled throughout the northwest, he would struggle to remain true to the austere piety of his early life. He was engaged as a clerk by the North West Company, was sent to Fort Alexandria on the Assiniboine River, and began in 1800 to keep a daily journal to record his frontier experiences. Despite initial apprehensions, he soon developed an admiration for the Native peoples of the west: "We met with more real politeness than is often shown to strangers in the civilized part of the world, and much more than I had expected to meet with from savages, as the Indians are generally called, but I think wrongfully."

Native hospitality contrasted sharply with the violence between rival traders. "This jarring of interests," Harmon complained, "keeps up continual misunderstandings, and occasions frequent broils between the contending parties…. Here a murderer escapes the Gallows, as there are no human laws that can reach or have any effect on the People of this Country." Most traders with the North West Company engaged in relationships with local Aboriginal women for companionship. These "country marriages" helped to cement trading alliances, offered practical assistance on fur trading expeditions, and provided relief from the isolation and loneliness of fur trade life. In 1802, a Cree chief offered Harmon one of his daughters. "He pressed me to keep her," Harmon confided in his journal, "and he almost persuaded me to accept her, for I was sure that while I had the daughter, I should not only have the father's hunts, but those of his relations also." But Harmon resisted the temptation: "Thanks be to God alone, if I have not been brought into a snare laid no doubt by the Devil himself."

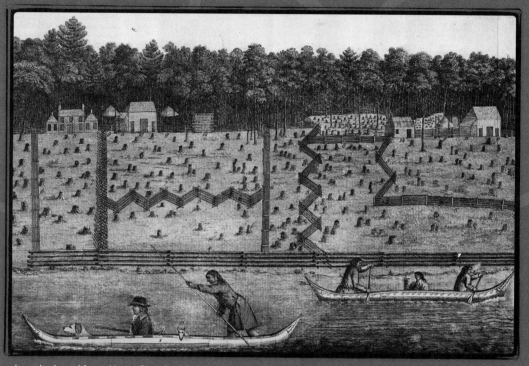

chapter 6

A newly cleared farm, Upper Canada, 1791.

Source: Library and Archives Canada, C-001529.

At last, in 1805, unbearably lonely and with only his books for company, Harmon entered into a country marriage with Lizette Duval, the attractive 14-year-old daughter of a French-Canadian voyageur and a Native mother. Harmon at first viewed the arrangement as temporary. He intended "to keep her as long as I remain in this uncivilized part of the world, but when I return to my native land, I shall endeavour to place her into the hands of some good honest man, with whom she can pass the remainder of her days in this country...."

Over the years, the two had a large family—between 10 to 14 children, although not all of them survived. The young Harmons were raised amid a mixture of English, French, and Cree influences as the family travelled together to fur-trading posts as far west as New Caledonia, beyond the Rocky Mountains in present-day British Columbia. After 19 years in the northwest, Harmon decided to return to Montreal. His conscience would not allow him to follow his earlier plan of leaving his family behind. "How could I spend my days in the civilized world, and leave my beloved children in the wilderness? The thought has in it the bitterness of death. How could I tear them from a mother's love and leave her to mourn over their absence to the day of her death?" Harmon married Lizette in a church wedding, and the family settled together in Montreal.[1]

After reading this chapter you will be able to:

1. Identify British strategies to administer and maintain the loyalty of its North American colonies.
2. Evaluate Lieutenant Governor John Graves Simcoe's efforts to create a "little Britain" in Upper Canada.
3. Assess the conflicting interests and cultures that shaped the economic and political development of Lower Canada.
4. Understand the sources of conflict in the western fur trade and their significance to the Natives and Métis.
5. Explain the British, American, and Native agendas during the War of 1812.

Introduction

The story of Daniel Harmon reveals much about the contest of identities that shaped and defined British North America between 1770 and 1815. This chapter examines the evolution of diverse and distinct societies in the Atlantic colonies after the American Revolution, the economic and political development of Lower Canada, the settlement of Upper Canada and the creation of public institutions, and conflict in the western fur trade and the beginnings of settlement at Red River. The chapter also considers the War of 1812, and the varying agendas of the British, the Americans, and the Aboriginal nations. In addition, it will look at events on the Pacific coast, as Spanish, British, Russian, and American explorers and traders attempted to claim the region for themselves.

The Atlantic Colonies after the American Revolution

Having suffered the loss of their American colonies, British authorities were determined to strengthen their hold over what remained of their other North American possessions. Britain's oldest North American colony, Newfoundland, presented a variety of challenges. Since 1729, the commanding officer of the naval squadron that accompanied the English fishing fleet to Newfoundland each summer had acted as governor. During his absence in the winter months, local justices of the peace attempted to maintain law and order among the small resident population. British authorities valued the colony primarily for its cod fishery, and had little interest in encouraging settlement or establishing the sort of colonial institutions that existed in the agricultural settlements to the south. Historian Jerry Bannister argues that "in strictly official terms, Newfoundland was not a colony, but rather a seasonal station for the migratory fishery operated from England." This does not mean it was a "failed society," as some might view it in looking to the lack of representative political institutions and the absence of social and economic diversity. Bannister maintains that the Royal Navy governors of Newfoundland, relying as they did upon customary and not statute (written) law, provided resilient governance that facilitated state formation, rather than impeding it. "State law in early Newfoundland relied extensively on unwritten law: custom and common law formed the foundation of governance; for most of the eighteenth century, statute law was of secondary importance." This was more widespread in English colonies than is generally supposed, Bannister notes.[2]

The resident population slowly grew in this "naval state." The early settlers consisted mostly of Protestants from southwest England who lived in small outports along the coast, and engaged in the local fishery. Irish Catholics, taken on by the English fishing fleet as extra labour while picking up supplies at Irish ports, often remained behind to engage in the local fishery, or were abandoned by their ships. By the 1770s, Irish Catholics accounted for nearly half of Newfoundland's 10 000 residents, resulting in growing tensions with the older English Protestant community. In fact, in 1762 when the French succeeded in capturing St. John's, near the close of the Seven Years War, the Irish sided with the French against English rule. Tensions also developed between the resident fishery, which enjoyed the advantages of proximity and a longer season, and the overseas fishers favoured by imperial authorities who doubled Newfoundland's population each summer. Relations were often turbulent among the overwhelmingly male population.

During the American Revolution, Newfoundlanders languished from the suspension of trade with New England, which was an important source of provisions and food-stuffs, and the offshore fishery suffered from the predations of American privateers. The population declined as residents fled the colony to escape starvation. The hardships that accompanied the war resulted in a significant restructuring of the Newfoundland economy. New England's trade embargo reoriented Newfoundland's trade to the West Indies, and contributed to the rise of a local shipbuilding industry and an increase in agricultural production. With the disruption of the migratory fishery by privateers, the resident fish-ery emerged as the mainstay of Newfoundland's economy and locals soon outnumbered the seasonal population. In the wake of the American Revolution, British authorities recognized the need to reduce tensions, and in 1784 religious toleration was extended to Roman Catholics and Protestant dissenters from the Church of England. A supreme court for the colony was established in 1791 and civilians joined naval officers as magistrates. Naval rule, however, did not end until 1825, when British authorities introduced a new constitution and appointed a civil governor.

1791: Judicial reform in Newfoundland introduces civilian magistrates and a supreme court.

Unlike Newfoundland, Nova Scotia and New Brunswick were governed by resident governors advised by appointed councils and elected assemblies that could make laws. Divisions between the "native Nova Scotians," who dominated Halifax society and the appointed councils, and Loyalist newcomers elected to the legislative assembly, defined Nova Scotia politics following the American Revolution. To the Loyalists, the old guard were simply Yankees who continued to enjoy the benefits of the British Empire without having endured any of the hardship or sacrifice that real loyalty demanded. To the Halifax elite, the Loyalists were quarrelsome and ungrateful refugees who held dangerous republican ideas. In the elections of 1785, 13 Loyalists were elected to the 39-person assembly. Although a minority, the Loyalist members tended to vote as a bloc, and successfully joined with rep-resentatives from other outlying areas in securing for the assembly the right to introduce money bills and to impeach corrupt and incompetent judges. Loyalist commitment to the cause of reform subsided when a fellow Loyalist, Sir John Wentworth, became governor in 1792. A former governor of New Hampshire, Wentworth was well-practised in the use of patronage, and placed Loyalist friends in his executive council and other administrative positions. This effectively stifled Loyalist opposition, although tensions between town and country continued to characterize Nova Scotia politics up to the War of 1812.

1792: The appointment of Sir John Wentworth as Nova Scotia's governor symbolizes Loyalist ascendancy.

In New Brunswick, Governor Thomas Carleton and a small group of Loyalist founders reigned over the colony's political affairs. A career military officer and the brother of Lord

Dorchester, Carleton shared the vision of Loyalists such as Ward Chipman and Edward Winslow, who sought to create a deferential, well-ordered society governed by a landed gentry that would be free of the faction and democratic excess found in the American states. "It will be best," Carleton insisted, "that the American Spirit of innovation should not be nursed among the Loyal Refugees by the introduction of Acts of Legislature, for purposes for which by the Common Law and the practice of the best regulated colonies, the Crown alone is acknowledged to be competent."[3]

The slow development of the colony—and charges that Carleton favoured a small Loyalist clique—contributed to growing discontent, especially among the merchants of Saint John. Opposition to Carleton and the Loyalist oligarchy was led by James Glenie. A young engineer in the Royal Artillery, Glenie was dispatched to Quebec during the Revolutionary War. Accused of treating the men placed under his command harshly, Glenie was brought before a court martial chaired by Thomas Carleton and found guilty of conduct unbecoming an officer. The ruling was later overturned, and Glenie returned to active duty. After the war, Glenie sought to settle in New Brunswick, and twice petitioned Carleton and the Loyalist-dominated council for large land grants with hopes of raising livestock. Both times he was offered nothing more than the standard 200-acre (80-hectare) grant. With his agrarian ambitions thwarted, Glenie turned to the timber trade and hoped to make his fortune supplying masts to the Royal Navy. Suspicious of commercial interests, Carleton and the council were less than supportive of Glenie and the merchant community emerging at Saint John. Given Glenie's previous history with Carleton and the reception of his land petitions and business operations by the council, it is hardly surprising that he sought a platform in the assembly to criticize Carleton's administration.

1795–1799: New Brunswick's executive and legislature are frequently at odds.

Elected to the assembly in a November 1789 by-election, Glenie led an increasingly bold opposition that attacked the policies of the ruling oligarchy, and championed the interests of pre-Loyalist settlers, the merchants of Saint John, and the growing number of Irish labourers working the colony's lumber camps and fishing grounds. Relations deteriorated, and between 1795 and 1799 there were frequent clashes, as the assembly used its power over money bills to refuse to approve defence expenditures, and the council in turn refused to give assent to other essential financial legislation. Frustrated by the criticism and increasing lack of deference shown by the assembly, Carleton returned to England in 1803. Although he continued as governor until 1817, a Crown-appointed administrator handled New Brunswick's affairs.

After the American Revolution, British authorities sought to maintain a loyal and stable population throughout the Maritime colonies by strengthening the position of the Church of England. The Anglican Church was established as the official Church in Nova Scotia in 1758, the same year that the colony was given representative government. An obligatory tithe to support the Church was also imposed, although Protestant dissenters were exempt. Similarly, the Church of England was established in New Brunswick in 1786, after the creation of the separate colony, and a similar act established the Anglican Church in Prince Edward Island in 1803.

In 1787, Charles Inglis, the loyalist rector of Trinity Church, New York, was appointed bishop of Nova Scotia, with jurisdiction over all of British North America. Inglis, having witnessed both the American and French revolutions, lamented the "times of democratic rage and delusion." He believed that the established church had a role in subduing "restlessness and discontent," and in teaching every individual to be "resigned to the will of God," and thankful for his allotted place in life. "Order," Inglis asserted, is essential to the well-being of every society. "Whenever the sacred law of Order—which indeed is Heaven's first law—wherever this Law is spurned, Confusion and Ruin must necessarily ensue." According to Inglis, the peace and order of society was threatened by "ambitious and self interested" individuals who were not "content with their proper rank in the scale of beings." A product of Enlightenment rationalism, Inglis had nothing but disdain for the emotional and experiential form of Christianity popular among the evangelical dissenters who dominated much of the countryside. The evangelicals' insistence that the humble individual could have a direct and personal relationship with God not only challenged the authority and position of the Church, but threatened the stability of society as a whole. Inglis, who insisted on the primacy of "rational doctrines purveyed by educated minds," attached great importance to the establishment of Anglican institutions of learning.[4] He secured a charter for King's College, Windsor, in 1788 and supported the creation of Fredericton's Academy of Arts and Sciences in 1800.

1788: King's College established in Nova Scotia.

Inglis's vision of a Nova Scotia society shaped by Anglicanism proved difficult to realize among an ethnically and religiously diverse population where Yankee planters, Loyal Americans, and recent immigrants from Scotland and Ireland outnumbered the English, and where Baptists, Methodists, and Roman Catholics were more plentiful than Anglicans. Despite repeated appeals from Inglis, Nova Scotia's assembly refused to vote funds to support the Church of England. In New Brunswick, James Glenie led a lively opposition to the prerogatives and privileges of the Anglican Church, and succeeded in amending the colony's marriage and divorce laws. The Church of England was not legally disestablished, however, until 1851 in Nova Scotia, 1854 in New Brunswick, and 1879 in Prince Edward Island.

In the years following the American Revolution, Nova Scotia, New Brunswick, and Prince Edward Island benefited from the arrival of new immigrants from overseas, who added to the ranks of Loyalists and pre-Revolutionary settlers. Between 1783 and 1812 some 17 000 Highland Scots, many of whom had been displaced by the enclosure of what had previously been common lands, or whose small holdings had been cleared by landlords converting tenant farms to sheep pasture, settled in Cape Breton and the Pictou area of Nova Scotia. Thomas Douglas, the Earl of Selkirk, settled 800 Highlanders from his Scottish estates on Prince Edward Island in 1803, nearly doubling its population.

1783–1812: 17 000 Highland Scots immigrate to Cape Breton.

Despite its rich red soil, Prince Edward Island was thinly populated due to the system of tenancy and absentee proprietorship established by British authorities. The island had been surveyed and divided into 8000-hectare lots in 1763. These estates were then granted to well-connected British men of rank, on the condition that they settle their lands with tenant farmers. Most of the proprietors took little interest in their lands, however, and few settlers wished to pay rent when plenty of freehold land was available elsewhere in British North America.

Highland Scots also added to the Loyalist and Acadian population of New Brunswick. They were recruited as labourers in the Miramichi by Scottish entrepreneurs, who recognized the value of the region's timber and its potential for shipbuilding. Mostly Gaelic-speaking and Roman Catholic, the Highland Scots added to the cultural diversity of the Atlantic colonies. So, too, did a growing number of Irish immigrants. Unlike the later famine migrants, this first wave of Irish settlers consisted mostly of individuals of at least modest means who arrived in the maritime colonies with resources and ambitions intact. Protestant Irish from Ulster frequently became farmers or fishers, and quickly integrated into the larger population. Irish Catholics tended to congregate in the larger ports and towns, where they formed the basis of a nascent working class. Differentiated by their religion and heritage from the Protestant majority, Irish Catholics often became the objects of charity and disdain, and understandably tended to stand apart.

The arrival of hundreds of Yorkshiremen and Presbyterian Lowland Scots further con-tributed to the cultural diversity of the Atlantic colonies. All of these immigrant groups exerted an influence that was perhaps enhanced by the low population densities of the areas into which they arrived. A much greater surge of immigration would further transform the British North American colonies by the mid-nineteenth century.

The *Constitutional Act of 1791* and the Age of Revolution

1791: The colony of Quebec is divided into Upper and Lower Canada.

In Quebec, British authorities faced the challenge of trying to satisfy the demands of Loyalist refugees for a representative assembly and English law, and the determination of the *Canadien* majority to preserve its language and culture. Britain's new colonial secretary, William Grenville, recognized that the demands of the Loyalists could not be ignored. He also understood that the concessions of the *Quebec Act* must be upheld to maintain French-Canadian allegiance. Overriding the opposition of the governor of Quebec, Lord Dorchester, Grenville arranged for an order in council in 1791 that divided Quebec at the boundary of the Ottawa River into two provinces—Upper and Lower Canada.

The *Constitutional Act of 1791*, or *Canada Act*, set out a plan of governance for the two new provinces that would attempt to satisfy the competing claims of *Canadiens* and Loyalists. Under the terms of the *Constitutional Act*, each province was provided with a separate government, each enjoying representative assemblies for the first time. The older and more populous Lower Canada would continue to be presided over by a governor general, and in Upper Canada a lieutenant governor would represent the Crown. Execu-tive councils were appointed to advise the governors; these were invariably drawn from the wealthy and socially prominent of the colony. In addition, each province would have an appointed upper house, or legislative council, with veto power over measures passed in the assembly. Beyond making the concession to representative government to answer the clamour from Loyalist newcomers, it was also understood that an elected assembly would be needed to levy taxes, thus relieving the burden on Britain's treasury.

To be eligible to vote, an individual had to own property or other assets of a specified value. Land was plentiful, however, ensuring a broad electorate. Women who held sufficient property were legally entitled to vote, although custom and social disapproval ensured that few exercised their franchise. Attempts by women, usually propertied widows, to vote were almost always contested by authorities. Members of the elected assemblies were not paid, and, as a result, most elected representatives were those with independent wealth. The

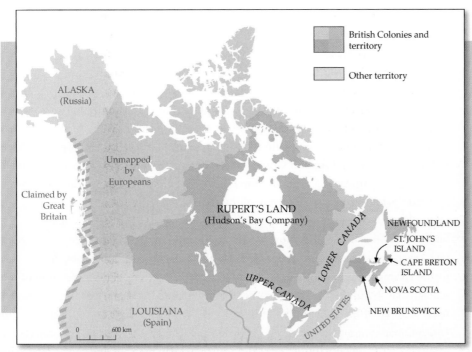

British Colonies and territory

Other territory

ALASKA
(Russia)

Unmapped
by
Europeans

Claimed by
Great
Britain

RUPERT'S LAND
(Hudson's Bay Company)

LOWER CANADA

NEWFOUNDLAND
ST. JOHN'S
ISLAND
CAPE BRETON
ISLAND
NOVA SCOTIA
NEW BRUNSWICK

UPPER CANADA

UNITED STATES

LOUISIANA
(Spain)

0   600 km

Map 6.1
British North America
in 1791.

Source: Map courtesy of Canadian Geographic.

creation of two provinces out of the old colony of Quebec ensured that duality became an entrenched Canadian reality. French civil law, the seigneurial system, and the rights of the Roman Catholic Church were preserved in Lower Canada, and English law and freehold land tenure were established in Upper Canada.

It is noteworthy that, as this bill came up for debate in Britain's houses of Parliament, the French Revolution was raging across the English Channel. The debate over the Constitutional Bill provided British parliamentarians with an opportunity to reflect on the merits of their own constitution at a time when it seemed critically important to defend it. In fact, political scientist Janet Azjenstat explains, "What we have in the 1791 Act is the British Constitution, the famous unwritten constitution itself, in legislative form. The *Constitutional Act, 1791* was to be a declaration about liberal freedoms that would compare well with the American Constitution and the French Declaration of the Rights of Man and Citizen."[5]

The debate in England's House of Commons on that occasion was famous, and led to a tearful rupture between long-time Whig colleagues and friends Charles James Fox and Edmund Burke. Both agreed on the need to avoid democratic tyranny, and to have a balanced constitution, consisting of monarchical, aristocratic, and democratic elements—in Britain, the king, the House of Lords, and the House of Commons—but disagreed about the relative power of each. Fox ridiculed the idea of introducing a hereditary aristocracy in North America: Should "those red and blue ribbons which had lost their lustre in the old world" be resurrected, "to shine forth again in the new?"[6] Burke's views, as expressed during this debate, and in his *Reflections on the Revolution in France* (1790), are often considered the quintessential statement of British conservatism.

1791: British parliamentarians fight a famous debate over the Constitutional Act.

To many conservatives, the Church was an essential safeguard against revolution and an important means to maintain a loyal and stable population. In Lower Canada, the *Constitutional Act* maintained state-enforced tithes to support the Catholic Church. In Upper Canada, the *Constitutional Act* empowered government authorities to appropriate one-seventh of all Crown lands "for the support and maintenance of a Protestant clergy," and to erect and endow within every township "one or more Parsonage or Rectory … according to the establishment of the Church of England."[7] Nonetheless, concerted attempts to make the Anglican faith the official, "established" Church of Upper Canada did not prove successful. John Graves Simcoe, the first lieutenant governor of Upper Canada, was an ardent supporter of church establishment. "All just government," Simcoe asserted, "is founded on the Morality of the People and such morality has no basis but when placed upon religious principles." For this reason, Simcoe was "extremely anxious, both from political as well as more worthy motives that the Church of England should be essentially established in Upper Canada."[8] The cause of church establishment was furthered by the creation of the diocese of Quebec in 1793 and the consecration of the scholarly Jacob Mountain as the first Anglican bishop of Quebec. The privileges accorded to the Church of England in the *Constitutional Act* aroused considerable resentment in Upper Canada among the non-Anglican majority, who resented not only Anglican claims to special status, but also the disruption of settlement and reduced land values created by the setting aside of substantial clergy land reserves.

Land and Loyalty in Upper Canada

John Graves Simcoe, Lieutenant Governor of Upper Canada, 1791–1799.

Source: Library and Archives Canada, C-008111.

Upper Canada's first lieutenant governor, John Graves Simcoe, brought with him high hopes for the colony. Simcoe had served with distinction during the American Revolution as an able field commander of the Queen's Rangers. Following the revolution, he retired to his estate in Britain, married, and was elected to the House of Commons, where he took part in the debate over the *Constitutional Act*. Simcoe aspired to be appointed governor general, but Lord Dorchester secured that position for himself. Simcoe was confident that Upper Canada, as a model of the merits of the imperial system, would demonstrate to Americans the folly of the Revolution and its republican ideas. "It will be with proper and honourable support," he predicted, "the most valuable possession out of the British Isles in population, commerce, and principles of the British Empire."[9] Indeed, Simcoe aimed to create a "little Britain" in Upper Canada. Even the place names he chose reflected this hope: Upper Canada soon had its own York, London, and Thames River.

When he arrived in Upper Canada, Simcoe's first priority was to establish a seat of government. He chose Newark (Niagara-on-the-Lake) as the location for the first legislative assembly. Newark was easily accessible and one of the few settled parts of the province. Simcoe's wife, Elizabeth, was not impressed with his choice, nor with "the miserable, unfinished, damp room, smelling atrociously of fresh paint and wet plaster" in which the assembly met.[10] Newark's location close to the American border made it unsuitable as a permanent capital for the new province. Convinced that war with the Americans was sure to come again, Simcoe set out in search of new and safer site. He believed he had found an ideal location at the forks of the Thames River (formerly La Tranche River) and had plans drawn up for a new capital, London. Although London was sufficiently removed from the American border to be secure, it was isolated from the rest of the province. Simcoe finally selected York (present-day Toronto), with its protected harbour on Lake Ontario, instead.

1793: John Graves Simcoe selects York as the capital of Upper Canada.

Simcoe also turned his attention to the settlement and development of Upper Canada. He ordered the construction a network of roads to link the province's disparate settlements, and to facilitate its defence and economic development, and then set about attracting settlers. Convinced that many Americans were dissatisfied with independence and republican institutions, Simcoe issued a proclamation in 1792 that offered free land grants to lure American settlers to the Upper Canadian wilderness. Among the Americans attracted to Upper Canada were a significant number of pacifist Quakers, Mennonites, and Dunkards, who had antagonized their Patriot neighbours by their refusal to take up arms during the revolution. Although these "late Loyalists" took an oath of allegiance before receiving title to their land grants, land, rather than loyalty, was the main attraction for many of the new settlers. The newcomers soon outnumbered Upper Canada's original Loyalist settlers, greatly reducing their power and influence.

1792: Governor Simcoe grants free land in Upper Canada to Americans willing to swear an oath of allegiance.

To ensure that republican notions of egalitarianism did not take root, Simcoe sought to transplant the "image and transcript of the British constitution" to Upper Canada.[11] This goal attracted criticism from both Loyalists and later arrivals. During the first session of Upper Canada's legislative assembly in 1793, Loyalist Richard Cartwright complained that the lieutenant governor "thinks every existing regulation in England would be proper here" and "seems bent on copying all the subordinate establishments without considering the great disparity of the two countries in every respect." Cartwright insisted that "a government should be formed for a Country and not a country strained and distorted for the Accommodation of a preconceived and speculative scheme of Government."[12] Simcoe, convinced that social and political stability demanded the reproduction of Britain's graduated social order, persisted with his efforts to engineer Upper Canadian society along British lines.

At the top of society, Simcoe envisioned a respectable aristocracy that was the natural governing class. To create such a class, Simcoe granted large tracts of lands to persons he deemed suitable, especially former military officers whose loyalty had been proven by service to the Crown. Although he was suspicious of merchants, Simcoe recognized the need and importance of a commercial class in a developing society, and appointed individuals from this class whom he believed had demonstrated merit, integrity, and ability to the legislative and executive councils. At the base of Simcoe's social order was "a happy yeomanry" of farmers and agricultural workers who knew their place and deferred to the judgment of their social superiors. To achieve the social stability he envisaged, Simcoe believed that all people should have access to a minimal level of education. Upper Canada, however, lacked the resources to implement Simcoe's plan and it would not be until the 1840s that a system of publicly supported common schools began to be implemented. Simcoe's vision of an ordered society never became a reality in Upper Canada. Land was too plentiful and the distance between social ranks too small to sustain a rigidly hierarchical society. Moreover, most settlers were Americans with liberal ideals of independence and social mobility, who chafed at Simcoe's conservative notions of deference and distinction.

Historian Jane Errington offers a balanced view of the Upper Canadian society that evolved in the early nineteenth century. Despite Simcoe's wish to replicate British ideals, and the influx of Loyalists, Upper Canada was a community with a "dual heritage," she explains.[13] The connection to the United States was as strong as the tie to Britain, with American society providing many of the economic models and social and ideological influences. Travellers frequently came to Upper Canada via the United States, and American newspapers, teachers, and ministers were prevalent. Then, as now, many worried about the shaping influence of American culture. Richard Cartwright noted with alarm that itinerant Methodist and Baptist preachers from the United States had "overrun the country." These "deplorable fanatics" were turning Upper Canadians away from the "rationale doctrines of the Church of England" and filling minds with "republican ideas of independence and individual freedom."[14]

Some conscientious British North Americans condemned the pervasiveness of slavery in the United States, and early steps toward abolition in Upper Canada may well be Simcoe's most important legacy. Several hundred slaves were brought to Upper Canada by Loyalists following the American Revolution. Most were employed as field hands in land clearing, or as domestic servants for wealthier families. Even before Simcoe became governor, he favoured abolition, and vowed to implement it: "The principles of the British Constitution do not admit of that slavery which Christianity condemns."[15] Simcoe was outraged when in March 1793, Chloe Cooley, an enslaved girl from Queenston, was beaten by her owner, bound, and sold to an American. Despite his personal opposition to slavery, Simcoe agreed to compromise legislation. He had little choice: six of the 16 members of the legislative assembly, and several members of both the legislative and executive councils, were slave owners determined to protect their property rights. In November 1793, Simcoe gave royal assent to an Act to Prevent the Further Introduction of Slaves. This Act, the first of its kind in the British Empire, permitted slave owners to keep their slaves until death, but prohibited new slaves from entering the province, and freed at age 25 the children born to slaves. Simcoe's progressive views on slavery did not mean that he welcomed immigrants of African descent. In 1794, Simcoe rejected a petition from 19 free blacks who had fought with the British during the American Revolution for a grant of land to establish an all-black settlement on the Niagara peninsula.

Although Simcoe was confident that Upper Canada's "superior, happier and more polished form of government" would convince Americans of the folly of independence, he recognized that the province's proximity to the United States made it vulnerable to American aggression.[16] Britain's policy to secure Upper Canada from the expanding United States depended upon an Indian buffer state in the Ohio Valley. To the Aboriginal nations of the area, this territory had not been won from them by conquest, nor had the British any right to sign it away to the Americans in the 1783 Treaty of Paris. Since this buffer state would in theory protect the frontiers of Upper Canada, it was in Britain's interest to lend some support to Ohio Valley Aboriginal nations in their quest to prevent American encroachment; such support, if overt, would likely provoke the Americans.

1793: An Act to Prevent the Further Introduction of Slaves is passed in Upper Canada.

Britain's diplomacy in the years after 1783 walked a precarious tightrope. "Since the Indian defence of the Ohio Valley was so intrinsically entwined with the survival of Canada," historian Robert Allen explains, "the British naturally and readily provided the necessaries to assist the chiefs and warriors." In late 1785, Secretary of State Lord Sydney met with Joseph Brant, who represented a Native confederacy, and vaguely assured him that His Majesty would be "at all times ready to attend to their future welfare." Nevertheless, Sydney privately warned colonial officials that any assistance should not be open; neither, however, should the tribes be left "to the mercy of the Americans, as from motives of resentment it is not unlikely that they might hereafter be led to interrupt the Peace and Prosperity of the Province."[17] Britain maintained a string of frontier garrisons at Niagara, Detroit, and Michilimackinac, in contravention of the terms of the 1783 treaty, on the grounds that the United States was also in violation by failing to compensate Loyalists and pay British creditors.

Open clashes between Britain's Aboriginal allies and Americans would threaten this carefully balanced diplomatic position. In November 1791, a Native force led by Little Turtle (Michikinikwa) of the Miami nation dealt a humiliating defeat to the American army in a battle on the Wabash River. But the Natives were becoming impatient with the limited support Britain was offering. If they were truly of one mind, some Algonquian chiefs demanded, "You will now give some proof of it."[18] In early 1794, Lord Dorchester told an Aboriginal delegation at Quebec that he would be very surprised if Britain was not at war with the United States within the year. To the delight of the Aboriginal allies, he followed up on this by advising Simcoe to construct a new fort, Fort Miami, on the Maumee River, at the south-western tip of Lake Erie, south of Detroit.

The Americans responded by sending a hero of the Revolutionary War, Major General "Mad Anthony" Wayne, to quell the Native resistance once and for all and to expel the British from Fort Miami. Convinced that Wayne would attack Upper Canada and fearing that "my character as a military officer must suffer in the extreme" if the province were lost, Simcoe set out for Detroit "with all the force I can muster."[19] On August 20, 1794, Wayne came upon a large party of Natives at Fallen Timbers—warriors from the Shawnee, Mingo, Delaware, Wyandot, Miami, Ottawa, Ojibwe, and Pottawatomie nations. In contrast to the fighting in 1791, this time the Natives were quickly routed. The survivors retreated and sought refuge at nearby Fort Miami, only to find the gates of the fort closed against them. Not wanting to risk war with the Americans, the young British commander, Major William Campbell, refused to give shelter to Britain's fleeing allies. Wayne's army marched up to Fort Miami but did not engage the small British garrison, choosing instead to destroy Native villages and fields. Wayne's reluctance to engage the British directly precluded any retaliatory action and left John Graves Simcoe at Detroit waiting for an attack that never came. The defeat at Fallen Timbers dealt a serious blow to the British dream of creating an Indian buffer state in the Ohio Valley.

There were other reasons, too, why Britain opted for a less aggressive policy in the interior. As had happened so often, European events also dictated events in North America. In January 1793, revolutionary France executed King Louis XVI. France's early hopeful, and perhaps naïve, revolutionary faith in human perfectibility and Enlightenment ideas was giving way to the guillotine. Days after the regicide, Britain and France were at war once again. In part, Britain acted in defence of monarchical ideals, and sought to prevent

1794: The Americans are victorious over Natives allied with the British at the Battle of Fallen Timbers.

1793: Britain and France are at war, and Simcoe organizes a militia for Upper Canada.

1794: Jay's Treaty seeks to resolve Anglo-American tensions in the interior.

revolution from spreading. But French expansion on the continent of Europe, and British designs on French colonial possessions, also played a role. Britain wished to avoid open war with the United States, which might then ally itself with France. In this atmosphere of heightened tensions, Lieutenant Governor Simcoe created a militia for Upper Canada, with all males between the ages of 16 and 60 liable for military service anywhere in the province during time of war. This, however, anticipated a worst-case scenario, and British foreign policy was directed to securing peaceful relations with the Americans.

In 1794, American Chief Justice John Jay travelled to London to meet with Britain's foreign minister, Lord Grenville. That November, they signed Jay's Treaty. The treaty resolved a number of outstanding Anglo-American differences, and provided for future international commissions to resolve others. Some reciprocal trade privileges between British North America and the United States were negotiated: trade would now be permitted freely by road, river, lake or canal, although the previous mercantilist limits on sea trade were retained. One of the key provisions of the treaty concerned the Ohio Valley and the Aboriginal nations living there. British authorities recognized that their Aboriginal allies had been faithful and had a strong claim, yet were compelled by other interests to agree to surrender the interior forts. As some measure of compromise, they secured American agreement to Article III, which recognized the Natives' right to cross freely over the border. "The reality was that the tribes were caught in the grip of two forces, an empire and a frontier. Neither side was particularly distinguished for mercy, and both were destined to resolve their differences by less costly methods than Indian wars," Robert Allen argues.[20]

By August 1796, the British had evacuated the forts. In the meantime, no longer able to count on British support and having endured a hungry winter, most of the Aboriginal nations of the Ohio Valley signed the Treaty of Greenville in 1795 with the United States, ceding the Ohio Valley. One veteran of the Battle of Fallen Timbers who did not sign the Greenville Treaty was a young Shawnee warrior, Tecumseh, who would later lead a new campaign of Native resistance.

After serving less than five years as Upper Canada's lieutenant governor, John Graves Simcoe was transferred to the West Indies in 1796. Perhaps in the new era of trans-border amity, Simcoe's vehement anti-Americanism would have been out of place. An early visitor to Upper Canada, the duc de la Rochefoucauld-Liancourt provides a fair assessment of Simcoe:

> But for his inveterate hatred of the United States, which he too loudly professes and which he carries too far, General Simcoe appears in the most advantageous light. He is just, active, brave, frank and possesses the confidence of the country, the troops and all those who join him in the administration of public affairs…. He preserves all the old friends of the King, and neglects no means to procure him new ones."[21]

Peter Hunter succeeded Simcoe as lieutenant governor of Upper Canada (1799–1805). A military officer drawn from the British landed gentry, Hunter had little experience in colonial administration, and set out to develop the province with the determination one might bring to a military campaign. His first priority was to implement a systematic reform of the province's land policies. To encourage more orderly settlement and to limit land speculation, Hunter discouraged the opening up of new townships until existing townships were filled. To facilitate the efficient processing of land grants, Hunter regularized procedures, hired additional clerks, and increased fees. The lieutenant governor alienated Loyalists when he ordered a review of Loyalist claims and purged nearly 900 names from the U.E. ("United Empire") list, the roll of all those who had served and sacrificed for the British cause during the American Revolution.

While colonial authorities were committed to populating Upper Canada, and eager to see land grants go to those who would actually bring property under cultivation, they also adhered to hierarchical social values which dictated that there ought to be a class of elite individuals with substantial property, able to assume the leading roles in society. Colonel Thomas Talbot (1771–1853) was an elite Anglo-Irish military officer who had served as Simcoe's secretary in Upper Canada from 1791 to 1794. In 1803, Talbot took up a land grant of 2000 hectares (5000 acres) along the north shore of Lake Erie. This sizeable land grant was a typical reward for service for a British military officer.

1803: Thomas Talbot begins settlement schemes that will ultimately grow to encompass 200 000 hectares (500 000 acres) of land in Upper Canada.

Talbot hatched a plan that he hoped would both bring personal wealth and promote the well-being and settlement of the colony. He recruited British settlers and granted them plots of 20 hectares (50 acres) from his own property, reserving for himself the 80 hectares (200 acres) to which each family would normally be entitled. In this way, he was able to lay claim to an additional 8000 hectares (20 000 acres) beyond his original grant. By 1807 he had begun to deviate from this plan and was settling his recruits outside his own property. Colonial officials permitted this, and also overlooked the fact that Talbot frequently failed to register land title transfers with the Surveyor General's Office. The lines between Talbot's personal interests and those of the province at large sometimes became blurred.

In addition to serving on the legislative council, in 1804 he had been named road commissioner in Upper Canada's London district, and oversaw the construction of the Talbot Road east, joining his substantial properties to the more densely settled areas of the Niagara district. Talbot's close personal friendship with Sir Francis Gore, who succeeded Peter Hunter as lieutenant governor of Upper Canada in 1806, was a further advantage: Gore authorized more roads, and granted Talbot settlement rights in still more new townships on vacant Crown lands. By 1838, almost 40 000 people had settled in the 27 townships Talbot had established.

Determined to replicate the social order of his family's Irish estates, Talbot sought to surround himself with "a comfortable and respectable tenantry."[22] His promise to authorities to recruit British, rather than American, newcomers increased support for his settlement scheme. He personally interviewed all potential settlers and pencilled in the names of those who met with his approval on one of his survey maps. Advocates of temperance or political reform had little chance of receiving land from Talbot, and the names of those who did anything to annoy or offend him were simply erased. Before settlers received a deed, they had to build a dwelling, bring the land under cultivation, and clear the road allowance, all within three years. Even after they had received title to the land, settlers remained bound to Talbot who managed his domain with a dextrous system of handouts, liquor, and preferment. Such behaviour was a classic example of the system of patronage and clientelism that was pervasive in Upper Canada.

Clearing the land was the foremost preoccupation of settlers to Upper Canada. A typical family could clear about two hectares of land a year. As a result, most families really operated a farm-in-the-making for a decade. Pioneer life was characterized by years of back-breaking labour, monotony, and isolation.

Wives attended to the domestic household business of raising children, cooking, cleaning, gardening, preparing preserves to get the family through long winters, and manufacturing essentials such as soap, candles and clothing. Children were not exempt from labour: they entered the world of work at an early age, girls helping their mothers with domestic chores and caring for younger siblings, and boys assisting their fathers clearing stumps or tending livestock and crops. The income generated by women and children, raising poultry and selling eggs, taking in boarders or doing laundry, often made the difference between getting ahead and a mere subsistence existence. Wives were frequently left to manage the farm on their own when their husbands took produce to market or sought employment in the winter months to earn cash. Additional income was also generated during the early years of settlement through the sale of potash, which was created by burning trees as the land was cleared.

Labour was in short supply, and cooperation was essential to survival on the frontier. Neighbours came together to assist each other in barn raising and land clearing bees. Doctors were few and far between, so women assisted at births and provided whatever medical care they could. Since schools were virtually non-existent outside the few towns, whatever education pioneer children received was provided by their parents in the home.

It was many years before pioneer farms produced a surplus crop, and those that did faced the problems of a small domestic market, poor transportation systems, and competition from cheaper American produce. As a result, most pioneer families were heavily dependent on credit from merchants to purchase supplies, seeds, and implements. This reliance on credit contributed to the rise of a "shopkeeper aristocracy" in Upper Canada. Merchants such as Robert Hamilton of Niagara and Richard Cartwright of Kingston acquired large fortunes by supplying settlers, transporting goods, investing in local industries, and securing government contracts and appointments. Both men invested their profits in land, motivated as much by the social status it carried as by its speculative value, and came to exercise considerable influence in both local and provincial politics. Despite the trials of pioneering, the population of Upper Canada climbed from just 10 000 in 1791 to about 60 000 in 1811. The outlines of a provincial economy had begun to take shape.

Sharpening Divisions in Lower Canada

When Lower Canada's legislative assembly met for the first time in 1792, French Canadians held 34 of the 50 seats. Anglophones, however, held a narrow majority of the seats in the appointed legislative and executive councils. *Canadien* domination of the assembly and Anglophone control of the councils institutionalized the divisions between French and English. The legislative assembly took three weeks to select a speaker, as both groups argued over whether the speaker should be English or French, and over which language should be used in debate. In the end, the assembly decided to alternate speakers, allowing debate to be conducted in either language.

The debate exposed tensions between the English newcomers and *Canadiens,* who feared that they were being treated as a conquered people rather than as partners. Other cleavages also became apparent as the assembly got down to business and considered its first bill. The merchant community in Lower Canada, which was dominated by recent arrivals from Scotland and the United States, sought support from the government for improvements to roads and canals to foster economic development. The government proposed that these improvements be funded through the introduction of a land tax, a tax that would fall primarily upon farmers, who were mostly *Canadiens.* The French-Canadian majority in the assembly scuttled the proposal, much to the annoyance of the English-speaking majority in the legislative and executive councils. Both these councils seemed to focus on policy that would serve the needs of the English merchant class, the so-called Château Clique.

The debate over improvements also unmasked divisions among the French Canadians themselves. Most of the *Canadiens* who had been appointed to the councils were part of the old seigneurial aristocracy, while many of the French Canadians elected to the assembly were drawn from a new class of professionals made up of lawyers, physicians, and journalists. Seigneurs regarded themselves as the traditional backbone of French-Canadian society. Looking down upon the upstart professionals with disdain, many seigneurs more readily identified with the Anglophones on the councils with whom they shared a conservative social vision.

The outbreak of the French Revolution, and the war with France after 1793, raised fears among British administrators that revolutionary ideas would spread to Canada. *Canadiens,* however, felt little, if any identification with old France, let alone revolutionary France. Nonetheless, this climate promoted the agenda of Anglophone leaders who wished to assimilate the *Canadiens* through immigration and the abrogation of the constitutional protection provided to their religion and legal system. Sensing an opportunity, the Anglican bishop of Quebec, Jacob Mountain, launched a concerted campaign to reduce the power and influence of the Roman Catholic Church and to achieve the legal establishment of the Church of England.

Mountain used his influence on the executive and legislative councils to prevent the division of Lower Canada into Roman Catholic parishes, and to block the entry of royalist Catholic priests who were fleeing revolutionary France. Mountain sought to have control over education placed firmly in the hands of Lower Canada's civil administrators, and, while several French-Canadian representatives in the assembly were absent, secured the passage of an 1801 act to establish the Royal Institution for the Advancement of Learning. Despite Mountain's intentions, a clause in the act permitting private schools left Catholic schools beyond the reach of this measure.

Mountain's agenda was shared by the governor of Lower Canada, Sir Robert Shore Milnes (1799–1805). Convinced that political stability required the creation of an English-speaking landed aristocracy, Milnes granted large tracts of land to prominent Anglophone merchants and office-holders. Such actions were widely perceived by *Canadiens* in the assembly as part of a general attack upon their culture and church. French-Canadian fears seemed to be confirmed by the appearance of the Quebec *Mercury,* an unabashedly anglophile and francophobe newspaper established late in 1804 to voice the aspirations of the British party in the assembly and councils. It began publication early the following year.

1804: The Quebec Mercury *is established as a voice for British Tories in Lower Canada.*

Pierre Bédard, Sir James Craig, and Reform Agitation in Lower Canada

At the same time, politically galvanized *Canadiens* in Lower Canada were growing more assertive about their own vision for the colony. Pierre-Stanislas Bédard was among the earliest members of Lower Canada's legislative assembly, serving from 1792 to 1812. Trained as a lawyer, Bédard was a contemplative man, who was inclined to be cynical about his chosen profession and preferred to immerse himself in philosophy and mathematics. He found much to admire in the *Constitutional Act of 1791*, recognizing that the British system offered considerably more liberty than under the French regime. He was not an advocate of untrammelled democracy. Like many late-eighteenth and early-nineteenth-century political philosophers, Bédard favoured a balanced constitution, one in which the democratic element would be held in check by the monarchical, in the form of the governor, and the aristocratic, in the form of the legislative council. Since taxing and spending—the "power of the purse"—was controlled by the elected assembly, that body's power could be considerable. Bédard believed that the executive council should be responsible to the majority of the elected assembly, a system known as "responsible government." But since it was only the majority whose views were represented in the elected branch, and not the entire people, the upper house and governor provided a necessary check on democratic excess. Under the British system, "the interests and rights of the various classes composing society are … carefully arranged,… wisely set off against one another and linked to one another as a whole," Bédard explained.[23]

1804: The reform-oriented Parti Canadien emerges in Lower Canada.

After 1804 Bédard emerged as leader of the newly formed Parti Canadien, a party advocating such reforms as responsible government and changes to the distribution of patronage. Patronage, the awarding of government contracts and official appointments, was firmly in the hands of the British-appointed governor. Speaker of the legislative assembly was the only position over which elected representatives had control. The Parti Canadien's newspaper, *Le Canadien,* began publication in Quebec City in 1806, partly as a foil to the English Quebec *Mercury.* Under its title, *Le Canadien* proudly bore its

1806: The newspaper Le Canadien *emerges as the voice of French-Canadian reform.*

nationalist slogan: "*Notre foi, notre langue, nos institutions*" (Our faith, our language, our institutions). The Roman Catholic religion, the French language, and such distinctive French-Canadian institutions as the civil law and seigneurial system were seen as essential bulwarks of French-Canadian cultural survival.

The cause of political reform in Lower Canada was thus intermixed with ethnic grievances. In the context of Britain's war with Revolutionary France, advocacy for the rights of French-Canadian nationhood seemed potentially seditious in the eyes of the new governor, Sir James Craig, who arrived in Lower Canada in 1807. Craig's temperament and outlook were shaped by his previous experience as a veteran of the American Revolutionary War and Napoleonic Wars. His reactionary conservatism, nurtured during the French Revolution, hardened into autocracy during a stint as a colonial administrator in southern Africa. Craig explained to the British Colonial Office that the *Canadiens* felt no tie to Britain, "on the contrary, viewing us with sentiments of mistrust and jealousy, with envy, and I believe I should not go too far, were I to say with hatred." "Indeed," he elaborated, "it seems to be a favourite object with them to be considered as [a] separate

Nation; La *Nation Canadienne* is their constant expression."[24] He even suspected that the *Canadiens* were prepared to support an American invasion of Lower Canada as a first step toward the creation of an independent republic.

The appointed legislative council had once contained many French Canadians, but increasingly the composition of both the legislative and executive councils had become more English. The gulf between the representative legislative assembly and the appointed councils was ever widening, since reformers in the assembly urged its members not to accept appointments to the executive council, lest they become corrupted by its systemic inequities. Yet, the French Canadians were gaining ground in the assembly, and the governor, when confronted by intransigent *Canadien* majorities, unsuccessfully attempted to interfere with its workings by dissolving the uncooperative assembly in hopes that elections might return more tractable members. After he dissolved the assembly for an election in 1809, an even stronger Parti Canadien majority was returned. Unsatisfied with the outcome of the autumn 1809 election, Craig again dissolved the legislative assembly for new elections in March 1810. Bishop Jacob Mountain and other prominent Anglophones supported the governor's heavy-handed approach.

1809: Lower Canadian Governor Sir James Craig is thwarted in his attempt to secure a conservative-dominated assembly.

In his anxiety to quash what he saw as seditious French-Canadian agitation, Governor Craig stopped the presses of *Le Canadien* that same month and ordered its operators, Pierre Bédard among them, imprisoned. While the others involved with the newspaper were released by that summer, Bédard insisted on a formal trial, or an unconditional discharge, and was not released until March 1811. By this time, he was dismayed to see that little was made of his triumphant return, and that others were taking over the Parti Canadien's leadership. Bédard bitterly noted that his former friends, Louis-Joseph Papineau and Denis-Benjamin Viger, both of whom were first elected to the legislative assembly in 1809, had seized control. For his part, Bédard accepted a judgeship in Trois Rivières. While he had always been contemptuous of *vendus*, or "sell-outs," who had acquiesced in the political regime by accepting patronage appointments, he decided that in his case it was just compensation for his imprisonment. Soon afterward, an ailing Craig returned to Britain, where he died a few months later.

1811: The pragmatic and personable Sir George Prevost succeeds Craig as governor-in-chief.

Lower Canada's new governor, Sir George Prevost, did much to heal the wounds left by Craig. An experienced, fluently bilingual diplomat of Swiss origin, Prevost was well-suited to task of reconciling French Canadians and the British administration. His wise governance may have played a role in preventing the feared alliance between *Canadiens* and the American invaders during the War of 1812.

Economic and Demographic Growth in Lower Canada

The factionalism of Lower Canadian politics was partly rooted in the province's social and economic evolution. Between 1791 and 1815, Lower Canada was transformed from a sparsely populated colony dependent on the fur trade and subsistence agriculture into an increasingly complex commercial society. In 1791, Lower Canada's population of 165 000 was predominantly French and overwhelmingly rural; by 1815, the population had more than doubled. Most of this increase was due to a high birth rate among French Canadians. The English-speaking population was bolstered by the arrival of some 9000 settlers from

The Forges at Saint-Maurice produced the engines for Canada's first steamship, the Accommodation.

Source: Library and Archives Canada, C-004356.

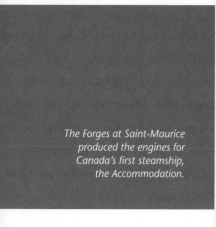

1806: British North America's timber industry undergoes rapid development with the closing of the Baltic to British trade.

New England who were part of the great flood of pioneers leaving the crowded states of the eastern seaboard in search of land and opportunity. Most of these new arrivals settled in the eastern townships, which were open to freehold tenure. (These new townships were in the western part of the province, but so named to distinguish them from newly settled areas in Upper Canada).

Commercial growth in Lower Canada was fed by new imperial legislation granting increased preference in the British market to exports from her colonies. Measures benefiting colonial grain production promoted the commercialization of agriculture. Other industries also flourished. John Molson, who came to Montreal at age 19 and established a brewery by 1786, watched his business expand amid population growth and increased prosperity. By 1809, he purchased Canada's first steamship, the *Accommodation*, built with engines produced locally at the Forges Saint-Maurice. Since the early eighteenth century, iron for naval purposes had been forged at Saint-Maurice, with the foundry soon expanding into producing stoves, farm implements, and pig iron for industry. Molson went on to establish a steamship service operating between Montreal and Quebec.

Perhaps the most profound growth was in the timber sector. War with France had a definitive impact on the development of a British North American timber industry. Napoleon Bonaparte, who had seized control of revolutionary France in a *coup d'etat* in 1799 and named himself emperor in 1804, devised a new economic weapon to strike at the British enemy. Late in 1806, Napoleon's Declaration of Berlin inaugurated his "Continental System": using France's command over most of continental Europe, Napoleon declared that the ports of Europe were closed to British trade. He followed this with an edict that all British goods and ships within Europe were to be confiscated. Britain countered by using its command of the seas to enforce a naval blockade, permitting only ships flying the British flag to penetrate the blockade to trade with Europe. Europe, in effect, was given the message that if they wished to have access to luxury goods from Asia, grain from the

United States, or other import commodities, they would have to defy Napoleon and trade with British merchants. Yet in the short term, Napoleon's measure deprived the British navy of the Baltic timber upon which it greatly depended.

The navy's appetite for wood seemed insatiable. A first-rate ship of the line such as British Admiral Horatio Nelson's *HMS Victory* required an incredible 6000 trees by the time of its completion in 1765, 90 percent of them oak trees. Mounting 100 guns, a first-rate ship was effectively a floating artillery battery. The floors of the gun decks on such a ship had to be built from as few pieces as possible to prevent the ship from being shaken to pieces while firing broadsides. Numerous joinings in the wood would compromise its strength. The design was not, therefore, one calculated to preserve precious wood. Admiral Nelson himself had spearheaded the planting of oak forests in Britain to provide for its future navy, but in the meantime, the loss of access to timber from Russia, Sweden, and Denmark made North America an attractive—indeed, an essential—source of supply.

Enterprising immigrants such as Philemon Wright from Massachusetts established highly profitable timber operations along the Ottawa and Saguenay rivers, employing hundreds of French-Canadian labourers. Wright had joined up at age 15 to fight for the rebel cause during the American Revolution, but like many others migrated north in search of economic opportunities. The city of Hull grew up around Wright's logging sites. The British government obligingly imposed tariffs to offer a protected market to colonial timber, and production surged. Exports of squared pine from Lower Canada increased 13-fold between 1808 and 1812.[25] New Brunswick would also share in this period of steep growth, and timber became a mainstay of that colony's economy.

Fur Trade Rivalry in the West

Despite the growth of the timber trade, furs were still an important staple in the British North American economy. In Rupert's Land, in the western interior, tensions between fur-trading factions had been growing since the late eighteenth century. Rupert's Land—all of the land drained by Hudson Bay—had been granted by the Crown to the Hudson's Bay Company (HBC) in 1670, and the company had established factories, or fur-trading posts, on the Hudson and James Bays. But after the conquest of New France by the British, a small, but vigorous, new merchant class had arrived in Quebec: newcomers from England, Scotland, and the American colonies to the south. The small fur-trading enterprises they established began to disrupt the HBC monopoly, pushing further inland to trade, through the St. Lawrence River-Great Lakes route. An ambitious and ill-tempered Connecticut veteran of the Seven Years War, Peter Pond, led the way, mapping and trading in the territories that lay beyond the reach of Hudson's Bay Company. Through the 1770s and 1780s, Pond pushed further west and north than any other non-Aboriginal trader, and produced an important map showing lakes and rivers west to the Rocky Mountains and north to the Arctic. A ruthless competitor, Pond intimidated rivals and was suspected of murdering two of his fellow traders.

The success of independent traders such as Pond forced the Hudson's Bay Company to take a more aggressive approach. Earlier, a critic of the Hudson's Bay Company had lamented that "the Company have for eighty years slept at the edge of a frozen sea," showing

1770–1772: Samuel Hearne explores north and west to reach the Arctic Coast.

1774: The Hudson's Bay Company expands inland by establishing Cumberland House.

1779: Montreal traders join together to form the North West Company.

no curiosity about further exploration and crushing that spirit in others, eager to keep the treasures of that territory a secret.[26] Native traders who had once brought furs to York Factory were now being intercepted by enterprising "pedlars" based out of Montreal. The HBC was forced to respond.

In December 1770, Samuel Hearne, a veteran of the Royal Navy who, like Pond, entered the fur trade after serving in the Seven Years War, undertook a trip on behalf of the HBC in search of new sources of revenue. He set out from Fort Prince of Wales (now Churchill, Manitoba) to follow up on reports of abundant copper to the north. Accompanied by a Chipewyan guide, Matonabbee, Hearne journeyed more than 2700 kilometres across the tundra, travelling north to the mouth of the Coppermine River on the Arctic coast. After enduring intense hunger and cold on the gruelling journey, a disappointed Hearne returned with only a two-kilogram lump of copper and an acknowledgment that little was likely to come from the expedition. It was clear that the shallow Coppermine River was not a viable commercial artery. As the first European to reach the shores of the Arctic Ocean overland, Hearne was at least able to raise serious doubts about the existence of the long-sought Northwest Passage through the continent.

Soon afterward, Hearne was assigned to establish the Hudson's Bay Company's first inland fur trading post, a measure that increased competition made imperative. Cumberland House, just north of the Saskatchewan River in what is today eastern Saskatchewan, was built in 1774. His strategically chosen spot commanded the junction of two main river systems; here the rivers connecting to Hudson Bay and the Arctic met with those of the plains. Growing competition made it increasingly difficult for independent traders to finance and supply their far-flung operations. To strengthen their hand against the HBC, a group of Montreal traders—Simon McTavish, Isaac Todd, James McGill, Peter Pond, and Benjamin and Joseph Frobisher among them—decided to consolidate their operations and formed the North West Company in 1779.

While the Hudson's Bay Company was administered from London by people with little knowledge of the fur trade, the North West Company (NWC) was run by men with firsthand experience. "Nor'Westers" such as McTavish and Pond had lived and worked in the west, and learned the fur trade from the bottom up. Highland Scots, many of them related to one another by birth or marriage, dominated the NWC. Simon McTavish, who would become the director, had been penniless on his arrival in New York from Scotland at the age of 14. When he died in Montreal in 1804, he was probably the city's wealthiest man, leaving an estate of £125 000. North West Company traders extended trade to the rich fur territory near Lake Athabasca, located in the northernmost part of what is now Saskatchewan and Alberta. Between 1774 and 1821, the two companies established a total of 601 trading posts throughout the west.

The establishment of new posts ushered in an era of cutthroat competition in the fur trade. An old HBC trader, R.M. Ballantyne, remembered that the brutal rivalry for furs plunged the country into "a state of constant turmoil and excitement" involving "fist fights" and "more deadly weapons. Spirits were distributed among the wretched natives to a dreadful extent, and the scenes that sometimes ensued were disgusting in the extreme." Each company vied to prevent cargoes of furs reaching the other.[27] Historian Arthur Ray puts a more positive construction on this competition, stressing that Native traders took

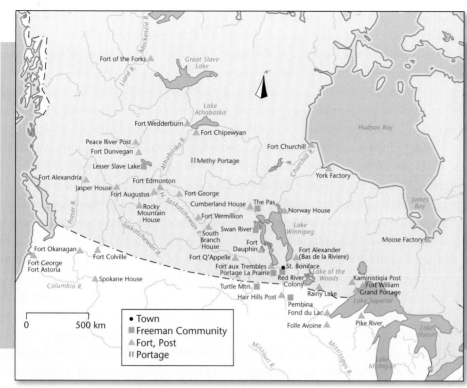

Map 6.2
Fur Trade Posts of the North West.

Source: Reproduced by *Making the Voyageur World: Travelers and Traders in the North American Fur Trade* by Carolyn Podruchny by permission of the University of Nebraska Press. Copyright © 2006 by the Board of Regents of the University of Nebraska.

advantage of the circumstances to force each company to offer better quality goods and higher prices for furs.[28] The fur trade was more than an exchange of goods—it was also a complex series of ceremonies whose objectives were social and political as much as economic. In trading with the Hudson's Bay and North West companies, Natives sought to create and to preserve an intricate system of alliances. Before trade began, Native leaders exchanged gifts with the chief factor, made speeches, and smoked peace pipes. Only after these ceremonies, which could extend over several days, did trade begin.

Trade was conducted through a window in the trade room at the posts, with only one Native permitted in the room at a time. An Aboriginal leader was allowed behind the trade window to ensure fair measure, to guard against company traders short-weighing and short-measuring goods and marking up the price of trade goods above the official company standard. Official standards of trade served only as points of reference that enabled traders to come to terms quickly. One HBC trader warned that the Natives "may be reckon'd a crafty sort of people…. They are cunning and sly to the last degree, the more you give the more they crave—the generality of them are loath to part with anything they have; if at any time they give, they expect double satisfaction."[29]

In spite of the rivalry between the Hudson's Bay Company and North West Company, Ballantyne noted an interesting paradox: each trading company tended to establish forts "within two hundred yards of each other in the wilds of North America," constantly visiting back and forth, and hosting frequent parties and entertainments. "More agreeable or friendly neighbours seldom came together," he remarked. Nevertheless, Ballantyne recalled that one North West Company ball was a ruse to distract HBC traders from the expected arrival of an Aboriginal trading party. As the liquor flowed and a Native fiddler played Scottish reels, a clandestine deal was struck by traders who lay in wait outside for the arriving dog sleds. The trading quickly concluded, the sleds vanished in a tinkling of bells, "and nothing was heard but the faint echoes of music and mirth, which floated on the frosty night-wind, giving token that the revellers still kept up the dance," ignorant of the missed opportunity.[30]

Two distinct social and labour structures evolved in the two fur-trading companies. The Hudson's Bay Company was structured as a joint-stock company with a highly centralized bureaucracy. The Annual General Court, or meeting of the stockholders, elected a governor to oversee the company's operations and policies. Organized along military lines, each Hudson's Bay Company post was commanded by a chief factor and his council of officers. Most of the workforce was made up of men recruited from the Orkney Islands of Scotland and drawn from the lower ranks of rural society. The Orkney Islands were the last stop for company vessels leaving England bound for Hudson Bay, and both workers and supplies could be taken on there. Scotland's superior educational system also made these workers attractive: in contrast to many English labourers of that class, they were generally literate and able to do arithmetic calculations. By 1799, three-quarters of the 529 "servants" employed by the HBC came from the Orkney Islands.[31] These labourers received an annual minimum wage of six pounds plus room, board, and clothing. Most of the men were employed in the fur trade for eight years or less. With few opportunities to rise in company ranks, many men saved their income to purchase farms back home.

Among those who saw work in the fur trade as a means to a better life was an adventurous woman, Isobel Gunn, who presented herself to the HBC as "John Fubbister" in 1806, and took ship from the Orkney Islands to distant Fort Albany on James Bay. The sturdily built Gunn worked alongside the men for two years, even undertaking a 2900-kilometre canoe journey to Pembina (in present-day North Dakota). Unfortunately, it was there that her ruse was discovered. When another company servant learned her true identity, and forced himself upon her, she become pregnant. On the night of December 29, 1807, Alexander Henry, the head of the North West Company post at Pembina answered a frantic knock at his door to find the distraught Gunn in childbirth. She gave birth to a son on the floor of Henry's lodging. Gunn was not permitted to return to her former employment, and worked for a time as a washerwoman for the HBC before returning to the Orkney Islands in the autumn of 1809.

Isobel Gunn was, of course, an exception, but women played important roles in the fur trade in other ways. A significant number of officers, and some labourers, had "country wives," often the daughters of Native leaders. Historian Sylvia Van Kirk has argued that Native women actively chose these liaisons, mindful of the benefits for themselves and their tribes. Secure provisions, access to European trade goods, and a lighter workload, were only some of the inducements. Valued as translators, guides, and brokers of trade, the women gained status both in their own communities and with the traders. They also brought to the relationship a host of essential practical skills, including the ability to make moccasins and snowshoes, preserve food, dress furs, and sew canoe seams. While the "women in between" were essential facilitators in the early days of the fur trade, officials in both the Hudson's Bay Company and the North West Company were ambivalent toward them. The HBC placed a strict prohibition on the practice of junior employees taking Native wives, unwilling to take responsibility for the growing populations surrounding the forts. The North West Company banned such marriages after 1806; such a policy may also have been motivated by the tendency of company employees to leave the fur trade to settle with their Aboriginal families. This loss of personnel could be costly and inconvenient. At the height of trade wars, women were used as pawns, kidnapped or abused by trade rivals. Conflicts between traders and tribes sometimes erupted over women, and "in between" status increasingly became a liability for the women.[32]

Unlike the Hudson's Bay Company, the North West Company consisted of a series of Anglo–Scots partnerships based on close personal and family associations. A clear line separated the senior partners from the French-Canadian voyageurs. There was a social hierarchy in the brigades of canoes that travelled from Montreal to the "great rendezvous" at Fort William (now Thunder Bay) at the head of Lake Superior. In time, a mixed-blood population, the Métis, came to dominate the middle rungs of the fur trade economy, acting as traders, brokers, guides, interpreters, provisioners, and labourers.

One advantage the North West Company possessed over its competition was superior adaptation to travel conditions in the interior. The HBC grudgingly praised the Nor'Westers as "natural water dogs," skilled at making and repairing birch bark canoes. These canoes were excellent vessels for negotiating the interior rivers and making arduous portages, but birch bark was unavailable on the shores of Hudson Bay, and HBC servants lacked the legendary skill of the voyageurs at paddling them over great distances. HBC traders relied on sturdy, but less manoeuvrable, York boats, long flat-bottomed boats with a steep-angled bow and stern, propelled by six to eight oarsmen working six metre long oars. The boats could be equipped with a mast and square sail for open water, and could carry about three tonnes of cargo, three times the capacity of the largest canoes. Each North West Company canoe was manned by a foreman, a steersman, and several middlemen; within the canoe, the foreman was in control. Each group of five to six canoes had a guide or pilot who had authority over the entire brigade.

In 1836 the American storyteller Washington Irving presented a vivid, if romanticized, picture of the Canadian voyageurs of the interior fur trade. They were, he reported, "prone to pass their time in idleness and revelry about the trading post or settlements; squandering their hard earnings in heedless indulgence, and an imprudent disregard of the morrow." Their dress was "half civilized, half savage." They wore an outer *capot*, or *surtout*, a garment that originated with French sailors at the time of contact, made from a blanket and closed with a sash. They might wear cloth trousers or leather leggings, moccasins of deerskin, and colourful belts made of variegated worsted, from which they hung their knives, tobacco pouches, and other necessities.

Irving praised the voyageurs' lightness of heart, predilection for stories, songs, and dance, noting that "instead of that hardness and grossness which men in laborious life are apt to indulge towards each other, they are mutually obliging and accommodating." They were remarkable in their civility, addressing one another as "brother" or "cousin."

On arduous journeys, they kept up their spirits by singing traditional French songs, and Irving found that this music, "echoed from mouth to mouth and transmitted from father to son, from the earliest days of the colony" added to the pleasing effect of seeing a fur-trading brigade. On a journey west, Irving thrilled "in a still golden summer evening, to see a *batteau* gliding across the bosom of a lake and dipping its oars to the cadence of these quaint old ditties, or sweeping along, in full chorus, on a bright sunny morning, down the transparent current of one of the Canadian rivers."[33]

Historian Carolyn Podruchny notes the centrality of songs to the voyageurs' world. Songs were a part of the rhythm of life on fur trading brigades, setting the pace of work, enjoyed in leisure time, and providing an outlet for creativity. Men sang while working on the canoes, loading and unloading cargo, paddling, running rapids, and portaging. They also sang to keep hunger and fatigue at bay. Perhaps this apparent light-heartedness added to the impression of the voyageurs' masters that these men were innately suited to such work, that it was somehow ingrained in French-Canadian culture. She notes an equivalent tendency by outsiders to see the voyageurs' work as "unskilled labour," rather than the incrementally acquired skills built up from boyhood.[34]

Explorations in the Pacific Northwest

1789: Alexander Mackenzie is disappointed to learn that the Mackenzie River flows to the Arctic, and not Pacific, Ocean.

In 1789, the North West Company commissioned one of its young and ambitious traders, Alexander Mackenzie, to find a new trade route to the Pacific. The Scottish-born Mackenzie had worked in the fur trade since the age of 15, and had served as second-in-command to Peter Pond in the Athabasca country. Pond was convinced that Cook Inlet (on the southwestern coast of Alaska) was the mouth of a great river flowing westward out of Great Slave Lake, which would provide a route through the interior to the Pacific Ocean. Mackenzie set out from Fort Chipewyan and travelled 2500 kilometres by canoe along the length of the river that now bears his name, only to find that it emptied into the Arctic Ocean and not the Pacific.

Before his next trip, Mackenzie studied surveying and map-making in England. Armed with a compass, sextant, and telescope, Mackenzie set out from Montreal on May 8, 1792, determined to reach the Pacific. He reached Peace River Landing in October where he spent the winter. The following May, he set out again with six voyageurs and two guides from the Beaver nation, managed to cross the Rockies, and reached the Fraser River in June. Persuaded by the local people that the Fraser was too hazardous to navigate, Mackenzie set out along the overland route that Natives used to carry their own trade goods to the coast. Nuxälk-Carrier guides led the party through 400 kilometres of portages. They were able to return to their canoes for the final leg of the journey down the Bella Coola River to the headwaters of the Dean Channel. At last, Mackenzie stood at the Pacific Ocean, the first European to reach it by an overland route. He recorded the momentous event with a bit of spontaneous graffiti: mixing some vermilion with melted grease he inscribed a rock with the words "Alexander Mackenzie, from Canada, by land, the twenty-second of July, one thousand seven hundred and ninety-three."

1793: Alexander Mackenzie becomes the first European to reach the Pacific coast by land.

In contrast to the assistance he had received from Natives throughout his journey, Mackenzie was surprised by the hostile reception he received from the local Bella Coola

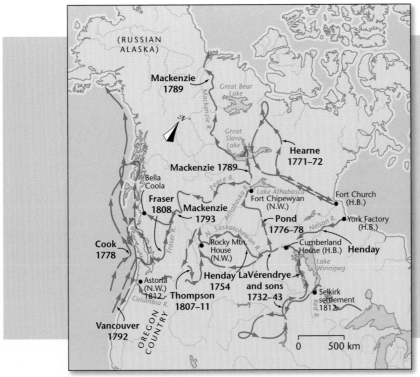

Map 6.3
Western Exploration before 1821.

Source: J.M.S. Careless, *Canada: a Story of Challenge* (Toronto: Macmillan, 1970), 140.

people, and felt compelled to retreat before he had an opportunity to survey the coastline. The Bella Coola had formed a poor opinion of Europeans from an encounter with the haughty British naval officer and explorer, George Vancouver, who had ventured into Dean Channel only a few weeks earlier. Mackenzie's achievement was of little immediate value to the North West Company, the overland route being too hazardous and the coastal Natives inhospitable to trade overtures. After a brief term as a member of the Lower Canadian assembly, Mackenzie returned to Scotland in 1799 where he wrote a popular book on his adventures and received a knighthood.

While the North West and Hudson's Bay companies competed to access new sources of furs, Spanish and English explorers jockeyed for position on North America's northern Pacific coast. In 1774, news that Russian traders had crossed the Aleutian Islands and landed on the North American mainland prompted Spanish authorities in Mexico to dispatch Juan Josef Pérez Hernández to travel north along the uncharted Pacific coast to search for signs of Russian activity and to protect Spanish claims to the territory. Hernández travelled as far north as the Queen Charlotte Islands (Haida Gwaii), where he traded cloth and beads for furs with the Haida. On the return voyage, he ventured into Nootka Sound on the west coast of Vancouver Island and found the Natives eager to trade.

Four years later, British explorer James Cook sailed east across the Pacific and ventured into Nootka Sound, seeking a western approach that would lead to a northwest passage. A veteran of the Royal Navy and the Seven Years War, Cook had helped guide the British fleet that captured Quebec up the St. Lawrence in 1759. He subsequently charted the

Source: Library and Archives Canada, C-011210.

Captain Cook's ships moored in Resolution Cove, Nootka Sound, Vancouver Island, March 1778.

coast of Newfoundland before embarking on his celebrated circumnavigations of the globe from 1768 to 1771, and then again from 1772 to 1775, greatly adding to knowledge of the South Pacific.

In 1775, the British government offered a reward of £20 000 to anyone who discovered the elusive Northwest Passage. Eager to claim the prize, Cook set out for the northern Pacific. Samuel Hearne's trip to the Coppermine River in 1771, and Russian reports that Alaska was an island, convinced him that such a passage existed. When Cook arrived in Nootka Sound in 1778, he traded iron goods to the local people for sea otter pelts. He was later able to sell the furs at Macao for a handsome price, setting off a rush of English adventurers eager to cash in on the lucrative pelts. But Cook's entry into the Bering Sea was thwarted when ice blocked further progress.

Spanish authorities, anxious to keep the British and the Russians at bay and to preserve their own claim to North America's Pacific coast, decided that the time had come to establish a presence there. They directed a junior naval officer, Esteban José Martínez, to establish a trading post and naval base on Nootka Sound in 1789. Martínez had accompanied Hernández on his explorations 15 years earlier. But Martínez behaved rashly, seizing British vessels at Nootka Sound and imprisoning their captains and crews. His blustering action brought Britain and Spain to the brink of war. To avoid this, the Spanish were compelled to sign the Nootka Convention of 1790. According to the terms of the agreement, Spain would return all seized property and recognize the right of any nation to explore, trade, and settle in the Pacific Northwest. For the next few years, both British and Spanish vessels plied the waters of the northern Pacific, trading with the Natives and seeking access to the fabled Northwest Passage.

1790: The Nootka Convention averts war between Spain and Britain over the Pacific Northwest.

British naval captain George Vancouver, who had accompanied Cook on earlier explorations, set out in the HMS *Discovery* in the spring of 1791 to systematically map the Pacific coastline between the latitudes of 30 and 60 degrees north, to definitively determine if any channel existed through the North American continent to Hudson Bay. Journeying by way of the Cape of Good Hope, New Zealand, Tahiti, and the Sandwich Islands (Hawaii), Vancouver reached North America's Pacific coast just north of present-day San Francisco in April 1792. He painstakingly charted territory northward—the Juan de Fuca Strait, Puget Sound, the Gulf of Georgia, Howe Sound, Jervis Inlet, and what is now the harbour of Vancouver. After circumnavigating Vancouver Island, he sailed north to the Queen Charlotte Sound, Burke Channel, and Nootka Sound. He then sailed south to California and to the Sandwich Islands where he spent the winter. In the spring of 1793, he returned to survey further, travelling north to 56 degrees latitude by September. His explorations of Dean Channel in June brought him close to the spot Alexander Mackenzie would reach by his overland travels a few weeks later. After another winter in the Sandwich Islands, Vancouver returned in 1794, sailing to Cook Inlet, Alaska, and concluding, after further explorations, that no northwest passage into the continent existed.

1792–1794: Captain George Vancouver maps North America's Pacific coast.

The Americans, too, had developed a keen interest in the Pacific Northwest, and the United States government sponsored an exploratory expedition led by U.S. Army officers Meriwether Lewis and William Clark. In May 1804, Lewis and Clark set out from St. Louis, Missouri, on an epic 12 800-kilometre journey to the Pacific coast. Among their companions were a Québécois former North West Company employee, Touissaint Charbonneau, and Sacagawea, his Shoshone wife, who was the source of valuable information for the mission. When the expedition reached the mouth of the Columbia River, Clark chose to commemorate the occasion much as Mackenzie had done: he carved in a tree, "William Clark December 3rd 1805. By land from the U. States in 1804 & 1805." This mission symbolized American ambitions for the "Oregon Territory," adding even greater urgency to the North West Company's goal of finding a viable trade route through the mountains. They feared that the Americans were poised to develop trade into the interior that would disrupt North West Company interests.

1805: American explorers Lewis and Clark reach the Pacific coast overland.

While Lewis and Clark were heading west, the North West Company was busy establishing a presence west of the Rocky Mountains. A young partner in the firm, Simon Fraser, took the lead in this. The New York-born Fraser had been born on the eve of the American Revolution. His Loyalist family relocated to the settlement of Cornwall on the St. Lawrence River at the war's end, and with the help of an uncle, he was apprenticed to the North West Company at the age of 16. Fraser founded the first newcomer settlements in what would later be British Columbia: Fort McLeod in 1805, Fort St. James and Fort Fraser in 1806, and Fort George (now Prince George) in 1807. Fraser gave the region the name "New Caledonia." In late May 1808, Fraser set out on a journey to explore the river now known as the Fraser River. The spring melt made the timing risky; water levels rose as much as 2.5 metres in a single day. Local people warned Fraser that the river's cascades and waterfalls would make it impossible to navigate safely, but portaging past rapids, carrying heavily laden canoes along slippery rock ledges was not always a tempting alternative. Sometimes it proved impossible to leave the river when conditions were risky: steep rock banks through the Fraser River Canyon forbade it. The canoes had to be cached above Lillooet, with the party carrying forward on foot. Canoes were borrowed, or even seized, from local people to traverse navigable sections of river. At times, Fraser recorded, "we had to pass where no human being should venture."[35] In early July, after a journey of more than 800 kilometres, Fraser reached a Musqueam village at the mouth of the river. Crowds numbering in excess of 1000 turned out to see the newcomers; most had never encountered Europeans. Fraser's goal of continuing on into the Strait of Georgia was thwarted by the suspicions of the Cowichan people.

1808: Simon Fraser arrives at the mouth of the Fraser River.

The main historical source traditionally used for this journey is Simon Fraser's own journal. But historian Wendy Wickwire has gone beyond this in her study of Fraser's encounters with the Nlaka'pamux (Thompson) people of the Fraser River canyon. She draws on oral accounts collected by early twentieth-century anthropologists, and on stories she herself has been told by Nlaka'pamux elders. Wickwire finds that these sources yield a "wider, deeper" history that goes beyond a single account in a dead document, offering a higher level of detail and specificity.[36] There is little doubt that without the hospitality, assistance, and guidance of Aboriginal communities, Fraser's expedition would not have succeeded. However, the mission was in many respects a disappointment: upon reaching the sea, it was evident that the river was not the Columbia, as Fraser had hoped, and the difficulties of the passage had killed any hopes of using the route for commercial purposes.

The North West Company's subsequent bid to be the first traders to establish a presence on the Columbia River came too late. David Thompson travelled through the continent to the mouth of the Columbia in 1811. Thompson was originally an HBC employee, having first been apprenticed to them at age 14. While recuperating from a serious leg injury sustained in a sled accident, Thompson learned surveying and cartography, greatly increasing his value to the company. In 1797, he left the HBC to join their rivals. He charted several routes through the Rockies, even bringing his family with him on occasion. In 1799, he took a country wife, Charlotte Small, the 13-year-old daughter of a North West Company partner and a Cree mother. The family would go on to have seven sons and six daughters. Charlotte Small, often pregnant during her canoe travels through the interior, traversed some 25 000 kilometres with her husband over the years, and her knowledge of Cree proved valuable in these journeys. The children also frequently came along. The family did not, however, accompany Thompson on the 1811 trip down the Columbia River. When Thompson arrived at the river's mouth in July, he discovered that John Jacob Astor's Pacific Fur Company had already constructed a post and had begun to trade with the Aboriginal people of the region. Although the Americans established operations on the Pacific first, Fraser and Thompson's efforts ensured that the British would later have grounds to claim an interest in British Columbia.

1811: Nor'Wester David Thompson reaches the mouth of the Columbia River.

Rise of the Métis

A lasting legacy of the interior fur trade was a new mixed-race population. French-Canadian voyageurs had been marrying Native wives *à la façon du pays* since late in the seventeenth century—the time of the French regime. Métis families—most often French and Ojibwe or Cree—had lived at trade crossroads such as Michilimackinac and Sault Ste Marie since the 1690s. They worked as voyageurs, traded with forts, hunted, fished, tapped trees for maple sugar, and practised small-scale agriculture. The colloquial label the Métis were given—*Bois Brûlés*, or burnt wood—referred to their cut-and-burn methods of clearing land for farming. Their faith was Roman Catholic, and the Métis language, Michif, combined elements of Cree and French. While the convention today is to use the label "Métis" for all those with mixed European and Aboriginal heritage, the term originally applied to those whose European stock was French Canadian. "Country born" or "half breed" (not then seen as a pejorative term) was the prevalent label for those who were descended from British—usually Scottish—fathers, and whose faith was usually Protestant.

After the 1794 Jay's Treaty confirmed American control over trade centres such as Detroit and Michilimackinac, the gradual influx of American settlers encouraged these Métis communities to migrate into the area of today's Prairie provinces. Other Métis, of course, would have been themselves born in the west. With this late-eighteenth-century migration, the Red River settlement, at the forks of the Red and Assiniboine Rivers, became a vital centre for supplying the interior fur trade, especially as the supply lines lengthened to serve a commerce that had extended into present-day Alberta.

The vital commodity that sustained the interior fur trade was pemmican. Made of dried buffalo meat mixed with fat and wild berries, pemmican was a nutritious and easily transported foodstuff. It did not require cooking and would keep for years. Pemmican was sewn into 40-kilogram bags made of buffalo hide; while some accounts describe it as palatable, one European observer noted that hair seemed to be a major ingredient.

At Red River, the Métis settled on narrow river lots, so as to ensure good access to vital transportation networks. This was rich agricultural land, but farming was a secondary activity to these traders and buffalo hunters. Unlike the Plains Cree, who hunted buffalo by driving the herd over the edge of a cliff or into sealed off areas, the Métis would spark a stampede, ride along with the herd on horseback, and use firearms to fell the buffalo. The hunt was a structured event, involving hundreds of families. The Métis met twice yearly to elect a president, captains, and sub-captains, a tradition that arguably politicized the Métis. The buffalo provided everything that was needed on the plains: even buffalo dung was valued as it could be burned for fuel, since wood was scarce on the grasslands.

For their part, the women organized themselves into work parties to process the meat, assisted by the children. Wasting nothing, the women made water bags from the bladder of the buffalo, drinking vessels or gunpowder containers from the horns, and other useful objects from the bones and teeth. The hide was used for tents, rope, saddles, clothing, and moccasins. The distinctive clothing fashioned by Métis women could be traded, and the women evolved their own unique designs to decorate their work. Métis women also drove the Red River carts to haul goods during the hunt. Pulled by an ox, a cart could travel about 30 kilometres a day, carrying 450 kilograms. Fashioned entirely of oak, the large wheels of the cart were angled to prevent tipping and to keep the wheels from sinking into the ground. If necessary, the wheels could be removed and the cart converted to a raft. Grease on the axles would have clogged with dust, so the most memorable characteristic of the Red River cart was the fingernails-on-a-blackboard screech of wooden wheels scraping wooden axles.

Selkirk's Settlement

The world of the Métis buffalo hunters of Red River would soon suffer complications. Thomas Douglas, the fifth Earl of Selkirk (1771–1820), was a Scottish aristocrat who had been considering measures to help landless Highland farmers. Selkirk, like many of his contemporaries, looked to emigration as a philanthropic solution for rural overpopulation and poverty. In 1803, he decided upon Prince Edward Island as a site for a settlement scheme, and recruited 800 migrants, mostly from the Isle of Skye. Selkirk himself visited the colony to oversee arrangements, and, while in North America, visited Canada's key commercial centre, Montreal. This proved to be a fateful trip.

Thomas Douglas,
Lord Selkirk.

Source: Library and Archives
Canada, C-001346.

1812: Lord Selkirk
launches a settlement
at Red River.

Early in the nineteenth century, Montreal's "Beaver Club" was the exclusive preserve of that city's business elite. Founded in 1785, the club was made up of North West Company partners who had wintered in the interior. Even at its peak in 1806, the club boasted a mere 55 members, plus 10 honorary members; admission depended on unanimous consent of current members. The club met at hotels and taverns every two weeks during the winter to dine on venison, quail, and partridge, drink prodigiously, share speeches, and relive adventures in the west. Guests included the military and political elite of the colony. Many of the club members—English, Scottish, French, and American—were related by blood, and the meetings helped cement family and commercial ties among Montreal's bourgeoisie.

Carolyn Podruchny notes that the club borrowed Native rituals, with war whoops and the ceremonial smoking of the *calumet,* or peace pipe, playing a key part in the festivities. They celebrated the exploits of the voyageurs through traditional songs and re-enactments of their exploits. Members "shot the rapids" by riding wine kegs from the table to the floor, and sat on the carpet armed with fire pokers or walking sticks to simulate paddling a canoe. Such posturing notwithstanding, membership in the club was restricted to the elite North West Company partners; working-class voyageurs and guides were not invited to join.[37]

During his 1803 visit to Montreal, Lord Selkirk enjoyed the hospitality of fellow Scots at the Beaver Club, and some members were struck by his attentiveness to all the details they shared about their exploits in the west. Selkirk had already been keenly interested in Alexander Mackenzie's 1801 published account of his journeys through the western interior, and by 1810 Selkirk had found a new focus for his emigration experiments: Assiniboia, the region where the Red and Assiniboine Rivers met, and where the Métis were already established. One year later, having acquired sufficient shares in the Hudson's Bay Company to give him controlling interest, Selkirk struck a deal to buy 300 000 square kilometres of territory in Rupert's Land. The price for what Lady Selkirk archly called her husband's "kingdom" was 10 shillings.

By 1812, Selkirk's settlers, many of them Hudson's Bay Company employees, began to arrive in Red River colony, under the governorship of Miles Macdonell, a loyalist officer in the Canadian militia, hand-picked by Selkirk. During the first difficult winter on the plains, the settlers were fortunate to receive assistance from the Saulteaux people, and especially Chief Peguis. The Saulteaux, an Ojibwe people who had moved west along with the fur-trading Métis in the 1790s, helped the Selkirk settlers procure buffalo meat when food supplies were low, and even provided ponies to transport the colony's children south to provisions at Pembina. Chief Peguis repeatedly proved himself to be a friend to the newcomers and the HBC later honoured him with a medal and annuity. He eventually converted to Christianity, under the influence of Anglican missionaries in Red River, and took the name William King. His descendants used the surname Prince, and included the much-decorated Manitoba World War II hero, Tommy Prince.

Selkirk's chosen settlement site was less than two kilometres from the North West Company's Fort Gibraltar. The arrival of agricultural settlers—initial plans called for

200 annually although the actual number was lower—threatened the Métis way of life. The new order of things quickly became apparent when Macdonell issued the Pemmican Proclamation early in 1814, forbidding the export of pemmican from the colony. The proclamation was ostensibly meant to ensure that the settlement would not run short of provisions, but it alarmed the partners of the North West Company, who had suspected all along that the colony's strategic location across their trade and supply routes was simply a Hudson's Bay Company ploy to disrupt their activities and to gain control of the fur trade. Determined to eliminate the threat, the North West Company offered to relocate the settlers to Upper Canada. Having suffered enough deprivation and adversity, many of the colonists jumped at the opportunity; only 60 remained behind. The proclamation also struck at the heart of the Métis' economy, and with North West Company encouragement, they were determined to fight back.

1814: Red River Governor Miles Macdonell's "Pemmican Proclamation" threatens to disrupt Métis trade.

The War of 1812 and the Contest for British North America

As these tensions intensified in the west, relations between Britain and the United States deteriorated. The British blockade of European ports, meant to counter Napoleon's 1806 "Continental System," prevented American ships from delivering their cargoes to the continent. The Americans were also provoked by Britain's heavy-handedness in seeking to stem the tide of deserters from the Royal Navy. An estimated 4000 sailors per year deserted British naval ships. Many of these had been the hapless victims of "press gangs," who used brutal tactics to keep up the supply of manpower in the fleet, rounding up men at will from British portside towns and pressing them into enforced service. The iron discipline of the cat-o'-nine tails, a diet of weevil-eaten sea biscuits, and years without shore leave prompted many "Jack Tars" to opt for the higher pay and better working conditions on board American vessels. The British navy intercepted American merchant ships at sea to search for deserters, an action the United States regarded as an illegal affront to American liberty. In the summer of 1807, the British warship *Leopard* fired upon the American naval frigate *Chesapeake*, killing three American sailors and wounding 18 others. The British then boarded the ship and removed five men suspected of desertion.

1807: The Chesapeake-Leopard *affair heightens Anglo–American tensions.*

The *Chesapeake* incident inflamed American opinion, but rather than declare war, President Thomas Jefferson chose to pursue a policy of "peaceful coercion," punishing the British by imposing an embargo on trade. While the British certainly felt the loss of American goods, the forfeiture of British trade imposed by the *Embargo Act* hit American merchants with equal force. With the implementation of the American embargo, the British declared Halifax, Shelburne, Saint John, and St. Andrews free ports. New England ships regularly came to call at these free ports to unload American cargo and take on British manufactured goods, thereby evading the embargo and contributing to an already expanding commercial economy in the Maritime colonies.

1807: Commerce flourishes in the Maritime colonies following the passage of the American Embargo Act.

Another source of enmity stemmed from American suspicions that the British were encouraging Native unrest in the interior. And indeed British policy had been to cultivate the friendship of Aboriginal nations and maintain them in a state of readiness to join in war against the Americans should it come. At the same time, the British Indian Depart-

1808: British officials at Amherstburg encourage Aboriginal readiness for war against the Americans.

Tecumseh joined his brother, Tenskwatawa, known as the Prophet, to unite the First Nations of the Ohio Country.

Source: Ohio Historical Society. State Archives Series 1018, AL00241.

1811: American forces destroy Tecumseh's village of Tippecanoe.

ment did not want the Natives to actually initiate activities against the United States. More than 5000 chiefs and warriors attended a great meeting in the autumn of 1808 with British officials at Fort Malden (Amherstburg), on the western shores of Lake Erie, not far from Detroit. Matthew Elliott exhorted those gathered to "keep your eyes fixed on me; my tomahawk is now up; be you ready, but do not strike until I give the signal."[38] As American settlers and land speculators pushed further west into the Ohio country, they encountered more systematic Aboriginal resistance.

A Shawnee warrior, Tecumseh (Tech-kum-thai), and his brother, Tenskwatawa, known as "the Prophet" played a vital role in organizing a concerted response to American settlement by the Aboriginal nations of the frontier. Realizing that unity offered the only hope for Native peoples to retain their territory, Tecumseh set out to establish a new Indian confederacy. Tenskwatawa provided a religious basis for unity, preaching a powerful message delivered to him by the Great Spirit in a series of visions. Historian Robert Allen describes the Prophet as an unlikely saviour, "a one-eyed, epileptic Shawnee with a drinking problem," yet acknowledges his captivating and charismatic oratorical skill. Tenskwatawa called for a rejection of the white man's alcohol and religion, and a return to a simple life. He argued that the land was a gift from the Great Spirit, which could not be sold or ceded. The Americans, he said, "grew from the scum of the great water, when it was troubled by the Evil Spirit.... They are numerous, but I hate them. They are unjust—they have taken your lands, which were not made for them."[39] Followers of the Prophet flocked to Tecumseh's capital at Tippecanoe in the Indiana Territory.

The American governor of the Indiana Territory, William Henry Harrison, recognized the danger posed by the combination of Tecumseh's political movement and Tenskwatawa's religious revival, although he believed the meddling British were at the root of it: "For who does not know that the tomahawk and the scalping knife of the savages are always employed as the instruments of British vengeance[?]"[40] Harrison prepared to attack Tippecanoe while Tecumseh was away visiting tribes to the south. Before leaving, Tecumseh advised his brother not to engage in any fighting during his absence. Tenskwatawa ignored the warning and attacked Harrison's forces on November 7, 1811. Although Harrison's troops suffered heavy casualties, Tippecanoe was destroyed during the battle and Tecumseh's followers dispersed. American apprehensions of British complicity in stirring up Native unrest seemed to be confirmed when Tecumseh and many of his supporters sought refuge in Upper Canada.

Within the United States Congress, an increasingly vocal group of "war hawks" demanded that the United States invade Canada, likening the contest to a second war for independence. This bold move, they reasoned, would restore America's national honour; avenge British harassment on the high seas and intrigue in the northwest; help eliminate the Native threat; provide new territory for expansion; and spread the blessings of American liberty across the continent. Of course, added to this catalogue of British injustices to be avenged was simple opportunism: with Britain preoccupied by war with Napoleonic

France, the time seemed ripe to pick off Britain's colonial possessions in North America. Persuaded by the rising tide of war fever, and convinced that the conquest of Canada was "a mere matter of marching," President James Madison declared war on Britain on June 18, 1812. A few days later, Britain revoked the ordinances that had disrupted American shipping and had caused such offence, but it was too late to turn back.

1812: The United States declares war on Britain on June 18.

Neither side was well prepared for war. At the start of the war, the American army had only 6500 poorly trained and ill-equipped men, and was commanded, for the most part, by aging veterans of the Revolutionary War. While support for the war was widespread in frontier states and in the south, there was strong opposition in the northeast. Flags even flew at half-mast in Boston when it was learned that war had been declared. The situation was not much better in British North America, which was defended by only 10 000 British regular troops spread from Newfoundland to Amherstburg in southwestern Upper Canada. The commander of British forces in Upper Canada, Sir Isaac Brock, questioned the loyalty of the general population and the reliability of the provincial militia. "My situation is most critical," Brock confided to Governor Prevost, "not from anything the enemy can do but from the disposition of the people. Most of the people have lost all confidence—I however speak loud and look big."[41] The sheer inequality of numbers was also a sobering reality: the population in all of the British North American colonies scarcely reached 500 000, in contrast to the 7.5 million people who now made up the United States.

The Americans developed a plan for a three-pronged attack to take the British North American heartland quickly. General Henry Dearborn would strike at Montreal via the Lake Champlain corridor; General Stephen Van Rensselaer would attack across the Niagara frontier; and General William Hull would drive northward from Detroit. The American strategy depended on timing and effective coordination of each of the assaults. However, long distances and rough terrain made communications difficult. As a result, each of the American commanders acted independently, launching poorly timed and ill-organized attacks.

In July 1812, William Hull moved to liberate western Upper Canada. Since the lion's share of Upper Canada's population consisted of post-Loyalist American immigrants, Hull confidently expected that Upper Canadians would welcome the American liberators. He crossed the border and issued a flamboyant proclamation inviting them to rise up and throw off their British overlords. At Sandwich (later Windsor), Hull assured the residents that they would be "emancipated from Tyranny and oppression and restored to the dignified station of freemen." He did not ask their assistance, he said, because "I come prepared for every contingency" with no doubt of success. Any resisters "will be … treated as enemies, and the horrors and calamities of war will stalk before you."[42] When his invitation failed to generate the expected response, Hull scurried back across the border to Detroit.

Tecumseh's help would prove vital to the British forces. Isaac Brock greatly admired the man he called the "Wellington of the Indians"[43] "A more sagacious or a more gallant Warrior does not I believe exist," he wrote.[44] Tecumseh returned the admiration. When Brock detailed a plan to attack the American position at Fort Detroit, Tecumseh reportedly exclaimed, "Ho-yo-o-e! This is a man!"[45] In the summer of 1812, Brock led a force of 1300 to Fort Detroit. British regulars made up only 300 of this contingent; the rest consisted of 400 militiamen, and about 600 Aboriginal warriors led by Tecumseh. Hull had a larger army inside the fort—a little over 2000 men—but Brock and Tecumseh managed to defeat him psychologically. The militia were clad in the uniforms of regulars, creating the appearance of a larger professional force. The Natives, with painted faces, lit bonfires and filled the air with the chilling sound of ceremonial war dances throughout the night. One of the Canadian militia thought that it looked as if the gates of hell had been opened, and all the demons let out to play. Tecumseh paraded the same warriors back and forth in front of the fort to create the impression of thousands of warriors massing for a devastating attack. In the morning, Brock sent Hull a note warning him that the Natives would soon be beyond his control. As Brock began the artillery bombardment of the fort, Hull's courage deserted him and on August 16, 1812, he sought terms for the surrender of Detroit. This improbable success buoyed Canadian morale.

1812: The British win a surprise victory at Detroit on August 16, 1812.

Brock hurried back to Fort George on the Niagara frontier where an imminent American invasion was rumoured. On the early morning of October 13, 1812, a confused American offensive was launched across the Niagara River from Lewiston, New York. The 1200 attackers had to cross the dangerous currents of the fast-moving river and then ascend an 80-metre embankment to Queenston Heights. Many boats lacked sufficient oars, and proper transport had not been arranged for the artillery pieces. Some New York militiamen, loath to engage with the Mohawk warriors who were massing on the heights, insisted on their right not to be deployed on foreign soil. Mohawk war chief John Norton (Teyoninhokovrawen), a Scottish-educated protégé of Joseph Brant, led the Native warriors. A few American detachments, however, ascended the heights, captured some British guns, and began to fire upon the town below. The gunfire awakened Brock, who immediately set out from Fort George with a force of 1000 British regulars and 600 Upper Canadian militiamen, including a detachment of former American slaves. Brock was determined to aggressively repel the invaders, convinced that the loss of Queenston Heights would augur the loss of all Upper Canada. But a sharp-eyed American sniper picked out the general's uniform, and took aim; Brock fell with a fatal bullet in his chest.

October 13, 1812: The victorious Major General Isaac Brock is killed by an American sharpshooter at the Battle of Queenston Heights.

Demoralized by the loss of their leader, the British troops and the militia fell back. But the arrival of reinforcements under Brock's second-in-command, Major General Roger Sheaffe, and a determined stand by the Mohawks, turned the tide of battle. Those among the American invaders who could, retreated back down the cliff face, but almost 1000 were left stranded on the wrong side of the Niagara River, and were taken as prisoners. The Americans lost an estimated 300 to 500 casualties, as opposed to fewer than 100 on the other side. The successful defence of Queenston Heights, added to the triumph at Detroit, did much to bolster Canadian confidence. Brock emerged as an iconic symbol, whose brave death had to be avenged.

The spring of 1813 brought a re-evaluation of American strategy. Control of the Great Lakes, American commanders reasoned, may be the key to taking Canada. While the American army was in poor shape, the navy had experienced officers and crew. The Americans struck quickly. On April 26, 1813, an American squadron of ships commanded by Commodore Isaac Chauncey landed a force of 1600, commanded by General Henry Dearborn and Brigadier Zebulon Pike, near York. With only four companies of British regulars defending the capital of Upper Canada, the commander of the British forces and

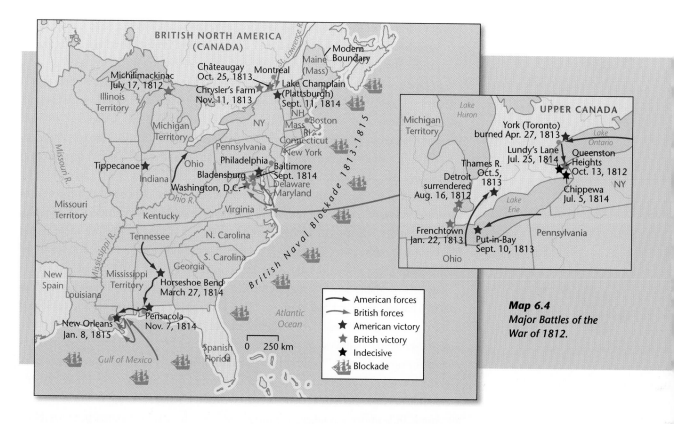

Map 6.4
Major Battles of the War of 1812.

civil administrator of the province, Major General Roger Sheaffe, decided upon a strategic withdrawal and retreated to Kingston. As the American troops advanced upon York, Chauncey's ships began to bombard the town's defences. Feeling abandoned by Sheaffe, a civilian delegation led by the Reverend John Strachan met with Dearborn to negotiate York's surrender. Strachan accused Dearborn of deliberately delaying the capitulation to permit his troops to loot and plunder. During the negotiations, the powder magazine at the fort exploded, killing Pike and inflicting heavy casualties on both sides.

Angry at the losses, American troops set fire to the legislative buildings and proceeded to pillage the town. The fallout from the loss of York was considerable. Although Sheaffe's decision to withdraw his forces was militarily prudent, public outrage forced his removal from his civil and military positions in Upper Canada. John Strachan's conduct during the siege added greatly to his reputation among the residents of York, and he emerged from the war an important and influential civil and religious figure. American arson and looting at York was cited as justification for the British burning of Washington a year later.

Emboldened by the fall of York, the Americans next struck at Fort George on the Niagara frontier. On May 25, 1813, the Americans began to bombard the British with hot shot (heated cannon balls) from their positions across the Niagara River, destroying much of the interior of Fort George. Having learned the lessons of the previous year's defeat at Queenston, the Americans used their naval superiority to land 2000 troops on the shores of Lake Ontario, rather than attempt another crossing of the Niagara River. Surprised by the American move, the commander of Fort George, Brigadier General John

April 1813: American forces capture and loot York, the capital of Upper Canada.

May 27, 1813: The Americans capture Fort George.

June 5–6, 1813: The British win a victory at Stoney Creek.

June 24, 1813: Advance warnings foil an American offensive at Beaver Dams.

September 10, 1813: Americans win a naval victory in the Battle of Lake Erie (or "Put-in-Bay").

Vincent, scrambled to meet the invaders on the beaches, but was forced to withdraw up the Niagara Peninsula to Burlington Heights. The cautious Dearborn waited for the arrival of reinforcements before setting out in pursuit of the retreating British forces.

On June 5, 1813, the Americans advanced toward Stoney Creek and set up their head-quarters at Gage Farm. Nineteen-year-old Billy Green learned the Americans' password, and immediately took news of the American position and signals to General Vincent. Vincent decided to launch a surprise attack that very night. A British force of 700 regulars and militia successfully overtook American sentries, and approached the main camp where some 3400 infantrymen were slumbering; the cry of a sentry who was struck by a tomahawk raised the alarm. In the confusion that followed, Vincent was thrown from his horse and wandered lost in the woods until daybreak. One of the American generals, William Winder, was captured when he mistook British troops for his own men. Seeing the capture of their leader, imagining that they faced a much larger force, and fearful of falling prey to Native warriors, the Americans retreated back to Fort George.

The British established two small outposts at Twelve Mile Creek and Beaver Dams from which to harass the Americans. With Fort George in ruins, American officers were billeted in the homes of nearby residents, including that of James and Laura Secord. When Laura Secord overheard the Americans discuss plans to attack the British outposts, she set out early on the morning of June 23 to alert the British commander, Lieutenant James Fitzgibbon. The risk was considerable: captured enemy spies could face summary execution. Secord's heroic journey later became the subject of myth and legend, although in the immediate aftermath, little notice was taken. She succeeded in reaching Beaver Dams, but Fitzgibbon had already been warned of American movements by Mohawk allies. The Mohawks, led by John Brant (Ahyouwaighs), the son of Joseph Brant, ambushed an American raiding party the following day. The Americans surrendered when Fitzgibbon warned that the Natives could not be restrained. The loss at Beaver Dams demoralized the Americans holed up at Fort George and returned effective control of most the Niagara frontier to the British.

The occupation of Fort George, however, permitted the Americans to transport additional ships to Lake Erie, where Commodore Oliver Perry, a veteran of the naval campaign at Tripoli, had already assembled an impressive fleet. On September 10, Perry defeated a squadron of British ships at Put-in-Bay, giving the Americans control of Lake Erie and making British control of Detroit and the surrounding frontier untenable.

The young and inexperienced British commander at Detroit, Major General Henry Procter (sometimes spelled "Proctor"), staged a strategic withdrawal. To Tecumseh and the Native allies, Procter was like "a fat animal that carries its tail upon its back but when affrighted, it drops it between its legs and runs off."[46] Tecumseh was determined to remain and fight, and pleaded with Procter to leave his arms and ammunition behind. Unmoved by Tecumseh's appeals, Procter's tired and hungry forces made a disorganized retreat up the Thames Valley, pursued by Tecumseh's old nemesis, William Henry Harrison and an American army of more than 3000. Tecumseh's warriors covered the rear, but the Americans caught up with Procter's retreating forces at Moraviantown. Exhausted and demoralized, the British fled in disarray, leaving Tecumseh's warriors to battle the Americans. Tecumseh's voice was heard above the din, exhorting his warriors on in pitched hand-to-hand combat.

Then, Tecumseh's voice fell silent. No one knows who killed Tecumseh or what became of his body. During William Henry Harrison's presidential campaign in 1840, supporters exploited his renown as an American "Indian fighter" by displaying what they claimed were Tecumseh's bones at political rallies.[47] Wherever his bones may lie, with the death of Tecumseh the dream of a pan-Indian nation to resist American expansion also received a mortal blow.

October 5, 1813: Tecumseh is killed at Moraviantown.

With their victory at Moraviantown, the Americans were well positioned to conquer Upper Canada. British commanders knew that they could not count on the militia or the civilian population to repel the Americans. Long periods of separation from family and livelihood, inadequate food, shelter, and supplies, and the threat of disease contributed to high rates of desertion and avoidance of service among the militia. One member of the militia warned his commanding officer of the "certain calamity that must befall us if the Militia are thus continued to be called from their families." Another wrote to his brother that "desertion has come to such height that 8 or 10 men go off daily."[48]

Relations between the military and the civilian population deteriorated as the war dragged on. Soldiers often complained that civilians charged exorbitant prices for food and supplies and participated in an illegal black market. Civilians resented the damage to their properties caused by soldiers who used fence rails for firewood and plundered their produce and livestock when supply systems broke down. Many residents of southwestern Upper Canada were themselves immigrants from the United States who quietly sympathized with the Americans; some even actively supported the enemy cause. Convinced that Upper Canada was about to fall to the Americans, Joseph Willcocks, a member of the legislative assembly, and one of the government's most vocal critics, began passing military intelligence to the Americans, accepted a commission in the United States army, and recruited a Canadian volunteer force to fight alongside the enemy. Despite signs of support among the local population, Harrison decided it was prudent to return to Detroit before the onset of winter rather than further his advance.

The American Secretary of War, John Armstrong, turned his attention to the east, and devised a plan for the capture of Montreal. Armstrong planned a two-pronged attack: one force would follow the traditional invasion route north from Lake Champlain, and another would proceed from Sackets Harbor, cross the St. Lawrence frontier, and move down the river to join up with the invading forces from Lake Champlain before falling upon Montreal. The Americans expected that few French Canadians would support the British defence. With rumours of an American invasion rampant, the commander of British outposts south of Montreal, Lieutenant Colonel Charles Michel de Salaberry, fortified a strategic position on the Châteauguay River from which to confront the attackers. With a force of just 500 *Canadien* volunteers, *Les Voltigeurs*, and two dozen Mohawk warriors, de Salaberry anxiously waited for the arrival of the American invasion force.

October 26, 1813: French-Canadian militia and Mohawk warriors repulse American invasion of Lower Canada at Châteauguay.

On October 26, 1813, the confident Americans, 4000 strong, opened fire on de Salaberry's small army. Protected by their well-placed defences, Les Voltigeurs and the Mohawks stood their ground. Unable to breach de Salaberry's barricades and vulnerable to enemy fire, the Americans withdrew. De Salaberry's men remained encamped in their makeshift fortifications for more than a week, enduring cold rains and depleted rations, lest the Americans regroup and renew the assault—but the Americans did not return. Dissension between American commanders, the refusal of the New York militia to cross the frontier, and the miserable weather conditions convinced Major General Wade Hampton to abandon the field and return to Plattsburg, New York.

Despite Hampton's withdrawal, the second prong of the American attack proceeded as planned. Successfully evading the British post at Prescott, an American force crossed the St. Lawrence on November 9, 1813. Two days later, at John Crysler's farm in Upper Canada, on the banks of the river near the Long Sault rapids, a force of British regulars and militia successfully repelled a much larger American force. With the approach of winter, the Americans ended their ill-fated St. Lawrence campaign.

Despite repeated attempts, the Americans had not succeeded in taking Canada, and to many the war appeared increasingly futile. The British also began to question the value of the war. Years of battling Napoleon had left the British war chest exhausted, and the commitment of Canadians to the war was doubtful. In November 1813, the British and Americans began peace negotiations. The British insisted that any peace should include the creation of a Native territory between Canada and the United States, the exclusive right to maintain a navy on the Great Lakes and to construct forts along the shores, and navigation rights on the Mississippi River. These terms were unacceptable to the Americans, and hostilities resumed in the spring of 1814.

With the defeat of Napoleon in Europe, experienced British troops began to arrive in North America in large numbers. These reinforcements strengthened British resolve to root out disloyalty and dislodge the Americans from Upper Canada. In the spring of 1814, 15 Upper Canadians were charged with treason and sentenced to hang. On July 20, 1814, eight men were publicly executed on Burlington Heights, their severed heads displayed on pikes as a warning to anyone who might consider helping the American enemies.

A couple of weeks before, on July 3, an American army under the command of Brigadier General Winfield Scott crossed the Niagara frontier and captured Fort Erie. Joseph Willcocks and his band of traitors set fire to Newark to clear the way for the advance of the American invaders. From Fort George, the lieutenant governor of Upper Canada, Lieutenant General Sir Gordon Drummond, took charge of the British forces and ordered an advance of troops to Lundy's Lane to repulse the Americans. There, in a graveyard, on July 25, 1814, the British and American forces met in the bloodiest battle of the war. The battle raged all day and continued until after midnight. Even the faint illumination of moonlight was lost amid the smoke from the guns, and many fell to friendly fire. The renegade Joseph Willcocks fled the battle scene around midnight and took refuge in Fort Erie, fearing the Americans had lost the battle and that he would be hanged if captured. He would later be killed during a raid on Fort Erie in September 1814.

By dawn, the rest of the American force had also retreated. By the battle's end, the Americans had lost 860 casualties, the British and Canadians 878. Dead and wounded lay in the dark among the tombstones. Having held their ground at Lundy's Lane, the British attempted to rout the Americans from Fort Erie. A long and costly siege ensued, but it was not until November that the Americans abandoned the fort, withdrawing across the Niagara River.

November 11, 1813: American invaders suffer defeat at John Crysler's farm in Upper Canada.

Spring 1814: Anglo–American peace negotiations break down.

July 25, 1814: The Americans are repelled in the bloodiest battle fought on Canadian soil at Lundy's Lane.

While the war had ground to a stalemate in Upper Canada, the British expanded the field of battle, launching a series of naval attacks around Chesapeake Bay in August. On August 24, 1814, the British marched on Washington, burning the White House and other public buildings. In September, the British attacked Baltimore, but failed to capture the city. Sunken American vessels in the harbour kept most of the British naval guns out of range of Baltimore's Fort McHenry. An American lawyer, Francis Scott Key, was on board a ship several kilometres from the fort, negotiating with the British over an exchange of prisoners. When dawn broke, he was relieved to see the American flag still fluttering from the ramparts of Fort McHenry. His much-celebrated anthem, "The Star Spangled Banner," thus commemorates a war in which the Americans failed to achieve most of their objectives.

By the autumn of 1814, the costs of the war pressed heavily on both sides, and the peace negotiations begun the previous year assumed a renewed urgency. On December 24, 1814 the Treaty of Ghent officially ended the conflict. It took several weeks for the news to reach North America, however, and the British and Americans still fought on in New Orleans from December 23 to January 8, 1815, unaware that the two nations were at peace. Hundreds more died in the Battle of New Orleans.

December 24, 1814: The Treaty of Ghent officially ends the War of 1812.

The Treaty of Ghent essentially restored matters to the status quo before the war, allowing the Americans, British, and Canadians to claim a measure of victory: the Americans failed to capture Canada, but neither had they lost any territory. The British had kept their British North American colonies. For their part, British North Americans could claim to have participated in their own defence against American aggression. Exaggerated claims of the importance of the militia in defending British North America from American aggression later provided the basis for a nascent English-Canadian nationalism. The First Nations, however, could not claim victory, regardless of their successes in battle—no Aboriginal nations were represented at the peace talks, nor did the British stand by their pledge to secure a territory for the Natives of the lower Great Lakes. The Treaty of Ghent simply affirmed the rights and privileges the Natives enjoyed before the war. The commitment was so vague as to be meaningless, as the First Nations of the region soon discovered.

Peace in Europe seemed to be secured with Napoleon's April 1814 exile to the Mediterranean island of Elba. He would escape early in 1815 and return to France, only to face final defeat in Belgium at the Battle of Waterloo on June 18, 1815. At last, after the November 20, 1815 Treaty of Paris, Britain could turn to the difficult task of restoring the nation to a peacetime basis after decades of warfare. The effects of this challenging transition would make themselves felt in British North America as well.

Historians have often credited the War of 1812 with unifying British North Americans, strengthening anti-American sentiment, and contributing to unprecedented economic growth and prosperity. Recent studies have painted a different and more complex picture. With communities isolated and diverse prior to the war, the conflict did little to draw the British North American colonies closer to each other. The Maritime colonies, removed from the fighting, continued to trade extensively with nearby American states. Besides profiting from this clandestine trade, Halifax derived benefits from the presence of 10 000 British regulars at the garrison.

Tensions between Francophones and Anglophones resurfaced as soon as the war ended, especially between French and English parties in Lower Canada's legislative assembly. In

Upper Canada, the war left a bitter legacy of discontent among the victims of the fighting. For many years following the war, veterans, widows, orphans, and property owners complained about delays in compensation and insufficient recognition of their contributions to the war effort. Among the Upper Canadian establishment, the war gave rise to a reactionary politics that was decidedly anti-American and that characterized any opposition to the province's administration as dangerous and disloyal. The war temporarily halted immigration to Upper Canada from the United States, and reoriented the recruitment of settlers to Britain. The fact that most Upper Canadian men avoided military service suggests that the majority of settlers did not feel strong attachments to either Britain or the United States. With demobilization and the end to wartime spending, many parts of British North America lapsed into economic recession. But the mere fact that the colonies had survived the war intact allowed them to continue to evolve and develop as diverse communities in the decades to come. Especially in Upper Canada, the War of 1812 provided the basis for a heroic past that contributed to an emerging sense of English-Canadian nationalism.

Conclusion

The years between the end of the American Revolution and the restoration of peace in 1815 were transformative ones in British North America. The difficult task of state formation in the Atlantic colonies and the new settlement of Upper Canada raised controversies over civil administration and religious privileges. The ambitions and anxieties of Aboriginal nations intersected, and at times conflicted, with Britain's imperial goals. New economic activity, often fuelled by protective tariffs in the mother country, transformed the colonies. The continuation of the old staple trade in furs brought growing conflict to the western interior. New knowledge of the continent's Pacific coast was emerging. A growing assertiveness on the part of the United States, coupled with provocative British policies, embroiled the colonies in a war not of their choosing. Throughout these difficult years, a new identity was beginning to take shape among the residents of British North America.

Questions to Consider

1. How successful were John Graves Simcoe's efforts to mould Upper Canada in the image of Britain?

2. What role did imperial tariff policy play in the development of the British North American economy?

3. Who were the Métis? What role did the Métis play in the fur trade and the development of the west?

4. What factors contributed to war in 1812? Who were the winners and the losers?

Critical Thinking Questions

1. What was the context of the 1791 *Constitutional Act*, and why is this significant?

2. What differences existed between the approach and organizational cultures of the Hudson's Bay Company and the North West Company? What accounts for these differences?

3. Did British policymakers deal fairly with their Aboriginal allies in North America in the years between 1783 and 1815? What constraints did they face?

4. The War of 1812 has been credited with contributing to a distinctive Upper Canadian and English-Canadian identity and nationalism. Was this emergent nationalism rooted in reality or myth? Explain.

Suggested Readings

The Atlantic Colonies

Bannister, Jerry. *The Rule of the Admirals: Law, Custom, and Naval Government in Newfoundland, 1699–1832.* Toronto: University of Toronto Press, 2003.

Bumsted, J.M. *The People's Clearance: Highland Emigration to British North America, 1770–1815.* Edinburgh: University of Edinburgh Press, 1982.

Cadigan, Sean. *Hope and Deception in Conception Bay: Merchant-Settler Relations in Newfoundland, 1785–1855.* Toronto: University of Toronto Press, 1995.

Conrad, Margaret, and James K. Hiller. *Atlantic Canada: A Region in the Making.* Toronto: Oxford University Press, 2001.

Fingard, Judith. *The Anglican Design in Loyalist Nova Scotia, 1783–1816.* London: Society for Promoting Christian Knowledge, 1972.

Gywn, Julian. *Excessive Expectations: Maritime Commerce and the Economic Development of Nova Scotia, 1740–1870.* Montreal and Kingston: McGill-Queen's University Press, 1998.

MacNutt, W.S. *The Atlantic Provinces: The Emergence of Colonial Society, 1712–1857.* Toronto: McClelland & Stewart, 1965.

Sager, Eric, and L.R. Fischer. *Shipping and Shipbuilding in Atlantic Canada.* Ottawa: Canadian Historical Association, 1986.

Wynn, Graeme. *Timber Colony: A Historical Geography of Early Nineteenth Century New Brunswick.* Toronto: University of Toronto Press, 1981.

Upper Canada

Allen, Robert. *His Majesty's Indian Allies: British Indian Policy in the Defence of Canada, 1774–1815.* Toronto: Dundurn, 1996.

Clarke, John. *Land, Power and Economics on the Frontier of Upper Canada.* Montreal and Kingston: McGill-Queen's University Press, 2001.

Craig, Gerald M. *Upper Canada: The Formative Years, 1784–1841.* Toronto: McClelland & Stewart, 1963.

Coates, Colin, and Morgan Cecilia. *Heroines and History: Representations of Madeline de Vercheres and Laura Secord.* Toronto: University of Toronto Press, 2002.

Errington, Jane. *The Lion, the Eagle and Upper Canada: A Developing Colonial Ideology.* Montreal and Kingston: McGill-Queen's University Press, 1987.

Errington, Jane. *Wives and Mothers, School Mistresses and Scullery Maids: Working Women in Upper Canada, 1790–1840*. Montreal and Kingston: McGill-Queen's University Press, 1995.

Fahey, Curtis. *In His Name: The Anglican Experience in Upper Canada, 1791–1854*. Ottawa: Carleton University Press, 1991.

Johnson, J.K. *Becoming Prominent: Regional Leadership in Upper Canada, 1791–1841*. Montreal and Kingston: McGill-Queen's University Press, 1989.

Johnson, J.K., ed. *Historical Essays on Upper Canada: New Perspectives*. Ottawa: Carleton University Press, 1989.

McCalla, Douglas. *Planting the Province: The Economic History of Upper Canada*. Toronto: University of Toronto Press, 1993.

McNairn, Jeffrey L. *The Capacity to Judge: Public Opinion and Deliberative Democracy in Upper Canada, 1791–1854*. Toronto: University of Toronto Press, 2000.

Mills, David. *The Idea of Loyalty in Upper Canada, 1784–1850*. Montreal and Kingston: McGill-Queen's University Press, 1988.

Morgan, Cecilia. *Public Men and Virtuous Women: The Gendered Language of Religion and Politics in Upper Canada, 1791–1850*. Toronto: University of Toronto Press, 1996.

Noel, S.J.R. *Patrons, Clients, Brokers: Ontario Society and Politics, 1791–1896*. Toronto: University of Toronto Press, 1990.

Wilson, Bruce G. *The Enterprises of Robert Hamilton: A Study of Wealth and Influence in Early Upper Canada, 1776–1812*. Ottawa: Carleton University Press, 1983.

Wilson, Catherine Anne. *Tenants in Time: Family Strategies, Land and Liberalism in Upper Canada, 1799–1871*. Montreal and Kingston: McGill-Queen's University Press, 2009.

Wise, S.F. *God's Peculiar Peoples: Essays on Political Culture in Nineteenth Century Canada*. A.B. McKillop and Paul Romney, eds. Ottawa: Carleton University Press, 1988.

Lower Canada

Coates, Colin M. *The Metamorphosis of Landscape and Memory in Early Quebec*. Montreal and Kingston: McGill-Queen's University Press, 2000.

Creighton, Donald. *The Empire of the St. Lawrence*. Toronto: Macmillan, 1956.

Greenwood, F. Murray. *Legacies of Fear: Law and Politics in Quebec in the Era of the French Revolution*. Toronto: University of Toronto Press, 1993.

Greer, Alan. *Peasant, Lord and Merchant: Rural Society in Three Quebec Parishes, 1740–1840*. Toronto: University of Toronto Press, 1985.

McCallum, John. *Unequal Beginnings: Agriculture and Economic Development in Quebec and Ontario until 1870*. Toronto: University of Toronto Press, 1980.

Ouellet, Fernand. *Economic and Social History of Quebec, 1760–1850*. Toronto: Macmillan, 1980.

Ouellet, Fernand. *Lower Canada, 1791–1840: Social Change and Nationalism.* Toronto: McClelland & Stewart, 1980.

The War of 1812

Benn, Carl. *The Iroquois in the War of 1812.* Toronto: University of Toronto Press, 1998.

Hitsman, J. Mackay. *The Incredible War of 1812: A Military History.* Updated by Donald E. Graves. Toronto: Robin Brass Studio, 1965. Revised Edition 1999.

Sheppard, George. *Plunder, Profits and Paroles: A Social History of the War of 1812 in Upper Canada.* Montreal and Kingston: McGill-Queen's University Press, 1994.

Stanley, G.F.G. *The War of 1812: Land Operations.* Toronto: Macmillan, 1983.

Sugden, John. *Tecumseh: A Life.* New York: Henry Holt. 1997.

Turner, Wesley B. *The War of 1812: The War That Both Sides Won.* Toronto: Dundurn, 2000.

Zuehlke, Mark. *For Honour's Sake: The War of 1812 and the Brokering of an Uneasy Peace.* Toronto: Random House, 2006.

The West and Fur Trade

Barman, Jean. *The West Beyond the West: A History of British Columbia.* Toronto: University of Toronto Press, 1991.

Binnema, Theodore. *Common and Contested Ground: A Human and Environmental History of the Northwestern Plains.* Norman: University of Oklahoma Press, 2001.

Brown, Jennifer S.H. *Strangers in Blood: Fur Trade Company Families in Indian Country.* Vancouver: University of British Columbia Press, 1980.

Bumsted, J.M. *Fur Trade Wars: The Founding of Western Canada.* Winnipeg: Great Plains, 1999.

Burley, Edith I. *Servants in the Honourable Company: Work, Discipline and Conflict in the Hudson's Bay Company, 1770–1879.* Toronto: Oxford University Press, 1997.

Clayton, Daniel. *Islands of Truth: The Imperial Fashioning of Vancouver Island.* Vancouver: University of British Columbia Press, 2000.

Ens, Gerhard J. *Homeland to Hinterland: The Changing Worlds of the Red River Métis in the Nineteenth Century.* Toronto: University of Toronto Press, 1996.

Friesen, Gerald. *The Canadian Prairies: A History.* Toronto: University of Toronto Press, 1984.

Gibson, James R. *Otter Skins, Boston Ships and China Goods: The Maritime Fur Trade of the Northwest Coast, 1785–1841.* Montreal and Kingston: McGill-Queen's University Press, 1992.

Gough, Barry. *The Northwest Coast: British Navigation, Trade and Discoveries to 1812.* Vancouver: University of British Columbia Press, 1992.

Mackie, Richard Somerset. *Trading Beyond the Mountains: The British Fur Trade on the Pacific, 1793–1843.* Vancouver: University of British Columbia Press, 1997.

Podruchny, Carolyn. *Making the Voyageur World: Travellers and Traders in the North American Fur Trade.* Toronto: University of Toronto Press, 2006.

Ray, Arthur. *Indians in the Fur Trade: Their Role as Trappers, Hunters and Middlemen in the Lands Southwest of Hudson Bay, 1680–1870.* Toronto: University of Toronto Press, 1998.

Rich, E.E. *The Fur Trade and the Northwest to 1857.* Toronto: McClelland & Stewart, 1967.

Morton, W.L. *Manitoba: A History.* Toronto: University of Toronto Press, 1957.

Van Kirk, Sylvia. *Many Tender Ties: Women in Fur-Trade Society, 1670–1870.* Toronto: Watson and Dwyer, 1980.

Notes

[1] William Kaye Lamb, ed. *Sixteen Years in Indian Country: The Journal of Daniel Williams Harmon, 1800–1816* (Toronto: University of Toronto Press, 1957). See also: Sylvia Van Kirk, *"Many Tender Ties" Women in Fur-Trade Society in Western Canada, 1670–1870* (Winnipeg: Watson & Dwyer Publishing, 1980); "'Women in Between': Indian Women in Fur Trade Society" *Canadian Historical Association Historical Papers* (1977), 30–47; *Canada: A People's History: The Pathfinders.*

[2] Jerry Bannister, *The Rule of the Admirals: Law, Custom, and Naval Government in Newfoundland, 1699–1832* (Toronto: University of Toronto Press, 2003), 4–15.

[3] W.G. Godfrey, "Thomas Carleton," *Dictionary of Canadian Biography*, http://www.biographi.ca.

[4] Charles Inglis in Thomas R. Millman and A.R. Kelly, *Atlantic Canada to 1900: A History of the Anglican Church* (Toronto: Anglican Book Centre, 1983), 52.

[5] Janet Azjenstat, "Celebrating 1791: Two Hundred Years of Representative Government," *Canadian Parliamentary Review* 14: 1 (1991), http://www2.parl.gc.ca/Sites/LOP/Infoparl/english/issue.asp?param=136&art=890.

[6] As quoted in Ibid.

[7] "The Constitution Act of 1791," J.H. Stewart Reid, Kenneth McNaught, and Harry S. Crowe, eds. *A Source-book of Canadian History: Selected Documents and Personal Papers* (Toronto: Longmans, Green & Co., 1959), 64–65.

[8] E.A. Cruikshank, ed., *The Correspondence of Lieut. Governor John Graves Simcoe*, vol. I (Toronto: 1923).

[9] E.A. Cruikshank, ed., *Correspondence of Simcoe*, vol. I.

[10] Mary Quayle Innis, ed., *Mrs. Simcoe's Diary* (New York: St. Martin's, 1965).

[11] John Graves Simcoe, *Journals of the House of Assembly*, 15 Oct. 1792, 18.

[12] Richard Cartwright quoted in Jane Errington, *The Lion, the Eagle and Upper Canada: A Developing Colonial Ideology* (Montreal and Kingston: McGill-Queen's University Press, 1987), 32, 30.

[13] Jane Errington, *The Lion, the Eagle, and Upper Canada*, 5.

[14] As quoted by Jane Errington, *The Lion, the Eagle, and Upper Canada*, 52.

[15] E.A. Cruikshank, ed., *Correspondence of Simcoe*, vol. I.

[16] E.A. Cruikshank, ed., *Correspondence of Simcoe*, vol. I.

[17] Robert Allen, *His Majesty's Indian Allies: British Indian Policy in the Defence of Canada, 1774–1815* (Toronto: Dundurn, 1996), 72–73, 66.

[18] Ibid., 76.

[19] E.A. Cruikshank, ed., *Correspondence of Simcoe*, vol. I.

[20] Robert Allen, *His Majesty's Indian Allies*, 85.

21 William Renwick Riddell, "La Rochefoucauld-Liancourt's travels in Canada, 1795," Archives of Ontario Report, 1916.

22 Alan G. Brunger, "Thomas Talbot," *Dictionary of Canadian Biography*, http://www.biographi.ca.

23 Fernand Ouellet, "Pierre Stanislas Bédard," *Dictionary of Canadian Biography*, http://www.biographi.ca.

24 Sir James Craig to Lord Liverpool, 1 May 1810, *Statutes, Treaties and Documents of the Canadian Constitution, 1713–1929*; W.P.M. Kennedy, ed. (Toronto: Oxford University Press, 1930), 226, 230.

25 R. Cole Harris and John Warkentin, Canada Before Confederation: A Study in Historical Geography (Toronto: Oxford University Press, 1974), 86.

26 Joseph Robson, *An Account of Six Years Residence in Hudson's Bay from 1733 to 1736, and 1744 to 1747* (London: J. Payne and J. Bouquet, 1752), 6. Full text available via Early Canadiana, http://www.canadiana.org/ECO/PageView/20155/0021?id=c541e4e2c1732385.

27 R.M. Ballantyne, *Hudson's Bay, or Everyday Life in the Wilds of North America: During Six Years' Residence in the Territories of the Honourable Hudson's Bay Company* (Edinburgh: W. Blackwood, 1848), 95–95. Available through Early Canadiana Online at http://www.canadiana.org.

28 Arthur Ray, "Fur Trade History as an Aspect of Native History," in Ian A.L. Getty and Donald B. Smith, ed., *One Century Later: Western Canadian Reserve Indians since Treaty 7* (Vancouver: UBC Press, 1978), 12.

29 James Isham, "Observations on Hudson's Bay," in Germaine Warkentin, *Canadian Exploration Literature* (Toronto: Oxford University Press, 1993), 58.

30 R.M. Ballantyne, *Hudson's Bay*, 96–97.

31 Jennifer S.H. Brown, *Strangers in Blood: Fur Trade Company Families in Indian Country* (Norman: University of Oklahoma Press, 1996), 27.

32 Sylvia Van Kirk, *"Many Tender Ties" Women in Fur-Trade Society in Western Canada, 1670–1870* (Winnipeg: Watson & Dwyer Publishing, 1980); "'Women in Between': Indian Women in Fur Trade Society" *Canadian Historical Association Historical Papers* (1977), 30–47.

33 Washington Irving, *Astoria*, in Jan Noel, ed. *Race and Gender in the Northern Colonies* (Toronto: Canadian Scholars' Press, 2000), 83–84.

34 Carolyn Podruchny, *Making the Voyageur World: Travellers and Traders in the North American Fur Trade* (Toronto: University of Toronto Press, 2006), 86–89.

35 As quoted by W. Kaye Lamb, "Simon Fraser," *Dictionary of Canadian Biography*, http://www.biographi.ca.

36 Wendy Wickwire, "To See Ourselves as the Other's Other: Nlaka'pamux Contact Narratives," *Canadian Historical Review* 75: 1 (March 1994), 20.

37 Carolyn Podruchny, "Festivities, Fortitude, and Fraternalism: Fur Trade Masculinity and the Beaver Club, 1785-1827" in Jan Noel, *Race and Gender in the Northern Colonies* (Toronto: Canadian Scholars' Press, 2000), 53–79; George Bryce, *Lord Selkirk: The Makers of Canada Series* (Toronto: Morang & Co.), 139–141.

38 As quoted by Robert Allen, *His Majesty's Indian Allies*, 116.

39 Ibid., 108–109.

40 Ibid., 110.

41 J. Mackay Hitsman, *The Incredible War of 1812: A Military History*, Revised ed. (Toronto: Robin Brass Studio, 1999), 67.

42 Ibid., 65.

43 As quoted by John Sugden, *Tecumseh: A Life* (New York: Henry Holt, 1997), 308.

44 As quoted by Herbert C.W. Goltz, "Tecumseh (Tech-kum-thai)," *Dictionary of Canadian Biography*, http://www.biographi.ca.

45 As quoted by John Sugden, *Tecumseh*, 300.

46 Court Martial of Major-General Henry Proctor, LAC, MG 13, War Office 71, vol. 243, 381–382, appendix 7.

47 Guy St-Denis, *Tecumseh's Bones* (Montreal and Kingston: McGill-Queen's University Press, 2005), 10–11.

48 Colonel Joel Stone to Colonel Lethbridge, 25 October 1812, Joel Stone Family Papers, Archives of Ontario, F 536, MU 2892; Thomas G. Ridout to George Ridout, 16 September 1813, Thomas Ridout Family Papers, AO, F 43, MU 2390.

7

Development *and* Diversity: *1815–1836*

*I*n the summer of 1820, a five-year-old boy arrived at Kingston in Upper Canada, along with his parents, brother, and two sisters. They had come from Scotland at the invitation of kinsmen of the boy's mother. Good fortune had proved elusive in Glasgow; the father was a merchant who had struggled in the economic depression that followed the end of the Napoleonic Wars in 1815. Like so many others, he decided to leave the British Isles for North America. Contradicting the stereotypical image of reluctant exiles driven from their land by oppressive landlords, these newcomers exemplified the proactive character of most migrants. With the help of extended family, they seized the initiative to better their prospects in Canada. Colonel Donald Macpherson, the relative who provided the family's bridge to the new world, had been an immigrant himself, and in the phenomenon known as "chain migration" enabled their transition. Macpherson had served in North America during the American Revolutionary War and had returned for garrison duty in Quebec in 1807. His service in the War of 1812 was rewarded with a pension and land grant in Kingston,

chapter 7

THE EMIGRANTS WELCOME TO CANADA.

This 1832 cartoon reflects the disillusionment experienced by some new arrivals to Canada.

Source: Library and Archives Canada, C-041067.

a town teeming with demobilized soldiers. The British government provided them with land grants both to prevent economic distress as thousands were released from duty, and to protect the colonies by settling experienced soldiers close to the American border. It was to Macpherson's comfortable two-storey stone house in Kingston that the newly arrived relatives were welcomed: Hugh and Helen Macdonald, and their children, Margaret, Louisa, James, and John Alexander. John A. Macdonald's arrival in Canada, utterly typical of that period's immigration, gave no hint of the vital role he would come to play in the nation's political life.

After reading this chapter you will be able to:

1. Understand the complex motives of conflicting parties in early-nineteenth-century Red River settlement.
2. Assess connections between political activism and land policy in Upper Canada.
3. Identify key early-nineteenth-century developments in the Atlantic colonies.
4. Identify important changes in economic activities in nineteenth-century British North America: shipping, the timber trade, and canal building.
5. Evaluate the impact of immigration to British North America after 1815.

Introduction

The years after the War of 1812 proved to be formative ones in the history of British North America. The disparate colonies did not form any integrated whole, and each faced particular challenges in this period of rapid change. In Rupert's Land in the western interior, fierce rivalry between the fur-trading empire of the Hudson's Bay Company and the Montreal-based Northwest Company would reach a climax at Seven Oaks in 1816, in a battle with lasting significance to the Métis people of the plains. The timber trade in the Maritimes and the Canadas, and rising wheat production in Upper Canada, launched increased diversification of the colonial economies. A flurry of canal building in the Canadas in the 1820s spurred economic growth aimed at meeting the American challenge. But the most profound changes of all occurred in Britain's newest North American colony, Upper Canada, in the early decades of the nineteenth century.

Earlier American immigrants, at one time the majority, were overwhelmed by a flood of newcomers from the British Isles. The population of Upper Canada swelled from 75 000 at the outbreak of the War of 1812 to 450 000 by 1842. Most immigrants landed at Montreal and Quebec, which bore the brunt of cholera epidemics and struggled to absorb landless wage labourers, but the majority of the new arrivals then travelled west to take up land in Upper Canada. Upper Canada became a society in transition, shaped by contending colonial settlement theories, transplanted old world social organizations, religious and cultural divisions, and the struggle of an established colonial elite to maintain hegemony.

In the years following the peace in 1815, new agreements between Britain and the United States settled some issues affecting British North America's security. The Rush-Bagot Agreement of 1817—named for its negotiators, American Secretary of State Richard Rush and Sir Charles Bagot, British minister at Washington—set limits for naval forces on the Great Lakes and Lake Champlain. The Convention of 1818, besides resolving fisheries disputes, set the border between the United States and British North America. The 49th parallel of latitude was now the boundary from Lake of the Woods to the summit of the Rocky Mountains.

1818: An Anglo–American convention sets the border at the 49th parallel.

Hudson's Bay Company and North West Company Rivalry and the Battle of Seven Oaks

Lord Selkirk's bid to establish an agricultural colony at Red River settlement in 1812 brought a focus to the escalating rivalry between the Hudson's Bay Company and their Montreal-based competitors, the North West Company. The settlement of Scottish and

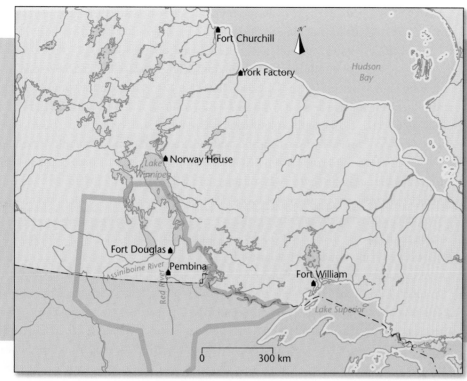

Map 7.1
Assiniboia and Red River Settlement.

Source: © Lucille Campey, *The Silver Chief*, p. 81.

Irish farmers at the junction of the Red and Assiniboine Rivers threatened the interests of Métis buffalo hunters, who had provided pemmican to sustain the North West Company's interior fur trade.

Cuthbert Grant, the son of a Scottish-born North West Company partner of the same name, had been "virtually born into the NWC," as George Woodcock puts it.[1] Grant had been born in the west, at Fort de la Rivière Tremblante in present-day Saskatchewan, had been educated at Montreal, and began work as a NWC clerk at a young age. He would have a vital role to play in the growing conflict with the HBC. Duncan Cameron, a North West Company partner with authority over the Red River district, encouraged the Métis in actions against the new settlers, and appointed the 21-year-old Grant one of four "Captains of the Métis" in the fall of 1814. Grant, who stood out among the others, would be later elevated to "Captain-General of all the Half-Breeds."

Grant and the Métis began a campaign of systematic harassment against the settlers, including the destruction of crops, theft of livestock, and the torching of buildings. Finding the area more akin to a war zone than the bucolic farming community they had been promised, the Selkirk settlers abandoned the colony in the spring of 1815, fleeing in boats up Lake Winnipeg. The HBC-appointed governor of the colony, Miles Macdonell, had been suffering under the constant strain of trying to protect the fledgling settlement, and suffered a nervous breakdown while at York Factory the previous summer, sending word to Selkirk that he should be replaced. Macdonell felt compelled to surrender himself to the NWC on the condition that the settlers not be harmed; they sent him to Montreal to answer for his supposed crimes. In the meantime, the dispossessed settlers were intercepted by Hudson's Bay Company officials at the top of the lake, and agreed to return to Red River only if the company promised to protect them from the Métis.

When news of the troubles reached London, Selkirk resolved to take charge of the situation himself, setting out for Canada in the fall of 1815. He spent the winter in Montreal, but his attempts to negotiate with the NWC were in vain. He was heartened, however, to learn in March 1816 that the colony had been re-established once more. This encouraging news was carried by Jean-Baptiste Lagimodière, who spent five months travelling 2900 kilometres on snowshoes from Red River to Montreal to reach Lord Selkirk. Recognizing that the fate of his settlers was still uncertain, Selkirk secured hired forces to defend them. These were the remnants of Swiss infantry regiments, the De Meurons and de Watteville, who had been disbanded after service in the War of 1812. An advance party set out for Red River in May 1816 under the command of Miles Macdonell, with Selkirk following with more men soon afterward.

As they were en route, however, events at Red River took an even more dramatic turn. On June 19, 1816, the HBC's new governor of the colony, Robert Semple, along with a band of settlers, confronted a party of Métis, led by Cuthbert Grant, at Seven Oaks. What began as a tense armed standoff and verbal exchange quickly ignited. When Governor Semple moved to grab the stock of a pointed gun, Métis riders sprang from their horses and opened fire; Semple was cut down along with 20 of his men. Only one Métis was killed. Grant's men, some decorated with war paint, capped their victory by stripping and mutilating the bodies of the vanquished. The surviving settlers fled the colony, and the Nor'Westers seized the local HBC headquarters at Fort Douglas.

1816: Fur trade rivalry culminates in the Battle of Seven Oaks.

These events are often described as the "Seven Oaks Massacre," a historical label that reflects the defeat of the forces of "civilization" and agricultural settlement. Gerald Friesen, professor of history at the University of Manitoba, also sees the conflict as pivotal to the historical identity of the Métis. Métis songs and stories commemorated the event, and the community grew more assertive in maintaining their right to hunt buffalo and live freely on the plains. The Native heritage of their mothers was central to that claim. "Seven Oaks was their ordeal by fire," Friesen explains. "It gave them a sense of nationhood that was to be reinforced by Riel and Dumont later in the century."[2] George Woodcock sees things differently, asserting that Grant "allowed himself to be used by the Nor'Westers," and was motivated by "vanity" and the desire for advancement in the company hierarchy. "There is nothing to suggest that before 1814 he saw the Métis as a nation, or gave any thought to their cause, or even identified himself with them," Woodcock argues.[3]

Red River resident Marie-Anne Gaboury Lagimodière, born near Trois Rivières, was the wife of messenger Jean-Baptiste Lagimodière. Her husband had not yet returned from his epic journey to Montreal when the violent crisis erupted at Seven Oaks. Fortunately, she and her children were rescued by Saulteaux Chief Peguis, who gave them shelter for several weeks at his camp. Peguis's protection yet again proved vital to those in the colony allied with the HBC. The chief vowed that he would always keep the colony under his care: "I shall hold it as an eagle keeps its prey in its talons."[4] Madame Lagimodiere would later be the grandmother of Métis leader Louis Riel.

Selkirk learned of the Seven Oaks killings as he and his forces approached Fort William, the North West Company's headquarters at the head of Lake Superior. Taking the law into his own hands, Selkirk captured the fort, released some prisoners taken by the NWC, arrested its director, William McGillivray, and seized the company's stores as compensation for the losses incurred at Red River. Selkirk's vigilante justice enraged Canadians, and warrants were issued for his arrest. The McGillivray family played a prominent role in the Montreal-based fur trade, and William himself was also a legislative councillor in Lower Canada.

Selkirk was approached with warrants for his arrest twice while at Fort William—in the autumn of 1816 and spring of 1817—but in each instance he resisted and had the constables apprehended. He believed that the warrants were forgeries, part of a NWC ploy to trap him. Selkirk set out for Red River on May 1, 1817, determined to overcome opposition and re-establish his colony. Peguis sent warnings that the NWC planned to waylay Selkirk's expedition as they neared Red River, and kept a force of his own warriors at Sturgeon Creek to discourage any further aggression by Grant's men. Selkirk arrived safely.

Also in Red River that summer was a commissioner appointed by Canadian authorities to enquire into the disturbing developments that had plagued the colony. William Bacheler Coltman, a Lower Canadian businessman and member of the executive council, brought a small detachment of troops with him, along with orders to collect evidence, re-establish peace and order, restore property seized by both sides, and arrest Selkirk, who had evaded earlier attempts to bring him to justice. Selkirk was alarmed to learn that Britain's Colonial Secretary, Lord Bathurst, who had sent instructions on what was to be done, had been getting his information from British Member of Parliament Edward Ellice, who was a partner in the North West Company. Selkirk was released on £6000 bail and travelled to Montreal to face trial, going first to Sandwich to address the earlier charges.

Although he was personally under a cloud of suspicion, before leaving Selkirk took the opportunity offered by Coltman's presence to conclude a land treaty with the local Cree and Ojibwe tribes. He hoped that the evidence of friendship and fair dealing would put to rest NWC claims that the Natives were resistant to an agricultural settlement. Selkirk had the authority of the Crown to conclude the treaties, and reassured Coltman that he need only act as a witness. On July 18, 1817, Chief Peguis and four other local chiefs, representing some Cree and Ojibwe tribes, gave their consent to a treaty that secured the colonists' right to settle two miles (3.2 kilometres) adjacent to the Red and Assiniboine Rivers in exchange for annual payments to each tribe of 100 pounds (45 kilograms) of tobacco or the equivalent. The terms of this treaty would be renegotiated in 1871 as "Treaty One," the first of a series of so-called "numbered treaties" made in Canada's interior in the post-Confederation era.[5]

The years of legal wrangling that followed over the fate of the Red River colony and Selkirk's own actions took a heavy toll on his health and reputation. Coltman's report appeared on May 4, 1818. Fair and balanced in his analysis, Coltman questioned the legality of the Red River colony and condemned Selkirk's actions at Fort William. Although he sympathized with the threat that the Red River colony presented to the trading interests of the North West Company and the way of life of the Métis, Coltman denounced the NWC's use of "intimidation and violence" and its inability to restrain the actions of the Métis. Coltman's report did little to ease the tensions in the northwest. The competition

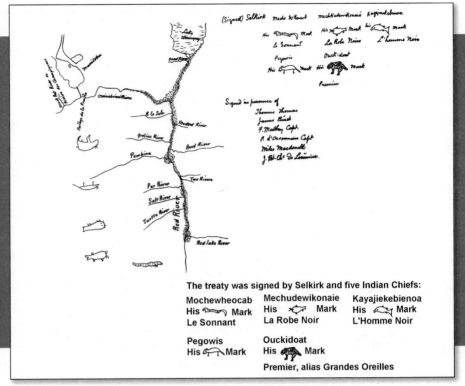

The treaty was signed by Selkirk and five Indian Chiefs:

Mochewheocab
His Mark
Le Sonnant

Mechudewikonaie
His Mark
La Robe Noir

Kayajiekebienoa
His Mark
L'Homme Noir

Pegowis
His Mark

Ouckidoat
His Mark
Premier, alias Grandes Oreilles

The 1817 Selkirk Treaty bears animal images, representing the marks of the chiefs who negotiated it.

Source: © Geoff Campey, 2003.

for furs simply shifted west to the Athabasca district where both the Hudson's Bay and North West companies established rival posts in close proximity to one another. The kidnappings, assaults, thefts, and court cases that followed exacted a heavy price from both companies.

Hudson's Bay Company and North West Company Merger, 1821

While devastating, the Battle of Seven Oaks was a blow from which Red River would eventually recover. Selkirk's interest in the colony's future included steps for a religious presence there, and the Roman Catholic Bishop of Quebec agreed to send priests: Father Joseph Norbert Provencher and Father Severe Dumoulin arrived in July 1818. Madame Lagimodière, who had had no access to the sacraments for 12 years, could hardly conceal her joy when the priests stepped from their canoe. Two days later, 100 children were brought forward to receive baptism. Madame Lagimodière, the only baptized woman in the colony, sponsored them all, becoming "ma Marraine," or godmother, to a generation of the colony's children.

Selkirk's reassertion of control over the colony and more aggressive Hudson's Bay Company tactics in the trade war were also beginning to tell on the fortunes of the North West Company. British colonial authorities pressed the trade rivals into a settlement. Selkirk's death in 1820 may have helped pave the way for an agreement between the two fur-trading enterprises. By 1821, negotiations were complete and the rivals merged all operations and personnel under the name Hudson's Bay Company. The new Hudson's Bay Company combined the financial and administrative stability of the old HBC with the field experience and adaptability of the North West Company. No longer a threat, the Red River settlement was now able to grow in peace, and the west stood on the verge of a new era in its development, an era that would seriously challenge the continued way of life of the Native peoples and the Métis.

1821: The long-warring Hudson's Bay and North West Companies are merged.

Rupert's Land Governor George Simpson and the HBC

Something of the culture of the HBC in the era after the 1821 merger may be gleaned from the story of the governor of Rupert's Land, George Simpson. His 18-year-old bride and cousin, Frances Simpson, recorded her impressions as she accompanied her 43-year-old husband on a canoe journey into the heart of the continent. In the spring of 1830, Frances Simpson left her home in England for the first time to travel thousands of kilometres, arriving at York Factory that summer. The new Mrs. Simpson was graciously received by the traders and factors at all the posts along the way, and praised for her gentility, civilizing influence, and "fascinating accomplishments," notably her skill on the pianoforte. Fort Frances, at the south of Rainy Lake, was named in her honour. But despite the warm welcomes she received, she was unaware that her arrival in the west had caused some consternation.

Frances Simpson.

Source: Hudson's Bay Company Archives, Archives of Manitoba.

George Simpson evidently had a somewhat callous attitude toward the successive "country wives" and consorts he maintained in the west. Even the seemingly cold-hearted custom of "turning off" one's country wife dictated some sense of responsibility: a trader might make provision for his wife by arranging her marriage to another. Simpson, on the other hand, simply turned up with his new young English wife a year after leaving his mixed-race wife, Margaret Taylor, in the care of Chief Factor John Stuart. Margaret Taylor and the two sons she bore by Simpson were quickly bundled out of the way.

While he did not dare to openly criticize the governor, Stuart wrote in strong terms to Chief Factor John George McTavish, who accompanied Simpson to Red River in 1830 with *his* new bride, Catherine: "[W]hat could be your aim in discarding her whom you clasped to your bosom in virgin purity and for 17 years with you. She was the Wife of your Choice and has born you seven Children, now Stigmatized with ignominy." The McTavish children had been eagerly watching the river for signs of their father's return.[6]

The two discarded wives were hastily married off to Company employees, Margaret Taylor to stonemason Amable Hogue, who had been one of Simpson's elite crew of voyageurs. While Hogue worked on the new headquarters being constructed at Lower Fort Garry, Margaret, living in the Métis labourers' camp, would have been able to see the governor and his new bride set up residence in their magnificent new home. Margaret Taylor had been born in 1805 on Hudson Bay and died in December 1885, a few weeks after the hanging of Louis Riel; her life thus spanned the formative years of the Métis nation.

George Simpson prided himself on his hardiness in travel, his ability to cover great distances in a canoe under the most rugged conditions. He sought to set new records for travel speed during his frequent river journeys through the interior of British North America to oversee operations in the Hudson's Bay Company's posts. His wife marvelled in her journal that he would rouse the voyageurs from sleep to commence the day's journey while it was still dark. His cry of "Lève, lève, lève!" might come at 4 a.m., 2 a.m., or even midnight, when there was an especially long way to go. It should be noted, however, that the "Little Emperor" slept while his crew paddled. Short and stout, Simpson swam daily, even in the coldest weather, and adapted equally well to feast or famine conditions. He could go without food for days, but on another occasion ate 22 geese and three ducks at a single session.

While Simpson came to dominate the fur trade after the merger between the North West Company and the HBC, his background was a comparatively modest one. He was born out of wedlock in Scotland and was raised by relatives, beginning work in the office of his uncle, a London sugar merchant, at the age of 13. A business partner in the sugar firm had a connection to Lord Selkirk by marriage and this tie provided Simpson with the opportunity to work for the HBC. Simpson's leadership after the 1821 merger was unquestioned, his style autocratic. He kept a confidential "Character Book" where he noted his impressions of company employees, including detailed descriptions of their personal faults.

On her journey west, Frances Simpson described the almost-10-metre-long canoes in which they travelled as "elegant beyond description." While they gamely negotiated many portages, Mrs. Simpson and Mrs. McTavish were carried over the most difficult passages. The burden of one portage proved too much for an elderly voyageur, and he pitched forward into a bog, sending the unfortunate Mrs. McTavish somersaulting over his head. Frances Simpson enjoyed the lively voyageur songs—neither cold nor fatigue dampened the spirits of the men who paddled, sang, laughed, and joked, as if on an excursion of pleasure. But nerves could be frayed on the long journey and when fisticuffs broke out, the suddenly awakened Governor Simpson seized a paddle to beat the combatants in the canoe.

Though liquor was carefully doled out along the way, Simpson fortified his crew for the last push toward the Red River settlement by allowing them to consume all that was left. Infused with new strength, the voyageurs completed a gruelling 24-hour shift. On the last portage, the crew shaved, freshened up, and decorated the canoe. They then made a grand entrance at the fort, with the company flag fluttering and a blast of bugle heralding the governor's arrival.[7]

Land Controversy in Upper Canada and the "Alien Question"

While Simpson and other Scots were making their way in the fur trade, and while the unwitting Scottish settlers in Red River were caught up in the early difficulties of that colony, another Scottish immigrant was at the centre of a growing controversy in Upper Canada. Far from a hapless victim of circumstance, Robert Gourlay deliberately plunged headlong into political agitation over Upper Canadian land policy. Gourlay was a Scottish-born writer, farmer, political reformer, and self-described enthusiast, who had already immersed himself in the cause of political reform in Britain, arguing for suffrage based upon literacy, and redistribution of land to the poor. When his wife inherited 350 hectares in Upper Canada, Gourlay saw an opportunity to make his fortune. He arrived in Upper Canada in 1817, but was quickly disillusioned by the reality of life in the new frontier. Besides being plagued by mosquitoes, Gourlay was dismayed to discover that the wild and forested land he now possessed could yield little immediate benefit, and would be unlikely to attract purchasers.

1817: The newly arrived Scottish immigrant Robert Gourlay takes up the cause of land rights for Americans.

Most recent immigrants to Upper Canada were American, and these "aliens" were denied the right to buy land. This had not always been the case. In the earliest days of Upper Canada, Lieutenant Governor John Graves Simcoe swallowed his own anti-American convictions, proclaiming in 1792 that land grants would be available without reference to national origins. By the time of the War of 1812, the population of Upper Canada was 80 percent American-born; at least three-quarters of these were neither Loyalists nor the descendants of Loyalists. Land policy changed after the War of 1812, with Americans no longer able to simply take an oath of allegiance to buy land—unless they had been resident in the province for seven years. This new provision upset the plans of land speculators who had acquired large tracts with the idea of selling land to immigrant—mostly American—newcomers. The rules were not uniformly followed and much uncertainty had surrounded the "alien" question, since British law had not foreseen the 1783 separation of the United States from the empire. No statute collectively stripped American residents of their status as British subjects.

For Robert Gourlay, as for others, only the extension of landholding rights to Americans, or large-scale British immigration, would make his extensive property saleable. The project also fit with Gourlay's other, more disinterested, goal of ensuring a broad base of land ownership. As historian David Mills puts it, "He envisioned an organic rural community dominated by virtuous yeoman farmers."[8] Sir Francis Gore, who had served as Upper Canada's lieutenant governor from 1806 to 1811, left the colony in charge of Sir Isaac Brock and other military administrators during the War of 1812. He returned to Upper Canada as lieutenant governor in September 1815 and would serve there until June 1817. Gore had already quashed a bill by which the legislative assembly hoped to extend land rights to Americans, so Gourlay poured his energies into a grand immigration scheme to recruit British settlers. He set out to prepare a statistical survey of Upper Canada, which would presumably generate some interest in the prospects of the colony.

Yet as Gourlay toured the province soliciting information from settlers, his design of launching a British settlement scheme began to unravel. Instead, he increasingly became a lightning rod for discontent. The questions he asked settlers encouraged them to air their grievances; they cited the lack of roads, the distance from markets, and Crown and clergy reserves that left desirable tracts of land scattered through each township, unavailable for settlement. Settlers were "cut off from each other," Gourlay reported, "left imprisoned in the woods. They cannot dispose of their farms: they cannot afford to abandon them; and so they pine on."[9]

Gourlay became convinced that more American settlers, and not British immigrants, were the key to prosperity for Upper Canada, and that a policy change to permit them property rights was essential. The tone of his writing intensified; he called for Gore's impeachment and implied that the province's fortunes would improve with annexation to the United States. In a series of newspaper articles and pamphlets, Gourlay, who had a history of making enemies, rashly and provocatively attacked the elite of Upper Canada, labelling them vile and loathsome vermin. He no doubt made a tactical error in singling out the influential Anglican minister and schoolmaster John Strachan for special ridicule and derision. Strachan's school was the hatchery of the colony's elite, and he reflected with satisfaction that "all my pupils now the leading characters in many parts of the Province opposed him sternly."[10] Politician Christopher Hagerman, whose brother's character had been maligned, took his revenge on Gourlay by beating him with a horsewhip in the streets of Kingston. By 1819, Gourlay was convicted of seditious libel and exiled from the province.

1819: Reform agitator Robert Gourlay exiled from Upper Canada.

His prospects only worsened: he lost his property to creditors, his wife died, and Gourlay spent time in an English asylum after striking a British parliamentarian with a riding crop. In later published work he likened himself to other persecuted historical greats—Christ, Socrates, and Galileo. Gourlay has sometimes been portrayed as an early martyr for the cause of political reform in Canada, but his influence is debatable; his tactics may have done as much to discredit as to advance the cause of reform.

More than land ownership was at stake in the issue over rights for American-born aliens. Participation in government, either as a voter or a member of the assembly, depended upon meeting a property qualification. The 1821 election of the Massachusetts-born Barnabas Bidwell to the legislative assembly of Upper Canada brought the alien controversy to a head. Bidwell had been attorney general in Massachusetts before his 1811 arrival in Upper Canada, but had left the United States amid allegations of embezzlement. His true loyalties were questioned during the War of 1812—he was suspected of being an agent for the Americans—and he was compelled to swear an oath of allegiance as a British subject. John Beverley Robinson, attorney general and leading member of Upper Canada's Tory elite, led the campaign to deny Bidwell a seat in the legislature, seizing upon his status as an "alien." Tory loyalty, David Mills explains, was "exclusive; it required adherence to the idea of Upper Canada as a special Loyalist bastion governed by a Tory elite."[11]

1821: The election of Barnabas Bidwell sparked political conflict over the "alien question" in Upper Canada.

Members of the assembly opposed to Bidwell marshalled more ammunition against him by raising the issue of his unsuitability on moral grounds. Since the fate of many others hung upon the disposition of the vote on Bidwell, this muddied the legal waters still further. The assembly at first rejected a motion to declare Bidwell ineligible, but then held a further vote in which he was ousted by a majority of one.

The British Colonial Office, to which the question was referred, ruled that American citizens, as aliens, were ineligible to stand for election. But recognizing that any ruling that jeopardized so many land titles would raise a storm in the province, the new lieutenant governor, Sir Peregrine Maitland (1818–1828), cast about for some means of compromise. Confusion grew when Bidwell's son, Marshall Spring Bidwell, who was likewise an American citizen, was permitted to stand for election in 1824, after having been twice blocked. The younger Bidwell won his seat and went on to become an active voice for reform in the assembly. While questions of naturalization fell under imperial jurisdiction, the Colonial Office agreed with Maitland that the provincial assembly might pass an act that would offer a compromise and reassure the many Americans in Upper Canada who already held property.

Unfortunately, this well-intentioned strategy provided the occasion for an open clash between the colony's Tory elite in the appointed legislative council, whom the younger Bidwell derisively labelled the "Family Compact," and reformers in the elected assembly. The latter insisted upon full citizenship rights for the American-born—in effect, a repudiation of the ruling from the British government. Their opponents were willing to make a concession, but insisted upon reiterating the alien status of American newcomers, a compromise that the assembly rejected. Only in 1828, after much ill-will had been generated, was the issue resolved. New legislation retroactively naturalized all who had arrived before 1820, or who had received a grant of land, or who held public office. Those who arrived afterward could become naturalized by taking an oath of allegiance after seven years' residence.

This acrimonious struggle brought the question of identity to the fore in Upper Canada and made manifest the clash between the ideal of a British colony and the reality of an American one. The conflict over citizenship in the 1820s raised the larger question of the meaning of "loyalty." While the immediate crisis had been put to rest, 1828 in some respects marked a watershed in Upper Canada's political life—for the first time, the assembly was dominated by reformers. Distinct political parties, in the modern sense, had not yet emerged, but a clash between the appointed executive and legislative councils and the elected legislative assembly loomed. The "alien question" was, historian Jane Errington suggests, "only a rehearsal for the vitriolic debates which would rock the colony in the 1830s."[12] The Tories, David Mills argues, "had more reason than before to distrust dissent." The appeal to the Colonial Office to resolve the "alien question" had undermined them, and the appeals to the population at large had been, in their eyes, "an organized and seditious appeal to the disloyal part of the electorate."[13] The very nature of the colony would change as the dominant American-born element would soon be dwarfed by a flood of British arrivals.

Land Speculation and Settlement in Upper Canada

Many facets of Upper Canada's early development turned on the question of land policy, and the early decades of the nineteenth century saw various philosophies and theories for land use contend for influence with British policymakers. In Upper Canada, those impatient for economic growth looked to the discouraging ratio of acres granted to acres actually brought under cultivation. By 1824, 3.2 million hectares (8 million acres) in Upper Canada had been granted to private individuals, but only 1.2 million hectares (3 million acres) were occupied, and only 200 000 hectares (500 000 acres) had been cultivated. Some of the earlier grants made to Loyalists had been long since traded away for a few gallons of whiskey or barrels of flour, with speculators now holding on to them until prices rose. Substantial grants to privileged favourites of the Crown, and vast tracts of clergy reserves, were part of the problem. As Gourlay's research had demonstrated, settlers were resentful about enormous expanses of vacant land that separated them from their neighbours and kept property values low.

Those offering solutions to populate the colonies readily found the ear of British authorities. In 1825, the Canada Company, led by the now obscure but once immensely popular Scottish novelist, John Galt, was granted a total of 1 million hectares (2.5 million acres). Half of the allocation was in the "Huron Tract" adjacent to Lake Huron, north of earlier settlements established by Thomas Talbot, and the rest consisted of Crown reserves

1824: Only a fraction of land grants in Upper Canada have been brought under cultivation.

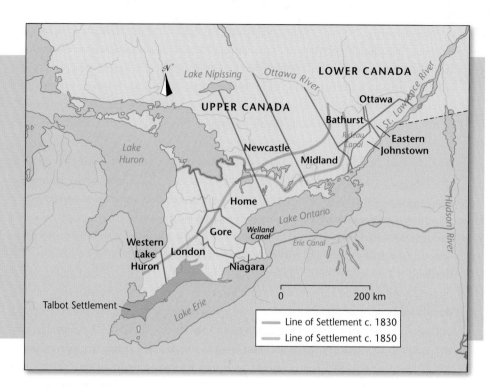

Map 7.2

Upper Canada districts, 1836, showing the Talbot Settlement, and extent of settlement by 1830 and 1850.

1826: Free land grants in Upper Canada eliminated.

throughout Upper Canada. The total price was £344 375, with liberal repayment terms and a generous policy for deducting expenses from the cost. John Galt's son, Alexander Tilloch Galt, was the principal agent of another similar enterprise, the British American Land Company, established in 1832, which took possession of 320 000 hectares (800 000 acres) at a cost of £120 000. This grant was in Lower Canada, in the Eastern Townships, south of Montreal. French-Canadian nationalist agitators denounced the grant as part of a policy aimed at swamping the French with British immigrants. Then, too, reformers in the colonial assemblies resented the fact that revenues from the companies' land sales were beyond the assembly's control, flowing directly to the executive council and governor. Any policy that afforded the executive financial independence from the elected representatives rankled.

Free grants of land were eliminated in 1826, except those awarded to military claimants. This seems to have been part of a general shift in colonial theory, promoted by British ideologue Edward Gibbon Wakefield. Wakefield opposed free grants, arguing that the sale of land at what he termed a "sufficient price" would ensure that it fell into the hands of those who had the resources to develop it. For a time, Wakefield exerted some influence on key figures in the British Colonial Office. The impact of Wakefield's ideas in Canada is difficult to gauge. On the other side of the world, the allocation of land in New South Wales and later New Zealand owed something to his theories, but his personal notoriety no doubt cost him credibility among British policymakers. Many were disgusted by his dastardly attempt to abduct the 15-year-old daughter of a wealthy manufacturer from her boarding school. Wakefield claimed to the credulous schoolgirl that he had been sent by the family's solicitor to hastily marry her in a bid to save her father from financial ruin.

Wakefield's influential work on colonial settlement policy, *Letter from Sydney* (1829), was in fact composed in Newgate prison.

The earlier land grants given to Thomas Talbot were also a magnet for controversy. Colonial officials grew increasingly concerned about his unorthodox methods. Some of the lands he was busy settling had already been allocated to others. What is more, potential provincial land revenues were being lost and control over huge tracts was slipping from the hands of Upper Canadian authorities. Further, Talbot's record keeping of land allocations was sloppy—he was even known to simply erase settlers' names from the map for capricious reasons. Talbot's energetic recruitment of settlers, construction of roads, mills, and other amenities may have hastened settlement in Upper Canada, but ultimately land allocation was too important to be left in the hands of an eccentric man who had become a reclusive alcoholic. In 1838, Talbot was compelled to turn his settlements over to the control of the province, retaining control over his personal holdings only.

The Atlantic Colonies: Challenges and Opportunities

Other challenges were confronting Britain's Atlantic colonies in North America in the years immediately following the Napoleonic Wars. Newfoundland had long been regarded by British policymakers as little more than a seasonal fishing station, a great ship anchored off the Grand Banks. By 1817, its population had grown to more than 40 000 inhabitants, and frequent clashes between Irish Roman Catholics and English residents clearly indicated the need for greater stability. A British parliamentary inquiry that year recommended the appointment of a permanently posted governor for the first time, although, in keeping with tradition, a naval officer filled the role.

1817: Francis Pickmore appointed as Newfoundland's first year-round governor.

Francis Pickmore became the first governor to winter in the colony, despite the fact that the governor's residence in Fort Townshend had not been fitted out for year-round occupation. The Colonial Office insisted that Pickmore commit to remaining in Newfoundland for the winter, but refused to authorize the expense of improvements to his accommodations. Pickmore was dismayed to see snow drifting into his bedroom. This proved to be the least of his worries. A fire late in 1817 destroyed 400 houses, leaving 2000 homeless. Provisions stored in warehouses had also been burned, and the winter of 1817 and 1818 became a nightmare of hunger, with the population torn by violence, vandalism, and looting. Pickmore struggled to keep order but, wracked by bronchitis, he died in February 1818. With Pickmore's corpse preserved in rum, work crews laboured for weeks to hack through the 1.5-metre-thick ice that choked St. John's harbour. At last, with a channel cut through the ice, Pickmore's remains could be shipped home to England. Despite his valiant efforts, his promise had been impossible to keep.

1817–1818: Newfoundland endures a difficult winter when fire destroys homes and supplies.

The appointment of Sir Thomas Cochrane as governor (1825–1834) ushered in a new era in the colony of Newfoundland. Cochrane, also a naval officer, immediately set to work remedying the deficiencies in the governor's residence. A grand Government House, originally meant to cost £8778, grew more and more ornate in its conception under Cochrane's direction, with the bill finally coming in at an embarrassing £36 000, sparking an inquiry at the Colonial Office. A cottage retreat by a placid lake five kilometres from Government House was part of the new governor's vision, and a special road was constructed to link the two. Cochrane saw to it that impoverished residents were given employment constructing an entire system of roads on the Avalon Peninsula. His largesse also extended to the more privileged elements of Newfoundland society, and a new era of ceremony and gracious entertaining began. In the early years, Cochrane governed with the sole assistance of an appointed council consisting of three judges and the commander of the garrison. Newfoundland did not have an elected assembly until 1832.

In the Maritime colonies, the peace in 1815 put an end to an expansive era of wartime prosperity. Shipbuilding and privateering had been growth industries during the war. Privateers received letters of marque from the British government authorizing them to capture enemy vessels, with captains and crew sharing the bounty. Nova Scotia's privateers took more than 100 American vessels as prizes of war in 1813 alone. While privateers were a key weapon in British warfare before the practice was abandoned in the mid-nineteenth century, historical perceptions of them vary—they are either gallant and daring heroes who protected the colonies from danger, or unscrupulous adventurers using the opportunity of war to amass personal fortunes through state-approved piracy. It should be noted, however, that rival nations' practices were similar, and harassment from American privateers was a constant menace to Maritime shipping during wartime.

There were other consolations when peace brought an end to this lucrative business. During the War of 1812, Americans had lost the privilege of sending their ships and cargoes to trade with Britain's Caribbean colonies. Nova Scotia and New Brunswick filled the void, and, with the preferential treatment they enjoyed under Britain's Navigation Acts, were able to carry American food products to supply the slave populations of West Indian sugar plantations, while carrying back Caribbean molasses to American rum distilleries.

American policymakers were not content to allow this valuable carrying trade to slip through their fingers, and responded in 1817 with an act that struck at British and British colonial rivals by denying them the right to carry West Indian cargoes to American ports. The following year, Congress closed American ports to British ships coming from any colonies not permitting American trade. Britain retaliated by relaxing the laws of mercantilism to allow Halifax, Nova Scotia, and Saint John, New Brunswick, to operate as free ports, open to American trade. An American countermove was quick to follow: in 1820, an American Navigation Act prohibited the importation of West Indian goods by way of Halifax or Saint John. Pressed by a powerful plantation owners' lobby group who resented higher prices for essential American foodstuffs to feed slave populations, Britain relented and permitted American vessels trade privileges in their Caribbean ports.

1820s: Freer trade policies open new opportunities for Nova Scotia mariners.

In Britain's cabinet, the president of the Board of Trade, William Huskisson, embraced free trade, an idea that was beginning to gain ground in the 1820s under the influence of Adam Smith's seminal book *The Wealth of Nations* (1776) and such prominent political economists as David Ricardo. The demands of British manufacturers that they ought to be permitted to buy in the cheapest market, and sell in the dearest, found a receptive audience in Huskisson. Britain was not ready to abandon protectionism entirely, but in 1825 Huskisson reduced tariffs on a wide range of products including wool, silk, cotton, linen, and, most significantly for the Maritime colonies, sugar. New Brunswick merchants, thriving under protective tariffs on timber, worried about what the future might hold if the doctrine of free trade should spread to that sector. For the moment, timber duties had not been adjusted. Huskisson, for all his commitment to tariff reform, was MP for Liverpool, an English port that owed a great deal of its traffic to the colonial timber trade. Nova Scotians, on the other hand, welcomed the new measures, confident in their ability to compete in an unfettered economy. For along with tariff reduction came reciprocal privileges that Huskisson negotiated with the Americans. Britain's North American colonies were now permitted to carry American cargoes to anywhere in the world. By the mid-nineteenth century, Nova Scotia's merchant shipping fleet was the world's fourth largest.

An Abortive Plan for Colonial Union, 1822

In the Canadas, trade was at the root of a thorny political and economic struggle that threatened the financial viability of the upper colony. The chief source of revenue for Upper Canada was customs duties; an 1821–22 committee of the legislature estimated that four-fifths of the colonial government's income came from that source. Since Upper Canada lacked a seaport, its imports had to come through the ports of the neighbouring province, Lower Canada. Customs agents at the key ports of Quebec and Montreal collected duties, and then paid a share to the colonial government of Upper Canada, on the understanding that some of the goods were destined for that province. A 1795 agreement stipulated a one-eighth share. The rapidly growing population of Upper Canada dictated an adjustment to one-fifth in 1817, but, even so, problems arose. Conflicts between Lower Canada's governor and its elected assembly at times paralyzed the colony's finances, with the assembly refusing to pass essential financial legislation. These conditions of chronic crisis made Upper Canada's revenue unreliable, prompting the British Colonial Office to consider systemic changes. The solution seemed simple: in 1822, Britain prepared a bill to unite the two colonies of Upper and Lower Canada. The bill failed to pass in England's House of Commons. Perhaps recognizing that the people of Canada ought to at least be consulted on such a substantial constitutional reorganization, the government withdrew the bill in the face of political opposition. As an interim solution, Britain passed the *Canada Trade Act*, which guaranteed Upper Canada a one-fifth share of all customs revenues collected, with provisions for adjustment every three years, dependent on what proportion of goods made its way to the upper province. British policymakers had not entirely given up on the idea of a union of the colonies, but this idea would have to wait.

New Economic Sectors

It was fortunate for the economies of British North America that the decline of the fur trade early in the nineteenth century coincided with a surge in the timber trade. Prominent Canadian political economist Harold Innis argued in the 1920s that Canada's historical evolution could be best understood in terms of the quest for successive staple products. From the earliest times of contact, Europeans exploited resources in North America that were not readily available at home, and this activity provided the rationale for imperialism. The exploitation of cod that began late in the fifteenth century has already been detailed; the fur trade was an outgrowth of this activity, followed by timber and Upper Canadian wheat production. While in many respects, Innis's "staples thesis" provides a useful paradigm around which Canada's economic history can be organized, later generations of historians have questioned its validity. Focusing on Upper Canada, Douglas McCalla argues that a focus on staples alone "yields an oversimplified and fundamentally inaccurate view." Factors other than export products shaped colonial economic development: population movements, the flow of ideas and information—including technological innovation—the policies of the imperial government, and even the American government, were among the dominant influences.[14]

Banking in the Canadas

1817: The Bank of Montreal and later the Bank of Upper Canada (1821) serve the needs of Canadian merchants.

The fur trade promoted new commercial institutions that would have a far-reaching effect: the Bank of Montreal, established in 1817, was largely a response to the needs of fur-trading merchants. The use of army bills as a form of currency during the War of 1812 provided a convenient alternative to hard currency, and perhaps helped to overcome psychological resistance to banknotes. Many forms of coinage circulated in British North America—English, Spanish, French, and American—with constantly shifting rates of exchange and frequent shortages of hard currency. A colonial bank was presumed to be the answer that would address these problems.

Although critics complained of the virtual monopoly the Bank of Montreal enjoyed, the fact that banking was concentrated in fewer hands resulted in greater stability and viability than was seen in the United States. In the upper province, the Bank of Upper Canada was founded in 1821, with control firmly in the hands of the colonial elite. The members of Upper Canada's Family Compact used their command of the legislative council to thwart the plans of upstart competitors who might wish to apply for bank charters that would challenge their ascendancy in the colony's business and political life.

The New Brunswick Timber Industry

In New Brunswick, the growth of the timber trade brought an influx of British capital, technology, and entrepreneurship. Saint John grew as an important commercial centre, and related industries, such as shipbuilding, flourished. Increased British demand for fish and agricultural produce benefited the fishers and farmers of Nova Scotia, New Brunswick, and Prince Edward Island. Halifax and St. John's profited from an increase in the size of their garrisons and a growing carrying trade with the Caribbean. While economic ties between the Atlantic colonies, Britain, and the Caribbean strengthened, there was little trade or commerce between the colonies. The lack of inter-colonial transportation links and the widely dispersed population ensured that the colonies largely developed in isolation from each other and formed distinct societies.

A timber industry in New Brunswick had followed Loyalist settlement at the end of the eighteenth century, but the introduction of protective British tariffs during the Napoleonic Wars brought a great surge of growth to the industry. Even after the war's end, high British tariffs on foreign wood were retained, benefiting colonial producers in that substantial market. As the exploitation of timber resources on Crown land in New Brunswick became more competitive, licences were introduced to regulate the activities of lumbermen. After 1819, a ton of timber could be taken for a fee of one shilling (one twentieth of a pound). Many Irish migrants bound for the popular destination of Boston took advantage of the burgeoning New Brunswick timber industry, stopping to work for wages that would help them establish themselves in the United States.

A nineteenth-century visitor to New Brunswick described the lumbermen he met near Grand Falls. On a "spree" at a nearby inn, the raucous woodcutters drank, sang, and tried their strength in competitive games of stone tossing. They wore red flannel shirts, homespun trousers, loose grey or green jackets that tied around the waists, straw or coarse felt hats, and brown moccasins or boots, the "moccasin or boot furnishing a ready napkin after a meal of salt pork and biscuit." He marvelled at the daring they showed in their work, using creeping irons, L-shaped medal devices that tied to their legs, with a sharp spike at the bottom "like the claw of a wild beast," to ascend the trees.[15]

1825: The Miramichi Fire killed hundreds and destroyed thousands of square kilometres of New Brunswick timber.

While the supply of timber must have seemed inexhaustible to colonial newcomers, devastating fires could claim huge swathes of woodland in a day. The Miramichi Fire of 1825, coming on the heels of a prolonged summer drought, devoured an estimated 10 000 to 20 000 square kilometres of timber in New Brunswick, including giants of the forest that had stood for centuries. Government House at Fredericton burned to the ground, and the fire claimed the lives of up to 300 people. Settlers in remote areas had been unaware of the fire until a terrifying roar was heard from the forest. Many fled to the Miramichi River in panic, hoping to outrun the flames, but some were asleep, or in bed suffering from an outbreak of fever, and were caught up in a hurricane of flame. Even those aboard ship in the Gulf of St. Lawrence felt the impact of the conflagration, the seas boiling and hissing, and the air thick with smoke and ash.

Fire in Saint John, 1825.

Source: Fitz Hugh Lane print: View of the Great Conflagration of the City of Saint John, New Brunswick, 1838. Hand coloured lithograph on woven paper support: 55.4 x 80.5 cm. Collection of the New Brunswick Museum, W6981.

Logging in the Canadas

For Lower Canada, timber provided an economic boost that softened the effect of the declining fur trade and diminishing yields in agriculture. Wheat production in Lower Canada continued to decline after crop failures in 1805, with yields not meeting the local demand, much less producing surplus for export. Long-established agricultural areas suffered from the effects of soil exhaustion, and newer more northerly areas of settlement tended to be marginal land, with soil and climate unsuited to wheat production. Further, Lower Canada's wheat producers began to face competition from Upper Canada where wheat production flourished on virgin land. By the 1830s, Lower Canada was a net importer of wheat, and farming families turned to subsistence agriculture, producing potatoes, barley, oats, and peas for their own consumption. In this environment, timber production became an important new staple—Lower Canada's "salvation," as historian Fernand Ouellet put it. The colony produced squared timber, essential for naval building, as well as processed lumber and barrel staves, and new sawmills sprang up, both in the Ottawa Valley and around Quebec. By 1831, these numbered 727. Activity in the ports of Lower Canada rose sharply: in 1812, 362 vessels cleared the port of Quebec; by 1834, the number had risen to 1213. While logging and its related industries offered work to Lower Canadians, most enterprises were British-owned.[16]

The historical focus has traditionally been on timber production for export, but much of the wood cut was consumed locally for fuel. A prodigious supply of wood was needed for heating homes, for cooking fires, to power industry, and for producing the charcoal used for smelting. Historical geographer J. David Wood estimates that in the decade before 1851 household use would have consumed 400 000 hectares (1 million acres) of Upper Canadian forest in that colony alone.[17] Unlike other seasonal occupations, logging offered winter work. Cold weather stilled the running sap, making trees easier to fell. With the first snowfall, logs could be moved, or "skidded," more easily, pulled by large draught horses or oxen along snow roads. Timber was cut and roughly squared by axe, a process that wasted about a third of the wood.

1850: Logging employs 10 000 in the Ottawa Valley.

By the early nineteenth century, the scramble to log the Ottawa Valley was on; by 1850, an estimated 10 000 loggers were at work there, living in hastily constructed shantytowns. When the spring thaw came to the tributaries of the Ottawa, the loggers would suddenly release the logs that had been stored in landings by the sides of the rivers to begin the drive downriver. Daring drivers broke up frequent jams by leaping from floating log to log in the swollen rivers. When the logs reached the Ottawa River from the tributaries, they were trapped by booms and then lashed together into cribs and rafts, without a single piece of iron used. Steered by raftsmen, these rafts could consist of over 2000 tonnes of timber, and were fitted out with small cabins for accommodating the crew, and cooking fires.

Enterprising logging companies, frustrated at frequent losses, constructed timber slides to bypass the roughest waters—large wooden chutes that could accommodate a crib built of 20 logs. The first of these, built at Chaudière Falls in 1829, became a popular draw for tourists.[18] The Prince of Wales, the future Edward VII, rode the Chaudière slide during an 1860 visit to Canada. Economic historian A.R.M. Lower noted that the best rapids-men were the Iroquois, closely rivalled by French Canadians. A journey through the rapids on

Timber slide, 150 feet high, Shawinigan, Quebec, about 1860.

a heavy mass of timber was, Lower enthused, "the most exhilarating of experiences, with the surge and roll of the waves, the grinding and bumping of the timbers, the perfect skill of the crew, the rocks missed by a hair's breadth, the terrific speed, and everywhere the consciousness of being in the grip of elemental forces."[19]

British Immigration after 1815

The growth of the timber industry in British North America was also a spur to immigration. Vessels carrying timber to the United Kingdom were hastily fitted out to carry immigrants on the return voyage to North America. Between 1815 and 1850, an astonishing 1 million immigrants made their way from Britain to British North America. The greatest number arrived via the St. Lawrence, disembarking at the port of Quebec City and then making their way on smaller vessels west to Upper Canada. Between 1825 and 1842, the population of Upper Canada tripled to 450 000; it would more than double again by 1851, swelling to close to a million.

A number of incentives motivated immigrants. The pull factors—the lure of higher wages or independent land ownership—were strong, yet the pushes—a wish to escape the burden of endemic poverty or to avoid slipping into it—exerted perhaps equal force. The end of the Napoleonic Wars in 1815 triggered a post-war depression, with demobilized soldiers swelling the ranks of the unemployed. Even the genteel families of officers felt the pinch of demobilization, and saw in emigration the answer to the problem of maintaining social status on half pay. Britain's Industrial Revolution had itself thrown many out

1815–1850: A million British immigrate to British North America.

of work, or reduced skilled crafts to machine-assisted unskilled jobs. The 1834 *Poor Law Amendment Act* instituted draconian conditions for poor relief in England and Wales. Parish subsidies for the working poor were no longer permitted. Instead of receiving "outdoor" relief, paupers were compelled to submit to virtual imprisonment in the parish workhouse. Besides heightening the incentive for paupers to choose immigration, the change in legislation made parish-assisted emigration more feasible for the rate-payers who looked for ways to reduce costs.

Most British newcomers to British North America in this era were from Ireland. Historian Donald Akenson notes that from 1815 to the mid-1850s, the number of Irish immigrants to British North America usually exceeded those from England, Wales, and Scotland combined. Even before the wave of Irish famine immigration in the second half of the 1840s, the Irish as an ethnic group made up at least a quarter of Upper Canada's population. These were not the stereotypical Roman Catholic Irish migrants; Akenson estimates the ratio of Protestants to Catholics at two to one. Nor were they predominantly urban dwellers, as they are so often portrayed; while Irish workers laboured on canals and in other industries, most took up farming.[20]

The precise number of Irish immigrants to British North America is difficult to discern. Records indicating a specific port of embarkation are not always available, and when they are, they can be misleading. Liverpool in England, and Greenock in Scotland were readily accessible ports from which Irish migrants frequently sailed. Immigrants might land at Quebec and make their way south to the United States, or do the reverse and reach British North America via New York. The 1842 census in Upper Canada showed that the Irish-born were the most numerous immigrant group, but the census only inquired about place of birth, which would distort the residents' true ethnicity. Consequently, children recently born in Canada would not be counted among the Irish.

The "Scots Irish" and the Orange Order

Considerations of ethnicity are further complicated by the confusing presence of the so-called Scots Irish, especially in what would become Ontario. While technically Irish, and counted as such, this was a group drawn from Ulster, most of which is Northern Ireland today. Their origins there date from attempts in the sixteenth and seventeenth centuries to transplant communities of loyal Scottish Protestants to subdue Catholic Ireland. By Confederation in 1867, Scots Irish made up three-eighths of Ontario's population. Historical geographers R. Cole Harris and John Warkentin see the influence of this group as decisive in shaping the character of Ontario: "It is not surprising that the small meeting hall of the Loyal Orange Lodge, a blatantly anti-Catholic society that had grown out of the Irish border tensions of the 1790s, had become a common sight in almost all parts of Ontario; … dourness, attachment to empire, and fierce anti-Catholicism were characteristics frequently ascribed to Ontarians."[21] Others see the Orange Order—this key social organization among Protestants in British North America—in a more positive light. Cecil J. Houston and William J. Smyth argue that the order was not solely a source of social divisiveness, but rather a "bulwark of colonial Protestantism" whose members emphasized loyalty to the Crown and the empire.[22]

The Orange Order accompanied colonial settlement in North America, quickly becoming, as Houston and Smyth argue, "an integral part of what might be called the Canadian colonial identity." An Orange Lodge may have been established among the military garrison at Halifax as early as 1799, and the organization took root soon afterward among settlers moving up the Saint John River in New Brunswick.

The 1829 arrival in Brockville of Ogle R. Gowan, the socially prominent son of a founding member of the Irish Grand Lodge, marked a watershed in the fortunes of the Orange Order in Upper Canada. A year later, a Grand Lodge of British North America was founded, and a flurry of new lodges followed. Besides affording an opportunity for male socializing—women were not included among its membership—the lodge offered valuable employment contacts and mutual aid, and solidified political connections. The rituals of membership were no doubt part of the appeal; colourful ceremonies, secret passwords, and the atmosphere of exclusiveness made the Order attractive. The climax of the Orange Order's social year, in both the old world and new, was the "Glorious Twelfth," the annual July 12 parade commemorating the Protestant William of Orange's 1690 victory over the Jacobite forces of the Catholic James II at the Battle of the Boyne in Ireland. A rider on a white horse, representing the heroic "King Billy" would be followed by Orangemen marchers. The fact that the march was provocative to Roman Catholics was no barrier; it almost certainly added to the appeal of the occasion.

1830: The Orange Order comes to Upper Canada.

Scottish Immigration to Canada

Another leading group of British immigrants after 1815 were the Scots, who roughly equalled the number from England in the pre-Confederation period. The English and the Scots each formed 20 percent of the arrivals at Quebec by 1829; by Confederation, the English and Scots made up one-quarter and one-fifth of Ontario's population, respectively. Mere numbers might mislead, however. The Scottish element exerted a disproportionate influence, holding key positions in colonial business and politics. This is attributable, in part, to a superior system of education in Scottish schools. Historian J.M. Bumsted suggests that the concept of a "democratic intellect," a focus on ability rather than advantages of class, contributed to Scottish success. The late-eighteenth-century Scottish Enlightenment, led by such figures as Adam Smith and David Hume, had a profound effect on shaping the ideas of the modern world.[23] Canada's political and business elite demonstrate the strength of this influence, with Scots prominent in politics, journalism, the fur trade, banking, railways, and other commercial endeavours. The tendency of well-placed Scottish families to lend assistance to relatives seeking to establish themselves was no doubt a factor as well.

Scottish immigration to British North America began well before 1815. A significant wave of Highland migration began as early as 1763, at the end of the Seven Years War, picking up momentum by the 1770s. An estimated 15 000 Highlanders came to British North America by 1815, driven mostly by economic motives. The population of Scotland rose dramatically in the eighteenth century, from 1 million in 1700 to 1.5 million in 1800. Rural overpopulation and the subdivision of tenant holdings were exacerbated by the notorious "clearances" of the late eighteenth and early nineteenth centuries. Tens of thousands of tenant farmers were displaced as "improving" estate managers evicted them to convert marginal cultivated land into sheep grazing areas and deer parks. The Duke of Sutherland's estates were among the worst examples, drawing commentary by Karl Marx. Marx's *Das Kapital* condemned the class robbery of conversion of 321 000 hectares (794 000 acres) of land "that had from time immemorial belonged to the clan" into "29 great sheep farms, each inhabited by a single family, for the most part imported English farm servants." British soldiers enforced the evictions, with "one old woman … burnt to death in the flames of the hut, which she refused to leave."[24] It is not surprising that such dramatic images should be seared into the collective memory as typifying Scottish migration. However, Scottish migrants to British North America were more frequently those who opted to leave of their own volition, confident that they could improve their prospects in a new land.

Short-Lived Experiments in Assisted Emigration

1823–1825:

Upper Canadian Peter Robinson organizes assisted emigration schemes in Ireland.

On a much smaller scale, schemes to enable the destitute to emigrate carried the important benefit of reducing the burden of poor relief in Britain. While Britain's surging population was once viewed in positive terms, attitudes were shifting under the influence of Malthusian principles. Thomas Malthus, in a famous 1798 essay on the "Principle of Population," posited gloomily that populations increased exponentially while food supplies could only grow arithmetically. In Britain's Colonial Office, Undersecretary Robert John Wilmot-Horton had been deeply influenced by Malthusian ideas, and grasped at a solution when in 1823 he met a visitor from Upper Canada.

Peter Robinson was the son of a loyalist family, and member of the colony's legislative assembly; Family Compact stalwart John Beverley Robinson, Upper Canada's attorney general, was his brother. Wilmot-Horton found that Robinson, presented as an authority on backwoods settlement, was the ideal vehicle through whom he could launch a migration scheme to assist destitute Irish. Robinson supervised the establishment of two Upper Canadian settlements, one at Scott's Mills, later Peterborough, and one at Shipman's Mills, later Almonte. At first, the Irish paupers to whom he publicized his plan regarded it as but a variation on the transportation schemes that were banishing criminals to Australia, but over time the idea of assisted emigration grew in appeal. Of the more than 50 000 impoverished residents of County Cork who applied for the scheme, some 2600 were selected for two group immigrations—one in 1823 and one in 1825. The migrants were given free passage and provisions, tools, and land grants of 70 acres (28 hectares) each. The assisted emigration program Robinson superintended was not unique. The Petworth scheme, a charitable enterprise sponsored by the Earl of Egremont, brought 1800 from the south of England between 1832 and 1837.[25] There were other similar initiatives, notably an 1835 to 1836 exodus of some 3800 unemployed English labourers from Norfolk and Suffolk.

Attitudes toward Immigration

Even while most immigrants made their way without organized assistance, the presence of these schemes gave rise to lingering impressions that the British North American colonies were dumping grounds for Britain's unwanted. Critics of the British government's assisted emigration program denounced the scheme as a means of "shovelling out paupers."[26]

Further, attempting to address Britain's social problems via an emigration safety valve was akin to trying to empty out the ocean with a thimble. The campaign was abandoned as impractical. Even at more elevated social levels, a perception that immigrants were the dregs of society persisted; an early-nineteenth-century observer asserted that "the scum of England is poured into the colonies: briefless barristers, broken down merchants, ruined debauchees, the offal of every calling and profession."[27]

The immigrants themselves were frequently disillusioned about the claims of those promoting British North America. While a map of Canada suggests an enormous expanse of land, newcomers to Upper Canada quickly discovered that this impression was illusory. The Canadian Shield, covering 90 percent of present-day Ontario, descends to within a couple of hundred kilometres of Toronto. Ontario's "cottage country" of picturesque lakes, birch forests—and ground of solid granite—was not an encouraging environment for aspiring farmers. Those who had not taken up land grants by the 1830s found the more northerly properties available to them utterly unsuitable for agriculture. In New Brunswick, colonists complained of unfertile stony soil overrun with thistles.

An 1832 political cartoon, "The Emigrant's Welcome to Canada," satirized the disillusionment felt by many. A heap of rock is labelled "Fine Land to grow wheat if you can plow it." Another sign advertises "Fine Grassland only 900 feet below the surface of the snow." By the 1840s, the dream of accessible, arable farmland would be beyond the reach of many new arrivals.

Some of the information prospective emigrants received was unbiased; after all, family members would hardly encourage others who might become dependent to join them in North America. Yet agents, like the well-known William Cattermole of the Canada Company, who gave lectures in England to promote migration, were paid a dividend for every immigrant recruited, and the temptation was obviously strong to present colonial life in glowing terms. Laudatory pamphlets, newspaper advertisements, immigrant letters read aloud from church pulpits, and published collections of testimonials by successful immigrants all extolled the superiority of life in the colonies. Historian Terry McDonald reveals that, even when such letters and testimonials were legitimate, their context was sometimes misrepresented. One example given was of Richard and Mary Barter of St. Stephen, New Brunswick, who congratulated themselves on having acquired 40 hectares (100 acres), a comfortable frame house, log barn filled with enough cut hay to keep their three cows through the winter, plus sufficient resources to pay passage for their parents and five other family members. When their letter was published with other immigrant success stories in 1833, the Barters had been in New Brunswick for 13 years, and not a mere two or three months as was implied.[28]

The New Brunswick and Nova Scotia Land Company

The New Brunswick and Nova Scotia Land Company was launched in 1834, and was modelled on the Canada Company and British North American Land Company active in Upper Canada. The New Brunswick Company, as it became known, purchased 238 000 hectares (589 000 acres) between the Saint John and Miramichi Rivers at a cost of approximately £60 000, spending another £80 000 to prepare two town sites. The enormous costs,

1834: The New Brunswick Company acquires 238 000 hectares (589 000 acres).

competition from other colonization schemes, and lukewarm response from prospective immigrants doomed the enterprise. The failure was not a blow for the shareholders alone. A party of several dozen recruits from Berwick-upon-Tweed in the north of England were supplemented by another larger contingent from the Isle of Skye later in 1836. But the Scottish settlers did not reach New Brunswick until late in the shipping season, and were consigned to unfinished houses with no chimneys yet built. Forty-one settlers died that cold winter.

The New Brunswick Company's schemes to boost immigrant numbers included one of the earliest experiments in assisted child immigration, an idea that would gain ground on a much larger scale in the post-Confederation era. While it might be imagined that objections to such a scheme would focus on the danger of exploitation of vulnerable children sent without guardians to those seeking tractable labourers, most contemporary critics worried about the infection of colonial society with a "moral leprosy." The *New Brunswick Courier* complained that the urchins, "the most depraved and vicious of the human race," were better suited for a convict colony. The children are sometimes remembered as the "Blue Boys," a commemoration of their supposed origins at the "Blue Coat School," Christ's Hospital in London. Historian Bruce Elliott speculates that this label may well have been meant to disguise the fact that the children were more likely drawn from humbler societies catering to vagrant juveniles.

John Harvey, one of a few dozen boys sent from London in 1836, was not actually an orphan. His mother remarried after the death of his father, and was convinced by the Children's Friend Society that her son would enjoy better prospects in New Brunswick. His mother only received one letter from him in many years, and its contents did not reassure her:

> [W]hen I arrived at Sergons [Saint John], I sailed up to Fredericton in a Stem bot, and then we cum up to Starley, and then we had to slep in a Barn amongst horses and lay in amongst straw, and then we was put out to the woods in a camp by ourselves, and the meet we got only fit for hogs; and der Mother we was sent out to work, and we Could not walk Because we was all Ragged like a Begger and starved with Cold, and then we last winter was took out farther to the woods, and Mister Foss Had us choping down his trees, and all the boys mostly Left him.

John Harvey managed to rise above his difficult youth, although with what psychological scars we can only guess. He became a farmer, married, and raised three children. Other immigrant children, like Edwin Foot, fared better. He was placed with a judge's family outside Fredericton who, he reported, treated him like a son. Some of the children later became prominent in New Brunswick society.[29]

Perhaps the greatest single factor in settler disillusionment was coming to grips with the enormity of the task of land clearing. Trees, to a pioneer farmer, were the enemy. With labour scarce and not all farmers having access to oxen or draught animals, this was a considerable obstacle. Once the trees had been felled, the removal of stumps was another problem. J. David Wood reminds us that "the massive challenge of clearing the woodland has diminished over time in the story of overall pioneer success, but it was *the* factor—usually combined with sickness, particularly the malarial 'fever and ague,' and isolation—that broke the settlers who gave up."[30]

1836: Dozens of impoverished child immigrants are sent to New Brunswick.

Immigration and Disease

Part of the reason for the ambivalence towards newcomers of those already resident in British North America was the fact that disease travelled along the same routes as the migrants. Steerage passengers, having endured a journey of up to nine weeks in crowded and filthy conditions, could be found exhausted and close to starvation, huddled on the wharves unable to afford shelter. Under such conditions, the immigrants' immune systems weakened by privation and overcrowding, contagious disease was virtually a certainty. Typhus, spread by the bite of lice or fleas, plagued those crowded into rat-infested dwellings. In 1827, 800 people died of typhus in the city of Halifax alone. In the narrow hilly streets below Citadel Hill, scores were packed into dirty ramshackle wooden houses. Authorities reported that one garret housed 47 paupers, with 48 living in the one next door.

1827: A typhus epidemic kills 800 in Halifax.

Cholera was an especially feared scourge. Spread via a micro-organism that enters the body through the mouth, the disease causes massive dehydration as victims vomit and suffer severe watery diarrhea—as much as a litre per hour. Drained of vital fluids, the mineral balance in a cholera victim's body is upset, disrupting the normal body processes; the victim becomes blue in complexion, husky-voiced, and suffers from cramps and spasms. Without effective treatment—impossible in an era when the usual recourse was to such measures as bleeding and turpentine enemas—death came within hours, or a few days at most. British North America was devastated by deadly epidemics in 1832 and 1834. An estimated 20 000 died of cholera in Canada during these years. Lower Canada was especially hard hit, as Quebec and Montreal were key points of disembarkation.

1832 and 1834: An estimated 20 000 died in cholera epidemics in the Canadas.

A newly established Board of Health failed to take adequate precautions, and fuelled local panic by attempting at first to deny the epidemic. Officials maintained silence while the public witnessed the daily spectacle of carts displaying yellow warning flags carrying away the dead. Convinced that the disease was air-borne, medical authorities organized the discharge of cannons and the burning of barrels of tar to create smoke to purify the air. Lower Canada's governor, Lord Alymer, encouraged residents to leave the city of Quebec, hopeful that a dispersal of population would inhibit the spread of disease. Instead, cholera travelled with fleeing town dwellers, infecting outlying communities. Suspicions grew among *Canadiens* that the influx of diseased immigrants from the British Isles was part of a deliberate bid to eradicate the French.

Early in 1832, the Quebec Board of Health established a quarantine station at Grosse Île, down the river from Quebec. Ships bearing immigrants were required to anchor at Grosse Île for inspection by a health officer. Vessels were either cleared to carry on to Quebec, or were required to serve a quarantine ranging from three to 30 days. The decision to quarantine was based on a visual inspection and the ship's masters' own report—hardly likely to be an objective one. Steerage passengers were required to land to clean themselves and their possessions, but more affluent cabin passengers were exempt. Those from infected ships mingled on the island with the healthy, and contact with shore was frequent, as supplies were carried from nearby towns. Not surprisingly, such a permeable quarantine failed to check cholera's spread.

Immigrant Impressions of British North America

Emigration literature was an important genre in nineteenth-century Britain, and this material leaves behind a record of contemporary attitudes about British North America. Of course, those with sufficient education and leisure to write and publish their impressions would hardly have been typical immigrants. The famous British pamphleteer and social reformer William Cobbett was very familiar with North America; he had been garrisoned as a soldier at New Brunswick shortly after the arrival of the Loyalists and later lived for a considerable period in Philadelphia and New York. Through his writings, Cobbett offered himself as a guide to the would-be emigrant: "To do this, I am, by mere accident, better qualified, perhaps, than any man in the world." He had taken up his duties in New Brunswick in 1785 and later boasted that he saw the first trees felled in the colony. It was in New Brunswick that Cobbett met the 13-year-old Anne Reid, and instantly decided that she should be his wife. Despite Cobbett's resolution that they should be instantly married, the nuptials were delayed for four years.

These pleasant associations did not endear Cobbett to the colony, however. He was a great advocate of emigration, but warned prospective settlers to go to the United States and not consider an English colony. For Cobbett, advocacy of emigration was bound up with criticism of English society at home, part of his larger social reform agenda. Cobbett proved to be influential among Canadian reformers as well. Robert Gourlay was reputed to be an admirer, and William Lyon Mackenzie dined with Cobbett in London in 1834 when he had come to present colonial grievances. The state of England, Cobbett lamented in 1829, was such that for the labouring classes, "hunger, and rags, and filth, are now become their uniform and inevitable lot. No toil, no frugality, can save them from these." Only through emigration, he urged, could labourers "save themselves from ruin, from degradation, from the poor-house, and finally, from the knives of the human butchers." He printed letters from successful emigrants and offered practical advice on such matters as booking passage on ship and how a would-be emigrant might "overcome the scruples … and wailings of his wife. Women, especially English women, transplant very badly," he cautioned.

The United States was the place to go, Cobbett advised. The population of British North America was scant, he asserted, most food had to be imported, and the colonial government suffered for being in a state of dependence. In short, he concluded, the British colonies are "the *offal* of North American; they are the head, the shins, the shanks and hoofs of that part of the world; while the UNITED STATES are the sir-loins, the well-covered and well-lined ribs, and the suet." Cobbett scoffed at the prevalent fear that Americans would eventually take over British North America: "This would be to act the wise part of a thief, who should come and steal a stone for the pleasure of carrying it about."[31]

Cobbett's admiration for all things American was not shared by his contemporary Susanna Moodie. Moodie's *Roughing it in the Bush* (1852) and *Life in the Clearings* (1853) offer personal accounts of a gentlewoman's migration and settlement in Upper Canada in the 1830s, and are among the most famous early Canadian immigrant accounts. No doubt some readers were swayed by her concluding remarks that "if these sketches should prove the means of deterring one family from sinking their property, and shipwrecking all their hopes, by going to reside in the backwoods of Canada, I shall consider myself amply repaid for revealing the secrets of the prison-house, and feel that I have not toiled and suffered in the wilderness in vain."

In the backwoods of Upper Canada, Moodie was dismayed to find herself surrounded by "semi-barbarous Yankee squatters" and sorely missed the civilities of polite society. "They think they can debase you to their level by disallowing all your claims to distinction," she fumed, while allowing that the "native-born Canadian is exempt." The pervasive spirit of democracy made it difficult for her to hire and retain household help. Workers brought from Britain "no sooner set foot upon the Canadian shores," Susanna Moodie found, "than they become possessed with this ultra-republican spirit.… They fancy themselves not only equal to you in rank, but that ignorance and vulgarity give them superior claims to notice." They demanded the highest wages, but shrank from hard work. If they were reprimanded, Moodie claimed, they would quit instantly, confident of another position: "away they bounce, leaving you to finish a large wash, or a heavy job of ironing, in the best way you can."

Moodie contrasted the conduct of the lower orders of American society, and new British arrivals of the same rank, with that of the First Nations. She wrote that, while she had heard much about the "savages" of Canada, and had seen "uncivilised life" during her residence in the bush, she found considerably more "delicacy of feeling" and "natural courtesy" among Aboriginal Canadians. "[T]he Indian," she asserted, "is one of Nature's gentlemen—he never says or does a rude or vulgar thing."[32] A Scottish immigrant, Robert MacDougall, made a similar observation in an 1841 publication, *The Emigrant's Guide to North America*. He praised the physical appearance and bravery of the Natives, and noted that "I do not ever expect to see men who are more respectful toward others." Their "slow, soft, pleasant, speech" he likened to his own Gaelic.[33]

Susanna Moodie's sister, Catharine Parr Traill, was also an accomplished author and immigrant to Canada; in fact, she seems to have encouraged Moodie to come to Canada. But Parr Traill positively relished the challenges of her circumstances. She painted landscapes, pressed wild flowers and wrote cloying illustrated children's stories set in the wilderness of Canada. The more prosaic and practical *The Backwoods of Canada* (1836) is Parr Traill's most famous work, but she also authored practical manuals that display an admirable spirit of improvisation and optimism. *The Canadian Emigrant Housekeeper's Guide* (1861) is a comprehensive domestic manual on an astonishing range of subjects, offering advice on what wild plants may yield substitutes for coffee and tea, how to make lard, cure meat, treat fevers and childhood diseases, make vinegar out of maple sap, and manage household servants.

Catherine Parr Traill.

Source: Library and Archives Canada, C-067337.

Her writings provide a fascinating window into the practicalities of pioneer life.[34] Parr Traill's prodigious energy seems all the more remarkable given her circumstances. Like her sister, she was married to a half-pay military officer, who had retired and accepted a Canadian land grant after falling on hard times at the end of the Napoleonic Wars. Thomas frequently sank into debilitating bouts of depression. Catharine Parr Traill's forbearance was also tested by the deaths of two of her nine children in infancy, and the loss of her home, along with unpublished manuscripts, in a devastating fire. She soldiered cheerily on, surviving her husband by 40 years and continuing to publish. She lived to age 97.

Transportation and Canal Building in the Canadas

Besides the challenge of land clearing, one of the chief difficulties faced by early British North American pioneers was travel. In central Canada, the railway age would begin in a modest way with the 26-kilometre-long Champlain and St. Lawrence Railroad in Lower Canada in 1836. Even so, by mid-century there would still be only a few dozen kilometres of railway track in all the British North American provinces. Before the advent of the railway age, road building had been similarly slow to progress, the source of perennial complaint by isolated farmers. In Upper Canada, settlers were compelled to clear lands for roads fronting their own lands. In swampy areas, "corduroy" roads were built, with logs laid in rows—a solution that made good use of available material but ensured that travellers would endure a jolting, bumpy ride. Smooth plank roads were a comparative luxury, but deteriorated quickly, and horse-drawn traffic was exposed to the perils of accidents, perhaps a hoof crashing through rotted planks. The first fall of winter snow brought relief: travellers bundled in layers of buffalo robes could enjoy swift sleighing through the frosty air, grain could be shipped overland to gristmills, and barrels of goods delivered to waiting merchants. In all other seasons, inland canals facilitated trade. Rapids at Lachine, up the river from Montreal, limited commercial navigation of the upper St. Lawrence, but the Lachine Canal, completed by 1825, bypassed the rapids and helped assure the commercial ascendancy of Montreal. Stimulated by protective British tariffs, the commerce of the Canadas flowed largely through that port. Further, the canal provided a source of hydraulic power and new industries clustered nearby to take advantage of that resource. A chartered company of merchants had provided the impetus for the Lachine Canal, but the government of Lower Canada bought out the project when it foundered.

1825: Lachine Canal completed.

1832: Rideau Canal completed.

The Rideau Canal, built between 1826 and 1832, and still used for small pleasure boats today, connected the Ottawa River to Lake Ontario. The Rideau Canal's primary purpose was military, rather than commercial: in the event of war with the Americans, it would be necessary to bypass the potentially vulnerable St. Lawrence route. Mindful of these defence considerations, the British government provided both the expertise and the capital for the Rideau Canal—at £1 million it was the most expensive defence project the British had ever undertaken in North America.

Lieutenant Colonel John By of the Royal Engineers supervised its construction. By established his camp at the junction of the Ottawa and Rideau Rivers; the site soon became known as Bytown, and in 1855 was renamed Ottawa. Two companies of the Royal Sappers and Miners worked on the canal project, but most of the 2000 workers were immigrant "navvies," frequently impoverished Irish newcomers who toiled barefoot 14, or even 16, hours a day, six days a week, using picks, chisels, shovels, and wheelbarrows. Illness and accidents stalked these overworked men, who were crowded together. They might be maimed or killed by gunpowder used for blasting, and hundreds succumbed to malaria, a disease more usually associated with tropical climates, but which flourished amid the boggy and pestilential conditions. Colonel By himself fell victim to malaria. Although he recovered sufficiently to complete the project, he returned to England in broken health to face a probe over excessive expenditure; he died soon afterward.

Other canal projects, notably the Welland Canal, proved to be of vital importance for Canada's future commerce. Commercial traffic between Lake Ontario and Lake Erie faced the formidable barrier of Niagara Falls. Before the construction of the canal, cargoes on Lake Erie destined for a seaport had to be transported over lengthy portages to bypass that obstacle. By 1825, the Americans had completed construction of an ambitious canal project of their own: the Erie Canal, linking Lake Erie to the Hudson River, provided an outlet to the Atlantic port of New York, which offered a commercial alternative to the St. Lawrence route.

The Welland Canal, constructed in 1829, met that challenge and also carried a considerable proportion of goods for the internal American market, goods travelling between Great Lakes ports. While construction began under the auspices of a private company, the government of Upper Canada purchased the Welland Canal and made improvements through the 1840s, replacing the old system of wooden locks that had already become obsolete with stone ones. Besides the obvious commercial advantages, such public works projects offered a kind of an economic safety valve, providing work for those for whom land ownership was a distant prospect.

1829: The Welland Canal is constructed to meet the commercial challenge of the American Erie Canal.

The Working Poor

Canal work drew thousands of labourers; many Irish navvies who had worked on the Erie Canal crowded into St. Catharines, Merriton, and Thorold to find work on the Welland Canal. Other immigrants unable to establish themselves on farms found wage labour cutting timber, working on the docks or in shipyards, or at other industries, especially in the Canadas' key commercial centre, Montreal. Molson's brewery, founded in 1786, as well as warehouses, factories, and foundries, drew job seekers to the city. Harsh conditions of work, long hours, and low pay made the plight of wage labourers a harsh one, but, for many, the onset of winter raised the spectre of genuine want. Not only was there no agricultural work, but winter halted public works projects and stilled commercial traffic on the ice-locked docks of Canada. Only the timber industry offered an outlet for those who could withstand the rigours of the work. The glut of workers in wintertime affected wages even for those whose work was not seasonal. The cruel dictates of supply and demand meant that January wages in Lower Canada for labourers were one-quarter to one-half less than what they were in August. Further, winter brought the need for firewood for fuel, not readily obtained in urban areas where the working poor congregated.

Maria Louisa Beleau, the child of a family with no male provider, died of exposure to cold in the harsh Quebec winter of 1816–17. Her home had been a hovel with open sides and a bare earth floor; there was no fuel for a fire. Staple foods were priced higher in winter; bread prices could rise by 50 percent. Relief efforts were piecemeal, and varied from one colony to another. New Brunswick and Nova Scotia had adopted English-style Poor Laws, with a system of poor rates and poorhouses; Upper Canada, more recently settled, did not have such programs. In Lower Canada, begging was regulated and licensed, and the religious orders oversaw most charitable and social programs. The St. Vincent de Paul Society, an international Roman Catholic association, founded in Paris in 1833 but only transplanted to British North America in 1846, was among the religious organizations that ministered to the needy. The Society's reports offer a glimpse into the state of life for the poorest. In St. John's, the Society visited fishermen's families and found that many had endured days without food. They found one desperate mother with nine starving children. While suffering the ravages of hunger herself, she continued breastfeeding her 18-month-old twins, as she had no other nourishment to give them.

Conclusion

Many sought and found a better life in Britain's North American colonies. Opportunities for independence and prosperity were more plentiful, but misfortune could appear in many guises. Some, like the ill-fated Selkirk settlers at Red River, found that their quest to begin a new life far from home carried with it risks they had never anticipated. For other immigrant newcomers, the opportunity to own land and move beyond the limits of old world constraints enabled them to rise from very humble circumstances to assume positions of real influence in a rapidly developing society. British North America's economy was being quickly transformed, with British tariff protection lending support for a variety of developing economic activities.

The foundation of Canada's modern identity as a nation of immigrants was being laid down in its early colonial history. In the years immediately following the Napoleonic Wars, the arrival of 1 million newcomers from the British Isles transformed British North America. In the colony of Upper Canada, these British—Irish, Scottish, and English—immigrants arrived into a population that had been previously dominated by the American-born. In Lower Canada, this new influx raised the spectre of cultural assimilation to the French Catholic population that had been established since the seventeenth century. The emergence of more populous colonies, and a growing assertiveness in those colonies that government should be responsive to their needs, contributed to a quest for political reform. Yet each colony had its own character and its own challenges. In no respect was there a unified sense of whole. The chapter that follows traces the emergence of new ideas for colonial government advanced by reformers, many of whom were fundamentally committed to British constitutional models. But increasing frustration at an inability to effect change by peaceful means led others to take up arms in rebellion. A dangerous crisis lay ahead for the Canadas.

Questions to Consider

1. What gave rise to the Battle of Seven Oaks in 1816?

2. What groups immigrated to British North America in the period following the Napoleonic Wars? Why?

3. Why was the status of American "aliens" controversial in Upper Canada?

4. What key economic developments can be identified in British North America in the early nineteenth century?

Critical Thinking Questions

1. Was Cuthbert Grant a heroic figure?

2. What problems plagued settlement in Upper Canada? How might these have been resolved?

3. Was assisted emigration to British North America a worthwhile scheme? Explain.

4. How reliable are contemporary immigrant accounts as an historical source?

Suggested Readings

Primary Sources

Alexander, James Edward. *L'Acadie, or Seven Years' Explorations in British America.* London: H. Colburn, 1849. Available through *Early Canadiana Online* at http://www.canadiana.org.

Ballantyne, R.M. *Hudson's Bay, or Everyday Life in the Wilds of North America: During Six Years' Residence in the Territories of the Honourable Hudson's Bay Company.* Edinburgh: W. Blackwood, 1848. Available through *Early Canadiana Online* at http://www.canadiana.org.

Cameron, Wendy, Sheila Haines, and Mary McDougall Maude, eds. *English Immigrant Voices, Labourers' Letters from Upper Canada in the 1830s.* Montreal and Kingston: McGill-Queen's University Press, 2000.

Cobbett, William. *The Emigrant's Guide; in Ten Letters Addressed to the Tax-Payers of England; Containing Information of Every Kind, Necessary to Persons Who Are About to Emigrate.* London: Mills, Jowett, and Mills, 1829. Available through *Early Canadiana Online* at http://www.canadiana.org.

Johnston, James Finlay Weir. *Notes on North America, Agricultural, Economical, and Social.* London: W. Blackwood and Sons, 1851.

MacDougall, Robert. *The Emigrant's Guide to North America.* Elizabeth Thompson, ed. Toronto: Natural Heritage, 1998.

Moodie, Susanna. *Roughing It in the Bush, or, Life in Canada.* Toronto: McClelland & Stewart, 1989. First published 1852. Available through *Early Canadiana Online* at http://www.canadiana.org.

Selkirk, Lord. *Lord Selkirk's Diary, 1803–1804: A Journal of His Travels in British North America and the Northeastern United States.* Patrick C. T. White, ed. Toronto: Champlain Society, 1958. Available online in Champlain Society digital collection, http://eir.library.utoronto.ca/champlain/search.cfm.

Useful Overview Sources

Craig, Gerald M. *Upper Canada, The Formative Years, 1784–1841.* Toronto: McClelland & Stewart, 1963.

Dickinson, John A., and Brian Young. *A Short History of Quebec.* Montreal and Kingston: McGill-Queen's University Press, 2002.

Friesen, Gerald. *The Canadian Prairies: A History.* Toronto: University of Toronto Press, 1984.

Innis, Harold A. *The Fur Trade in Canada.* Toronto: University of Toronto Press, 1962.

Harris, R. Cole, and John Warkentin. *Canada before Confederation: A Study in Historical Geography.* Toronto: Oxford University Press, 1974.

Harris, Cole. The Reluctant Land Society, Space, and Environment in Canada before Confederation. Vancouver: University of British Columbia Press, 2008.

MacNutt, W.S. *The Atlantic Provinces: The Emergence of Colonial Society, 1712–1857.* Toronto: McClelland & Stewart, 1965.

Magocsi, Paul Robert, ed. *Encyclopedia of Canada's Peoples.* Toronto: University of Toronto Press, 1999. Contains historical details on key immigrant groups, along with useful readings suggestions. Available online at http://www.multicultural canada.ca/ecp/.

McCalla, Douglas. *Planting the Province: The Economic History of Upper Canada.* Toronto: University of Toronto Press, 1993.

Ouellet, Fernand. *Lower Canada, 1791–1840: Social Change and Nationalism.* Toronto: McClelland & Stewart, 1980.

Pannekoek, Frits. *The Fur Trade and Western Canadian Society, 1670 – 1870.* Ottawa: Canadian Historical Association, 1987.

Ray, Arthur. *Indians in the Fur Trade.* Toronto: University of Toronto Press, 1983.

Wood, David. *Making Ontario: Agricultural Colonization and Landscape Recreation before the Railway.* Montreal and Kingston: McGill-Queen's University Press, 2000.

Wynn, Graeme. *Timber Colony: A Historical Geography of Nineteenth Century New Brunswick.* Toronto: University of Toronto Press, 1981.

Special Topics

Backhouse, Constance. *Petticoats and Prejudice: Women and Law in Nineteenth Century Canada.* Toronto: Osgoode Society, 1991.

Bilson, Geoffrey. *A Darkened House: Cholera in Nineteenth-Century Canada.* Toronto: University of Toronto Press, 1980.

Bumsted, J.M. *The Scots in Canada.* Ottawa: Canadian Historical Association, 1982. This booklet, and a variety of other Canadian Historical Association booklets on other topics, including the Ethnic Groups series, are available online through the Library and Archives Canada website at http://www.collectionscanada.ca/cha-shc/002013-111.01-e.php?q1=E&interval=100.

Bumsted, J.M. *Lord Selkirk: A Life.* Winnipeg: University of Manitoba Press, 2008.

Cadigan, Sean. *Hope and Conception in Deception Bay: Merchant—Settler Relations in Newfoundland, 1785–1855.* Toronto: University of Toronto Press, 1995.

Cameron, Wendy, and Mary McDougall Maude. *Assisting Emigration to Upper Canada: The Petworth Project.* Montreal and Kingston: McGill-Queens University Press, 2000.

Campey, Lucille H. *An Unstoppable Force: The Scottish Exodus to Canada.* Toronto: Dundurn, 2008.

Campey, Lucille H. *The Silver Chief: Lord Selkirk and the Scottish Pioneers of Belfast, Baldoon and Red River.* Toronto: National Heritage, 2003.

Clarke, John. *Land, Power, and Economics on the Frontier of Upper Canada.* Montreal and Kingston: McGill-Queen's University Press, 2002.

Dick, Lyle. "The Seven Oaks Incident and the Construction of a Historical Tradition, 1816 to 1970" *Journal of the Canadian Historical Association* (1991): 91–113.

Dictionary of Canadian Biography. Online at http://www.biographi.ca.

Elliott, Bruce. "The New Brunswick Land Company and the Settlement of Stanley and Harvey," http://history.earthsci.carleton.ca/company/history/elliott1.htm.

Elliott, Bruce. "Regional Patterns of English Immigration and Settlement in Upper Canada" in *Canadian Migration Patterns from Britain and North America.* Barbara J. Messamore, ed. Ottawa: University of Ottawa Press, 2004.

Errington, Jane. *The Lion, the Eagle, and Upper Canada: A Developing Colonial Ideology.* Montreal and Kingston: McGill-Queen's University Press, 1987.

Fingard, Judith. "The Winter's Tale: The Seasonal Contours of Pre-industrial Poverty in British North America, 1815–1860." *Canadian Historical Association Historical Papers* (1974): 65–94.

Gray, Charlotte. *Sisters in the Wilderness: The Lives of Susanna Moodie and Catherine Parr Traill.* Toronto: Penguin, 2008.

Greer, Allan, and Ian Radforth, eds. *Colonial Leviathan: State Formation in Mid-Nineteenth Century Canada.* Toronto: University of Toronto Press, 1992.

Harper, Marjory, and Michael E. Vance, eds. *Myth, Migration, and the Making of Memory: Scotia and Nova Scotia, c. 1700–1990.* Edinburgh: John Donald, 1999.

Houston, Cecil J., and William J. Smyth. *The Sash Canada Wore: A Historical Geography of the Orange Order in Canada.* Toronto: University of Toronto Press, 1980.

Houston, Cecil J., and William J. Smyth. *Irish Emigration and Canadian Settlement: Patterns, Links, & Letters.* Toronto: University of Toronto Press, 1990.

Johnston, H.J.M. *British Emigration Policy, 1815–1830: "Shovelling Out Paupers."* Oxford: Clarendon Press, 1972.

Karr, Clarence. *The Canada Company.* Ottawa: Ontario Historical Society, 1974.

Kealey, Gregory S. "The Orange Order in Toronto: Religious Riot and the Working Class" in *Essays in Canadian Working Class History.* Gregory S. Kealey and Peter Warrian, eds. Toronto: McClelland & Stewart, 1976.

Little, J.L. "Feast or Famine: The British American Land Company and the Colonization of the St Francis Tract." In *Nationalism, Capitalism, and Colonization in Nineteenth-Century Quebec: The Upper St Francis District.* J.L. Little, ed. Montreal and Kingston: McGill-Queen's University Press, 1989.

McCallum, John. *Unequal Beginnings: Agriculture and Economic Development in Quebec and Ontario until 1870.* Toronto: University of Toronto Press, 1983.

McDonald, Terry. "'A Door of Escape': Letters Home from Wiltshire and Somerset Emigrants to Upper Canada, 1830–1832." In *Canadian Migration Patterns from Britain and North America.* Barbara J. Messamore, ed. Ottawa: University of Ottawa Press, 2004.

McNairn, Jeffrey L. *The Capacity to Judge: Public Opinion and Deliberative Democracy in Upper Canada, 1791–1854.* Toronto: University of Toronto Press, 2000.

Mills, David. *The Idea of Loyalty in Upper Canada, 1784–1850.* Montreal and Kingston: McGill-Queen's University Press, 1988.

Noel, Jan, ed. *Race and Gender in the Northern Colonies.* Toronto: Canadian Scholars' Press, 2000.

Peterman, Michael. *Sisters in Two Worlds: A Visual Biography of Susanna Moodie and Catherine Parr Traill.* Toronto: Doubleday, 2008.

Podruchny, Carolyn. *Making the Voyageur World: Travellers and Traders in the North American Fur Trade.* Toronto: University of Toronto Press, 2006.

Romney, Paul. "Re-inventing Upper Canada: American Immigrants, Upper Canadian History, English Law, and the Alien Question" *Patterns of the Past: Interpreting Ontario's History.* Roger Hall, William Westfall and Lauren Sefton MacDowell, eds. Toronto: Dundurn Press, 1988.

Tulchinsky, Gerald, ed. *Immigration in Canada: Historical Perspectives.* Toronto: Copp Clark Longman, 1994.

Van Kirk, Sylvia. *"Many Tender Ties": Women in Fur-Trade Society in Western Canada, 1670–1870.* Winnipeg: Watson & Dwyer Publishing, 1980.

Warkentin, Germaine, ed. *Canadian Exploration Literature.* Toronto: Oxford University Press, 1993. (Excerpts from Frances Simpson's journal are included in this source.)

Welsh, Christine. "Voices of the Grandmothers: Reclaiming a Métis Heritage" *Canadian Literature* 131 (Winter 1991): 15–24. (The author, who relies upon collected oral histories, is the great-great-great granddaughter of George Simpson's wife, Margaret Taylor.)

Notes

[1] George Woodcock, "Cuthbert Grant," *Dictionary of Canadian Biography.* Online at http://www.biographi.ca.

[2] Gerald Friesen, *The Canadian Prairies: A History* (Toronto: University of Toronto Press, 1984), 76–80.

[3] George Woodcock, "Cuthbert Grant."

[4] As quoted by Lucille H. Campey, The Silver Chief: Lord Selkirk and the Scottish Pioneers of Belfast, Baldoon and Red River (Toronto: National Heritage, 2003), 106.

[5] More information on the 1817 Selkirk Treaty may be obtained in Arthur J. Ray, Jim Miller, and Frank Tough, *Bounty and Benevolence: A History of Saskatchewan Treaties* (Montreal and Kingston: McGill-Queen's University Press, 2000), Chapter 2, "The Selkirk Treaty, 1817." The treaty itself is available online though the Manitoba Historical Society at http://www.mhs.mb.ca/docs/pageant/21/lordselkirktreaty.shtml.

[6] Sylvia Van Kirk, *"Many Tender Ties": Women in Fur-Trade Society in Western Canada, 1670–1870* (Winnipeg: Watson & Dwyer Publishing, 1980), 188.

[7] Frances Simpson, excerpt from "Journal of a Voyage from Montreal thro' the Interior of Canada, to York Factory on the Shores of Hudson's Bay, 1830" in Germaine Warkentin, ed. *Canadian Exploration Literature* (Toronto: Oxford University Press, 1993), 384–395.

[8] David Mills, *The Idea of Loyalty in Upper Canada, 1784–1850* (Montreal and Kingston: McGill-Queen's University Press, 1988), 29.

[9] As quoted by J. David Wood, *Making Ontario: Agricultural Colonization and Landscape Re-creation before the Railway* (Montreal and Kingston: McGill-Queen's University Press, 2000), 4.

[10] As quoted by G.M. Craig, "John Strachan," *Dictionary of Canadian Biography,* http://www.biographi.ca.

[11] David Mills, *The Idea of Loyalty,* 35–36.

[12] Jane Errington, *The Lion, the Eagle, and Upper Canada: A Developing Colonial Ideology* (Montreal and Kingston: McGill-Queen's University Press, 1987), 188.

[13] David Mills, *The Idea of Loyalty,* 46.

[14] Harold A. Innis, *The Fur Trade in Canada* (Toronto: University of Toronto Press, 1962); Douglas McCalla, *Planting the Province: The Economic History of Upper Canada* (Toronto: University of Toronto Press, 1993), 5.

[15] James Edward Alexander, *L'Acadie, or Seven Years' Explorations in British America* (London: H. Colburn, 1849), 74–76, *Early Canadiana Online*, http://www.canadiana.org.

[16] Fernand Ouellet, *Lower Canada, 1791–1840: Social Change and Nationalism* (Toronto: McClelland & Stewart, 1980), 56–58, 127–129; John McCallum, *Unequal Beginnings: Agriculture and Economic Development in Quebec and Ontario until 1870* (Toronto: University of Toronto Press, 1983), 4–5.

[17] J. David Wood, *Making Ontario*, 14.

[18] Graeme Wynn, *Timber Colony: A Historical Geography of Early Nineteenth Century New Brunswick* (Toronto: University of Toronto Press, 1981), 67.

[19] A.R.M. Lower, "The Trade in Square Timber" *Contributions to Canadian Economics* 6 (1933), 56.

[20] Donald Akenson, "Ontario: Whatever Happened to the Irish?" *Immigration in Canada: Historical Perspectives*, Gerald Tulchinsky, ed. (Toronto: Copp Clark Longman, 1994), 87, 96, 100.

[21] R. Cole Harris and John Warkentin, *Canada Before Confederation: A Study in Historical Geography* (Toronto: Oxford University Press, 1974), 118.

[22] Cecil J. Houston and William J. Smyth, *The Sash Canada Wore: A Historical Geography of the Orange Order in Canada* (Toronto: University of Toronto Press, 1980), 3, 7; see also Gregory S. Kealey, "The Orange Order in Toronto: Religious Riot and the Working Class" *Essays in Canadian Working Class History*, Gregory S. Kealey and Peter Warrian, eds. (Toronto: McClelland & Stewart, 1976), 13–34.

[23] J.M. Bumsted, *The Scots in Canada* (Ottawa: Canadian Historical Association. Canada's Ethnic Groups. Booklet 1, 1982), 2–4.

[24] Karl Marx, "Expropriation of the Agricultural Population from the Land," *Das Kapital*, http://www.bibliomania.com/2/1/261/1294/frameset.html.

[25] See Wendy Cameron and Mary McDougall Maude, *Assisting Emigration to Upper Canada: The Petworth Project* (Montreal and Kingston: McGill-Queens University Press, 2000); see also Wendy Cameron, Wendy, Sheila Haines, and Mary McDougall Maude, eds., *English Immigrant Voices, Labourers' Letters from Upper Canada in the 1830s* (Montreal and Kingston: McGill-Queen's University Press, 2000).

[26] H.J.M. Johnston, *British Emigration Policy, 1815–1830: "Shovelling Out Paupers"* (Oxford: Clarendon Press, 1972).

[27] George Cornewall Lewis to Sir Edmund Head, 3 October 1837, *Letters of the Right Hon. Sir George Cornewall Lewis, Bart. to Various Friends.* Gilbert Franklin Lewis, ed. (London: Longmans, Green & Co., 1870), 90.

[28] Terry McDonald, "'A Door of Escape': Letters Home from Wiltshire and Somerset Emigrants to Upper Canada, 1830–1832," *Canadian Migration Patterns from Britain and North America*, Barbara J. Messamore, ed. (Ottawa: University of Ottawa Press, 2004), 115.

[29] Bruce Elliott, "The New Brunswick Land Company and the Settlement of Stanley and Harvey," http://history.earthsci.carleton.ca/company/history/elliott1.htm.

[30] J. David Wood, *Making Ontario*, 85.

[31] Greg Gatenby, ed., *The Very Richness of that Past: Canada Through the Eyes of Foreign Writers*, Vol II. (Toronto: Alfred A. Knopf, 1995), 174 –191, contains an account of Cobbett's Canadian associations. Quotations are drawn from this source and from William Cobbett, *The Emigrant's Guide; in Ten Letters addressed to the Tax-Payers of England; Containing Information of Every Kind, Necessary to Persons Who are About to Emigrate* (London: Mills, Jowett, and Mills, 1829), 7–41, available through *Early Canadiana Online* at http://www.canadiana.org.

[32] Susanna Moodie, *Roughing It in the Bush, or Life in Canada* (Toronto: McClelland and Stewart, 1989. First published 1852), 489, 197–201, 29, also available through *Early Canadiana Online* at http://www.canadiana.org.

[33] Robert MacDougall, *The Emigrant's Guide to North America.* Elizabeth Thompson, ed. (Toronto: Natural Heritage, 1998 ed.), 31, 39.

[34] The guide is available through *Early Canadiana Online* at http://www.canadiana.org/ECO/ItemRecord/41581?id=201406c1b4339b6c.

8

Rebellion *in the* Canadas: *1826–1838*

On November 25, 1837, Lower Canadian patriotes massed at Saint Charles to take up a defensive position against Colonel George Wetherall's advancing force of some 350 British regulars. Only two days before, the rebels had routed British and Loyalist militia forces at Saint-Denis, and they busily prepared for another victory. Leading the patriotes was Thomas Brown, a bankrupt hardware merchant who had lost an eye in earlier clashes between Loyalists and the rebel Fils de la Liberté in the streets of Montreal. The idea of risking his life in a contest where he had everything to lose and little to gain held a perversely romantic appeal to Brown. His forces at Saint Charles ransacked the nearby manor house of seigneur Pierre-Dominique Debartzch, seizing it as a rebel stronghold, and commandeering grain, cattle, and muskets from the surrounding countryside. Copying the American rebels of 1776, some rebels wore homespun cloth, straw hats, and crude homemade "beef shoes," a symbol that they were boycotting British imports.

But Saint Charles lacked the natural defences that had served the patriotes at Saint-Denis so well. Worse, an intercepted message led Brown to believe that Wetherall's troops had been ordered back to Montreal. The sound of artillery shattering the steeple of the village church signalled that he had been misinformed. Only a few dozen patriotes were at the ready to do battle. Wetherall's forces set homes and barns ablaze, targeting buildings from which musket fire had emanated. Some patriotes

Henri Julien of the Montreal Star *created this image in 1887 to commemorate the* patriotes *of 1837. It was also used by the Front de Libération du Quebec in 1970.*

drowned attempting to escape across the Richelieu River, and Brown himself fled the scene of battle. By the evening, the small rebel forces had been overwhelmed and 56 patriotes lay dead in the grass. Burning buildings ignited the dry grass surrounding the battle scene, and the air was filled with the smell of roasted flesh and the burnt remnants of the coarse homespun fabric in which the patriotes had been clad.

After reading this chapter you will be able to:

1. Identify the source of reformers' dissatisfaction with the forms of government in British North America.
2. Understand moderate voices for reform in Nova Scotia.
3. Assess Britain's response to colonial grievances.
4. Explain the nature and causes of the rebellions in 1837 and 1838 in Lower and Upper Canada.

Introduction

In the autumn of 1837, both Lower and Upper Canada were embroiled in armed uprisings aimed at overthrowing British rule. Political dissenters complained that, while the colonies had representative government, all effective power was wielded by the non-elected legislative and executive councils and the British-appointed governors. Yet the grievances that would ignite rebellion were more complicated than simple dissatisfaction with oligarchical rule. In Lower Canada, nationalist goals also animated reformers who, as they drifted toward more radical positions, began to refer to themselves as *patriotes*; some found inspiration in the American Revolution. Louis Joseph Papineau, the acknowledged leader of Lower Canada's *patriotes*, embraced other values that were fundamentally conservative, aimed at preserving French Canada's distinct institutions. In Upper Canada, William Lyon Mackenzie spearheaded the radical reform cause, and he found an especially receptive audience among American-born newcomers. Faced with intransigence on the part of British authorities, rebels in both colonies took up arms.

Representative Government in the British North American Colonies

Since 1791, there had been representative government—an elected assembly—in the Canadas, the two colonies of Upper and Lower Canada. This was not an innovation in British North America: Nova Scotia had had such an assembly since 1758, Prince Edward Island from 1773, and New Brunswick from 1784. The 13 British colonies that rebelled to become the United States had also had representative institutions, some since the early seventeenth century. The introduction of representative government in the Canadas had been sparked by the arrival by 1784 of the Loyalists into the colony of Quebec: it had been necessary to implement a form of government that would be more congenial to English-speaking, largely Protestant, newcomers than the 1774 *Quebec Act*. The *Constitutional Act*, or *Canada Act*, of 1791 introduced into each of the now-separate colonies of Upper and Lower Canada a constitution that was meant to echo the British form of government. The governor represented the Crown—the governor-in-chief was based in the more populous and long-established colony of Lower Canada, while Upper Canada's administration was presided over by a lieutenant governor. In each colony, an upper house, or legislative council, was modelled on the British House of Lords, and a legislative assembly was based on the House of Commons. The governor's appointed executive council resembled a cabinet, although it functioned in a different way. As political scientist Janet Ajzenstat has pointed out, the "bones" of our modern constitution can be seen in the 1791 Act.[1]

From its very beginning, though, the more astute observers of Canadian politics recognized that the constitution's resemblance to British models was superficial. While the colony enjoyed representative institutions, and those who possessed sufficient property were eligible to vote, the wishes of the legislative assembly could be, and frequently were, thwarted by the legislative council and the British-appointed governor. What is more, the executive council was appointed by the governor, without reference to the wishes of the assembly. The governor simply selected as his advisors men who were likely to be loyal to him, and whose prominence generally implied deeply conservative views. Today, of course, ministers—the cabinet—are appointed based on which party commands a majority in the House of Commons. It is understood that the leader of the party with majority support in the Commons will be appointed prime minister, and that the prime minister will advise the governor general about who should be appointed to cabinet. If the cabinet ceases to command the support of the Commons, the government is considered defeated, which would usually signal an election. But the form of government introduced in the Canadas in 1791 did not operate according to this principle of ministerial responsibility. The struggle to obtain such a system—variously referred to as *responsible government*, *cabinet government*, *colonial self-government*, or even simply *home rule*—engaged political activists in both Lower and Upper Canada, and ultimately engulfed the colonies in rebellion.

Louis Joseph Papineau Takes Up the Cause of Reform in Lower Canada

The lawyer and member of the legislative assembly Pierre Bédard was an early moderate voice for reform in Lower Canada. After 1804, Bédard emerged as the leader of the Parti Canadien. This new political party, along with the 1806 appearance of the reform-oriented French-language newspaper *Le Canadien*, signalled the intermingling of ethnic nationalist aspirations with the drive for constitutional reform. Bédard's place as leader of the Parti Canadien was supplanted by 1811 by his former friends, Louis-Joseph Papineau and Denis-Benjamin Viger. Papineau was a complex figure, who in many respects embodied the ideological crosscurrents of reform in Lower Canada. While his political views were on the radical end of the reform spectrum—he urged wholesale, systemic political change—he believed in the preservation of what he saw as the core traditions of French Canada.

His family had risen from humbler origins to the ranks of the elite with his father's purchase of the seigneurie of Petite-Nation. His education was exclusively Roman Catholic, first at the College of Montreal, and then the Petite Séminaire of Quebec, where more than half of his classmates were destined for the priesthood. Young French Canadians in this era might also opt to enter the professions—to become doctors, lawyers, or perhaps politicians; commerce was increasingly the preserve of an assertive English-Canadian

Louis Joseph Papineau.

Source: Library and Archives Canada, C-005462.

minority. Papineau's education culminated with training in law at the Montreal offices of his cousin, Denis-Benjamin Viger. He qualified as a lawyer in 1810, by which time he had already begun a lifelong career in politics.

Perhaps politics was a natural vocation for Papineau, whose eloquence was remarkable even at an early age—he was not yet 30 when he was chosen to be speaker of the legislative assembly. During the War of 1812, Papineau took up arms to defend the colony against American invaders. He was a militia captain with the victorious British forces at Fort Detroit. In this respect, he followed in his father's footsteps—Joseph Papineau fought on the side of the British when the Americans invaded Montreal in 1775 during the American Revolution. They were hardly unique in this respect, but their military service to Britain reveals that Papineau's later opposition was motivated by resentment at perceived British misrule, not the authority of the Crown in and of itself. Papineau—like Pierre Bédard—ascribed many positive advantages to British rule. On the occasion of the accession to the throne of King George IV in 1820, Papineau reflected on "our present happy situation," enumerating the benefits of British rule: the protection of the British navy and army; religious tolerance; trial by jury, which he described as the "wisest of safeguards ever devised for the protection of innocence"; security against arbitrary imprisonment; security of person and property; and "the right to obey no other laws than those of our own making and choice, expressed through our representatives."[2]

1820s: The Parti Canadien *use the assembly's control over financial legislation to attempt to force constitutional concessions.*

By the early 1820s, reformers in Lower Canada's assembly, led by Papineau, decided to use their majority to thwart the dominance of the English merchant class. Their chief weapon was obstructionism. Money bills, those concerned with taxation revenue and spending, such as the civil list (the salaries of paid public servants and officials), had to be initiated in the assembly, despite the other limitations on the power of that body. Refusal to pass essential financial measures became a key strategy in the reformers' quest to pressure Britain into conceding constitutional change.

The abortive 1822 Bill in Britain's Parliament that had sought to unite the Canadas was aimed largely at overcoming the intransigence of Lower Canada's assembly by ensuring that government revenues and expenditures could not be thus held ransom for political ends. Furthermore, commercial interests, preoccupied with meeting the American challenge, were concerned that legislative jurisdiction over the vitally important St. Lawrence River was divided between two colonies. Merchants in Lower Canada favoured the union bill, although some in Upper Canada worried about the possibility of being linked to the still more numerous French in the lower colony, with a capital established at Montreal or Quebec. British parliamentarians had not accepted the principle that colonial consultation should be sought before enacting legislation affecting them, but, when they were attacked for their haste in pushing the measure through, they decided to shelve the bill. Papineau and John Neilson had been chosen by the assembly of Lower Canada to go to London to submit a 60 000 signature petition against it; the reformers' reputation rose when British authorities abandoned the proposed bill.

John Neilson exemplifies the fact that not all reformers in Lower Canada were French Canadian: some did not see the struggle primarily in terms of cultural survival. Scottish born, John Neilson had come to Quebec as a youth to work in his older brother's printing business, and later built it up into a thriving publishing empire. He married a French-

Canadian woman, and spoke French as comfortably as he did his own native tongue. Neilson and his wife had 10 children, and reached a very Canadian sort of compromise: their sons would be raised as Presbyterian, their daughters as Roman Catholic.

In 1828, Neilson would again be among the petitioners who laid complaints before a Select Committee of the British House of Commons. This time, a petition containing 87 000 signatures accompanied the resolutions of the assembly, although Papineau worried that opponents of reform would make political capital out of the fact that 78 000 of the signatories could only mark the petition with crosses. Political agitators who were not sufficiently literate to sign their own names would hardly make an impressive case.

Neilson complained of abuses by the governor Lord Dalhousie (1820–1828), who had been hastily appointed when his predecessor, the Duke of Richmond (1818–1819), was bitten by his pet fox and died of rabies. Dalhousie, who had been serving as lieutenant governor of Nova Scotia, was a crusty veteran of Waterloo who had been in the British army since the age of 17. He had no inclination to finesse his obstreperous assembly, and the constant struggle over that body's unwillingness to vote supply reached an impasse in 1826–27. Dalhousie illegally appropriated funds in the provincial treasury to meet costs without bothering to obtain the consent of the legislature. Moreover, he had a legitimate alternative source of funds, in the form of the Crown land reserves, the sale of which traditionally came under the control of the governor and his council. Dalhousie dissolved his uncooperative assembly in 1827, but in the ensuing election an even stronger and more radical reform element came to the fore. Dalhousie refused to accept the assembly's nomination of Papineau as their speaker, the assembly refused to reconsider, and the thwarted governor expressed his displeasure by proroguing it—in other words, ending the session of the legislature—before it had even properly begun. Complaints about Dalhousie to the Commons committee in Britain undoubtedly played a role in his recall. He was sent to be commander in chief of the British forces in India, a position eminently more suited to his disposition. In addition to complaints about the governor's abuses, Neilson and his fellow petitioners warned against plans to do away with French Canada's unique civil law and to replace seigneurial land tenure with one with which the people of Lower Canada were unfamiliar.

The presence of Neilson helped reassure Britain's policymakers that the grievances of Lower Canadian reformers were not purely nationalistic, aimed at French-Canadian autonomy. The Commons select committee helped statesmen in the mother country come to a clearer understanding of the realities of colonial politics, and to better grasp the extent to which colonial practice deviated from the British pattern as laid out in the 1791 *Constitutional Act*. The committee conceded that the assembly alone should have control over the colony's income and expenditures, but insisted that control over official salaries should not be subject to annual votes by the assembly. Historian John Manning Ward credits the debates in Britain's Parliament on the occasion of the select committee's report with introducing the concept of self-governing colonies, a concept that would ultimately come to fruition in the 1840s.[3]

1828: Lower Canadian reform petitioners appear before a British Commons committee.

Growing Radicalization in Lower Canada

In the meantime, clashes with uncompromising governors and the growing assertiveness of the Château Clique had pushed reformers into a more radical posture. Moderates

1826: The Parti Canadien becomes more radical and is renamed the Parti Patriote.

1828: The Vindicator is founded as a voice for Irish radical reformers.

such as John Neilson were being crowded out of a Parti Canadien that was transforming. The name of the party had already been changed: in 1826 it became the Parti Patriote, a name that had echoes of the American Revolution. Louis-Joseph Papineau's previous admiration of British institutions had been steadily waning, and he increasingly looked to the republican United States for political models to admire.

By the early 1830s, Papineau was openly republican in his views, and had become won over by the ideas of Thomas Jefferson. He praised what he saw as a more egalitarian society in the United States, the greater fluidity through social ranks. Much as he admired American democracy, Papineau wanted Canada to avoid the excessive reliance of Americans on commerce; he hoped Lower Canada could retain its agricultural character. Papineau also emphasized the separation of church and state, and freedom of religion, a platform that guaranteed he would be opposed by Roman Catholic authorities. However, his anti-clerical stance was tempered with the conviction that the Roman Catholic religion could be an important part of the distinct French-Canadian nation that he wished to preserve. "It is understandable that his contemporaries became lost in this tangled skein of thinking, so full of contradictions," historian Fernand Ouellet wryly observed.[4] A new newspaper, *La Minerve*, was launched in 1826 to be the organ of the new party.

A radical Irish reformer based in Montreal, Daniel Tracey, founded an English-language newspaper in 1828, *The Vindicator,* which supported the *patriote* cause and the rights of Irish immigrants. Irish migrants to Canada were a substantial group, and many brought with them the deep-seated disaffection for British rule that pervaded political life in their home country. The voice of Irish dissidents also encouraged the swing to a more radical outlook.

The French political philosopher Alexis de Tocqueville visited Lower Canada in 1831 during a journey to the United States. In addition to his famous *Democracy in America*, de Tocqueville recorded his views about that colony in his travel diary, *Journey to America.* He noted that while the French showed every sign of being a conquered people, subject to commercial and political domination by the English, he expected that this would not long be the case. He observed that the 1822 plan for union was "designed completely to break up the French Canadian nation, so the whole people rose at once and it is from that time that it knows its strength." French and English can never merge, he predicted, nor could "an indissoluble union … exist between them."[5]

William Lyon Mackenzie and Reform in Upper Canada

Agitation for reform had long been a feature of Upper Canadian politics as well. The activities of Robert Gourlay, who had arrived in the colony in 1817, and the controversy over the "alien question" that had caused such upheaval in the 1820s, demonstrated that Upper Canadian reform politics emanated from a different impulse. While the "nationalist" motives that inspired some of Lower Canada's reformers were absent in the upper colony, the quest for constitutional reform was common to both.

William Lyon Mackenzie, a journalist and printer who had arrived in Upper Canada from Scotland in 1820, was among the most vocal champions of political reform in that province. Slight of stature, with a contentious disposition, Mackenzie did not show promise in his early years. When he was only three weeks old, his father died, and his mother was left to raise him alone. Financial troubles plagued him from an early age, and this would prove to be a constant theme in his life. His first business venture in Scotland collapsed in bankruptcy. He was also inclined to quarrel with business partners; more than one promising association dissolved amid acrimony. In his late teens, he led what he later admitted was a life of dissipation—drinking, gambling, and fathering a child out of wedlock. Mackenzie lost his hair as the result of a fever, but wore an untidy looking flame-red wig to mask the fact. In fits of excitement he was known to tear off his wig, or even to throw it at bystanders. In 1824, soon after his arrival in Canada, Mackenzie moved to York (Toronto) from Queenston, taking with him his newly established newspaper, *The Colonial Advocate.* Launching a series of attacks on the Tory elite of Upper Canada, Mackenzie was making a name for himself among reformers, but the paper's circulation was modest. Mackenzie, unable to pay his creditors, fled to New York in May of 1826 to avoid arrest for debt.

William Lyon Mackenzie.
Source: Library and Archives Canada, C-001993.

Weeks later, his salvation came—in an unexpected guise. A gang of young men, resentful of Mackenzie's printed attacks on their elite families, descended upon his printing office. Unconvincingly disguised as Indians, they smashed Mackenzie's presses and threw his printing type into the bay. Local authorities stood idly by, in no way attempting to prevent the daylight raid. Yet Mackenzie was able to turn the episode to his advantage, suing the wrongdoers and winning £625 in damages in a jury trial—a sum that far exceeded the actual damages and enabled him to make a fresh start. Reformers jubilantly enjoyed the irony.

1828: William Lyon Mackenzie enters politics in Upper Canada.

Mackenzie won election to Upper Canada's legislative assembly in 1828 as member for York, one of a reform majority elected to the assembly that year. This signalled Mackenzie's formal entry into politics, but it was undoubtedly through his newspaper writings, public meetings, and petitioning that he made his greatest impact.

Political Life in British North America

Mackenzie's activities and career demonstrate a sometimes forgotten feature of political life in colonial North America. While it is customary to refer to Conservatives, or Tories, and Reformers, the fact is that disciplined political parties, as we know them in the modern sense, did not yet exist in the early years of the nineteenth century. Historian Carol Wilton notes that, like most political figures of his day, Mackenzie "did not think in terms of parties that might legitimately differ on questions relating to the public good. On the contrary, he stigmatized his opponents as members of 'factions' motivated by no grander objective than pure self-interest." The idea of an "opposition," so crucial to politics today, could not, in the minds of many, be separated from the notion of disloyalty.

Furthermore, political participation in the formal sense was restricted to men who possessed sufficient property to be eligible to vote—an estimated 10 to 12 percent of the population in early-nineteenth-century Upper Canada.[6] In Lower Canada, habitants had enjoyed a wide franchise since the 1791 *Constitutional Act*, yet subdivisions of ever-smaller holdings, shortages of land, and a drift away from agricultural occupations meant that the

1834: Lower Canada eliminates votes for women.

percentage who enjoyed the franchise was actually shrinking in the early nineteenth century. Nevertheless, with as many as 70 percent of heads of families eligible to vote, Lower Canada enjoyed an enviable degree of popular participation. Historian Allan Greer points out that such "would have been unheard of in Britain, in most of the United States, and even in revolutionary France."[7] Some female heads of families in Lower Canada even exercised the franchise until a *patriote*-dominated assembly specifically disenfranchised them in 1834. Papineau, for all his political progressiveness, was deeply conservative about entrenched social traditions, and his struggle for full political rights was not meant to include women. He was probably also mindful of the fact that women did not tend to support the Parti Patriote.

Beyond limits on voter eligibility, the democratic character of the elected assembly was also undercut by the very method in which the franchise was exercised. Elections did not take place within a single day, but could last over the course of weeks, and, even more significantly, were not done by secret ballot. Elections were "manly" occasions on which voters openly declared their support for candidates, giving their opponents the opportunity to pelt them with rocks and bottles. Intimidation, bribery, and liquor-induced persuasion were key features of early-nineteenth-century elections. Newspapers frequently printed lists of the names, addresses, and occupations of voters, along with a record of whom they had voted for. The lightly populated colony of Newfoundland, having been granted representative government for the first time in 1832, was plagued by violence at the polls. At the height of the troubles in 1835, Protestant newspaper editor Henry Winton, who had railed against the influence of Roman Catholic priests in local politics, was seized upon by masked men who mutilated his ears. Fearful of growing violence, the Colonial Office implemented a change in constitution in 1842. Newfoundland's elected legislative assembly and appointed legislative council were amalgamated into one body until 1848, with some elected members and some appointed.

In addition to a property qualification for prospective members of the assembly, there were other factors that limited direct participation in government. Members of the assembly were not paid a salary, making a political career the exclusive preserve of those with independent means. In New Brunswick in 1786, Upper Canada in 1793, and Lower Canada in 1831, legislation was introduced to pay members a daily wage for attending sittings, but these payments could hardly stretch to cover the costs of travel and accommodations for members who lived away from the seat of government. "That a member should be paid a salary large enough to live on apparently occurred to nobody; his living was his own affair," political scientist Norman Ward noted. Even such modest payments were considered, in the words of one Colonial Secretary, "derogatory to the dignity of the House." Members of Parliament in Britain were not paid until 1911. The nineteenth-century British political philosopher John Stuart Mill worried that if members were paid, "the business of a member of Parliament would … become an occupation in itself, carried on, like other professions, with a view chiefly to its pecuniary returns…."[8]

Given these limitations, it is perhaps fortunate that nineteenth-century political action did not take place exclusively in the realm of elections and in the activities of the legislature. Petitioning was an essential feature of early-nineteenth-century politics, in the colonies and the mother country alike. In Britain, some 645 petitions in favour of parliamentary reform reached the House of Commons between November 1830 and March 1831. Thus, Papineau and Neilson's voyages to Britain in 1822 and 1828 were by no means unique. Upper Canadian agitation against the Alien Bill in 1827 was another example of successful petitioning. In *The Colonial Advocate,* Mackenzie defended petitioning as a British tradition with no taint of disloyalty.

Influences on Canadian Reformers

In 1829, Mackenzie travelled to the United States and met the newly elected president, Andrew Jackson. The 1828 election of Andrew Jackson was one in a series of events from which radical reformers drew inspiration. It seemed to herald a new shift toward a more democratic polity. As Jackson was not a member of the eastern political elite, his supporters saw his election as the triumph of popular forces over entrenched privilege. Moreover, numerous individual states had moved toward universal—or, rather universal white male—suffrage. Mackenzie's favourable views of Jackson would have accorded well with those of his many American-born constituents in Upper Canada, and American democracy became a key influence on his views. Jackson's idea that "to the victor belong the spoils"—that a victorious administration should have control over patronage—struck a responsive chord in Mackenzie. So too did Jackson's opposition to the power of big banks. The monopoly of the Bank of Upper Canada had been a particular provocation to reformers in that province who saw it as yet another symbol of the unbreakable power of a cadre of colonial elite.

1830: France's "July Revolution" inspires radical reformers in Canada.

Beyond events in the United States, radical reformers also drew encouragement from other signs around the world auguring a new age in politics. The success in 1830 of the July Revolution in France was one example. The Bourbon monarchy, restored at the end of the Napoleonic Wars, was ousted in a short-lived uprising in Paris. In its place was established the more moderate and modern constitutional regime of Louis-Philippe, formerly the duc d'Orléans, who ruled not as the King of France, but as King of the French. The success of the July Revolution offered encouragement to revolutionary movements in Belgium and Poland that same year.

Britain did not experience a revolution, but radical reform movements flourished in the years following the Napoleonic Wars. Unemployment caused by demobilization and mechanization of industry fed discontent. In addition, the presence of active and compelling voices for reform—people like William Cobbett and Henry Hunt—exerted pressure. Cobbett was a bold spokesman for the condition of the agricultural poor, and exposed corruption in the British parliamentary system. Entrenched privilege meant that notorious "rotten boroughs" like Old Sarum could elect two members of Parliament when by 1831 it had only three houses. By contrast, burgeoning new urban centres like Birmingham and Manchester had no representation at all. Henry Hunt advocated universal adult suffrage and is best known for his role in an 1819 political rally at St. Peter's Fields, Manchester. The rally attracted a crowd estimated at 60 000 to 80 000. When authorities moved in to put a stop to what was seen as a seditious gathering and to arrest its leaders, a riot ensued. Eleven people were killed in the so-called "Peterloo massacre." Early reformers in the Canadas, such as Upper Canada's Robert Gourlay and William Lyon Mackenzie, drew inspiration from Cobbett and Hunt. No doubt events on the continent sent a chill over

1832: Britain's
Great Reform Act
has a fundamentally
conservative goal.

British policymakers, and made reform of the worst abuses a matter of greater urgency. The climate of fear was exacerbated by the Swing riots in rural England in the early 1830s. Agricultural workers, made desperate by falling wages, unemployment, and the introduction of mechanized harvesting, burned barns and houses, destroyed machinery, and raised the spectre of a wider uprising.

The *Great Reform Act* of 1832 introduced in Britain by the Whig government of Earl Grey was seen as a necessary concession with the fundamentally conservative goal of preserving the existing system. The Act widened the political franchise to include more of the middle classes, and reallocated Commons seats to eliminate small boroughs and give representation to new industrial cities. Despite the hyperbolic label given to the measure, it should be noted that after the *Great Reform Act* had been passed an estimated one in seven adult males, and no females, were eligible to vote. Even so, colonial reformers saw it as an encouraging sign.

Buoyed by growing optimism, throughout 1831 Mackenzie travelled around Upper Canada to gather signatures on a petition, and also met with reformers in Lower Canada. His attacks on the Tory elite in the *Colonial Advocate* became bolder than ever, exposing Mackenzie to accusations of libel. Britain had in 1831 offered an olive branch to the Canadian colonies, relinquishing to the assemblies control over customs duties—a key part of provincial revenues—in exchange for a permanent civil list. A permanent civil list meant that salaries paid to public officials could not be held ransom by a legislative assembly using obstructionist tactics. The assembly of Lower Canada refused to comply with this compromise, but Upper Canada's legislature, dominated again by Tories at this point, accepted the offer, voting a civil list in exchange for control over customs revenues. Mackenzie, in vocal opposition, sputtered in indignation at what he termed the "Everlasting Salary Bill," seeing in it another way to entrench the privilege of elite office holders. He insisted that any changes should be accompanied by substantial constitutional concessions. By December 1831, the Tory majority in the assembly voted to expel him.

1831: William Lyon
Mackenzie expelled from
the legislative assembly.

A mob of several hundred turned out to protest, but, finding no satisfaction, voiced their views in a more effective manner: Mackenzie's constituents re-elected him in a by-election in January 1832. This was only the first of five occasions on which Mackenzie's expulsion from the assembly would be followed by immediate re-election. A victory procession of 134 sleighs bore the triumphant Mackenzie—adorned with a valuable gold medal awarded him by his constituents—down Yonge Street to the accompaniment of bagpipes. He was buoyed up in a tide of personal popularity, and the movement toward reform seemed inexorable. Mackenzie's ideas were making themselves felt in imperial corridors of power as well. In 1832, he travelled to London to present grievances and to meet leading political reformers in Britain. The Secretary of State for the Colonies, Lord Goderich, was evidently swayed by Mackenzie's entreaties, and wrote to Lieutenant Governor John Colborne to urge a more conciliatory policy. Upper Canadian Tories were outraged.

Growing Radicalization in Upper Canada

Mackenzie's optimism about the redress of colonial grievances was soon to suffer a series of blows. In Britain, the progressive Goderich was succeeded as colonial secretary in 1833 by the more conservative Lord Stanley. The new reactionary climate was all the harder to bear given the tantalizing promise of reform that had seemed so close. Mackenzie's convictions about ultimate success through petitioning and peaceful means began to waver; his admiration for American politics deepened. His attacks on the colonial elite, the Family Compact, became more acrimonious and personal. The September 26, 1833, edition of *The Colonial Advocate* listed the patronage posts enjoyed by key members of Upper Canadian society, their salaries, and the names of the prominent figures to whom they were related. Mackenzie's growing radicalism alienated moderate reformers such as Egerton Ryerson, a leading Methodist minister who had opposed the claims of the Anglican elite to be the sole beneficiaries of the provincial clergy reserves. Ryerson's influence with the substantial Methodist population of Upper Canada would have been valuable to Mackenzie, but the latter's uncompromising spirit drove many potential supporters into opposition. Similarly, Mackenzie's brief foray into municipal politics—he was mayor of Toronto between 1834 and 1835—showed his inability to adapt his ideas to practice. Those who might have endorsed moderate, incremental constitutional reform took alarm at Mackenzie's increasingly extreme position.

Growing Crisis in Lower Canada

In Lower Canada, meanwhile, the reformer-dominated legislative assembly's unwillingness to pass essential financial legislation, and the similar obstructionism of the non-elected legislative council over other bills, had produced a condition of paralysis. Between 1822 and 1836, some 234 bills passed by the assembly were refused in the upper house. By 1828, Papineau had made an elective legislative council a chief plank in his reform platform, attacking the existing appointed upper house as "a putrid cadaver." Lower Canada's councillors were driven by "passionate hatred of Canadians and unbridled love of money … of gold which they have made their god." The British-appointed governors also came under attack. In *La Minerve*, Papineau denounced them as natural promoters of monarchical and aristocratic values, who chose colonial service as a means to revive their flagging personal fortunes. At least one appointee sought in Canada "the wherewithal to repair his dilapidated old castle," he sneered.[9]

Added to the purely political complaints that Lower Canada shared with its neighbouring colony were persistent economic woes. In contrast to soaring wheat production in Upper Canada, Lower Canadian agriculture was in a persistent state of crisis from early in the nineteenth century. Shrinking land holdings were a product of a population that exceeded half a million by the 1830s. While some historians have cited inefficient agricultural techniques among the habitants—the reluctance to use crop rotation and failure to fertilize with manure—little could be done to prevent unseasonable frosts, droughts, and wheat fly plagues that devastated successive harvests. Lower Canada became a net importer of wheat, and habitants turned increasingly to subsistence crops—oats, barley, and peas—while lapsing into chronic debt. Between 1834 and 1846, the journals of Lower Canada's legislative assembly were crowded with references to parishes in distress. In 1833, it was reported that in most parishes of the District of Quebec one-third of the population had nothing to eat, with a further one-third not having enough to last to the next harvest. To make things worse, there was inadequate seed to sow next year's crop. By 1837, instances of actual starvation were reported.

1833: Inadequate harvests threaten hunger in many parishes of Lower Canada.

1832: Montreal's cholera epidemic serves to avert an immediate political crisis.

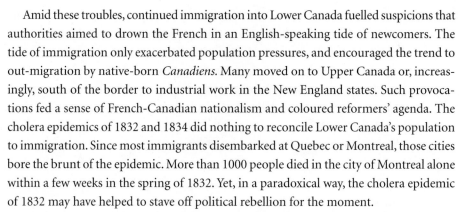

Amid these troubles, continued immigration into Lower Canada fuelled suspicions that authorities aimed to drown the French in an English-speaking tide of newcomers. The tide of immigration only exacerbated population pressures, and encouraged the trend to out-migration by native-born *Canadiens*. Many moved on to Upper Canada or, increasingly, south of the border to industrial work in the New England states. Such provocations fed a sense of French-Canadian nationalism and coloured reformers' agenda. The cholera epidemics of 1832 and 1834 did nothing to reconcile Lower Canada's population to immigration. Since most immigrants disembarked at Quebec or Montreal, those cities bore the brunt of the epidemic. More than 1000 people died in the city of Montreal alone within a few weeks in the spring of 1832. Yet, in a paradoxical way, the cholera epidemic of 1832 may have helped to stave off political rebellion for the moment.

The spring of 1832 was marked by an especially contentious by-election to fill a vacancy in the west ward of the city of Montreal. Daniel Tracey, an Irish medical doctor, and the editor of *The Vindicator,* was the reform candidate. Tracey, along with Ludger Duvernay, editor of *La Minerve,* had only recently served jail terms for libellous attacks on the legislative council in their respective newspapers. Tracey's stock among reformers—both Irish and *Canadien*—was high, and, as the election progressed, he gained a narrow lead over Stanley Bagg, an American-born merchant favoured by the Tories. The poll was held at Place d'Armes from April 28 to May 22. Feelings ran high, occasionally bubbling over into violence, and, as a precaution, the militia was called out. On the second-to-last day, a crowd of Tracey's supporters accompanied him home at the close of the day's poll, flushed with what appeared to be a hard-fought triumph: Tracey was ahead by three votes.

The spectacle of the lately imprisoned Irish radical flanked by jubilant comrades anticipating victory was too much for Bagg's disappointed partisans. They rained stones on their opponents, who responded in the same way. The militia following the rival mobs were caught up in the hail of stones, and opened fire. Three of Tracey's supporters fell dead, with another 20 wounded. The events sparked bitter indignation in the ranks of reformers: "The Governor sleeps in his château, and they leave us with these murderers," Papineau said to Neilson, fuming over the events.[10] Mass meetings were hastily summoned to fan the flames of disaffection. The event strangely echoed the Boston Massacre in 1770, where troops who had been goaded by a stone-throwing mob killed five. The event in Boston is traditionally seen as a watershed in the steady march toward the American Revolution. In Montreal, though, momentum was diverted.

The cholera struck with the first immigrant ships arriving that spring. Those who could fled the city of Montreal amid the raging epidemic; public meetings were out of the question. Dr. Tracey, whose victory had been anticlimactically declared the day after the shootings, bravely ministered to the sick of the stricken city. On July 17, 1832, less than two months after his election, he himself fell ill with cholera. By the next day, he was dead.

New Nationalist Symbols Emerge in Lower Canada

A new organization, the Saint Jean-Baptiste Society, formed in 1834, symbolized the growing national consciousness of Lower Canada's *patriotes*. The feast day of Saint Jean-Baptiste had long been culturally significant in the old world. Medieval Catholic authorities

1834: The Saint Jean-Baptiste Society emerges as a symbol of French Canadian nationalism.

in France had grafted the feast day celebrating the birth of John the Baptist on June 24 onto an existing pagan holiday celebrating the summer solstice. The traditions surrounding this Catholic holiday were transplanted to Canada, and seventeenth-century New France enjoyed the traditional bonfires and celebrations. Even interior fur traders would mark the day with boisterous gatherings. The festival coincided with the days of summer fur collection, and fiddle music, dancing, and spectacular bonfires on June 24 were a popular highlight of summer trading. The festival became less important after the conquest, but Ludger Duvernay, *patriote* and publisher of *La Minerve*, resurrected it in 1834, seeing in it an opportunity to celebrate French Canada's growing cultural identity and to rally support to the *patriote* cause. Many of Canada's earliest cultural symbols were adopted by the society, including the maple leaf. An early contender for a national anthem, George-Etienne Cartier's "Ô Canada! Mon Pays! Mes Amours!" was sung at the association's first gathering. St. Jean-Baptiste Day gained momentum as a lively part of that province's cultural life— villages along the St. Lawrence would be illuminated with a chain of bonfires.

St. Jean-Baptiste emblem, showing maple leaves and a beaver.

Source: © McCord Museum, M930.50.1.949.

Reformers' Complaints to Britain: The 92 Resolutions and Seventh Report on Grievances

By 1834, the same year in which the St. Jean-Baptiste celebration was resurrected, reformers in both Lower and Upper Canada had achieved a majority in their respective assemblies. Each assembly busied itself preparing a statement for the imperial government setting out key grievances. Lower Canada's *patriote*-dominated assembly produced the "92 Resolutions" in 1834; the following year, a committee of Upper Canada's assembly, chaired by William Lyon Mackenzie, presented the "Seventh Report on Grievances."

1834: Lower Canada's 92 Resolutions are sent to Britain's Parliament.

The 92 Resolutions reflected the pent-up frustration of Lower Canadian *patriotes*. The resolutions complained that the Colonial Office erroneously asserted that the Canadas had been granted the same constitutional institutions as Great Britain when such was not the case. The executive council was entirely irresponsible to the elected assembly. The resolutions alleged that the Crown's power was exorbitant and unbalanced, controlling an entire branch of the legislature, the legislative council. Exclusion of the French was also a cause for complaint, especially since France "has never been behind the British nation … in the cause of liberty and of the science of Government." Further, the resolutions expressed admiration for American models: "The constitution and form of government which would best suit this colony are not to be sought solely in the analogies offered by the institutions of Great Britain, where the state of society is altogether different from our own." More specific causes of complaint included the fact that a substantial portion of revenues were still controlled by the executive, rather than by the assembly, and that extensive Crown lands were unavailable for settlement. In addition, patronage posts were being disproportionately awarded to those of British origin, and especially to members of the same elite families.[11]

John Neilson, who had now broken entirely with the radical reformers of the lower province, condemned the resolutions. He is believed to have penned an attack on them in the Quebec *Mercury*. This published critique acknowledged that "eleven stood true," but dismissed the bulk of the resolutions: "Six contained both truth and falsehood; sixteen stood wholly false; seventeen seemed doubtful and twelve ridiculous; seven were repetitions; fourteen consisted only of abuse; four were false and seditious; and the remainder were indifferent."[12] Members of the British cabinet found many of the complaints simply impenetrable: "Such is the copiousness and warmth of expression ... that in many cases it is difficult to discern what is the subject matter to which the writers refer," one complained.[13] The list of resolutions ran to dozens of closely written pages, in a torrential style that hardly encouraged a close and systematic reading of the grievances.

From the governor's chateau in Lower Canada, Lord Aylmer condemned the resolutions as tantamount to a Declaration of Independence. He had served as governor since 1830 and, although his credentials were primarily military and did not include any marked political skills, he had begun his term by earnestly seeking reconciliation, even offering seats on his executive council to Louis-Joseph Papineau and John Neilson in 1831. Both had refused on principle, but Aylmer had managed to secure a few francophone appointees with reform leanings. His early optimism soon gave way to bitter frustration, however, and, after the bloodshed of the 1832 by-elections, relations between governor and reformers seemed beyond redemption. Sessions in Lower Canada's legislative assembly were stalled in complete paralysis, the members unwilling to vote supply, and the governor asserting his prerogative to block other legislation in a vain attempt to exert pressure.

Leading Montreal Tories were prompted by the growing assertiveness of Lower Canada's legislative assembly to form a "Constitutional Association" in 1834, along with rifle clubs whose real purpose was ominously military. The Constitutional Association declared its goal of using every effort to maintain the imperial connection. One of the association's leading spokesmen was John Molson, Jr. Molson's father, of the same name, was founder of the Molson's brewing enterprise, had interests in a steamboat, hotels, and railways, was president of the Bank of Montreal, and was a legislative councillor. His son followed him in many of these enterprises, and became a key leader of Montreal's business elite. He spoke for many of the colony's privileged when he warned that "recent events have roused us to a sense of impending danger." The French, he intimated, might be ill-equipped to defend themselves "against the awakened energies of an insulted and oppressed people."[14] That he should regard the privileged Château clique as "oppressed" emphasizes how wide the gulf of understanding had grown between Tories and Reformers.

In Upper Canada, a committee of the assembly chaired by William Lyon Mackenzie produced the Seventh Report on Grievances to give voice to their complaints. The 1835 report referred to earlier grievances and petitions placed before British authorities, and the colonists' earlier expectations that constitutional change would have been forthcoming. Instead, their key demands remained unmet. They complained of the "almost unlimited extent of the patronage of the Crown" and the fact that the assembly's power over expenditure was limited by "a system that admits its officers to take and apply the funds of the Colonists without any legislative vote whatever." Judges, appointed by the Crown, were in a position of dependency. The Canada Company, with vast control over land reserves, and banking and canal companies "unite their patronage with that of the local government, and steadily strive to increase the influence of the Crown." Further, they complained about the awarding of public funds to such companies without proper scrutiny. The appointed legislative council continually rejected "many valuable measures earnestly prayed for by the people." The report cited the "great excellence of the English constitution" but complained that the system had not been properly adapted in Canada, leaving the elected assembly "powerless and dependent." "At the root of all the evils" was the appointed legislative council: an elected upper house was a favourite remedy of Mackenzie's.

Echoing a sentiment expressed by the earliest colonial reformers, the report insisted that their present form of government was "ever against the spirit of the Constitutional Act." More boldly, they complained of the injurious effect of the interference of "a succession of Colonial ministers in England who have never visited the country, and can never possibly become acquainted" with "the affairs of people 4000 miles off." The report cited the phenomenal growth of Upper Canada, which doubled its population every 12 years, and insisted that its growth "requires that there should be an entire confidence between the Executive and the Commons House of Assembly"—in other words, responsible government.[15]

Britain's Response to Colonial Complaints

It might have been predicted that such complaints would not fall on especially fertile ground in Britain. Long-range policy was difficult to plan at the Colonial Office. A total of 10 ministers filled the portfolio of Secretary of State for War and the Colonies between April 1827 and April 1835 (only after 1854 did the Colonial Office become a separate ministry). The complaint in the Seventh Report on Grievances about "a succession of Colonial ministers" who had never set foot in the colonies was thus close to the mark. During a somewhat later period, British Prime Minister Lord Palmerston is supposed to have proposed taking the Colonial Office portfolio himself when none of his ministers wanted it: "Just come upstairs and show me on the map where these damned places are."[16] The story may be apocryphal but it exemplifies the simple truth that the colonies were not always accorded a high priority in British policy, and cabinet ministers could be called upon to make critical decisions about far-removed places of which they knew little. Greater stability was achieved when in April 1835 the newly returned Whig administration of Lord Melbourne placed Lord Glenelg at the head of the Colonial Office, a post he would hold until 1839. Glenelg proved unequal to the task of finding a solution to Canada's grievances, which is perhaps enough to explain the scant regard with which historians have condemned him. But the man contemporary critics called "His Somnolency" made an easy target in other ways: he was apt to fall asleep at inopportune moments. Even Queen Victoria's coronation in 1838 was not enough to keep Glenelg awake. He slumped forward in sleep, his coronet rolling beneath his chair in Westminster Abbey.

Glenelg's predecessors in the Colonial Office had already bowed to pressure and taken some steps aimed at addressing the growing crisis in the Canadas. While the appointed governors were not wholly to blame for the chronic dysfunction, some tangible evidence of action was necessary. Aylmer found himself recalled to Britain, his early attempts at reconciliation having ended in acknowledged failure, his partisanship toward the English elite now open. As he departed Lower Canada, he gave a wistful speech on the wharf, acknowledging that his "anxious endeavours" had fallen far short of his hopes. Overcome by emotion at the cheers of a small crowd of supporters, Aylmer burst into tears.

In a bid to placate Canadian reformers, Lord Gosford was named governor in Aylmer's stead, and was appointed to preside over a three-person commission of inquiry into Canadian affairs. An Irish peer who had long supported a policy of conciliation and tolerance for Ireland's Roman Catholic majority living under British rule, Gosford was perceived by many as possessing the right qualities to arrive at solutions acceptable to French Canadians.

In Upper Canada, lieutenant governor Sir John Colborne was likewise recalled. His controversial decision to grant 6000 hectares (15 000 acres) of clergy reserves, set aside in the 1791 *Constitutional Act* for the Protestant clergy, plus another 2670 hectares (6600 acres) of Crown land, wholly to the Anglican Church sparked indignation among Upper Canada's numerous Presbyterians and Methodists, and seemed especially ill-advised in the tense political atmosphere of 1836. Colborne, a towering soldierly man whose long hooked nose gave him a patrician bearing, had been a hero among the Duke of Wellington's forces at the Battle of Waterloo, where he sustained a serious wound to his arm. Colborne's sudden recall as lieutenant governor was tempered by his speedy appointment as commander-in-chief of the forces in the Canadas.

Sir Francis Bond Head Confronts Reformers in Upper Canada

Sir Francis Bond Head arrived to succeed Colborne as lieutenant governor of Upper Canada early in 1836. Historians long cherished the intriguing notion that the British Colonial Office inadvertently appointed the wrong man—that they intended to commission Sir Edmund Head, who would eventually be named governor general in 1854. This historical myth has proved very persistent, but if Bond Head was not literally the wrong man for the job, he may have proved to be the wrong man just the same. He had no political experience whatsoever, and no colonial experience, but had vague associations with reform based upon a short stint as an assistant Poor Law commissioner in England. Torontonians generously gave him the benefit of the doubt, welcoming him as "A Tried Reformer." But Bond Head's true colours could not be concealed for long.

Bond Head was dismayed to find that, in his view, the province of Upper Canada was in the grip of "demagogues" like William Lyon Mackenzie, Dr. Charles Duncombe, Robert Baldwin, Marshall Bidwell, and Dr. John Rolph. Bond Head refused to believe that the views of this reform contingent were representative and "occupied myself in ascertaining the real sentiments of the people." He reserved special contempt for Mackenzie, and made no secret of his feelings. With alarm, he followed the activities of the fiery Scottish journalist who drew considerable crowds to "Monster Meetings": Mackenzie "wrote, and then he printed, and then he rode, and then he spoke, stamped, foamed, wiped his sedi-tious little mouth, and then spoke again," keeping up feverish revolutionary activity "like a squirrel in a cage." Especially worrisome to Bond Head was the influence of Americans, an influence he saw as central to dissent in Upper Canada. He believed it was necessary both to "suppress rebellion, and, above all, to resist the smallest attempt to introduce that odious principle of 'responsible government' which a few republicans in the province had been desirous to force upon them."[17]

This idea that an uneducated public could be dupes to unscrupulous partisans was a pervasive one. Historian Jeffrey L. McNairn argues that early-nineteenth-century Upper Canadians examined contending ideas in an atmosphere of "deliberative democracy." Through the press, and through reasoned public debate, McNairn argues, public opinion emerged. To McNairn, "public opinion" means more than simply the aggregate of every-one's views: not all ideas were of equal weight. Education and exposure to rationally sound notions of governance were meant to ensure intellectual independence and the flourishing of sound principles for the common good. He maintains, however, that in the tumultuous 1830s, "conservatives had yet to integrate public opinion into their constitutional outlook."[18]

Bond Head appointed some reform-oriented men to his executive council, including Robert Baldwin, a moderate lawyer whose Irish-born father William—both a doctor and a lawyer—had played a key role in the political development of Upper Canada since his arrival there late in the eighteenth century. But Bond Head was unprepared to listen to the counsel of even a moderate reformer like Baldwin, and the executive council resigned in protest in March 1836.

Further, Bond Head succeeded in poisoning the atmosphere of conciliation that Gos-ford was attempting to create in Lower Canada. Gosford disliked the presumptuousness of the colonial oligarchy, privately characterizing them as a little group of old men jealously protecting their privileges, and hoped to inculcate a spirit of greater inclusiveness. He planned to use aristocratic hospitality as a means of breaking down divisions, and came equipped with prodigious supplies of claret, champagne, and sherry. However, the opti-mism of colonial reformers was shattered when Bond Head foolishly released documents detailing the terms of Gosford's commission. They saw at once that the much-vaunted commission was charged only with making inquiries, and was powerless to implement the structural changes that many were convinced were essential—an elected legislative council, or the surrender of revenues controlled independently by the Crown.

1836: Sir Francis Bond Head manipulates a Tory victory in Upper Canada's election.

In Upper Canada, Bond Head called an election soon after his arrival in 1836, and, not leaving matters to chance, openly supported the Tory side. He hinted darkly that Upper Canada's security was jeopardized by outside threats, and maintained that the contest was between such outsiders bent on pursuing selfish ends, and those committed to loyalty, law, and order. As added insurance, Orange Order gangs intimidated those who might have supported reform candidates. The result was a resounding defeat for the reformers.

Historian Sean T. Cadigan cautions against seeing Bond Head's success in manipulating this election as a "simple function of his own political personality." Adopting a class-based analysis, Cadigan emphasizes instead the lieutenant governor's role "as a nexus between the high-ranking Tories and their lower-ranking Orange allies."[19] William Lyon Mackenzie was dismayed to lose his seat, and his frustration grew at his inability to achieve reform through peaceful political means. Within days, he had launched a new newspaper, *The Constitution.* Symbolically, it was inaugurated on July 4, 1836, the 60th anniversary of the American Declaration of Independence.

Even as Mackenzie moved toward a more violent and uncompromising stance, the actions of such Upper Canadian reformers as Robert Baldwin demonstrated that political reform was a continuum, consisting of radical and moderate elements. While Bond Head was inclined to lump all reformers together as trouble-making demagogues, Baldwin's strategies to win reform were patient and measured. In July 1836, having been refused a meeting with Lord Glenelg, Baldwin wrote to the colonial secretary with a proposed solution to the constitutional impasse. He rejected reforms proposed by others, such as the elimination of the legislative council, or a change to an elected legislative council. Instead, he insisted simply that the remedy lay in the transformation of the executive council into a true provincial cabinet on the British model. This would require no legislative interference, he pointed out, nor any "sacrifice of any constitutional principle" or "diminution of the paramount authority of the Mother Country." Indeed, since ministerial responsibility was "an English principle," it would "strengthen the attachment of the people to the connection with the Mother Country."[20] Yet the moderate and respectful tone of Baldwin's entreaties proved no more effective than Mackenzie's incendiary and provocative ones. And Baldwin's absence from Upper Canada's political scene during his extended stay in Ireland and England meant that reformers were denied the benefit of a voice of moderation and reason.

Joseph Howe and the Early Reform Movement in Nova Scotia

The nature of reform politics in the colony of Nova Scotia also demonstrated that even those with the deepest commitment to Britain sought constitutional change. Joseph Howe was a case in point. Born in Halifax, the descendant of Loyalists, Howe had been educated by his father, and from an early age was inculcated with a reverence for the imperial connection. Howe became the influential editor of the *Novascotian* in 1827, and used his newspaper to educate Nova Scotians about the workings of their colonial government. He published the assembly's debates in detail, and also closely followed events in other parts of North America, Britain, and Europe. Howe's editorial activities attracted attention, but, as with William Lyon Mackenzie, it was adversity that brought Howe his greatest opportunity for prominence. In 1835, his newspaper published an anonymous letter complaining that the police and magistrates of Halifax had extracted over £30 000 from the pockets of the people through excessive fines in the past 30 years. The publication resulted in Howe facing charges of criminal libel.

Lawyers did not hold out much hope of a successful defence, so Howe decided to carry on without legal representation. He pleaded his own case before a jury, and it was here that Howe's talent for oratory came to full fruition. For six hours he spoke, detailing systemic corruption in Nova Scotia's penal system. A Halifax magistrate, he revealed, milked personal profit from prisoners by working them in their cells, requiring them even to make shoes for his own family. In his stirring speech, Howe appealed to the jury to leave to their children the legacy of an unshackled press. While the chief justice pointedly reminded the jury of Howe's guilt before their short deliberation, they returned with an acquittal.

Buoyed by a surge of personal popularity, Howe was elected to Nova Scotia's legislative assembly in 1836. Howe was typical of many inherently conservative political thinkers of the early nineteenth century in his distaste for the concept of party politics. He considered the idea of an "opposition" to the government to be inimical to loyalty, yet ironically he would be the figure around whom a reform party in Nova Scotia's legislature was organized.

1836: Joseph Howe enters Nova Scotia politics.

Nova Scotia's ruling oligarchy, colloquially known as the "Council of Twelve" consisted of Halifax's business and social elite, people of prominent families who filled the top ranks in shipping, banking, and merchant activities, or who were substantial landowners. These individuals monopolized places in the governor's appointed council, but in Nova Scotia, unlike other colonies, the executive council and legislative council was one and the same body. Five council members controlled a banking monopoly that unsuccessfully attempted to thwart the establishment of the rival Bank of Nova Scotia in 1832. It is not surprising that the Council of Twelve represented a tempting target for reform.

Joseph Howe, forming the nucleus of a reform party in Nova Scotia's assembly, drafted in 1837 the "Twelve Resolutions" to present the colony's grievances to the Colonial Office. The resolutions insisted that Nova Scotia was grateful for their prosperity and happiness, and revered British institutions. "They know that the spirit of that constitution—the genius of those Institutions is a complete responsibility to the people by whose resources and for whose benefit they are maintained. But sad experience has taught them that in this Colony, the People and their Representatives are powerless, exercising upon the local Government very little influence, and possessing no effectual control." This was very different from the way the constitution functioned in England, the resolutions maintained. The resolutions called for a separation of the executive and legislative councils, with the latter body to be elected. In this respect, Howe's remedy more resembled Mackenzie's early demands—each focused primarily on the power of the unelected legislative council as the chief evil. The Colonial Office was not prepared to concede an elected upper house, but did in 1837 introduce one important change for Nova Scotia: the executive and legislative councils were divided into two bodies.[21]

1837: Nova Scotia produces the "Twelve Resolutions."

New Brunswick's Demands for Reform

Similarly, the Colonial Office responded positively to complaints in New Brunswick. In that colony, the chief grievance was a comparatively modest one: the elected assembly wanted control over timber leases on Crown lands, which were often unfairly awarded to those with connections to the appointed council. Thomas Baillie, a 28-year-old military officer, had been sent from Britain as Crown lands commissioner in 1824, a position second only to that of the lieutenant governor of the colony. Baillie was determined that sufficient revenues should be raised from Crown lands to meet the colony's expenses, something that would have made the elected assembly entirely impotent. Moreover, his arrogant and self-important demeanour made him a particular target of complaints. By 1837, the Colonial Office succumbed to pressure from New Brunswick and reduced Baillie's powers, giving the assembly the control they sought over timber revenues.

1837: Colonial Office makes modest concessions to reform in New Brunswick.

Russell's Resolutions

1837: Russell's Resolutions reject colonial demands for reform.

These modest concessions in New Brunswick and Nova Scotia were not indicative of any new willingness in the Colonial Office to embrace constitutional change. The reports made by the Gosford Commission in 1836 were, as Bond Head unwisely intimated they would be, modest in scope, rejecting any of the remedies favoured by Canada's reformers. By the spring of 1837, Britain's cabinet had had time to reflect on the commission's recommendations and issued a response to colonial demands.

Lord John Russell, home secretary in Lord Melbourne's Whig ministry, was the architect of this response. The diminutive Russell, who weighed 112 pounds and stood a little over 5 feet 4 inches, had been active in the drafting of the Great Reform Bill of 1832. A fellow MP had remarked that Russell had shrunk to his present size by being so consistently in hot water. Yet Russell's Ten Resolutions represented a complete denial of the reformers' aspirations for the Canadian colonies. The resolutions rejected an elected legislative council, dismissed responsible government as "inadvisable," and undercut one of the key principles of representative government: to address the ongoing financial crisis, especially arrears in civil servants' salaries, the governor was authorized to spend provincial funds without the consent of the assembly. Even British newspapers condemned this as an act of robbery.

1837: Economic and social disturbances add to the political disquiet.

A worldwide economic recession cast its shadow over Canada, too, adding to the growing political tumult. The era of heady financial expansion, the boom of excessive speculation and of railway and canal construction, had ended, and Britain and the United States were in the grip of a severe commercial crisis. American President Andrew Jackson, in an attempt to curb the power of the Bank of the United States, set off a financial panic; bank notes lost their value, and investors clamoured for scarce hard currency. Canada's banking industry also suffered. By disastrous coincidence, harsh weather and insect plagues reduced Lower Canada's already inadequate wheat yields still further, and crop failures now extended to the upper colony. Grain prices soared, and declining trade dried up traffic at the ports, throwing many into unemployment. Unemployment in the lumber camps and canal building sites ignited clashes between rival gangs of Irish and French-Canadian workers. Brawls broke out in Bytown (Ottawa) among the "Shiners," lumbermen whose name was probably derived from the French word *cheneur,* or "oak man."

Russell's Resolutions reached Canada in the spring of 1837, sparking renewed outcry and a flurry of protest meetings. The death of William IV late in June, and the accession to the throne of Queen Victoria, was accompanied by an announcement that the Resolutions would be suspended, but the momentum was not to be diverted.

The Road to Rebellion

Radicals in both provinces had been devising common strategies. William Lyon Mackenzie was in communication with Wolfred Nelson, one of Lower Canada's most vehement protesters. Wolfred Nelson's radical agenda is in some respects surprising. Both he and his brother, Robert, were medical doctors, born in Montreal, the sons of an English schoolteacher and a Loyalist mother. Wolfred Nelson married a French woman, Charlotte-Josephte Noyelle de Fleurimont, and lived immersed in French-Canadian culture and language. Robert kept a respectable surgical practice in Montreal, but had a secret passageway in his home to accommodate meetings with *patriote* associates. Wolfred Nelson and William Lyon Mackenzie supported a policy of boycotting British goods, with Mackenzie urging *The Constitution*'s readers to avoid buying, wearing, or using British manufactured goods or British West Indian liquors. Wearing homespun cloth, straw hats, and crude homemade shoes—subject to no import duties—became a symbol of patriotism in Lower Canada, ominously copying the tactics used in the rebellious Thirteen Colonies. A group of Papineau's followers answered their leader's call and showed up at the August session of the assembly wearing the suggested attire. Papineau's dignity would not permit him to abandon his usual meticulous dress.

This symbolic nod to the American Revolution was not the only such gesture. Mackenzie arranged a printing of Thomas Paine's *Common Sense,* the book whose 1776 appearance in the rebellious colonies has been credited with converting agitation for reform into a drive toward independence. Reformers in Upper Canada issued the "Declaration of Toronto," a derivative document that drew heavily on the American Declaration of Independence, with overtones of John Locke, and a smattering of the utilitarian ideas of British philosophers Jeremy Bentham and John Stuart Mill. "Government is founded on the authority, and is instituted for the benefit, of a people," the Declaration asserted. "When, therefore, any Government long and systematically ceases to answer the great ends of its foundation, the people have a natural right given them by their Creator to seek after and establish such institutions as will yield the greatest quantity of happiness to the greatest number."[22]

In the lower province, the *Société des Fils de la Liberté* (Sons of Liberty) modelled themselves on the American Revolutionary movement of the same name. Even more alarmingly, the society organized a military branch to give its members militia training. In Upper Canada, Mackenzie hinted that manpower, as well as ideological inspiration, could be drawn from south of the border. "There are thousands, aye tens of thousands of Englishmen, Scotchmen, and above all, of Irishmen, now in the United States, who only wait till the standard be planted in Lower Canada, to throw their strength and numbers to the side of democracy," he claimed.[23]

During the summer of 1837, political meetings organized by Lower Canada's *patriotes* were drawing ever-larger crowds. Throughout the parishes and towns of Lower Canada, thousands thronged to massive political demonstrations. By mid-June, Gosford was sufficiently alarmed to forbid meetings "having for their objects the resistance of the lawful authority of the King and Parliament, and the subversion of the laws." But notices carrying the governor's proclamation were torn down, and the decree proved unenforceable. Gosford exerted pressure by dismissing any magistrates or militia officers who were found to have attended the banned meetings. Others voluntarily resigned their posts in protest.

On October 23, 1837, at Saint-Charles, 5000 people turned out to hear Papineau speak for two-and-a-half hours. The demonstration had the air of a national celebration, with the singing of hymns, volleys of musketry, and booming cannon. A column was erected, called the "liberty pole," crowned with a red cap of liberty, with an inscription dedicated to Papineau. There were tricolour flags, the symbol of the French Revolution, and banners carrying revolutionary messages: "Fly Gosford, Persecutor of the Canadians" and "Liberty! We'll Conquer or Die for Her." Other banners bore the American eagle carrying a maple leaf

1837: Governor Gosford outlaws radical political demonstrations.

in its mouth, and a skull with the slogan "Death to the Legislative Council." But Papineau gave signs of wishing to rein in the revolutionary fervour his activism had helped to unleash. The night before the Saint-Charles demonstration, he had worked with like-minded supporters to prepare an "Address of the Confederation of the Six Counties to the People of Lower Canada," urging the replacement of the administration with "men worthy of confidence." Papineau's words at the rally were measured and cautious, hardly a call to arms. Others, though, showed no such scruples. Wolfred Nelson jumped to his feet, exclaiming, "I differ from Mr. Papineau! The time has come," he roared, "to melt our spoons into bullets." Another *patriote*, Dr. Cyrille Côté, called on the crowd to throw lead at their enemies.[24]

Through the autumn of 1837, ardent *patriotes* roamed the countryside, applying pressure to those who still retained government posts as militia officers or justices of the peace. They used the time-honoured tactic of the *charivari*, a French folk custom, which was a night-time nuisance raid customarily used to voice social disapproval for unconventional marriages. Traditionally, a widow who married too soon after her husband's death, a couple whose ages were separated by too wide a gulf or whose social standing was too different, or a mixed race couple, might find themselves the objects of an unwelcome nocturnal visit by local rowdies disguised in costumes, banging pots, and rudely serenading the newlyweds with raucous music. This medieval custom, known in English Canada as the "shivaree," could continue for several consecutive nights. The revellers were often dispersed with a good-natured gift of money for drink, or with an invitation to come inside for refreshment. But some charivaris ended in violence, and in the tense atmosphere of 1837, the prospect of drunken raiders, their faces blackened to ensure anonymity, roaming the countryside unchecked for more sinister purposes alarmed authorities.

The Roman Catholic clergy had already condemned revolution from the pulpit. The Bishop of Montreal, Jean-Jacques Lartigue, ordered priests to read a pastoral letter citing the Pope's message of obedience to political authority. Resentment had already been simmering since the occasion of 18-year-old Victoria's accession to the throne, when church authorities offered praise to the British monarch and ordered the *Te Deum* to be sung in near-empty churches.

Gosford poured out his frustration with *patriote* tactics in a letter to his chief at the Colonial Office. He had prorogued the assembly in August 1837 after its fruitless meeting, the representatives having once more refused to vote supply. He decided that no terms were possible with Papineau, declaring to Glenelg that he would be forced to submit to Papineau if he was not put down. An open clash on November 6 between the Fils de la Liberté and the Loyalist Doric Club brought fighting to the streets of Montreal.

Troops had earlier been moved from Halifax to Lower Canada, and more were being called for, but Gosford feared that inadequate numbers of British regulars would be available. He unofficially sanctioned the use of volunteer militia—many of whom would have been the same Doric Club Loyalists who had been pelting their *patriote* rivals with rocks in the streets. Moreover, he diverted troops from Upper Canada to the lower colony. Lieutenant governor Bond Head knew that Mackenzie and his followers were fomenting rebellion, but decided, as he reflected in his memoir, "the more I encouraged [the rebels] to consider me defenceless, the better." He acknowledged to Colborne that he would be issuing a challenge to the rebels by moving the troops, and insisted to the acting adjutant-general of militia,

James Fitzgibbon, who had urged better defence preparations, that "nothing can be more satisfactory than the present political state of this province." John Beverley Robinson, the loyal and conservative chief justice of Upper Canada, later marvelled that "any quiet Englishmen will be apt to say that man would make a rebellion anywhere." Bond Head later revised his memoir to suggest that Colborne had ordered the troops moved without consultation.[25]

Far from being tranquil, events in Upper Canada had been moving steadily toward open revolt. On November 15, 1837, Mackenzie drafted a Constitution "in case the British system of government shall be positively denied us." Days later, a broadside "Appeal to the People" appeared under the bold heading "Independence." Mackenzie exhorted his followers: "Canadians! Do you love freedom? I know you do. Do you hate oppression? Who dare deny it? … Then buckle on your armour, and put down the villains who oppress and enslave our country—put them down in the name of that God who goes forth with the armies of his people." Mackenzie's move to a bolder stance was inspired by events in the lower province where, he asserted, "the vile hirelings of our unlawful oppressors have already bit the dust in hundreds." The reformers in Lower Canada were, he claimed, "united as one man" and outnumbered their opponents 100 to 1.[26] Clearly, this was wishful thinking.

November 1837: Mackenzie calls for open revolt.

Rebellion in Lower Canada

Days after the street fighting in Montreal, Gosford issued arrest warrants for 26 of Lower Canada's rebel leaders. A few smaller fish were scooped up, but Papineau and others moved quickly to Saint-Denis on the Richelieu River to join Wolfred Nelson. While Nelson assumed military leadership of the *patriote* forces, Papineau, according to his later explanation, retreated to a safe place in order to be available to oversee negotiations in the event of a defeat. Nelson's rebel forces at Saint-Denis learned that British troops under Colonel Charles Gore were marching against them on the morning of November 23, and bravely prepared to defend their position. Nelson was able to secure a superior tactical position, using sharpshooters behind stone walls, and Gore's forces, having marched all night in freezing November rain, were forced to retreat.

November 23, 1837: Rebel forces win a victory at the Battle of Saint-Denis.

The *patriote* victory at Saint-Denis swelled the rebels' confidence and transformed Wolfred Nelson into a hero. His triumph was tempered by the discovery that Papineau had left them "in the lurch," as he later put it. Papineau wandered through Lower Canada for several days after the battle, at last making his way to the United States. Nelson was also dismayed by the flight of many of his other supporters, who did not welcome the prospect of a return engagement with the British. His forces having melted away, a discouraged Nelson fled south. Separated from a small band of supporters, Nelson roamed the countryside, enduring ten days without food. But a worse fate was in store: he was captured by militia forces, and sent to prison to await trial. Martial law had just been declared, and the penalty for high treason was death.

Two days after the rebel victory at Saint-Denis, another *patriote* force clashed with Colonel George Wetherall's troops at Saint-Charles. Poor natural defences and faulty intelligence plagued rebel leader Thomas Brown and his wavering force. As General Wetherall's troops pounded the village church with artillery and burned buildings, a number of *patriotes* tried to escape across the Richelieu River, some drowning in the attempt. Brown fled, and

November 25, 1837: The rebels suffer defeat at the Battle of Saint-Charles.

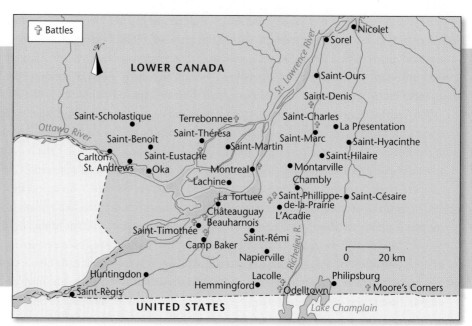

Map 8.1
Lower Canadian battle sites.

Source: Reprinted with permission of the Osgoode Society for Canadian Legal History and the University of Toronto Press.
© Osgoode Society for Canadian Legal History, 2002.

by the day's end 56 rebels lay dead on the burning grass. Wetherall led his forces back to Montreal, and within the week was marching through the city's streets leading 30 prisoners. A red-capped liberty pole captured from Saint-Charles completed the sorry procession.

Further west, in the Deux Montagnes area, *patriotes* Jean-Joseph Girouard, an Acadian notary, and Amury Girod, a Swiss-born farmer and author, were attempting to organize the rebel forces in their stronghold of Saint-Eustache, but their ill-disciplined forces varied in strength from day to day. Sometimes 200 were available; other days, 1500 swelled the camp. The parish priest, Curé Jacques Paquin, thrown into house arrest by the insurgents, sneeringly dismissed any notion of discipline among the rebels: "These men would recognize no rules and believed themselves masters to do anything they pleased. This is how they conceived of the freedom of patriotism."[27] While Girod styled himself "General," both he and Girouard were men better suited to a war of words than actual battle. Early in December 1837, Sir John Colborne, leading a force of 1280 British regulars and 220 volunteer militia, prepared to march against Saint-Eustache. Militia from Lachine were heartened by the sound of wild war whoops as 200 Iroquois warriors from Caughnawaga answered the call for volunteers. The militia cheered at the sight of the St. Lawrence filled with Iroquois canoes.

On the morning of December 14, 300 *patriotes* moved out to confront what they believed was Colborne's force. It soon became apparent that the small force of about 80 Crown troops was only a diversion; the main force caught the rebels by surprise. Girod fled across the ice in a pre-prepared sleigh; he eventually shot himself rather than face capture. Girouard, leading the resistance at nearby Saint-Benoît, encouraged his forces to surrender when Colborne's troops advanced there the day after the Saint-Eustache engagement. He himself fled to Coteau-du-Lac, where he ultimately gave himself up as prisoner. At Saint-Eustache on December 14, Jean-Olivier Chénier, a medical doctor, assumed command

December 14, 1837:
The Battle of Saint-Eustache
deals a definitive blow
to the rebel cause.

after Girod's flight. Girod had originally rejected Chénier as poor leadership material, claiming that he was too talkative. The other *patriote* leaders having fled, Chénier led a group of 50 insurgents to the village church. From that position, they held Colborne's men back for a time with sniper fire, while a howitzer in the main street kept up an artillery barrage against them. At last, the Crown forces were able to advance under a smokescreen, entered the rear of the church, and set a fire behind the altar. Chénier and most of the other rebels were killed as they tried to make their escape from the flaming church. By the afternoon, the main force of the rebellion had been broken.

At Saint-Eustache, 70 insurgents had been killed, 15 wounded and 118 taken prisoner. All told, in all engagements during the Lower Canadian rebellions of 1837 and 1838, the death toll reached 325, of whom some 27 fought on the side of the Crown. A dozen more rebels would die on the gallows. Chénier's heroic death lent an iconic image to the cause of French-Canadian resistance, a much-needed martyr, in contrast to the many who had fled to the United States. More than a century later, the Front de Libération du Québec, or FLQ, who attempted to secure Quebec independence and a Marxist revolution through terrorist activities in 1970, adopted the symbols of the rebellion. A sector of their organization was named the Chénier cell, and the publicized FLQ manifesto was illustrated with an image of an armed 1837 *patriote*.

Rebellion in Upper Canada

Events in Upper Canada late in the autumn of 1837 reveal a pattern of wilful misunderstanding. Lieutenant Governor Bond Head had been insistent that stripping the upper colony of military forces was perfectly safe; William Lyon Mackenzie believed that Lower Canada would fall to the *patriotes*, encouraging the people of Upper Canada to likewise embrace the cause of revolution. Both were mistaken.

Upper Canadian rebels had made little actual military preparation, and conflicting reports of plans for rebellion made for an atmosphere of confusion. Mackenzie originally planned to stage a *coup d'état* on December 7, 1837, counting on American military intervention to force a political union with the United States. He rallied reluctant rebels to the cause by implying that outside forces were marching to Upper Canada to throw their support behind the insurrection. Some supporters of rebellion were equivocal, keeping their convictions quiet until sure that the uprising was successful. Dr. John Rolph, an English-born lawyer and medical doctor who had previously been a member of the legislative assembly and an advocate for the property rights of American "aliens" in the 1820s, was a case in point. He was loath to have his name openly linked to the radicals, yet he had reportedly struck a secret agreement with Mackenzie to take a leading role in government once the coup had succeeded.

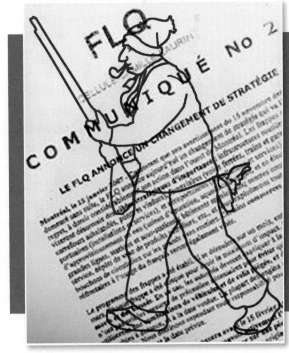

The manifesto of the FLQ, issued during the 1970 "October Crisis," was illustrated with an image of a patriote of 1837.

When Rolph learned that authorities were planning to arrest Mackenzie, he urged other rebels to move the date of the planned rebellion forward.

Although Mackenzie realized that military arrangements were far from adequate, his hand had been forced. Having assured supporters that the tide toward rebellion was inexorable, that Lower Canada was successfully throwing off imperial oppression, and that aid from the United States was assured, Mackenzie was forced to confront the consequences of his rhetorical wishful thinking. He hastily met with Rolph, who proposed that the rebellion be abandoned when he learned the true state of preparations. It was too late. That same day, December 4, rebels who had answered Mackenzie's call were beginning to assemble at Montgomery's Tavern just outside Toronto. By the next day, several hundred rebels were marching down Toronto's Yonge Street in drill formation, and Lieutenant Governor Bond Head, like Mackenzie, was belatedly coming to terms with the consequences of his actions.

The day before, Bond Head had hastily bundled his own family aboard a steamer at Toronto to protect them from harm, but he was left with little hope of repelling an effective attack upon the colony. Lieutenant James Fitzgibbon, who had earlier urged better military preparations, was left with only 300 militia and no regular troops to oppose any rebellion. On December 5, Bond Head used Robert Baldwin and John Rolph—thought to be a moderate—to carry a message to the rebels, promising that they would be pardoned if they laid down their arms. Rolph carried out his duties as if a neutral arbiter, but gave the rebels a secretive wink. Mackenzie refused to surrender. It was fortunate that lack of preparation on the part of the government was met with even poorer preparation on the rebel side.

Mackenzie's several hundred supporters were reinforced by the arrival of another 700 rebels on the evening of December 5. These new rebel reinforcements were led by Samuel Lount, a Pennsylvania-born blacksmith, who was, surprisingly, a Quaker. There were numerous Quakers—as the adherents of the Society of Friends are colloquially called—among the rebel ranks. Since Quakers are traditionally pacifists, these rebels' lack of military training may in part explain the almost farcical events of that evening.

Only a minority of the rebel forces were armed; the rest made do with pikes and pitchforks. A small defence force of two dozen, commanded by Sheriff William Jarvis, fired at the rebels advancing down Toronto's Yonge Street, but then fled in the darkness and smoke. Lount ordered the fire returned, but when the rear ranks of his rebel forces saw the front ranks drop to the ground—to allow a volley to be fired over their heads—his inexperienced troops assumed the front line had been cut down by enemy fire and took to their heels. One rebel lay dead, two dying. The first clash of arms in what Mackenzie believed would be a sweeping revolution fizzled out in ignoble failure.

The conflict awakened the energies of Upper Canada's volunteers, and a force of more than 1000 flocked to Toronto to suppress the uprising. John Wedderburn Dunbar Moodie, husband of author Susanna Moodie, although suffering from a broken leg and weakened from a long bout of fever, struggled from his bed to answer the call. Rumours reached the Moodies at their isolated cabin in Upper Canada's backwoods that Canada and the United States were at war and Toronto besieged by 60 000 men. Many others joined the standard, including the future prime minister, John A. Macdonald. A 22-year-old lawyer based in Kingston, Macdonald was a member of the Sedentary Militia, a force supposed to encompass every able-bodied male in the province between 18 and 60. The Sedentary Militia was aptly named: its training consisted of an annual drill on King George III's birthday that combined military preparation with games, picnics, and boisterous socializing. Amid the growing crisis, the acting adjutant-general, James Fitzgibbon, who had battled with Bond Head about the need for proper military preparation, was dismayed when the lieutenant governor placed an inexperienced, but socially prominent, colonel of the militia, Allan MacNab, in overall command. Humiliated, Fitzgibbon protested to Bond Head, who relented at the last moment and returned Fitzgibbon to command.

Meanwhile, more than half of the rebels at Montgomery's Tavern deserted the cause, alarmed by evidence of poor planning and disorganization, leaving a force of approximately 500. Mackenzie's conduct during the crisis seemed hardly calculated to inspire confidence. He was busily pursuing personal vendettas, burning the home of the manager of the Bank of Upper Canada, and threatening to put the sheriff's and postmaster's homes to the torch, and he had robbed a mail coach before being stopped by supporters.

On December 7, Anthony Van Egmond belatedly arrived to command the rebels, not knowing that the date for the uprising had changed. The Dutch-born Van Egmond had adopted his aristocratic surname while a fugitive from the law, and invented a dazzling military résumé that impressed his fellow conspirators. Van Egmond attempted to impose some order on the band of insurgents at Montgomery's Tavern, but quickly despaired of any success; Mackenzie sharpened his resolve to continue by levelling a pistol at his head. Fitzgibbon likewise was suffering a crisis of confidence. He sank to his knees in prayer,

December 7, 1837: Upper Canadian rebels are ill-prepared at the Battle of Montgomery's Tavern.

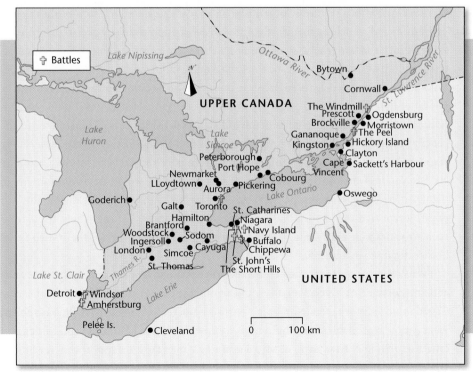

Map 8.2
Upper Canadian battle sites.

Source: Reprinted with permission of the Osgoode Society for Canadian Legal History and the University of Toronto Press. © Osgoode Society for Canadian Legal History, 2002.

marshalled his courage, and resolved to attack. Fitzgibbon led his troops up Yonge Street to the accompaniment of martial bands and the cheers of Toronto's loyal citizens. A cannon blast through the roof of Montgomery's Tavern sent a stream of rebels rushing from their shelter, and the assault quickly became a rout. Some of Mackenzie's fleeing supporters were pursued through the woods, but the rebellion had been crushed in under 20 minutes. One rebel was dead and several were wounded; five militiamen were wounded.

The Aftermath of the Rebellions

As the skirmish collapsed, Van Egmond was captured. Cast into a cold dank Upper Canadian jail in December, Van Egmond sickened and died in prison less than a month later. Fitzgibbon resigned as adjutant general the day after the successful defence of the colony, deeply embittered by Bond Head's actions. Mackenzie, like so many of the rebel leaders in both provinces, fled to the United States, a price of a £1000 on his head. He later boasted that "I had risked much for Canadians, and served them long, and as faithfully as I could, and now, when a fugitive, I found them ready to risk life and property to aid me—far more ready to risk the dungeon, by harbouring me, than to accept Sir Francis Head's thousand pounds." Many supporters helped him as he made his way to American soil. Perhaps the hardest part of Mackenzie's journey—"the most cruel and intense sensation of pain I ever endured"—was a neck-deep crossing of the icy Sixteen Mile Creek on a bitter December night, his clothes held above his head to keep them dry.[28]

December 13, 1837:
Dr. Charles Duncombe
leads an uprising
near Brantford.

Trouble further west in Upper Canada demonstrated that not all spirit of rebellion had yet been crushed. In the London district, west of Brantford, the American-born Dr. Charles Duncombe was hastily organizing an uprising, inspired by word of the clash at Toronto. As well as being a medical doctor—an occupation strangely over-represented in the ranks of Canadian rebels—Duncombe had been a member of Upper Canada's legislative assembly. At first a moderate, he was driven into a more radical posture when, in 1836, Colonial Secretary Glenelg refused to even meet with a delegation of Canadian reformers. His bitter mindset worsened under the influence of personal tragedy that same year: his house burned down and his only son was killed in a fall from a horse. Duncombe's insurgence attracted several hundred supporters, but Bond Head ordered Colonel MacNab to command a militia force to confront them. By December 13, MacNab's troops, including 100 Six Nations warriors from the Grand River area, put the would-be revolutionaries to flight. American newspapers, perhaps recalling clashes with the Natives during the War of 1812, reported that Aboriginal warriors scalped some retreating rebels, though no such atrocities were ever verified. Duncombe reputedly escaped across the United States border disguised as a woman.

Even as this sputtering flame of rebellion was doused in Upper Canada, the sad events at Saint-Eustache on December 14 would signify the all-but-inevitable defeat of Lower Canada's bid for independence. Yet Mackenzie was not temperamentally inclined to accept what a more reasonable man would have acknowledged was failure. He had earlier sent letters to a Buffalo, New York, newspaper urging Americans to support the freedom of Upper Canada. As Duncombe's uprising was crushed, Mackenzie proclaimed a provisional government from his base on Navy Island, Canadian territory close to the American side of the Niagara River. He was aided by a hard-drinking Dutch-American adventurer, Rensselaer Van Rensselaer, but the two men quickly became embroiled in quarrels over tactics. On Christmas night, Colonel MacNab left his palatial home, the 72-room Dundurn Castle at Burlington Heights, and marshalled a force of volunteers loyal to the government cause, including Six Nations warriors once again. Also among MacNab's force of 2500 was a company of 50 blacks from St. Catharines, organized by James H. Sears and Thomas Runchey. Mackenzie later insisted that black Canadians had been misguided in their allegiances, expressing his regret that "an unfounded fear of a union with the United States on the part of the coloured population should have induced them to oppose reform and free institutions in this colony."[29]

MacNab's forces watched the rebel encampment on Navy Island from the shore near Chippawa but wished to move cautiously, as Bond Head had warned against provoking the Americans. On the night of December 29, MacNab instructed Royal Navy Commander Andrew Drew to intercept a steamer, the *Caroline,* that was ferrying supplies and weapons to Navy Island. Drew and his crew of 50 rowed in seven boats across the fast current three kilometres above Niagara Falls to find that the *Caroline* was gone. Investigating further, they continued across the river and detected the vessel tied up at Fort Schlosser, New York, under the guard of American guns. They boarded the steamer, drove off the 30 or so crew who were sleeping on board, cut loose the lines, and set the *Caroline* ablaze. The flames lit up the sky as Drew and his crew made their way back to the safety of Canadian territory. One American lay dead, shot through the head. The burning *Caroline* ran aground and broke apart, and the current carried the pieces over the falls.

December 29, 1837: The Caroline *affair sparks intense reaction in the United States.*

A dramatized representation of the Caroline *incident*

Source: Library and Archives Canada, C-004788.

The *Caroline* affair outraged Americans: during peacetime, British and Canadian forces had destroyed an American ship in American territory, violating United States sovereignty. American newspapers reported the massacre of dozens, and included fanciful accounts of the anguished cries of passengers trapped aboard the burning vessel as it plunged over the falls. A fresh infusion of American recruits crowded Navy Island in the wake of the incident, eager to avenge the insult. Yet all semblance of military discipline was breaking down there. Rolph visited the island but left within the hour, disgusted by the filth, disorder, and drunken bickering between Van Rensselaer and Mackenzie. Mackenzie himself left the island shortly afterward to take his wife to a doctor in Buffalo, where American authorities seized him and laid charges of violating neutrality laws. He was allowed out on bail, and returned briefly to Navy Island before abandoning that doomed enterprise and settling in New York City. Mackenzie resumed his journalism career in the United States, but ultimately served a year in jail. He made his way back to Canada in 1850, when a pardon ended his exile. Although he would re-enter political life, he never again achieved his former prominence. His grandson, William Lyon Mackenzie King, would later become Canada's longest-serving prime minister.

The fizzling end to the squalid settlement at Navy Island did not mean a return to complete security for Canada's frontiers. The year 1838 began with a series of skirmishes along the border, as rebels who had fled south the previous autumn continued their quest for revolution. Among them was Robert Nelson. Unlike his brother, Wolfred, who had taken a leading role in the Battle of Saint-Denis only to be captured shortly afterward, Robert had been arrested immediately when the authorities began to move against those suspected of sedition. He spent one day in jail, released on a technicality, but scrawled on the wall of his cell, "The English government will remember Robt. Nelson." It was no idle boast.

When a conference of exiled rebels met in Vermont in January 1838, Papineau disavowed the goal of launching a retaliatory expedition from the United States, largely because radicals were now dedicated to the overthrow of the seigneurial system and breaking the influence of the Catholic Church, objectives that he opposed. Robert Nelson now dismissed Papineau as a selfish man, a man of words and not action. Papineau abandoned the revolutionary enterprise, went to New York, and later to Paris, where he would stay until an amnesty permitted his return to Canada in 1845. His departure left a leadership vacuum into which stepped Robert Nelson, elected by his co-conspirators as president of the future Canadian republic. Back in Lower Canada, Lord Gosford had proclaimed that February 26, 1838, was to be a day of general thanksgiving to mark the restoration of tranquillity, but, south of the border, events revealed that that tranquillity would be short-lived. Rifles and cannons had been stolen from the militia arsenal at Elizabethtown, New York, and on the night of February 28, Nelson led several hundred armed men across the border to proclaim the independence of Lower Canada. This lofty goal was thwarted by the sudden melting away of many of the American supporters. The muster of *patriotes* the next morning revealed only 160 troops. Furthermore, Lower Canadian militia quickly assembled to drive the invaders back across the border, where American army troops were waiting. Nelson, along with other key figures in the raid, was quickly arrested.

Militia units had been called out all along the Canadian frontier, both in Lower Canada and the upper province, as far west as Windsor, across the river from Detroit. Among

March 1, 1838: A cross-border raid on Lower Canada is thwarted.

the Canadians who answered the call to defend the frontier against filibusters from the United States was the Reverend Josiah Henson, who had been living at Windsor. Henson, a black Methodist preacher who had been born into slavery in Maryland, rallied to the cause of Canada's defence, taking command of a small company of other black newcomers to Canada. Sir John Colborne preferred to keep militia units, rather than regular troops, concentrated near the border. Underpaid and harshly disciplined career soldiers often found the temptation to desert to the United States irresistible. This would not be a factor for home-based militia, and certainly not for black militia; Josiah Henson remembered that when his feet first touched Canadian soil after his escape from slavery in 1830, "I threw myself on the ground, rolled in the sand, seized handfuls of it and kissed them and danced around, till, in the eyes of several who were present, I passed for a madman."[30]

1838: Black militia units help to defend the border against American-based rebels.

The failure of Nelson's abortive raid, and the signs of a spirited defence by militia units across the two colonies, suggested to the exiled rebels that other tactics were necessary. Through the summer of 1838, agitators on both sides of the border were busy forming mysterious secret societies, known in English as the Hunters' Lodge, and in French as the *Frères Chasseurs*.

The Hunters' Lodge in the United States sprang from radical elements in the Democratic party; Ohio was a particular hotbed of Hunters' Lodge activism centred on working men's rights and bank reform. The republican sentiments of radicals in Canada appealed to American adventurers bent on finishing the tasks of 1775 and 1812. Estimates as to the number of adherents these secret societies attracted varied wildly. Colborne believed that tens of thousands were involved, yet the actual number of active members who posed a threat to Canadian sovereignty was more likely a matter of hundreds. The societies maintained complete secrecy, relying on passwords, initiation rites, and a quasi-military organization. In the *Frères Chasseurs* a Grand Eagle (*Grand Aigle*) was at the top of the hierarchy, with a series of *Castors,* or Beavers, each commanding a company.

1838: The Hunters' Lodge and Frères Chasseurs *emerge as new threats to security.*

Conclusion

Despite the looming disquiet these secret organizations threatened, authorities in both Canadian colonies had succeeded in dealing with the immediate military threat. It was evident, however, that some more profound solution to the instability would have to be found. The constitution of Lower Canada had been suspended in February 1838, and a new "special council," along with the executive council, was governing the colony. "The seriousness of the crisis can be gauged not only in the far-reaching challenges to the existing order, but also in the extraordinary measures taken to preserve British rule," historian Allan Greer explains. In Lower Canada, "martial law was imposed, habeas corpus suspended, and arrests were carried out on a massive scale and largely without charges being laid." The curtailment of legal rights in Upper Canada was more modest in scope, but did include later immunity to Loyalists whose zeal to apprehend rebels may have involved breaking the law.[31] Gosford, having tendered his resignation as governor-in-chief in November 1837, learned in January 1838 that it had been accepted. A fall on the ice delayed his departure from Canada, but he was at last sailing home to Britain by the end of February 1838. Sir John Colborne, as commander of the forces, stood in until a replacement arrived. In Upper Canada, Sir Francis Bond Head's resignation, tendered months earlier, was likewise accepted, and he left the colony early in 1838. Sir George Arthur arrived to become the colony's new lieutenant governor in March 1838.

The prisons were filled with rebels awaiting their fate. Sir George Arthur moved quickly to make examples of two captured rebels, Samuel Lount and Peter Matthews, who were tried, convicted, and, on April 12, 1838, hanged. This act of swift justice disturbed even those who had taken up arms to oppose the rebellion. Sheriff William Jarvis, who had led the band of defenders confronting Lount's forces on Yonge Street, wept as he prepared the prisoners for execution. Lount and Matthews embraced him, assuring him that they were prepared to meet their judgment in heaven. They dropped through the trapdoor of the gallows reciting the Lord's Prayer.

Sir John Colborne, acting as administrator of Lower Canada, recognized that the situation was even more volatile in that colony, where more than 500 languished in the jails. He released the majority, leaving only 161 of those whose apparent crimes could not be ignored. The explosive issue of justice for imprisoned *patriotes* awaiting death for treason would have to wait. The newly appointed governor-in-chief would be handed the unenviable task of meting out justice in an atmosphere where fresh threats to the colony's security bubbled just below the surface. He was also charged with the duty of inquiring into the causes and remedies for colonial discontent. A heavy burden lay on Lord Durham as he arrived in Canada in May 1838.

Questions to Consider

1. What had been the intention of the 1791 *Constitutional Act*? In what way were political reformers in the Canadas dissatisfied with the way that it had been implemented?

2. Rebellions in Lower and Upper Canada in 1837 were linked in some respects, yet emanated from different causes. What were some of the key goals of the rebels in each of the two colonies?

3. Louis Joseph Papineau has been characterized as a "divided soul." In what sense is this an accurate assessment?

4. How successful was William Lyon Mackenzie as a voice for reform in Upper Canada?

Critical Thinking Questions

1. To what extent is it important to study context outside the Canadas in order to fully understand the rebellions? What outside factors might be relevant?

2. How likely were the rebellions to succeed?

3. How well did British authorities respond to the growing evidence of discontent in the colonies?

4. How might you account for the decision of the Iroquois to take up arms to oppose the rebellion?

Suggested Readings
General Histories

Beck, J. Murray. *Joseph Howe. Vol.1: Conservative Reformer, 1804–1848.* Montreal and Kingston: McGill-Queen's University Press, 1982.

Bond Head, Francis. *The Emigrant.* London: John Murray, 1846.

Bonthius, Andrew. "The Patriot War of 1837–1838: Locofocoism with a Gun?," *Labour/Le Travail* (Fall 2003). http://www.historycooperative.org/journals/llt/52/bonthius.html.

Burroughs, Peter. *The Colonial Reformers and Canada, 1830–1849.* Toronto: McClelland & Stewart, 1969.

Dictionary of Canadian Biography. Online at http://www.biographi.ca. Contains detailed, scholarly articles on all of the key figures.

Greenwood, F. Murray, and Barry Wright, eds. *Canadian State Trials. Vol.2: Rebellion and Invasion in the Canadas, 1837–1839.* Toronto: The Osgoode Society and University of Toronto Press, 2002.

Greer, Allan. "1837–38: Rebellion Reconsidered," *Canadian Historical Review* 76 (March 1995): 1–18.

Kennedy, W.P.M., ed. *Statutes, Treaties and Documents of the Canadian Constitution, 1713–1929.* Toronto: Oxford University Press, 1930.

McCallum, John. *Unequal Beginnings: Agriculture and Economic Development in Quebec and Ontario until 1870.* Toronto: University of Toronto Press, 1980.

Ward, John Manning. *Colonial Self-Government: The British Experience, 1759–1856.* London: Macmillan, 1976.

Webb, Jeff A. "Representative Government, 1832–1855." Newfoundland and Labrador Heritage, Memorial University. http://www.heritage.nf.ca/law/representative.html.

Lower Canada

Bernard, Jean-Paul. *The Rebellions of 1837 and 1838 in Lower Canada.* Ottawa: Canadian Historical Association, 1996.

Boissery, Beverly. A Deep Sense of Wrong: The Treason, Trials, and Transportation to New South Wales of Lower Canadian Rebels after the 1838 Rebellion. Toronto: Dundurn, 1995.

Bulletin d'Histoire politique 2003, 12 (1) and 1998, 7 (1). These editions are entirely devoted to French language articles on the *patriotes* of 1837 and 1838.

Coates, Colin M., "The Rebellions of 1837–38, and Other Bourgeois Revolutions in Quebec Historiography" *International Journal of Canadian Studies* 1999 (20): 19–34.

DeCelles, Alfred. *Louis-Joseph Papineau.* Toronto: Morang & Co, 1911.

Greenwood, F. Murray, and Barry Wright, eds. *Canadian State Trials: Rebellion and Invasion in the Canadas, 1837–1839.* Vol. 2. Toronto: Osgoode Law Society, 2002.

Greer, Allan. *The Patriots and the People: The Rebellion of 1837 in Rural Lower Canada.* Toronto: University of Toronto Press, 1993.

Mullally, Emmet J. "Dr Daniel Tracey, A Pioneer Worker for Responsible Government" *Canadian Historical Association Report* 2 (1934–35): 33–45.

Ouellet, Fernand. *Lower Canada, 1791–1840: Social Change and Nationalism.* Toronto: McClelland & Stewart, 1980.

Senior, Elinor Kyte. *Redcoats and Patriotes: The Rebellions in Lower Canada, 1837–1838.* Stittsville, Ontario: Canada's Wings, 1985.

Upper Canada

Cadigan, Sean. "Paternalism and Politics: Sir Francis Bond Head, the Orange Order, and the Election of 1836" *Canadian Historical Review* 72 (1991): 319–347.

Craig, Gerald M. *Upper Canada: The Formative Years, 1784–1841.* Toronto: McClelland & Stewart, 1963.

Dent, John Charles. *The Story of the Upper Canadian Rebellion.* 2 vols. Toronto: C.B. Robinson, 1885.

Fryer, Mary Beacock. *Volunteers and Redcoats, Rebels and Raiders: A Military History of the Rebellions in Upper Canada.* Toronto: Dundurn, 1987.

Greenwood, F. Murray and Barry Wright, eds. *Canadian State Trials: Rebellion and Invasion in the Canadas, 1837–1839.* Vol 2. Toronto: Osgoode Law Society, 2002.

Healey, Robynne Rogers. *From Quaker to Upper Canadian: Faith and Community among Yonge Street Friends, 1801–1850.* Montreal and Kingston: McGill-Queen's University Press, 2006.

Kelly, Wayne Edward. "Canada's Black Defenders" *The Beaver* 1997 77 (2): 31–34.

Kilbourn, William. *The Firebrand: William Lyon Mackenzie and the Rebellion in Upper Canada.* Toronto: Clarke, Irwin and Company, 1956.

McNairn, Jeffrey L. *The Capacity to Judge: Public Opinion and Deliberative Democracy in Upper Canada, 1791–1854.* Toronto: University of Toronto Press, 2000.

Mills, David. *The Idea of Loyalty in Upper Canada, 1784–1850.* Montreal and Kingston: McGill-Queen's University Press, 1988.

Palmer, Bryan. "Popular Radicalism and the Theatrics of Rebellion: the Hybrid Discourse of Dissent in Upper Canada in the 1830s." *Transatlantic Subjects: Ideas, Institutions, and Social Experience in Post-Revolutionary British North America.* Nancy Christie, ed. Montreal and Kingston: McGill-Queen's University Press, 2008.

Read, Colin. *The Rising in Western Upper Canada, 1837–8: The Duncombe Revolt and After.* Toronto: University of Toronto Press, 1982.

Read, Colin. *The Rebellion of 1837 in Upper Canada.* Ottawa: Canadian Historical Association booklet, 1988.

Read, Colin, and Ronald Stagg, eds. *The Rebellion of 1837 in Upper Canada: A Collection of Documents.* Toronto: Champlain Society, 1985.

Sewell, John. *Mackenzie: A Political Biography of William Lyon Mackenzie.* Toronto: James Lorimer, 2002.

Wilton, Carol. *Popular Politics and Political Culture in Upper Canada, 1800–1850.* Montreal and Kingston: McGill-Queen's University Press, 2000.

Notes

1. Janet Ajzenstat, "Celebrating 1791: Two Hundred Years of Representative Government," *Canadian Parliamentary Review* 14, 1 (Spring 1991), 26–30.

2. As quoted by Alfred D. DeCelles, *Louis-Joseph Papineau* (Toronto: Morang & Co, 1911), 5, 35–7.

3. John Manning Ward, Colonial Self-Government The British Experience, 1759–1856 (London: Macmillan, 1976), 32.

4. Fernand Ouellet, *Louis Joseph Papineau: A Divided Soul* (Ottawa: Canadian Historical Association Booklet, 1961), 11–13.

5. Alexis de Tocqueville, *Journey to America*, http://english.republiquelibre.org/notes-of-alexis-de-tocqueville-in-lower-canada.html.

6. Carol Wilton, *Popular Politics and Political Culture in Upper Canada, 1800–1850* (Montreal and Kingston: McGill-Queen's University Press, 2000), 248, n. 43.

7. Allan Greer, *The Patriots and the People: The Rebellion of 1837 in Rural Lower Canada* (Toronto: University of Toronto Press, 1993), 114.

8. Norman Ward, *The Canadian House of Commons: Representation* (Toronto: University of Toronto, 1963), 98–99.

9. Fernand Ouellet, *Lower Canada*, 216, 223, 221.

10. As quoted in Jospeh Schull, *Rebellion: The Rising in French Canada, 1837* (Toronto: Macmillan, 1971), 19.

11. The 92 Resolutions appear in full in W.P.M. Kennedy, ed. *Statutes, Treaties and Documents of the Canadian Constitution, 1713–1929* (Toronto: Oxford University Press, 1930), 270–290.

12. As quoted by Alfred D. Decelles, *The 'Patriotes' of '37* (Toronto: Glasgow, Brook & Co., 1916), 39.

13. As quoted in Joseph Schull, Rebellion, 37.

14. John Molson, Jr. "An Address by the Constitutionalists of Montreal to Men of British or Irish Origin, 1834," *Statutes, Treaties and Documents*, 291–294.

15. "The Seventh Report on Grievances, 1835" *Statutes, Treaties and Documents*, 295–307.

16. Palmerston, as quoted in Donald Creighton, "The Victorians and the Empire" *Canadian Historical Review* 19 (June 1938), 143.

17. Sir Francis Bond Head, *The Emigrant* (London: John Murray, 1846), 154–157. Available via *Early Canadiana Online*, http://www.canadiana.org.

18. Jeffrey L. McNairn, *The Capacity to Judge: Public Opinion and Deliberative Democracy in Upper Canada, 1791–1854* (Toronto: University of Toronto Press, 2000), 211.

19. Sean T. Cadigan, "Paternalism and Politics: Sir Francis Bond Head, the Orange Order, and the Election of 1836," *Canadian Historical Review* 72 (1991), 320.

20. Robert Baldwin to Lord Glenelg, 13 July 1836, Appendix No. 5, *Journals of the House of Assembly of Upper Canada from the 8th day of November, 1836 to the 4th day of March, 1837* (Toronto: W. L. Mackenzie, 1837). Available via Early Canadiana Online, http://www.canadiana.org/ECO/PageView/9_00942_13/0177?id=22d80bec117b6744.

21. A copy of the Twelve Resolutions may be read at http://www.gov.ns.ca/legislature/Facts/TwelveResolutions.htm.

22. R.A. Mackay, "The Political Ideas of William Lyon Mackenzie," *The Canadian Journal of Economics and Political Science* 3 (February 1937), 17.

23. As quoted in Gerald Craig, *Upper Canada: The Formative Years, 1784–1841* (Toronto: McClelland & Stewart, 1963), 244–245.

24. As quoted in Joseph Schull, *Rebellion*, 58.

25. As quoted in S.F. Wise, "Sir Francis Bond Head," *Dictionary of Canadian Biography*, http://www.biographi.ca.

26. As quoted by John Sewell, *Mackenzie: A Political Biography of William Lyon Mackenzie* (Toronto: James Lorimer, 2002), 146–148.

27. As quoted in Allan Greer, *The Patriots and the People*, 319.

28. As quoted in Charles Lindsey, *William Lyon Mackenzie* (Toronto: Morang, 1911), 386.

29. As quoted in Owen A. Thomas, *Niagara's Freedom Trail: A Guide to African-Canadian History on the Niagara Peninsula* (Thorold: Niagara Region Tourist Council, c. 1995), 15.

30. Josiah Henson, *Father Henson's Story of His own Life* (Boston: John P. Jewett & Co., 1858), 126–127.

31. Allan Greer, "1837–38: Rebellion Reconsidered," *Canadian Historical Review* 76 (March 1995), 16.

9

The Fate of British North America: 1838–1846

In 1936, Old Pierre, of the Katzie nation along the Pitt River in British Columbia's lower mainland, told an anthropologist his people's story. While Native oral traditions do not always allow events to be pinpointed chronologically, Old Pierre clearly recalled his great-grandfather's account of events that probably date from the epidemic of smallpox that devastated British Columbia Aboriginal nations in the 1830s:

> My great-grandfather happened to be roaming the mountains at this period, for his wife had recently given birth to twins, and, according to the custom, both parents had to remain in isolation for several months. The children were just beginning to walk when he returned to his village at the entrance of Pitt Lake, knowing nothing of the calamity that had overtaken its inhabitants. All his kinsmen and relatives lay dead inside their homes; only in one house did there survive a baby boy, who was vainly sucking at its dead mother's breast. They rescued the child, burned all the houses, together with the corpses that lay inside them, and built a new home for themselves several miles away. If you dig today on the site of any of the old villages you will uncover countless bones, the remains of the Indians who perished during this epidemic of smallpox.[1]

chapter 9

Source: Library and Archives Canada C-121846.

John George Lambton, first Earl of Durham, arrived in Canada as governor and commissioner in 1838.

> **After reading this chapter you will be able to:**
>
> 1. Appreciate the threat posed by 1838 border raids against Upper and Lower Canada.
> 2. Explain Lord Durham's mission and his 1839 Report.
> 3. Assess the success of the Baldwin–La Fontaine alliance after the 1840 Act of Union.
> 4. Understand the background of the "Aroostook War" in New Brunswick and the 1842 Ashburton–Webster Treaty.
> 5. Identify key early-nineteenth-century British activities in the Pacific Northwest, and the context of the 1846 Oregon Treaty.
> 6. Explain the nature of Arctic exploration in the first half of the nineteenth century.

Introduction

The tragic account preserved in Katzie oral history as told by Old Pierre reveals some of the terrible costs associated with growing imperial interest in the Pacific Northwest in the nineteenth century. In the wake of the 1821 merger of the Hudson's Bay and North West Companies, the jurisdiction of the HBC was extended beyond the Rockies, and small newcomer settlements began to appear in what would later be known as British Columbia. This growing interest was matched by a more assertive American presence centred around the mouth of the Columbia River. The ambitions of the United States extended beyond this, however, with some insisting that all territory west of the Rockies to the northern latitude of 54°40' should be in American hands. Britain's tenuous foothold in the Pacific Northwest hung in the balance. Similarly, border tensions arose in the east, with lumbermen from New Brunswick and Maine contending over rights in the Aroostook Valley. This era was also one of renewed interest in northern explorations. The most famous example is John Franklin's ill-fated 1845 expedition to the Arctic. Before considering these important events, though, it is necessary to first continue the story in Lower and Upper Canada.

The rebellions of 1837 had been crushed and the prisons were full of failed adventurers and *patriotes* awaiting the noose. Lord Durham, a British statesman of enormous prestige, whose days were numbered by the ravages of tuberculosis, faced the unenviable task of meting out justice in an explosive atmosphere of simmering discontent. Durham's 1839 Report on the Affairs of British North America would emerge as a controversial milestone in Canada's constitutional evolution. The forced union of Upper and Lower Canada was intended to assimilate the French, but was a catalyst that helped usher in a new and positive political era. The Baldwin–La Fontaine alliance emerging out of such an unpromising climate would lay the groundwork for a flexible and constructive federalism.

Lord Durham Comes to Canada

Reformers in Canada welcomed the appointment of John George Lambton, first Earl of Durham, as governor and commissioner. The man heralded as "Radical Jack" in Britain would surely have a progressive approach to Canadian policy. Durham was a major player in British politics, a man of tremendous wealth and prestige, someone who had taken a leading role in the drafting of the Great Reform Bill of 1832. The Lambton family coalmines in the north of England employed more than 2000 men and generated an income estimated at £80 000 per year in the early nineteenth century, an era in which a comfortable home might rent for £20 per year.

Durham was handsome and youthful in appearance, dark-haired and dark-eyed, likened by one observer to a young Spanish Jesuit. Yet these advantages had not shielded him from experiencing more than his share of life's inevitable sorrows. He was only five when he lost his father to tuberculosis; when his mother remarried, her two sons were banished and sent to live with a family friend. Durham's health was never robust, and he suffered from nosebleeds, swollen glands, and migraine headaches. At the age of 19, he eloped with a woman of whom his family disapproved, but tuberculosis claimed his young wife after three years. He remarried, but a further series of tragedies struck. His oldest son died on Christmas Eve 1831 at the age of 13, and within a four-year period all three daughters of Durham's first marriage died.

Durham had just returned to England after serving as ambassador to Russia when in July of 1837 Lord Melbourne, the British prime minister, proposed he accept a mission to Canada. Melbourne cynically mused to Durham that separation of the Canadian colonies might not hurt the Mother Country, but recognized that the loss of the colony could prove fatal to his ministry. Durham at first declined the post; he had recently left Russia amid concerns about the effect of the cold climate on his health. Only after the rebellions, when Melbourne pressed him to reconsider the appointment, did he relent.

Unfortunately, the position served to showcase some less laudable features of Durham's character. His arrogance, vanity, tendency toward petulance, and love of ostentation—defects that may explain his failure to reach his potential within the Whig party—now manifested themselves as he began to make elaborate preparations to be governor general of Canada. *The Times,* alluding to Durham's late Russian post, dubbed him "the Czar of all the Canadas," declaring him as "open as a schoolgirl to skillful flattery." One fellow Whig was a guest at an extravagant dinner party at Durham's London home, and noted the printed French menu cards announcing "Dinner with His Excellency." The guest caught the eye of a friend and recalled that he thought he "should burst out laughing" at Durham's self-importance. Further, complaints were raised in Britain's Parliament about the expenses Durham was racking up, and the Whigs narrowly survived a confidence vote on the issue.

Melbourne confided to Queen Victoria that Durham had brought the criticism on himself: "he has gone to such expense, and has made such an amazing fuss and show about everything; people going to see his harness at this place and his carriage at another." Critics wondered why it was necessary for him to be accompanied by eight aides-de-camp, although Durham himself paid the salaries of four of them, and took no salary himself. His meticulous attention to the details of his elaborate uniform ensured that he cut a splendid figure upon a white horse. Durham ultimately claimed to have spent £35 000 of his own money during his short mission to Canada. This is easy to believe: it allegedly took days to unload the crystal, plate, wine, and other luxuries that made up Durham's baggage when he arrived in Canada.[2]

Historian Bruce Curtis argues that the grandeur of Durham's elaborate domestic arrangements while in Canada was "political theatre," part of a strategy of "condescension." Durham used aristocratic hospitality to reach down into the social ranks, in a carefully orchestrated way, for political ends.[3] But the criticism before he left home stung, and Durham came close to abandoning the whole idea of serving in Canada. He was, a visitor reported, "in a dreadful way about it, deadly pale, frightened and wanting to write a letter to Lord Melbourne throwing it all up."[4] The earliest indications seemed to suggest that Durham was not made of stern enough stuff to be Canada's governor general.

Durham made other preparations before leaving Britain. He delved into Colonial Office files and met with leading experts on Canadian affairs, including moderate Lower Canadian reformer Louis-Hippolyte La Fontaine. He also selected aides to accompany him to Canada, and these men were very significant to Durham's mission. Among them was Edward Ellice, the son of Edward "Bear" Ellice. The elder Ellice was a Whig member of Britain's Parliament, a sometime cabinet minister, and a substantial Hudson's Bay Company shareholder. He had engineered the 1821 merger of the Hudson's Bay and North West Companies, attempted to push through the bill to unite the Canadas in 1822, and was a significant influence on Britain's Canadian policy. Further, Ellice owned a substantial Canadian seigneurie at Beauharnois. Ellice's son may well have proved a conduit for his father's ideas, many of which would ultimately appear in Durham's report on Canada.

In addition to the younger Ellice, other aides included the colonial theorist Edward Gibbon Wakefield whose infamous conduct in attempting to kidnap a 15-year-old heiress prompted Melbourne to warn Durham not to "touch him with a pair of tongs." Melbourne was no more impressed with another one of "scamps and rogues" bound for Canada: Thomas Turton was a pariah in polite society since his wife had sued for divorce, citing Turton's adultery with her sister. On the other hand, Charles Buller, an MP and journalist, was a great asset to the mission, and held sound ideas on responsible government. Buller's views on the Canadian rebellions were considered radical by British parliamentarians: he privately attributed the rebellions to "the deplorable imbecility of our colonial policy" and insisted that the government should "set a memorable example by not shedding one drop of blood."[5]

May 27, 1838: Durham arrives in Canada.

When Durham arrived in Canada in May 1838, he proclaimed his intention to show fairness and open-mindedness, and to act as a friend to the people of Canada. Aristocratic hospitality was a vital part of this, and Lady Durham wrote home to her mother that they hosted large dinner parties daily at Quebec's Government House. She found the French-Canadian ladies the most pleasant and refined; by contrast, she gossiped, one of the most prominent English women invited used her knife to eat jelly.

Despite Durham's successes in the social realm, the looming question of justice for imprisoned rebels remained. F. Murray Greenwood and Barry Wright describe the events of 1837–38 as "arguably the most serious state-security crisis in Canadian history. It is certainly the largest one when measured by legal proceedings: over 350 persons were tried for treason and equivalent political offences punishable by death." In January 1838, a Tory-dominated Upper Canadian legislature passed new statutes to deal with the insurrection.[6] By one act, habeas corpus was suspended. "Habeas corpus" is the traditional right, enshrined in a 1679 British statute, that safeguards individual liberty by requiring that the grounds for someone's imprisonment be shown before a court of law.[7] Needless to say, the suspension of habeas corpus during a military crisis opens the door to the risk of arbitrary imprisonment of legitimate political dissidents.

Another new Upper Canadian law passed as a temporary expedient in 1838, usually referred to as the *Pardoning Act*, allowed the accused to petition for a pardon before undergoing a jury trial. This was meant to streamline justice, with so many treason cases looming. The understanding was that a prisoner would confess in return for a likely grant of clemency. The two Upper Canadian rebels hanged in April 1838, Peter Matthews and Samuel Lount, had their petitions denied, only to later face trials that, as Greenwood and Wright put it, "had become mere formalities because of their earlier confessions."[8] In Lower Canada, any such swift retribution would have almost certainly invited disaster: support for the *patriote* cause was both deep and wide.

New Raids on Upper Canada by Rebel Forces

Nor was the immediate crisis past. Rumours of fresh insurrection abounded. Rebel agitators south of the border had been coordinating plans for new attacks on British North American soil. In March 1838, an organization with the misleadingly benign name of the Canadian Refugee Relief Association was established at Lockport, New York. Members plotted a raid against the Short Hills area of Pelham Township in Upper Canada—present-day Fonthill, Ontario. They launched an invasion in early June under the leadership of an American-born tanner of Irish descent, whose illiteracy may be inferred from variances in his name, which appears as James Morreau, Morrow, Munro or Munroe.

Only 26 rallied to the cause, perhaps lured by promises of fortune and assurances that 25 000 men in Upper Canada were waiting to join in and throw off imperial rule. Authorities worried that Pelham Township was a hotbed of rebel sympathizers and that the Niagara Escarpment would afford invaders a natural hideout. When the raiders moved into the Short Hills area with vague notions of "liberating" Canada, they found little support for their enterprise. Delegates from the United States approached them on June 15, asking them to abandon the scheme, fearing it would compromise a larger invasion planned for July 4. Unwilling to retreat without having made any show of defiance, the insurgents made the symbolic gesture of attacking the village of St. Johns, stopping first to rob the home of Abraham Overholt, a 90-year-old veteran. After a brief skirmish with a small troop of British regulars stationed in St. Johns, the force dispersed. Iroquois warriors from the Six Nations reserve hunted them down, promised rewards for the capture of rebels. The Tory-supported Toronto *Patriot* wholeheartedly approved, asserting that the insurgents "ought to be treated like mad dogs" and hoping that none escaped "the halter, the rifle, or the tomahawk." Morreau, for one, did not escape: he was captured and later hanged on July 30, 1838.[9]

1838: Six Nations warriors capture rebel raiders in Upper Canada.

Morreau was alone among the most recent crop of rebel invaders in suffering this ultimate penalty for his crimes. His co-conspirators, and those who had offered them assistance, were subject to milder penalties—imprisonment or transportation to penal colonies. A total of 102 of these offenders were sent to British penal colonies in the antipodes, most to Van Diemen's Land (later Tasmania), the colony over which Sir George Arthur had earlier presided as governor. Most of those transported were American citizens, although for some their national status was complicated by the fact that they had been resident in Canada as well.[10]

One of the other Upper Canadian statutes passed in January 1838, the *Lawless Aggression Act*, was meant to apply to hostile invaders from outside, rather than British subjects guilty

Satirical American representation of British warfare in 1812, 1837–38.

Source: Library and Archives Canada, C-040831.

of treason. Authorities in the United States appealed to Canada for lenient treatment of American subjects found guilty. Governor W.L. Marcy of New York protested that those captured were "unreflecting young men who have been deluded in the cause they have taken by false notions and by gross misrepresentations." There was no danger in mercy, he urged, since the American government had already taken steps to deal with threats emanating from south of the border. Upper Canada's executive council treated these calls for clemency with disdain: "None was shown for the innocent and peaceful Inhabitants of the Province who were threatened with the miseries of Civil War. None for those whom the rifles belonging to the United States Government were to murder. None for the widows and orphans to be left destitute in Canada."[11] The Americans had made no effort to warn or aid Canada, the council charged.

The strain on relations between the United States and British North America had been a primary concern to Lord Durham; episodes such as the *Caroline* incident and the formation of seditious Hunters Lodge societies on American soil ensured an atmosphere of tension. The American press also criticized British authorities for their strategy of "using" Aboriginal warriors as a potent weapon against invasions, failing to recognize that Native groups acted in what they perceived to be their own best interests.

While on a visit to Upper Canada in July 1838, Durham saw an opportunity to promote accord with the neighbouring republic. He had been visiting Niagara Falls—a spectacle that Lady Durham believed almost made the sacrifice of coming to Canada worthwhile—when he took the unprecedented step of crossing the border to visit the United States. The trip paid important diplomatic dividends, won praise in the American press, and contributed to more cordial relations. As a further precaution to deal with the continued threat of rebel instigators from south of the border, Durham selected his wife's brother, Colonel Charles Grey, for a special mission to the United States. Grey succeeded in convincing American authorities to step up the border patrols.

Durham also believed he had found a solution to the explosive question of justice for imprisoned rebels awaiting their fate in Lower Canada's jails. With almost no prospect of finding an impartial jury to try the prisoners, Durham settled upon another expedient: making promises of mercy, he persuaded eight of the key instigators—including Wolfred Nelson—to acknowledge their guilt in writing. This plan was put in place through the special council governing Lower Canada. Durham had already reconstituted the special council after his arrival, shrinking it to a mere seven members, mostly military officers or members of his entourage. Now, it was, in Steven Watt's words, transformed "to full-time judge and policeman."[12] Buller was dismayed that the first confessions of guilt read more like political manifestos. "If there be guilt in high aspirations, then we confess our guilt," declared one.[13] Buller pointed out to the prisoners that, while Durham was disposed to be merciful, there were limits to his forbearance. The prisoners substituted more moderate versions. Spared the noose, they would instead be transported to Bermuda; only those convicted of the most egregious acts of bloodshed were condemned to death.

On July 3, 1838, the eight exiles sailed for Bermuda, after giving their word that they would not attempt to escape. Charles Buller reportedly saw to it that the ship was properly equipped for a comfortable journey, and the prisoners toasted Durham's health en route. Sixteen of the rebels who had fled south of the border, Louis-Joseph Papineau and Cyrille Côté among them, were to be banished from Canada, subject to execution if they should return.

July 1838: Durham compromises by exiling captured rebels.

Although Durham's expedient violated some central British legal principles, many in Canada applauded it as a just and conciliatory approach. Throughout both colonies, a great number who had not supported the rebellions were ambivalent toward those who had. In Upper Canada, where the execution of Samuel Lount and Peter Matthews had caused so much agony in the spring of 1838, other convicted rebels were awaiting transportation to penal colonies.

On the night of July 29, 1838, amid a violent thunderstorm, 15 rebel prisoners escaped from custody at Fort Henry in Kingston, and all indications were that someone in the fort had given them the tools they needed for their breakout. They loosened stones from the mortar of their cell's walls with an iron bar, and scaled the outer walls of the fort with a crude ladder. While three of the fugitives were recaptured, 12 reached St. Vincent, New York, where sympathetic Americans welcomed them. A plaque in that town commemorates the house that sheltered the rebels during the "Patriot War" of 1838.

July 29, 1838: 15 rebel prisoners escape in Upper Canada.

Despite the distraction of periodic alarms in the summer of 1838, Durham progressed in his larger task as commissioner, inquiring into the general causes of colonial discontent. Relying heavily on the expertise of the aides he had brought with him to Canada, Durham established working groups to investigate settlement and Crown lands, immigration, education, municipal institutions, the seigneurial system, and justice issues. Durham implemented Canada's first urban police force, copying the metropolitan police model implemented in London in 1829 under Sir Robert Peel. Peel's London "bobbies" had proved such a success that Durham implemented a similar system in Canada's cities to replace the outdated town-watch system. All new legislation, of course, was enacted by the special council, and not by an elected assembly.

1838: First police force is instituted in Lower Canada.

To address political grievances, Durham offered an olive branch to moderate reformers in Canada whose voices had been hitherto unheard. Among the leading moderates were the father and son team William and Robert Baldwin of Toronto. Durham granted the Baldwins a private interview, inviting them to explain their ideas on constitutional reform to the governor. Durham also encouraged them to follow up with more detail in writing, and the report Robert Baldwin had tried in vain to present to Lord Glenelg in 1836 at last found a more receptive audience.

Yet Durham was exhibiting signs of that same susceptibility to criticism that had dogged him when he had been criticized in England over his expenses. The storm over his selection of Edward Gibbon Wakefield and Thomas Turton to accompany his mission had not abated, and Durham was distressed by the failure of the home government to rally to his defence. Charles Buller put aside his usual genial light-heartedness to deliver a stinging rebuke to the governor general, who had by the autumn suddenly lapsed into sulkiness, abandoning his early spirit of initiative. Buller acknowledged Durham's health problems, but charged that "be your bodily disorders what they may, the real cause of your sufferings is in your mind…. You have no chance of recovery without raising yourself from your present morbid state of feeling." This was hardly fair—Durham's early death in 1840 would have vindicated him on that score. He had suffered greatly with chronic illness, and the looming onset of a harsh Quebec winter would not have been a welcome prospect. Lady Durham was frequently alarmed about the toll the Canadian appointment was taking on her husband's frail health; his illness made him increasingly irritable, a constant complaint of those close to him. Charles Grey confided to his father that "I daily thank my stars that I have nothing to do with him. It is astonishing, taking everything of importance as coolly as he does, to observe how trifles upset him."[14]

Durham Resigns

If Durham was having difficulty ignoring the lack of support he had received from British quarters, and becoming distressed by critical accounts in Britain's newspapers, a much greater challenge lay ahead of him. The compromise he had reached to deal with imprisoned *patriotes* found favour in Canada, but he learned on September 19, 1838, that the home government, tottering on the brink of parliamentary defeat, had disallowed his ordinance dealing with the rebels. Even fellow Whigs in Britain condemned his actions, pointing out that he had exiled men who had not had the benefit of a proper trial, and had pronounced sentences on fugitives. Further, they argued, Bermuda was beyond Durham's jurisdiction, and he could not legally send anyone there. *The Times* of London accused the Whig government of throwing Durham overboard to save itself. Perhaps the most difficult thing to bear was that Durham only learned of the British government's disavowal of his policy by reading it in the New York newspapers. Melbourne, in an earlier letter, had congratulated Durham on settling the difficult affair so well, and expressed his complete approval. Feeling betrayed, Durham decided that same night to resign.

Durham's indignation had not subsided in the month it took for the official notice of the imperial government's disallowance of his ordinance to cross the Atlantic. His official resignation on October 9, 1838, signalled his unwillingness to shrink meekly from the Canadian scene. Instead, he issued a public proclamation to the peoples of the two Canadas. Traditionally, the governor general's dignity would prevent him from defending his own position or criticizing his home government or colonial administration. But Durham recklessly shattered this tradition of vice-regal reserve. His proclamation complained of "incessant criticism" of the most minute aspects of his administration from the mother country, where the imperial government was legislating for Canada in a state of "ignorance and indifference." His ordinance for the exile of prisoners having been disavowed, "no impediment therefore exists to the return of the persons who have made the most distinct admission of guilt." He also pointed out that the prerogative of the Queen's mercy to those whose lives he had spared could not be cancelled. In essence, the rebels were invited to consider themselves completely exonerated from guilt. In Britain, *The Times* howled its indignation at the "Lord High Seditioner" who vented his pique by inviting rebellion in

October 1838: Durham resigns and lashes out at his home government.

Canada.[15] Critics saw in Durham's dramatic gesture another exhibition of his vanity and petulance. His sudden abandonment of his post amidst rumours of insurrection suggested that Durham placed his own fragile dignity above the safety of the colony.

Just before midnight on All Hallows' Eve 1838, as the *Inconstant* lay at anchor at Quebec waiting to bear him home to England the next day, Durham wrapped up the last tasks necessary before his departure. Then, bundling up against the chilly night, he climbed to the tower overlooking the city for a last long look at Quebec. The night wind carried with it the knell of midnight church bells and the first flurries of snow. The next morning, the coach bore a pale and solemn Durham, flanked by his wife and children, through streets crowded with spectators, all standing in funereal silence. Few could have been hopeful about Canada's fate.

New Rebel Uprisings, 1838

Fresh military crises erupted almost immediately on the heels of Durham's departure. Robert Nelson had led a failed raid against Lower Canada in February 1838, declaring the colony's independence. In the aftermath, he had been arrested in the United States, but had been acquitted by an American jury. Nelson immediately set to work on renewed schemes to further his revolutionary agenda. In the autumn of 1838, Durham's sudden resignation offered an ideal opportunity. *Patriotes* in Napierville, Lacolle, and Châteauguay awaited the arrival of reinforcements from the United States, and Dr. Cyrille Côté, who had crossed over into Lower Canada earlier, busily garnered resources; £327 was seized from Napierville's parish church. On November 3, 1838, Nelson and the *Frères Chasseurs* launched an invasion, carrying 250 American muskets provided by a sympathetic American colonel. Nelson proclaimed himself president of the provisional government, and read aloud a declaration of independence before an audience of more than 3000.[16] Throughout the vicinity, an estimated 4000 joined the ranks of the insurgents, and bands of rebels attacked Loyalist homes, seizing arms, ammunition, or other property.

November 3, 1838: A fresh rebellion erupts at Napierville.

Nelson's nominal leadership of the rebels could not disguise the fact that the *patriotes* embraced a wide variety of dangerous and radical schemes. One rebel from Saint-Mathias targeted priests, announcing his plan to take several "black pigs" prisoners. Others called for the confiscation of the Lachine canal, a forced levy from brewing magnate John Molson, the murder of all bureaucrats, and a raid on bank assets. Another plot called for all of Montreal's Jews to be strangled and their property confiscated;[17] seigneur and magistrate Benjamin Hart was a special target.

It is noteworthy that Jewish citizens served as militia in the bid to suppress the rebellion. Eleazar David, the scion of a prominent Jewish merchant family established in Montreal since shortly after the conquest, had commanded a militia unit with great distinction at the 1837 Battle of Saint-Eustache. The small Jewish community of Lower Canada had earlier been involved in a controversy over political rights. In 1807, Ezekiel Hart of Trois-Rivières won election to the legislative assembly, but was prevented from taking his seat on the grounds that he could not swear a Christian oath. Early the next year, the assembly passed a vote confirming this refusal. Pierre Bédard argued in the Lower Canadian reform newspaper *Le Canadien* that Jews ought not to be allowed the rights of citizens because they themselves did not wish to be citizens of any country, but rather only to live "where they could do good business." Historian Gerald Tulchinsky maintains that this bid to deny rights to Jews was a "political, not religious decision." Many Francophone reformers anticipated that the interests of Lower Canadian Jews would mirror those of the Anglophone business community. Jews were vulnerable in a "struggle between French Canada's pursuit of cultural distinctiveness, and the Anglo-Saxon forces of economic progress," Tulchinsky asserts.[18] At last, in 1832, a *patriote*-dominated assembly voted to extend full political rights to Jewish citizens, decades before such progressive legislation had been adopted elsewhere in the empire. The 1838 call for action against Jews, presumably a fringe view, was a troubling return to anti-Semitism amid an extraordinarily strained economic and political climate.

Patriote forces in the November 1838 rising sealed off the village of Châteauguay to ensure that its terrified residents could not flee to raise a general alarm. But the nearby Aboriginal settlement of Caughnawaga (Kahnawake) was still cause for worry—the Iroquois were feared warriors with a tradition of loyalty to the Crown. The insurgents attempted to convince the Natives that they had a force of 20 000 and had already taken control of large sections of the province; if the Iroquois gave up their arms and stayed neutral they would be allowed to keep their land under the new regime. Instead of being taken in by this ruse, the Iroquois captured 64 rebels and brought them by canoe to Lachine, where a grateful militia—who had not been aware of the uprising—took the prisoners into captivity.

In the meantime, 150 to 300 *Chasseurs* prepared to move against Beauharnois, where the younger Edward Ellice, aide to Lord Durham, slept in his manor house. Ellice's wife, Jane, had been disturbed in her sleep by the sound of barking dogs and the shrieking of turkeys in the yard. A sudden bang on the door alerted the family to trouble, but the warning by the militia came too late for escape. Insurgents surrounded the house and carried Ellice off to be imprisoned at Châteauguay. Jane Ellice and her sister huddled together in their nightgowns while ruffians carrying guns, knives, and pikes looted the family wine cellars, growing drunker as the night wore on. At last, a parish priest persuaded the rebels to allow the women to take refuge in the presbytery, where others were being held under guard by the *Chasseurs*.

The *Chasseurs'* bold beginning did not culminate in a successful revolution. Sir John Colborne, commander of the forces and administrator of the colony after Durham's hasty departure, reacted to the crisis with energy and severity: he declared a renewal of martial law, and Montreal authorities moved swiftly to apprehend those suspected of complicity in the uprisings. Colborne quickly mustered all the troops at his disposal, including the local Iroquois.

Anthropologist Matthieu Sossoyan explains that prowess in warfare was central to the identity of the Iroquois. Aboriginal veterans of the War of 1812 shared stories of military exploits with younger generations, and their status as warriors enhanced the prestige of communities such as Caughnawaga. Beyond merely supporting British interests, Natives had their own resentments against some of the same locals swelling the *patriote* ranks. Growing pressure for agricultural land in Lower Canada had led to persistent problems of incursions into Native villages by habitants. Disputes flared over illegal taking of firewood, non-payment of rents, and other trespasses. Colborne was quick to recognize the military value of the Iroquois. The merest chance of confronting Native warriors sometimes caused rebel forces to simply melt away. While they served with British troops, Iroquois warriors remained distinct by decorating themselves with red and black war paint and dressing in Native combat gear. The sounds of Iroquois war whoops mingled with the bagpipes of the Highland regiments produced a terrifying cacophony.[19]

Robert Nelson faced other difficulties, too. Canadian volunteers intercepted an American schooner bringing rebel reinforcements and arms. In addition, American troops foiled rebel attempts to retrieve arms and ammunition that had been cached south of the border. On November 8, Nelson abandoned Napierville, announcing his intention to clear the way for an invasion from the south. His sudden flight toward the border looked suspiciously like desertion in the face of looming defeat. He was seized by rebels at Odelltown, just inside Lower Canada's borders, but explained to his skeptical followers that he had been making an inspection tour. Amid a blinding snowstorm on the morning of November 9, the rebel forces were resoundingly defeated at Odelltown, with 50 *patriotes* killed. Amid the battle, both Nelson and Cyrille Côté slipped south to the United States. Nelson would continue to be buffeted about by the winds of fortune. Impecunious and discouraged, he made his way to California, gained an instant fortune in the gold rush, but lost it all at the hands of a dishonest agent.

November 9, 1838: The rebel forces suffer a defeat at Odelltown.

The night after the rebel defeat, British troops, along with volunteers and Aboriginal allies, sought for the enemy at their former stronghold of Châteauguay. Disappointed to find it deserted, the troops spent their rage by burning and looting the town. Such retribution was exacted throughout the countryside as hundreds of homes were put to the torch and untold atrocities perpetuated. The Glengarry regiment boasted of having cut a swath six miles (nine kilometres) wide through rebel territory, and vowed that they would be sure to burn any homes left standing on their return march. The savagery with which the last vestiges of rebellion were crushed left a legacy of bitterness among *Canadiens*. Colborne's direct responsibility for the wanton destruction is questionable, yet he long afterward remained a hated symbol of British military brutality. His elevation to the peerage in 1839 as Lord Seaton was greeted with derision by *Canadiens* who preferred the epithet "Lord Satan."

Upper Canadian Invasion Led by Nils Von Schoultz, November 1838

As in 1837, the 1838 insurrection in Lower Canada provided an opportunity for a coordinated uprising in the upper province. A band of insurgents crossed the St. Lawrence River from New York into Prescott, Upper Canada, led by a Swedish-born New Yorker, Nils von Schoultz, who claimed to be an officer in the Polish army. He was a romantic figure who had served in the French Foreign Legion and left a trail of gambling debts, abandoned children, and broken hearts as he moved throughout Europe. Von Schoultz likened Canada's struggle against British rule to Poland's slavery under the tyranny of the Russian Empire. On November 11, 1838, he and 150 to 200 supporters took up a defensive position in a stone windmill and several stone houses near Prescott. Von Schoultz looked forward to an infusion of sympathetic Upper Canadians eager to support the cause of rebellion, but was dismayed to discover that the crowd of several hundred he spied approaching was an attacking force, not his anticipated reinforcements. British regular and Canadian militia forces pounded the position for several days, and at last Von Schoultz—his forces reduced to firing cannon loaded with hinges, bolts, and scrap metal—was compelled to surrender. The "Battle of the Windmill" ended with a defeat of the rebel forces, perhaps 30 of whom had been killed, among many more wounded. An estimated 16 British regulars and Canadian militia paid with their lives for the victory. By the night of November 17, 131 prisoners, a ragged Von Schoultz at the head of them, were jeered as they marched through the streets to Fort Henry, bound with rope.

Von Schoultz's court martial defence was conducted by John A. Macdonald, who at 23 was beginning to make a name for himself as a rising young Kingston lawyer. Macdonald was captivated by his client's patrician manners, exotic accent, and the air he gave of a short and tragic life led in the pursuit of romantic lost causes. Von Schoultz did not attempt to deny his guilt, but spoke only to reject allegations that he had permitted the mutilation of a slain British lieutenant's body. He was one of a dozen condemned to death by Canadian authorities whose patience with constant alarms along their borders had been exhausted.

November 17, 1838: Nils von Schoultz's rebel force is defeated at the Battle of the Windmill near Prescott, Upper Canada.

December 4, 1838: At Windsor, Upper Canada, five rebel invaders are executed without trial.

Rebel Raiders Attack Windsor

A few short days before Von Schoultz's execution on December 4, 1838, another band of some 150 would-be revolutionaries crossed the Detroit River at Windsor, killing four Upper Canadian militiamen and setting fire to the barracks. Neighbouring loyal militia forces converged on Windsor, killing 27 invaders and taking another 44 prisoner. John Prince, a colonel in Upper Canada's militia, and member of the legislative assembly, rushed to the defence of the colony, but was dismayed to see that a close friend who had been among the defenders had been killed with an axe and bayonet in the melee. In his rage, Prince ordered the summary execution of five rebel prisoners. Upper Canada's lieutenant governor, Sir George Arthur, was shocked by this flagrant violation of the rules of warfare, and alarmed by the potential risk to Anglo–American relations. Nevertheless, he conceded that Prince's rash and illegal act won wide approval among Upper Canada's beleaguered population, and seemed to work as a "deterring example" to other adventurers.

Despite Durham's earlier resolve to be merciful, the latest round of insurrections demonstrated the limits of conciliation. Approximately 850 Lower Canadians were swept up and imprisoned under the provisions of martial law; of these, 106 would ultimately face trial, with 90 condemned to death. Most did not hang, though—58 were transported to penal colonies. But mercy was not extended to all. At Pied du Courant in Montreal, the sound of the rushing current and swirling eddies of the St. Lawrence echoes coldly from the grim stone walls of the prison. Here, for 12 patriots, the clanging iron door of an opened cell heralded only a short walk to the winter prison yard and execution.

Durham's Report on the Affairs of British North America

Even as the last of these dozen prisoners met their sad fate at the end of a hangman's noose, Britain's Parliament was coming to grips with a report that Durham had laid before them. While Durham's precipitous departure seemed to suggest that he was abandoning any concern for Canada, he had, upon his return to England, busied himself in synthesizing the work of his aides, producing a report on Canada and its troubles. Having already resigned his position, Durham's drive to write this report may have been inspired by a deep commitment to British North America and its problems, or perhaps more cynically, by his wish to vindicate his position after the cabinet's disavowal of him. The Durham Report is an enduring document in Canadian history, historian Gerald Craig explained, perhaps paradoxically because, "like so many great ideas, it was extremely simple, not very original, indeed almost obvious." Others had already proposed the very things at the heart of the report.

The two key recommendations of the Durham Report were union of the colonies of Upper and Lower Canada—the measure abandoned by British policymakers in 1822—and responsible government. Responsible government simply meant that the well-tested practices and principles of the British constitution would be used. The governor would select as his executive council men who commanded the support of a majority of the legislative assembly and, in internal matters, act upon their advice. Since responsible government was already the model in Britain, the system required "no change in the principles of government, no invention of a new constitutional theory," Durham explained. The imperial government could continue to oversee those matters that fell outside the colony's domestic jurisdiction—matters such as relations with foreign governments, regulation of foreign trade, and the constitution itself. Where internal matters were concerned, the colonists had a "greater interest in coming to a right judgment on these points, and will take greater pains to do so than those whose welfare is very remotely and slightly affected," Durham insisted. What is more, responsible government necessarily followed from representative institutions.[20] It did little good to permit elected assemblies if the will of those bodies was constantly thwarted: "It is better to be without a fire, than to have a fire without a chimney," as Charles Buller later put it.[21]

One of Durham's other recommendations concerned the contentious question of the clergy reserves; the section of the report dealing with Upper Canada described the issue as "the question of the greatest importance." In the report, Durham lamented how the elite of the province who "possessed almost all the highest public offices" in government, the legal system, and the Church of England, had "acquired nearly the whole of the waste lands of the Province." Not surprisingly, this group had used its domination to ensure that the Anglican Church, that Protestant denomination of which they were adherents, claimed exclusive control over the substantial land reserves set aside for the Protestant Church in the 1791 *Constitutional Act*. The numerous Methodists and Presbyterians of the province could hardly be expected to "acquiesce quietly" in this, Durham pointed out; yet reformer-dominated assemblies had found their measures to redress the situation constantly thwarted by upper councils dominated by the Anglican elite.[22] Durham urged that the reserves be portioned out among the Protestant sects.

Despite the recommendation of responsible government, reformers in Lower Canada found aspects of the report highly objectionable. Durham's guiding principle was the assimilation of the French Canadians into the "great race" of the British Empire. He looked forward to the day when a vigorous English majority would make it apparent that the "vain endeavour to preserve a French Canadian nationality" must be abandoned. Indeed, he attributed the rebellions primarily to ethnic causes. In a famous phrase, Durham declared, "I expected to find a contest between a government and a people: I found two nations warring in the bosom of a single state: I found a struggle, not of principles, but of races." Any "amelioration of laws or institutions" would depend on first "terminating the deadly animosity" between French and English. It is hardly surprising that the Durham Report—which seems to contain a blueprint for extinguishing the French-Canadian nation in North America—triggers visceral antipathy in Quebec. Durham himself seemed to anticipate this response to what he acknowledged was a "hard measure." Some no doubt would point out, he admitted, that "the English are new-comers who have no right to demand the extinction of the nationality of a people." It might also be said, he argued, that the French "are not so civilized, so energetic, or so money-making a race," although they could be described as amiable and virtuous, not copying "the spirit of accumulation, which influences their neighbours."[23]

Durham's recourse to ethnic stereotypes and his prescription for cultural assimilation make him an easy target—he almost seems a parody of the ethnocentric nineteenth-century imperial administrator. Yet political scientist Janet Ajzenstat rejects the simple explanation that Durham was illiberal, suggesting instead that Durham's rejection of group identity and group rights is entirely consistent with liberalism, which puts paramount emphasis on individual rights. He believed that responsible government would put English and French Canadians on an equal footing, with the appointed elements of the constitution—the legislative council and the governor—the protectors of minority groups who might suffer at the hands of those elected democratically by the dominant group. The ideal was a balanced constitution.[24]

The intentions of the report aside, the extent to which it guided imperial policy is open to question. Traditionally seen as a formative document in British colonial history, the Durham Report was long cited as a definitive turning point of the empire. After all, its key recommendations—the union of the two Canadas and responsible government—would ultimately become policy. Yet in a revisionist study, historian Ged Martin points out that the report's reception was hampered by Durham's deep unpopularity in Britain's political world. Durham had quarrelled even with fellow Whigs, and had deeply embarrassed his government by throwing up his post on the eve of fresh rebellions. The British press was almost unanimous in debunking the report and Durham's exaggerated claims of its importance. The *Morning Post* ridiculed Durham's "bundle of balderdash" and the fact that Wakefield had arranged to have "bragging and fantastical lies about it" written up as if it were a miracle pimple plaster.[25] Then, too, British policymakers were awash in proposed solutions to the Canadian conundrum, and none of Durham's vaunted solutions were his own original ideas.

Of course the sense of cause and effect is sharpened by the fact that British policymakers *did* legislate the union of the Canadas in 1840, one of the main planks of Durham's report. Responsible government was still years away. The 1840 *Act of Union* deviated from Durham's recommendation in a critical way, however: it provided for one legislature for the hitherto separate colonies of Lower and Upper Canada, but then divided the representation in half, with an equal number of members for each segment of the province. Equal representation was hardly fair representation: Upper Canada's population stood at 450 000, Lower Canada's at 650 000. Durham in fact had specifically cautioned against any such attempt to rig a system of unequal representation.

Union was intended to solve the vexing problem of apportioning between Upper and Lower Canada customs revenue collected at Quebec City and Montreal. Moreover, it would give the commercial sector of both provinces a united voice to push for the canal-building projects they had hoped to see financed out of public funds; such public works would help merchants fully exploit the commercial potential of the St. Lawrence River. Those whose interests would not be served by such costly enterprises had long resisted these commercial schemes; men like Papineau had articulated their fundamentally conservative vision in Lower Canada's assembly. Durham had remarked on this crucial cleavage: the great natural channel of trade "concerns not only those who happen to have made their settlements along the narrow line which borders it" he insisted. He looked to the inevitable immigration of substantial numbers of English speakers into Canada's interior, and asked rhetorically: "Is it just that the prosperity of this great majority … should be for ever, or even for a while, impeded by the artificial bar which the backward laws and civilization of a part, and part only, of Lower Canada, would place between them and the ocean?"[26]

Durham's recommendation for a more equitable distribution of the clergy reserves in Upper Canada also came to fruition in 1840. His successor as governor, Charles Poulett Thomson, later Lord Sydenham, agreed with Durham's assessment, describing the clergy reserves as "the one great overwhelming grievance—the root of all the troubles of the Province—the cause of the Rebellion—the never failing watchword at the hustings—the perpetual source of discord, strife and hatred." The "greatest boon which would be conferred on the Country would be that they could be swept into the Atlantic and that nobody should get them," Thomson pronounced. By early 1840, he had deftly managed to coerce his Upper Canadian government into a settlement whereby the reserves would be divided among the Protestant sects, but warned the British colonial secretary to expect complaints from prominent Anglicans. Bishop Strachan "has excited his clergy to petition against it…. You will remember that it is [to] Dr. Strachan that we owe this matter still being open—15 years ago he might have settled it, if he would have given anything to the Church of Scotland."[27]

Act of Union Implemented in Canada, 1841

Charles Poulett Thomson arrived in Quebec to take up his position as governor on October 19, 1839. The government in place in Lower Canada still consisted of an appointed council, and not a representative assembly. This authoritarian regime had, in historian Allan Greer's words, "a free hand to govern Lower Canada without regard to the views of the population." Far from being merely a "neutral caretaker" government, "instead, it enacted far-reaching programs of political, legal, and institutional reform, with changes … that favoured the interests of the urban business community."[28] The new governor was untroubled by this. "If it were possible," he wrote, "the best thing for Lower Canada would be a despotism for ten years more."[29] Thomson moved promptly to impose the plan for union, giving Lower Canada's special council only two days to debate it. Even that small and unrepresentative body could not fully consider the measure; many members were prevented by a snowstorm from taking part in the discussion.

The formal "consent" of Lower Canada having been thus secured, Thomson quickly carried forward to Upper Canada, where on November 22, 1839, he took on the office of governor in that province as well. Lower Canadians protested the union, and support for the measure was far from complete in Upper Canada. Thomson's swearing in was greeted, in the words of one witness, "with an abortion of a cheer which was worse than silence." The promise of an imperial loan guarantee for £1 500 000 to finance public works projects and to pay off the accumulated colonial debts helped to sugar-coat the measure. Thomson managed to resist the "unjust and oppressive" conditions Upper Canada's legislature attempted to impose—that the seat of government be permanently in Upper Canada, that the language of the courts be exclusively English, and that the Upper Canadian half of the legislature be allocated more seats.[30] He was rewarded by the home government for his success in implementing union with an elevation to the peerage in 1840 as Baron Sydenham.

February 10, 1841: The Act of Union is proclaimed, uniting Upper and Lower Canada.

On February 10, 1841, as the 21-year old Queen Victoria celebrated both her first wedding anniversary and the christening of her first child, across the ocean in British North America, the Act of Union was proclaimed. Three years earlier to the day—on February 10, 1838—Lower Canada's constitution had been suspended amid constant alarms of invasion and domestic insurrection. Now, a new constitution was put in place to revamp the plan of 1791. A single apparatus of government would serve the now united colony. One governor would preside over the united Canadas, and there would be one executive council, and one upper house, or legislative council, both of these bodies appointed as before. There would be one elected legislative assembly.

The allocation of an equal number of seats in the single legislative assembly for Canada East (as Lower Canada would now be known) and Canada West (formerly Upper Canada) was plainly an injustice to the more populous French-dominated eastern half. This division of representation in an ostensibly united province seemed also to suggest a proto-federal arrangement. In a federal constitution, each element retains some degree of separation and autonomy even as they submit to an overall umbrella authority governing all. While the new united colony was not technically a federation, the Act of Union's provision of equal seats for each section of the colony—a measure meant to reduce the influence of more populous French Canada—paradoxically set the tone for a long tradition of federalism in Canada.

The Act of Union also provided for a permanent civil list; the salaries of officials could not be withheld by the legislature for political reasons. In exchange, the Crown relinquished any control over revenues, ending the independence the governor enjoyed through control of the proceeds of land sales. Further, it was enacted that only the elected legislature had the power to initiate money bills, confirming that body's traditional "power of the purse." Duties and other revenues would flow into a single treasury. Unhappily for Lower Canada, all existing provincial debt was also to be pooled. The upper colony's more aggressive public works program for canals and other infrastructure had left it with a debt exceeding $5 million. By contrast, Lower Canada had accumulated a surplus. The act made no specific provision for responsible government, stipulating only in vague terms that the governor would act with the advice, or advice and consent, of his executive council and offering no guidelines as to how that executive council should be selected. Responsible government—a key demand of reformers and one of Durham's central recommendations—remained an unrealized goal.

The rebellions had been quashed and the most radical reformers tainted with an image of treasonous disloyalty. A succession of colonial governors in the years following Durham's tenure seemed hopelessly intransigent about any concession of constitutional reform, either because of their own convictions or because of instructions from Britain. Nonetheless, the 1840s proved to be a fruitful period of political maturation for the British North American colonies. And new political alliances, born out of the assimilationist Act of Union, demonstrated that Durham had been fundamentally wrong about one important aspect of Canadian political life: reform principles, and not ethnicity, would be the motivating force drawing colonial politicians together.

The Baldwin–La Fontaine Alliance

The midwife of the new political alliance emerging in the 1840s was Francis Hincks, an Irish-born merchant who had come to Canada in 1832, becoming a wine and dry goods wholesaler. Hincks rented a warehouse in York from William Baldwin, an earlier Irish immigrant, and his son Robert, and this business relationship blossomed into a significant friendship. By the time of the Act of Union, Hincks was an important voice for reform in Canada West, making his ideas known through his Toronto-based newspaper, the *Examiner*, launched in 1838. The words "Responsible Government" appeared as a motto under the newspaper's title, and Hincks published weekly articles elucidating the concept for his readers. When Durham's report reached Canada in April 1839, Hincks immediately seized the initiative and set in motion events that would culminate in one of the greatest partnerships in Canadian history.

Hincks wrote to leading French-Canadian reformer Louis-Hippolyte La Fontaine to convince him that union of the provinces could be made to work: "Lord Durham ascribes to you national objects. If he is right, union would be ruin to you, if he is wrong, & that you are really desirous of liberal institutions & economical government, the union would in my opinion give you all you desire." This letter was only the first in which Hincks encouraged La Fontaine to lay aside ethnic differences and embrace an alliance with his English-Canadian reform counterpart, Robert Baldwin. He personally vouched for Baldwin's character, goodwill, and sense of public duty, insisting that "Mr. Rob[er]t Baldwin is *incorruptible*."

Most of Baldwin's acquaintances would have agreed, even if he was not a man to inspire affection. Baldwin's cold and distant manner masked an acutely sensitive poetic temperament, and he loathed the life of a public figure. He was a poor orator and his stooped posture, radiating defeatism and gloom, did not render him a charismatic leader of men. Robert Baldwin had followed his father William into the study of law as a profession. This was only one of the elder Baldwin's proficiencies; he was at various times a doctor, lawyer, architect, and militia officer, as well as operating a small school offering young Upper Canadian gentlemen a classical education, before turning his attention to politics and public service. The Baldwins, father and son, shared a deep conviction about the necessity of responsible govern-

Robert Baldwin.

Source: Library and Archives Canada, C-031493.

ment, but the senior Baldwin's advancing age dictated that Robert Baldwin would have to overcome his distaste for political life to work for its achievement.

Beyond his political convictions, Robert Baldwin, after a youthful stint as a skeptic, embraced a deep religious faith. No doubt part of Baldwin's earlier emotional turmoil had been the result of a forbidden love for his 16-year-old first cousin, Eliza. "The heart," he insisted in one of his passionate letters to her, "cannot be *divided*. [M]ine is wholly my Eliza's." Pleading that a separation from her would leave his heart a "leafless desert," Baldwin married Eliza just before her 18th birthday. Their happiness proved short-lived: the caesarean birth of their fourth child harmed Eliza's health, and she died in 1836 at the age of 25. Her despondent husband left written instructions that, when he died, the abdomen of his corpse should be cut with a caesarean incision like Eliza's, and his coffin chained to hers. Baldwin's eldest daughter Maria sacrificed her youth ministering to her father's demands through the rest of his life. Depression and other attendant disorders rendered him an invalid while he was still in his early 50s. Baldwin's youngest son, disabled by polio, also remained at home. Maria was compelled to refuse two offers of marriage in order to continue to serve as hostess and chatelaine of her father's Spadina estate. When Baldwin died in 1858, her patience perhaps exhausted, Maria ignored her father's bizarre final wishes. Upon discovering the oversight a month after the burial, Baldwin's eldest son insisted upon exhuming the body and carrying out his father's request.[31]

Baldwin's tormented personal life did not prevent him from playing a pivotal role in Canada's political evolution, but his success in doing so within the new united Canadas depended upon an alliance with the man who emerged as a dominant political figure after the failure of the rebellions. Louis-Hippolyte La Fontaine had seemed destined to do great things from an early age; his schoolmates dubbed him "the big brain." His family had deep roots in Lower Canada, and his grandfather had been a member of the legislative assembly from 1796. By the age of 21, La Fontaine was qualified to practise law, and two years later he began a career in active politics, winning election to the assembly as the member from Terrebonne in 1830. Despite his intellectual gifts, the socially withdrawn and uncommunicative La Fontaine was not a natural politician. Indeed, it is fortunate that Hincks should have brought together two men who might neither have reached out to the other.

La Fontaine was also noteworthy for his resemblance to Napoleon Bonaparte. His steady black eyes and carefully copied hairstyle echoed Napoleon's, and La Fontaine adopted the imitative habit of thrusting one hand between the buttons of his waistcoat. During a visit to Paris, his sudden appearance at the Invalides reportedly caused a sensation among the old soldiers who marvelled at the sight of their dead emperor.

La Fontaine had long been active in the *patriote* cause; he had been wounded in the clash of arms that accompanied the stormy 1832 Montreal by-election of Daniel Tracey. Later, he had shown his solidarity with the cause by wearing the homespun garments that *patriotes* adopted as a symbol of their boycott of British imports. La Fontaine ultimately eschewed violence and, while *patriote* forces confronted

Louis-Hippolyte La Fontaine.

Source: Library and Archives Canada, C-005961.

British and colonial troops in the fall of 1837, La Fontaine was making his way to England to lay his case before Colonial Office officials. In his absence, his wife Adèle visited imprisoned rebels and ensured that their families would not want for anything. On his return journey, La Fontaine visited with the exiled Papineau in New York. This apparent endorsement of the rebel cause, coupled with his long-standing activity on the fringes of the *patriote* movement, deepened suspicions surrounding La Fontaine and, amid fresh rumours of insurrection in 1838, he was cast into prison.

Ultimately, La Fontaine was recognized as a moderate, and his incarceration proved short-lived. Durham and his aides depended upon La Fontaine's integrity as a negotiator and his pragmatic approach to Canadian politics—it was La Fontaine who successfully secured amnesty for a number of captured rebels.

Lower Canadian *patriotes* had insisted that to cooperate in any way with the Act of Union was to sell out. Indeed, when the governor offered La Fontaine the post of solicitor general in 1840 he had refused it on principle. But the French-Canadian reformer listened receptively to Hincks's overtures. Hincks's message, "You want our help as much as we do yours," struck a chord with La Fontaine, whose thoughts had been along the same lines. He had earlier written to Edward Ellice that "it is a great mistake to suppose that there is no means of rapprochement between the two parties … their interests are the same." On another occasion, La Fontaine recalled his conviction that "the rod"—union— "unjustly designed to punish" and "destroy my countrymen" could instead be used to save them.[32]

A Climate of Uncertainty

Such clarity of objectives and spirit of cooperation were essential preconditions for the achievement of responsible government. The constructive Baldwin–La Fontaine alliance kept the idea alive in the confused climate that surrounded Britain's colonial policy in the period after Durham's departure. Durham's place had been filled by a succession of colonial governors, all of whom shared certain characteristics. Charles Edward Poulett Thomson, Lord Sydenham, held office from 1839 until his sudden death in 1841. His successor, Sir Charles Bagot, who arrived early in 1842, likewise succumbed to illness after a little more than a year in office. Charles Metcalfe, Lord Metcalfe, served from 1843 to 1845 until cancer forced his retirement to England. Charles Cathcart, Earl Cathcart, commander of the British forces in North America, stepped in as governor from 1845 to 1846.

Beyond the coincidence of being named Charles, their short terms of office, and, in the case of three of them, their ill health, a more significant common thread tied these governors together. None had been given a clear mandate to implement responsible government.

British Secretary of State Lord John Russell gave Durham's successor a warning that the principles of British cabinet government were not readily transferable to a colony: "It may happen … that the Governor receives at one and the same time instructions from the Queen, and advice from his executive council, totally at variance with each other." Nevertheless, Russell instructed Sydenham in a somewhat contradictory vein two days later, appointments to council should not be indefinite but instead "such officers [should] be called upon to retire from the public service as often as any sufficient motives of public policy may suggest the expediency of that measure."[33] In other words, Russell seemed to be suggesting that an executive council should resign if they lost the confidence of the assembly, a key plank of responsible government.

Sydenham ridiculed the "absurdity of claiming to put the council over the head of the governor…. Either the governor is the sovereign or the minister."[34] Even as he dismissed the idea of responsible government for a colony, in some respects he copied the conventions of cabinet government as it functioned in Britain. In this climate of ambiguity, reformers nurtured hopes that responsible government could be achieved.

In the summer of 1840, Louis-Hippolyte La Fontaine travelled to Toronto to meet with Robert Baldwin. John Ralston Saul has argued that the Baldwin–La Fontaine handshake inaugurated a defining political tradition in Canada "capable of including a multifaceted culture and two languages." The effect was immediate, and upon his return, La Fontaine explained his political epiphany to his constituents. His August 25, 1840, address to the electors of Terrebonne acknowledged the defects of union, but declared his "common cause" with reformers of the upper province, urging a "spirit of peace, union, friendship and fraternity." Only through the principle of responsible government—possible if they worked together—could the colony achieve constitutional and effective government and control of its own affairs.[35]

Much work remained to be done. Sydenham was busily taking steps to ensure that in the first election following the Act of Union, a cooperative legislative assembly would be returned. Strategically placed polling booths, patronage rewards, and blatant intimidation of voters kept reformers from winning a victory. La Fontaine, appalled by the violent spectacle in his own riding, withdrew from the contest, proclaiming bitterly that the "LAW OF THE BLUDGEON HAS PREVAILED." But a governor's manipulation of Canadian politics could only achieve temporary results. Lord Seaton (formerly Sir John Colborne), who had been commander of the forces and who now sat in the British House of Lords, was a shrewd observer of the Canadian political scene. He noted that support for the governor's policies in the assembly was likely to be fragile, "unless the machine is constantly worked by an Artist as clever and unscrupulous as the one that contrived to secure the majority of the first session," a pointed reference to Sydenham.[36]

Sydenham denounced La Fontaine as "a scoundrel," claiming that in the recent election the French-Canadian reformer "after arming his people with dirks and bludgeons loaded with lead was scared away by a few Irishmen." The French Canadians were no more impressed with the governor. His family name, Poulett Thomson, offered too tempting a target—Sydenham's detractors labelled him "le poulet" (the chicken). Sydenham also ridiculed La Fontaine's assertion that the governor had tried to buy his support: "He is a cantankerous fellow without talent & not worth buying or I would have had him when I pleased," he boasted to Lord John Russell.[37]

Robert Baldwin accepted Sydenham's appointment as solicitor general and also agreed to serve on the Tory-dominated executive council, along with other moderate reformers. Immediately, though, he clashed with the governor by insisting that Sydenham should govern on the advice of a truly responsible cabinet, that the executive council should be held responsible to the assembly. Sydenham had little patience for Baldwin's stubborn idealism: "Was there ever such an ass!" was his exasperated verdict.[38] To the colonial sec-

August 25, 1840: La Fontaine addresses the electors of Terrebonne, inaugurating a new spirit in Canadian politics.

retary Sydenham denounced Baldwin as "the most crotchety impracticable enthusiast I ever had to deal with." The newly elected legislature met at Kingston in June 1841 and Baldwin was quick to go on the attack.

His bold move to gain responsible government did not gain wide support in the legislature. Sydenham was able to stave off a ministerial crisis and Baldwin was compelled to resign from the council. The governor crowed to Russell that he had "gained the most complete victory. I have got rid of Baldwin and finished him as a public man for ever."[39] Moreover, the important alliance between Francis Hincks and Baldwin had begun to unravel. Hincks, a pragmatist, did not have Baldwin's deep sense of principle, and decided that Sydenham's commitment to the economic progress of the united Canadas was more important than constitutional niceties. Although Sydenham had not conceded responsible government, "we have *practical* responsibility," Hincks insisted.[40] Sydenham's triumph over Baldwin and the principle of responsible government did not last. Ill health forced him to resign the following month and, as he awaited his return to England, Sydenham suffered a further mishap. In September 1841 he fell from his horse and broke his leg. The wound became infected and within days Sydenham had died of lockjaw.

Sydenham's unscrupulous machinations had tempted Baldwin to give up politics altogether. He confided to his father that he was coming to the conclusion that he was not made for it. Yet Baldwin soon rebounded with a new plan and approached his father with a suggestion. Both Baldwins had recently been elected in Toronto ridings. The younger Baldwin wondered if his father's constituents would accept his retirement and vote for La Fontaine, "if he will accept the nomination instead of you." Nothing, he predicted, "would have a better effect." His father graciously agreed to stand aside.[41]

September 23, 1841:
La Fontaine is elected in
a Toronto constituency.

On September 23, 1841, the Fourth Riding of North York elected La Fontaine in a by-election. Upper Canadian voters had proved that, despite Durham's views, ethnic differences were incidental: they were committed to political reform and happy to select a leading French Canadian to win it for them. La Fontaine was later able to repay the favour: in 1843, he arranged a safe seat for Robert Baldwin in the riding of Rimouski, Canada East.

The new governor, Sir Charles Bagot, arrived in January 1842. His instructions from the colonial office were similar to Sydenham's, even though a Conservative administration had now taken power in Britain: responsible government was not to be conceded. But, by September 1842, Bagot felt compelled to appoint both Baldwin and La Fontaine to his executive council. The only alternative, he explained, was to appoint men "prepared to act without the sympathy and against an overwhelming majority of the House of Assembly." He recognized that that would be "disastrous." Realizing the significance of what he had done, Bagot explained to the colonial secretary, "whether the doctrine of responsible government is openly acknowledged, or is only tacitly acquiesced in, virtually it exists."[42] If these developments seemed to herald a new and hopeful era for Canadian political reformers, their hopes were soon dashed: not only did Britain's policymakers heartily disapprove, but Bagot's ill health forced his resignation six months later. He died in Kingston in May 1843.

Bagot's successor was determined to turn back the clock on reform. Charles, Baron Metcalfe came to Canada against his own better judgment: "I never undertook anything with so much reluctance, or so little hope of doing good," he confided to a friend. Decades

1843: In the "Metcalfe Crisis" late that year, almost all of the governor's council resigns.

1846: Lord Cathcart is commissioned as governor.

of imperial service in India and Jamaica had hardly equipped Lord Metcalfe for the demands of an assertive representative government. He especially dreaded the possibility of a clash with his Canadian ministry if their policies should conflict with the interests of the mother country: "This ought to have been well considered before … Responsible Government was established. It is now, perhaps, too late to remedy the evil," he wrote sourly to his superior in London.[43]

By November 1843, Metcalfe was embroiled in an open clash with his executive council, and all but one resigned. Metcalfe disavowed responsible government by refusing assent to legislation of which he disapproved, and by making appointments without cabinet approval. Like Sydenham, Metcalfe openly interfered with the elections that followed in 1844, and won a conservative victory by equating reform with disloyalty. By November 1845, Metcalfe too was forced from office by illness. Even his detractors were moved to pity and admiration at Metcalfe's brave stoicism as a painful and disfiguring facial tumour opened a gaping hole in his cheek. Scarcely able to speak or eat, blind in one eye, Metcalfe returned to England to die.

During a period of interregnum (when Canada was temporarily without a governor), it was usual for the commander of the forces to assume the administration of the colony. Today, the chief justice of Canada's Supreme Court would fill this role. With Metcalfe's sudden departure, Lord Cathcart, commander of the forces, took over the governor's responsibilities, and was himself commissioned in that role in April 1846. British authorities evidently decided that a governor with military credentials might be useful, given the increasingly strained relations with the United States.

Mid-Nineteenth-Century Tensions with the United States

New Brunswick and Alarms along the Border

Tensions between Britain's North American colonies and the United States were nothing new. In the decades following the War of 1812, numerous irritants along the border ensured that Anglo–American accord could never be taken for granted. Long before Sir Charles Bagot served as governor, he had acted as a special envoy to the United States, negotiating the Rush–Bagot agreement of 1817 and the Convention of 1818. The former limited armed vessels on the Great Lakes, while the latter set the boundary from Lake of the Woods to the Rocky Mountains at the 49th parallel and clarified fishing rights. However, other issues remained unresolved, and the strained atmosphere during the rebellions of 1837–38, with frequent alarms along the border, stretched the demands of Anglo–American diplomacy to the limit.

By 1839, a conflict over the boundary between the colony of New Brunswick and the state of Maine was reaching the point of crisis. According to the 1783 Treaty of Paris ending the American Revolutionary War, the border ran north from the St. Croix River. The wording that described this boundary was ambiguous, and the burgeoning timber industry in New Brunswick and Maine raised the stakes. In Madawaska, Americans from Maine tried to encourage Acadians and *Canadiens* to renounce British authority, while timbermen from New Brunswick encroached into the Aroostook Valley surrounding a tributary of the Saint John River in their quest for big trees. An intransigent American senate rejected an arbitrated agreement, and clashes between rival woodsmen during the "Aroostook War" of 1839 led both sides to send troops into the area. Despite the label, the conflict was more a war of words. At one point, American lumberjacks taunted their New Brunswick rivals across the river by singing:

> Britannia shall not rule the Maine,
> Nor shall she rule the water;
> They've sung that song full long enough,
> Much longer than they oughter.[44]

1839: New Brunswick and Maine lumbermen confront one another in the "Aroostook War."

In addition to the conflict over the Maine–New Brunswick border, unfinished business from the *Caroline* affair still embittered relations with the United States, with British authorities insisting that the Americans release Alexander McLeod, an Upper Canadian who faced murder charges stemming from the incident. While a drunken McLeod had boasted of his role in the destruction of the *Caroline*, British authorities insisted that his execution would be deemed an act of war. "I don't think that you sufficiently understand the character of Jonathan," Sydenham wrote home to Lord John Russell (Jonathan was a nickname for the United States that predated the better-known "Uncle Sam"). "He will never be fair or just unless he is compelled, but he will always yield if you are firm."[45] Fortunately, McLeod was acquitted after a trial and the other outstanding differences between the United States and Britain and her North American colonies were resolved in the Ashburton–Webster Treaty of 1842.

1842: Ashburton–Webster Treaty sets boundary between New Brunswick and Maine.

Among other matters, the Ashburton–Webster Treaty settled the international boundary from Lake Huron to Lake of the Woods, and contained provisions for better enforcement of the ban on slave trading. Both Britain and the United States had banned the slave trade early in the nineteenth century—that is, the importation of slaves—although slavery continued in many American states. Since 1820, American law had defined slave trading as piracy, punishable by death, but the United States resisted joint international action toward enforcement, reluctant to surrender freedom of the seas and permit the British to board and inspect American vessels. The British were thwarted in their efforts to curtail the clandestine trade by the fact that wily slavers would inevitably run up the Stars and Stripes when confronted by a patrol. Daniel Webster, the American secretary of state, agreed in 1842 that American vessels would patrol the African coast to prevent the illegal trade.

For British North America, the most controversial element of the treaty settlement was the question of the Maine–New Brunswick border. Some of New Brunswick's Acadian population would now live under the American flag, and suspicions abounded in British North America that British Foreign Secretary Lord Ashburton had fallen victim to smart Yankee manipulation and failed to protect colonial interests. Accusations of British indifference to colonial concerns were sharpened by the fact that the British House of Commons could not even muster a quorum when the treaty came up for debate. A "quorum" is the minimum number of members who must be present to conduct business. The final settlement left only a narrow strip of British territory on the south shore of the St. Lawrence. A later historian complained that Canadian territorial interests had long been "treated by England as a fund from which she can make payments at her own discretion

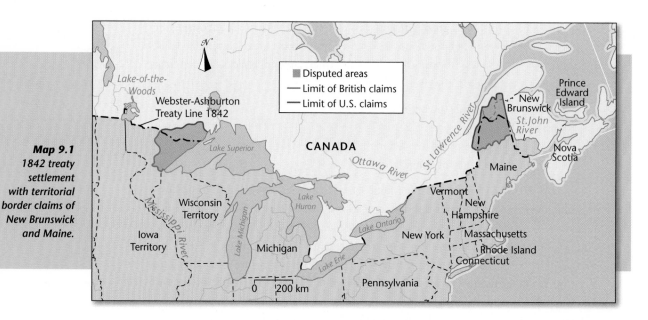

Map 9.1
1842 treaty settlement with territorial border claims of New Brunswick and Maine.

to purchase the goodwill of the United States." "The state of Maine," he elaborated, "runs like a wedge into the heart of Canadian territory," necessitating a costly detour for railway traffic bound for a Canadian Atlantic port.[46]

Unfortunately, this same sentiment would be echoed when British diplomatic authorities confronted the Americans over the issue of the border on the Pacific coast. The settlement of the Ashburton–Webster Treaty in 1842 had only temporarily patched up Anglo–American differences, and only a few years elapsed before a fresh controversy arose over the Oregon territory.

The Pacific Northwest and Renewed Border Tensions

European exploitation of the future province of British Columbia was a comparatively late phenomenon. From the second half of the eighteenth-century, explorations aimed at finding the elusive Northwest Passage through the continent, and commercially motivated voyages seeking sea otter pelts, whales, and other marine resources, brought rival mariners—Russian, Spanish, British, and American—to the Pacific coast. The overland explorations of Northwest Company traders Alexander Mackenzie, Simon Fraser, and David Thompson late in the eighteenth and early in the nineteenth century inaugurated an era of closer contact with diverse coastal and interior Aboriginal communities.

As in earlier generations in eastern and central North America, this contact devastated Aboriginal nations as newcomers unwittingly spread diseases to which Native people had no immunity. The earliest European explorers observed the scourge of smallpox, measles, tuberculosis, and other ailments, sometimes spread via travelling Natives whose home nations had earlier made contact with newcomers. The occasional elder's pockmarked skin bore witness to earlier smallpox plagues. David Thompson estimated the mortality on the northern plains at one-half to three-fifths, and recounted tales told by an Orcadian fur trader. On the plains, the Orkney man had stumbled upon "stinking tents in which all were dead," the bodies partly devoured by wolves and wild dogs.[47] In present-day British Columbia, smallpox epidemics through the 1830s killed an estimated one-third of the Tsimshian people and probably even more of the Haida. Other villages were completely swept away, as the oral history recollection of a Katzie elder that opens this chapter reveals.

Despite the accidental introduction of disease, most traders had little desire to alter Aboriginal patterns of life. The impact of the fur trade on Native culture and ways of life was less profoundly disruptive than settlement would later prove to be. Because traders required Aboriginal cooperation, they were compelled to make adaptations themselves. Up to the mid-nineteenth century, newcomers in northwest coastal areas numbered at best a few hundred. As in Rupert's Land, trade ties were often cemented with marital alliances. Unlike the short-term unions arising out of the maritime-based trade, the establishment of permanent coastal forts and incursions into the interior led to the growth of mixed-race families.

In the wake of the 1821 merger between the Hudson's Bay Company and Northwest Company, the British government extended the HBC's jurisdiction to the Pacific coast. George Simpson, the company's dictatorial governor, made canoe journeys to the Pacific Northwest in 1824, 1828, and 1841. One chief factor, who dreaded the visits, grumbled that Simpson's methods combined the despotism of a military tyrant with a miserly scrutiny of accounts. But even the hard-driving governor enjoyed occasional moments of lightheartedness: during one trip, Simpson attempted to impress a group of Carrier Natives by pretending that the sounds emanating from a music box were being made by his dog. Some concerns transcended the balance sheet: during his 1841 journey, noting that the Kwakiutl (Kwakwaka'wakw) Natives of Port Neil on northern Vancouver Island had so far been spared the smallpox that devastated other Aboriginal communities, Simpson pleaded with the chief to allow the tribe's children to be vaccinated.

Simpson's main goal was to determine the profit potential west of the Rockies. The area at the mouth of the Columbia River, an arterial waterway that today divides the American states of Washington and Oregon, attracted rival American and British traders in the early nineteenth century. The overland American Lewis and Clark expedition of 1804–1806 had spurred growing interest in the United States. The Convention of 1818 had allowed for joint British and American occupation of the territory between the Rockies and the Strait of Georgia, and by the 1820s, the Columbia River emerged as the unofficial dividing line between British and American activities. The HBC was not altogether convinced that trade in the Columbia River area was worthwhile—not least because malaria was frequent and vessels were apt to founder on sandbars at the river estuary—but the British Foreign Office insisted a presence be maintained on the north shore to strengthen any possible claim. Fort Vancouver, the site of present-day Vancouver, Washington, was established there in 1825. Simpson continued to hope that the Fraser River would prove a viable trade route; the establishment of Fort Langley on the lower Fraser River in 1827 reflected this optimism.

Simpson placed the management of Fort Langley in the hands of Archibald McDonald, who had led a group of Selkirk's Scottish settlers to Red River in 1813 and joined the HBC several years later. McDonald married Princess Sunday (Koale Koa), the daughter of a prominent west-coast Chinook chief, but she died soon afterward in childbirth. Their son, Ranald MacDonald (father and son spelled their names differently), raised by his

1827: Hudson's Bay Company establishes Fort Langley on the Fraser River.

Fort Langley, established on the lower Fraser River in 1827, has been preserved as a historic site.

Source: Image © 2008, www.settestudio.com.

1830s: HBC establishes more northerly west-coast trading posts.

Chinook aunts, would go on to live a life of great adventure: at age 24 he travelled with a whaling vessel to Japan where he taught English to Japanese officials in an era when most foreigners were barred entry into Japan.

From Fort Langley, Archibald McDonald tackled the perennial problem of the fort's reliance on imported European supplies. He began a vigorous trade in salmon, procured from the Natives and dried or preserved in locally made barrels. Salmon preserved at Fort Langley found markets as far away as Hawaii and Japan. Hawaii, then known as the Sandwich Islands, was a key source of the salt needed for salmon preservation. The islands also supplied hundreds of workers, known as Kanakas, whom the HBC brought to the Pacific Northwest as a more cost-effective alternative to Scottish and Canadian employees. McDonald's spirit of initiative impressed Simpson and lent new purpose to Fort Langley. Simpson, after a hair-raising journey through the Fraser River canyon, had ruefully conceded that "Frazers River can no longer be thought of as a practicable communication with the interior; it was never wholly passed by water before, and in all probability never will again."[48]

The Hudson's Bay Company took aim at their American rivals by establishing trading posts along the northern coast: Fort Simpson in 1831 at the mouth of the Nass River, just south of the Alaska panhandle, and Fort McLoughlin in 1833 further south on the mainland coast just across from the southern tip of the Queen Charlotte Islands (Haida Gwaii). The launching of the wood-burning steamship SS Beaver in 1836 further expanded trade. This paddlewheel steamer was able to enter narrow waterways and won for the HBC the contract to provision Russian posts. In 1839, Simpson successfully negotiated a lease of the Alaska panhandle from the Russians for the HBC.

The HBC's 1840 launch of a subsidiary, the Puget Sound Agricultural Company, posed another potential threat to American interests. The company imported large numbers of sheep and cattle for grazing into an area that had been suddenly depopulated a few years before. A devastating malaria epidemic in 1830–33 wiped out more than 75 percent of the Aboriginal population in the area south of the lower Columbia River. Yet the settlement of the Puget Sound would ultimately strengthen American, rather than British, claims to the area.

John McLoughlin, chief factor at Fort Vancouver, gave a warm welcome to American pioneer farmers, even extending generous credit terms for seed and implements, a policy that horrified the parsimonious Simpson. The Scottish-born McLoughlin, who apprenticed with a medical doctor at age 14, and himself qualified as a physician at 19, was a formidable force at Fort Vancouver. Standing six foot four inches tall, with a shock of white hair that inspired the Natives to call him Pee-kin, "the white-headed eagle of the whites," McLoughlin was perhaps more American than British in his attitudes; he later became an American citizen and is celebrated as the "father of Oregon." McLoughlin admired the Canadian rebels of 1837–38 and applauded their stand against "despotism." Hudson Bay Company governor George Simpson noted in his "character book" that McLoughlin's "violent temper and turbulent disposition" would make him "a Radical in

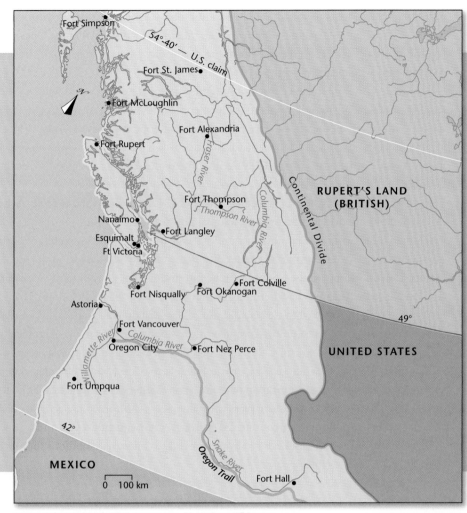

Map 9.2
HBC fur trading posts in the northwest, mid-nineteenth century.

Source: Colonies, Canada 1867, Bercuson, p. 78. McGraw-Hill Ryerson.

any Country—under any Government and under any circumstances." A young Oxford-educated Anglican minister, Herbert Beaver, sent to Fort Vancouver in 1836, was quick to learn about McLoughlin's temper. When Reverend Beaver made the mistake of denigrating McLoughlin's country-born wife, Marguerite Waddens, as "a female of notoriously loose character," McLoughlin administered a sound thrashing in the public courtyard.[49]

Perhaps anticipating that the area surrounding the Columbia River would fall into American hands, George Simpson directed the establishment of a new HBC fort on the southern tip of Vancouver Island. The building of Fort Camosun, later renamed Fort Victoria, was commenced in 1843. James Douglas, sent to establish the HBC presence there, enthused that the site was a perfect Eden.

Simpson's reservations about long-term British control of the area proved correct: within a few years, American policy toward the Pacific Northwest became more bellicose. Democratic presidential candidate James Polk fought a vigorous election campaign in 1844 on the platform "Fifty-four forty or Fight!" The northern latitude of 54°40' was the

1843: Hudson's Bay Company extends operations to Vancouver Island with the establishment of Fort Victoria.

beginning of the Alaska panhandle and the southernmost limit of Russian territory (see Map 9.2). Exponents of "manifest destiny" in the United States insisted that the American flag was one day destined to fly over the entire North American continent, and viewed control of the whole Pacific Northwest as inevitable.

Fortunately, the Americans chose not to fight—they were preoccupied with war on another front. Having recently annexed the former Mexican possession of Texas, by 1846 the Americans were in the midst of war with their neighbour to the south. The prospect of simultaneous hostilities with Britain was too much even for an expansionist president like Polk, and by the terms of the 1846 Oregon Treaty the Americans agreed to set the boundary at the 49th parallel.

As in the case of the Ashburton–Webster Treaty of 1842, suspicions abounded that the British had not pursued justice for their colonial possession as vigorously as they might have done. John Gordon, a naval officer and brother to British foreign secretary Lord Aberdeen, sent to investigate the area under dispute, reportedly dismissed it as worthless. Finding salmon fishing on the Columbia to be inferior to what he enjoyed in Scotland, Gordon allegedly declared that there was no value in a river where the salmon would not rise to take a fly. Yet even those who did not believe Britain had abandoned colonial claims on such a light pretext pointed out that the new boundary was not geographically logical: the Columbia River formed the natural boundary, and was the simplest means of gaining inland access. With that river in American hands, the Coast Mountain range posed a formidable barrier to communication with the colony's interior. The practical difficulties would prove enormous in future years when engineers confronted the geographical challenge of constructing a transcontinental railway. As subsequent events would show, the conclusion of the treaty did not finally put an end to American ambitions for more territory in the Pacific Northwest.

1846: The Oregon Treaty sets the border at the 49th parallel in the Pacific Northwest.

Sir John Franklin and Northern Exploration

The increase in British activity on North America's Pacific coast in the first half of the nineteenth century gave fresh impetus to a long-cherished dream of finding a Northwest Passage from the Atlantic to the Pacific Ocean. Such a route would shave months from the tortuous journey around Cape Horn or across the pestilential Isthmus of Panama. It would also be a means of consolidating Britain's claims to the Pacific coast in the face of growing American interest. All earlier explorations had ended in failure. At the end of the Napoleonic Wars in 1815, members of the British Admiralty saw Arctic exploration as a worthy pursuit for naval officers left idle by the peace. Two expeditions launched in 1818, under Commander John Ross and Commander David Buchan, had to be abandoned when they encountered impenetrable ice north of Spitsbergen. The following year, William Parry's expedition was able to sail through Lancaster Sound almost as far west as the 114th meridian. Not only was Parry able to boast that all but one of his crew of 94 remained in robust health, relying entirely on provisions they had brought with them, but the expedition earned a reward of £5000 offered by the British Crown to anyone able to traverse further west through the Arctic than 110° longitude. Parry's successful organization became a model for future Arctic expeditions; he had kept up the morale of his crew with musical and theatrical entertainments, classes, hunting parties, scientific observation, and even a weekly newsletter.

Concurrent with Parry's voyage was an overland expedition led by John Franklin. The Franklin party was to travel overland from York Factory on the Hudson Bay to chart the north coast of North America east of the mouth of the Coppermine River. John Franklin had already been part of the abortive 1818 Arctic expedition. This was by no means the first of his adventures. He had joined the navy at the age of 12, saw action in Admiral Nelson's famous victory at the 1801 Battle of Copenhagen, and by 16 was en route to Australia with his uncle, under whose tutelage Franklin learned navigation. On the return voyage from Sydney, their ship was wrecked on a reef and the crew spent six weeks stranded on a sandbar before being rescued by a merchant ship that took them to China. Franklin served as a midshipman on the *Bellerophon,* overseeing flag signals for the vessel during the critical 1805 Battle of Trafalgar. He was wounded in action during the 1814–1815 Battle of New Orleans, and returned home to peace and to reduced circumstances as a half-pay officer.

Franklin's 1819 mission to explore the Arctic coastline posed a number of problems: only two Europeans had previously sighted the territory he would be travelling—Samuel Hearne and Alexander Mackenzie, in separate eighteenth-century expeditions. He would be forced to rely on the assistance of traders of the Hudson's Bay Company and North West Company, who were then at the height of an acrimonious trade war. Franklin was unable to secure transport from the HBC for some of his supplies, and shortages ensured that his mission would be plagued by hunger and poor morale. The expedition travelled by heavily laden boat from York Factory to Cumberland House along the fur trade route. As most of the party wintered at Cumberland House, Franklin led a small group on snowshoes to Fort Chipewan in search of more information about the area.

The two parties met up in the spring and, by August 1820, reached Winter Lake, north of Great Slave Lake. Any goodwill Franklin had with the Natives, voyageurs, and traders was steadily eroded as quarrels erupted over short supplies. At last able to secure transport of their abandoned supplies from York Factory, the expedition continued down to the mouth of the Coppermine River. The success of the mission depended upon the cooperation of the Inuit, but the local people took alarm at the party's approach. By late summer 1821, with supplies exhausted, their canoes too damaged to travel in icy seas, and 10 of the party dead—nine of hunger or exposure and one shot for cannibalism—a discouraged Franklin was forced to turn back. They returned to England in the autumn of 1822. Hudson's Bay Company governor George Simpson contemptuously blamed the mission's failure on Franklin's physical limitations, sneering that Franklin was the sort of man who insisted on three meals a day washed down with regular cups of tea.

Simpson's assessment was clearly unfair: even after such an ordeal, Franklin did not shrink from beginning to organize a fresh expedition within the year. By the time the mission was launched early in 1825, Franklin had married and become the father of a baby girl. Sadly, news of his wife's death reached him as he landed at New York. Despite that inauspicious start, Franklin's 1825–1827 expedition, much better planned than the first, was able to chart 640 kilometres of the Arctic shore.

Upon his return, Franklin was much feted in British and continental society. His two published narratives of his journeys raised his profile, and he was knighted and received an honorary doctorate from Oxford University and a gold medal from the Société de Géographie de Paris. He also remarried. After another stint of naval service, he accepted a post as governor of Van Diemen's Land, where he arrived with Lady Franklin in 1837 to succeed Sir George Arthur, who was headed to Upper Canada.

By 1845, renewed British interest in the Northwest Passage provided Franklin with the opportunity to try again at the age of 58. He persuaded the Admiralty to entrust him with command of a new expedition. Two steam-powered vessels with iron-reinforced hulls, the *Erebus* and the *Terror*, carried a crew of 134, along with every imaginable necessity, including tinned food, which was a new innovation. First developed in 1811, the process was not yet very practical for ordinary purposes, as each can had to be produced by hand and could only be opened with a hammer and chisel. But to Franklin, who remembered the starvation and misery of his 1820s mission, the technology must have seemed a godsend. He laid in a supply of thousands of tins of food, enough to last at least three years. Franklin's objective was to chart the remaining area of the mainland coast between where he had explored earlier and where two HBC traders, Peter Warren Dease and Thomas Simpson, had mapped. Whalers in northern Baffin Bay encountered Franklin's party setting out late in July 1845. They were the last to see them alive.

The disappearance of Franklin's expedition was one of the great mysteries of the Victorian age. Between 1847 and 1859, some 30 separate search missions were launched. The British Admiralty offered a reward of £20 000, and Lady Franklin travelled the Empire, keeping the cause of her husband's rescue prominent in the public mind. From York Factory, Letitia Mactavish Hargrave, wife of the chief factor, noted that while the HBC traders kept up a façade of encouragement for the Admiralty's search, they privately laughed at the idea of anyone undertaking such a futile plan. Hope dimmed with the 1850

1845: Sir John Franklin's Arctic expedition vanishes.

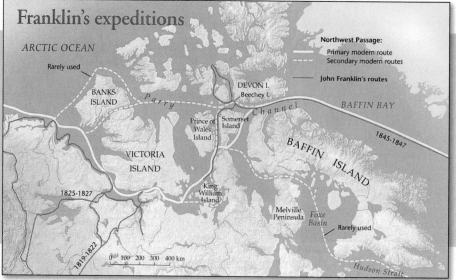

Map 9.3
Arctic exploration.

Source: Map courtesy of Canadian Geographic.

discovery by Inuit hunters of the mutilated bodies of 30 men; worse, the remaining evidence pointed to cannibalism. The discovery in 1859 of more human remains and relics of the expedition, including notebooks, confirmed the worst fears. While Franklin's body was not found, the notes confirmed that he died aboard his ship in 1847 and that the survivors abandoned the ice-locked vessels.

University of Alberta anthropologists, still fascinated by the Franklin mystery, exhumed some of the bodies in 1984 and 1986, and, besides detecting scurvy, raised the new theory that the lead solder used to seal up the tins of food used on the expedition may have been a factor in the explorers' deaths. Further analysis of more remains in the 1990s confirmed elevated lead levels. The lead poisoning theory, while by no means universally accepted, might also explain some of the bizarre behaviour of the Arctic castaways in their final months: relics found reveal that the weakened and starving men burdened themselves with all manner of unnecessary tools, soap, towels, slippers, and other sundry items as they trekked overland. Unfortunately, the macabre details of the final days of Franklin's crew deflect attention from the explorer's tangible achievements. By charting unknown territory, Sir John Franklin added more to the coastal map of what would later be Canada than any other explorer, except for George Vancouver. Still, the key objective had not succeeded: no Northwest Passage was found that would enable Britain to consolidate her hold on the imperial periphery beyond the Rocky Mountains.

Skulls of members of the Franklin expedition.

Source: Library and Archives Canada, PA-147732.

Conclusion

In the middle decades of the nineteenth century, Britain was about to enter into a new era of empire. The settlement of the looming boundary questions in North America that had complicated Anglo–American relations had been resolved—even if the settlements were not as generous as some colonists might have wished. The resolution of border questions for New Brunswick and then the Pacific coast brought a new, if temporary, security to international relations. Cathcart was recalled as governor in chief of British North America, his military credentials no longer being the most important qualification for office. A fresh administrative approach would be needed as centuries of mercantilist doctrine was dismantled and a shift to free trade would inaugurate a new theory of colonial governance. The colonies of Nova Scotia, and then Canada, would in 1848 be at the vanguard of an experiment that would someday culminate in the Commonwealth of Nations. The goals of reformers like Howe, Baldwin, and La Fontaine would at last be achieved. For the united Canadas, violence and the flames of destruction punctuated this critical transition.

Questions to Consider

1. What key concerns did authorities have about the restoration of order after the 1837–38 rebellions?

2. What were the key features of the Durham Report?

3. What factors inspired the 1840 Act of Union, and how did Canadian reformers respond to it?

4. Why were some reformers critical of La Fontaine's alliance with reformers in Canada West?

Critical Thinking Questions

1. How do you assess the official response to the rebellions? Was it just? Was it effective?

2. How successfully did Britain protect the interests of its North American colonies in treaty negotiations with the Americans? What factors had to be taken into consideration?

3. How might you explain the fascination with the lost Franklin expedition?

Suggested Readings
Primary Sources

Ajzenstat, Janet, and Gerald M. Craig, eds. *Lord Durham's Report*, new ed. Montreal and Kingston: McGill-Queen's University Press, 2006.

Buller, Charles. "Responsible Government for Colonies" in *Charles Buller and Responsible Government*, E.M. Wrong, ed. Oxford: Clarendon Press, 1926.

Cole, Jean M., ed. *This Blessed Wilderness: Archibald McDonald's Letters from the Columbia, 1822–44*. Vancouver: University of British Columbia Press, 2001.

Franklin, Sir John. *Sir John Franklin's Journals and Correspondence: The first Arctic Land Expedition, 1819–1822.* Richard C. Davis, ed. Toronto: The Champlain Society, 1995. Available online in Champlain Society Digital Collection, http://eir.library.utoronto. ca/champlain/search.cfm.

Franklin, Sir John. *Sir John Franklin's Journals and Correspondence: The Second Arctic Land Expedition, 1825–1827.* Richard C. Davis, ed. Toronto: The Champlain Society, 1998. Available online in Champlain Society Digital Collection, http://eir.library. utoronto.ca/champlain/search.cfm.

Godsell, Patricia, ed. *The Diary of Jane Ellice.* Toronto: Oberon Press, 1975.

Greenwood, F. Murray, ed./trans. *Land of a Thousand Sorrows: The Australian Prison Journal, 1840–2 of the Exiled Canadien Patriote, François-Maurice Lapailleur.* Vancouver: University of British Columbia Press, 1980.

Hargraves, James. *The Hargrave Correspondence, 1821–1843.* G.P. de T. Glazebrook, ed. Toronto: The Champlain Society, 1938. Available online in Champlain Society Digital Collection, http://eir.library.utoronto.ca/champlain/search.cfm.

Hargraves, Letitia. *The Letters of Letitia Hargrave.* Margaret Arnett MacLeod, ed. Toronto: The Champlain Society, 1947. Available online in Champlain Society Digital Collection, http://eir.library.utoronto.ca/champlain/search.cfm.

Knaplund, Paul, ed. *Letters from Lord Sydenham, Governor-General of Canada, 1839–1841, to Lord John Russell.* Clifton, NJ: Augustus M. Kelley, 1973.

Little, J.L., ed. *The Child Letters: Public and Private Life in a Canadian Merchant Politician's Family, 1841–1845.* Montreal and Kingston: McGill-Queen's University Press, 1995.

McLoughlin, John. *The Letters of John McLoughlin from Fort Vancouver to the Governor and Committee: First Series, 1825–38.* E.E. Rich, ed. Toronto: The Champlain Society, 1941. Available online in Champlain Society Digital Collection, http://eir.library. utoronto.ca/champlain/search.cfm.

McLoughlin, John. *The Letters of John McLoughlin from Fort Vancouver to the Governor and Committee: Second Series, 1839–44.* E.E. Rich, ed. Toronto: The Champlain Society, 1943. Available online in Champlain Society Digital Collection.

McLoughlin, John. *The Letters of John McLoughlin from Fort Vancouver to the Governor and Committee: Third Series, 1844–46.* E.E. Rich, ed. Toronto: The Champlain Society, 1944. Available online in Champlain Society Digital Collection, http://eir. library.utoronto.ca/champlain/search.cfm.

Maclachlan, Morag. *The Fort Langley Journals, 1827–30.* Vancouver: University of British Columbia Press, 1998.

Useful Overview Sources

Barman, Jean. *The West Beyond the West: A History of British Columbia.* Toronto: University of Toronto Press, 1991.

Buckner, Phillip and John Reid, eds. *The Atlantic Region to Confederation: A History.* Toronto: University of Toronto Press, 1994.

Careless, J.M.S. *The Union of the Canadas: The Growth of Canadian Institutions, 1841–1857.* Toronto: McClelland & Stewart, 1967.

Mackie, Richard Somerset. *Trading Beyond the Mountains: The British Fur Trade on the Pacific, 1793–1843.* Vancouver: University of British Columbia Press, 1997.

MacNutt, W. S. *New Brunswick: A History, 1784–1867.* Toronto: Macmillan, 1963.

MacNutt, W.S. *The Atlantic Provinces: The Emergence of Colonial Society, 1712–1857.* Toronto: McClelland & Stewart, 1965.

Morrell, W.P. *British Colonial Policy in the Age of Peel and Russell.* London: Frank Cass & Co, 1966.

Ouellet, Fernand. *Lower Canada, 1791–1840: Social Change and Nationalism.* Toronto: McClelland & Stewart, 1980.

Special Topics

Ajzenstat, Janet. *The Political Thought of Lord Durham.* Montreal and Kingston: McGill-Queen's University Press, 1988.

Barman, Jean, and Bruce McIntyre Watson. *Leaving Paradise: Indigenous Hawaiians in the Pacific Northwest, 1787–1898.* Honolulu: University of Hawai'i Press, 2006.

Boissery, Beverley. *A Deep Sense of Wrong: The Treason, Trials, and Transportation to New South Wales of Lower Canadian Rebels after the 1838 Rebellion.* Toronto: Osgoode Society, 1995.

Boyd, Robert. "Commentary on Early Contact-Era Smallpox in the Pacific Northwest." *Ethnohistory* 43 (Spring 1996): 307–328.

Buckner, P.A. and David Frank, eds. *The Acadiensis Reader: Atlantic Canada before Confederation.* Fredericton: Acadiensis Press, 1988.

Carroll, Francis M. *A Good and Wise Measure: The Search for the Canadian–American Boundary, 1783–1842.* Toronto: University of Toronto Press, 2001.

Cooper, Leonard. *Radical Jack: The Life of John George Lambton, First Earl of Durham.* London: Cresset Press, 1959.

Dictionary of Canadian Biography. Online at http://www.biographi.ca. Contains detailed scholarly articles on all of the key figures.

Ducharme, Michel. "L'état selon Lord Durham Liberté et Nationalité dans l'Empire Britannique" *cahiers d'historire.* Université de Montreal (Fall 1998): 39–63.

Eldridge, C.C., ed. *Kith and Kin: Canada, Britain and the United States from the Revolution to the Cold War.* Cardiff: University of Wales Press, 1997.

Fryer, Mary Beacock. *Volunteers and Redcoats, Rebels and Raiders: A Military History of the Rebellions in Upper Canada.* Toronto: Dundurn, 1987.

Gibson, James R. "Smallpox on the Northwest Coast, 1835–1838." *BC Studies* 56 (Winter 1982–1983): 61–81.

Glazebrook, G.P. de T. *Sir Charles Bagot in Canada.* London: Oxford University Press, 1929.

Greer, Allan. "The Birth of the Police in Canada" in *Colonial Leviathan: State Formation in Mid-Nineteenth Century Canada.* Toronto: University of Toronto Press, 1992, 17–49.

Leacock, Stephen. *Baldwin, La Fontaine, Hincks: Responsible Government.* Toronto: Morang, 1910.

Martin, Ged. *The Durham Report and British Policy: A Critical Essay.* Cambridge: Cambridge University Press, 1972.

Martin, Ged. "Attacking the Durham Myth: Seventeen Years on" *Journal of Canadian Studies* 25 (Spring 1990), 39–59.

Monet, Jacques. *The Last Cannon Shot: A Study of French-Canadian Nationalism, 1837–1850.* Toronto: University of Toronto Press, 1964.

Morgan, Cecilia. *Public Men and Virtuous Women: The Gendered Languages of Religion and Politics in Upper Canada, 1791–1850.* Toronto: University of Toronto Press, 1996.

New, Chester. *Lord Durham's Mission to Canada.* Toronto: McClelland & Stewart, 1963.

Radforth, Ian. "Sydenham and Utilitarian Reform" in *Colonial Leviathan: State Formation in Mid-Nineteenth-Century Canada.* Allan Greer and Ian Radforth, eds. Toronto: University of Toronto Press, 1992, 64–102.

Read, Colin. "The Short Hills Raid of June, 1838, and Its Aftermath," *Ontario History* 68 (June 1976): 93–115.

Reimer, Chad. "Borders of the Past: The Oregon Boundary Dispute and the Beginnings of Northwest Historiography" in *Parallel Destinies: Canadian-American Relations West of the Rockies.* John M. Findlay and Ken S. Coates, eds. Montreal and Kingston: McGill-Queen's University Press, 2002, 221–245.

Saul, John Ralston. *Reflections of a Siamese Twin: Canada at the End of the Twentieth Century.* Toronto: Penguin, 1997.

Notes

[1] As quoted in Cole Harris, "Voices of Disaster: Smallpox around the Strait of Georgia in 1782," *Ethnohistory* 41 (Fall 1994).

[2] Quotation from *The Times* is from Ged Martin, *The Durham Report and British Policy: A Critical Essay* (Cambridge: Cambridge University Press, 1972), 15; Ged Martin, "Attacking the Durham Myth: Seventeen Years on," *Journal of Canadian Studies* 25 (Spring 1990), 50–51; Chester New, *Lord Durham's Mission to Canada* (Toronto: McClelland & Stewart, 1963).

[3] Bruce Curtis, "The 'Most Splendid Pageant Ever Seen': Grandeur, the Domestic, and Condescension in Lord Durham's Political Theatre," *Canadian Historical Review* 89 (March 2008): 55–88.

[4] Chester New, *Lord Durham's Mission to Canada*, 166.

[5] As quoted in Chester New, *Lord Durham's Mission to Canada*, 59, 69, 43, 50.

[6] F. Murray Greenwood and Barry Wright, "Introduction: Rebellion, Invasion, and the Crisis of the Colonial State in the Canadas, 1837–9," *Canadian State Trials: Rebellion and Invasion in the Canadas, 1837–1838*, F. Murray and Barry Wright, eds., Vol 2. (Toronto: Osgoode Law Society, 2002), 3, 25–26. The statutes may be read in Appendix D of this work.

[7] A.V. Dicey, *An Introduction to the Study of the Law of the Constitution* (London: Macmillan, 1965), 215.

[8] F. Murray Greenwood and Barry Wright, *Canadian State Trials*, 26.

[9] Colin Read, "The Short Hills Raid of June, 1838, and Its Aftermath," *Ontario History* 68 (June 1976): 93–115.

[10] See Cassandra Pybus, "Patriot Exiles in Van Diemen's Land," *Canadian State Trials*, II, 188–204. See also Barry Wright, "The Kingston and London Courts Martial," *Canadian State Trials*, II, 130–159.

[11] As quoted in Colin Read, "The Short Hills Raid," 106–107.

[12] Steven Watt, "State Trial by Legislature: The Special Council of Lower Canada, 1838–41," *Canadian State Trials*, 253, 255.

[13] As quoted in Leonard Cooper, *Radical Jack: The Life of John George Lambton, First Earl of Durham* (London: Cresset Press, 1959), 243.

[14] As quoted in Chester New, *Lord Durham's Mission*, 104, 88.

[15] As quoted in Leonard Cooper, *Radical Jack*, 268.

[16] F. Murray Greenwood and Barry Wright, *Canadian State Trials*, 15.

[17] Gerald Tulchinsky, *Taking Root: The Origins of the Canadian Jewish Community* (Lebanon, NH: University Press of New England for Brandeis University Press, 1993), 37.

[18] Ibid., 27–28, 37.

[19] Matthieu Sossoyan, "The Iroquois and the Lower-Canadian Rebellions, 1837–1838," Department of Anthropology, McGill University, Montréal, July 1999.

[20] Lord Durham, *Report on the Affairs of British North America*, Gerald M. Craig, ed. (Toronto: McClelland & Stewart, 1963), 139–142.

[21] Charles Buller, "Responsible Government for Colonies" in *Charles Buller and Responsible Government*, E.M. Wrong, ed. (Oxford: Clarendon Press, 1926), 93.

[22] Durham Report, 79–80, 94–95.

[23] Durham Report, 50, 22–25, 146.

[24] Janet Ajzenstat, *The Political Thought of Lord Durham* (Montreal and Kingston: McGill-Queen's University Press, 1988), 4–12.

[25] As quoted in Ged Martin, *The Durham Report*, 36.

[26] Durham Report, 147.

[27] C. Poulett Thomson to Lord John Russell, private, 23 January 1840, in Paul Knaplund, ed. *Letters from Lord Sydenham, Governor General of Canada, 1839–1841 to Lord John Russell* (Clifton, NJ: Augustus M. Kelley, 1973), 44.

28 Allan Greer, The Patriots and the People: The Rebellion of 1837 in Rural Lower Canada (Toronto: University of Toronto Press, 1993), 356–357.

29 Phillip Buckner, "Charles Edward Poulett Thoson, 1rst Baron Sydenham," *Dictionary of Canadian Biography*, http://www.biographi.ca.

30 Ibid.

31 Michael S. Cross and Robert L. Fraser, "The Waste That Lies before Me," 169, 177. See also Robert L. Fraser, "Robert Baldwin" *Dictionary of Canadian Biography*, http://www.biographi.ca.

32 As quoted in Jacques Monet, "Louis-Hippolyte La Fontaine," *Dictionary of Canadian Biography*, http://www.biographi.ca.

33 Lord John Russell to Poulett Thomson, 14 October 1839, and Lord John Russell to Poulett Thomson, 16 October 1839, in W.P.M. Kennedy, ed. *Statutes, Treaties and Documents of the Canadian Constitution, 1713–1929*, 2nd ed. (Toronto: Oxford University Press, 1930), 421–423.

34 Ibid., Poulett Thomson to a Friend, 12 December 1839, 430.

35 John Ralston Saul, *Reflections of a Siamese Twin: Canada at the End of the Twentieth Century* (Toronto: Penguin, 1997), 177; quoted passage: Louis-Hippolyte La Fontaine in Jacques Monet, "Louis-Hippolyte La Fontaine" *Dictionary of Canadian Biography*, http://www.biographi.ca.

36 J.M.S. Careless, *Union of the Canadas*, 44; Lord Seaton's words are quoted in Phillip Buckner, "Charles Edward Poulett Thomson, first Baron Sydenham" *Dictionary of Canadian Biography*, http://www.biographi.ca.

37 C. Poulett Thomson to Lord John Russell, private, 10 April 1841, in Paul Knaplund, ed., *Letters from Lord Sydenham, Governor General of Canada, 1839–1841 to Lord John Russell* (Clifton, NJ: Augustus M. Kelley, 1973), 130.

38 J.M.S. Careless, *Union of the Canadas*, 40.

39 Sydenham to Russell, private, 27 June 1841 in Knaplund, ed., *Letters from Lord Sydenham*, 145.

40 As quoted in J.M.S. Careless, *Union of the Canadas*, 53.

41 As quoted in *Canada: A People's History*. Episode 7, "Rebellion and Reform," http://history.cbc.ca/history.

42 Bagot to Stanley, 26 September 1842, *Statutes, Treaties and Documents*, 478–482; Bagot to Stanley, 28 October 1842, as quoted in W.P. Morrell, *British Colonial Policy in the Age of Peel and Russell* (London: Frank Cass & Co, 1966), 56.

43 Metcalfe, as quoted in Jacques Monet, *The Last Cannon Shot: A Study of French-Canadian Nationalism, 1837–1850* (Toronto: University of Toronto Press, 1964), 137; Metcalfe to Stanley, 5 August 1843, *Statutes, Treaties and Documents*, 489–493.

44 M.E. Chamberlain, "Canadian Boundaries in Anglo-American Relations," *Kith and Kin: Canada, Britain and the United States from the Revolution to the Cold War*, C.C. Eldridge, ed. (Cardiff: University of Wales Press, 1997), 51. See also W.S. MacNutt, *The Atlantic Provinces: The Emergence of Colonial Society, 1712–1857* (Toronto: McClelland & Stewart, 1965), 216–217.

45 Sydenham to Russell, private, 25 May 1841, *Letters from Lord Sydenham*, 138–139.

46 Richard Jebb, *Studies in Colonial Nationalism* (London: Edward Arnold, 1905), 20.

47 Cole Harris, "Voices of Disaster: Smallpox around the Strait of Georgia in 1782," *Ethnohistory* 41 (Fall 1994), 604.

48 As quoted in Margaret Ormsby, *British Columbia: A History* (Toronto: MacMillan, 1971), 65.

49 W. Kaye Lamb, "John McLoughlin" *Dictionary of Canadian Biography*, http://www.biographi.ca; Stephen Woolworth, "The School is under my Direction: The Politics of Education at Fort Vancouver, 1836–1838," *Oregon Historical Quarterly* 104 (Summer 2003), http://www.historycooperative.org/journals/ohq/104.2/woolworth.html. It is noteworthy that Marguerite Waddens's father was Jean-Étienne Waddens, one of the men purported to have been killed by early fur trader and western explorer Peter Pond (see Chapter 6).

The Hinge *of the* Imperial Relationship: *1846–1849*

*B*ryan Prior rented a five-acre (two-hectare) plot in Drumreilly, County Leitrim. This holding was comparatively large for an Irish tenant's farm, three or four times the size of most, suggesting Prior was somewhat prosperous. But the potato crop failed in 1845 and again in 1846, and by the spring of 1847, two successive years of no harvests left Prior destitute. His rent in arrears, his family without food, Prior grasped desperately at a solution offered by his landlord's agent: if the family would vacate their land and cottage, the landlord would pay their passage to North America, and they could start again in a new land, as so many others were doing. With work crews standing ready to pull down the cottage, Prior gave his consent, his wife and four children standing watching in the field. As the cottage crumbled, the agent made some calculations, and announced that the value of the land was only sufficient to cover the cost of one passage. It was quite expensive enough to send him, Prior was told, and he might be thankful for it. Prior agonized over the decision, finally accepting passage for himself. He was shipped to Quebec, the heavy knowledge weighing on him that, for all he knew, his wife and children were now starving and homeless in Ireland.[1]

Burning of the parliament buildings, Montreal, 1849.

Introduction

The rebellions of the 1830s had failed and the two Canadas had been forced into an uneasy union, a union aimed at the assimilation of French Canada. Moderate and constructive reform elements, led by two unlikely leaders—the melancholic and withdrawn Robert Baldwin and the brilliant but diffident Louis-Hippolyte La Fontaine—struggled to achieve responsible government for Canada. A series of hostile or ambivalent governors in the united Canadas, and a fundamental resistance in the British cabinet to the notion of colonial self-government frustrated their efforts. Yet sentiment was shifting in Britain after decades of mercantilist doctrine. Free trade would become the lodestar of Britain's new economic and political policy.

At first, this shift would be cataclysmic in its effect on British North America's economy, and all of the staples that buttressed colonial prosperity would see their protected markets swept away as tariffs tumbled down. This global change affected the Caribbean sugar islands, dealing a blow to Nova Scotia shipping interests, and dramatically undercut markets for British North American wood and wheat. Even as the colonies struggled to recover, an unprecedented surge of immigration strained resources to the breaking point. Black '47—the peak year of the devastating Irish potato famine—brought more than 90 000 immigrants to British North America. Contagious diseases carried by hunger-weakened victims of the famine stalked the port cities of Quebec and Montreal, and thousands fell dead of cholera, typhus, and other illnesses. Amid this misery, warehouses full of unsold wheat convinced Canadian merchants that Britain had abandoned them.

Nevertheless, along with free trade came a new willingness in Britain to permit the colonies the privilege of governing themselves. In Nova Scotia, Joseph Howe had long been working toward this goal; that colony became the first in the British Empire to win self-government in internal matters. Lord Elgin's arrival in Canada in 1847 signalled the beginning of a new era for that colony and the realization of Baldwin and La Fontaine's goal. But those who had previously enjoyed the perquisites of privilege vented their frustrated rage in an attack on Montreal's parliament buildings. The Tory Rebellion of 1849 saw the legislature consumed by flames in a futile bid to hold back the tide of reform and the beginning of a new era.

British Abandonment of Imperial Protection

A momentous political and economic change was sweeping Britain in the mid-nineteenth century, and the impact on its North American colonies would be profound. Britain's overseas colonies owed their very foundation to the widespread doctrine of mercantilism, an economic theory practised by all the great European colonial powers since the seventeenth century. Mercantilism was not a single system, but many complex interrelated laws regulating trade. The idea was that a nation could only be enriched at the expense of rivals, and the goal was to prevent the outflow of currency to other countries through a system of protective tariffs. Colonies played an important role in this system, benefiting the mother country by supplying such goods as could not be produced domestically—ensuring that these would not have to be bought from competing nations—and serving as a market for its manufactured goods. In concert with these protective tariffs, Britain's Navigation Laws restricted the carrying of most cargoes to British or British colonial ships, also ensuring that the merchant marine would be a nursery for sailors for the Royal Navy.

In the West Indies, or Caribbean islands, Britain's theory of mercantilism achieved almost perfect expression. These sugar-producing islands became a main source of overseas revenue for Britain. In the late eighteenth century, Prime Minister William Pitt (the younger) estimated that four-fifths of Britain's overseas income originated in the West Indies. While British preferential tariffs made this activity profitable, it was the cancer of slavery that made it possible. An estimated 2 million Africans had been shipped across the Atlantic to British colonies between 1680 and 1786.

Merchants in Britain's American colonies had filled the vital role of provisioning the sugar islands, but after the American Revolution the new republic of the United States was severed from Britain's closed mercantilist network. Nova Scotian merchants rushed to fill the gap, carrying preserved fish to feed the slave populations of the Caribbean, and British North American timber, and taking cargoes of molasses away to be processed into sugar or rum. The lucrative privilege of continuing to trade in the British West Indies was in itself a powerful incentive to loyalism among New England traders during the American Revolution.

1833: Britain abolishes slavery.

In 1833, the privileged world of Britain's Caribbean planters was dealt a blow with the abolition of slavery. Decades of work towards emancipation, much of it spearheaded by Quakers (the Society of Friends) and Methodists, educated Britons on the evils of slavery. The abolition of the slave trade in 1807 had not freed those already in bondage, and had prompted a new evil as outlaw slave traders, subject to a £100 fine per slave found on board their vessels, were known to throw their captives overboard when threatened with detection. Evangelical Christian William Wilberforce led the fight for abolition in Britain's House of Commons, aided by a burgeoning humanitarian movement. Susanna Moodie, who was soon to take up residence in Canada, contributed her talents to the cause; her narrative of the life of Ashton Warner, a 24-year-old slave in St. Vincent, is a moving indictment of the system.

Yet the long-awaited dawn of freedom in Britain's empire brought far-reaching economic consequences. It is hardly surprising that the Caribbean colonies, raised to wealth on the lacerated backs of the enslaved, should suffer a cataclysmic decline in its fortunes. When emancipated slaves had finished serving the four-year "apprenticeship" dictated by law, they—unsurprisingly—fled the scene of their oppression, disinclined to work for wages for their former masters when squatting on vacant land was an attractive alternative. Victorian essayist Thomas Carlyle sneered at the image of "our beautiful black darlings … sitting yonder with their beautiful muzzles up to the ears in pumpkins, imbibing sweet pulps and juices … while the sugar crops rot around them uncut, because labour cannot be hired, so cheap are the pumpkins."[2]

Another blow to the colonial economy was still to come. In 1846, Britain's Parliament, under Conservative Prime Minister Sir Robert Peel, voted for the elimination of the protective tariffs on British colonial sugar. Free trade sentiment in Britain had increasingly dictated that lower prices for consumers at home was a higher priority than the subsidization of the profits of merchants overseas through artificial protection in the market. The British public, having condemned the evil of slavery, now opted to buy the cheaper sugar produced by Spanish and Portuguese colonies that still permitted slavery.

Once the cash cow of empire, the West Indies spiralled into economic ruin. Property values plummeted: Bog Estate in Jamaica, valued at £80 000 in the 1830s, sold for £500 in 1849; some plantations could not be sold at any price. By 1852, 240 estates in Jamaica had been abandoned. Those plantation owners who might have hung on found that they could no longer secure credit, as West Indian banks failed and dozens of merchant houses in England, their livelihood dependent upon the sugar trade, succumbed to bankruptcy. Nova Scotia, which had reaped benefits under the old system, was not immune to effects of the devastation. Between 1832 and 1836, the value of British North American exports to the British Caribbean, which had consisted largely of fish for slave rations and timber coming from Nova Scotia ports, fell by almost 90 percent, from £268 000 to £25 000.[3]

1846: Repeal of the sugar duties damages Nova Scotia shipping interests.

Britain's removal of preferential tariffs on sugar was only one in a series of moves toward free trade. British tariffs protecting colonial timber had already been reduced in 1841 and, as the free trade movement continued to gain momentum, new legislation in 1846 cut tariffs on foreign timber still further. By 1860, differential tariffs on timber that had protected colonial suppliers since the Napoleonic Wars would be eliminated altogether. The prominent Nova Scotian writer and judge Thomas Chandler Haliburton had retired to England, becoming a Tory member of Britain's Parliament in 1859. From this position, he fought a futile rearguard action against the elimination of the final vestige of imperial protection on colonial timber in 1860, arguing that the measure would cut the cable that bound the colonies to the mother country. "Those who begot children were bound to protect and support them," he insisted.[4] By this time, though, free trade was clearly the new orthodoxy.

The increased competition from Baltic timber suppliers in the wake of reduced tariffs endangered British North American timber interests. But the danger was partly offset by surging demand for wooden railway ties in the 1840s as Britain entered a railway building boom. Canadian economic historian A.R.M. Lower argued, however, that uncertainty over the looming change to tariff policy led British North American timber producers to flood the British market with a glut of wood, precipitating the very conditions they had feared: oversupply and falling prices.[5]

Historical geographer Graeme Wynn attributes New Brunswick's growth in the first half of the nineteenth century, "from an undeveloped backwater of 25,000 people to a bustling colony of 190,000," to the timber industry.[6] But the sudden loss of imperial protection in the 1840s meant ruin for many of the colony's timber producers. According to Joseph Howe, who looked from Nova Scotia across the Bay of Fundy, there was "scarcely a solvent house from Saint John to Grand Falls."[7] Emigration from the colony surged, with some setting off for better fortunes in Australia or New Zealand, and other unemployed lumbermen opting for the United States. Disenchantment with the British Empire and its perceived indifference to its colonies inspired a closer sense of identification with the American republic. In 1849, New Brunswick authorities noted with alarm that Independence Day was being celebrated in Miramichi towns.

Britain's inexorable embrace of free trade principles in the mid-nineteenth century undercut another key colonial staple: the repeal of the Corn Laws in 1846 was a watershed in British politics and colonial policy. Britain's Parliament, dominated by landowners, had for centuries protected domestic wheat prices by legislating tariffs (despite the misleading label, the Corn Laws were concerned with wheat, rather than maize). The earlier movement toward freer trade spearheaded by British cabinet minister William Huskisson included a change in 1828 to the Corn Laws, although the voices against their repeal were still too many and too powerful. Huskisson's measure inaugurated a sliding scale system of duties: when wheat prices dropped below a certain level, tariffs would rise to restrict supply and ensure British farmers would not be undercut by a flood of competing wheat. Colonial wheat producers were beneficiaries of Huskisson's new sliding scale Corn Law: tariffs on colonial wheat were always a fraction of those levied against foreign imports. For example, in 1828 the duty on colonial wheat was five shillings per quarter ton (227 kilograms), while foreign wheat faced a tariff of more than 32 shillings. The Corn Laws were intensely unpopular with reformers in England, who insisted that food prices should not be kept artificially high to guarantee the profits of privileged landowners. Moreover, a growing number of industrialists in Britain, recognizing that lower cost bread would mean that wages could be reduced and British manufactures made more competitive, lobbied for the repeal of the Corn Laws. Since the 1832 Great Reform Act, the commercial class in Britain enjoyed new political clout.

Under the protective shelter of imperial preference, wheat production had soared in the rich virgin soil of Canada West (Upper Canada). Economic historian John McCallum remarked that "a more classic case of a staple product would be difficult to imagine," noting that the province's economy was even more specialized in wheat production than late-twentieth-century Saskatchewan's. Three quarters of Canada West's cash income before 1860 flowed from wheat exports. By contrast, Canada East (Lower Canada), plagued by crop failures, soil exhaustion, and population pressure on agricultural land, had been a net importer of wheat since the 1830s.[8] Nevertheless, Canada East shared in the agricultural bounty as the port of Montreal became the united Canadas' largest city and its decided leader in commerce. Its population doubled in the 20 years after 1825, quickly overtaking Quebec City and swelling to more than 44 000. Canal building to improve navigation on the St. Lawrence, and construction of the Welland Canal in 1829, made Montreal, with its closer proximity to booming Canada West, the natural seaport. Banking, brokerage, and insurance companies, whose businesses were linked to trade, established headquarters in Montreal, as did a host of other industries—foundries, brickyards, distilleries, breweries, shoe factories, manufacturers of soap and candles—drawn by the availability of labour and access to water power and transportation.

1846: Britain's repeal of the Corn Laws ends protective tariffs for the colonies on wheat.

Paradoxically, just before the devastating repeal of the Corn Laws in 1846, Montreal's successful wheat trade had been given a boost with Britain's Canada Corn Act of 1843, which reduced still further the tariff on colonial grain reaching Britain. In retrospect, it seems clear that this reduction was only a step toward the ultimate sweeping aside of protective tariffs in favour of free trade, but for the moment, the measure seemed heaven sent to Montreal's merchants, a sign of Britain's continued commitment to imperial preference. American wheat producers even found it worth their while to ship their grain to Montreal for export, and the Welland Canal helped Canada capture the agricultural produce of the United States Midwest. Ground into flour in Montreal mills, this American wheat found its way to the British market as protected colonial grain. It has been estimated that the lion's share of the "Canadian" wheat exported to Britain in some years actually originated in the United States. In 1841, for example, Canada imported 210 000 quarter tons (47.7 million kilograms) of wheat from the United States and exported a total of 280 000 quarter tons (63.6 million kilograms). Montreal's warehousing, milling, and transport capacity boomed. A spirit of expansive optimism fed continued improvements to the province's network of roads and canals. Britain encouraged this expansion with an imperial loan guarantee of £1 500 000 for canal building.

Sir Robert Peel's government's repeal of the Corn Laws in 1846 has often been historically linked with the great Irish famine in the same era. The widespread failure of the staple Irish potato crop in 1845, which would be followed by a total failure the following year, made any policy that taxed food especially indefensible. It has been said that the unseasonably wet summer of 1845 brought the rain that rained away the Corn Laws. Wheat production suffered along with the potato crop. Indeed, when he introduced his measure to sweep away the Corn Laws, Prime Minister Peel admitted that the famine in Ireland had left him with no alternative. Still, he denied that the temporary scarcity was the fundamental point. Nor was he prepared to be swayed by the mere interests of the landlords, which he described as important, but subordinate.

Peel was a committed free trader on simple grounds of social justice, and was prepared to watch Britain's Conservative party torn in two over the issue. Tory landowners and wheat producers, whose interests Peel had airily dismissed as secondary, withdrew their support, and, although Peel's bill repealing the Corn Laws passed in Britain's Parliament with the support of Liberals, his government was defeated on another bill that same day. As he acknowledged parliamentary defeat, Peel mused aloud that he hoped he would be "sometimes remembered with expressions of good will in the abodes of those whose lot it is to labour, and to earn their daily bread by the sweat of their brow, when they shall recruit their exhausted strength with abundant and untaxed food, the sweeter because it is no longer leavened by a sense of injustice."[9] When the Whig (or Liberal) administration of Lord John Russell took office in 1846, Britain's Conservative opposition was left divided between the old supporters of protectionism and free traders who took on the party label of "Peelites."

The Tragedy of the Irish Potato Famine

While Peel denied that the Irish famine was the fundamental factor in his free trade policy, it seems clear that the tragedy put the final nail in the coffin of protectionism.

The widespread failure of the Irish potato crop in 1845 was only a precursor to the total devastation the following year. Ireland's complete dependence on the potato had fuelled a surge in population during the first half of the nineteenth century. Between 1779 and 1841, Ireland's population grew by 172 percent to reach 8.2 million. A small plot of land planted with potatoes could sustain a large family—one-quarter to one-sixth of the size needed for the production of an equivalent grain crop. Potatoes could easily be cultivated in boggy or hilly ground, offering a nutritious staple that could also be used for animal feed. English agriculturalist Arthur Young compared the Irish diet favourably with the English farm worker's staple of bread and cheese. He noted the "well-formed vigorous bodies" of the Irish, and "their cottages swarming with children." "When I see their men athletic, and their women beautiful, I know not how to believe them subsisting on an unwholesome diet."[10] Yet the potato was a treacherous friend. Ireland's dangerous dependence on it meant that if the crop failed, no alternative food supply was available.

The potato crop of 1845 at first promised to be especially abundant. But reports began to emerge of a blight that had first struck North American crops, causing the plants to turn black, wither, and die. A man in Sligo on Ireland's northwest coast described the eerie first inklings of the cataclysm that would take hold of Ireland: "A mist rose up out of the sea, and you could hear a voice talking near a mile off across the stillness of the earth. You could begin to see the tops of the stalks lying over as if the life was gone out of them. And that was the beginning of the great trouble and famine that destroyed Ireland." Even more alarmingly, potatoes that had already been harvested were not immune to the air-borne fungus. Overnight, a crop of healthy potatoes could be reduced to stinking black liquid putrefaction. One-third to one-half of Ireland's potato crop was destroyed in 1845, yet in an unpredictable patchwork pattern that saw some areas totally affected and others mysteriously spared.[11]

British authorities, who had directly governed Ireland since the union of 1801, struggled to ameliorate the disaster, yet clung to *laissez faire* convictions that market forces ought not to be hampered. Too much assistance would carry the danger that the Irish might "relax in their exertions to provide for themselves," one statesman worried.[12] Maize, or Indian corn, was imported in a vain attempt to fill the gap, but mills to grind the flint hard corn were in short supply. Some of the Irish, made desperate by hunger, consumed the corn unground, and were seized with searing abdominal pain and bloody diarrhea as the coarse grains moved through their intestines. A Quaker relief worker operating a charitable soup kitchen in County Leitrim saw children wasted to "skeletons, their features sharpened with hunger," their arms and legs so emaciated they looked like mere bones, and "the happy expression of infancy gone from their faces, leaving the anxious look of premature old age."[13]

Stubborn faith in free market principles meant that shiploads of Ireland's other agricultural produce—wheat, barley, oats, cattle, pigs, eggs, and butter—continued to leave the country as its population lapsed into starvation. Military escorts stood guard to keep back the crowds as food was carried away to export. "It was a sight which the Irish people found impossible to understand and impossible to forget," historian Cecil Woodham Smith reflected. Even before the famine, Ireland's burgeoning population consisted of many who were chronically underfed and dependent upon charity—almost 2.4 million according to the Poor Inquiry Commission. "This hopeless, wretched multitude, already starving, already diseased, unemployed beggars, dispossessed squatters, evicted persons, penniless widows, starving children, snatched at every offer of relief, swamped every scheme, and formed a hard core of destitution whose numbers could be reduced only by death," Woodham Smith explained.[14]

Clinging to the folk belief that crop failures never struck in successive years, people looked forward to a fresh potato harvest in 1846. Yet early signs of a luxuriant yield late that summer soon gave way to stunned disbelief as disease reappeared. Early reassurances that the blight was less severe and less widespread were soon discounted. In fact, it was far worse—the failure of the 1846 crop was total. "Almost in a night, every potato in Ireland was lost," Woodham Smith wrote simply.[15]

1845 and 1846: Failures in the Irish potato crop lead to widespread famine.

What we would today call "donor fatigue" began to hamper British relief efforts: "It is possible to have heard the tale of sorrow too often," *The Times* callously proclaimed. Subsequent articles complained of Ireland's "indolent preference of relief to labour," and contemptuously explained that the Irish had been taught to repeat the same mistakes and to look to the state for assistance: "Unless a Baron Munchausen will immediately plant the Emerald Island with ten million quartern-loaf trees, and the same number of roast beef and leg of mutton trees, all in full bearing, we see not the least hope of appeasing a clamour which makes it a merit to be unreasonable."[16]

As the winter of 1846–47 came on, even scarce supplies of nettles, edible roots, and cabbage leaves upon which the people had subsisted were gone. Starving people pawned their bedding and the very rags they wore for scraps of whatever food they could get. Nature's cruelty to suffering Ireland was unremitting as the cold struck early and with unaccustomed severity, bringing snow in November. Ill-clad men left the warmth of a peat fire to labour on government public works projects, breaking rocks and building roads. Many fell down dead of hunger and exposure to cold, rain, and snow.

People whose constitutions had been weakened by protracted hunger died of diseases that accompany famine—cholera, typhus, and various fevers and bowel disorders. Throughout "Black '47" worsening conditions brought a rising death toll. It is estimated that Ireland's population fell by almost 2 million during the famine years—1 million emigrating and another million lost to death. Alarming reports came daily. At a farm in County Cork, visiting authorities found a woman and her two children dead in a cottage, their bodies half-eaten by dogs; in another home, the parish priest found a man still living lying in bed with his dead wife and two dead children, while a cat devoured a dead infant nearby. A woman with three children, deserted by her husband, was too weak from hunger to move the body of her dead mother that lay in the house. Many died of typhus, called "Black fever" by the Irish because its symptoms included circulatory problems that caused the skin to darken. Gangrene was frequent, and the progress of the disease often includes the loss of fingers, toes, and feet. The odious presence of Black fever in a cottage announced itself before visitors even reached the door—the stench of putrefaction permeated the dwelling. One medical officer complained of being forcibly driven back, retching, by the smell.

British officials despaired of their inability to collect the poor rates during this time when demand upon government assistance was heaviest. Despite the use of troops to collect the tax, Poor Law Unions were faced with enormous arrears in the sums owed to them, and some workhouses simply had to shut their doors, sending the local poor to starve in the ditches. Landlords, unable to collect rents owing, faced cries for clemency, but many hardened their hearts against defaulting tenants. For many who had endured habitual arrears, the famine was simply the breaking point. Doubtful that Ireland's crop would ever recover sufficiently to enable the collection of arrears, some landlords opted to evict their tenants instead. To guard against the likelihood that the homeless and starving would simply choose to squat in their former homes, landlords ordered vacated cottages demolished. Troops grimly enforced this heartbreaking policy, keeping the anguished tenants at bay while crews pulled down their cottages. Some evicting landlords offered the philanthropic inducement of emigration, but the British government rejected the idea of a systematic program to assist emigration as a way of dealing with the crisis. "There is no use in sending them from starving at Skibbereen to starving at Montreal," the prime minister explained.[17]

Impact of the Famine Migration on British North America

Even without government assistance, immigrants surged into British North America. The first six months of the 1847 shipping season saw approximately 90 000 immigrants arrive—almost triple the number of the years immediately preceding.

The ports of Quebec and Montreal bore the brunt, and officials there reeled at the enormity of the task that lay ahead of them. The more prosperous Irish tended to make up the bulk of immigration in the pre-famine years, and historian Donald Akenson has demonstrated that, contrary to popular belief, this continued to be the case in the famine years.[18] But to officials in Canada, the number of indigent arrivals in 1847 was staggering. Ships were crowded with "the decrepit, the maimed, the lame, the subjects of chronic disease, widows with large families of tender age, and others, who from their infirmities or confirmed habits were incapable of maintaining themselves at home by their own labour," Canada's executive council complained. Montreal alone had more than 1000 orphaned children.[19] The French-Canadian people opened their homes and their hearts to these unfortunates, and many Irish immigrant children were raised as *Canadiens*.

In New Brunswick, the quarantine station at Partridge Island, near the mouth of the harbour at Saint John, had been established in 1785, around the time of the Loyalist migration, but over the years had fallen into neglect. With crude hospital facilities to accommodate 200 people at most, the island was ill prepared for the onslaught it was about to face as almost 15 000 people would land there in 1847. In that year alone, 1195 died on Partridge Island. Sometimes called "Canada's Emerald Isle," the island's sad history lends a bitter flavour to its colourful nickname—it echoed Ireland's suffering. Dr. James Patrick Collins, only 23 years old, newly married, with a baby on the way, was himself an immigrant who had come to Saint John from County Cork as a youth ten years earlier. The inducements to accept an appointment as physician on Partridge Island must have been strong. Not only would he be helping his fellow Irish immigrants, but the salary of £50 per month was ten times what Collins might otherwise earn, a powerful temptation with a growing family. Sadly, the decision was a costly one; he was dead within weeks.

1847: 90 000 immigrants arrive in British North America.

1847: 1195 die at New Brunswick's Partridge Island.

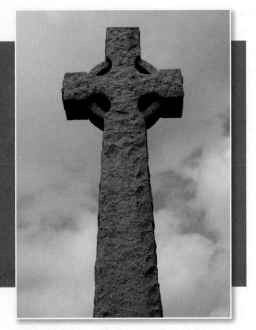

Celtic cross memorial at Middle Island, New Brunswick.

Source: Fintastique/ Dreamstime.com.

Middle Island in the Miramichi River had not been intended as a quarantine station, but in early June 1847 typhus struck the *Looshtauk* (sometimes spelled *Loosthauk*), a vessel carrying 462 immigrants, mostly Irish, sailing from Liverpool to Quebec. With 146 already dead, the desperate captain made for the port of Miramichi and the vessel was quarantined on nearby Middle Island. Two more ships whose passengers were also suffering outbreaks of disease were likewise detained there. A young Miramichi-born doctor, John Vondy, who had trained in London at the Royal College of Surgeons, had no qualified assistance and staggered under the burden of caring for so many dying people. A further 96 passengers died on the island, and within weeks Vondy himself was seized by typhus. His sister risked death by hurrying to the island to nurse him, but it was too late—he died at age 28, on the same day as Dr. Collins on Partridge Island. All the ships in the harbour lowered their flags to half mast as Vondy's double-sealed lead-lined casket left the island.

Grosse Île, converted into a quarantine station during the cholera epidemic of 1832, was downriver from Quebec, and was the first port of call for vessels bound for ports in Canada East. In the 1847 shipping season, queues of vessels miles long waited to discharge their passengers there. The frantic reports emanating from the island offer some of the most poignant glimpses of the tide of human misery arriving on Canadian shores. The Montreal Emigrant Society described Grosse Île as a "great charnel pit of victimized humanity."[20] During the 1847 shipping season, Dr. George Douglas, the medical superintendent at Grosse Île, reported that more than 10 000 had died either en route to British North America or soon after arrival. A further 30 000 were sick, and 38 000 completely destitute. The *Virginius* sailing from Liverpool—a common point of embarkation for Irish migrants—told a story that was becoming all too familiar, as "coffin ships" carried famine-weakened emigrants fleeing tragic Ireland. There had been 476 passengers when the ship set sail; fever and dysentery took 158 lives during the passage, and of those remaining, 106 were seriously ill. "The few that were able to come on deck were ghastly yellow looking spectres, unshaven and hollow cheeked," medical inspectors reported. Inspecting the vessels' holds was a grim duty: the dirt and filth "creates such an effluvium as to make it difficult to breathe." Ships' crews dragged bodies out of the berths of the living with boat hooks. More than 2000 dead had to be removed from arriving vessels.[21]

Thousands among Canada's existing population became infected with disease, especially in the lower province. The mayor of Montreal, John Mills, and the Roman Catholic Bishop of Toronto, Dr. Michael Power, were among the many who succumbed to fever caught while visiting the sick. Dr. Wolfred Nelson, who had once led Lower Canada's disaffected in rebellion, now risked his life to minister to the sick at Montreal's waterfront. Authorities desperately grasped at any straws of hope offered. A Colonel Calvert claimed to have developed a disinfecting fluid that would stop the spread of illness, and Colonial Secretary Lord Grey enthused about this "really wonderful" antidote. Calvert was dispatched to Canada where he amazed Dr. George Douglas, medical superintendent at

Grosse Île, with a demonstration. He filled barrels with human excrement, sprinkled the disinfecting fluid around, and waved wet sheets to disperse the effects. Douglas was less amazed when Calvert died of fever, and he himself became ill. Douglas would recover from his illness, although it permanently damaged his health. Living and working amid constant sorrow marked him in other ways, too. Douglas had been on the front line in Canada's bid to help the victims of the Irish famine. He had a monument raised to his medical colleagues and all other victims who died at Grosse Île: "In this secluded spot lie the mortal remains of 5,425 persons who, flying from pestilence and famine in the year 1847, found in North America but a grave." Some time later, at his home near the site, Douglas committed suicide.[22] Today, this picturesque, but inexpressibly sad, place is maintained by Parks Canada, a Celtic cross commemorating the many who died there.

To make matters worse, Montreal was gripped by a heat wave in the summer of 1847; in June, three people dropped down dead in the streets from the effects. The spread of typhus, which had infected thousands, brought simmering resentment. In Montreal alone, it had claimed 924 residents before the summer ended. Claims that Britain was simply transferring responsibility for its poor and indigent were fuelled by reports that some of the worst examples of landlord-assisted emigration had originated on the estates of British members of Parliament. One vessel, the *Lord Ashburton*, which arrived at Quebec very late in the shipping season, contained 174 passengers from Lord Palmerston's estate—only a fraction of the more than 2000 that his agents acknowledged they had sent to British North America. Emigration agents in Canada reported that 87 of Palmerston's former tenants aboard the *Lord Ashburton* had no clothing at all, with naked infants huddled together under a coarse canvas sail, shivering in the biting winds of a November Atlantic crossing.

Economic Crisis in the Canadas

Canada's sense of having been abandoned by indifferent and callous imperial legislators was sharpened by the staggering economic slump caused by the loss of imperial preference. The surging optimism that had been fed by continued tariffs favouring colonial wheat, and especially by the 1843 Canada Corn Act, which afforded even more generous treatment in the markets of the mother country, had been suddenly undercut by the repeal of the Corn Laws in 1846. Montreal warehouses, once part of a bustling trade in colonial grain, were full of unsold wheat. In a disastrous chain of events, the Americans had also earlier made a bold move toward capturing some of the grain trade of Upper Canada. In 1845 and 1846 they introduced two Drawback Acts, which eliminated duties on goods crossing through the United States for re-export. Goods travelling to or from British North America would face no disadvantage if they took the American route. The Erie Canal, linking Lake Erie to the Hudson River and thus to the port of New York, became an even more appealing alternative to the St. Lawrence since it did not face the prolonged freeze that hampered the Canadian route. Canadian wheat producers in Canada West were quick to respond to this opportunity for quicker, cheaper transportation, especially since American-shipped wheat would now face no disadvantage in the British market. In 1847, the value of Canadian wheat exported to the United States was £34 000; by the very next year it had risen to £374 000.[23] "Peel's bill of 1846," Canada's governor-general

1845 and 1846: Two American Drawback Acts challenge the St. Lawrence commercial trade route.

explained, "drives the whole of this Produce down the New York channels … destroying the Revenue which Canada expected to derive from Canal dues, & ruining at once Mill owners, Forwarders, and Merchants. The consequence is that Private Property is unsaleable in Canada, and not a shilling can be raised on the credit of the Province."[24]

Even as Britain eliminated mercantilist tariff protection for colonial products, they kept in place the restrictive Navigation Acts, a system of laws requiring that most seagoing cargoes leaving Britain and her possessions be carried in imperial vessels. These laws, originally intended to protect the British carrying trade and to ensure that the merchant marine would continue to be a training ground for sailors for the Royal Navy, now seemed harshly restrictive. British ships were not always available when needed during the short Canadian shipping season, and rates were far lower from American ports. The *Canadian Economist* complained that "the *benefits* [of the imperial connection] are destroyed; but the *burdens* are left to oppress and gall the industry of our hard-working people."[25]

While it had been Peel's Conservative government that had presided over the dismantling of Britain's mercantilist system, the Whigs, or Liberals, who took power in 1846 would continue the trend toward a laissez-faire economic system. The French phrase *laissez-faire* means to allow to do, to let something go its own way. In economics, this term denotes a lack of government intervention, a willingness to allow market forces to dictate prices, supply, and the mechanics of trade. This was the very system (or, more properly, *lack* of system) that Scottish economist Adam Smith famously advocated, and that was becoming the new political and economic orthodoxy of the mid-nineteenth century.

Britain's Government Embraces Colonial Self-Rule

In such a climate, the value of colonial possessions was increasingly called into question. It is not that Britain wished to divest itself of its far-flung empire: there were, after all, important considerations of territorial strategy and international prestige to consider. Prime Minister Lord John Russell explained that "the loss of any great portion of our Colonies w[oul]d diminish our importance in the world, and the vultures w[oul]d soon gather together to despoil us of other parts of our Empire, or to offer insults to us as we c[oul]d not bear."[26] But political reformers in Britain persisted in asking why English taxpayers should be burdened with the defence costs of colonies, especially when thriving colonies would be better able to meet those costs themselves. Nor was it necessary for mature colonies with traditions of representative government to be directly governed by Britain in matters that had no bearing on the larger empire. As British Colonial Office official Herman Merivale archly put it: "We give them commercial advantages, and tax ourselves for their benefit, in order to give them interest in remaining under our supremacy, that we may have the pleasure of governing them."[27]

The new secretary of state for the colonies, the third Earl Grey, was firmly committed both to free trade and to a loosening of imperial control over colonies with representative government. New legislation in 1846 gave colonial legislatures the power to reduce or remove tariffs that the imperial government had placed on foreign imports, a significant move that one opponent in the British House of Commons complained would topple the entire colonial system. (The colonies, however, were not yet permitted to impose protective tariffs.) The next step remained to be taken: where domestic matters were concerned—matters not affecting the empire as a whole—Britain's Whig government prepared to embrace the dramatic shift of granting self-government to those colonies with elected legislatures. In November 1846, Grey set out his ideas about colonial governance in a dispatch to the British-appointed governor of Nova Scotia, Sir John Harvey. This dispatch has become one of the key documents in the constitutional history of British North America.

November 1846: Colonial Secretary Earl Grey issues instructions concerning responsible government.

Grey explained in this dispatch that the government of the colony should be modelled on that of the mother country. The governor should follow the wishes of his executive council as long as they possessed the confidence of the legislative assembly. He should be politically neutral, not favouring any one party over another. If the council lost the support of the assembly, they would normally resign, and the governor should show equal willingness to grant to their opponents the privilege of forming a government. Grey's words encapsulated the very essence of responsible government: "It cannot be too distinctly acknowledged that it is neither possible nor desirable to carry on the government of any of the British Provinces in North America in opposition to the opinion of the inhabitants."[28]

Responsible Government Achieved in Nova Scotia first

Unfortunately, Sir John Harvey did not entirely share Grey's convictions. He could hardly be blamed: the idea of responsible government for a colony was new—to many observers, the notion that a colony could be self-governing was a logical absurdity. Even Lord John Russell, under whose administration the principle would be conceded, had earlier pronounced it inconsistent with colonial status. "It would be better to say at once, 'Let the two countries separate' than for us to pretend to govern the colony afterwards."[29] Harvey had considerable experience in colonial governance—nearing 70, he had been a successful lieutenant governor of Prince Edward Island, Newfoundland, and New Brunswick, before being sent to Nova Scotia in 1846. But Harvey was resistant to the introduction of partisan politics in Nova Scotia and—like many of his contemporaries—failed to grasp that responsible government depended upon parties. Harvey believed that it would be best for the province if a coalition of leading politicians could be brought together, and he seized hold of Grey's dispatch as evidence that the Colonial Secretary supported the idea. After all, had Grey not said that the governor should be neutral, not favouring any one party?

Joseph Howe.

Source: Library and Archives Canada, pa025486.

Behind the scenes, Nova Scotia journalist and politician Joseph Howe was busy working toward a true form of responsible government for the colony. He struck up a correspondence with Charles Buller, one of Lord Durham's former aides, who was now a British member of Parliament and judge advocate for the Colonial Office. Buller's ideas about how responsible government could be made to work were sound and even prescient, and in him Howe found a receptive audience for his views. What is more, Buller was able to show Howe that the British cabinet was firmly committed to responsible government. This fortified Howe in his fight against Governor

Harvey's strategy of attempting to force men of opposite parties into awkward coalitions. Howe complained that his Liberals had clearly won the election held in Nova Scotia in August 1847, but their Tory opponents refused to resign and Harvey was not summoning an executive council of the Liberals who had the support of the majority of the assembly.

Buller in turn had the ear of Grey, the colonial secretary, and this gave Grey a window into Nova Scotia politics that was missing from Harvey's official dispatches. Howe was grateful that Buller should act as a conduit in this way, telling him that "I never dreamed that you had troubled Earl Grey … with any explanation of my private sentiments."[30] Grey supplied Harvey with another dispatch that clarified Colonial Office policy; it helped him understand that under responsible government, his duty was not to force his unwilling advisors into a coalition, but to respect the wishes of a majority of the assembly. Grey reflected that "as every free government necessarily is a party government, I think it is better that Nova Scotia should submit to the evils of party government rather than be without the privileges of freedom."[31]

By the end of January 1848, the Conservative executive councillors who had clung to office were compelled to resign, and Lieutenant Governor Harvey called upon Liberal leader James B. Uniacke to form a government in Nova Scotia. Uniacke's cabinet, including Joseph Howe, was sworn in early in February 1848. Scarcely concealing his excitement now that the long-sought goal of responsible government had been won, Howe wrote to Buller: "The scene was a novel one, and to us Colonial Anglo Saxons, very interesting. We were conscious of having achieved a Revolution, without bloodshed." Howe was proud that the colony of Nova Scotia was the first in the Empire to achieve self-government, and boasted to Buller that Nova Scotia would be a "Normal School" for the rest of the colonies.[32] Buller responded in kind, expressing confidence in Howe's moderation and wisdom. He had, he said, seldom been so gratified by any letter as he was by Howe's news of the advent of responsible government. Sadly, this fruitful correspondence was cut short—at the age of 41, Buller suddenly succumbed to typhus.

1848: The first responsible cabinet in a British colony is sworn into office in Nova Scotia.

1847: Elgin arrives in Canada as governor.

Lord Elgin and Responsible Government in Canada

Elsewhere in British North America, the transition to responsible government would not be so peaceful. James Bruce, the eighth Earl of Elgin, had arrived early in 1847 to take up his new post as governor of the united Canadas. Unlike the elderly Sir John Harvey in Nova Scotia, and unlike the four frail "Charleses"— Charles Poulett Thomson, Baron Sydenham; Sir Charles Bagot; Charles, Baron Metcalfe, and Charles, Earl Cathcart—who preceded him, Elgin was in excellent health and only 36 years old when he came to Canada.

Despite a tendency to corpulence and prematurely thinning hair, Elgin was vigorous and energetic, with bright dark eyes. He was fond of snow-shoeing the five kilometres from his viceregal residence to the Montreal legislature. Government House was now full of merry little voices as the governor was raising a young family in Canada. Near the end of Elgin's term in 1854, he returned from travels on a quiet Sunday to what was then his official residence at Spencer Wood in Quebec. As he passed by one house, he was warmly greeted by an old lady who put her head out of a window and whispered, "Welcome home again!" Elgin, whose nature was sentimental, found himself strangely moved by her words, and by the beauty of his surroundings. He even mused to his wife that he dreamed of remaining in Canada permanently. Instead, after serving as a diplomat and in the British cabinet, Elgin accepted the governorship of India. It was a prestigious post, but a deadly one; like his two predecessors in office, Elgin was buried there.

Part of Elgin's rationale in accepting the later appointment to India had been financial. His father, the seventh Earl, who had been ambassador to Constantinople, enthusiastically studied and collected Greek antiquities. He had severely damaged the family fortune by spending more than £62 000 of his own money to have the so-called "Elgin Marbles" removed from the Parthenon at Athens and transported to Britain, concerned that they were falling into ruin, neglected by the ruling Turks. These treasures are now housed at the British Museum despite recent efforts to have them returned to Greece. The enormous debt encumbering the Elgin estate had compelled his heir, the eighth Earl, to seek a salaried post overseas, but Elgin's hope of improving his family's precarious financial footing in Canada was soon dashed. He quickly discovered that he was responsible for meeting a host of expenses from his own salary—travel outside Montreal, large dinner parties several times a week, and even snow clearing for the road to his estate. He was especially alarmed to learn that his predecessor, Metcalfe, spent almost double his salary to maintain the dignity of the office.

James Bruce, Earl of Elgin and Kincardine.

Source: © McCord Museum, M22464.

Even if the Canadian post did not help Elgin achieve the elusive financial stability he craved for his family, it would secure his place in history. Here, he was able to make a profound contribution to the constitutional development of the empire. Unlike Governor Harvey in Nova Scotia, who only acquiesced in responsible government when it became clear that all other avenues had been exhausted, Elgin came to Canada with a firm conviction of the necessity of that change. Grey had given Elgin a copy of his dispatch to Harvey explaining Britain's new commitment to responsible government, and Elgin himself strongly believed in the principle. Elgin's wife Mary was the daughter of Lord Durham, and the new governor assured her that he would adopt her "father's system" in Canada. The beautiful and gracious Mary Lambton proved a great asset to Elgin in his duties and, as Durham's daughter, found a warm welcome from many in Canada. She was also the niece of the colonial secretary, Earl Grey; in letters to Mary, Elgin mischievously referred to her uncle as "King Henry."

Elgin's determination to impose a system of colonial self-government was not immediately obvious in Canada. An election was not yet due, and Elgin explained to Grey that he wanted "to avoid if possible giving the impression that I am ready to jump down every body's throat the moment I touch the soil of Canada."[33] The transition to responsible government was not marked by the passage of any new law. Instead, like many key aspects of Canada's constitution, it was a matter of convention. Constitutional conventions are unwritten rules that dictate parliamentary and political practices, and that have evolved through history. Elgin simply began a new practice for colonial governors in Canada. After elections had been held early in 1848, and after it became clear that the former

1848: The formation of the "Great Ministry" of La Fontaine and Baldwin signals the advent of responsible government in Canada.

1848 is a year of revolutions throughout Europe.

administration had lost the confidence of the assembly, he called upon the leaders of those whose party had won a majority of the seats in the legislature to form a government. It was now understood that the executive council must enjoy the support of the assembly, and that, under normal circumstances, the governor would act on the advice of his executive council. The Tories, brought to office by Metcalfe's machinations, had been defeated, and on March 7, 1848, Elgin sent for Reformers Robert Baldwin and Louis-Hippolyte La Fontaine to ask them to form a government.

Britain's colonial secretary, Lord Grey, had been watching Canadian events with anxiety, kept abreast of Elgin's "great experiment" of responsible government with frequent personal letters. His interest was that much more acute, given world events. The year 1848 engulfed Europe in a wave of revolution. Republicans in Paris threw up barricades and once again, amid bloodshed, a French monarchy was toppled. Alexis de Tocqueville had looked to the wind of revolution blowing on the horizon and warned France's Chamber of Deputies that they were sleeping on a volcano. The same wind blew through the cities of Italy, Germany, Prussia, Galicia, Bohemia, and Hungary. Uprisings in the Austrian Empire drove Chancellor Metternich from Vienna to safety in England. An abortive 1848 uprising in Ireland, fuelled by the disaster of the potato famine, threatened British rule. England itself, having made modest concessions to reform a few years before, was able to keep the boiling forces of revolution from spilling over. Yet Britain's earlier concessions, coupled with the success of bold revolutionaries on the continent, lent courage to those who demanded more sweeping changes. Chartists, demanding the extension of political rights to the working classes, collected more than 2 million signatures on a monster petition and carried the 225-kilogram document to the House of Commons in three coaches. It was in this inflammatory climate that Karl Marx and Friedrich Engels produced *The Communist Manifesto*, calling upon workers of the world to unite. Grey was increasingly uneasy about the "monstrous absurdities" he saw taking place across the channel in France, and throughout Europe.[34]

Grey's worries about Elgin's success in his experiment of responsible government were fed by his conviction that the very survival of the imperial connection in Canada was at stake. To many Canadian reformers, a republican system like that of the Americans or the French was an attractive model; the lure of what Grey called "extreme democracy" was strong. But Elgin was adamant that his concession of responsible government was not a step toward the American system: "On the contrary," he predicted, it would "draw the Colonist the other way." It "slakes that thirst for self Gov[ernmen]t," offering a system "intrinsically superior to that of the Yankees." Canada's government would retain "the check of the Crown," a means of preventing the representative legislature from lapsing into "a reckless and overbearing tyranny." Borrowing Tocqueville's phrase, Elgin insisted that "a tyranny of the majority" was "not the more tolerable because it is capricious & wielded by a Tyrant with many heads."[35] The ideal was a balanced constitution, in which the popular will would be kept in check, affording protection to the rights of minorities that might be otherwise trampled by majority rule.

Elgin's ideas about constitutional reform fit well with the convictions of moderate reformers in the united Canadas. The achievement of responsible government in 1848 saw fulfilled the long-standing vision to which Robert Baldwin had tried to convert Colonial

Office authorities in 1836. While the rebellions that convulsed the Canadas in 1837 and 1838 are often seen as a necessary baptism by fire accompanying the birth of colonial self-government, revisionist historians like Colin Read reject such a view. Read notes that apologists for the rebellions err in believing that the violence hastened the advent of responsible government. Instead, he suggests, the violence discredited all reformers. In Upper Canada in particular, he points out, it took years for the reform movement to recover.[36]

On March 11, 1848, the Baldwin–La Fontaine administration, sometimes known as the "Great Ministry" because of the watershed in constitutional principle that it represented, was sworn into office. The leading role in the executive council, the office that most approximated what we would call prime minister today, was that of the attorney general. La Fontaine was appointed attorney general for Canada East, and Baldwin, attorney general for Canada West. The maintenance of separate civil and common law traditions in the two sections of the united province necessitated this dual appointment. The legislative session itself did not begin until January 1849.

1849: Parliament is officially bilingual.

The governor-general's traditional speech from the throne beginning the session was read in French as well as English. Lord Elgin, having spent much of his youth in Paris, spoke French comfortably, and he informed the legislature that the imperial Parliament had repealed that offensive provision of the Act of Union that had declared English to be the official language of Canada's legislature. La Fontaine had for years made the language issue a central plank in Canada East's reform platform, and had insisted on speaking French in the legislature over the jeers and protests of some English-speaking members.

The new legislative session in 1849 also saw the return of diehard *patriotes* and Upper Canadian rebels to the legislature. The "Great Ministry" introduced a bill granting a general amnesty to those rebels in exile who had not yet been pardoned. William Lyon Mackenzie took advantage of the opportunity to return. He wrote the governor-general a contrite letter in which he confessed that he had been wrong to advocate "Worship of the Idol enthroned at Washington."[37]

1849: Amnesty is extended to exiled rebels of 1837–1838.

Wolfred Nelson, who had earlier returned from exile with La Fontaine's help, had been active again in Canadian politics for a few years. Louis Joseph Papineau had returned to Canada in 1845 under an amnesty negotiated by La Fontaine, and far from being grateful, now returned to the legislature to sneer at "*vendus*" who had sold out to cooperate with union. Nelson, concerned about Papineau's intemperate attacks on La Fontaine's leadership, worried that the old rebel leader would split the ranks of French-Canadian reformers. Nelson attacked Papineau for his cowardice in deserting the rebel standard on the eve of battle, but reflected bitterly that it was perhaps fortunate that Papineau did not have the opportunity to seize power, "persuaded as I am at present that you would have governed with a rod of iron." La Fontaine could not resist denouncing Papineau when the latter accused him of seeking office out of self-interest. Had La Fontaine not pursued a policy of cooperation, Papineau "would be at Paris, fraternizing, I suppose, with the red republicans, the white republicans, or the black republicans, and approving, one after the other, the fluctuating constitutions of France."[38]

In the face of these concerted attacks, Papineau's reputation with reformers began to fall. La Fontaine offered an attractive alternative: someone able to bear the responsibility of power, rather than churlishly denouncing those who did. Moreover, as historian Jacques Monet pointed out, Lord and Lady Elgin provided French Canadians with "an alternative focus of loyalty." The Elgin family spent the summer of 1848 at Beaumont in the countryside outside Quebec and mingled frequently with the local residents. Even such small gestures as an informal *levée* at Chambly on Saint-Jean-Baptiste day, and speeches delivered in impeccable French served as a reminder of the essential function of the Crown as a guardian of their historic rights.[39] Elgin consciously recognized this. "Contact with those precious specimens of Anglo Saxondom, who are ignorant of his language, despise his intellect, ridicule his customs, and swindle him in every transaction" would hardly win over any French Canadian. But Elgin believed that if French-Canadian national sentiment were nourished instead of suppressed, it might ultimately "furnish the best remaining security against annexation to the States." This phrase echoed an earlier pronouncement by cabinet minister Étienne-Paschal Taché, who during the era of strained Anglo–American relations in 1846 had declared that the last cannon shot to defend British power in America would be fired by a French Canadian.[40]

The Rebellion Losses Bill and the Tory Rebellion of 1849

1849: La Fontaine introduces the controversial Rebellion Losses Bill.

The real test of the Baldwin–La Fontaine alliance was yet to come. Early in the legislative session of 1849, La Fontaine introduced the controversial Rebellion Losses Bill. The rebellions of 1837–38 had reduced many farms, homes, and other buildings to smoking ruins. The damage was heavier by far in Lower Canada, and legislation in 1845 had already compensated those in Upper Canada whose property had been damaged. But the bill to compensate Lower Canadians whose property had been damaged during the Rebellions of 1837–38 was controversial for reasons beyond the amount of money involved.

Suspicions abounded that many who would be compensated by the bill had been active in the rebellions themselves—it would hardly do to reward treason. Wolfred Nelson, for example, was claiming more than £12 000 in compensation. While neither Baldwin nor La Fontaine had endorsed violent methods, they knew that many members of the assembly had supported the rebellion, and shied away from openly denying that the bill would compensate rebels. The bill itself specified only that those who had been convicted by a court of law would be barred from receiving compensation, and it was well known that many rebels did not fall into that category, having received amnesty, or having fled across the border.

The Rebellion Losses Bill became a critical test, both of the French–English political coalition that La Fontaine and Baldwin had forged, and of responsible government itself. The Tory element in the assembly was not willing to meekly accept the new order of things—and the stormy debates in the assembly over the bill were just the beginning. The member for Hamilton, Sir Allan MacNab, knighted for his role in helping to suppress the rebellions, vehemently denounced the proposed measure, and, warming to his subject, extended his condemnation to all French Canadians, whom he characterized as rebels and aliens. John Prince, who had summarily executed five rebel invaders at Windsor in 1838, now represented Essex as a Tory member, and joined in the vocal opposition to the bill. The most eloquent defender of the Rebellion Losses legislation was Reformer William Hume Blake, solicitor general for Canada West. The Irish-born Blake, a successful lawyer, spoke for almost three hours, alternately impassioned, sarcastic, and dogmatic. He had no sympathy, he said, for "the would be loyalty of honorable gentlemen opposite, which, whilst it affects at all times peculiar zeal for the prerogative of the Crown, is ever ready to sacrifice the liberty of the subject.… True British loyalty owes allegiance alike to the Crown and the constitution." He ridiculed the opposition, suggesting that they erect a gibbet before the door of every French Canadian.

Blake singled out Allan MacNab in particular, denouncing him as a rebel to the constitution and the country.[41] Outraged, MacNab leapt up in a fury, shouting that the words were a lie. Blake refused to retract them. The house erupted in chaos, with the visitors' gallery a seething riot of fistfights and taunts. Ladies present there had to be escorted to safety on the floor of the house, and several spectators were arrested. Blake and MacNab were on the point of blows, only separated from each other by the sergeant-at-arms. The controversy resumed the following day, February 16, with Blake renewing his arguments. John A. Macdonald, Tory member for Kingston, who had held his tongue for as long as he could, at last gave vent to his pent-up wrath, challenging that Blake had deliberately misrepresented some of the legal and historical documents from which he quoted. "I should feel obliged by the honourable member reading all the words," he said pointedly. Blake retorted that he would read any part that he liked. The Speaker quashed the renewed uproar, but the enraged Macdonald demanded satisfaction: he sent a note to Blake challenging him to a duel. Perhaps fortunately, Blake did not appear to fight Macdonald. He later admitted that his language had not been as "measured" as it ought to have been.[42]

But amid all the mayhem, the bill passed its first critical test. Both sections of the Reform-dominated legislative assembly—predominantly English Canada West and predominantly French Canada East—gave majority support to the measure, and it passed by 47 votes to 18. English Canadian reformers showed their commitment to the interests of their opposite numbers in French Canada. The bill subsequently passed by a vote of 20 to 14 in the legislative council. It remained to be seen if it would pass the second test. Elgin found much about the bill distasteful and had been subject to a torrent of petitions and covert threats from Tories demanding that he refuse royal assent to it. On the cold morning of April 25, 1849, Elgin travelled in his carriage from his residence at Monklands to Montreal's parliament buildings. Hostile spectators crowded the visitors' gallery, waiting to see what the governor-general would do.

Elgin pronounced his assent. He recognized that, under responsible government, his own feelings about the bill were not the issue—this was an internal measure, not a matter that touched upon foreign affairs or any imperial question. Hisses and groans rose up from the visitors' gallery, and the crowd rushed down the stairs to the street where Elgin was making his way back to his carriage. The mob shouted insults and spattered the governor with rotten eggs. Elgin escaped the wrath of the protesters, but their rage was not yet spent. Ringing fire bells drew larger crowds into the streets, and hastily printed handbills exhorted them to gather at a public meeting that evening at Montreal's Champ de Mars. A crowd of 1500 poured into the square.

This was not a mob of the poor and disenfranchised. Their dress revealed that many were well-to-do merchants, the respectable classes whose loyalty to the Crown had always

1849: Elgin's assent to the Rebellion Losses Bill triggers the "Tory Rebellion of 1849."

been assured. The crowd pressed through the narrow streets and descended upon the parliament buildings where the legislators were still sitting. The mob smashed windows and tore up furniture and wall hangings. Stones lobbed through the broken windows shattered the gas lamps, and flames, fed by escaping gas, soon began to spread. From the Speaker's chair, the dull but dignified Augustin-Norbert Morin, long-time member of the legislative assembly, solemnly pronounced the adjournment of the House before leading the members in an orderly procession from the riotous chamber. Not all Tories condoned this recourse to violence. Sir Allan MacNab braved the flames to rescue a portrait of his beloved Queen. Meanwhile, a member of the mob declared his own dissolution of "this French house," and another seized the parliamentary mace and paraded it through the streets outside. Fire swept through the building. The crowd grew savage, greeting rumours that some of the French members of parliament were trapped in the cellar with cheers and jubilation. The fire raged unchecked, water hoses having been cut and firemen prevented by the mob from intervening. Montreal's parliament buildings were reduced to ruins, and a valuable library of 20 000 volumes and irreplaceable documents was lost to the flames.

In the days of rioting that followed, the mob descended upon La Fontaine's house, smashing furniture and china, tearing up floorboards and woodwork, burning the stables and uprooting trees in the orchard. La Fontaine's enemies assaulted him in the street, and threats of assassination dogged him all summer. Months after the passage of the bill, when some of the earlier rioters were arrested, La Fontaine's friends, anticipating further trouble, stood guard with guns to protect their leader's house. They killed a would-be attacker, and wounded six others. Baldwin did not offer his opponents so tempting a target: his home was in Toronto, and he stayed at a Montreal boarding house during the parliamentary session. A crowd of attackers laid siege to the house, but Baldwin was not there.

Elgin and his supporters continued to suffer the assaults of the mob. The ladies of the viceregal household were rudely jeered as they went to church. Elgin and his brother, Colonel Bruce, faced a volley of paving stones that protesters had pried up from the streets while their cavalry escort, many of whom were the sons of Montreal's disappointed merchant class, stood by watching with amusement. The panels of Elgin's carriage were

Political cartoon of Elgin, mocking egg-throwing attacks on him.

Source: Artist: J. W. Bengough, *Punch*, 1849.

"Thrown at the Gov: Gen:
Montreal - April 30.
1849"

Source: Office of the Secretary to the Governor General, 2003.

smashed by the onslaught, and the governor had to cover his face for protection. A large rock hit him in the chest. Elgin knew, however, that his duty was clear. As much as it would be unpopular with the formerly privileged classes—those who had enjoyed the economic perquisites of protectionism and a monopoly on political power—he must not interfere with the will of the colony's majority expressed through their own government.

He remained in isolation in his home outside Montreal, determined to do nothing to provoke further violence. Detractors jeered his absence, accusing him of cowardice. Despite the public unrest—the events Elgin described as "the Tory rebellion of 1849"—Elgin refused to use his royal prerogative to thwart the will of the legislature. He thus began the important constitutional convention of colonial self-government in Canada, the convention that would one day culminate in the Commonwealth of Nations: self-governing members of the former British Empire who had won independence not through revolution but through constitutional evolution. Lady Elgin saved the stone that struck her husband, noting its significance in neat writing on the side, and the Elgin family has recently returned it for display in Canada. Elgin's great grandson, the eleventh Earl, while visiting Canada, mused that the souvenir stone was the rock upon which the Commonwealth was founded.

Deepening Economic Troubles and Social Disorder in British North America

Those who had reacted violently were only partially motivated by politics; their grievances were fundamentally economic. Just before the riots had broken out in Montreal, Elgin had written to Grey to assure him that "political discontent, properly so called there is none." Instead, he painted a gloomy picture of Canada's economic state: "The downward progress of events! These are ominous words! But look at the facts," he remonstrated. Property values in most Canadian towns, especially Montreal, had dropped 50 percent in three years. Three quarters of the commercial men were bankrupt. Britain's abandonment of protectionism meant that colonists were forced to seek markets for Canadian wheat in the United States, where their produce faced a tariff of 20 percent.[43]

Elgin had been keeping up a steady stream of letters to Grey in which he pleaded for British help in meeting the costs of the flood of Irish migration, and appealed for a repeal of the restrictive Navigation Acts hampering Canadian trade. "I do not think that you are blind to the hardships which Canada is now enduring," he reasoned, but he doubted whether Grey was aware of how directly they were traceable to British policy. Public officials, including the governor-general himself, had to take their pay in government bonds, which could not be accepted at face value. "My Ministers have No Money," Elgin bluntly exclaimed.[44]

Formerly prosperous merchants and disappointed land speculators were not the only ones bearing the brunt of harsh economic times. Many of the main canal-building projects were substantially complete by the late 1840s, and falling traffic because of American competition had dampened enthusiasm for new schemes. At peak times throughout the 1840s, as many as 10 000 workers at once had found work in canal construction, usually the newly arrived Irish who lacked the resources to farm. Contractors drew labourers as needed from those crowded into nearby shanties who were desperate for wages. To the burgeoning pool of newly arrived Irish competing for work was added an influx from the United States who migrated north when canal-building opportunities in that country began to dry up. Authorities in the Niagara district complained that construction sites for the Welland Canal acted "as beacon lights to the whole redundant and transient population of not only British America, but the United States."[45] A 14-hour day would pay a wage barely sufficient to provide food for two people, leaving families in want even during times of full employment. Some unscrupulous contractors paid workers in scrip only redeemable at contractor-owned stores. Dr. Wolfred Nelson, tending to the medical needs of this distressed population, found himself unable to prescribe the thing most needed: adequate nourishment. With such conditions the norm, the crisis of the 1840s hit especially hard. Diminished traffic at Canadian ports and a glut of timber flooding the market closed off other opportunities for wage labour.

1849: Economic grievances heighten violence among canal labourers.

Harsh economic times exacerbated the existing tensions between rival groups of canal workers that had erupted in occasional violence. During a strike on the Lachine canals in 1843, Irish workers had attacked gangs of French-Canadian strike-breakers; similar confrontations occurred between Scottish stonecutters and their Irish rivals on the Welland Canal in 1844. But not all rivalry was interethnic. Workers from the provinces of Munster and Connaught, which encompass the southern and western counties of Ireland, were divided by sharp rivalries and united by fierce allegiances. Clashes between Roman Catholics and Protestant Orangemen were frequent, but competing Roman Catholic groups also resorted to violence. Shantytowns housing Irish canal workers had long drawn the condemnation of nearby communities; merchants and farmers were sometimes the target of thefts of food and firewood by their impoverished neighbours. Beyond this, residents complained of the drunkenness and senseless brawling that made the canal sites "war zones," according to historian Ruth Bleasdale. One St. Catharines newspaper condemned the canallers as "strange and mad belligerent factions—brothers and countrymen, thirsting like savages for each other's blood."[46]

In such an incendiary climate, lurid stories of revolutions in Europe fed worries that Irish and French agitators would join forces to foment revolution in Canada. Papineau, it has been noted, drew inspiration from his time spent among Paris republicans planning revolution. On his return to Canada, he and his supporters founded the radical republican Parti Rouge in 1848. In Ireland, the disaster of the famine and the inadequacy of Britain's remedies to deal with it spawned the Young Ireland movement, a revolutionary agitation against British rule. Some of the movement's leaders escaped to Paris in the aftermath of the crushed uprising, and by the early 1850s would be active in recruiting supporters in the United States. These republican movements also captured wide support in Canada, and the Irish flocked to monster meetings held to garner adherents and raise funds for the cause. The spectre of Irish republicans taking up arms against British North America from bases in the United States was never far from the minds of authorities in Canada, and fears were fed by a steady stream of dark rumours. One letter from a Boston inform- ant to the governor-general late in 1848 warned of a force of 5000 men, armed and ready to invade; another warning from New York spoke of 50 000.

The violence—actual and potential—among the "Green," or Roman Catholic Irish, was met by equal turbulence on the part of the "Orange" Protestant groups throughout the British North American colonies. Historian Scott W. See, in a study of the Orange Order in New Brunswick, rejects the simple explanation that these competing groups transplanted their rivalries from Ireland. Instead, he sees mid-nineteenth century escalations in violence as a product of social tensions wrought by surging immigration and commercial distress.

In 1849 on the "Glorious Twelfth" of July—the anniversary of the 1690 defeat of the Catholic supporters of James II by the forces of Protestant William of Orange at Ireland's river Boyne—Saint John was convulsed with rioting. Several hundred New Brunswick Catholics turned out to confront a roughly equal number of Protestant marchers, under the eyes of British troops. At least 12 were killed in the melee, and many more injured.[47] The Orange Order in Canada included many of the merchant class—those hard hit by Britain's shift to free trade, and who felt betrayed by the change to responsible government and consequent growth in the power of French-Canadian Roman Catholics. Looking to the chaos in Montreal after the passage of the Rebellion Losses Bill, Elgin speculated that all of the trouble was the work of the Orange societies.

1849: Orange and Green forces clash in riots in Saint John.

Disenchantment with Britain Fuels a Turning toward the United States

Some Orange Order members had already formed a core part of the "British American League," which had begun meeting in the spring of 1849. In April, the League issued a manifesto that was ardent in its protestation of loyalty to the Crown, but which neverthe- less vaguely asserted that the political system required modification and improvement. The manifesto complained that Canada's diversity of national origins was a potent impedi- ment to progress. For his part, Elgin was convinced that the League aimed at annexation of Canada to the United States. Annexation, Elgin ruefully remarked, was invoked as the remedy for all ills, imaginary or real.

By the autumn of 1849, the more rash elements of the British American League had seized the agenda and were now openly advocating a political union of Canada with the United States. On October 11, 1849, the Montreal Annexation Association published an

1849: Montreal Annexation Association publishes manifesto.

Annexation Manifesto, signed by more than 300 people. Signatories included some of the leading businessmen of Montreal, whose loyalty to the Crown had once seemed inviolate. John and William Molson, of the prominent brewing family, were among those who declared their eagerness to cease being "Canadian." John J.C. Abbott, who would in 1891 succeed John A. Macdonald as Conservative prime minister, was among the supporters of the manifesto. He later excused his action by protesting that the annexationists had "no more serious idea of seeking annexation with the United States than a petulant child who strikes his nurse has of deliberately murdering her." Perhaps surprisingly, these Tory annexationists, many of whom decried French Catholic domination, were joined in their cause by radical Rouge adherents. Some Rouge signatories to the manifesto believed that the nationalist aspirations of French Canada could be better realized in a union with the United States. Politics does indeed make strange bedfellows.

Historian Jeffrey McNairn emphasizes that, even among Tories who did not advocate annexation to the American republic, there were many who looked to the United States for constitutional models. "Conservative annexationists wanted to replace parliamentary government with American republicanism by joining the … [United States]. A significantly larger number of conservatives wanted to do the same without joining the union," McNairn argues. They feared that the establishment of responsible government would mean that the power of the legislative assembly would be unchecked. They contemplated such innovations as an elected governor with a legislative veto, or an elected upper house, on the grounds that the British parliamentary system could not be readily transferred to North American society, which lacked its social stratification. William H. Boulton, Toronto's mayor, member of the elite "Family Compact," and denizen of the gracious residence "The Grange" (now part of the Art Gallery of Ontario), was open in his advocacy of an American-style republic. The state of New York, he suggested, had a system of checks, while Canada's constitution was "a rampant democracy." Of course, in Boulton's case, fear of French-Canadian domination was at the heart of his politics. He captured the support of his fellow Orange order stalwarts in his successful election to the legislative assembly in 1848 by vowing his opposition to "Tobacco-smoking, Dram Drinking, Garlick Eating Frenchmen."[48]

Conclusion

In time, remedies for some of Canada's economic woes undercut the lure of the United States—and the fierce American internal divisions that would in the 1860s culminate in civil war made that model less and less appealing. Canada's key economic grievance could not be redressed: no return to imperial protectionism was in the cards. But Britain, in its continued embrace of *laissez-faire* principles, in 1849 repealed the Navigation Acts that had been a source of irritation to Canadian commercial interests. Vessels at London docks lowered their flags to half mast to mourn the end of an era. In the 1850s, the economy of British North America would move in a more determined way toward a continental orientation, with the United States becoming the dominant trade partner. New transportation networks would develop in the railway age to reinforce this economic continentalism.

Politically, new alliances would develop in the 1850s. The 1848 achievement of responsible government, while a major step in British North American constitutional maturity, would not resolve every issue. The precarious balance between French and English in the United Canadas at the close of the 1840s would soon be overturned by burgeoning population growth in Canada West. An equal partnership between French and English satisfied English-Canadian reformers when French numbers were greater. But explosive growth in the numbers of English Canadians would raise crucial questions about political representation and national aspirations.

Questions to Consider

1. What factors led the British government to abandon protectionism?

2. What was the impact of the Irish potato famine on British North America?

3. Who was Joseph Howe and what role did he play in the transition to colonial self-government in Nova Scotia?

4. What was the significance of the Rebellion Losses Bill?

5. What was the Annexation Manifesto?

Critical Thinking Questions

1. What factor was the most significant in Canada's achievement of responsible government?

2. Why did critics of the new system of responsible government look to American models of government? What defects did they think had been introduced?

3. What best explains the surge in social violence in British North America in 1849?

Suggested Readings

Primary Sources

British Parliamentary Papers Relating to Canada, 1847–48, Vol. 17. Shannon: Irish University Press, 1968. Contains details on the Irish famine migration.

British Parliamentary Papers Relating to Canada, 1849, vol. 18. Shannon: Irish University Press. Contains details on the Rebellion Losses Bill, including a complete list of the claimants and amounts claimed.

Doughty, Sir Arthur G., ed. *The Elgin-Grey Papers, 1846–1852*. 4 Vols. Ottawa: J.O. Patenaude, 1937.

Grey, Earl. *The Colonial Policy of Lord John Russell's Administration. 2 Vols.* London: R. Bentley, 1853.

Kennedy, W.P.M., ed. *Statutes, Treaties and Documents of the Canadian Constitution, 1713–1929*, 2nd ed. Toronto: Oxford University Press, 1930. Online through Early Canadiana, http://www.canadiana.org/ECO/ItemRecord/9_03428?id= 5a27814275435f34.

Martin, Chester. "The Correspondence between Joseph Howe and Charles Buller, 1845–1848" *Canadian Historical Review* 6 (1925): 310–331.

The Ships List at http://www.theshipslist.com/ contains a wealth of primary material related to immigration.

Useful Overview Sources

Buckner, Phillip A. *The Transition to Responsible Government: British Policy in British North America, 1815–1850.* Westport, Connecticut: Greenwood Press, 1985.

Buckner, Phillip A. *Canada and the British Empire.* Toronto: Oxford University Press, 2008.

Gwyn, Julian. *Excessive Expectations: Maritime Commerce and the Economic Development of Nova Scotia, 1740–1870.* Montreal and Kingston: McGill-Queen's University Press, 1998.

Harris, R. Cole and John Warkentin. *Canada before Confederation: A Study in Historical Geography.* Toronto: Oxford University Press, 1974.

Knorr, Klaus E. *British Colonial Theories 1570–1850.* Toronto: University of Toronto Press, 1944.

McCallum, John. *Unequal Beginnings: Agriculture and Economic Development in Quebec and Ontario until 1870.* Toronto: University of Toronto Press, 1980.

Messamore, Barbara J. *Canada's Governors General, 1847–1878: Biography and Constitutional Evolution.* Toronto: University of Toronto Press, 2006.

Monet, Jacques. *The Last Cannon Shot: A Study of French-Canadian Nationalism, 1837–1850.* Toronto: University of Toronto Press, 1964.

Ward, John Manning. *Colonial Self-Government. The British Experience, 1759–1856.* Toronto: University of Toronto Press, 1976.

Wynn, Graeme. *Timber Colony: A Historical Geography of Early Nineteenth Century New Brunswick.* Toronto: University of Toronto Press, 1981.

Special Topics

Acheson, T.W. *Saint John: The Making of a Colonial Urban Community.* Toronto: University of Toronto Press, 1993.

Akenson, Donald. "Ontario: Whatever Happened to the Irish?" in *Immigration in Canada: Historical Perspectives.* Gerald Tulchinsky, ed. Toronto: Copp Clark Longman, 1994.

Bleasdale, Ruth. "Class Conflict on the Canals of Upper Canada in the 1840s." *Labour/ Le Travail* 7 (1981): 9–39.

Burn, D.L. "Canada and the Repeal of the Corn Laws." *Cambridge Historical Journal* 2 (1928): 252–272.

Checkland, Sydney. *The Elgins, 1766–1917: A Tale of Aristocrats, Proconsuls and Their Wives*. Aberdeen: Aberdeen University Press, 1988.

Cuccioletta, Donald. "The Montreal Annexation Manifesto of 1849: An Appeal for Liberal Democracy in the Canadas and the rise of French Canadian Liberalism" in *Canada 1849*. Derek Pollard and Ged Martin, eds. Edinburgh: University of Edinburgh Centre of Canadian Studies, 2001, 70–80.

Fecteau, Jean-Marie. *La Liberté du Pauvre. Sur la Régulation du Crime et de la Pauvreté au XIXᵉ Siècle Québécois*. Montréal: VLB Editeur, 2004.

MacKay, Donald. *Flight from Famine: The Coming of the Irish to Canada*. Toronto: McClelland & Stewart, 1990.

Martin, Ged. "The Canadian Rebellion Losses Bill of 1849 in British Politics." *Journal of Imperial and Commonwealth History* 6 (October 1977): 3–22.

McGowan, Mark. *Creating Canadian Historical Memory: The Case of the Famine Migration of 1847*. Ottawa: Canadian Historical Association, 2006.

McNairn, Jeffrey L. "Publius of the North: Tory Republicanism and the American Constitution in Upper Canada, 1848–54." *Canadian Historical Review* 77 (December 1996): 504–537.

Sager, Eric. *Seafaring Labour: The Merchant Marine of Atlantic Canada, 1820–1914*. Montreal and Kingston: McGill-Queen's University Press, 1989.

See, Scott W. *Riots in New Brunswick: Orange Nativism and Social Violence in the 1840s*. Toronto: University of Toronto Press, 1993.

Schuyler, Robert Livingston. "The Abolition of British Imperial Preference, 1846–1860." *Political Science Quarterly* 33 (March 1918): 77–92.

Tucker, Gilbert. "The Famine Immigration to Canada, 1847." *American Historical Review* 36 (April 1931): 533–549.

Tucker, Gilbert. *The Canadian Commercial Revolution, 1845–1851*. New Haven: Yale University Press, 1936.

Way, Peter. "The Canadian Tory Rebellion of 1849 and the Demise of Street Politics in Toronto." *British Journal of Canadian Studies* 10 (1995): 10–30.

Way, Peter. "Evil Humors and Ardent Spirits: The Rough Culture of Canal Construction Labourers." *Journal of American History* 79 (1993): 1397–1428.

Woodham-Smith, Cecil. *The Great Hunger: Ireland, 1845–1849*. New York: Harper & Row, 1962.

Wrong, George. *The Earl of Elgin*. London: Methuen & Co., 1905.

Notes

1   Enclosure 3 in Elgin to Grey, Dispatch no. 91, 27 October 1847, *British Parliamentary Papers Relating to Canada, 1847–48*, vol. 17, 218.

2   Thomas Carlyle, as quoted by James Morris, *Heaven's Command* (Markham, Ontario: Penguin Books, 1979), 305.

3   William A. Green, *British Slave Emancipation* (Oxford: Clarendon Press, 1976), 234–235; Cyril Hamshere, The British in the Caribbean (London: Weidenfeld and Nicolson, 1972), 157; Julian Gwyn, *Excessive Expectations: Maritime Commerce and the Economic Development of Nova Scotia, 1740–1870* (Montreal and Kingston: McGill-Queen's University Press, 1998), 54–56.

4   Thomas Chandler Haliburton as quoted by Robert Livingston Schuyler, "Abolition of British Imperial Preference, 1846–1860," *Political Science Quarterly* 33 (March 1918), 91.

5   A.R.M. Lower, "The Trade in Square Timber," *Contributions to Canadian Economics* 6 (1933), 45.

6   Graeme Wynn, *Timber Colony: A Historical Geography of Early Nineteenth Century New Brunswick* (Toronto: University of Toronto Press, 1981), 33.

7   As quoted by W.S. MacNutt, *The Atlantic Provinces: The Emergence of Colonial Society, 1712–1857* (Toronto: McClelland & Stewart, 1965), 236.

8   John McCallum, *Unequal Beginnings: Agriculture and Economic Development in Quebec and Ontario until 1870* (Toronto: University of Toronto Press, 1980), 4.

9   Extract from Sir Robert Peel's final ministerial speech in the House of Commons, 29 June 1846, http://www.victorianweb.org/history/pms/peel/peel7.html.

10 As quoted by Donald MacKay, *Flight from Famine: The Coming of the Irish to Canada* (Toronto: McClelland and Stewart, 1990), 217. See also Cecil Woodham-Smith, *The Great Hunger: Ireland, 1845–1849* (New York: Harper & Row, 1962).

11 As quoted by Donald MacKay, *Flight from Famine*, 220, 224–225.

12 Grey to Elgin, dispatch 109, 19 July 1847, *British Parliamentary Papers Relating to Canada*, 1847–48, vol. 17, 202.

13 As quoted by Donald MacKay, *Flight from Famine*, 237.

14 Woodham-Smith, *The Great Hunger*, 77, 165.

15 Woodham-Smith, *The Great Hunger*, 91.

16 *The Times* [of London], 3 August 1846, 22 September 1846, 2 September 1846, 15 September 1846.

17 Lord John Russell to Bessborough, as quoted in W.P. Morrell, *British Colonial Policy in the Age of Peel and Russell* (London: Frank Cass & Co, 1966), 430.

18 Donald Akenson, "Ontario: Whatever Happened to the Irish?" *Immigration in Canada: Historical Perspectives*, Gerald Tulchinsky, ed. (Toronto: Copp Clark Longman, 1994), 108–109.

19 "Extract from a Report of a Committee of the Executive Council," 7 December 1847, *British Parliamentary Papers Relating to Canada*, 1847–48, vol. 17, 384.

20 As quoted by J.M.S. Careless, *The Union of the Canadas, 1841–1857* (Toronto: McClelland & Stewart, 1967), 113.

21 "Extract from Report of G.M. Douglas, Medical Superintendent, Grosse Île," and "Extract from Report of A.C. Buchanan, Chief Emigration Agent, 8 December 1847," *British Parliamentary Papers Relating to Canada*, 1847–48, vol. 17, 385, 201.

22 Donald MacKay, *Flight from Famine*, 270–271, 291.

23 D.L. Burn, "Canada and the Repeal of the Corn Laws," *Cambridge Historical Journal* 2 (1928), 264.

24 Elgin to Grey, private, 16 November 1848, *The Elgin-Grey Papers, 1846–1852*, vol. 1, Sir Arthur G. Doughty, ed. (Ottawa: J.O. Patenaude, 1937), 256.

25 "Necessity for Repeal of the Navigation Laws," *Canadian Economist*, 25 July 1846, in H.A. Innis and A.R.M. Lower, *Select Documents in Canadian Economic History, 1783–1885* (Philadelphia, 1977), 349.

26 Lord John Russell to Earl Grey, 19 August 1849, as quoted in Phillip Buckner, *The Transition to Responsible Government: British Policy in British North America, 1815–1850* (Westport, Connecticut: Greenwood Press, 1985), 7.

27 As quoted in Klaus E. Knorr, *British Colonial Theories 1570–1850* (Toronto: University of Toronto Press, 1944), 340.

28 Grey to Sir John Harvey, dispatch, 3 November 1846, *Statutes, Treaties and Document of the Canadian Constitution, 1713–1929*, 2nd ed., W.P.M. Kennedy, ed. (Toronto: Oxford University Press, 1930), 494–496.

29 Lord John Russell, speech of 16 May 1836, as quoted in Stephen Leacock, *Baldwin, La Fontaine, Hincks: Responsible Government* (Toronto: Morand, 1912), 273, n. 2.

30 Joseph Howe to Charles Buller, 4 May 1848, Chester Martin "The Correspondence between Joseph Howe and Charles Buller, 1845–1848" *Canadian Historical Review* 6 (1925), 328.

31 Grey to Harvey, draft dispatch on responsible government, Doughty, Sir Arthur G., ed. *The Elgin-Grey Papers, 1846–1852*, vol. 3 (Ottawa: J.O. Patenaude, 1937), 1151–1155.

32 A "normal school" was a training college for teachers. Howe to Buller, 12 February 1848, Chester Martin, "Correspondence between Howe and Buller," 324.

33 *Elgin-Grey Papers*, I, Elgin to Grey, secret, 24 February 1847, 13.

34 *Elgin-Grey Papers*, I, Grey to Elgin, private, 22 March 1848, 125.

35 *Elgin-Grey Papers*, II, Elgin to Grey, private, 17 December 1850, 775–776.

36 Colin Read, *The Rising in Western Upper Canada, 1837–8: The Duncombe Revolt and After* (Toronto: University of Toronto Press, 1982), 211.

37 W.L. Mackenzie to Lord Elgin, New York, 14 February 1848, in *E-G*, I, 226–234.

38 Wolfred Nelson, as quoted in John Beswarick Thompson, "Wolfred Nelson," *Dictionary of Canadian Biography*, http://www.biographi.ca; Louis Hippolyle La Fontaine, speech of 23 January 1849, as quoted in Stephen Leacock, *Baldwin, La Fontaine, Hincks*, 292.

39 Jacques Monet, *The Last Cannon Shot: A Study of French-Canadian Nationalism, 1837–1850* (Toronto: University of Toronto Press, 1964), 327,

40 *Elgin-Grey Papers*, I, Elgin to Grey, private, 29 June 1848, 191.

41 As quoted by Donald Swainson, "William Hume Blake," *Dictionary of Canadian Biography*, http://www.biographi.ca.

42 Quoted material is from Donald Creighton, *John A. Macdonald: The Young Politician* (Toronto: Macmillan, 1952), 136–138. See also John Charles Dent, *The Last Forty Years: Canada Since the Union of 1841*, vol. II (Toronto: George Virtue, 1881), 149–155.

43 *Elgin-Grey Papers*, Elgin to Grey, private, 23 April 1849, I, 349.

44 *Elgin-Grey Papers*, Elgin to Grey, private, 16 November 1848, I, 256; *Elgin-Grey Papers*, I, Elgin to Grey, 17 February 1848, 124.

45 Ruth Bleasdale, "Class Conflict on the Canals of Upper Canada in the 1840s" *Pre-Industrial Canada, 1760–1849*, Michael S. Cross and Gregory S. Kealey, eds. (Toronto: McClelland & Stewart, 1982), 102.

46 Ruth Bleasdale, "Class Conflict on the Canals," 102–107, 111. See also Peter Way, "Evil Humors and Ardent Spirits: The Rough Culture of Canal Construction Labourers," *Journal of American History* 79 (1993), 1397–1428.

47 Scott W. See, "The Orange Order and Social Violence in Mid-Nineteenth Century Saint John," *Acadiensis* 13 (1983), 68–92.

48 McNairn, Jeffrey L. "Publius of the North: Tory Republicanism and the American Constitution in Upper Canada, 1848–54" *Canadian Historical Review* 77 (December 1996), 520, 522; Quotation by Boulton appears in Hereward Senior, "William Henry Boulton" *Dictionary of Canadian Biography*.

11

Colonial Societies *in* Transition: *1849–1864*

The five Douglas girls, daughters of British Columbia Governor James Douglas, were raised to take their places at the very pinnacle of colonial society. Like all the social leaders in Victoria, the Douglas family was part Aboriginal. Schooled in the kind of refined accomplishments expected of young ladies of their rank, the girls learned dancing, drawing, singing, elegant handwriting, and the art of gracious entertaining. Formal family portraits reveal young ladies attired in the latest fashions of Victorian Britain—elegant silks with demur lace collars and elaborate flounces. For the youngest daughter, Martha, finishing school in England would "get rid of the cobwebs of colonial training," as her father put it. Mother Amelia, born in the western interior to a Scottish fur trader and his Cree wife, was shy about her English skills, and while she won the praise of visitors for her modesty and simple kindness, was content to let her daughters set the tone for hospitality at Government House. The girls' social attainments were showcased at dances, parties, and elaborate weddings, as each in turn was married to a prominent colonial newcomer. One visitor to British Columbia noted with surprise that the girls' Native heritage was even more prominent in their features than in their mother's. But, traditionally, social class, and not race, was the basis of imperial hierarchy, and this would only begin to change by mid-century. Young Agnes Douglas spurned an invitation to dance at a ball in the 1850s because her prospective partner was a mere midshipman. "What would Papa say if I were to dance with a middy?" she protested. The sailor's retort speaks volumes about the shift in colonial society: "What would Mama say if I were to dance with a squaw?"[1]

chapter 11

Source: © McCord Museum, MP-0000.1323.7.

The Cariboo Road, near Chapman's Bar, Upper Fraser River, BC, 1890–1900, by E. Roper.

After reading this chapter you will be able to:

1. Explain the events that led to the Underground Railroad and heightened black migration to Upper Canada.
2. Explain key features of educational reform in the mid-nineteenth century.
3. Account for the rise of Canada West's Clear Grits and new party alliances.
4. Understand the development of a new continental economy.
5. Identify important mid-nineteenth century technological innovations.
6. Assess mid-nineteenth century developments in Rupert's Land and the 1849 breaking of the HBC monopoly.
7. Explain the reasons for changing native policy in the mid-nineteenth century.
8. Assess the impact of newcomers to the Pacific Coast and the causes of the Fraser River War in 1858.

Introduction

By the middle decades of the nineteenth century, the colonies of British North America were in the midst of a far-reaching transition. The great wave of immigration that began after the Napoleonic Wars had worked a transformation in the colonies. The three Maritime colonies—Nova Scotia, New Brunswick, and Prince Edward Island—had grown from a collective total of approximately 80 000 inhabitants at the start of the nineteenth century to over half a million by mid-century. Over the same period, Newfoundland had grown from about 20 000 to 100 000. The decades of the 1850s and 1860s would mark the beginnings of substantial settler population growth in the westernmost parts of British North America—Rupert's Land and the Pacific coast. The gold rush in British Columbia and the challenge to Hudson's Bay Company hegemony in Rupert's Land inaugurated sweeping changes.

British North America's most dramatic growth was in the united Canadas. Canada East's population more than doubled between 1825 and 1851, reaching 890 000. Much of this growth was attributable to natural increase, but immigration was also substantial. By 1861, 260 000 people in Canada East, approximately 22 percent of the population, were not French Canadians. Canada West was the destination of most nineteenth-century newcomers, and by 1851 its population had soared to 952 000. This demographic shift, and the revelation that Canada's English-speaking population had outstripped the French, had profound implications in the decades ahead. An increasingly vocal Protestant majority demanded an end to what they perceived as domination by Roman Catholic interests. In addition to this demographic change, the end of the old mercantilist colonial system in the 1840s prompted a growing continental orientation in the British North American economy. The 1854 Reciprocity Treaty with the United States set out a new pattern of trade, and the emerging use of railways enabled the British North American colonies to exploit it.

Following the North Star to Freedom

Among the new communities springing up in Upper Canada were havens for black immigrants fleeing slavery south of the border. Approximately 3500 blacks had come north as Loyalists in the wake of the American Revolution—Nova Scotia was their prime destination—and in 1793, Upper Canada's Lieutenant Governor John Graves Simcoe took the first steps toward the outright abolition of slavery on Canadian soil, the first limitation on slavery in the British Empire.[2] Upper Canada's legislature passed the *Anti-Slavery Act* in 1793, forbidding the importation of slaves into that province. Some slave-owning members of the assembly resisted outright emancipation—besides black Loyalists, some 2000 enslaved blacks had been brought north at the time of the revolution—but the Act curtailed slavery and stipulated that children born to slaves would be freed at age 25. The British Parliament banned the slave trade throughout the empire in 1807 and legislated an end to slavery in 1833—measures that made British North America a beacon to slaves in the United States following the North Star to freedom.

Josiah Henson was born into slavery in Maryland in 1789. Rough treatment at the hands of a cruel master who broke his arm and both shoulder blades left him permanently disabled. The intelligent and conscientious Henson became indispensable to a new master in Kentucky, trusted to travel on his master's business and spurning the temptation to cross into Ohio, a free state. Henson's travels exposed him to the teachings of Methodist preachers, and by 1828 he began preaching himself, an activity that enabled him to raise the $350 needed to buy his own freedom. But his unscrupulous owner bilked Henson of his savings, refused to honour a previous agreement to free him, and ordered him to be sold in New Orleans. Being "sold down the river" to servitude in the deep south was every slave's worst fear. Henson resolved to trust God and not to despair, but he did not leave things entirely in the hands of the Almighty. His master's son became ill while transporting him south, and the unscheduled return to Kentucky presented Henson with an opportunity to escape. He seized his wife and four children and bolted for Upper Canada in October 1830.

As a farm labourer in Canada, Henson patiently learned to read by each evening's dim light with his 12-year-old son Tom's tutelage. Henson's memoir recalled that the gift of reading, while a great comfort, made him "comprehend better the terrible abyss of ignorance in which I had been plunged all my previous life. It made me also feel more deeply and bitterly the oppression under which I had toiled and groaned; but the crushing and cruel nature of which I had not appreciated, till I found out, in some slight degree, from what I had been debarred."[3] This appreciation made Henson determined to do something to help those still mired in degradation and ignorance.

In 1841, with the help of American missionary Hiram Wilson and Quaker philanthropists, Henson organized a community for black fugitive slaves at Dawn Settlement in Upper Canada. The community had a school, farms, a gristmill, sawmill, brickyard, and rope-making facility. At its peak, 500 lived and worked at the Dawn Settlement. Henson himself became the model for Harriet Beecher Stowe's *Uncle Tom's Cabin*, published in 1852, a novel that gave great impetus to the American emancipation crusade. The Dawn Settlement was not unique; there were a number of communities in Canada for fugitive slaves before the 1865 abolition of slavery in the United States led many to return south. The Elgin Settlement, not far from Dawn, was a community whose educational attainments were truly remarkable. A number of the black pupils of Irish-born Presbyterian minister William King went on to university studies. Dr. Anderson Abbott was among three who became medical doctors; he studied at the University of Toronto and qualified to practise medicine in 1861.

1841: Fugitive slave Josiah Henson establishes Dawn Settlement in Canada West.

*1850: The Underground
Railroad becomes
especially important
after the passage of the
Fugitive Slave Act in
the United States.*

*1851: St. Catharines in
Canada West becomes an
important base for Harriet
Tubman, "conductor" on
the Underground Railroad.*

These thriving communities, and other centres such as Sandwich (now Windsor) and St. Catharines in Upper Canada, became terminal points on the "Underground Railroad," a clandestine network of safe houses and sympathetic friends offering help to runaway slaves. Coded messages in songs, including well-known spirituals, offered direction and encouragement, and black oral history suggests that pictorial symbols in quilt patterns were used to relay secret messages to those on the run, most of whom could not read. An image of flying geese would remind slaves to follow migrating birds north; a log cabin symbol would signify the presence of sympathetic hosts who would provide shelter. Some historians dispute the story of coded quilts as legend, finding no evidence that any such system of communication existed.

The Underground Railroad functioned from 1840 to approximately 1860, bringing as many as 30 000 slaves to freedom in Canada. The passage of the *Fugitive Slave Act* in the United States in 1850 spurred even more desertions to north of the border, since it ended the tradition of sanctuary north of the Ohio River. With the Act's passage, American slave hunters could apprehend their quarry even in free states.

The story of the Underground Railroad is rife with tales of extraordinary individuals, such as Harriet Tubman, a remarkable woman who was known as the Moses of her people because of her role in leading so many to freedom. Born into slavery in Maryland, Tubman suffered a severe blow to the head as a child during an altercation in which an overseer tried to apprehend an escaping slave. The injury left her with epilepsy for the rest of her life. Tubman fled north to freedom in Philadelphia in 1849, leaving behind her free husband; her hopes of reconciliation were dashed when he took another wife.

Tubman established a base of operations in St. Catharines, Upper Canada, in 1851, and escorted an estimated 300 slaves there over the course of the next several years. The British Methodist Episcopal Church known as Salem Chapel, established in St. Catharines by these newcomers, became a centre of Underground Railroad activities and fundraising. As one of the most famous and bold "conductors" on the Underground Railroad, Tubman risked capture to return to the south again and again, employing a variety of clever disguises. She used draconian tactics to stiffen the resolve of slaves tempted to abandon the journey en route; knowing that even one defector could put the entire party at risk, Tubman carried a gun and warned her "passengers" that they would be free or die. But she later reflected with pride that she never lost a passenger.

Harriet Tubman.

The Systemization of Education

The arrival of newcomers into British North America, and the consequent demographic growth, brought with it a more systematic approach to education. The history of Canadian education is closely bound up with the career of Egerton Ryerson, superintendent of schools in Canada West from 1844 to 1876. Born into a Loyalist family, Ryerson was one of five brothers to become a Methodist minister. In his mid-20s, he began to edit the widely influential Methodist newspaper, the *Christian Guardian*. Ryerson worked tirelessly to counter the impression spread by the Anglican elite that the main agents of the Methodist faith were ill-educated American preachers. Education was, to Ryerson, the key to man's achievement of God's purposes, and he saw his appointment as school superintendent as a means to promote Christian virtue in society.

In Canada West, Ryerson inherited a system that included more than 2500 elementary schools. While some of these received government support, most charged fees, attendance was voluntary, and standards were lax. Only in 1871 would education be free and compulsory. To tackle Canada's educational needs, Ryerson compared practices throughout Europe. He was particularly impressed by the system of mass education put in place in Ireland in 1831, and he adopted the Irish National Readers for use in Canada West in the 1840s. In the face of American political and social influences, a curriculum tailored to the Irish Protestant majority of Canada West could be used to reinforce loyalty to British cultural and political values. Ryerson also copied the Irish system of a strong centralized authority controlling what was taught, and how it was taught, instituting "normal" schools to train teachers. Day-to-day control and the hiring of teachers were in the hands of locally elected school trustees sitting on school boards. The system Ryerson implemented in Canada West would in the post-Confederation era influence education in British Columbia, Manitoba, and the Northwest Territories (which in the nineteenth century encompassed Canada's prairies).

By 1853, Ryerson had also tackled the problem of education beyond the elementary level: new legislation established central control over grammar schools, as high schools or collegiate institutes were then known. These secondary schools would be part of the larger educational system, would receive government funding, and would be subject to regular inspection. Overseen by a headmaster who was required to have a university degree, grammar schools were intended for the minority of students continuing on after age 12.

Ryerson also took an active interest in post-secondary education. In 1841, he became the first principal of Victoria College, a Methodist university that became part of the University of Toronto. The University of Toronto had begun its life in 1827 as King's College, an Anglican institution, but the university's association with the elite Church of England made it a target for reformers' demands for a secular institution, and by 1850 legislation transformed it into a non-denominational university.

Anglicans established their own Trinity College in response, which remained a separate institution until early in the twentieth century. The same year that Victoria College was created, Queen's University in Kingston was established by the Presbyterian Church. The growth of these institutions reflected the maturation of Canada West. Other parts of British North America had long since had universities catering to their more established populations: King's College in Windsor, Nova Scotia—English Canada's oldest university—had been established in 1788, shortly after the arrival of the Loyalists. New Brunswick's Provincial Academy of Arts and Sciences received a university charter in 1800 as the College of New Brunswick. It was later known as King's College before becoming the University of New Brunswick. Dalhousie in Halifax followed in 1818, Montreal's McGill University in 1821, and two more institutions in Atlantic Canada in the 1830s—Mount Allison in Sackville, New Brunswick, and Acadia in Wolfville, Nova Scotia. St. Francis-

1844: Egerton Ryerson is appointed superintendent of schools in Canada West and begins ambitious reforms.

1853: New regulations are introduced for grammar schools (high schools).

1850: The University of Toronto becomes a non-denominational university.

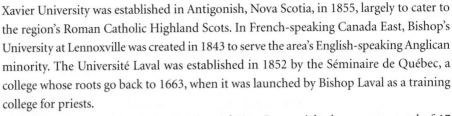

Xavier University was established in Antigonish, Nova Scotia, in 1855, largely to cater to the region's Roman Catholic Highland Scots. In French-speaking Canada East, Bishop's University at Lennoxville was created in 1843 to serve the area's English-speaking Anglican minority. The Université Laval was established in 1852 by the Séminaire de Québec, a college whose roots go back to 1663, when it was launched by Bishop Laval as a training college for priests.

In the united Canadas, Nova Scotia, and New Brunswick, there were a total of 17 degree-granting institutions by the time of Confederation. Most of these were controlled by specific religious denominations, with only Dalhousie, McGill, the University of New Brunswick, and the University of Toronto non-denominational. Despite the multiplication of institutions of higher learning in the first half of the nineteenth century, these colleges were tiny by modern standards, few serving a student body of over 100. While only a minority pursued education to the level of grammar school, university education was truly the exclusive preserve of a privileged elite.

New Political Alliances in the United Canadas

1851: Canada West's population exceeds that of Canada East.

Changing demographics in the united Canadas would have a far-reaching effect on the cooperative balance struck in the 1840s by Robert Baldwin and Louis-Hippolyte La Fontaine. By 1851, both of these political reformers had resigned from office, their places taken by Francis Hincks in Canada West and Augustin-Norbert Morin in Canada East. But a new political force was on the rise in Canada West, partly inspired by the revelation of the 1851 census that the population in that section of the united colony was marginally larger.

The 1840 Act of Union's provision for equal representation for each half of the colony had been unfair to the French when their numbers were greater—now it was unfair to the English, and Upper Canada's Clear Grit party made representation by population, or "rep by pop," their rallying cry. This rising element disapproved of the drift toward moderate conciliatory politics among reformers. One of the party's founding members, Scottish-born farmer and politician David Christie, objected to the inclusion of a man who was thought to be too yielding, and his protestation gave the party its name. "We don't want him!" Christie exclaimed. "We want only men who are clear grit."[4]

These Upper Canadian agrarian radicals urged more American-style political systems, and criticized the alliance between French and English reformers that had been carefully nurtured under Baldwin and La Fontaine. Besides representation by population, they sought universal manhood suffrage, more elective institutions, and the secularization of the clergy reserves—the land that had been set aside for the support of Upper Canada's Protestant clergy. Tension between the Anglican Church and other Protestant denominations had led to an agreement for the sharing of the reserves in the 1840s. But the Clear Grits now demanded something more. Embracing the idea of "voluntaryism"—the notion that churches ought to be purely voluntary organizations, without government support or political influence—this party wanted the reserves withdrawn from church control altogether and placed in the hands of local municipalities. This issue indirectly touched Canada East as well—any talk of curtailing the influence of the church in politics was deeply threatening to the Roman Catholic Church in French Canada.

The Clear Grit political faction had an influential voice in George Brown, an Edinburgh-raised reforming journalist, who founded the Toronto newspaper *The Globe* in 1844. Brown won election to the assembly in 1851. Brown's entry into politics, and his emerging leadership of the Clear Grit faction, split the ranks of reformers. His adamant stance on voluntaryism, and his eagerness to curtail what he perceived as undue French-Canadian influence in government, ensured that no acceptable compromise could be reached with reformers in the eastern half of the province. The 1853 *School Act*—a concession to Catholic demands for state-funded education in Canada West—was to Brown evidence of the "entering wedge of priestly encroachment," and he was determined to fight back.

1851: Globe *editor George Brown enters politics as a voice for Canada West's Clear Grit reformers.*

Heightened Religious Antagonisms

Events in the wider world were also playing into Brown's anti-Catholic agenda. Italian nationalists Giuseppe Mazzini and Giuseppe Garibaldi had in 1848 made a bold bid to unify Italy by wresting it away from the control of the Austrian empire and breaking the control of the Vatican in the Papal States. While the 1848 Revolution did not succeed, their temporary success in driving Pope Pius IX into exile emboldened anti-Catholic activists the world over. Once restored to the Vatican, Pius IX's vehement anti-liberalism further stimulated international anti-Catholic forces. Especially provocative was Pius's aggressive bid to recapture the Catholic Church's lost influence in England, symbolized by his 1850 appointment of bishops to bishoprics vacant since the Elizabethan age. Orange Order membership in North America surged in this period.

1853: The Gavazzi riots were sparked by an ex-priest's anti-Catholic speaking tour.

In the summer of 1853, Protestant–Catholic tensions reached a flashpoint in Canada. Protestants flocked to hear the wild rantings of former Catholic priest Alessandro Gavazzi, who launched an incendiary speaking tour throughout North America. A supporter of Garibaldi's patriot movement, Gavazzi broke with Rome during the 1848 Revolution and condemned the evils of popery to Protestant audiences who needed little convincing. On the night of June 6, 1853, Gavazzi was in full rhetorical flight in Quebec's Free Presbyterian

Gavazzi riots, 1853.

Source: © McCord Museum, MP-0000812.2.

Church when a shower of stones shattered the window and an angry mob burst through the doors. Gavazzi's supporters managed to fend off the largely Irish attackers, who then surged forward to Quebec's parliament buildings, where they hoped to confront George Brown. More than anyone else, Brown was seen to personify anti-Catholicism in Canada. But the mob was disappointed: Brown had not arrived for that evening's sitting of parliament. Russell's Hotel, where Gavazzi was lodging, withstood a virtual state of siege, protected with armed guards until the renegade priest was escorted to the docks for his journey on to Montreal.

At Montreal's Zion Church on June 9, Gavazzi's anti-Catholic tirade took place in the shadow of troops called out from the local garrison, with incensed Catholic protestors clashing with Gavazzi's Protestant audience, many of whom were members of the Orange Order. But as the Protestant congregation was leaving the church, in the riotous confusion, troops opened fire. Ten people were killed and dozens wounded. The "martyrdom" of these Canadian Protestants fuelled the already strong anti-Catholic sentiment in Canada West and helped further George Brown's cause. Brown's resistance to political compromise to accommodate Roman Catholics now seemed to his supporters to be evidence of a principled refusal to be intimidated by violence.

Shifting Party Politics

In the aftermath of the Gavazzi riots, Brown's influence continued to grow, and he launched a successful attack on Reform leader Francis Hincks, who exemplified the spirit of pragmatic compromise that Brown had so denounced. Evidence of corruption on Hincks's part gave Brown further ammunition: *The Globe* helped to drive Hincks from office in 1854 with allegations that he had personally profited from a variety of investment schemes that took advantage of his insider status.

1854: A new Liberal–Conservative coalition emerges after the collapse of the old Baldwin–La Fontaine reform alliance.

Hincks's political downfall and division among reformers paved the way for a new alliance in the 1850s. Hincks had once brokered the understanding between Baldwin and La Fontaine, an alliance that successfully won responsible government. That alliance had unravelled amidst the aggressive and uncompromising stance of Canada West's Clear Grit reformers, but the 1848 achievement of responsible government pointed a way for other former antagonists to come together. At one time, responsible government had been the great dividing issue between Canadian Tories and Reformers. Since that milestone had been achieved, the ideological gulf between parties was beginning to close, and moderate Tories and moderate Reformers found they had much in common.

1854: Canada East's seigneurial system ends; in Canada West, the clergy reserves are secularized.

In 1854 a Liberal–Conservative coalition under Sir Allan MacNab and Augustin-Norbert Morin was sworn into office. This ministry carried forward many of the long-standing goals of political moderates. Canada West's clergy reserves were secularized, and turned over to the municipalities. Canada East's seigneurial system was abolished, with the seigneurs paid compensation for the loss of their traditional privileges.

Morin was forced to step down due to ill health and was replaced in Canada East by Étienne-Paschal Taché in 1855, continuing the proto-federal tradition of having co-premiers, one French and one English. Some reformers wished to carry the federal idea still further: John Sandfield Macdonald in Canada West made "double majority" his platform.

According to this principle, any measure passed in the united Canadas would have to have majority support in each half of the united legislature, rather than a simple overall majority. While appealing on a philosophical level, the political compromises necessary to carry on government made this a near impossibility. In the meantime, the MacNab–Taché administration took further steps to meet Reformers' demands through the introduction of an elected legislative council (the precursor of the modern senate). In 1856, this measure was put in place, although existing appointed councillors had the right to continue in office. The experiment in an elected upper house would prove short-lived.

1856: Canada implements an elected upper house.

That same year, Conservative John A. Macdonald replaced the aging MacNab as leader in Canada West. In 1857, Taché's place as leader for Canada East was filled by George-Étienne Cartier, who led what was now known as the Bleu party. The Macdonald–Cartier Conservative partnership would ultimately become a dominant force in Canadian politics, yet for the moment, George Brown's Clear Grit stranglehold on Canada West kept the Conservatives in a minority position in that portion of the united Canadas. At the same time, Brown could not hope to command any support in Canada East, where French Catholics naturally recoiled from his vehement stance on voluntaryism. In the years to come, a more fundamental political reorganization would have to take place in order to overcome the fractured factionalism that now characterized Canadian statecraft.

1857: The long-lived Macdonald–Cartier political partnership begins.

A Continental Economy

By the 1850s, British North America's economic orientation was increasingly a continental one. The loss of imperial tariff protection and the advent of responsible government diminished ties to Britain. The resolution in the 1840s of some of the residual tensions between the Britain and the United States over territory paved the way for strengthened economic ties across the border. The 1842 Ashburton–Webster Treaty had settled the boundary between New Brunswick and Maine, ending conflict over lumbering in the area. The 1846 Oregon Boundary Treaty had set the Pacific coast border at the 49th parallel. With these cross-border differences settled, progress was possible toward a trade agreement. The economic devastation wrought by the loss of imperial preference in the 1840s lent urgency to this goal.

The promotion of closer trade ties with the United States always raised the spectre of outright political annexation, yet proponents of a reciprocity treaty argued that improved economic prospects in British North America would instead dampen enthusiasm for union with the Americans. One of the most enthusiastic advocates of free trade was Canada West politician William Hamilton Merritt, who had also been the driving force behind the Welland Canal. Merritt bombarded the governor general, Lord Elgin, with arguments in favour of liberalized trade with the United States, and communicated with like-minded politicians in the Maritimes as well. Elgin had the task of negotiating with the Americans on behalf of the British colonies, a difficult undertaking since the Americans were lukewarm about free trade. It seemed clear that the benefits would be mainly felt on the northern side of the border, where commercial interests could enjoy access to a market in the United States that was 10 times the size of their own. Moreover, the Americans were preoccupied with the question of slavery, and especially the precarious balance

1854: Reciprocity Treaty establishes free trade in natural products between the United States and British North America.

1852: New Brunswick is the first of the British North American colonies to convert from pounds to dollars.

1840: Nova Scotian Samuel Cunard begins a transatlantic steamer service for the British Royal Mail.

between slave and free states in the union. Elgin craftily convinced southern senators that reciprocity would help stave off political annexation, thus avoiding the addition of more slave-free territory. To northern senators, Elgin reversed his pitch, presenting free trade as a step *toward* a future political union.

The tactic succeeded and the Reciprocity Treaty was concluded in 1854. The treaty was to be in place for ten years, subject to cancellation with a year's notice by either side. Tariffs would be eliminated on a long list of natural products, and the coastal waters of each nation would be open to fishers from either side of the border, a powerful inducement to the United States. Additionally, access to the St. Lawrence–Great Lakes waterways would be shared.

Whether attributable to the Reciprocity Treaty alone, or to general economic improvement, exports from Canada to the United States surged—from a value of $8 million in 1854 to $18 million in 1856. Imports into British North America from the United States also rose sharply, reflecting a growing continental orientation in trade.

While not in itself a product of the treaty, currency reform in the British North American provinces simplified trade through the adoption of a decimal-based currency. The united Canada's *Currency Act* of 1853, proclaimed the following year, permitted provincial accounts to be kept in dollars and cents—valued on par with American currency—as well as the more complex British system of pounds, shillings, and pence.[5] New Brunswick had already adopted a decimalized system in 1852. In 1857, Canada revised its *Currency Act* so as to convert to dollars entirely, and the province's first coins were struck in 1858. Other provinces followed suit in the early 1860s.

"The Ringing Grooves of Change": Mid-Nineteenth-Century Technology

The mid-nineteenth century seemed an age of technological marvels. Developments in transportation, communication, and engineering were among the hopeful signs of modern progress. British North America was poised to overcome the challenges of great distances and limited infrastructure with technical innovation.

Nova Scotia-born Samuel Cunard was among the earliest to recognize the full potential of steamship navigation. Cunard had little formal education, but as a teenager helped to expand his father's merchant activities, moving from timber sales to trade in coal, iron, West Indian sugar, molasses, and spirits, making shrewd investments in Halifax waterfront property and branching into shipping. A. Cunard and Son shipping agents, launched in 1813, would grow to become the world-famous Cunard Shipping Line. While the beginning of the railway age in the 1830s made water transportation seem hopelessly old-fashioned, Cunard recognized that the advent of steam would enable ships to operate as punctually as if on an ocean railway. In 1839, Cunard and his partners successfully bid to provide the British Royal Mail with regular steam service between Liverpool, Halifax, Quebec, and Boston, risking the perils of repeated North Atlantic crossings through the winter season. The service commenced in 1840, with the company's first steamer, the *Britannia*, making the crossing in 14 days. Cunard's innovations included the use of shipping navigation lights—red on a vessel's port side, green on the starboard—an idea that has since been adopted the world over.

The city of Halifax looked forward to an economic boom and envisaged a future as the primary terminus for transatlantic traffic, but business interests dictated that most vessels travel directly to Boston and New York. By 1867, Cunard's service to Halifax ended altogether. While Nova Scotia was thus left behind, Cunard Lines continued to prosper, meeting the challenge of American competitors who set new standards in speed by emphasizing Cunard's spotless safety record in passenger traffic. Indeed, the 1915 loss of the *Lusitania,* torpedoed by a World War I German submarine, marked the first loss of passengers on a Cunard vessel. The need for speed did, however, dictate a shift from paddle-wheels to screw-driven propellers, and from wooden to iron-hulled vessels, beginning in the mid-1850s. This technological shift dealt a profound blow to Nova Scotia's shipbuilders and New Brunswick's timber trade. The era of wind, wood, and water was drawing to a close.

Mid-1850s: The shift from wooden sailing ships to iron-hulled steamers signals the end of an era in the Maritimes.

Among the marvels of new technological innovation was the telegraph, launched by American painter Samuel Morse in 1844. Morse's first test message, sent from Washington to Baltimore, reflects the breathless wonder of the age: "What Hath God Wrought!" Canada's first telegram was sent from Toronto to Hamilton in 1846, and within a couple of years telegraph lines following railway routes connected Canadian cities.

1846: Canada enters the age of the telegraph.

Frederick Gisborne, who had emigrated from England in 1845, was an early promoter of telegraph technology, organizing an overland link from Nova Scotia through New Brunswick to the United States, and then in 1852 an insulated underwater cable between New Brunswick and Prince Edward Island—the world's first submarine telegraph system.

1852: The world's first submerged telegraph cable is laid between New Brunswick and Prince Edward Island.

Another submerged cable, this time between Cape Ray, Newfoundland, and Cape Breton Island, followed in 1856. Gisborne's success inspired a far more ambitious plan. For the British North American colonies, the slow rate of communication with Britain was often a great inconvenience—sometimes more than an inconvenience: the British forces at the 1815 Battle of New Orleans lost thousands of casualties without knowing that the War of 1812 had ended two weeks before. After a number of unsuccessful attempts, in 1858 British and American entrepreneurs of the Atlantic Telegraph Company laid a submerged transatlantic cable between Ireland and Trinity Bay, Newfoundland. Unfortunately, excessive voltage damaged the cable and it stopped working within three weeks. But by 1866 the project was renewed, with cable laid between Valencia, Ireland, and Heart's Content, Newfoundland. Within 20 years, more than 160 000 kilometres (100 000 miles) of undersea cable would link all the parts of the world.

Perhaps the most far-reaching technological change for Canada was the growth of railways. The railway age had already arrived in Great Britain—in fact, British cabinet minister William Huskisson, the great advocate of free trade, was an early railway casualty: at the official opening of the Liverpool and Manchester Railway in 1830, Huskisson was run over by the locomotive while crossing the tracks. Forward-thinking British North Americans were clamouring aboard the railway mania, seeing in this new technology a means to exploit the growing continental orientation of trade, but also a civilizing influence that would break down narrow parochial views. Thomas Keefer of Montreal and Thomas Chandler Haliburton of Nova Scotia saw railways as essential to colonial progress. Keefer's 1849 pamphlet, "The Philosophy of Railroads," lamented the fact that a reliance on water transportation meant that much commercial life in Canada ground to a standstill with the onset of winter: "The animation of business is suspended, the life blood of commerce is curdled and stagnant in the St. Lawrence—the great aorta of the North." Haliburton's writings sounded a similar note, even presciently calling for "a safe, easy, and expeditious route to Frazer's River on the Pacific," something that would not be realized until 1885.[6]

Some of Canada's leading politicians actively promoted railway-building schemes. In an age before clear conflict-of-interest regulations had been enacted, the line between the demands of public service and personal interests were sometimes blurred. Francis Hincks reaped handsome profits in railway stocks while overseeing legislation affecting the value of those same stocks. George-Étienne Cartier both introduced the bill to charter the Grand Trunk Railway and acted as the company's solicitor. Sir Allan MacNab acted as director of both the Great Western Railway and the Grand Trunk, and used his political influence to extort thousands of pounds in personal profit. MacNab is supposed to have confessed after "one or two bottles of good port" that "all my politics are railroads."[7]

1836: Canada's first railway is built.

Railway building in Canada began with the 1836 opening of the 26-kilometre-long (16-mile) Champlain and St. Lawrence Railroad between La Prairie on the St. Lawrence and St. Jean on the Richelieu River. Among the many who turned out for the gala opening celebration was future rebel leader Louis-Joseph Papineau. Despite the excitement surrounding this brave beginning, and a couple of other small-scale railways in Canada and Nova Scotia, there were only 106 kilometres (66 miles) of railway track in all the British North American provinces by 1850. Within ten years that number multiplied to over 3200 kilometres (2000 miles).

The Grand Trunk Railway, begun in 1853, quickly became the largest project, incorporating a number of existing smaller lines, including one running from Longueuil, Quebec to Portland, Maine. To these routes was added track from Montreal to Toronto, and then further west to Sarnia. By 1860, track extended from Quebec to Rivière du Loup. The challenge of spanning the St. Lawrence in Montreal, the hub of nineteenth-century commerce, spurred Canada's proudest technological showpiece of the age: the Victoria Bridge, billed as the eighth wonder of the modern world. Spanning 2.7 kilometres and able to withstand the vibrations of rail traffic, the strong current of the St. Lawrence, and the pressure of ice jams, the Victoria Bridge's tubular steel design represented state-of-the-art engineering technology and set the standard for thousands of rail bridges to follow.

1860: Montreal's Victoria Bridge is heralded as the eighth wonder of the modern world.

The Prince of Wales, later to become King Edward VII, formally opened the bridge named in his mother's honour in August 1860, presiding over a dazzling spectacle of Victorian self-congratulation, which included fireworks, banquets, concerts, and gala balls for several thousand celebrants. The Prince, making the first official royal tour to British North America, had earlier toured Newfoundland and the Maritimes, touching off what historian Bonnie Huskins shows was a frenzy of competitive civic boosterism between the rival cities of Saint John and Halifax.[8] On September 1, 1860, close to the end of the two-month royal progress, the Prince laid the cornerstone of the new gothic-revival style Parliament building in Ottawa.

September 1, 1860: The Prince of Wales lays the cornerstone of Ottawa's new Parliament buildings.

After the 1849 destruction of Montreal's legislative building, the unsatisfactory system of moving the capital between Toronto and Quebec had been settled by referring the question to Queen Victoria in 1857. Her choice of Ottawa (formerly Bytown) began the transformation of a rough lumber town with muddy unpaved roads into Canada's political nerve centre.

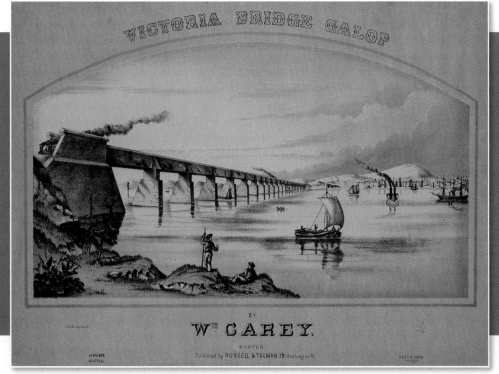

Source: © McCord Museum, M981.130.1-4.

Sheet music composed to commemorate the opening of the Victoria Bridge.

The Changing World of the Métis

Isolated in Rupert's Land on the western prairies, the settlement at Red River established earlier in the century was entering a period of profound change. Métis families on the prairies lived by means of the buffalo hunt, small-scale agriculture, and seasonal work for the Hudson's Bay Company, which since 1821 held monopoly trade rights on the prairies. But the hegemony of the company on the prairies would not survive the challenges of the mid-nineteenth century. The wider world was coming to Red River.

As early as the days of Selkirk, Roman Catholic missionaries had begun their work in the colony; Joseph-Norbert Provencher and two other priests had arrived in 1818. Although Provencher had initially shrunk from the task, protesting that he was not the right man for the job, he would go on to devote his life's work to Red River, becoming the first Bishop of St. Boniface in 1847. The presence of a vigorous Roman Catholic community in the future province of Manitoba ensured the persistence of French culture there.

In 1844, four Grey nuns arrived in Red River. They had made an arduous journey west from Montreal, enduring cold and rain, travelling with voyageurs using the fur trading brigade routes. In late June of that year, Governor George Simpson at Lower Fort Garry had been surprised to hear boisterous singing on the Red River as a flotilla of canoes approached. The tune was a familiar boatman's song, but the words were different—a song of praise and worship taught to the voyageurs by 38-year-old Sister Marie-Eulalie Lagrave, one of the Grey nuns headed west. Within two weeks, these energetic women established an elementary class for girls in the settlement. Bishop Provencher had also

1844: Grey nuns arrive to join Roman Catholic missionaries already working in Red River.

requested more priests from Montreal, but was dismayed at what he was sent: among the arrivals were 24-year-old Louis-François Richer Laflèche—he had been born the year Bishop Provencher first came to Red River—and a youthful-looking novice, Alexandre Taché, just 21 years old. "I have asked for priests, and what do they send me? Children!" Provencher burst out. He later amended his judgment, assuring authorities that "you can send me, without fear, more of these Tachés and Laflèches."[9] Despite being disabled by severe rheumatism, Father Laflèche, whose own family background was part Métis, spent 12 years in the northwest, establishing a base further afield in Ile-à-la-Crosse (Saskatchewan), and extending his missionary work to Reindeer Lake and Lake Athabasca.

While Roman Catholic orders were the first to begin missionary work on the prairies, Protestants followed soon afterward. The Reverend John West, a Church of England missionary, arrived in Red River in 1820 and began work on the church that would become St. John's Cathedral. Unfortunately, West's approach to his evangelical work was less than a resounding success. The community of Red River was already experiencing strain—to the residual conflicts between Nor'Westers and employees of the HBC were added new sources of division. West stubbornly adhered to a program of "civilizing" his parishioners and alienated much of his flock by insisting that marriages contracted *à la façon du pays* be solemnized. In some instances, this had an unintended effect, as men who had been given the message that their country marriages were not valid discarded their Native and mixed-race wives; Aboriginal families were increasingly seen as a social impediment in a changing northwest. Unfortunately, West's successor at Red River, Reverend William Cockran, who arrived in 1825, similarly promoted divisiveness in the colony as opposed to social harmony. He enjoyed little success in his program to encourage Natives and mixed-race traders to abandon hunting and trade in favour of a settled agricultural life. Not surprisingly, curtailing the influence of Roman Catholic missionaries in Red River was also part of the agenda. St. Andrew's Church, built in the 1840s, remains a visible symbol of the missionaries' earnest wish to re-create the familiar world of an English parish. Historian and travel writer James Morris remarked that "there could hardly be a more homesick church than the Anglican church of St. Andrew's, peaceful beside the river, with its imported English trees doing well in the churchyard, its authentic English smells of church must and hassock (though the hassocks were made of buffalo hide)," and even soaring skylarks imported from England.[10]

The multiplying conflicts between those who wished to live a traditional plains lifestyle, and those who followed the missionaries' prompting to adopt European ways were also part of larger divisions over the future of the colony. As Red River's isolation decreased, it was becoming apparent that rule by the Hudson's Bay Company was an anachronism. What was less certain was the form any new authority in the colony would take.

Another aspect of Red River's integration into a wider world was the expansion of trade to the south. The establishment in the 1840s of a trading post at Pembina, just south of Red River in American territory, opened up the American market to Métis traders in Rupert's Land. Métis families were all the more inclined to focus their attention on trade rather than agriculture, since harvests had been bad for several successive years. Buffalo robes, once used predominantly by the Indians and traders, were increasingly popular in the eastern market, and durable buffalo hide was also valued for industrial purposes:

it made ideal belting for steam-driven equipment. Cuthbert Grant, who in 1816 had led Métis traders in a bloody confrontation with HBC authorities at Seven Oaks, now served that same company as Warden of the Plains of Red River. From his estate at White Horse Plain (west of present-day Winnipeg) he worked to prevent illicit trading, served as sheriff, and was a member of the Council of Assiniboia, which since 1835 had helped to administer Red River for the HBC. Grant also worked to make peace with the Dakota, a Sioux nation to the south of Red River, when the expansion of the Métis buffalo hunt into traditional Dakota territory triggered skirmishes between the two groups in 1844. But Grant's status as an HBC employee ultimately undercut his credibility with the Métis, and, in the second half of the nineteenth century, the cooperative pragmatic approach he embraced would give way to a more militant stance under other leaders who wished to challenge the continued trade monopoly of the Hudson's Bay Company.

While the philosophical shift in British government quarters toward free trade suggested that the days of the company monopoly were numbered, immediate events in the west lent greater urgency to the change. In 1846, 300 British regular troops had been stationed in the vicinity of Red River; HBC Governor George Simpson had convinced British authorities that extra defence precautions against American invasion were necessary in the strained atmosphere of the Oregon Boundary crisis. The removal of the troops in 1848 now emboldened Métis traders who wished to flout the authority of the HBC.

1849: The Sayer trial marks the effective end to the HBC trade monopoly in Rupert's Land.

In the spring of 1849, HBC Chief Factor John Ballenden arrested four Métis traders for illegal trafficking in furs and liquor. Among the four was Pierre-Guillaume Sayer, whose case would mark a major turning point in Rupert's Land history. The day of the trial was Ascension Day, and the Métis who had attended mass at St. Boniface Cathedral gathered at the church steps to listen to a stirring and impassioned appeal for trade freedom by Louis Riel senior. That afternoon, over 200 Métis congregated noisily outside the courthouse. Sayer had clearly violated the law, and the jury found him guilty, but recommended mercy on the grounds that Sayer had not believed his actions to be illegal. Charges against the other three traders were dropped. In the presence of an armed band—and the absence of any alternative force—Ballenden recognized that enforcement of the company monopoly was impossible. When Sayer appeared outside the court a free man, a chorus of celebratory gunfire resounded and a cry rose up from the exultant crowd: "Vive la liberté! La commerce est libre!" (Long live liberty! The trade is free!).

With the Hudson's Bay Company monopoly effectively broken, traffic in Red River carts carrying buffalo hides south picked up sharply. In 1844, six carts carried cargoes south to St. Paul; by 1855, this had risen to 400, and by 1858 the level of trade had doubled again to 800.

1851: A clash between Métis and Saulteaux allies and the Sioux consolidates Métis dominance of the plains.

The steady stream of carting traffic, and the more aggressive pursuit of buffalo in wider areas brought the Métis and their Saulteaux allies into conflict with the Sioux again in 1851. That summer, bands of Métis hunters from Saint Boniface, Saint Francois-Xavier (White Horse Plain), and Pembina to the south, met up for the hunt, working together so as to be prepared for any confrontation with the Sioux.[11]

The structured and organized Métis hunting groups were accompanied by Roman Catholic priests, Father Laflèche and Father Albert Lacombe. At Grand Coteau, in present-day North Dakota, on July 13, 1851, the Métis clashed with a war party of some 2000 Sioux.

Three Métis scouts had been taken prisoner the day before by the Natives, who then attempted to open negotiations for their release. Father Laflèche was among those in the Métis camp who feared a trap and argued for bold military action, even if it meant the captives would be killed. As the Métis prepared for battle that night, an eclipse of the moon seemed an eerie portent. Laflèche administered the sacrament so that the Métis fighters might die well.

The next morning, the Métis, having prepared a defensive position behind overturned carts, and having armed every male over the age of 12—77 fighters in all—dealt a devastating defeat to the formidable Sioux. Jean-Baptiste Falcon watched the Sioux approach, a young chief riding at their head. The warrior was "so beautiful," Falcon remembered, "that my heart revolted at the necessity of killing him." He fired his weapon and shot the warrior off his horse. From his place at the middle of the circle of wagons, Father Laflèche, clad in a flowing white surplice and holding a crucifix high, exhorted the Métis warriors to victory, soothed the children, and prayed. He did not join the battle, but kept a hatchet nearby, determined to use it if the Sioux broke through their defences. One of the captured scouts named Malaterre made a desperate bid to escape from the Sioux camp; he was felled by a flurry of arrows and musket balls. The Natives brandished his torn and mutilated body to demoralize the Métis encampment.

After six hours of battle, the Sioux were unable to prevail against steady Métis defensive fire, and broke off the fight. A chief, seeing Laflèche's courage under fire, was heard to cry that the French had a Manitou (spirit) with them and could not be defeated. The next day, the Métis retreated to join up with the other branch of their hunting party and their Saulteaux allies, bringing the number of warriors to 700. Fresh hostilities broke out and the day ended with some 80 Sioux dead, many more wounded, and 65 horses lost. Only one, the captive Malaterre, was lost on the Métis side. A drenching thunderstorm rolled in across the coteau, adding to the sorrowful spectacle for the Sioux whose warriors lay dead on the prairie. The Métis, historian William Morton argued, now became "masters of the plain." The battle ended the protracted war between the Métis and their Sioux rivals, and added another tale of legendary valour to the growing national consciousness of the Métis people.[12]

Yet events had been set in motion that would bring an end to the Métis way of life. Paradoxically, the breaking of the power of the HBC—a development welcomed by the free trading Métis—brought wider change to the plains. The Métis would be supplanted in turn by newcomers coming to the west not to hunt but to farm. The population of Assiniboia, which included Red River Settlement, had already been climbing slowly from its modest beginnings. From 2751 in 1832, the population had risen to 6691 in 1856.[13]

By 1855, the supply of available frontier farmland in Upper Canada was becoming exhausted. Expansion-minded Canadians, such as *Globe* editor George Brown, advocated the acquisition of Rupert's Land as an outlet for further settlement. The Hudson's Bay Company had long maintained the fiction that Rupert's Land was unsuitable for farming, but in 1857 a Select Committee of the British House of Commons investigated the company's continued hold over the northwest.

Annexation to Canada was not the inevitable alternative: the Colonial Office might have opted to end HBC rule and create a Crown colony in the area. Hudson Bay Company Governor George Simpson's bleak picture of the area's agricultural prospects was chal-

1857: Britain's House of Commons launches a committee to plan the future of Rupert's Land.

lenged when a member of the committee flourished Simpson's own ghost-written auto-biography, *Journey Round the World* (1847). This work inconveniently enthused about bumper crops of luxuriant wheat and other grains grown on the prairies, and beef, mut-ton, pork, butter, cheese, and wool in abundance. Called upon to explain these passages, Simpson backtracked awkwardly, explaining that he was referring to "merely a few small alluvial points occupied by the Scotch farmers." One committee member remembered that Simpson "in answering our questions had to call in the aid of incessant coughing."[14]

The British government attempted to shed more light on the question with an 1857 geological expedition to the prairies of Rupert's Land. Gentleman adventurer and fellow of the Royal Geographical Society John Palliser was granted £5000 to explore the terri-tory and report on its potential. The Colonial Office also wanted knowledge of any passes through the Rocky Mountains on British territory, and to assess the possibility of finding a transportation route from Canada to Red River that would not require traversing American territory. The old North West Company canoe routes from Lake Superior were explored for this purpose, although the predictable conclusion was that routes on the American side of the border were more viable. Palliser's explorations revealed that there was a semi-arid area—"Palliser's Triangle"—in the southern part of what is today Saskatchewan and

1857: Geological expeditions led by Palliser and Hind reveal the agricultural potential of the western interior.

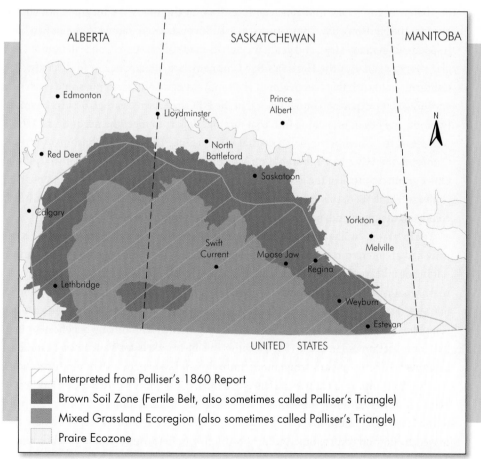

Interpreted from Palliser's 1860 Report

Brown Soil Zone (Fertile Belt, also sometimes called Palliser's Triangle)

Mixed Grassland Ecoregion (also sometimes called Palliser's Triangle)

Praire Ecozone

Map 11.1
Palliser's Triangle and the Canadian prairies. (Modern provincial boundaries and place names added for reference.)

Source: Canadian Plains Research Centre, University of Regina.

Alberta, an area that has proved to be prone to drought. But there was also territory he termed the "fertile belt," whose agricultural potential was excellent.[15] Palliser publicized his findings in a series of reports from 1859 on, with a comprehensive map released in 1865.

Similar exploratory missions were launched in 1857 and 1858 by the expansionist-minded government of the united Canadas. These surveys were led by Henry Hind, a chemistry professor from Trinity College (University of Toronto) who lacked scientific training, but who wrote captivating exploration literature, and was an enthusiastic advocate of annexation. Historian of science Richard A. Jarrell notes that Hind "possessed sound journalistic skills," but describes his scientific publications as "less than brilliant," and at times even "scientifically weak."[16] The consensus that flowed from these reports was that Rupert's Land should be acquired by Canada, although this would not happen for more than a decade. The consolidating spirit that would bring about Confederation in 1867 would prompt Canada's acquisition of the prairies. The Métis people would soon face their greatest challenge to date.

Newcomers on the Pacific Coast

While Red River was experiencing modest growth, and the population of the province of Canada was multiplying dramatically, newcomer settlement in the Pacific Northwest had barely begun by the mid-nineteenth century. By the 1840s, the fur trade, which had brought the Hudson's Bay Company to the Pacific coast, was in retreat. Animals had been trapped out in many areas, and gentlemen's hats made of beaver felt, once in fashion, had given way to silk. But the Hudson's Bay Company had already begun to diversify. The California gold rush that had begun in 1848 spurred demand for supplies, and especially encouraged the expansion into lumber that the HBC had started earlier. Besides sawmills, the company began branching into coal mining, in part to meet the needs of the HBC's own steamers, which were plying coastal waters. Since the 1843 establishment of Fort Camosun, the HBC had a foothold on Vancouver Island. In 1849, the British Colonial Office granted control of the island to the company for 10 years, at an annual rent of seven shillings. Until 1866, this colony would be separate from the other HBC-administered colony on the mainland, named New Caledonia by Simon Fraser in 1805.

The Kwakwaka'wakw people living on northern Vancouver Island, finding that the company had an interest in the coal resources for fuel, seized the initiative and began surface mining near Beaver Harbour in the mid-1830s. The Kwakwaka'wakw traditionally used the coal primarily as a dye. They would not permit the HBC to take control of the coal resources, but agreed to sell the coal that they had mined themselves at the rate of one Hudson's Bay Company blanket for every two tons. This arrangement was mutually beneficial at first, but complications soon arose. The growth of viable markets for Vancouver Island coal prompted the company to attempt more controlled and systematic coal mining operations.

The HBC imported eight experienced Scottish coalminers to Fort Rupert on Beaver Harbour in 1849. Almost immediately, however, the Scottish miners began to complain to the HBC that conditions were not what they had been led to expect. They were dismayed to find no shafts sunk and no productive underground seams yet discovered. The Kwakwaka'wakw miners did not welcome their Scottish rivals, and launched an

1849: The HBC begins coal-mining operations on Vancouver Island.

effective campaign of harassment that included physical threats and the theft of supplies and equipment. The Scottish miners expressed their grievances in a strike.

The simmering atmosphere at Fort Rupert was brought to the boil by the arrival in June 1850 of the *England,* a vessel bound for California, bearing four sailors who had deserted from an HBC ship with dreams of the riches to be found in the California gold fields. Tales of gold rush wealth deepened the dissatisfaction of the Scottish miners at Fort Rupert, and the company feared widespread defection. Given the lately strained relations with the Kwakwa̱ka̱'wakw, any diminishment of the fledgling British population arrayed against thousands of Aboriginal people would be dangerous—in fact, an American warship, *Massachusetts,* which had taken on coal at Fort Rupert, agreed to linger there a little longer in case extra support was needed. Dr. John Sebastian Helmcken, a surgeon employed by the HBC, who was named magistrate at the height of the 1850 crisis, reported on "dangers within; dangers outside; danger all around."[17] Despite HBC attempts to prevent it, most of the miners fled the settlement. Three of the deserting sailors also slipped away from the departing *England* when they learned that they were about to be apprehended.

Coal Tyee (Ki-el-sa-kun) alerted the HBC to coal resources in Nanaimo. Photograph c. 1860.

Source: Image F-09838 courtesy of Royal BC Museum, BC Archives.

The fate of these seamen threatened to derail the HBC's entire colonial enterprise on the Pacific coast. Rumours soon surfaced that the three had been killed by the Newitty (or Nahwitti), members of the Kwakwa̱ka̱'wakw nation who were rivals of the coal-mining Kwagiulth. Helmcken set out with a party to investigate, and discovered two bodies in hollow trees, and a third that had been weighed down and dropped into the sea. The newly appointed governor, Richard Blanshard, eager to assert the company's fragile authority, decided that a show of force was essential. He instructed Helmcken to warn the Newitty that "white man's blood never dries."[18] Blanshard launched two punitive raids against the Newitty, in October 1850 and again the following July. The Natives fled their villages in advance of the attacks, but eventually offered up the bodies of the three purported murderers, who may have simply been warriors killed in the engagement with the British, who could now render greater service by helping to appease the clamour for justice.

1850: HBC Governor Richard Blanshard launches a retaliatory raid against the Newitty.

The tiny population of 30 or 40 newcomers at Fort Rupert were part of a non-Native Pacific coast population in British North America that numbered only a few hundred in the early 1850s, most of that population on the southern tip of Vancouver Island. Only a few scattered and very small fur trading posts, such as Fort Langley, dotted the mainland. The devastating epidemics wrought by first contact had tragically reduced Aboriginal populations, but they still outnumbered the newcomers by more than 50-to-1. Despite the clemency of the Pacific coast weather, other considerations kept would-be settlers away. The journey itself was a powerful disincentive: prior to the twentieth-century opening of the Panama Canal, Europeans bound for the North American west coast faced a five-month journey round Cape Horn, or the risky crossing of the Isthmus of Panama, a region in which travellers were apt to fall victim to deadly yellow fever. The HBC's land sales policy also was unattractive. The company set a substantial price for land, hoping to lure those who had the capital to develop their holdings. Anyone purchasing 100 acres (40 hectares) was required to bring labourers to cultivate it, and investors shrank from purchasing land that they had never seen and that had not even been surveyed, especially since American land just over the border could be had at a quarter of the price.

1852: The Hudson's Bay Company begins coal-mining operations at Nanaimo.

The growth of Nanaimo as a newcomer settlement was prompted by a visit by Ki-el-sa-kun (Chi-wech-i-kan), or Coal Tyee, to Fort Victoria to have his rifle repaired at the blacksmith. He alerted HBC authorities to rich deposits of coal at Nanaimo that were far superior to that being mined at Fort Rupert. The company moved operations south in 1852. Two dozen new miners from Britain were added to a workforce consisting largely of Aboriginal women, and the company began shipping Nanaimo coal to San Francisco. While the company would sell off its coal-mining operations in 1862, by the turn of the century there would be more than 3000 coalminers at work in Nanaimo, a workforce that included not only British miners, but also Chinese and workers drawn from the Pennsylvania coalfields.

Further south, British naval crews soon began surveying the excellent natural harbour of Esquimalt. The plan was to provide the British Royal Navy with a base of operations during the Crimean War against the Russians (1854–1856). A few hospital sheds were constructed in 1855, although a decade later, Esquimalt, a convenient coaling station, would replace Valparaiso, Chile, as a base for the navy's Pacific Squadron.

1855: Esquimalt is established as a Royal Navy base on Vancouver Island.

In the main settlement of Victoria, colonial growth was slow. Governor Blanshard accepted the advice of the Colonial Office to appoint an advisory council, but almost all possible appointees to the council had HBC ties. All life in Victoria revolved around the company. By 1851, Blanshard tendered his resignation, having wearied of life in a colonial outpost, and HBC chief factor James Douglas, long recognized as the real power in the colony, was appointed in his stead. Douglas was instructed to expand Vancouver Island's government further, and introduced a representative assembly in 1856. This was hardly a blow for democracy: only 43 residents possessed the 20 acres (8 hectares) in property that would qualify them to vote, and most of the seven members of the assembly had HBC ties.

James Douglas was born into the second family of a Scottish sugar merchant operating in British Guiana. His mother was a Creole woman, probably of mixed African and European heritage. James was sent to Scotland to be educated, and by the age of 16 was on his way to Canada to apprentice with the North West Company. Intelligent, steady, and known for good judgment, Douglas made a positive impression on his superiors and rose quickly in the ranks of the fur trade, especially after the merger with the Hudson's Bay Company. He almost abandoned his fur-trading career after a harsh and hungry winter spent at Bear Lake in the isolated interior of present-day British Columbia, but by the

Source: Courtesy of the Office of the Lieutenant Governor of British Columbia.

Source: Image H-04909 courtesy of Royal BC Museum, BC Archives.

James and Amelia Douglas.

spring had changed his mind. In April 1828, he married 16-year-old Amelia Connolly, the daughter of chief factor William Connolly and his Cree wife, Suzanne (Miyo Nipiy).

James and Amelia Douglas would become the leaders of an inner circle of families who first settled Victoria after 1849. Martha, one of the Douglas's surviving daughters—only 6 of 13 children lived to adulthood—married engineer Dennis Reginald Harris, and in 1901 published a book of her mother's Cowichan stories. By this time, both of Martha's parents were dead. Earlier, when she had been at finishing school in England, her father had warned her that he had no objection to her sharing the stories but "pray do not tell the world they are Mamma's." As the white population of British Columbia grew, Native heritage was increasingly seen as a social liability. Historian Sylvia Van Kirk notes the irony of the fact that Victoria, a city long seen as quintessentially English, should have been established primarily by mixed-race families. The earliest town lots were claimed by James Douglas, William H. McNeill, John Work, John Tod, and Charles Ross, all of whom were HBC officers, and all of whom had Native wives.[19]

Native–Newcomer Relations and Policy in British North America

Historians have pointed to a hardening of racial attitudes in the second half of the nineteenth century, not only in the Pacific Northwest, but elsewhere in the British empire. Fur traders did not usually express negative feelings about the Aboriginal peoples with whom they came into contact. Besides frequent mixed-race marriages, there tended to be a spirit of grudging respect toward Natives, who were tough bargainers in trade deals. Not surprisingly, settlers—whose goals were centred on the acquisition of Native land, as opposed to trade—tended to have more negative views. One nineteenth-century visitor to the Pacific Northwest concluded that the Natives' existence on the earth must have been intended by providence as temporary, until "races of greater capacity were ready to occupy the soil. A succession of races, like a rotation of crops, may be necessary to turn the earth to the best possible account." The "indolent, contented savage must give place to the bustling sons of civilization and toil."[20] This expectation pervaded policy toward Aboriginal peoples throughout British North America, and indeed elsewhere. Historian Elizabeth Vibert urges a careful handling of the written accounts of fur traders and others, which have so often been privileged as fact. In particular, Vibert warns that ideas presented in these accounts, such as the "indolence" of indigenous peoples, must be interrogated. Impressions of newcomers often betrayed a deep assumption that fishing-hunting-gathering societies occupied the lowest rung on the social evolutionary ladder.[21]

The flourishing humanitarian movement of the early nineteenth century that had dictated more enlightened racial attitudes had lost some of its force with the successful elimination of slavery. Then, too, some dark chapters in Britain's imperial adventure had produced a reactionary climate—the Indian Mutiny of 1857–1858 and the bloody reprisals that followed; wars between New Zealand settlers and the indigenous Maori in the 1860s; and an 1865 uprising at Morant Bay, Jamaica, were all pivotal events in this respect. Even the 1859 publication of Charles Darwin's *The Origin of Species* contributed to popular perceptions that some peoples of the earth were destined to give way to others. Pseudoscientific theories, such as phrenology, which categorized human potential according to head shape, reinforced race prejudices.

In British North America, key developments in the middle decades of the nineteenth century had already augured a shift in Native status "from alliance to irrelevance," as historian J.R. Miller puts it.[22] The 1821 Hudson's Bay Company and North West Company merger ended the Montreal-based fur trade in favour of a maritime trade centred on Hudson Bay, and thus ended the commercial cooperation that had existed between eastern Natives and newcomers. It undercut Native power elsewhere by eliminating fur trade competition. The advent of peace with the United States eliminated the need to cultivate military alliances with Aboriginal nations, although episodes such as the 1837–38 rebellions saw the Natives' martial role temporarily resurrected. In 1830, the administration of Native issues was transferred from military authorities to civilian ones, a change that reflected the reality that Aboriginal people were no longer deemed necessary as military allies, and were seen as a burdensome social responsibility. The overall goal now shifted from the maintenance of military alliances to what was perceived as the practical and humanitarian goal of "civilizing" Natives.

1830: Responsibility for Native affairs moves from military authorities to civilian ones.

Indian affairs were administered in different ways in the three large regions into which British North America was divided. In Rupert's Land and the Pacific coast, matters were left to the devices of the HBC, a policy that for British Columbia merely forestalled resolution of most questions until the era of comprehensive treaty settlements in the twenty-first century. On the plains, vast "numbered treaties" would be made in the post-Confederation era, in the decades after Rupert's Land was acquired by the Dominion of Canada. In the North Atlantic region, the colonies of New Brunswick, Nova Scotia, Prince Edward Island,

and Newfoundland, the areas in which Native–newcomer contact had first been made, ineffectual attempts had been made to protect Aboriginal nations from the depredations of settlers, but there was little systematic recognition of any inherent Aboriginal title. By the early decades of the nineteenth century, many Aboriginal nations were in sharp demographic decline. The Beothuk had vanished from Newfoundland, most succumbing to disease: Shanawdithit, a Beothuk woman thought to be the last of her people, died of tuberculosis in 1829. Settlers routinely alienated Native land in the Atlantic region, a practice that betrayed a general expectation that the original occupants were a dying race.

1829: The Beothuk vanish.

In the Canadas, the overarching goal was amalgamation, the blending of Natives into the settler population through intermarriage, and education to promote European-style agricultural life. The Royal Proclamation of 1763 established the principle that Native land could not be alienated except by treaty with the Crown. The high ideals of the proclamation were not always met, but in the years from the British conquest to 1836, some 27 substantial land transfers had taken place in Upper Canada under this treaty system. Reserves had usually been set aside for surrendered territory in practice, but after 1830, consistent with the goal of "civilization," a more systematic provision of reserves was inaugurated. The reserves were to function as a kind of social laboratory, paradoxically separating the Natives for their own protection from unscrupulous newcomers, so that they might be gradually trained to blend into the larger population. Missionaries were often at the vanguard of efforts to inculcate Natives in European ways, and worked to assist them in establishing housing, farms, schools, mills, and all that was needed for European-style self-sufficiency.

1836: Governor Bond Head proposes to relocate all Upper Canadian Natives to Manitoulin.

Upper Canadian lieutenant governor Francis Bond Head in 1836 proposed a plan that ran counter to the general policy of assimilation, suggesting that all Upper Canadian Natives be relocated to the islands of the Manitoulin area between Lake Huron and Georgian Bay. This rocky land was not sufficiently attractive to newcomers to cause any conflict over the area, Bond Head believed. While misguided, Bond Head seems to have been motivated by humanitarian concerns. He had visited most of the Native communities in Upper Canada and clung to the notion that Aboriginal societies could remain frozen in time. Peter Jones (also known as "Sacred Feathers," Kahkewaquonaby, or Desagondensta in Mohawk) was a Mississauga Ojibwe chief and Methodist minister who objected to the plan to relocate his Credit River community. Jones embraced the ways of the newcomers and believed that the surest route to success for the Mississauga lay in Christian education and a settled agricultural life. He travelled to London to register his protest against Bond Head's plan, and in 1838 was granted an audience with the young Queen Victoria. Other Methodist missionaries added their voices to the protest, and Bond Head's scheme was abandoned.

A number of pre-Confederation measures had lasting significance for Canadian Natives. On the recommendation of a British parliamentary committee, the *Crown Lands Protection Act* of 1839 declared Aboriginal lands to be Crown lands, making the Crown the guardian of the land Natives held in common. The fact that the Natives held their lands in common, and not as individuals, also debarred them from exercising a vote: the franchise depended upon the possession of property. The Bagot Commission, established in 1842 by Governor General Sir Charles Bagot, laid the groundwork for much of Canada's future Native policy.

1842: The Bagot Commission recommends systematic schooling of Natives.

1844: New Brunswick's Indian Act *provides for sale of reserve land.*

1846: Chief Shinguakouse confronts Great Lakes mining party.

The Bagot Commission confirmed the Crown's obligations to Aboriginal people, as set out in the Royal Proclamation, but articulated the goal of reducing costs, a policy that was consistent with the overall mid-nineteenth-century curtailment of imperial financial obligations. Annual presents traditionally given to indigenous nations amounted to some £20 000 per year after 1830 (in itself a reduction from the £50 000 annual cost in the era of the War of 1812). The commission recommended the gradual discontinuation of this practice, which was put into effect in 1858. The Bagot Commission's plan to replace Native communal landholding systems with one of individual freehold ownership met vigorous resistance by Natives and had to be abandoned. Perhaps the furthest-reaching recommendation was the plan to implement residential and industrial training schools for Native children, a recommendation that at first had some appeal to Aboriginal leaders but which became the basis of practices that scarred generations of Aboriginal children. A series of enactments in the 1850s sought to define who was Indian, in part with a view to limiting the scope of responsibility. This set the stage for an ever-narrowing definition that would go on to exclude Aboriginal women marrying non-Native men.

In the Atlantic region, demographic decline among Aboriginal populations led local officials to ignore eighteenth-century treaties, and settler convenience rather than fundamental justice dictated the disposition of land. In New Brunswick, an 1844 *Indian Act* showed the disastrous consequences of permitting elected assemblies of newcomers to act as wardens over Native land. The Act proposed that Native reserve land could be sold, with the proceeds used to further the goal of "civilization" of the Natives. Revenues proved to be very low and most of the funds were swallowed up in administrative costs. Moreover, non-Native squatters often simply occupied Indian land without purchase. Moses Perley, New Brunswick's commissioner of Indian affairs, was a respected advocate for the Mi'kmaq and Maliseet people, who named him an honorary chief. Perley's attempts to win redress for New Brunswick's Natives succeeded only in getting him bounced from his position for his criticism of the colony's administration.

While overall Native policy was being bent to the urgent clamour of settlers for farmland, the quest for minerals raised further complications. On the north shore of Lake Superior, the northern Ojibwe traditionally mined copper along the shoreline, each band maintaining control over its own areas. As with traditional fishing stations, these sites were occupied seasonally by bands who lived further inland. In 1845, mining entrepreneurs, wishing to duplicate the success of those who were finding rich mineral deposits on the shores of Lake Michigan, sought mining permits for the Lake Huron and Lake Superior areas from the Crown Lands Department of the united Canadas. Provincial surveyors and geologists compiled data, and the Montreal Mining Company, having acquired 466 square kilometres (180 square miles) for mining, recovered an encouraging 1.34 million kilograms (1475 tons) of copper from Bruce Mines on Lake Huron. These activities threatened Natives' traditional rights, and in the spring of 1846, Chief Shinguakouse (Shingwaukonse) of Garden River, near Sault Ste Marie, confronted and threatened a provincial land surveyor.

Chief Shinguakouse appealed to the governor, Lord Elgin, for justice, citing his personal history of service to the Crown, which included military service during the War of 1812. Elgin was disappointed that his executive council did not consider the Natives' claim worthy of consideration. Denis-Benjamin Papineau, Commissioner of Crown Lands (and brother of Louis-Joseph), asserted that Shinguakouse's people's residency in the area was not of sufficient duration, nor did he consider the bands in the region to be nations capable of negotiating a territorial claim. Elgin bided his time, and when a new administration came into office in 1848, he raised the issue again, this time with greater success.

Unfortunately, before matters could be resolved, a new disturbance escalated the situation. In November 1849 at Mica Bay on eastern Lake Superior, a force of Natives and Métis, led by a Hamilton lawyer and mining entrepreneur Allan Macdonell, succeeded in driving off mine workers. Macdonell's detractors accused him of manipulating the Natives out of self-interest, and scoffed at his romantic references to "my people" and buckskin attire, although others applauded his championing of the Natives' resource rights. Elgin reported the incident to the Colonial Office, explaining that a force of 100 troops had to be dispatched to quell the threat. He could not resist adding the crisp observation that "it is much to be regretted that steps were not taken to investigate thoroughly and extinguish all Indian claims before licences of exploration or grants of land were conceded."[23]

1849: Troops sent to quell the Mica Bay disturbance over mining rights.

Elgin himself made a visit to the area late in the summer of 1850. This evidence of the Crown's scrutiny and concern had a reassuring effect; Elgin also extended pardons to the Native and Métis leaders of the Mica Bay disturbance. When Canadian colonial authorities sent an investigative party a short time later, the commissioners took pains to ensure that no non-Aboriginal intermediary claimed to speak for the Natives. They believed that a Jesuit priest in the area had ulterior motives for attempting to influence negotiations, and also convinced the Natives that Macdonell's mediation had not been disinterested. Chief Augustin, the son of Shinguakouse, was dismayed when he learned that Macdonell's words to Governor Elgin, purporting to be a translation of the Natives' speeches, were highly disrespectful. "An Indian could not speak such words," Augustin declared.[24] The commission of investigation paved the way for treaty negotiations by William Benjamin Robinson, brother of Canadian Chief Justice John Beverley Robinson and emigration organizer Peter Robinson. The 1850 "Robinson Treaties" alienated 130 000 square kilometres of territory north of the Great Lakes, established 21 reserves, and included the provision that Natives could continue to hunt and fish in the ceded territories as before.

1850: The "Robinson Treaties" negotiated for territory north of the Great Lakes.

The 1857 *Act for the Gradual Civilization of Indian Tribes* in the Canadas laid the groundwork for a series of Indian Acts in the post-Confederation era. The Act fully embraced the principle that Aboriginal people ought to assimilate into the society of newcomers, and set out ways that natives might shed their Indian status to gain enfranchisement and become full citizens. Residential schools were seen as a necessary means to achieve this. Once educated and literate in French or English, if a Native could prove he was of sound moral character and free of debt, he might surrender his Indian status and gain full citizenship rights. He would be given freehold tenure over 20 hectares of reserve land. Ultimately, the idea was that the reserves would disappear, carved up piecemeal among enfranchised Natives who would, over time, blend into non-Aboriginal society. While Natives would prove resistant to its goal, rejecting enfranchisement, many provisions of the Act would remain in place until 1960.

1857: The Act for Gradual Civilization of Indian Tribes *provides the model for subsequent Indian Acts.*

1860: Responsibility for Indian affairs transferred from imperial authorities to the colony of Canada.

Most Native leaders embraced opportunities for education, but opposed wholesale assimilation, and campaigned to have the 1857 Act repealed. This did not happen, and in 1860 responsibility for Native affairs was transferred from the imperial government to the colonial administration of the united Canadas. This meant that there would no longer be a disinterested arbiter overseeing questions of Native policy, scrutinizing it to ensure just treatment. Instead, those who answered to the political will of enfranchised settlers would legislate for the Natives. "Potentially, here was the 'dark side' of responsible government," historian David McNab explains.[25] Alarmed Natives placed their grievances before the Prince of Wales when he came to North America on his 1860 royal tour, and lobbied in other ways, but with Britain eagerly divesting itself of many of the burdens of empire, it was to no avail.

The Gold Rush Transforms the Pacific Northwest

By the early 1850s, colonies on the west coast administered by the Hudson's Bay Company had made only very modest inroads toward colonization—small toeholds in Victoria, Nanaimo, and Esquimalt. In 1858, this state of things would change and it would change "dramatically between breakfast and dinner on a single day," as George Woodcock put it. The small settler population of Victoria emerged from church one Sunday in April 1858 to see an American side-wheeler, the *Commodore,* unloading 450 passengers in the harbour. These new arrivals, fresh from the gold fields of California, were eager to buy up supplies in Victoria before making their way across the strait to the mainland and up the Fraser River. Word of the discovery of gold on the Thompson River in 1857, along with rumours of finds along the Fraser, had filtered down to the United States. Three weeks before the miners descended upon Victoria, a consignment of British Columbia gold had reached the San Francisco assay office, and opportunists who had wearied of the crowded California fields were determined to get in on the new strike early.[26]

James Douglas has often been regarded as the ideal representative of British authority on the west coast. Historians have emphasized that his firm measures sent an unmistakable message to eager gold seekers: this was not a new American wild west frontier. Historian Barry Gough describes Douglas as "a master of crisis management."[27] Douglas proclaimed the Crown's authority over all mineral rights, and required miners to take out licences. Recognizing the efficacy of what has sometimes been called "gunboat diplomacy," Douglas arranged that a Royal Navy vessel be stationed at the mouth of the Fraser River to ensure that all who sought passage up the Fraser possessed the necessary licences. Even a single vessel carried with it the message that newcomers were under the watchful eye of British imperial authority, and would presumably forestall any American dreams of annexing territory north of the 49th parallel.

Douglas also had the advantage of long experience with the Aboriginal nations, and had earlier recognized that some provision had to be made for the legitimate acquisition of Native land. Douglas's 1849 query to Hudson's Bay Company authorities did not provide much guidance. The Royal Proclamation of 1763 recognized the principle that Aboriginal peoples had an inherent right to the land they occupied, and had influenced the terms of British occupation elsewhere. In New Zealand, the 1840 Treaty of Waitangi with the indigenous Maori people was concluded on the same understanding. Yet Company officials advised Douglas to consider Native land that was not actually settled and cultivated to be "waste" land, available for occupation. The Natives were deemed to have only a "qualified Dominion" over their land.

Left to his own discretion on Vancouver Island, Douglas concluded a number of small-scale treaties before permitting newcomer occupation of land, 11 of these treaties in the Victoria area, two at Fort Rupert, and one in Nanaimo. Ironically, some of the land set aside for reserves was encroached upon a few years later when construction of British Columbia's legislative buildings began in Victoria in 1854. Only in 2006 was a settlement reached between British Columbia's government and the Esquimalt and Songhees First Nations to resolve the long-standing embarrassment of the provincial legislature standing illegally on Native land.

As governor, James Douglas took a different approach to justice questions than had Richard Blanshard, his predecessor. Blanshard had been eager to make a show of force to bolster Britain's shaky prestige with the much larger Aboriginal population, and this agenda had informed his approach to the reprisals made in 1850 and 1851 against the Newitty for the alleged murder of three deserting British sailors. Douglas, by contrast, believed that Aboriginal confidence in British justice could best be maintained if the rule of law were emphasized; only individuals, and not entire tribes, would be punished for any wrongdoings. Douglas thought Blanshard's actions had been "as unpolitick as unjust"— after all, the coastal Native nations had strong martial traditions and it would be unwise for the tiny population of newcomers to behave provocatively. An incident in 1852 reveals how much Douglas differed from Blanshard in his approach. A shepherd employed by the HBC, Peter Brown, had been killed by two Natives in the Cowichan Valley, reportedly in retaliation for Brown's insults to Native women. Rather than exacting retribution from the entire community, Douglas ensured that only the perpetrators were brought to justice. There was a period of tension with the Cowichan and Nanaimo peoples, whom Douglas described as "the most numerous and warlike" on Vancouver Island, but at last a captive— possibly a hapless slave—was offered up, the other suspect was captured, and both were punished, something Douglas saw an "an epoch in the history of our Indian relations."[28]

The 1858 Fraser River gold rush presented much more challenging conditions. As many as 30 000 gold seekers flooded into the Pacific Northwest, most of them bound for the areas between Hope and Lillooet on the Fraser River. Tiny Victoria instantly became a booming tent city, as miners converged upon the settlement to purchase supplies and obtain the necessary licences. More than 200 buildings sprang up in six weeks during the tumultuous summer of 1858. Businesses catering to stereotypical masculine amusements—drinking, gambling, and other vices—proliferated. Historian Adele Perry observes that the overwhelmingly male nature of west coast colonial society raised concerns among reformers who believed that the unruliness of the men and their tendency to form relationships with Native women would be detrimental to the creation of a "stable, respectable" British colony. Between 1849 and 1871, organizations such as the Columbia Emigration Society, organized by the Anglican Church, assisted the emigration of white women who might help forge a respectable British colony by "taming" the men. In light

1858: Some 30 000 miners descend upon the Fraser River in search of gold.

of this, Perry suggests that gender should be a "central category of analysis" in seeking to understand the goals and ideals of west coast British colonialism.[29]

Enterprising Natives transported newly arrived miners across the Strait of Georgia to the mainland in cedar dugout canoes, while some impatient miners lashed together rafts for the journey. This still left the prospect of travelling up the Fraser River, and Douglas arranged for American stern-wheelers in addition to HBC vessels to provide this service. He quickly put plans in hand to construct a road along the Harrison River to Lillooet, and a track for mule trains from Yale to Lytton along the Fraser. Lytton, incidentally, was named for the British colonial secretary, Sir Edward Bulwer-Lytton (later Lord Lytton), who also won fame as a novelist. He is chiefly remembered today for having begun one of his works with the much-parodied line "It was a dark and stormy night...."

While most of the first wave of arrivals came directly from California, not all were Americans. An early visitor to Victoria marvelled at its polyglot population, in which "almost every nationality is represented. Greek fishermen, Jewish and Scottish merchants, Chinese washermen, French, German and Yankee officeholders and butchers, Negro waiters and sweeps, Australian farmers and other varieties of the race, rub against each other, apparently in the most friendly way." Black pioneers in British Columbia established mercantile houses, barbershops, restaurants, and other enterprises, and were among the earliest non-Aboriginal settlers of Saltspring Island. Their commitment to the empire was demonstrated through the organization of a volunteer militia unit, the Victoria Pioneer Rifle Corps.[30]

One of the new arrivals during the summer of 1858 was Amor De Cosmos, a flamboyant Nova Scotia businessman who had earlier travelled to California to make a living photographing miners. Born William Smith, De Cosmos chose to rename himself to

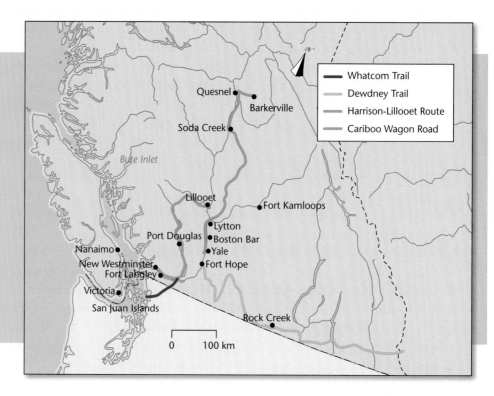

Map 11.3
Gold rush area.

symbolize his love for the universe, and to ensure his mail did not get mixed up with all the other Bill Smiths who populated the California gold fields. De Cosmos quickly established a newspaper in Victoria, the *British Colonist*, which frequently levelled attacks at the colonial elite of families with Hudson's Bay Company connections; he derisively called these dominant individuals the Family-Company-Compact, paraphrasing the epithet preferred by earlier Upper Canadian agitator and journalist William Lyon Mackenzie. The political reformer and journalist De Cosmos most admired was fellow Nova Scotian Joseph Howe. Both began their political careers as journalists, owning and editing their own newspapers. Both were effective orators, and were elected to their colony's legislatures where they fought for responsible government. De Cosmos served as a member of Vancouver Island's legislative assembly from 1863. Each would ultimately become premier of his province, and a federal member of Parliament.[31]

The miners who arrived in that watershed year of 1858 worked sandy bars along the Fraser River, using either picks and pans, or rocker cradles or sluice boxes that they hastily constructed of local wood. The object of both methods was the same: to churn up sand and gravel in the water so that the heavier gold would be sifted to the bottom. The usual haul was fine dust or small particles, although some found nuggets of several grams. An average daily yield of 80 to 100 grams had a value of $50 to $65—a considerable sum in the nineteenth century. Costs were also high, though, a reflection of transportation costs, given the distance from commercial centres. A bag of flour worth $16 in Whatcom, in American territory, would cost more than double that in Hope, and as much as $100 in the most northerly miners' camps.

1858: HBC authority ends in mainland British Columbia.

In July 1858, Britain ended the authority of the HBC on the Pacific coast mainland and created a Crown colony. This would theoretically dispel any thoughts that the Americans might have that there was a political vacuum in the Pacific Northwest. The name "New Caledonia" was abandoned, since a French Pacific island colony had the same name, and the colony became British Columbia. James Douglas, having relinquished all ties to the HBC, became the new colony's governor. The HBC's lease on the Vancouver Island colony did not expire until the following year; in 1859, Vancouver Island also came directly under British control as a separate colony, with Douglas continuing as governor there as well.

The Fraser River War, 1858

Even before the announcement of direct British colonial control over the mainland, Douglas had undertaken the first of a series of visits he made during the summer of 1858 to the main gold-mining sites on the Fraser River. The pervasive historical perception that Douglas firmly established British control over the area, and successfully quashed any frontier turmoil before it had a chance to begin, may stem from Douglas's own letters to the British Colonial Office describing these visits. In June, Douglas explained, he "spoke with great plainness" to the miners, warning them that they were there "merely on sufferance." He further admonished them "that no abuses would be tolerated," stressing that "the Laws would protect the rights of the Indians no less than those of the white men." After his August visit, Douglas marvelled to the colonial secretary that he had never seen "a crowd of more ruffianly looking men." On his command, they gave three cheers for the Queen "with a bad grace."[32]

Historian Daniel P. Marshall has challenged the historical impression of British security in the area under Douglas's firm hand, arguing that during the "Fraser River War of 1858" British control over the region was negligible. Though Douglas may have wanted to protect Aboriginal interests against rapacious foreign gold seekers, Marshall describes a scenario in which Natives were compelled to accept terms forced upon them by a virtual army of invasion. California mining culture, he argues, transcended the 49th parallel.

Many miners made their way north by land, using the old HBC brigade trails in Oregon and Washington. Following open clashes between the United States Army and several Native tribes south of the border, miners travelling to the Fraser River rush banded together in companies as large as 200 or 300, electing their own officers. A German miner among the party, H.F. Reinhart, was dismayed to see that the object was not to travel safely through Native territory, but to "clean out all the Indians in the land." At Okanagan Lake, trekkers helped themselves to a cache of nuts and berries stored at an Aboriginal village, dumping the remainder into the lake so as to destroy the Natives' winter provisions. A group of 25 invaders concealed themselves in a gulch and confronted the unarmed Okanagan people when they returned. Reinhart estimated that 10 to 12 of those unable to get away were killed by gunfire, and as many wounded: "It was a brutal affair, but the perpetrators of the outrage thought they were heroes, and were victors in some well-fought battle," he reported disgustedly.[33] Native couriers spread word of atrocities throughout the Pacific Northwest. Attempts by the Natives to buy arms and ammunition to prepare for the conflict were thwarted, however; HBC authorities refused to sell weapons either to the Natives or the invading miners.

The presence of miners along the upper Fraser River disrupted age-old traditions in which certain Aboriginal families, often from some distance away, returned year after year to the same fishing rocks along the river—sites chosen because they were optimal areas to catch salmon at their peak and to set up drying racks positioned to take full advantage of the sun's rays trapped in the canyon. Such traditional claims were important to the Stó:lō nations of the Fraser River; one of the purposes of the potlatch celebration was to pass on fishing rights to a designated spot. The *sia:teleq* (loosely pronounced "see-at-el-uk") was the Stó:lō arbiter of any conflicting fishing claims.[34]

1858: Dozens were reported killed during the "Fraser River War" between miners and the Nlaka'pamux.

Further upriver from Stó:lō territory, the Nlaka'pamux (Thompson) Natives sought to limit incursions into their territory and maintain control over gold resources. Edward Stout, a veteran of the California rush of 1849, was a member of a party that arrived just beyond the junction of the Fraser and Thompson Rivers to find themselves suddenly in the midst of open warfare between the Nlaka'pamux and an earlier group of miners. Stout and the newly arrived miners quickly joined in the fight. Mutilated and headless corpses of miners drifted down the river past Yale. As many as 36 Natives had been killed in this "Fraser River War," including five chiefs, and Stout claimed that the same number of white miners had been massacred. American newspapers circulating in the west fanned the flames, exaggerating the death count of white miners, and implying that the HBC had incited Native resistance.

By late August 1858, the U.S. Army had reinforced Washington territory with additional troops, transferring almost all forces in California northward. The Okanagan people south of the border fled north into British territory, while other tribes from Washington and Idaho made a defiant, but futile, stand before the howitzers of Colonel George Wright's U.S. Ninth Infantry. Insisting on unconditional surrender, Wright sealed his victory by burning Native grain crops and destroying livestock.

Following this confrontation on American soil, volunteer militia, primarily from among the ranks of the miners, marched north to extend this policy of pacification above the 49th parallel. One militia company, the Pike Guards, led by San Francisco journalist Captain H. M. Snyder, compelled Native tribes in British territory from Yale to Lytton to conclude peace treaties under threat of force, and distributed white flags, which the Indian communities were required to fly. The Nlaka'pamux were warned that if the white men came again, it would not be by the hundreds but by the thousands, and that they would drive the Natives from the river forever. Historian Keith Carlson notes, however, that Aboriginal oral history offers another perspective on these events. A Stó:lō elder, Patrick Charlie, speaking in the 1950s, reported that Stó:lō chief Liquitem played a positive role by preventing further violence during that dangerous summer of 1858. Liquitem reportedly held council with Snyder, accepted a white flag offered to him as a symbol of peace, and then travelled up river to Spences Bridge to encourage a similar policy of non-violence in neighbouring Native communities.[35]

A short while later, at the end of August 1858, Douglas travelled to the Fraser River area with the goal of making peace treaties with the Natives. Marshall explains that Douglas's official communication to British authorities very much downplayed what occurred, not mentioning that British sovereignty had been threatened by foreign newcomers taking the law into their own hands. For a while, British Columbia had become an extension of the American west. Moreover, Douglas meted out no punishment to the American adventurers who had usurped British control. Instead, he approached them in a conciliatory manner, his eagerness to ingratiate himself a sign of the power imbalance implied by such large numbers of foreign miners. Snyder was congratulated on his restoration of peace to the region.

By the close of 1858, the immediate crisis had passed. Most of the miners had returned south for the winter, and the spring saw fewer adventurers seeking wealth in British Columbia's gold fields. No doubt the troubles of the previous season, along with disappointing yields and frequent high waters along the Fraser, which sometimes made mining impossible, contributed to the declining numbers. However, the change to the Pacific Northwest was permanent.

After the uneasy days of American conflicts with Aboriginal nations, a more secure footing was achieved with the arrival of British troops in the autumn of 1858 and spring of 1859. These troops, the Royal Engineers, had a usefulness that transcended their value in the colony's defence. They tackled civilian tasks, surveying the area and constructing roads. Colonial Secretary Bulwer-Lytton urged colonial authorities to avoid any overt military display, fearing that it would be provocative to the Americans. Commanding officer Colonel Richard Clement Moody chose a capital for the mainland colony at the mouth of the Fraser River, which was named New Westminster, in honour of the British seat of government in London. Sappers and marines under Moody's command began the arduous work of clearing old-growth timber stands. A "sapper" is a military engineer, named for the French word *sappe* (trench); their traditional role was to undermine an enemy's fortifications by digging trenches. When their service in British Columbia ended, most of these soldiers accepted land grants and settled in Sapperton, now part of New Westminster.

The administration of British justice was also taken in hand with the 1858 appointment of Cambridge-educated barrister Matthew Baillie Begbie. As British Columbia's first judge, Begbie approached his duties with a sense of occasion, conducting circuit court sessions in a tent while wearing judicial robes and a wig. Historian Tina Loo sees the establishment of law in British Columbia as an essential phase in colonial state formation, a process driven by classical liberal ideology, which emphasizes individual rights and protects the pursuit of one's self-interest, a goal that is assumed to be both rational and universal.[36]

New Anglo–American Tensions on the Pacific Coast

1859: The "Pig War" stems from competing claims in the San Juan Islands.

These measures to secure the British presence in the northwest were important in light of fresh strains in Anglo–American relations in 1859. This time, the cross-border tension flared over what has earned the tongue-in-cheek historical label "The Pig War."

The 1846 Oregon Treaty dividing British from American territory on the Pacific coast at the 49th parallel was plagued with ambiguities. The border cut through the channel to the south of Vancouver Island, but more than one channel fit the treaty description: the British claimed that the border ran through the more easterly Rosario Strait, while the United States claimed it was through the more westerly Haro Strait. At issue was possession of several of the San Juan Islands between Vancouver Island and the American mainland— Orcas, Lopez, San Juan, Shaw, and others. In July 1859, a minor dispute flared up among San Juan Island residents that was actually a lightning rod for the larger issue of political authority on the island. An American farmer, Lyman Cutlar, shot a pig that had broken through the fence from a neighbouring HBC-owned farm to root in his garden. Hudson's Bay Company officials demanded compensation, and threatened to have Cutlar arrested. The 18 or so American residents demanded protection of their rights as citizens, and were obliged with a company of U.S. troops under Captain George E. Pickett—later famous for the doomed Confederate "Pickett's Charge" on Union forces during the American Civil War.

The British countered this American move to show the flag, and dispatched warships of the British Royal Navy to the area. By the end of August, 461 American soldiers and 14 artillery pieces defended American interests on the tiny island, ranged against three British warships mounting 70 guns and manned by more than 2000. Newspapers on both sides of the border raised the emotional temperature with inflammatory accusations that national rights were being trampled. By October, an agreement was struck for joint military occupation of the island, a status that remained in place until 1871, when international arbitration settled the dispute in the Americans' favour. Throughout the period of joint occupancy, other crises in British–American relations added to the atmosphere of hostility, especially during the American Civil War (1861–65), when war between the two countries seemed imminent. But on remote San Juan Island, the pig proved to be the only casualty. American disinclination to pursue an aggressive approach to the Pacific coast in the future was perhaps also attributable to the precipitous decline in the American population north of the 49th parallel after the high-water mark of the summer of 1858.

Chinese Migrants to the Pacific Coast

This declining interest in British Columbia on the part of American miners was offset by a new surge in Chinese arrivals. A visitor reported that Victoria was "crowded with Celestials bound for the … mines." Governor Douglas's view was that "they are certainly not a desirable class of people, as a permanent population, but are for the present useful as labourers, and, as consumers, of a revenue-paying character."[37] While few Chinese lived east of the Rockies before the twentieth century, Chinese Canadians have deep historic roots in the Pacific province. Canada's modern population of Chinese origin is diverse in origins, but this was not the case in the nineteenth century: almost all of the earliest migrants from China came from Guangdong province on China's southeast coast, or from nearby Hong Kong.

The city of Guangzhou, or Canton, at the mouth of the Pearl River in Guangdong province, had long been China's only port open to trade with western foreigners, so residents learned about opportunities in the new world. By 1850, Guangdong's population had swollen to 28 million, and the pressure on agricultural resources was acute. In 1842, a humiliating defeat by the British in the first Opium War compelled the Chinese to expand the number of ports open to foreign trade, and frustrated their efforts to limit the influx of opium brought into the country by British traders. This meant that the city of Guangzhou no longer enjoyed a monopoly on foreign trade, and many workers in that port city were thrown out of work. A flood of cheap foreign imports undercut the produce of local manufacturers. Still worse, the Taiping Rebellion claimed millions of lives in the 1850s and 60s, disrupting farming and bringing social upheaval in its wake. Guangdong was also plagued by a series of natural disasters—floods, droughts, earthquakes, and typhoons—that brought starvation to the already famine-plagued region.

Labour contractors who filled the demand for workers created by the decline of slavery found a readily exploitable pool of labourers in Guangdong, and recruited heavily there for overseas workers. Naturally, migration would be a solution that would occur more obviously to those living in this coastal province. Between 1845 and 1873, more than 300 000 contract labourers left the region. Only a minority came as far as Canada, but by 1860, an estimated 7000 Chinese—an almost exclusively male population—were resident in British Columbia.

The earliest significant wave of Chinese migrants to British Columbia came by way of California, where they had been drawn by the gold rush a decade before. Experience in California had taught the Chinese that any perceived challenge for mining stakes would be met with hostility by white miners. Instead, in British Columbia, the Chinese kept their expectations modest and often took up sites already abandoned by discouraged white miners. Besides mining, the burgeoning gold rush economy offered job opportunities in laundries, restaurants, and vegetable farming. British Columbia's developing resource extraction opened the possibility of work in fish canneries and coalmines. A thousand Chinese workers were employed on the construction of the Cariboo Wagon road between Harrison Lake and Williams Lake after 1863. Another 500 strung telegraph wires between New Westminster and Quesnel in 1866.

In addition to the stereotypical miners and "coolies," as contract labourers were known, comparatively prosperous merchants came to British Columbia as well. Chu Lai, a merchant from Guangdong province, was not a member of China's majority Han ethnic group, but

Hakka, a group whose prominence and wide influence belied their minority numbers. The Hakka have been likened to dandelions, scattered by the winds and able to thrive in the least promising soil. Dr. Sun Yat Sen, who led China's 1911 revolution was Hakka; it is also part of the background of Canada's former governor general (1999–2005) Adrienne Clarkson. Chu arrived in British Columbia in the 1860s, and by 1876 opened the Wing Chong Company in Victoria, selling general merchandise and importing Chinese goods. Chu exemplified one of the other features of Chinese immigrant society: only members of the merchant class had the resources to establish wives and families in Canada. Chu had four wives, two in Canada, and two in China who oversaw the family's interests there. By the time of his death, Chu had amassed a fortune of $500 000, and was probably British Columbia's most prominent Chinese merchant. Merchants shared with their working-class counterparts the goal of enriching their families and clans in China. Overseas remittances became enormously important to the Chinese economy. Merchant activities went beyond a quest for wealth; they played a key part in the development of an overseas Chinese community in British Columbia, acting as labour contractors and bankers, and organizing Chinese-language schools and fraternal and philanthropic organizations.

The Cariboo Gold Rush

The waning of the Fraser River gold rush coincided with new discoveries deeper in British Columbia's wild interior. The Cariboo gold rush began in 1860 with the discovery of gold on Horsefly River and in the surrounding area. Gold fever, fanned by stories of lucky strikes, drew thousands to the area. But this was not simple placer mining—the mining of alluvial sand and gravel deposits by a river; instead, the process required considerable capital and the sinking of deep shafts into the rock. Hydraulic systems were used to direct pressurized jets of water into the rock, which would then wash into a system of sluice boxes. Even though the effort was daunting, some miners did get rich: Billy Barker, for whom the main settlement of Barkerville was named, exemplified the classic rags to riches—and back again—saga. An English canal labourer who first tried his luck in California, Barker struck it rich by doggedly working 12-metre deep shafts to unearth gold deposits. The legend is that Barker made, but then lost, a fortune estimated at $600 000 to a "calculating woman." The more probable and prosaic explanation seems to be that Barker continued to invest in unproductive mines and was simply too generous in his spending. He was located in his 70s living in a one-room shack with several other miners, and ended his life as a pauper.

Governor Douglas proved to be as energetic in supplying the necessary infrastructure for the Cariboo strike as he had for the Fraser. The Royal Engineers organized the construction of a 600-kilometre trail, paved with logs, from Yale to Barkerville. By 1863, stagecoaches and ox-drawn wagon trains rattled over the high wooden trestle bridges and hairpin turns of the Cariboo trail, and innkeepers offered accommodations for travellers along the way. One imaginative entrepreneur hit upon the idea of importing 23 camels to carry freight, but unfortunately these beasts caused panic in other animals hauling goods along the route. Met with a storm of opposition, the disgusted owner of the camels simply turned them loose. For years afterward, travellers to British Columbia might find themselves confronted by the unlikely sight of a camel wandering free.

By the time of the Cariboo rush in the 1860s, British Columbia's population was changing. Domination by Americans had given way to new arrivals from Canada, the Atlantic colonies, and Britain. Judge Begbie noted with approval that eastern and British families were sending their best sons to the Cariboo. Settlement of newcomers on the lower mainland of British Columbia—the future greater Vancouver area—began early in the 1860s, with the exploitation of coal near the entrance of the Burrard Inlet, and the establishment of sawmills nearby soon afterward.

Early 1860s: Sawmills begin operations in area of future Vancouver.

Hastings Mill on the south shore of the inlet, and Moody's Mill on the north, were steam-powered operations that employed Squamish and Musqueam people living nearby, supplemented with the occasional runaway sailor. The elite of the sawmill workforces were the skilled teamsters who coaxed teams of oxen to drag enormously heavy logs over greased skids to reach the water. The settlement of Granville on the south shore began with Yorkshireman Jack Deighton's Globe Saloon in 1867. Deighton's loquacious nature—seemingly an indispensable attribute in a barkeeper—earned him the epithet "Gassy Jack," a nickname commemorated in Vancouver's trendy Gastown.

Rivalry developed between the growing settlement of New Westminster and Victoria, especially since Victoria enjoyed the perquisites associated with being the seat of colonial government. Trade also flowed primarily through Vancouver Island, since Victoria had been named a free port in 1860. Just as in another Victoria, far across the Pacific in the British possession of Hong Kong, the absence of any tariffs on imports conferred an enormous advantage in capturing commercial trade. Governor Douglas had made some concession to New Westminster's increasingly vocal demands for participation in their own government. In 1860, that mainland centre was incorporated as a city with a municipal

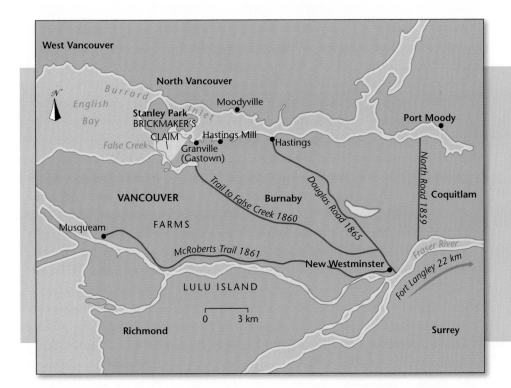

Map 11.4
Early settlement in Vancouver area.

1861: A convention in Hope demands responsible government for British Columbia.

council. But a flurry of petitions to the British Colonial Office and, more ominously, an 1861 convention in Hope which met to demand responsible government, signified that the mainland population was still not satisfied. John Robson, the Upper Canadian-born editor of the mainland newspaper *British Columbian*, angrily likened their condition to "serfdom." Douglas was a particular target of attacks in Robson's newspaper, as he was in the Vancouver Island newspaper of the like-minded Amor de Cosmos, and he considered the malcontents a clique of troublemakers from California and Canada. Nonetheless, in 1862 he recommended the introduction of a representative chamber on the mainland, with one-third of the members elected.

By 1863, a torrent of complaints about the dictatorial Douglas, and the fact that he had already served as governor for 12 years—about twice the usual term of office—prompted the Colonial Office to relieve Douglas of his duties in both Pacific colonies. The colonial secretary assured him that his retirement would be carried out in such a way as to avoid giving any occasion for triumph to his enemies, and he offered Douglas the consolation of a knighthood. In the spring of 1864, Douglas stepped down as governor, his reputation as the "father of British Columbia" assured by the myriad challenges he had met with unfailing dignity and resourcefulness.

With Douglas's retirement, an era ended in British Columbia. His two successors—Arthur Edward Kennedy on Vancouver Island, and Frederick Seymour on the mainland—had no HBC connections. Instead, both were Northern Ireland aristocrats with colonial service all over the globe—Kennedy in Sierra Leone and Western Australia, and Seymour in Van Diemen's Land, Antigua, Nevis, and British Honduras.

Mid-Nineteenth-Century Missionaries in British Columbia

As this HBC influence waned, other forces were beginning to leave their mark on the Pacific coast. A male Roman Catholic religious order, the Missionary Oblates of Mary Immaculate, had been active in the Oregon territory since the 1840s, and began work on Vancouver Island alongside the earliest permanent European settlers in 1849. The order had been founded in France and came to the diocese of Montreal in 1841, ministering to the surrounding lumber camps and the local Indians. The college that the Oblates founded at Bytown would later become the University of Ottawa. On Vancouver Island, Oblate father Honoré-Timothée Lempfrit began a school in Fort Victoria for wives and children of fur traders. He enjoyed some success in Victoria where settlement was beginning, but his early attempts to extend the reach of his mission further north up the coast of Vancouver Island were abortive. Confronted by the Cowichan people, who were hostile to his mission, Lempfrit had to be rescued by a party sent by Governor James Douglas.

Despite this inauspicious start, the order would go on to expand into British Columbia's interior and north by the end of the century. The work of these missionaries was made easier by the settled condition of their potential converts. Unlike some Aboriginal nations whose quest for scant resources dictated constant mobility, the more prosperous Natives of the Pacific coast, who enjoyed abundant resources of salmon, cedar, and indigenous berries, occupied permanent sites. Further, the hierarchical nature of coastal Native societies enhanced the ability of the missionaries to claim authority, and this grafting of Christianity onto existing structures was unwittingly helped along by the loss of traditional spiritual leaders, shamans and elders, through rampant disease. By 1861, the Oblates had established the residential school of St. Mary's for Native children at Mission on the Fraser River. This enterprise, begun with such hopeful optimism and positive spirit, would sadly culminate in a history of tragic abuse.

Historian Jacqueline Gresko notes that although official records tend to celebrate the achievements of male missionaries, the female religious orders also played a key role in the life of the colony. The Sisters of Saint Ann, an order founded in Montreal, began their work on the Pacific coast in 1858, teaching children, ministering to the poor, and working in orphanages and hospitals. Some of the early sisters sent to teach in the west were hampered by the fact that they were French speakers and lacked sufficient command of English. This was not the case for Sister Mary Providence, who was born Eleanor McTucker in Ireland. Her birthplace of Sligo was among the areas hardest hit during the Irish potato famine, and like so many others, the McTucker family emigrated to Montreal. At the age of 16, Eleanor entered the noviciate of the Sisters of Saint Ann. While she quickly learned French, her fluency in English made her a great asset to the Order. By 22, Sister Mary Providence was heading west as the Sisters' western directress. During her long administrative term, which lasted from her arrival in 1859 through to 1881, Sister Mary Providence became known and respected along the Pacific coast.[38]

1857: Anglican missionary William Duncan arrives to work among the Tsimshian.

As the Roman Catholic orders were beginning their work in the northwest, Protestant missionaries—chiefly Anglican and Methodist—also commenced activities. William Duncan, an Anglican lay missionary, arrived on Vancouver Island in 1857, and his activities among the Tsimshian people make up one of the most famous chapters in missionary activity in Canada's west. Duncan was born out of wedlock in England and began work in a tannery at age 14. He took evening classes at the Mechanics' Institute, and came under the influence of Victorian social reformer Samuel Smiles, who preached the idea of individual self-help through thrift, industry, and the cultivation of a virtuous orderly life. Duncan taught Sunday school, and by 22 was training with the Church Missionary Society to be a missionary teacher. When a British Royal Navy captain suggested to the CMS that British Columbia's Nass River would be a promising field for missionary work, the organization sent Duncan to undertake it.

At Port Simpson, Duncan was housed at the Hudson's Bay Company post and, while struggling with feelings of isolation, loneliness, and despair at the enormity of his task, began to learn the Tsimshian language, and to teach the Natives. He soon noted with pride that they could sing hymns along with "God Save the Queen." Duncan aimed not only to Christianize the Natives, but to inculcate the same Victorian spirit of progress that had so shaped his own life. In order to do this most effectively, Duncan believed, he would have to separate the Christianized Natives from the corrupting influence of traders and non-Christians who surrounded them. In 1862—providentially just before a devastating outbreak of smallpox would sweep the Pacific coast—Duncan led Tsimshian converts to a new home at their former village site of Metlakatla. The fortunate timing seemed to confirm that Divine Providence smiled upon their enterprises, sparing them from the disease that killed so many others.

1862: Model village of Metlakatla is established.

From 1862 until 1887, when the community would again move to a new Metlakatla in Alaska, Duncan and over 900 Tsimshian Christians established a utopian model village.

It boasted orderly Victorian homes, workshops, gardens, a brass band and uniformed police force, substantial public buildings—including a school, museum, reading room, and jail—and a range of commercial activities: a salmon cannery, blacksmith, trading post, sawmill, and furniture and soap factories. The Native-built church at the mission was capable of seating over 1000 worshippers. Residents renounced alcohol and gambling, abandoned traditional face painting and the Potlatch—ceremonial giveaways of property—and vowed to educate their children and to observe the Sabbath.

William Duncan was not alone as a Protestant missionary on the Pacific coast. Methodist Thomas Crosby was among the other important arrivals. He began work at Nanaimo in 1862, later moving on to Chilliwack on the Fraser River, and then to Port Simpson, where he served Christian converts who found Duncan's brand of evangelism too oppressive. Needless to say, if rivalries between different brands of Protestant missions were prevalent, those between Protestants and Catholics were that much more acute. "Paganism was preferable to the heresy of conversion to the wrong form of Christianity," historian Keith Carlson wryly observes. Crosby complained that the Oblate fathers instructed their converts by means of a "Catholic Ladder," an illustration that showed Catholic Indians ascending to heaven while Crosby and the Methodists went head-first into hell. The Methodists fought back with a "Protestant Ladder," in which even the Pope himself was dropped into hell's burning flames.[39]

As settlement advanced on the Pacific coast, opportunities for conflict between Natives and newcomers increased and the greater prevalence of whisky as an item of trade contributed to outbreaks of violence. Bishop D'Herbomez of the Roman Catholic Oblate order at Mission lamented that "nearly all the Chiefs have been victims of this corrosive destroyer of civilization." Another priest agreed, heaping scorn on the "shameless men … trafficking poisons." Some of the Natives were "never sober," he reported. "That relatives, even friends should fight and kill each other was nothing unusual; we saw drunken fathers stab their innocent children."[40]

Native–Newcomer Conflict on the Pacific Coast

The principle that Governor James Douglas had worked to establish—that individual Natives, rather than entire Native communities, would be punished for any crimes—was sometimes complicated by the fact that Aboriginal communities might shelter those whose crimes were considered justifiable responses to provocation. On several occasions, both under Douglas's term and during the tenure of his successors, colonial authorities used military force—notably the Royal Navy—to compel cooperation with colonial law enforcement.

In 1861, a British Royal Navy gunboat, the *Forward*, used its cannons to bombard a site near Cape Mudge on Quadra Island to which a Haida party had fled after stealing tools, blankets, rum, and other goods in Victoria. The Natives had also plundered vessels in the Gulf and terrorized settlers on Saltspring Island. Four of the Haida were killed in the *Forward's* attack, and five others taken to Victoria for trial. The *Forward* also launched a retaliatory attack with three other vessels against Kuper Island in 1863. Lamalchi village on Kuper Island was thought to be protecting those who had earlier killed settler Frederick Marks on Saturna Island and then hacked his daughter Caroline Harvey to death. Lamalchi was destroyed in the naval attack before four men were captured and brought to trial. These prisoners were later executed; a fifth had already been killed by the Natives of Kuper Island.

Another incident involved the sloop *Kingfisher,* which had been involved in illicit whisky trading with Pacific coast Natives; in 1863, the vessel had been seized by colonial authorities, the contraband alcohol it was plying poured out, and its captain fined. But the very next year, the *Kingfisher* was at the centre of a virtual war between coastal Natives and the Royal Navy. In 1864 the Ahousat of Clayoquot Sound raided the *Kingfisher,* killing its crew of three and leaving the sloop a smouldering wreck. The climate of escalating violence led naval officials at Esquimalt to respond in unmistakable terms. The flagship *Sutlej,* along with the aptly named *Devastation,* launched a retaliatory attack, killing 15 Natives, torching nine villages, and sinking 64 Native canoes. A group of Natives taken prisoner during the incident were later acquitted by a jury in Victoria.

1864: The Chilcotin War erupts over incursions by newcomers.

While the alcohol trade may have been a factor in native–newcomer clashes, some incidents stemmed from other causes. The "Chilcotin War" of 1864 was sparked when road crews at Bute Inlet on the mainland coast, who were building a route to the Cariboo mines, were attacked by Natives.

Beyond the immediate provocation of road building through traditional Tsilhqot'in (Chilcotin) territory was the building resentment over the influx of European diseases. Smallpox and measles had already ravaged the Pacific coast in earlier generations, but an especially devastating smallpox epidemic in 1862—coinciding with the influx of newcomers during the Cariboo gold rush—dealt a deadly blow. An estimated 20 000 British Columbia Natives died, reducing still further a population that had fallen to approximately 60 000 by mid-century. In some especially hard-hit pockets, the mortality rate reached 90 percent. The Haida, once numbering some 8000, were reduced to a mere 800 after the 1860s epidemics.

Amid this atmosphere of aggrieved anger, the Tsilhqot'in lashed out at the road builders, killing 19. Some were attacked as they lay sleeping in tents. Mainland governor Seymour had just hosted some 3500 Native visitors at a New Westminster celebration of Queen Victoria's birthday; the spectacle included a vast flotilla of Aboriginal canoes on the Fraser River, Native songs and drumming, and gifts of Union Jacks and gilt-headed canes to the Natives. Seymour had been confident that he could build a spirit of goodwill with the Natives similar to that enjoyed by Douglas. But immediately on the heels of the celebration, Seymour had to accompany a militia force to Bute Inlet to deal with the crisis. The powerful Chilcotin chief Alexis cooperated in the apprehension of suspects, and, after a trial presided over by Judge Begbie at Quesnel, five Native men were hanged. Among these was a Tsilhqot'in chief known as Klatsassin, which translates as "we do not know his name," a man who won the admiration of Judge Begbie. Questions long remained over these punishments meted out for the killings, over the fact that the Natives regarded the killings not as murder but as acts of war, and especially over promises of amnesty allegedly made to induce the fugitives to surrender. The Cariboo–Chilcotin Justice Inquiry in 1993 led to an apology by British Columbia's government, and the Tsilhqot'in people today celebrate Klatsassin Memorial Day to mark the anniversary of the chief's execution. One victim's descendant wondered who would apologize for shooting his great-grandfather in the back.

Demands for Political Reform on the Pacific Coast

Besides contending with sporadic outbreaks of warfare, the colonial governors who succeeded Douglas had the challenging duty of managing their fledgling assemblies. While the principle of responsible government had not yet been conceded, the assemblies enjoyed the traditional privilege of controlling the provincial treasury. On Vancouver Island, Arthur Kennedy immediately became caught up in a struggle with the island's assertive assembly, dominated by Amor De Cosmos, over that body's frequent refusal to vote necessary funds. Kennedy, who dourly concluded that Vancouver Island consisted of "those who are convicts and those who ought to be convicts," was dismayed to see his assembly vote to repeal a real estate tax when seven members of the assembly's own personal tax bills were in arrears.[41]

Financial struggles were only part of the rationale for the decision to merge Britain's two Pacific coastal colonies. Just as the Colonial Office was trying to bring about a union of its colonies on North America's Atlantic coast, a similar scheme for the western-most colonies seemed to promise more efficient and cost-effective colonial government. While Seymour, the mainland governor, was resistant to the idea of union, agitation by Amor De Cosmos and other islanders, and the lobbying of bankers and investors alarmed by the perilous state of colonial finances, clinched the decision.

1866: Vancouver Island and mainland British Columbia merge as a single colony.

In 1866, the two colonies were combined as British Columbia, with Seymour serving as governor of both. Victoria lost its status as a free port, and the single legislative assembly, in which only nine of the 23 members were elected, was briefly located at New Westminster before being moved to Victoria in 1868. Needless to say, this half-hearted concession to colonial self-government would not slake the thirst of reformers. In the years to come, Confederation offered the chance for British Columbia to at last win responsible government.

Conclusion

British North American territory west of the Rocky Mountains was the scene of some of the most profound changes of the mid-nineteenth century. The earlier small-scale settlement dictated by the Hudson's Bay Company's exploitation of resources was dwarfed by the sudden influx of thousands of miners in the summer of 1858. Change in the other, more-established colonial possessions was perhaps less dramatic, but nevertheless significant. The Métis people of Red River and environs saw new opportunities arise in the era of liberalized trade, but would soon be faced with a serious challenge in the form of new agricultural settlers. Many of these newcomers would be from the growing province of Canada, and particularly from Canada West, whose population by mid-century outstripped the older Canada East. This new demographic reality also exerted its influence on political discourse.

A more radical reform element, the Clear Grit party, added complexity to partisan politics in the united Canadas. In Canada East, the Parti Rouge became a new voice for French-Canadian sovereignty by mid-century. Religious sectarianism, and more antagonistic Catholic–Protestant relations embittered many aspects of public life. At the same time, British North America was transformed by technological change—the shift from wooden sailing ships to iron-hulled steamers, and the advent of the telegraph and the railway. The conclusion of a free trade treaty with the Americans after the loss of imperial protection also reoriented economic life in the colonies. The decades of the mid-nineteenth century brought significant alterations to life in the British North American colonies. It is not surprising, then, that in the 1860s demands for political reform would bring even more far-reaching change.

Questions to Consider

1. What examples can be cited of conflict over religious sectarianism in mid-nineteenth-century British North America?

2. What important technological changes emerged in the middle decades of the nineteenth century?

3. What developments in the 1840s and 1850s contributed to the rising power of the Métis?

4. What general assumptions underlay Aboriginal policy and practice in British North America?

5. In what ways did the 1858 gold rush bring changes to the Pacific coast?

Critical Thinking Questions

1. How and why did political alliances change in the united Canadas during the 1850s?

2. To what extent were sectarian tensions in British North America driven by external factors?

3. What prompted the governments of Britain and Canada to undertake geological surveys of the continent's interior?

4. What basic philosophical differences characterized the approach taken by Governors Blanshard and Douglas to the administration of justice among Natives in the Pacific Northwest?

5. Is James Douglas's reputation as the "father of British Columbia" merited? How successful was he in meeting the challenges he faced?

Suggested Readings
Primary Sources

Doughty, Sir Arthur G., ed. *The Elgin-Grey Papers, 1846–1852*. 4 vols. Ottawa: J.O. Patenaude, 1937.

Harris, Martha Douglas. *History and Folklore of the Cowichan Indians*. Introduction by Paul Lindholdt. Spokane, Washington: Marquette Books, 2004.

Henson, Josiah. *The Life of Josiah Henson, Formerly a Slave, Now an Inhabitant of Canada. Narrated by Himself*. Boston: Arthur D. Phelps, 1849.

Merivale, Herman. *Lectures on Colonization and Colonies*. London: Longman and Green, 1842.

Spry, Irene M. *The Papers of the Palliser Expedition, 1857–1860*. Toronto: The Champlain Society, 1968.

Useful for Overview

Careless, J.M.S. *The Union of the Canadas: The Growth of Canadian Institutions, 1841–1857.* Toronto: McClelland & Stewart, 1967.

Friesen, Gerald. *The Canadian Prairies: A History.* Toronto: University of Toronto Press, 1984.

Harris, R. Cole, and John Warkentin. *Canada Before Confederation: A Study in Historical Geography.* Toronto: Oxford University Press, 1974.

Morton, W.L. *Manitoba, A History.* Toronto: University of Toronto Press, 1957.

Native–Newcomer Relations

Chris Arnett. *The Terror of the Coast: Land Alienation and Colonial War on Vancouver Island and the Gulf Islands, 1849–1863.* Burnaby, BC: Talon Books, 1991.

Binnema, Theodore and Kevin Hutchings. "The Emigrant and the Noble Savage: Sir Francis Bond Head's Romantic Approach to Aboriginal Policy in Upper Canada, 1836–1838." *Journal of Canadian Studies* 39 (Winter 2005): 115–138.

Bolt, Clarence R. *Thomas Crosby and the Tsimshian: Small Shoes for Feet Too Large.* Vancouver: University of British Columbia Press, 1992.

Cannadine, David. *Ornamentalism: How the British Saw Their Empire.* Toronto: Oxford University Press, 2001.

Carlson, Keith, ed. *You Are Asked to Witness: The Stó:lô in Canada's Pacific Coast History.* Chilliwack, BC: Stó:lô Heritage Trust, 1997.

Carlson, Keith. "The Power of Place, The Problem of Time: A Study of History and Aboriginal Collective Identity." Ph.D. Dissertation. University of British Columbia, 2003.

Carlson, Keith, ed. *A Sto:lo Coast Salish Historical Atlas.* Vancouver: Douglas and McIntyre, 2006.

Carter, Sarah. *Aboriginal People and Colonizers of Western Canada to 1900.* Toronto: University of Toronto Press, 1999.

"Great Unsolved Mysteries in Canadian History" *Canadian Mysteries* online at http://canadianmysteries.uvic.ca. For the Chilcotin War, see "We Do Not Know His Name: Klatsassin and the Chilcotin War," *Canadian Mysteries* online at http://canadian mysteries.uvic.ca/sites/klatsassin//home/indexen.html.

Harring, Sidney L. *White Man's Law: Native People in Nineteenth-Century Canadian Jurisprudence.* Toronto: University of Toronto Press, 1998.

Harris, Cole. *Making Native Space: Colonialism, Resistance, and Reserves in British Columbia.* Vancouver: University of British Columbia Press, 2002.

Kelm, Mary-Ellen, and Lorna Townsend. *In the Days of our Grandmothers: A Reader in Aboriginal Women's History in Canada.* Toronto: University of Toronto Press, 2006.

Knight, Alan, and Janet E. Chute. "A Visionary on the Edge: Allan Macdonell and the Championing of Native Resource Rights" in *With Good Intentions: Euro-Canadian and Aboriginal Relations in Colonial Canada.* Celia Haig-Brown, ed. Vancouver: University of British Columbia Press, 2006, pp. 87–105.

Marshall, Daniel P. "No Parallel: American Miner-soldiers at War with the Nlaka'pamux of the Canadian West" in *Parallel Destinies: Canadian–American Relations West of the Rockies.* John M. Findlay and Ken S. Coates, eds. Montreal and Kingston: McGill-Queen's University Press, 2002, pp. 31–79.

McNab, David T. "Herman Merivale and Colonial Office Policy in the Mid-Nineteenth Century." In *As Long as the Sun Shines and Water Flows: A Reader in Canadian Native Studies.* Ian A.L. Getty and Antoine S. Lussier, eds. Vancouver: UBC Press, 1983, pp. 85–103.

Miller, J.R. *Skyscrapers Hide the Heavens: A History of Indian–White Relations in Canada,* 3rd ed. Toronto: University of Toronto Press, 2000.

Milloy, John S. "The Early Indian Acts: Developmental Strategy and Constitutional Change." In *As Long as the Sun Shines and Water Flows: A Reader in Canadian Native Studies.* Ian A.L. Getty and Antoine S. Lussier, eds. Vancouver: University of British Columbia Press, 1983, pp. 56–64.

Neylan, Susan. *The Heavens are Changing Nineteenth-Century Protestant Missions and Tsimshian Christianity.* Montreal and Kingston: McGill-Queen's University Press, 2003.

Smith, Donald B. *Sacred Feathers: The Reverend Peter Jones (Kahkewaquonaby) and the Mississauga Indians.* Toronto: University of Toronto Press, 1987.

Tobias, John L. "Protection, Civilization, Assimilation: An Outline History of Canada's Indian Policy." In *As Long as the Sun Shines and Water Flows: A Reader in Canadian Native Studies.* Ian A.L. Getty and Antoine S. Lussier, eds. Vancouver: University of British Columbia Press, 1983, 39–55.

Upton, L.F.S. "The Origins of Canadian Indian Policy." *Journal of Canadian Studies* 8 (November 1973): 51–61.

Upton, L.F.S. *Micmacs and Colonists: Indian–White Relations in the Maritimes, 1713–1867.* Vancouver: University of British Columbia Press, 1979.

Vibert, Elizabeth. *Traders' Tales: Narratives of Cultural Encounters in the Columbia Plateau, 1807–1846.* Norman: University of Oklahoma Press, 1997.

British Columbia

Barman, Jean. *The West Beyond the West: A History of British Columbia.* Toronto: University of Toronto Press, 1991.

Belshaw, John Douglas. *Colonization and Community: The Vancouver Island Coalfield and the making of the British Columbian Working Class.* Montreal and Kingston: McGill-Queen's University Press, 2002.

Ficken, Robert E. *Unsettled Boundaries: Fraser Gold and the British–American Northwest.* Pullman, Washington: Washington State University Press, 2003.

Gough, Barry. Gunboat Frontier: British Maritime Authority and Northwest Coast Indians, 1846–1890. Vancouver: University of British Columbia Press, 1984.

Johnston, Hugh J. M., ed. *The Pacific Province: A History of British Columbia.* Vancouver: Douglas & McIntyre, 1996.

Loo, Tina. *Making Law, Order, and Authority in British Columbia, 1821–1871.* Toronto: University of Toronto Press, 1994.

Ormsby, Margaret. *British Columbia: A History.* Toronto: Macmillan, 1958.

Perry, Adele. *On the Edge of Empire: Gender, Race, and the Making of British Columbia, 1849–1871.* Toronto: University of Toronto Press, 2001.

Van Kirk, Sylvia. "Tracing the Fortunes of Five Founding Families of Victoria." *BC Studies* 115/116 (Autumn/Winter 1997–1998): 149–179.

Woodcock, George. *Amor de Cosmos: Journalist and Reformer.* Toronto: Oxford University Press, 1975.

Woodcock, George. *British Columbia: A History of the Province.* Vancouver: Douglas & McIntyre, 1990.

Yee, Paul. *Saltwater City: An Illustrated History of the Chinese in Vancouver.* Vancouver: Douglas & McIntyre, 1988.

Other Special Topics

Axelrod, Paul. *The Promise of Schooling: Education in Canada, 1800–1914.* Toronto: University of Toronto Press, 1997.

Curtis, Bruce. "Class Culture and Administration: Educational Inspection in Canada West." In *Colonial Leviathan: State Formation in Mid-Nineteenth Century Canada.* Allan Greer and Ian Radforth, eds. Toronto: University of Toronto Press, 1992, pp. 103–133.

Curtis, Bruce. *Building the Education State: Canada West, 1836–1871.* London, ON: The Althouse Press, 1988.

Curtis, Bruce. *The Politics of Population: State Formation, Statistics, and the Census of Canada, 1840–1875.* Toronto: University of Toronto Press, 2001.

den Otter, A.A. "The 1849 Sayer Trial: An Ecological Perspective." In *Canada 1849.* Derek Pollard and Ged Martin, eds. Edinburgh: University of Edinburgh Centre of Canadian Studies, 2001, pp. 129–150.

Ens, Gerhard. "Dispossession or Adaptation: Migration and Persistence of the Red River Metis, 1835–1890." In *The Prairie West: Historical Readings.* R. Douglas Francis and Howard Palmer, eds. (Edmonton: Pica Press/ University of Alberta, 1992).

Francis, R. Douglas Francis. "'The Iron Civilizer': T.C. Keefer and T.C. Haliburton, Two Canadian 'Philosophers of Railroads.'" In *Canada 1849*. Derek Pollard and Ged Martin, eds. Edinburgh: University of Edinburgh Centre of Canadian Studies, 2001, pp. 117–128.

Huskins, Bonnie. "'A Tale of Two Cities:' Boosterism and the Imagination of Community during the Visit of the Prince of Wales to Saint John and Halifax in 1860." *Urban History Review* 28 (October 1999): 31–46.

Jin Tan, and Patricia Roy, *The Chinese in Canada*. Ottawa: Canadian Historical Association, 1985.

MacLeod, Margaret Arnett. *Cuthbert Grant of Grantown: Warden of the Plains of Red River*. Toronto: McClelland & Stewart, 1963.

Morton, W.L. "The Battle at the Grand Coteau, July 13 and 14, 1851." *Transactions of the Manitoba Historical Society*, Series 3, 1959–60 season.

Pannekoek, Frits. "The Anglican Church and the Disintegration of Red River Society, 1818–1870." In *The West and the Nation: Essays in Honour of W. L. Morton*. Carl Berger and Ramsay Cook, eds. Toronto: McClelland and Stewart Limited, 1976, pp. 72–90.

Prentice, Alison. *The School Promoters: Education and Social Class in Mid-Nineteenth Century Upper Canada*. Toronto: McClelland & Stewart, 1977.

Prud'homme, Maurice. "The Life and Times of Archibishop Taché." Transactions of the Manitoba Historical Society, series 3, 1954–1955 season.

Radforth, Ian. Royal Spectacle: The 1860 Visit of the Prince of Wales to Canada and the United States. Toronto: University of Toronto Press, 2004.

Tulchinsky, Gerald. *The River Barons: Montreal Businessmen and the Growth of Industry and Transportation, 1837–1853*. Toronto: University of Toronto Press, 1977.

Zeller, Suzanne. *Land of Promise, Promised Land: The Culture of Victorian Science in Canada*. Ottawa: Canadian Historical Association booklet number 56, 1996.

Zeller, Suzanne. *Inventing Canada: Early Victorian Science and the Idea of a Transcontinental Nation*. Toronto: University of Toronto Press, 1987.

Notes

[1]   Sylvia Van Kirk, "Colonized Lives: The Native Wives and Daughters of the Five Founding Families of Victoria," in Mary-Ellen Kelm and Lorna Townsend, eds., *In the Days of Our Grandmothers: A Reader in Aboriginal Women's History in Canada* (Toronto: University of Toronto Press, 2006).

[2]   James W. St. G. Walker, "African Canadians," in *Encyclopedia of Canada's Peoples.* Available online at http://www.multiculturalcanada.ca/ecp/. This encyclopedia contains in-depth, authoritative material on all of Canada's main immigrant groups.

[3]   Josiah Henson, *The Life of Josiah Henson, Formerly a Slave, Now an Inhabitant of Canada. Narrated by Himself* (Boston: Arthur D. Phelps, 1849), 65–66.

[4]   John Charles Dent, *The Last Forty Years: Canada Since the Union of 1841,* vol. II (Toronto: George Virtue, 1881), 190, n.

[5]   In the system used in the United Kingdom prior to the 1971 currency reform, there were twelve pence to a shilling and twenty shillings to a pound. The system was further complicated by the use sundry coins such as the farthing (worth a quarter of a penny) and the half crown (worth two shillings, six pence), among many others.

[6]   As quoted in R. Douglas Francis, "'The Iron Civilizer': T.C. Keefer and T.C. Haliburton, Two Canadian 'Philosopers of Railroads,'" *Canada 1849,* Derek Pollard and Ged Martin, eds. (Edinburgh: University of Edinburgh Centre of Canadian Studies, 2001), 119,125.

[7]   As quoted by Peter Baskerville, "Sir Allan Napier MacNab," *Dictionary of Canadian Biography,* http://www.biographi.ca.

[8]   Bonnie Huskins, "'A Tale of Two Cities:' Boosterism and the Imagination of Community during the Visit of the Prince of Wales to Saint John and Halifax in 1860," *Urban History Review* 28 (October 1999): 31–46.

[9]   Maurice Prud'homme, "The Life and Times of Archibishop Taché" Transactions of the Manitoba Historical Society, series 3, 1954–1955 season. Online at http://www.mhs.mb.ca/docs/transactions/3/tache.shtml.

[10] James Morris, *Heaven's Command: An Imperial Progress* (New York: Harcourt, Brace, Jovanovich, 1973), 340.

[11] Historian David G. McCrady has raised doubts about the identity of the Sioux group that the Métis confronted in 1851. Others have asserted that these were Dakota, but this has not been definitively established, according to McCrady. See David G. McCrady, *Living with Strangers: the Nineteenth-Century Sioux and the Canadian-American Borderlands* (Lincoln: University of Nebraska Press, 2006), 13.

[12] As quoted in William Morton, "The Battle at the Grand Coteau, July 13 and 14, 1851," Transactions of the Manitoba Historical Society, Series 3, 1959–60 season. Online at http://www.mhs.mb.ca/docs/transactions/3/grandcouteau.shtml.

[13] R. Cole Harris and John Warkentin, *Canada Before Confederation* (Toronto: Oxford University Press, 1974), 248.

[14] As quoted in James Morris, *Heaven's Command: An Imperial Progress* (New York: Harcourt, Brace, Jovanovich, 1973), 128.

[15] Henry Hind also used the term "fertile belt" in his report. For more detail, see entries on "Fertile Belt," and "Palliser's Triangle," in Encyclopedia of the Great Plains. David J. Wishart, ed. (Lincoln: Center for Great Plains Studies, University of Nebraska, 2004).

[16] Richard A. Jarrell, "Henry Youle Hind," *Dictionary of Canadian Biography,* http://www.biographi.ca.

[17] As quoted in Barry M. Gough, *Gunboat Frontier: British Maritime Authority and Northwest Coast Indians, 1846–1890* (Vancouver: University of British Columbia Press, 1984), 41.

[18] As quoted in Robin Fisher, *Contact and Conflict: Indian-European Relations in British Columbia, 1774–1890* (Vancouver: University of British Columbia Press, 1992), 52.

[19] Sylvia Van Kirk, "Tracing the Fortunes of Five Founding Families of Victoria," *BC Studies* 115/116 (Autumn/Winter 1997–1998): 149–179.

[20] As quoted in Robin Fisher, *Contact and Conflict,* 88.

21 Elizabeth Vibert, T*raders' Tales: Narratives of Cultural Encounters in the Columbia Plateau, 1807–1846* (Norman: University of Oklahoma Press, 1997), 5.

22 J.R. Miller, *Skyscrapers Hide the Heavens: A History of Indian-White Relations in Canada*, 3rd ed. (Toronto: University of Toronto Press, 2000), 103.

23 Elgin to Grey, dispatch 118, 23 November 1849, *The Elgin-Grey Papers, 1846-1852*, vol. 4, Sir Arthur G. Doughty, ed. (Ottawa: J.O. Patenaude, 1937), 1486.

24 As quoted in Robert J. Surtees, "Treaty Research Report: The Robinson Treaties (1850)," Government of Canada, Indian and Northern Affairs, http://www.ainc-inac.gc.ca/pr/trts/hti/trob/hist_e.html. See also Alan Knight and Janet E. Chute, "A Visionary on the Edge: Allan Macdonell and the Championing of Native Resource Rights," in *With Good Intentions: Euro-Canadian and Aboriginal Relations in Colonial Canada*, Celia Haig-Brown, ed. (Vancouver: University of British Columbia Press, 2006), 87–105.

25 David T. McNab, "Herman Merivale and Colonial Office Indian Policy in the Mid-Nineteenth Century," in *As Long as the Sun Shines and Water Flows: A Reader in Canadian Native Studies*, Ian A.L. Getty and Antoine S. Lussier, eds. (Vancouver: University of British Columbia Press, 1983), 99.

26 George Woodcock, *British Columbia: A History of the Province* (Vancouver: Douglas & McIntyre, 1990), 92.

27 See, for example, Barry Gough, *Gunboat Frontier: British Maritime Authority and Northwest Coast Indians, 1846–1890* (Vancouver: University of British Columbia Press, 1984), 78.

28 As quoted in Fisher, Contact and Conflict, 53, 55. See also Chris Arnett, *The Terror of the Coast: Land Alienation and Colonial War on Vancouver Island and the Gulf Islands, 1849–1863* (Burnaby, BC: Talon Books, 1991), 43–45.

29 Adele Perry, *On the Edge of Empire: Gender, Race, and the Making of British Colombia, 1849–1871* (Toronto: University of Toronto Press, 2001), 4, 9, 17, 150, 138.

30 Woodcock, *British Columbia,* 100. The quoted passage is by George Munro Grant.

31 George Woodcock, *Amor de Cosmos: Journalist and Reformer* (Toronto: Oxford University Press, 1975), 5.

32 As quoted in Margaret Ormsby, "James Douglas," *Dictionary of Canadian Biography,* http://www.biographi.ca.

33 As quoted in Daniel P. Marshall, "No Parallel: American Miner-soldiers at War with the Nlaka'pamux of the Canadian West," in John M. Findlay and Ken S. Coates, eds., *Parallel Destinies: Canadian-American Relations West of the Rockies* (Montreal and Kingston: McGill-Queen's University Press, 2002), 38.

34 We thank Stó:lō cultural advisor Albert "Sonny" McHalsie for information about the role of the sia:teleq.

35 Keith Carlson, "The Power of Place: The Problem of Time: A Study of History and Aboriginal Collective Identity," Ph.D. Dissertation (Vancouver: University of British Columbia, 2003), 209.

36 Tina Loo, *Making Law, Order, and Authority in British Columbia, 1821–1871* (Toronto: University of Toronto Press, 1994).

37 As quoted in Robert E. Ficken, *Unsettled Boundaries: Fraser Gold and the British–American Northwest* (Pullman, WA: Washington State University Press, 2003),151.

38 Jacqueline Gresko, "Gender and Mission: The Founding Generations of the Sisters of Saint Ann and the Oblates of Mary Immaculate in British Columbia, 1858–1914," Ph.D. Dissertation (Vancouver: University of British Columbia, 1999).

39 Carlson, "The Power of Place," 241.

40 Carlson, "The Power of Place," 231–232.

41 As quoted in Margaret Ormsby, *British Columbia: A History* (Toronto: Macmillan, 1958), 214, 216.

12

*T*hree Weddings *and a* Divorce: Confederation: *1858–1867*

*I*n early September 1864, Confederation delegates at Charlottetown, Prince Edward Island, took a break from the tedious business of discussing federal fiscal arrangements. The delegates from the united colony of Canada invited their Maritime hosts to lunch with them aboard the steamer *Queen Victoria*. It was a golden autumn afternoon, and the vessel rode lightly at anchor on the sun-dappled waves as the Canadians plied their guests with copious quantities of champagne. Canada West Reformer George Brown, once a shrill critic of Conservative John A. Macdonald, now joined him in seeking to win over Atlantic colonists to the idea of a wider union. "Whether as the result of our eloquence or of the goodness of our champagne," Brown wrote to his new wife, "the ice became completely broken, the tongues of the delegates wagged merrily. If any one can show just cause or impediment why the Colonies should not be united in matrimonial alliance," one delegate boomed, "let him now express it or for ever hold his peace." None of those present forbade the banns, Brown reported, "and the union was thereupon formally completed and proclaimed!"[1]

Frances Monck, sister-in-law of the governor general, was a keen observer of Canadian life.
Photograph by William Notman, 1864.

Introduction

By the early 1860s, the "united" Canadas were anything but. The colony was at the point of being ungovernable, and the conviction was growing that some fundamental structural reform was needed. At the same time, a bloody civil war south of the border introduced new strains in Anglo–American relations. The peaceful resolution of North American border questions in the 1840s and the conclusion of the 1854 free trade deal had barely begun to usher in a new era of cross-border amity when a series of crises erupted to shatter colonial security. If war should erupt, it seemed doubtful that Britain—eagerly divesting itself of colonial responsibilities—would launch a concerted defence to confront the powerful United States. Confederation in 1867 was not the inevitable result of a sense of cohesive national identity, but rather one possible—if imperfect—solution to various problems.

The Political World of the United Canadas

George Brown.

Source: © McCord Museum, I-16559.1.

The 1854 emergence of a new coalition between moderate conservatives and liberals to supplant the old Baldwin–La Fontaine alliance of the 1840s did not resolve all of the united Canadas' political difficulties. Even the new partnership struck in 1857 between new Canada West Conservative leader John A. Macdonald and Canada East Bleu chief George-Étienne Cartier could not consistently rally majority support. The strong voice of Clear Grit leader George Brown in Canada West, and a vocal minority of Rouge members in Canada East, led by Antoine-Aimé Dorion, ensured that the politics of the united Canadas would be more complicated than a simple English–French dichotomy.

As editor of the reform newspaper Toronto's *Globe,* George Brown exerted an enormous influence on public opinion. Born in Scotland, Brown collaborated with his Presbyterian merchant father on several journalistic projects meant to advance the cause of political reform, first in New York and then in Toronto. Sober and industrious, Brown was driven principally by ideals rather than pragmatism, making him better suited to be an opposition leader than head of a governing party. Brown was convinced that the existing equal allocation of seats in the single legislature of the united Canadas was an injustice to the more populous Canada West. As of 1861, that portion of the colony had grown in numbers to 1.4 million, as opposed to 1.1 million in Canada East. Brown maintained that Catholic interests were thus able to dominate. Brown's personal characteristics and overall style made him an unnatural politician: unlike his archrival Macdonald, Brown was inflexible and standoffish, had trouble remembering names and faces, and failed to nurture the personal connections upon which political allegiances often rest.

While John A. Macdonald would go on to dominate nine-teenth-century Canadian political life, his early life and family background did not especially augur a powerful political career: his family emigrated from Scotland when he was a child, and they struggled financially as father Hugh Macdonald failed as a merchant in a string of ill-fated enterprises. Macdonald attended school to the age of 15, and his intelligence and character, coupled with fortuitous circumstances, brought him to the pinnacle of Canada's political world. He articled as a lawyer with a Kingston firm, and by 17 was running a branch law office in Napanee. While still in his early 20s, he attracted attention as a defence lawyer in several high-profile cases, including that of Nils von Schoultz, who had led a raid into Upper Canada in 1838. Gradually, more of Macdonald's legal practice was devoted to corporate clients, and he built powerful business connections with banking and land companies. At 19, Macdonald ventured into public life, first serving on a local Board of Education, and then becoming an alderman on Kingston's town council. By 1844, at age 29, he had won election to the Canadian provincial assembly as a Conservative member for Kingston.

John A. Macdonald.
Source: McCord Museum, I-7952.1.

While it is tempting to ascribe strong guiding principles and steely convictions to the statesman who would come to loom so large in the country's history, in truth the secret to Macdonald's political longevity may lie more in his pragmatic flexibility. Never a political ideologue, Macdonald was adept at compromise. Macdonald's later strategy in attempting to lure Michael Foley, a leading Reform politician, into cabinet speaks volumes. Foley objected that he did not know what the policies of the new administration would be. "D—n it, Foley, join the Government and then help to make the policy," Macdonald improvised, slapping him on the knee.[2] Tactics of delay were also a staple ingredient in Macdonald's winning formula. An awkward or unpopular decision could always wait. In later years, a Native chief, frustrated by the government's inaction in addressing grievances, was reportedly first to nickname Macdonald "Old Tomorrow," a name that stuck. However, Macdonald had a remarkable gift for friendship, a knack for cultivating the social connections that grease the wheels of political life. Even opposition members fell under the persuasive spell of Macdonald's personal charm: one Liberal remembered delivering a plodding maiden speech in the House of Commons. While the new member's own party colleagues yawned and fidgeted impatiently, Macdonald turned his chair to face the stumbling neophyte, greeted the speech with applause and shouts of "Hear! Hear!" and made a point of congratulating the young parliamentarian later in the House dining room. Such gestures helped Macdonald capture the loyalty of wavering partisans.

Of course, many of the social connections that bound political allies together were lubricated with alcohol. Legislative sittings took place in the evening, and members often fortified themselves with strong drink. This was by no means an exclusively Canadian practice: British statesman Lord Kimberley remembered what he called "the good old times of two bottle men, when one of the duties of the Secretary to the Treasury is said to have been to hold his hat on occasion for the convenience of the First Lord when 'clearing himself' for his speech."[3]

Even amid a culture that permitted immoderate drinking, Macdonald's habits attracted notice. One of the best-known anecdotes concerns an especially embarrassing lapse when Macdonald was campaigning in northern Ontario. Having heavily imbibed throughout a bumpy ride to the hustings, Macdonald became queasy when he rose to offer a rebuttal to his opponent's campaign speech. To the horror of his supporters, he vomited all over the platform. He recovered the situation, though, and quickly explained to the crowd that hearing the Liberal candidate speak had turned his stomach. At times, however, damage control was more difficult, and Macdonald's frequent drunkenness had real political consequences for his party. During the spring of 1862, his government went down to defeat over a proposed Militia Bill while Macdonald was absent from the House for a week, reportedly on a prolonged drinking binge. Political friends and supporters tried to shield him when possible. On one occasion, a newspaper reporter sympathetic to the Conservatives hesitated to report the contents of a speech Macdonald gave at a lively and festive public dinner, since the prime minister's incoherent rambling made his impaired condition obvious. The reporter called on Macdonald privately the next day, and tactfully explained that he was unsure whether he had obtained an accurate transcript of the speech. Macdonald kindly repeated his remarks in a more sensible form for the reporter, but then scolded the young man, warning him to never again attempt to take notes while drunk.[4]

In Canada East, George-Étienne Cartier was emerging as the dominant political force, the other half of a fruitful partnership; Macdonald called Cartier "my second self." Cartier's family were prosperous merchants in Quebec's Richelieu Valley. George-Étienne's father, Jacques Cartier III, had inherited a substantial estate, which included a grand 17-room stone house and contents, plus capital that exceeded £120 000. Yet within 15 years he was bankrupt, a victim of Lower Canada's agricultural decline coupled with his own profligate habits. He reportedly had a taste for fine clothes, music, and liquor, and, despite being the father of eight children and husband of a pious family-oriented wife, was given to extravagant socializing and a life of dissipation. The insolvency of a merchant father was thus a theme in both Macdonald's and Cartier's lives, although the Cartier family had further to fall.

Another common element was an early career in law: Cartier began work as a clerk in a Montreal law firm at age 17. Cartier also shared Macdonald's reputation for sociability—he was the life of any party, a jovial singer and an enthusiastic dancer. When visiting London, he reportedly juggled five invitations per day. Handsome and impeccably dressed in imported silk shirts and fashionably tailored suits, he was of short stature—Governor-General Lord Monck privately called him "little Cartier"—with a large head, intense gaze, and luxuriant mane of hair swept back from a receding hairline. Neither Macdonald nor Cartier found particular felicity in marriage. Since Cartier was known to describe "love" as one of his hobbies, it is not surprising that he soon became estranged from his wife. His long alliance with Luce Cuvillier, with whom he later lived, was an open secret in Ottawa society. Like Macdonald, as a lawyer Cartier took on prominent corporate clients; in fact, he continued to act as solicitor for the Grand Trunk Railway even after becoming a cabinet minister, and used his place in government to advance his client's interests. These many similarities notwithstanding, there were important distinctions between the two men's early lives—where Macdonald was a member of the militia that sought to suppress the 1837–38 rebellions in Upper Canada, in Lower Canada Cartier joined in the insurrection. He composed an anthem, "O Canada, mon pays, mes amours," for the nationalist Jean Baptiste organization in 1834, was active in the *patriote* cause, and even took up arms with the rebels at Saint Denis in 1837. He was forced into hiding in the aftermath, and was later smuggled across the American border in a barrel. Cartier later attempted to explain this youthful ardour for rebellion by explaining that he was loyal to the Crown, but only opposed a corrupt minority who sought to exploit government for their own ends. Cartier had first entered politics as a moderate reform member in 1848, before moving toward a Liberal–Conservative (Bleu) coalition in partnership with Macdonald in 1857.

1857: Conservative John A. Macdonald and Bleu counterpart George-Étienne Cartier establish a lasting partnership.

George-Étienne Cartier's lower historical profile—compared to his English-Canadian counterpart, Macdonald—is no doubt attributable to the fact that he is a problematic hero for French Canada. His cooperation with English-Canadian politicians and his pragmatic spirit of compromise do not sit well with those who would like to see an unambiguous champion of French-Canadian nationality. Historian Brian Young describes Cartier as "a confirmed anglophile who turned increasingly to London for his clothes, his status symbols, and his ideology." This tradition evidently ran deep in Cartier's family: he was named for the British king George III, and he himself named one of his daughters Reine-Victoria. Cartier saw Canada as united by a "political nationality," rather than divided by ethnic nationality, and in his view, the monarchy was an important element in preserving this. In English-Canadian historiographical tradition, a Whiggish view of Cartier prevails, according to Young: Cartier is often seen as an "intemperate French Canadian rebel in 1837" who successfully evolved into "a leader who had come to his senses."[5]

George-Étienne Cartier.
Source: McCord Museum, I-7956.1.

Cartier and Macdonald had an approach to politics that differed sharply from that of the conscientious and principled George Brown, who sought to institute systemic reforms and clean up corruption. To the basic philosophical and practical differences between these political antagonists was soon added personal grounds for enmity. The unstable political environment of the 1850s gave rise to a particularly acrimonious episode that would leave behind an atmosphere of bitterness in Canada's public life.

In July 1858, the Macdonald–Cartier ministry lost a vote in the legislative assembly connected to the recent decision to situate Canada's capital at Ottawa. The government had opted to refer the question to the Queen, and some members voiced their disapproval of the royal choice. Of course not every legislative vote is considered a confidence measure: an adverse vote does not necessarily imply the defeat of a government. In this instance, Macdonald rejected Brown's insistence that a want of confidence had been shown in the Conservative administration, but agreed that adjournment of the house should be moved as a test. His government survived the confidence vote, but Macdonald saw an opportunity to make political capital out of the controversy—he could both vindicate the Conservative party and humiliate Brown. Having just survived a test of confidence, the Macdonald–Cartier ministry nonetheless presented their resignation to the governor-general, Sir Edmund Head (1854–1861). Brown's ability to command enough support to form a government would be put to the test. Perhaps unwisely, Brown's *Globe* had two months before speculated that if a government should resign, and a rival party fail to successfully form an alternative government, "the old set would come back again and … they would succeed better than they had done before, because it would be evident that they were the only parties who could govern the country."[6] Macdonald evidently believed this prediction as well. He gleefully reported to a Conservative newspaper that "the fish scarcely waited till the bait was let down. He jumped out of the water to catch it."[7] Brown advised Head that he would need a couple of days to assemble his supporters, but that he was willing to form a government.

Brown turned to Canada East's Rouge leader Antoine-Aimé Dorion to achieve an alliance. Antoine-Aimé Dorion's career and ideas offer a historical corrective for the tendency to oversimplify and homogenize French-Canadian political thought. Radical political allegiances were part of the Dorion family legacy: his father had been a supporter of Papineau. The all-too-familiar theme of family reversals of fortune also shaped Dorion's background. His father suffered financial ruin, and the 20-year-old Antoine-Aimé, already articling in a law office, had to become a law clerk to earn his living. He qualified as a lawyer and began to practise in Montreal, although he preferred to devote his subtle mind to philosophical and political questions. His energetic and contentious younger brother, Jean-Baptiste-Eric Dorion, nicknamed *l'enfant terrible*, similarly immersed himself in the world of ideas, founding the radical newspaper *L'Avenir* in 1847 to disseminate the Rouge ideas that Papineau carried back from Paris. The younger Dorion also took part in the founding of the *Institut Canadien,* an organization devoted to liberal ideas, which soon earned the condemnation of the Vatican. While a devout Catholic, Antoine-Aimé joined the *Institut*, although later the organization's increasingly strident anti-clericalism would drive him from it. In 1851, Dorion became leader of Canada East's Rouge party. The inauguration of a new newspaper, *Le Pays*, the following year also heralded the party's shift to a more moderate position. Dorion first won a seat in the assembly in 1854.

On the face of it, any alliance between the vehemently voluntaryist—even anti-Catholic—Brown and the French-Canadian nationalist Dorion might seem astonishing. After all, curtailing what he perceived as undue French-Canadian political domination was a key part of Brown's platform. However, the two did have some liberal elements in common:

Dorion championed measures that he believed would promote a more democratic polity, measures such as universal manhood suffrage, fixed election dates, and a secret ballot. Like Brown, Dorion condemned government corruption. The fact that Dorion had proposed federation of the united Canadas as early as 1856 reveals a pragmatic streak. While his goal was the promotion of French-Canadian national autonomy, he believed that the federation option was a viable alternative to outright separation, and preferable to the more worrisome alternative of representation by population proposed by the Clear Grits of Canada West. Dorion enjoyed the support of much of Montreal's English-speaking business elite. His friendship with brewing magnate John Molson dated from their mutual support of the 1849 Annexation Manifesto. The support of Thomas D'Arcy McGee is perhaps less surprising: Montreal liberal politician McGee had taken part in the abortive Irish uprising of 1848 that had won the approval of Paris republicans. Dorion, the champion of French-Canadian nationalism, allegedly spent so much time immersed in the company of English speakers that his own French language skills became rusty.

Unfortunately for Dorion and Brown, their stab at cooperation in 1858 was a mortifying failure. Their administration was sworn into office at noon on August 2, 1858, and was defeated in a confidence vote some time after midnight. Despite this outcome, historian Ged Martin remarks on the success Brown enjoyed in drawing supporters from across partisan lines—even Bleu member F.X. Lemieux, who had previously sat in Macdonald's cabinet, defected from Conservative ranks to join Brown. A record six Roman Catholics had been appointed to Brown's cabinet. "Macdonald and his allies faced an urgent need to strangle the new ministry at birth," Martin suggests.[8]

1858: A short-lived coalition between the Clear Grits and Parti Rouge exemplifies Canada's unstable political atmosphere.

Brown cried foul, arguing that his new ministry had lost a confidence vote because many of his supporters were absent from the House. The law required that any member accepting a cabinet post have the decision ratified by his constituents. This need to stand for by-election meant that key members were not present in the legislature to vote in support of Dorion and Brown's administration, and the latter insisted that the Conservatives, by forcing the vote, were abandoning parliamentary courtesy in order to drive them from office unfairly. In reality, the presence of those few missing members would not have sufficiently swelled the ranks of supporters to ensure the administration's survival, but the episode fuelled partisan bitterness. John A. Macdonald enjoyed his triumph, but would be left to pay for it with a poisonous atmosphere of political acrimony.

Brown's humiliation was sealed when he appealed to Sir Edmund Head, the governor-general, for a dissolution of Parliament and a new election, but was refused. Recognizing that there had been an election only the previous winter, and that the Conservative administration had resigned without actually losing a direct vote of confidence, Head

Antoine-Aimé Dorion.

Source: © McCord Museum, I-6442.

chose instead to simply call upon another set of ministers to see if they could command sufficient support. This was the first occasion since the advent of responsible government in 1848 that the governor-general found it necessary to refuse the advice of his ministers. It demonstrated that in rare circumstances the governor-general still had a critical role to play in safeguarding the constitution. Head first called upon Alexander Galt, a moderate independent who favoured federation—something Head himself was convinced could resolve the chronic instability of Canadian politics. Galt declined the offer and proposed that George-Étienne Cartier be chosen. Cartier accepted, sought the support of his ally, Macdonald, and the two returned to office amid an atmosphere of festering ill will.

Another controversy followed fresh on the heels of the Brown–Dorion humiliation. The same rule required cabinet ministers in the new Cartier–Macdonald administration to seek a new mandate from their constituents, yet it was a certainty that the opposition would not extend the newly returned ministry any parliamentary courtesy on that score. In this instance, the new government's fear that the absence of these members during the necessary by-elections might cause them to lose a vote was probably well founded. Unwilling to take the chance, the Conservatives made use of a slick legal loophole. Since the law allowed ministers to change portfolios without a by-election, ministers who had held office before the Brown–Dorion debacle were simply sworn into new offices, and then sworn back into their original portfolios the following day. This manoeuvre came within the letter, if not the spirit, of the law, as these cabinet ministers had held office within the last 30 days. As governor, Head evidently felt that he had little choice but to acquiesce in this shady transaction. The so-called "double shuffle" brought howls of indignation from Brown's reformers, and the *Globe* was shrill in its condemnation of both Macdonald and the governor-general.

In the aftermath of the Brown–Dorion defeat and the sordid "double shuffle," Head busied himself in drawing up a plan for federation of the British North American colonies, and he alluded to that plan later that year in a speech as he closed the legislative session. No doubt the fractious and unstable political environment of the united Canadas added urgency to what had been a long-discussed policy alternative. Head had an academic and philosophical cast of mind, and he had been working on such ideas earlier when he had been lieutenant governor of New Brunswick.

Various ideas of some kind of British North American union had been openly discussed by others for years—even before the American Revolution, in fact. Historian L.F.S. Upton suggests that the 1754 Albany Conference on union organized by influential statesman, inventor, and writer Benjamin Franklin was a continued "source of inspiration to many Loyalists as the great might-have-been that could have averted revolution." Numerous alternative plans were proposed throughout the mid-nineteenth century. Some theorists favoured federation—a joining together of autonomous individual colonies under some umbrella authority, with each retaining a local legislature. Others believed in simple union, without another layer of government at the provincial level. In 1850, former attorney general of Canada West Henry Sherwood published a series of letters in *The British Colonist* outlining a plan for a "Federative Union of the British North American Provinces." He had been advocating this as early as 1838 when he chaired a committee of the Upper Canadian assembly, and Upton describes Sherwood's work as

1858: John A. Macdonald out-manoeuvres opponent George Brown in the notorious "double shuffle."

"a most valuable contribution to the literature of confederation." He had even prepared a draft act for the imperial parliament to put it into effect.

In Nova Scotia, J.W. Johnston made an impassioned case for union in 1854, reminding members of that colony's assembly that in union was strength and calling for "the realization of a dream as old as the English presence in America." Johnston pointed to the railways as a solution to the impediment of distance, the wider scope for local talents that union would offer, and the fact that, as he saw it, municipal governments would be sufficient to protect local interests and make provincial legislatures redundant. Canada East politician Joseph-Charles Taché published a series of articles on the question in 1857 followed by *Des Provinces de l'Amérique du Nord et d'une Union Fédérale* in 1858, in which he compared various alternatives before urging confederation rather than union. That same year, Alexander Galt, member for Sherbrooke, proposed resolutions in the assembly to create a federal system, but there was little enthusiasm. "They had heard it all before," Upton explains. "Theirs was not the indifference of hostility but of over-familiarity. By then there was such an accumulation of writings on the idea of confederation that no literate person could be ignorant of the topic." Confederation was a long-standing "solution in search of a problem" and only the pressure of outside events would make it sufficiently attractive.[9]

1858: Governor-General Sir Edmund Head speaks out in favour of federating the North American colonies.

Just as British North American politicians at first rejected these much discussed innovations, British policymakers threw cold water on the scheme in 1858, and privately rebuked Sir Edmund Head for having openly shown support for it. Such initiatives should come from the imperial government, he was reminded. Colonial matters were not always accorded a high priority in the British political agenda—unless of course some immediate crisis was erupting. During the course of Sir Edmund Head's seven-year tenure as Canada's governor, there were some eight successive secretaries of state for the colonies in office in Britain. Long-range policy was practically impossible, and cabinet ministers were apt to disavow, or be in ignorance of, policies that their predecessors had endorsed. Possible union or federation schemes for British North America were a case in point.

1861: Lord Monck arrives as governor-general, and will hold office until the end of 1868.

In November 1861 a new governor-general arrived in Canada to take Head's place. Lord Monck was an affable Irish aristocrat who brought with him an extended family, not to mention a menagerie of animals. Including the pets kept by the staff at Government House, the count was 15 dogs, seven cats, numerous horses for the family to ride, and various birds, including a tame owl. The butler made the best of the situation by keeping a flea circus. The animals sometimes disrupted the household's decorum: an amorous dog, Fuss, jumped on the back of the British ambassador to Washington as he knelt to join family prayers in the chapel.

Monck was an unpretentious easygoing man who proved to be remarkably adept at smoothing over political wrangles among warring Canadian parliamentarians. His wife, who was also his first cousin, unfortunately lacked his down-to-earth nature, and proved to be less successful than other vicereines at extending gracious hospitality. Lady Monck privately complained about the "drove of horrid people" who came to Government House receptions. She had difficulty adjusting to North American customs, and, as an aristocrat, did not welcome presumption: "My back gets quite stiff—drawing myself up lest they should insist on shaking hands with me."[10] Lord Monck's brother Richard acted as his military secretary, and was accompanied by his wife, Frances Elizabeth Owen Monck, "Feo," as she was known to the family. Feo Monck was the daughter of Lady Monck's older sister, and thus the cousin, niece, and sister-in-law of the governor-general. Her gossipy account of her stay in Canada, later published, provides a fascinating window into mid-nineteenth-century social customs. At the governor-general's traditional New Year's levee, Feo Monck hid behind a door to watch the parade of well-wishers and was appalled to see mere tradesmen welcomed into polite society: "You cannot conceive the people that came—a watch maker, a glover, a sleigh maker, two photographers.... Some of them spit before they went in, and many came out munching food." She suspected that for some the food had been the chief attraction. Lord Monck "had to shake hands with *everyone* of the dirty people."[11]

The Effects of the American Civil War

1861: The outbreak of the civil war in the United States provokes a colonial defence crisis.

Monck soon had a much greater challenge than negotiating Canadian social customs. In the very month he arrived in Canada, a serious military crisis threatened the country's peace. As governor-general, Monck was nominal commander-in-chief, but had no military experience, and took up his place in a colony that was utterly unprepared for war against a powerful and well-armed neighbour. By the spring of 1861, the newly formed Confederate States of America, consisting of 11 southern states, had seceded from the union and touched off a bloody and divisive civil war. President Abraham Lincoln's declared opposition to slavery had threatened the autonomy of the southern states and their continued right to maintain their "peculiar institution." While it might be expected that Britain, having abandoned slavery, would support the north, British textile mills depended on a supply of cotton from the American south, and the Union navy's strategy of blockading southern ports dealt a devastating blow to this trade. Britain did not openly avow support for the Confederate states, but Britain's declared neutrality was in itself a provocation to the Union, as it implied recognition of the Confederacy as a legitimate combatant. More than this, however, northern forces suspected Britain of covert aid to the south, and Anglo–American relations became increasingly strained as the war went on. Should war between Britain and the now fractured United States break out, the likely battleground would be Britain's North American colonies. Colonial defences were in no state to withstand a determined Union invasion.

The same imperial laissez-faire philosophy that had in the 1840s led to the dismantling of centuries of mercantilist legislation and the decision to grant self-government to those colonies with representative institutions had also dictated the curbing of military aid. Beyond this philosophical principle, the immediate demands of the Crimean War triggered a reduction of imperial troops in British North America, and the Canadian legislative assembly passed a Militia Bill in 1855 as a gesture toward filling the void. But cost-conscious colonial politicians did not always accord military spending the high priority imperial authorities might have wished, and the result was that, by the outbreak of the American Civil War, there were fewer than 5000 Canadian volunteers in the colony's militia. The number of imperial regulars stood at 4300 in all of British North America, with only 2200 of these in Canada itself.

In November 1861, a sudden crisis sharpened anxieties about the dismal state of colonial defences. Union navy Captain Charles Wilkes, commanding the frigate *San Jacinto,* intercepted a British mail steamer, the *Trent,* in neutral Atlantic waters, and seized two Confederate commissioners who were on board—James Murray Mason and John Sliddell. The southerners were ostensibly en route to London to negotiate British aid for the Confederate cause. In an ironic reversal of the rhetoric surrounding the War of 1812, British authorities indignantly condemned American interference with their freedom of the seas. The British press demanded that the insult by the "pirate Wilkes" be avenged. Britain rushed to reinforce their troops in British North America, bringing the number of regulars to 14 000 in anticipation of possible war with the United States. Unfortunately, the onset of winter meant that only one of the 18 transport vessels could travel up the freezing St. Lawrence to reach the terminus of the Grand Trunk Railway at Rivière-du-Loup. There was no Atlantic coastal railway terminus on British North American soil: the nearest one was at Portland, Maine. Clearly, the Americans would never permit the passage of potentially hostile forces through their territory to reinforce the small garrison in Canada.

Meanwhile, the other troop ships pitched and rolled in a violent gale and snowstorm in the wintry Atlantic before making for Halifax and Saint John. Newly arrived British officers undertook the daunting task of arranging overland sleigh transport to Rivière-du-Loup and en route barrack accommodation for this huge contingent, while statesmen on each side rattled their sabres. Across the Atlantic, Queen Victoria's beloved husband Prince Albert lay desperately ill with typhoid fever. From his deathbed, he prevailed upon Prime Minister Lord Palmerston to tone down the provocative language of an ultimatum demanding the Confederate prisoners be released. The gentler tactic won, and Lincoln wisely decided that one war at a time was all he was willing to fight. The Union released the Confederate prisoners and the immediate crisis was averted.

The emergency demonstrated that more systematic military planning was essential. A Canadian cabinet portfolio devoted to control of the militia was created for the first time late in 1861, with John A. Macdonald the first to assume those duties. By the spring of 1862, the British government was calculating the costs of the urgent reinforcements to British North America during the *Trent* incident: the total estimate for land and naval forces was a staggering £843 000. It is little wonder that British authorities prevailed upon Monck to keep defence considerations foremost in the minds of his ministers. By March 1862, a Canadian commission was ready to report their findings on the state of the colony's defences. This commission, on which both Macdonald and Cartier sat, also had experienced British military representation. Colonel Daniel Lysons had overseen the details of the *Trent* incident reinforcement, and had a long military career with distinguished service throughout the British Empire. Lysons had been a young lieutenant with Colonel Charles Gore's forces fighting against the *patriotes* at Saint-Denis in 1837. He and Cartier, having once fought on opposite sides, now sat at the same table discussing defence planning. The commission recommended a dramatic improvement to Canada's militia forces, proposing an increase to 50 000 active and 50 000 reserve members. These recommendations formed the basis of the 1862 Militia Bill, the terms of which would have consumed one-tenth of provincial revenue and contained provisions to allow conscription if volunteer enlistment fell short.

1861: The Trent *crisis brings Britain to the brink of war with the United States.*

Further Political Difficulties in Canada

Macdonald cautiously presented the bill to the assembly as an "enabling" measure that would permit, but not require, the government to put the commission's recommendations into action. Support for the Cartier–Macdonald ministry hung by a thread when Monck opened the parliamentary session in March 1862, and Liberal and Rouge members saw in the controversial Militia Bill an opportunity to topple the government. They also brandished apparent evidence of financial wrongdoing—notably the conspicuous link of key cabinet ministers to the Grand Trunk Railway—and, in the face of this concerted assault, Macdonald abandoned his duties and took to the bottle, oblivious to the fate of his wavering administration. The ministry was defeated in May of 1862.

Monck was deeply concerned on several levels. He would have to find a new set of ministers. But, beyond this, the biggest worry was the impression that these events would make in the United States. Canada had signalled a disregard for military preparedness, and this apparent sign of weakness might embolden Union war hawks. British public opinion, too, was a concern. The high cost of defending the colonies had already been questioned, and this sent an unmistakable message that Canadian authorities had no wish to take responsibility for their own defence.

Monck's selection of an alternative ministry was complicated by George Brown's absence from the legislature. Brown had been defeated in the last election and was about to go to Britain to recover his strength after a long bout of illness and a series of draining financial reversals. The nominal head of the Liberal party was Michael Foley, yet Monck exercised a degree of personal discretion and did not call upon Foley to form a new government. Foley had been an outspoken critic of the volunteer militia, and Monck wanted someone fully committed to improving defence to take over the reins of government. Moreover, Foley was busy drinking himself to death, something he would accomplish by 1870. After the debacle of the previous government's defeat, Monck may have been impatient with anyone who exhibited that particular failing.

Monck called upon Liberal John Sandfield Macdonald to head his administration; Louis-Victor Sicotte joined the ministry as the leader in Canada East. Sandfield, as he is often called to distinguish him from the more famous John A. Macdonald, was an adherent of the constitutional principle of "double majority," rather than the representation by population favoured by Brown. This meant that measures passed in the assembly of the united Canadas would have to have a majority in each half of the house, something that would ensure that neither English nor French Canadians could impose their will on the other section of the province. In some ways, this idea of double majority anticipated a federal system: each half of the single legislature was viewed as having separate interests. The fact that Canadian ministries were typically led by joint attorneys general—one from Canada East and one from Canada West—was also indicative of this proto-federal system, as were the distinct judicial systems in each half of the province and the fact that some legislation was only applicable in one section.

While Sandfield Macdonald's ideal of double majority was appealing, in practice recent events had demonstrated that even a simple majority was difficult to obtain. In fact, the Sandfield Macdonald–Sicotte government was quick to abandon this defining principle of their administration when Richard W. Scott introduced a bill that would grant Roman Catholic schools in Canada West a full share of provincial funding and give their trustees the same freedoms as public school trustees. This 1863 *Separate Schools Act* (sometimes referred to as the *Scott Act*) was warmly supported by the members for Canada East. While the bill passed with an overall majority, it did not receive a majority of votes in the Canada West section of the legislature. Sandfield Macdonald's administration, despite its commitment to "double majority," did not treat this sectional defeat as an expression of non-confidence. To Protestant "voluntaryists" of Canada West, this was more evidence that French-Canadian Roman Catholics were able to have a definitive effect on policy in the western half of the province. Sandfield Macdonald's government clung to office during the passage of the *Scott Act*, but was defeated a short while later—after less than a year in power.

Atlantic Colonial Concerns

A Plan for an Intercolonial Railway to the Maritimes

While the united Canadas were preoccupied with the inability of any administration to form a stable government, the Maritime colonies had other priorities, and the concerns of these colonies would soon intersect. The idea of an intercolonial railway to connect British North America's Maritime colonies with each other and with the Canadas had been long discussed. Nova Scotia's Joseph Howe had been one of the chief boosters of such a scheme, and in 1850 he had travelled to Britain to discuss an imperial loan guarantee for the project, plus a grand plan of imperial immigration and settlement that would follow—an idea he promoted to enthusiastic crowds in England and British North America. Unfortunately, the British financing that he sought fell through when imperial authorities declined to underwrite a planned connection to Portland, Maine, something many Maritimers saw as the most economically advantageous part of the scheme. This killed any immediate hope for a large-scale intercolonial railway. In spite of this setback, numerous smaller-scale railway projects were steadily being constructed in the Maritimes. But the vital link to central Canada remained an unrealized dream.

Howe's 1850 mission was only one of a series of attempts to secure British assistance. In the autumn of 1861, he was back en route to London, this time with the support of the premier of New Brunswick, druggist and prohibitionist Samuel Leonard Tilley, who also endorsed an intercolonial railway. Their entreaties again came to nothing, and the sudden eruption of the *Trent* crisis triggered a hasty return across the Atlantic. Back at home, Tilley faced a series of personal trials—he had grown ill on the return journey and then, in March 1862, lost his wife to cancer. Howe urged him to submerge his grief in work, advice Tilley appears to have followed. Within a few months, he had secured Canadian agreement for a conference on constructing the intercolonial railway, over the objections of his Reform colleague, Albert James Smith, who opposed any publicly financed railway projects and split the party over the issue. When Britain at last agreed to guarantee a loan for the purpose, hopes for an agreement between the colonies were high.

1862: Canadian and Maritime delegates meet to plan an intercolonial railway.

The September 1862 intercolonial railway conference at Quebec, chaired by Canadian politician Thomas D'Arcy McGee, seemed to reach a substantial agreement over the apportioning of costs. But the details of Britain's loan guarantee proved unpalatable to the Canadians, and Sandfield Macdonald's fragile administration had been unable to marshal sufficient support for a publicly financed scheme. The Canadians put up a show of continuing the plan, including hiring railway engineer Sandford Fleming to undertake surveys for a route. But it quickly became apparent that the deal was off, and resentment grew in the Maritime colonies that the Canadian politicians had acted in bad faith.

Ironically, this resentment would spark events that would ultimately lead to Confederation. The British-appointed governor of New Brunswick, Arthur Hamilton Gordon, was a keen advocate of a railway link between the colonies, in part because he saw it as a precursor to colonial union, either of all of the British North American colonies, or—as a halfway measure—the Maritime colonies alone. Gordon, a self-important aristocratic young bachelor, came to New Brunswick as governor in 1861. Although his own political experience was limited, he had served as private secretary to his father, the fourth Earl of Aberdeen, during the latter's term as Britain's prime minister, and was on intimate terms with Britain's ruling inner circle. In the summer of 1863, with the Canadian about-face on the intercolonial project, Gordon actively began to promote Maritime union.

Prince Edward Island's Land Tenure Question

Prince Edward Island was the Maritime colony that had seemed most resistant to the idea of a wider union, but a meeting with some of the island's leading political figures during a visit to Charlottetown gave Gordon grounds for hope. Prince Edward Island's Conservative premier, Colonel John Hamilton Gray, and the provincial secretary, W.H. Pope, were supportive of such a scheme. Their Liberal rival, George Coles, who had been instrumental in Prince Edward Island's fight to win responsible government in 1851, had a more immediate agenda. He wished to bring about an end to the island's oligarchic system of land distribution. Since 1767, Prince Edward Island had been controlled by a coterie of largely absentee landowners. At that time, the island had been divided into 67 townships of 20 000 acres (8000 hectares) each, and these parcels were awarded by lottery to military officials and other favourites of the Crown. Settlers ever since had rented farms on these vast estates without the security of tenure enjoyed by their counterparts in other British North American colonies. There had been a limited move in the 1840s to provide government assistance to buy out parcels from absentee landlords, but, as historians Rusty Bitterman and Margaret McCallum point out, the issue ran deeper than money alone. The rights of property owners were fundamental, and any move to compel the sale of land violated core British principles.

Investigations of the land question in Prince Edward Island were bound up with similar questions elsewhere, notably Ireland. British policymakers had long been wrestling with the question of a more just land policy for Ireland, where long-standing disabilities against Roman Catholics seemed impossible to redress while still respecting Protestant property rights. In Prince Edward Island, agitation by an organized Tenant League, and a commission of investigation in 1860, had failed to break the impasse.[12]

1863: Prince Edward Island's George Coles speaks out in favour of colonial union.

Now, in the summer of 1863, Arthur Gordon noted optimistically that Liberal leader George Coles seemed warmer to the idea of a union between Prince Edward Island and other British North American colonies. In a speech, Coles had suggested that this might provide the means by which Prince Edward Island could break the power of its monopoly landowners.

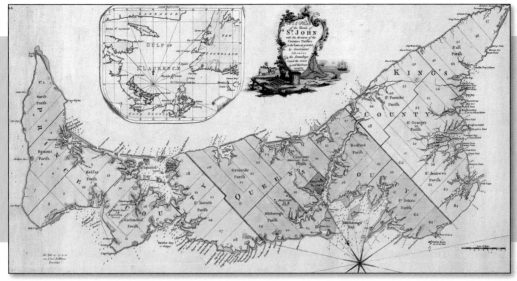

Map 12.1
Prince Edward
Island
by surveyor
Samuel
Holland, 1764.

Source: Library and Archives Canada, nmc-23350.

Lieutenant Governor Arthur Gordon and Dreams of Colonial Union

Buoyed by this evidence of support in Prince Edward Island, Gordon pressed New Brunswick Premier Tilley about the idea. Historian Donald Creighton suggested that Tilley, a businessman whose fortune had been built on patent medicines, had "something of the counting-house approach to politics." The slight and clean-shaven Tilley was energetic and practical, with a shopkeeper's affability. "He treated politics as a series of concrete, prosaic problems which could best be solved in a matter-of-fact, business-like way." He was not captivated by grand ideas of nation building, but by the opportunities for expanded commerce and improved communications that a wider union would offer.[13]

In Nova Scotia, the election of a new Conservative ministry under Charles Tupper in the summer of 1863 augured well for Gordon's pet project of a wider union. Tupper, a third generation Nova Scotian, who trained as a medical doctor in Edinburgh, had earlier expressed his convictions about the need for railway building to advance civilization. He extolled the advantages to Nova Scotia of colonial union, seeing both commercial opportunities and a means to make Nova Scotia's influence more widely felt. Perhaps it went without saying that it would offer a more promising platform for his personal influence as well.

The Duke of Newcastle, Britain's secretary of state for the colonies, encouraged Gordon to press ahead in promoting the union of the colonies, and was encouraged when Gordon advised him in the summer of 1863 that a Maritime union seemed to be within reach. Dramatic events south of the border added urgency to the idea for defence reasons. In July 1863, Confederate General Robert E. Lee suffered a devastating defeat at Gettysburg, Pennsylvania. A few days later, the Union's capture of Vicksburg, Mississippi, gave the north control of the vitally strategic Mississippi River. The cause of the South turned irrevocably with these two successive defeats in the summer of 1863, and to the British North American colonies, the prospect of a Northern victory raised the spectre of invasion.

1863: Conservative Dr. Charles Tupper, an advocate of Confederation, is elected in Nova Scotia.

1863: A series of Southern defeats over the course of the summer renews colonial anxiety about invasion by Union forces.

Anglo–American relations had not appreciably mended since the tense days of the *Trent* crisis. Among the fresh provocations was Britain's tacit consent for the building and arming of Confederate vessels in English ports. One of these, the cruiser *Alabama,* commissioned in the summer of 1862, proved a devastating menace to Union shipping, capturing some 68 prizes of war over the next two years. Indeed, after the war's end, the Americans pursued a claim for damages against the British, and figures as high as $2–8 billion were bandied about, on the grounds that the vessel had been so successful that it prolonged the war. The chair of the United States Senate Foreign Relations Committee even proposed that Britain might wish to simply hand over its North American colonies in lieu of the cash.

The Marriage of the Canadas in Crisis

During the summer of 1863 in the united Canadas, Governor-General Monck was wrestling with his colony's political instability. This was a serious problem in itself, but the need to have a stable administration take decisive control of the colony's militia and make a clear commitment to building its strength was now critical. With the defeat of the administration of John Sandfield Macdonald and Louis-Victor Sicotte in May 1863, Monck might have opted to simply call upon another set of ministers, to give the Conservative opposition a chance to form a government—after all, the 1861 election had been held less than two years ago. Monck was nevertheless mindful of the fact that Liberals still smarted from the events of 1858, when his predecessor, Sir Edmund Head, had refused Brown and Dorion a dissolution and called upon the Conservatives. Monck privately maintained that there was no basis for their suspicions of a Conservative bias, but felt that it was better to leave no opening for such an accusation. With Sandfield Macdonald's Liberals defeated, he did not insist upon the government's resignation, but agreed that fresh elections should be held.

Monck also busied himself behind the scenes trying to assuage some of the bitterness that had characterized public life. He had had some experience in political coalitions during his own backbench parliamentary career under Lord Aberdeen in Britain. Aberdeen had managed to build Britain's Liberal party by bringing together Peelite Conservatives and Whigs. Monck recognized that George Brown, while out of office, held the key to a huge support base in Canada West. The governor-general requested a private interview with Brown, and urged him to try to build a coalition once again with Dorion. He also expressed general approval of some of the constitutional principles that Brown embraced, and hinted that the influential Brown was essential to lasting political stability in Canada. Such words must surely have been a balm to Brown's wounded dignity after the difficulties of 1858. A clear signal of viceregal support would be especially welcome to the Liberals, since they had suspected Monck's predecessor of being manipulated by the wily Conservatives.

It is tempting, too, to ascribe personal factors to Brown's increasingly conciliatory position. After limping away to Britain in the summer of 1862 to lick his wounds, having suffered electoral defeat, ill health, and financial losses, Brown unexpectedly fell in love at the age of 43. While visiting an old school friend in Edinburgh, he met Anne Nelson of the prominent Edinburgh publishing family. Nelson was in her early 30s—past prime marrying age in the Victorian era—but had travelled widely in Europe, was intelligent, cultivated and socially gifted, with a warm, affectionate nature. She was also attractive, with dark glossy hair, a fair complexion, and bright eyes. The fact that she came from a wealthy family and brought a dowry of $120 000 was certainly helpful as well, although Brown himself was later able to recover his financial footing by selling some substantial land holdings. Within weeks of meeting, the pair had reached a swift and confident decision to marry. By the beginning of December 1862, Mr. and Mrs. Brown set sail to return to Canada. Brown found in his wife an insightful supporter in whom he could confide all the trying details of political life. They would quickly have three children and their happy home became a much-needed refuge for Brown. When business took him away, Brown poured out his thoughts in letters, confessing that he counted the days until they could be together.

1862: George Brown marries Anne Nelson.

In the early summer of 1863, Brown, who had just won a new seat in the legislature in a by-election, decided against plunging back into a coalition as urged by Monck, but the process of reconciliation had begun. The June 1863 election returned another shaky ministry presided over by Sandfield Macdonald, and, what was most important to Monck, a modified Militia Bill was passed that autumn. Support for the administration gradually dwindled, however and, despite Sandfield Macdonald's attempts to negotiate the support of moderate Conservatives Étienne-Paschal Taché, John A. Macdonald, and George-Étienne Cartier, it became clear that the ministry did not have sufficient support to carry on. They resigned in March 1864 without waiting for a vote of non-confidence.

Once again, Monck faced the prospect of trying to find a new set of advisors who could command majority support. He called upon a succession of prominent parliamentarians, but found that none was able to gather enough supporters. At last, Étienne-Paschal Taché, who in turn sought the assistance of John A. Macdonald and Cartier, agreed to take over the reins of government. But this proved a short-lived expedient, and by June 1864 the new ministry was defeated by a margin of only two votes.

March 1864: The resignation of the John Sandfield Macdonald ministry signals continued political instability in the province of Canada.

Taché approached Monck with a request for dissolution and new elections, but Monck hesitated. Four ministries had collapsed within three years, and two general elections within this period had not broken the deadlock. Monck was convinced that there was no great principle that should prevent Canada's political antagonists from working together. He assured Taché that he was willing to follow his advice, but hoped that a new election could be avoided. He played for time, admitting privately that he was overstepping the strict lines of his constitutional role, and appealed directly to George Brown to come into a coalition cabinet. The success or failure of political negotiations hung directly on Brown's decision, he urged. These were flattering words, but spoken out of firm conviction. Monck's campaign to win Brown over included social invitations, and Brown was a guest at a lively dinner party at Government House that featured group sing-alongs in English and in French, and an impromptu solo by Cartier. The groundwork for rapprochement having been laid by Monck earlier, Brown was persuaded.

As it happened, before the Sandfield Macdonald ministry had fallen in March of 1864, George Brown had proposed a committee of the legislature to review Canada's constitutional options. This 20-member committee, by coincidence, delivered its report the same day the administration of Taché and John A. Macdonald was defeated. They laid out no concrete plan, but recommended one of two options: a federal system for the province of Canada alone, or one that took in all of the British North American colonies. For Brown, the chance of working toward the goal of breaking the forced connection between Canada East and Canada West made a coalition appealing.

June 1864: The defeat of four Canadian ministries within three years points to the need for systemic change.

The 1864 Great Coalition and Plans for a New Federal System

Late in June 1864, the so-called "Great Coalition" came together. Besides George Brown, the unlikely partnership included John A. Macdonald, George-Étienne Cartier, Alexander Galt, William McDougall, Thomas D'Arcy McGee, Oliver Mowat, Étienne-Pascal Taché, Hector Langevin, Alexander Campbell, James Cockburn, and J.C. Chapais. The coalition thus brought together the key political elements of the united Canadas, with the notable exception of Rouge representation. The elderly Étienne-Pascal Taché remained head of the administration, perhaps because he was least likely to be objectionable to any of the others. An agreement was reached that the coalition would pursue federation, and Brown himself insisted that, to satisfy Canada West, representation by population would have to be a part of any new formula. The admission into the federation of British territory in the Maritimes and the west would also be considered. For Brown's supporters in Canada West, annexation of the prairies as an outlet for expansion had long been an aim, and this popular objective no doubt sealed his approval of the overall plan.

Historian Ged Martin rejects the "unhelpful myth" that for one shining moment these men were able to put aside their differences in pursuit of the nobler object of Confederation. "The arch-enemies John A. Macdonald and George Brown attempted to seize each other not by the hand but rather by the throat," he argues. Brown saw federation as a way to make representation by population palatable, a way to curb French Canada's influence. Martin speculates that, for Macdonald, a wider union offered more scope for "his political talents of balancing and blandishment." Before the Great Coalition, Canada's administration was mired in what has often been described as "political deadlock," with no administration able to command majority support for any reasonable period of time. Martin prefers to think of the situation as a temporary logjam, and cautions against seeing Confederation as the only, and inevitable, solution to the problem.[14] Brown carefully justified his decision to enter into the coalition, knowing that supporters might believe he had been duped by the wily Macdonald. Indeed one Conservative triumphantly characterized the coalition as "one of John A.'s *coups*."[15]

The plan for federation that the Great Coalition embraced was helped along by fortunate circumstances. The colonies of Prince Edward Island, New Brunswick, and Nova Scotia, contemplating a Maritime union, had scheduled a conference at Charlottetown for the beginning of September 1864. Lord Monck wrote to the lieutenant governors of the Maritime colonies to see if Canadian delegates could wangle an invitation to the upcoming conference. In the meantime, as Canadian ministers were discussing the broad strokes of possible new constitutional arrangements among themselves, a group of 100 other prominent Canadians set out on a tour of New Brunswick and Nova Scotia. The tour included members of Canada's legislative assembly, members of the legislative council, journalists, and other interested parties. It was all unofficial, not connected to the Charlottetown conference, but the timing made it significant.

One of the chief organizers of the tour was Thomas D'Arcy McGee, a member of Canada's new political coalition who would do much to promote a sense of national consciousness. The Irish-born McGee had once been an ardent republican, who in a Boston Fourth of July speech at age 17 had denounced British rule as "heartless, bigoted, [and] despotic" and British people as "born slaves." McGee's incendiary words won the approval of many of the city's Irish Catholic immigrants, and by 19, he was editor of a popular Catholic newspaper, the *Boston Pilot,* and was working to promote Irish independence and Canada's annexation to the United States. McGee returned to Ireland in time to take up the cause of the Young Ireland movement, and to play a role in the abortive Irish rebellion of 1848. In the aftermath, he proudly described himself as a "traitor to the British government."[16] But like William Lyon Mackenzie and George Brown before him, McGee found that actually living in the United States markedly reduced his enthusiasm for American institutions. In 1857, McGee came to Montreal and became a Reform member of the assembly, and later a Conservative. His split with Brown's reformers came in 1863 because of his support for R.W. Scott's bill for separate Catholic schools in Canada West. McGee's youthful anticlericalism gave way to an obedient and observant Catholicism, and he also abandoned ideas of Canada's annexation to the United States. He became a favourite visitor to the viceregal household during Monck's term as governor-general, even winning favour with the standoffish Lady Monck, whom he affectionately called "my governess general." McGee was reportedly fond of drink, but it was rumoured that John A. Macdonald took him aside and confided that the party could only stand one drunk, and the position had already been filled. Historian David Shanahan rejects the simple conclusion that McGee was a former militant who "sold out to British gold." Instead, he sees in McGee a vision of a new kind of nationalism, one that could encompass multiple ethnicities and religions, rather than being a homogenizing force. "McGee's Irishness was not abandoned in favour of Canada but was subsumed into the new nationality," he explains. "[I]t was an essential ingredient in the mix."[17]

The Maritime tour that McGee helped organize was partly an exercise in this kind of consolidation of identity, and his approach to it was almost evangelical. The Canadian visitors were feted throughout the Maritimes. A breathless Halifax newspaper story reported on all the entertainments, including voyageur music meant to make the French-speaking visitors welcome, and applauded the "most inspiring effect." Those present "hugged each other … affectionately," laughed, slapped backs, and exclaimed, "Nous thankez-vous tres much indeed!" and "Jolly Good Fellow, Johnny Kanuck" to one another.[18] Banquets, picnics, speeches, Scottish highland dancing, and even games of Leapfrog were on the agenda.

Besides this unofficial mission aimed at building feelings of fellowship across British North America, McGee kept in communication with Tilley about the prospects for an agreement on the intercolonial railway. "Hold on to the Intercolonial," he had written to Tilley that spring. "You have now men in power in Canada who will resume the project with perfect sincerity."[19] Tilley had just introduced legislation in New Brunswick to subsidize railway lines heading in multiple directions. He evidently hoped that this so-called "Lobster Bill" would satisfy all constituents by suggesting that their communities would enjoy rail access. For residents of the Saint John Valley and the North Shore, the intercolonial route was but one more flashpoint in systemic political rivalry. One exasperated critic later confronted the premier in verse about his unwillingness to commit his government to any one route: "Mr. Tilley, will you stop your puffing and blowing/ And tell us which way the railway is going?"[20] Both Tilley and McGee hoped that the planned Charlottetown conference would put the intercolonial railway back on the agenda.

The Confederation Conferences

On August 29, 1864, seven of the members of Canada's coalition government set out on the steamer *Queen Victoria* bound for Prince Edward Island, ready to pitch the idea of a broader federal union to their opposite numbers in the Maritime colonies. On the morning of September 1, the Canadian delegates arrived, a day behind delegates from Nova Scotia and New Brunswick. The arrival of so many dignitaries at once, coupled with a long-awaited circus tour which had just arrived in Charlottetown, meant that the island hosts had to deliver some embarrassing news: there was no accommodation to be had, and several of the Canadians would have to sleep on board the vessel that had brought them. An indignant island reporter noted that, after a long delay, the provincial secretary rowed out to meet the *Queen Victoria* "in a canoe or a flat-bottomed boat, with a barrel of flour in the bow, and two jars of molasses in the stern, and with a lusty fisherman as his only companion.... The Canadians were under the necessity—as were the Nova Scotians—of hunting up quarters for themselves, some of whom found their way into Eckstadt's Oyster Saloon."[21]

The conference arrangements made up for this lapse. While the original agenda had been to discuss Maritime union, the Atlantic delegates decided to hear what the Canadians had to say on the issue of a larger scheme. The visitors were permitted to lay out their plan, explaining how a broader federal union might work. The ostensible agenda for which the conference had been convened was abandoned when it became clear that Prince Edward Island was against any arrangement in which Charlottetown would not be the capital of an Atlantic federation. The conference provided some opportunities for socializing, and the abundant drink at a lunch hosted by the Canadian delegates on board the steamer *Queen Victoria* broke down the delegates' reserves, and advanced the Confederation project immeasurably. "Canada, like many a child, was conceived under the influence of alcohol," Will Ferguson quipped."[22] A week of meetings at Charlottetown was capped by a ball at Government House. The event got under way at nine in the evening, with a midnight supper where the refreshments included beef, ham, salmon, lobster, oysters, salad, pastry, fruits, and wine. This was followed by elaborate toasts and speeches honouring the Queen, the royal family, the colonial governors, the army and navy, and all the visitors in turn. After the night's exhausting round of dancing, drinking, and eating, the parade of speakers kept everyone prisoner until close to four in the morning. After this contest of endurance, the delegates travelled on to Nova Scotia and then crossed over to New Brunswick. Further discussion of Maritime union having foundered, representatives from the Atlantic colonies accepted an invitation to a follow-up conference in Quebec the following month.

No Newfoundland delegates had been included in the Charlottetown conference, but, as historian James K. Hiller put it, "in the summer of 1864 the mainland architects of confederation remembered Newfoundland's existence and invited the Hoyles government to send representatives to the Quebec conference."[23] Conservative Frederic B.T. Carter was the speaker of the assembly in Hugh William Hoyles's Conservative government, and J. Ambrose Shea was the leader of the Liberal opposition. These two delegates would ensure that Newfoundland's delegation had a bipartisan character and represented both Protestants and Catholics. It was understood, however, that neither was empowered to make a binding agreement.

1864: The September conference in Charlottetown is followed by an October conference in Quebec.

In October, Atlantic politicians began to gather in Quebec, some bringing their wives and daughters along to take part in the social whirl surrounding the 18-day conference. Feo Monck recorded her impressions of the many visitors to Government House, and was especially shocked by the behaviour of those attending a delegates' ball. One of her cousins who stayed late reported that the guests' conduct deteriorated as the evening wore on: "Such drunkenness, pushing, kicking, and tearing, he says, he never saw; his own coat-tails were nearly torn off; the supper room floor was covered with meat, drink, and broken bottles." She reported that the elderly Étienne-Paschal Taché was to be her partner for the quadrille, but she caught him "hiding behind a screen to escape from me." Worst of all, John A. Macdonald "is always drunk now," she noted, and was found "in his night shirt, with a railway rug thrown over him, practising Hamlet before a looking-glass." He told one lady guest at dinner that he wanted to blow up Sir Richard Macdonnell, the governor of Nova Scotia, with gunpowder. Macdonnell, who had just been appointed to Nova Scotia earlier that year had supported the idea of a Maritime union, but opposed a wider federation. "You shall not make a Mayor of me, I can tell you," he blustered to Macdonald. Macdonald laughed behind Macdonnell's back, confiding that he had won him over by making Lady Macdonnell believe that her husband would be the new governor-general.[24] Britain's colonial office reassigned Macdonnell to Hong Kong the following year, appointing a successor, Sir William Fenwick Williams, who had a clearer grasp of Britain's wish to encourage the scheme for a wider union. Williams liked to dismissively refer to his Irish-born predecessor as "Governor McPotato."[25] The Nova Scotia-born Williams was rumoured to have been the half-brother of Queen Victoria. Edward Augustus, later the Duke of Kent and Queen Victoria's father, had once commanded the Halifax garrison, and Williams was born four months after his departure.

New Cross-Border Tensions

At the height of the Quebec conference, fresh developments brought renewed alarms along the border and ensured that defence questions were never far from anyone's mind. On October 19, 1864, a group of Confederate agents launched a raid against St. Albans, Vermont, from their base on Canadian soil. They killed one citizen, robbed the town's banks of more than $200 000, attempted to set some buildings alight, and stole horses to make an escape back across the Canadian border. Two among the group never made it: Union authorities caught them before they crossed the border. Canadian authorities apprehended 14, and seized $19 000. When the raiders were brought to trial in Montreal two months later, they

1864: The St. Alban's Raid is another crisis in foreign relations with the United States.

were released on a technicality, and the judge ordered the money returned to them. Americans were outraged. The *New York Times* proclaimed: "We were never in better condition for a war with England." Amid this threatening atmosphere, news of a sharply reduced British budget for North American defence in 1865 reached Canadian officials. John A. Macdonald wondered aloud if the projected figures had a zero omitted by mistake.[26]

This cross-border tension found expression in a number of ways. The American State Department declared that British North Americans would require passports to cross into the United States, a ruling that affected each of the colonies. More important, the Americans struck back at their northern neighbours economically. The Reciprocity Treaty of 1854 had inaugurated mutual free trade in natural products between the United States and British North America. In December 1864, amid an atmosphere of growing hostility, Americans opted to cancel the treaty, which was up for renewal after ten years. This decision was not entirely a product of the diplomatic deterioration: American economists argued that the benefits of reciprocity had mainly fallen to British North America and that the United States had accumulated a trade deficit of some $30 million over the course of the treaty. The loss of this vital trade connection posed a serious economic threat to the British North American colonies and fuelled arguments in favour of a colonial union or federation to facilitate trade.

1864: The Americans give notice of the cancellation of the Reciprocity Treaty.

Terms of Confederation

The delegates at Quebec hammered out 72 resolutions that would form the basis of the *British North America Act* passed in 1867 by Britain's Parliament. While some Canadians today mistakenly imagine that Confederation heralded a sort of separation from Britain, this is far from the case. The resolutions insisted upon the continued connection to the Crown, and "the perpetuation of our connection with the Mother Country." It was no way a declaration of independence. Colonial self-government had already been achieved in 1848, with respect to internal matters. Autonomy in foreign policy was still decades away, and Canada would continue to depend on Britain for protection. Executive power remained vested in the hands of the Queen. In the general government, the governor-general would act as the representative of the Crown—indeed Lord Monck continued in office as governor-general of the confederated provinces—while in the provincial governments, lieutenant governors would fulfill that function.

The Quebec Resolutions called for a federal system, with a general government that would deal with matters common to all, and local legislatures for each province. The two Canadas were able to break out of their unhappy union to become the separately governed provinces of Quebec and Ontario. There would also be provincial legislatures for Nova Scotia, New Brunswick, and Prince Edward Island, which the resolutions anticipated would join. The resolutions provided for later admission of other colonies, including Newfoundland, the prairie west currently under Hudson's Bay Company control, and the two westernmost colonies of British Columbia and Vancouver Island (united as one colony in 1866). The initial federation included only the four provinces of Quebec, Ontario, Nova Scotia, and New Brunswick.

According to the terms agreed upon, the central parliament would have a bicameral (two house) structure—that is, an elected House of Commons and an appointed legislative council, or Senate. The seats in the House of Commons were to be apportioned according to population. It was here that George Brown's wish for "rep by pop" found expression. The representation in the Senate would in theory partly address the resultant central Canadian domination by allowing 24 seats for each of Quebec and Ontario, and 24 for the Maritime region as a whole (ten for Nova Scotia, ten for New Brunswick, and ultimately four for Prince Edward Island). There would still be a preponderance of central Canadian representation, but the Atlantic provinces were given a larger voice than their numbers alone would warrant. Besides helping to offset the regional imbalance, the Senate was also meant to provide a check on any potential democratic excess in the House of Commons. As an appointed body, the Senate was meant to allow for a kind of "sober second thought," perhaps to protect propertied interests, but also to protect minorities from the vagaries of crude majority rule. The short-lived experiment of an elected legislative council, as implemented in Canada in 1856, came to an end.

The Quebec Resolutions also set out the division of powers between the general Parliament and the provincial ones. This apportioning of responsibility was especially delicate, and laid the foundations for long-standing tensions between these levels of government. That this was so is no indictment of the so-called "fathers of Confederation." The goal was to secure substantial agreement for a federation, a way for both Canada East and Canada West to achieve greater autonomy than they had had under the 1840 Act of Union, and for the Maritime colonies to gain new economic opportunities and improved defence. If a general agreement could be reached, the fine points could be worked out in practice, like a roughly sewn garment awaiting tailoring for the wearer.

Indeed, the British constitution itself presented an example in which there need be no core written document at all—Britain's history illustrates that the accumulated statutes, common law precepts, judicial interpretations, and simple constitutional conventions, or established practices, when taken together, yield a flexible yet firm political framework. Coming as they did from this largely unwritten tradition, the architects of the Quebec Resolutions took a great deal of constitutional practice for granted. The relationship between government and Parliament was not spelled out, nor was the role of the prime minister, or the convention that a ministry needed the confidence of Parliament to carry on government.

John A. Macdonald would have preferred a simple union to a federation, and pointed to the bloody American civil war as an object lesson in what could happen when the individual constituent parts of any union were too powerful. Others, incidentally, drew the opposite lesson, seeing the war as a result of a central government impinging on the states' claim to autonomy. While Macdonald was forced to compromise his vision for a centralized union, he believed that the provincial levels of government would eventually wither away, although he privately acknowledged that it would "not do to adopt this point of view when discussing the subject in Lower Canada."[27]

Later interpreters of the constitution would see Confederation in an entirely different light. Britain's highest court, the Judicial Committee of the Privy Council, would, in the decades ahead, have to rule repeatedly on questions of federal versus provincial jurisdiction. Most often, they tended to see Confederation as a classic federation, with the individual provinces retaining considerable autonomy. There are certainly elements that would support both visions in the terms agreed upon at Quebec—cross-currents of centralized authority and provincial autonomy.

The terms set out some of the key areas of jurisdiction to be assumed by each level of government. The general parliament was given apparently broad powers to "make laws for the peace, welfare and good government" of the federated provinces. By the time these resolutions were translated into the final draft of the *British North America Act*, this phrase became "peace, order, and good government," something political scientists like to call the POGG clause. Some have seen in the phrase "peace, order, and good government" a quintessential encapsulation of Canadian values, perhaps our somewhat duller version of the ringing French slogan "*liberté, égalité, fraternité*" or the American "life, liberty, and the pursuit of happiness." As tempting as it might be to elevate the phrase to a statement of national identity, it should be remembered that British policymakers inserted the same tripartite slogan into the New Zealand constitution in 1852. In Canada, the POGG clause applied to all matters that were not designated to be under provincial jurisdiction. Some of the key matters specifically assigned to the federal government include criminal law, justice, defence, currency, postal service, Indian affairs, plus important taxation powers, notably over customs revenue. The provinces were to have jurisdiction over such questions as property, civil law (bearing in mind Quebec's distinct system), Crown lands, hospitals, and education. The following provides details of the specific powers assigned to the federal and provincial governments in the final version of the *British North America Act* passed in 1867.

The *British North America Act*, 1867, designated these specific powers to the federal government exclusively:

1. The Public Debt and Property.
2. The Regulation of Trade and Commerce.
3. The raising of Money by any Mode or System of Taxation.
4. The borrowing of Money on the Public Credit.
5. Postal Service.
6. The Census and Statistics.
7. Militia, Military and Naval Service, and Defence.
8. The fixing of and providing for the Salaries and Allowances of Civil and other Officers of the Government of Canada.
9. Beacons, Buoys, Lighthouses, and Sable Island.
10. Navigation and Shipping.
11. Quarantine and the Establishment and Maintenance of Marine Hospitals.
12. Sea Coast and Inland Fisheries.
13. Ferries between a Province and any British or Foreign Country or between Two Provinces.
14. Currency and Coinage.
15. Banking, Incorporation of Banks, and the Issue of Paper Money.
16. Savings Banks.
17. Weights and Measures.
18. Bills of Exchange and Promissory Notes.
19. Interest.
20. Legal Tender.

21. Bankruptcy and Insolvency.
22. Patents of Invention and Discovery.
23. Copyrights.
24. Indians, and Lands reserved for the Indians.
25. Naturalization and Aliens.
26. Marriage and Divorce.
27. The Criminal Law, except the Constitution of Courts of Criminal Jurisdiction, but including the Procedure in Criminal Matters.
28. The Establishment, Maintenance, and Management of Penitentiaries.
29. Such Classes of Subjects as are expressly excepted in the Enumeration of the Classes of Subjects by this Act assigned exclusively to the Legislatures of the Provinces.

These were the powers designated exclusively to the provincial governments:

1. The Amendment from Time to Time, notwithstanding anything in this Act, of the Constitution of the Province, except as regards the Office of Lieutenant Governor.
2. Direct Taxation within the Province in order to the raising of a Revenue for Provincial Purposes. [sic]
3. The borrowing of Money on the sole Credit of the Province.
4. The Establishment and Tenure of Provincial Offices and the Appointment and Payment of Provincial Officers.
5. The Management and Sale of the Public Lands belonging to the Province and of the Timber and Wood thereon.
6. The Establishment, Maintenance, and Management of Public and Reformatory Prisons in and for the Province.
7. The Establishment, Maintenance, and Management of Hospitals, Asylums, Charities, and Eleemosynary Institutions in and for the Province, other than Marine Hospitals.
8. Municipal Institutions in the Province.
9. Shop, Saloon, Tavern, Auctioneer, and other Licences in order to the raising of a Revenue for Provincial, Local, or Municipal Purposes. [sic]
10. Local Works and Undertakings other than such as are of the following Classes,—
    a. Lines of Steam or other Ships, Railways, Canals, Telegraphs, and other Works and Undertakings connecting the Province with any other or others of the Provinces, or extending beyond the Limits of the Province:
    b. Lines of Steam Ships between the Province and any British or Foreign Country:
    c. Such Works as, although wholly situate within the Province, are before or after their Execution declared by the Parliament of Canada to be for the general Advantage of Canada or for the Advantage of Two or more of the Provinces.
11. The Incorporation of Companies with Provincial Objects.
12. The Solemnization of Marriage in the Province.
13. Property and Civil Rights in the Province.
14. The Administration of Justice in the Province, including the Constitution, Maintenance, and Organization of Provincial Courts, both of Civil and of Criminal Jurisdiction, and including Procedure in Civil Matters in those Courts.

15. The Imposition of Punishment by Fine, Penalty, or Imprisonment for enforcing any Law of the Province made in relation to any Matter coming within any of the Classes of Subjects enumerated in this Section.

16. Generally all Matters of a merely local or private Nature in the Province

A separate section of the *British North America Act* provided for the establishment of a Supreme Court, although this would not be put into place until 1875, and appeals would continue to Britain's highest court, the Judicial Committee of the Privy Council, until 1949. Further, a separate section with respect to education made it clear that this was a matter under provincial jurisdiction, subject only to the proviso that the rights of denominational—that is, religious—schools could not be undercut from what existed by law at the time of Confederation. This was meant to protect the rights of the Protestant minority in Quebec, and Roman Catholic minorities in Ontario and New Brunswick. The general government could thus intervene in provincial affairs if necessary to protect these minority rights. The general government agreed to assume the debts of the individual colonies at the time of Confederation, and, in view of the concentration of taxation power in the central government, to allocate funds on a population basis to the provinces for their local expenditures. There was also a clear commitment to construct the intercolonial railway to link Halifax to the St. Lawrence.

Those who saw in the terms a classic federal arrangement, as opposed to a centralizing union, could point to the fact that provinces had some authority with respect to their own constitutions, and initially, both Quebec and New Brunswick opted to have a bicameral (two house) system at the provincial level. In the eyes of their defenders, these provincial senates seemed to imply a substantial, dignified level of government at the provincial level, not something resembling a mere municipality. And, despite the use of the phrase "merely local or private" in the final point on the list of provincial powers, these did represent significant powers over substantial matters.

Others saw troubling signs that suggested Macdonald's wish for a centralized union had prevailed, that the agreement for what was ostensibly a federation was, in the words of Rouge critic A.A. Dorion, "union in disguise."[28] The power of disallowance was a potential threat. The central government would have the power to disallow provincial legislation, suggesting that its relationship to the provinces resembled an imperial power more than anything else. Indeed, in the early years of Confederation, the federal government did wield that now-lapsed power quite capriciously. Then, too, there was the troubling issue of "residual" powers—that is, those not specifically designated to either level of government. The final draft of the *British North America Act* put under the control of the central government "all Matters not coming within the Classes of Subjects by this Act assigned exclusively to the Legislatures of the Provinces."

Historian Paul Romney has argued that this was not what the delegates at Quebec agreed upon. He points out that in the Quebec Resolutions both the central and the provincial governments had residual powers. Somehow, between the conference of the colonial representatives at Quebec in the autumn of 1864, and the final drafting of the 1867 Act, significant changes were introduced, something Romney sees as the work of the cagey Macdonald and British authorities who also favoured a more centralized union. Referring to the clause that would have acknowledged provincial residual powers as well as federal ones, Romney argues that, as successive versions were written, the clause "flickered like a candle in a draft" before being extinguished altogether. The final Act "made it possible to say not only that the residual power had been vested in the federal government, but that the federal power was *wholly* residuary—it comprised everything that was not specifically allotted to the provinces."[29]

The conversion of the Quebec Resolutions into the final terms of the *British North America Act* took place primarily during the course of the London Conference in late 1866 and early 1867. But before this could happen, the delegates had to work to promote acceptance of the Confederation scheme in their own colonies. It was not a formally understood rule that a new constitution, passed in Britain, would require colonial consent. But winning popular support, or at least the appearance of it, was good policy and British statesmen would be more inclined to hear the proposals colonial politicians put forth if it was understood that they had the support of their constituents.

Reactions to the Proposed Confederation

Prince Edward Island's delegates met a storm of political opposition from those who denounced the scheme as opening the door to increased taxation and the drafting of islanders for the defence of distant Canada. Historian Peter Waite points out that many islanders feared that they might be compelled to join a larger union, as they were mindful that British policy favoured colonial consolidation. For them, a nearby analogy would be the colony of Cape Breton Island, which had been merged with Nova Scotia in 1820. Alexander Anderson, a legislative councillor on Prince Edward Island, probably spoke the concerns of many when he voiced his objections, fearing that they had no chance of gaining anything, but many chances to lose:

> I think the offer is something like this: if we will give up to one-half of our revenue to the Canadians, and allow them to tax us as much as they please, they would then take charge of us. We fought hard and contended long for responsible government, and are we now going to give up our constitution and say we are not able to govern ourselves? I do not think that any man or any body of men in Canada can know the wishes or wants of the people of this island as well as we do ourselves.[30]

Thus, while Charlottetown was the cradle of the Confederation scheme, Prince Edward Island initially opted against it. Financial pressures arising from overly ambitious railway building schemes later compelled the island to join in 1873.

Similarly, Newfoundland, while sending delegates to Quebec, opted not to join Confederation in 1867, and held off until 1949. Newfoundland had been in the grip of devastating economic decline, with famine conditions triggered by poor fishing yields and disappointing results from the seal hunt, gale force winds, and a blight on the potato crop. The pro-Confederation F.B.T. Carter had succeeded Hoyles as premier and brought the Roman Catholic Liberal, and fellow supporter of the scheme, J. Ambrose Shea, into his cabinet. Carter saw in Confederation an answer to the colony's endemic poverty: a quarter of Newfoundland's revenues were being consumed in direct relief to the poor. Others pointed to the fact that the Confederation scheme rested on a protective economic system, hardly likely to benefit Newfoundland, which was separated from the mainland by hundreds of miles of sea, and which was dependent upon imports to feed its population, and upon an export market for fish, seals, and similar resources. Newfoundland's orientation was to the British Isles, especially with the 1866 advent of the first trans-Atlantic cable connecting Newfoundland to Ireland. Historian Andrew Smith sees Newfoundland's rejection of Confederation as consistent with the "libertarian, anti-statist streak in Newfoundland's political culture." A manifestation of this might be seen in the lower per capita debt load in Newfoundland, where public debt amounted to £1.44 per person in 1864, in contrast to £5.20 in Canada.[31]

The Confederation proposal was not considered in isolation in the island's politics, and Carter came to the conclusion that the issue could not be pressed. The 1869 election drove Carter's administration from office. Arguably, forces other than opposition to Confederation were at play: Carter's policies aimed at reducing relief to the able-bodied poor were alarming to those for whom outright starvation was the alternative. Moreover, Protestant political opponents, disapproving of Carter's coalition with Catholics, worked to intensify Orange Order suspicions of papists, and promoted rumours of subversive activities by Irish radicals. Tory anti-Confederation agitator Charles Fox Bennett found it easy to convince Roman Catholics that rule from Canada would be as disastrous for Newfoundland as rule from England had proved for Ireland. Interestingly, a pro-Confederation member of the assembly, D.W. Prowse, had earlier drawn a different lesson from history, pointing to the prosperity Scotland had enjoyed after its 1707 union with England.[32]

Debate over Confederation in the Canadas

In the Canadas, Thomas D'Arcy McGee played up the nation-building rhetoric, describing his vision of "one great nationality bound like the shield of Achilles, by the blue of ocean" but which was nonetheless "quartered into many communities—each disposing of its internal affairs."[33] It would be a distortion, however, to suggest that nation-building was the foremost consideration, even in the minds of those who favoured the Quebec Resolutions. Instead, political debate revolved around practical considerations, and practical objections.

In Canada East, Rouge members, who had been left out of the Great Coalition and the Confederation conferences, raised sensible concerns about the proposed scheme. Antoine-Aimé Dorion had favoured some new federal arrangement to break the unworkable legislative union of 1840, but found the Quebec Resolutions untenable. He laid out his views in *La Minerve* late in 1864 and reiterated these in the February and March 1865 debates on Confederation in the assembly of the united Canadas. He recalled his earlier advocacy of some form of federation, "but the Confederation I advocated was a real confederation" he insisted. The scheme currently under debate would give the provincial governments "the smallest possible amount of freedom of action." Dorion also ridiculed the idea of an intercolonial railway for improved defence: "A railway lying in some places not more than fifteen or twenty miles from the frontier, will be of no use whatever…. An enemy could destroy miles of it before it would be possible to resist him, and in time of difficulty it would be a mere trap for the troops passing along it, unless we had almost an army to keep it open."[34] Fellow Rouge member Henri Joly added that the Americans already understood that an attack on any one British North American colony would prompt a spirited resistance by all: Confederation was not necessary to ensure united defence. Moreover, expansion to include the west would create "the outward form of a giant, but with the strength of a child," Joly pointed out.[35]

Cartier defended the Quebec Resolutions, promising that union with the Maritime colonies could help to break the dominance of Canada West. He also maintained that the proposed system would protect the rights of minorities, including Quebec's English-speaking Protestants. He also claimed that the clergy, and the Pope himself, approved of the plan. The maintenance of the connection to the Crown would ensure that the executive was respectable and beyond the tumult of political abuse, he insisted, something that he saw as an inherent defect in the American system.

English-speaking Canadians were not unanimous in their support for Confederation either, despite John A. Macdonald's skilful management of the 1865 debates and George Brown's considerable moral authority. Legislative councillor James Currie sensibly reasoned that British North America's limited manpower and pecuniary resources would not multiply under Confederation. Joining with the Maritimes "was like tying a small twine at the end of a long rope and saying it strengthened the whole line," he said.[36] Yet the prospect of achieving representation by population, and breaking the unworkable union of 1840, was appealing in Canada West. The positive votes of Canada West Reformers would ensure the resolutions' adoption.

March 11, 1865: The assembly of the province of Canada votes to adopt the Confederation resolutions.

By the wee hours of Saturday, March 11, 1865, the Confederation debates in the Canadian legislature were winding down. A Canada West newspaper described the state of the house as "seedy," with members stretched out sleeping on the benches, having exhausted the saloonkeeper's stores of food and liquor, and others expressing their impatience by rattling their desks and making birdcalls. "Men with the strongest constitutions for Parliamentary twaddle were sick of the debate, and the great bulk of the members were scattered about the building, with an up-all-night, get-tight-in-the-morning air, impatient for the sound of the division bell." At last, at quarter past four in the morning, the members were called to vote.[37] A majority of members supported the resolutions, with 91 in favour and 33 opposed; there were sectional majorities in Canada West, with 54 in favour and 8 opposed, and, more narrowly, in Canada East, where the vote was 37 to 25.

An Uncertain Verdict in Nova Scotia and New Brunswick

As the Canadians debated the Quebec Resolutions, colonists in Nova Scotia and New Brunswick also considered their options. Joseph Howe was out of office in Nova Scotia, serving as a fisheries commissioner, but expressed his disapproval of Confederation anonymously in the published "Botheration" letters of early 1865. Howe ridiculed the clichéd conviction that "something must be done." The one thing that certainly ought to be done, he countered, was that Nova Scotians, the freest people on the earth, having won self-government in 1848, "ought all to go down on our knees and thank the Almighty for the abundant blessings he has showered upon us." They ought to resist the serpent in the garden. As for Canada, "If they are in trouble let them get out of it; but don't let them involve us in distractions with which we have nothing to do. Are not the Canadians always in trouble? Did not Papineau keep Lower Canada in trouble for twenty years, and McKenzie [sic] disturb the Upper Province for about the same period?" he asked.[38] The idea of Nova Scotians being called from their own frontiers to defend Canada was far from appealing. Yarmouth merchant, ship owner, and politician Thomas Killam objected to the idea of limiting potential markets for Nova Scotia commerce: "We will hedge ourselves in as it were, and shut ourselves out from the markets that are now open to us." He saw in Confederation the ruin of Nova Scotia's shipping interests.[39]

Historian Phillip Buckner rejects the idea that those Maritimers who resisted Confederation were inherently conservative or motivated by simple parochialism. For some, Buckner explains, the real issue was not a wider union but the specific terms of the Quebec resolutions.[40] Del Muise has emphasized economic factors, arguing that the old Nova Scotia economy based on wooden ships was giving way to a new continentally based model which favoured industrial growth, coal, and railway transportation.[41] Those whose interests lay with the latter would be most inclined to support the Confederation scheme. Voters in Nova Scotia would be denied the chance to participate in an election on the question, however.

Just as the Canadian legislature pronounced its support for Confederation, the project faced a reversal in New Brunswick. Tilley's government sought a mandate on the Confederation issue, and during the election that lasted from February 28 to March 18, 1865, Albert Smith's anti-Confederation forces ran a lively campaign. Echoing Nova Scotian Joseph Howe's arguments, Smith characterized Canada as convulsed by anarchy and disquiet, in contrast to the peace and contentment that reigned in New Brunswick. Irish journalist Timothy Warren Anglin, whose Saint John newspaper the *Morning Freeman* had long been an influential voice among New Brunswick Roman Catholics, maintained that Canada, and not New Brunswick, would reap any economic and political advantages. He rejected arguments centred on defence, insisting that the British North American colonies were but innocent bystanders in Britain's quarrels with the Americans and should thus not be expected to bear the burden of increased military expenses. Anglin also argued that New Brunswick's administration was more cost-effective than that of the province of Canada, and that the residents of New Brunswick enjoyed more free services. Toll roads and bridges were more pervasive in Canada, he wrote, because the politicians had spent public money on grandiose parliament buildings.[42]

Smith's anti-Confederates swept Tilley and his supporters from office, a result that some disappointed partisans blamed on an organized Roman Catholic conspiracy. Lieutenant Governor Arthur Gordon was compelled to call upon Smith to form a government—a man he personally despised and had earlier scolded for abusing his position as attorney general. But matters would not rest here. A little more than a year later, Gordon would be the instrument through whom British policymakers would exert pressure to see Confederation enacted.

British Pressure for Confederation

While the British government had once quashed discussion of colonial union or federation, by 1865 policy strongly favoured it. Consolidated colonies would be better able to

March 18, 1865: Samuel Leonard Tilley's pro-Confederation government is defeated in New Brunswick.

provide for themselves, especially with respect to defence, and be less apt to be a burden on British taxpayers. While Confederation was in no sense a separation of the colonies from the mother country, it ideally would serve to help the mother country divest itself of onerous obligations. Edward Cardwell, Britain's secretary of state for the colonies, urged his colonial governors to do everything in their power to promote acceptance of the Quebec Resolutions. "I need scarcely assure you that here there is but one desire—which is to promote to the utmost the work in which you are engaged," he wrote privately to Lord Monck.[43] London's banking community also lobbied in favour of Confederation, seeing in it a means to secure investments in British North America. "Had a group of politically powerful investors disliked the Quebec Resolutions, it is doubtful whether the imperial parliament would have implemented them," historian Andrew Smith argues.[44]

George Brown travelled almost straight from the Quebec Conference to London where in December 1864 he had a private conversation with Cardwell about the Confederation scheme, and about the wish of Canadians to acquire the Hudson's Bay Company holdings in Rupert's Land to provide an outlet for western expansion. This idea was appealing to British policymakers, as it offered the prospect of transferring responsibility for the northwest onto other shoulders. Soon after the passage of the Quebec Resolutions in Canada's legislature in the spring of 1865, Brown returned to London for further negotiations, this time accompanied by fellow members of the Great Coalition government—Macdonald, Cartier, and Alexander Galt. Cardwell attempted to resist arguments that Britain should continue to bear considerable costs for naval and land defences, but for the most part, British statesmen flattered the visiting colonials with invitations to dinner parties, balls, horse races, and other delights of the London social whirl. Macdonald even accepted an honorary Oxford doctorate. Beneath this cajolery, though, was the underlying agenda to promote the Confederation scheme, seemingly at risk with Tilley's electoral defeat in New Brunswick. In London, *The Times* proclaimed, "If, in short, these colonies ever wish us to defend their whole soil, they must combine in a general organization … the House of Commons ought to have the courage, if necessary, to enforce it upon the colonies." A later editorial comment put it even more baldly: "We look to Confederation as the means of relieving this country from much expense and much embarrassment…. We appreciate the goodwill of the Canadians and their desire to maintain their relations with the British Crown. But a people of four million ought to be able to keep up their own defences."[45]

April 1865: The Confederate forces are defeated, ending the American Civil War.

In April 1865 the American Civil War was over. Confederate General Robert E. Lee offered his surrender to Union General Ulysses S. Grant at the village of Appomattox Court House in Virginia. Before long, British North America would face fresh threats to their security—and again, the threat would be based upon a quarrel not truly their own.

The Fenian Danger

In 1857, Irish republicans who had fled to the United States in the wake of the failed 1848 uprising formed a new society, the Fenian Brotherhood—an early version of the Irish Republican Army—aimed at securing Irish independence from British rule. American Fenians coordinated activities with their counterparts in Ireland, and drew some 10 000 supporters from the ranks of battle-hardened American Civil War veterans. The organization boosted recruitment by offering new enlistees a $100 incentive. Many demobilized soldiers also took advantage of a United States Army offer to buy their own rifles for six dollars. Much of the Fenians' funding originated in the United States, too: Irish expatriates drawn to the republican cause donated almost $500 000. Yet some supporters of Irish independence might well have shrunk from the terrorist tactics the Fenians employed on both sides of the Atlantic. Political assassinations, or threats of them, kept authorities throughout the British empire on constant alert. Among the most serious incidents in this era was an 1867 bomb explosion in London that killed six and injured many more. While actual attacks were rare, shared intelligence told of secret caches of weapons, and tracked the movement of those under suspicion. A would-be assassin who claimed to be a Fenian shot and wounded Prince Alfred, the son of Queen Victoria, while the Prince made the first ever royal visit to Australia in 1868. Queen Victoria herself was the target of alleged Fenian conspiracies, and in 1872, a 17-year-old youth leapt at her carriage, waving a pistol and demanding the release of Fenian prisoners. Canada's first secret service was established for the purpose of monitoring the Fenian threat, a precursor to a later branch of the North West Mounted Police. Thomas D'Arcy McGee, who had once espoused the cause of Irish republicanism, but was now denounced as a turncoat, was a hated target with a price on his head of $1000. In April 1868, as he returned to his rooming house from a late-night parliamentary session, he was shot dead in the streets of Ottawa. His assassin, Patrick Whelan, was rewarded with the noose.

Some Fenians believed that an attack on Britain's North American colonies would be an effective way to deliver a blow to Britain, a way to exert pressure for Irish independence. Colonial officials had been monitoring rumours of an attack on St. Patrick's Day, 1866, and called out militia units to prepare. The day passed without incident. Then, early in April, reports surfaced that about 1000 Fenians had descended upon Eastport, Maine, bound for an attack on New Brunswick. British troops and colonial militia, backed by the Royal Navy, soon put the would-be invaders to flight, leaving, it was said, unpaid hotel bills behind them.

In June of that year, fresh assaults came against British North American territory, this time at Ridgeway in Canada West, and Missisquoi Bay in Canada East. The Fenian forces succeeded in overwhelming the Canadian militia, but withdrew when their anticipated reinforcements failed to arrive. Nine militiamen were killed in the engagement or died of wounds soon afterward, including three young students from the University of Toronto, and dozens were wounded. Fenian losses were fewer, but many were apprehended as they fled back across the United States border.

1866: Fenian raids are launched on New Brunswick and Canada.

This monument was erected at the University of Toronto in 1870 to commemorate those killed in the Fenian raids.

Source: Archive on Ontario, I0001819.

In the meantime, the Fenian crisis exerted a powerful influence in New Brunswick. Albert Smith's administration held an uncertain majority, and wavered on the issue of Confederation. The sudden presence of an overt military threat to the colony sharpened apprehensions about defence, and Lieutenant Governor Arthur Gordon moved quickly to capitalize on it. He manoeuvred the Smith government from office and called an election, a little more than a year since the previous one. As he had hoped, Samuel Leonard Tilley and the pro-Confederation Liberals were swept into office in June 1866, in a campaign subsidized with Canadian money.

A pro-Confederation resolution was quickly passed. A couple of months before this, Charles Tupper had introduced a resolution in Nova Scotia for Confederation, which was carried, although he did not risk seeking a mandate from voters on the question. To Joseph Howe, the coincidental timing of the raids provoked questions: "The proceedings from beginning to end, were the very best possible to subserve the ends of the Confederates," he pointed out. "The Fenians made their appearance at Eastport, and forthwith the Confederation resolution was tabled in our House of Assembly. A few days after the resolution was carried, and presto! the Fenians had evaporated and gone."[46]

1866: Both New Brunswick and Nova Scotia pass resolutions in favour of Confederation.

American authorities seemed loath to deal with the Fenian threat; the fact that a society dedicated to terrorist tactics was able to fundraise, recruit, and drill on American soil all pointed to the fact that no administration wanted to alienate Irish-American voters. Meting out justice to Fenian raiders would prove a political dilemma for Canadian officials, who faced American pressure for lenient treatment, and who feared creating martyrs with executions. Knowing that Fenian hangings would infuse fresh blood into the cause of Irish republicanism, yet reluctant to provoke Orange Order reaction, Canadian authorities quietly released the prisoners one at a time. Ironically, a supposedly contrite "General" John O'Neill, Fenian commander at Ridgeway, was released from a Canadian prison in 1870, only to take part in a fresh raid against Manitoba in 1871. This abortive project anticipated the assistance of Riel and the Métis, a hope that was not realized.

Some American observers believed that the Fenian raids would force the inevitable annexation of Canada, and in this light it is easy to see that, while the military crises themselves quickly blew over, the attacks added urgency to the Confederation project. An American takeover was not an entirely far-fetched notion. In July 1866 a bill was introduced into the United States House of Representatives providing for the admission of Nova Scotia, New Brunswick, the united Canadas, and the western territories into the union. This proposed legislation, denounced as impudent by the Canadian press, did not move beyond the committee stage.

1866: American House of Representatives entertains a bill for annexation.

The Ideological Context of Confederation

The focus thus far has been on the pragmatic—on a Confederation driven by practical realities, rather than any nationalist ideals. Yet some political scientists and historians do emphasize an ideological component in analyzing the debates that took place around the measure. Janet Ajzenstat, Paul Romney, Ian Gentiles, and William D. Gairdner, in their introduction to the published Canadian Confederation debates, remark that "too often" the label "pragmatist" is taken to mean that the Fathers of Confederation had no strong interest in, or commitment to, political ideology. They acknowledge that these were practical men with practical goals, but reject the notion that "Canada was created as a mere framework—an empty shell, waiting to be filled with whatever political content Canadians chose."[47]

Political scientist Peter J. Smith traces the ideological origins of the Canadian federal state to debates over the state's role in society that were part of British, American, and French political culture in the eighteenth and nineteenth centuries. Smith argues that debates over commercial capitalism, and its supposed risk to agrarian virtue were important in Canada as well.[48] In considering what ideological currents were influential, Janet Ajzenstat disputes the long-standing idea, articulated by Louis Hartz and Gad Horowitz in the 1960s, that Canada was shaped at the time of the Loyalists' arrival by a "Tory touch"—a belief in the value of collectivism, that, paradoxically, explains our tolerance for policies and institutions that our American neighbours might view as socialist. Instead, Ajzenstat sees the Fathers of Confederation as "John Locke's disciples, students of modernity's most ardent opponent of elitism and oligarchy." Canada was not a Tory invention, in Ajzenstat's view. There was no inherent preference for a regulatory state, and Confederation was not a "formula for oligarchy." Indeed, there was no monolithic definition of normative Canadian values.[49]

Historian Andrew Smith likewise discounts the notion that ideology was insignificant in the process of Confederation, but he sees no Lockian liberal consensus, and maintains that those who see in Confederation the triumph of classical liberal ideas of individualism and free enterprise are mistaken. "It is far more accurate to describe 1867 as the birth of a 'Tory-interventionist order' in Canada than of a liberal one," he argues, noting that the strongest supporters of such classical liberal values as free trade and low taxes can be found among the anti-Confederates. He notes that "today, when the interventionist or Red Tory tradition in Canadian conservatism has been largely eclipsed by neo-liberalism (i.e., modernized classical liberalism), it is sometimes difficult to conceive of the days when Canada's Conservatives were the main proponents of greater state intervention in the economy." But he believes that the "intellectual archaeology" of recovering these ideas is essential to an understanding of the politics of Confederation.[50]

Ideology is indeed an important aspect of the Confederation process, and it is fruitful to consider the intellectual climate in which British North American politicians were immersed. That said, one must be cautious in using political debates and speeches in the assembly as a reliable guide to the most deeply held convictions of politicians. Then, as now, utterances intended for public consumption tended to be carefully tailored to the audience and particular context.

Legislating Confederation: The London Conference, 1866–1867

With Confederation approved in the united Canadas, Nova Scotia, and New Brunswick, a final step remained: the Quebec Resolutions would have to be drafted into legislation to be passed by Britain's Parliament. Not until 1982, with the "patriation," or bringing home, of the Constitution, would Canada have the authority to legislate changes to its own constitution. British policymakers generally approved of the plan to federate the colonies, encouraging colonial governors to advance the project, and looking to Confederation as a means to reduce expenditures. A change in government in 1866 brought Britain's Conservatives into power, but support for Confederation did not falter. Lord Stanley, the foreign secretary, privately explained: "The Colonies will remain Colonies, only confederated for the sake of convenience. If they choose to separate, we on this side shall not object: it is they who protest against the idea. In England separation would be generally popular."[51] He may have overstated the latter point, although enthusiasm for colonial possessions was especially low in Britain by the middle decades of the nineteenth century.

December 1866 to March 1867: The London Conference finalizes Confederation details with the imperial government.

From December 1866 to March 1867, British North American delegates met with their imperial counterparts at the Westminster Palace Hotel in London. The London Conference finalized the details of Confederation legislation. Canada's Great Coalition government had lost the leadership of Étienne-Pascal Taché, who had died in the summer of 1865. George Brown had withdrawn from the cabinet in December 1865, having already played his part in launching the Confederation project. A Canadian delegation led by Macdonald, and a smaller Maritime contingent, which included Charles Tupper from Nova Scotia and Samuel Leonard Tilley from New Brunswick, travelled to Britain. Nova Scotia's Joseph Howe was also on hand to continue his fight against the Quebec Resolutions, but the force of momentum, plus British government support, was too formidable a tide for him to overcome. The Earl of Carnarvon was now Britain's secretary of state for the colonies, and he flattered Howe by seeking out his views, but had no intention of abandoning the project.

Like George Brown a few years before, Macdonald found that his sojourn in Britain involved a whirlwind courtship. Not too long after the conference began, Macdonald happened to meet the sister of his private secretary Hewitt Bernard, while walking in London. The 52-year old Macdonald had lost his first wife, Isabella, to tuberculosis nine years earlier. Agnes Bernard was a tall, commanding woman of 31, with angular features and an austere manner. They married in February 1867. Despite reassuring Hewitt Bernard that he had curtailed his drinking, rumours persisted that Macdonald was frequently "indisposed" during the days of the conference. Such rumours were no doubt fed by a frightening episode that occurred shortly before his marriage: Macdonald awoke in his hotel bedroom to discover the bedding and curtains on fire. He sustained burns to his hair, face, and shoulder. Perhaps Macdonald hoped that Agnes could save him from himself. She may have tried, but her success was always qualified.[52]

February 1867: John A. Macdonald marries Agnes Bernard.

Conclusion

In the same month that John and Agnes Macdonald's marriage was solemnized, the bill to unite the British North American colonies was passed in the House of Commons in London. The new federated colony of four separate provinces was to be named the "Dominion" of Canada. Tilley wrote to his son that the term occurred to him during his daily Bible reading, when he stumbled upon it in Psalm 72: "He shall have dominion also from sea to sea, and from the river unto the ends of the earth." Macdonald favoured the "Kingdom" of Canada, but the more neutral "Dominion" seemed less potentially provocative to the Americans. In March 1867, Carnarvon shepherded the bill through the House of Lords, and the Queen pronounced her Royal Assent on March 29.

1867: The British North America Act is passed in Britain's Parliament.

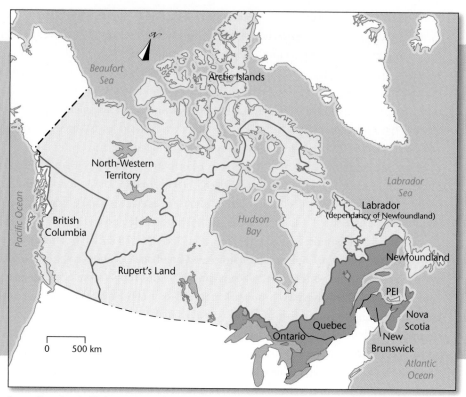

Map 12.2
Canada in 1867.

Source: Reproduced with the permission of Natural Resources Canada 2010, courtesy of the Atlas of Canada.

Macdonald bristled at the fact that British parliamentarians had shown general indifference to the measure, treating it like "a private bill uniting two or three English parishes." Indeed, Governor-General Lord Monck's letter to his son describing his plans for July 1, 1867, the day Confederation was to be proclaimed in Canada, speaks volumes. He blandly noted that he would be "obliged to go to Ottawa for a few days for some business."[53] Monck disappointed those expecting a sense of grand occasion: rather than wearing his cocked hat and ceremonial uniform trimmed with gold braid, he simply turned up in his ordinary street clothes. In Halifax, Joseph Howe reported on a Confederation Day crowd of about 600, the number that might be expected for a decent funeral, he said sourly.

For the Maritime colonies, Confederation was a marriage of convenience: there was scant enthusiasm, but imperial pressure and the absence of other practical alternatives all exerted their force for a union. For Canada East and Canada West, united since 1840, Confederation was not so much a marriage as a divorce. There was no divorce from Britain, but rather from each other. Now each section of the once-united colony would be a separate province, able to legislate over questions where autonomy mattered most. If any nationalist agenda was at work, it influenced the breaking of the unworkable union that had bound the Canadas unwillingly together, freeing the provinces of Ontario and Quebec to govern themselves more effectively. A sense of wider national identity could not be forced, but rather would have to be built incrementally as Canadians shared challenges and triumphs in the years to come.

Questions to Consider

1. What made the united Canadas difficult to govern in the 1850s and 1860s?

2. How did the Civil War in the United States affect British North America?

3. What influence did the Fenian raids exert?

4. What was the general policy of the British government towards Confederation?

Critical Thinking Questions

1. Why did Nova Scotia and New Brunswick join Confederation?

2. What criticisms of Confederation were raised in the Atlantic colonies?

3. Why did some French-Canadian critics of the Quebec Resolutions see them as a plan for "union in disguise"?

4. How significant were the individual political actors in the British North American colonies in bringing about the scheme for Confederation?

5. How did the *British North America Act* contain crosscurrents of centralization and provincial autonomy?

Suggested Readings

Primary Sources

Ajzenstat, Janet, Paul Romney, Ian Gentles, and William D. Gairdner, eds. *Canada's Founding Debates.* Toronto: University of Toronto Press, 2003.

British North America Act, 1867. Government of Canada. Department of Justice. Online at http://www.justice.gc.ca/en/ps/const/loireg/p1t1-1.html.

Monck, F.E.O. *My Canadian Leaves: An Account of a Visit to Canada in 1864-1865.* London: R. Bentley, 1891. Available online via Early Canadiana Online, http://www.canadiana.org/ECO/mtq?doc=10127.

Morton. W.L, ed. *Monck Letters and Journals, 1863–1868: Canada from Government House at Confederation.* Toronto: McClelland & Stewart, 1970.

"The Quebec Resolutions, 1864." *Documents on the Confederation of British North America.* Toronto: McClelland & Stewart Ltd., 1969: 154–165. Online at http://www.collectionscanada.ca/confederation/023001-245-e.html.

Smith, Cynthia M., and Jack McLeod, eds. *Sir John A.: An Anecdotal Life of John A. Macdonald.* Toronto: Oxford University Press, 1989.

Waite, P.B., ed. *The Confederation Debates in the Province of Canada, 1865.* Montreal and Kingston: McGill-Queen's University Press, 2006.

Waite, P.B., ed. *Confederation, 1854–1867. Canadian History Through the Press Series.* Toronto: Holt, Rinehart and Winston, 1972.

Secondary Sources

Ajzenstat, Janet. "The Conservatism of the Canadian Founders." In *After Liberalism: Essays in Search of Freedom, Virtue and Order.* William Gairdner, ed. Toronto: Stoddart, 1998.

Ajzenstat, Janet. *The Canadian Founding: John Locke and Parliament.* Montreal and Kingston: McGill-Queen's University Press, 2007.

Baker, William M. *Timothy Warren Anglin, 1822–1896: Irish Catholic Canadian.* Toronto: University of Toronto Press, 1977.

Bittermann, Rusty, and Margaret McCallum. "Upholding the Land Legislation of a 'Communistic and Socialist Assembly': The Benefits of Confederation for Prince Edward Island." *Canadian Historical Review* 87 (March 2006): 1–28.

Buckner, Phillip A. "The Maritimes and Confederation: A Reassessment." In Ged Martin, ed. *The Causes of Canadian Confederation.* Fredericton: Acadiensis Press, 1990.

Buckner, Phillip A., and John G. Reid. *The Atlantic Region to Confederation: A History.* Toronto: University of Toronto Press, 1994.

Careless, J.M.S. *Brown of the Globe.* 2 vols. Toronto: Macmillan, 1959, 1963.

Cornell, Paul G. *The Great Coalition of 1864.* Ottawa: The Canadian Historical Association Booklets, 19, 1966.

Cook, Ramsay, Craig Brown, and Carl Berger, eds. *Confederation.* Toronto: University of Toronto Press, 1967.

Creighton, Donald. *The Road to Confederation: The Emergence of Canada, 1863–1867.* Toronto: Macmillan, 1964.

Creighton, Donald. *John A. Macdonald. I. The Young Politician.* Toronto: Macmillan, 1952.

den Otter, A.A. *The Philosophy of Railways: The Transcontinental Idea in British North America.* Toronto: University of Toronto Press, 1997.

Dictionary of Canadian Biography, online at http//www.biographi.ca, is an excellent sources of in-depth biographical entries on all the key figures.

Forbes, E.R. and D. A. Muise. *The Atlantic Provinces in Confederation.* Toronto: University of Toronto Press, 1993.

Gwyn, Richard. *John A. The Man Who Made Us.* Toronto: Random House, 2007.

Hamilton, C.F. "The Canadian Militia: from the Crimean War to 1861." *Canadian Defence Quarterly* 6 (October 1928): 36–48.

Hamilton, C.F. "The Canadian Militia: from 1861 to Confederation." *Canadian Defence Quarterly* 6 (January 1929): 199–211.

Hiller, James. "Confederation Defeated: the Newfoundland Election of 1869." In James Hiller and Peter Neary, eds. *Newfoundland in the Nineteenth and Twentieth Centuries: Essays in Interpretation.* Toronto: University of Toronto Press, 1980, pp. 67–94.

Hitsman, J. Mackay. "Winter Troop Movement to Canada, 1862." *Canadian Historical Review* 43 (June 1962): 127–135.

Hodgins, Bruce W. *John Sandfield Macdonald.* Toronto: University of Toronto Press, 1971.

Keshen, Jeff. "Cloak and Dagger: Canada West's Secret Police, 1864–1867." *Ontario History* 79 (December 1987): 353–381.

MacKinnon, Frank. *The Government of Prince Edward Island.* Toronto: University of Toronto Press, 1951.

Martin, Ged, ed. *The Causes of Canadian Confederation.* Fredericton: Acadiensis Press, 1990.

Martin, Ged. *Fact and Faction in Canada's Great Coalition of 1864.* Sackville, New Brunswick: Centre for Canadian Studies, Mount Allison University, 1993.

Martin, Ged. *Britain and the Origins of Canadian Confederation, 1837–67.* London: Macmillan, 1995.

Martin, Ged. "John A. Macdonald and the Bottle." *Journal of Canadian Studies* 40 (Fall 2006): 162–185.

Moore, Christopher. *1867: How the Fathers Made a Deal.* Toronto: McClelland & Stewart, 1997.

Morton, W.L., ed. *The Shield of Achilles: Aspects of Canada in the Victorian Age.* Toronto: McClelland & Stewart, 1968.

Morton, W.L. *The Critical Years: The Union of British North America, 1857–1873.* Toronto: McClelland & Stewart, 1964.

Neidhardt, W.S. "The Fenian Trials in the Province of Canada, 1866–7: A Case Study of Law and Politics in Action." *Ontario History* 66 (1974): 23–36.

Robertson, Ian Ross. "Political Realignment in Pre-Confederation Prince Edward Island, 1863–1870." In P.A. Buckner and David Frank, eds. *Atlantic Canada Before Confederation.* Fredericton: Acadiensis, 1990.

Romney, Paul. *Getting It Wrong: How Canadians Forgot their Past and Imperilled Confederation.* Toronto: University of Toronto Press, 1999.

Rothney, G.O. *Newfoundland: A History.* Ottawa: Canadian Historical Association booklet no. 10, 1964.

Shanahan, David. "Young Ireland in a Young Canada: Thomas D'Arcy McGee and the New Nationality." *British Journal of Canadian Studies.* 12: 1 (1997): 1–8.

Silver, A.I. *The French Canadian Idea of Confederation.* Toronto: University of Toronto Press, 1997.

Smith, Andrew. "The Reaction of the City of London to the Quebec Resolutions, 1864–1866." *Journal of the Canadian Historical Association* 17 (2007): 1–24.

Smith, Andrew. "Toryism, Classical Liberalism, and Capitalism: The Politics of Taxation and the Struggle for Canadian Confederation." *Canadian Historical Review* 89 (March 2008): 1–25.

Smith, Andrew. *British Businessmen and Canadian Confederation: Constitution Making in an Era of Anglo-Globalization.* Montreal and Kingston: McGill-Queen's University Press, 2008.

Smith, Peter J. "The Ideological Origins of Canadian Confederation" *Canadian Journal of Political Science* 20 (March 1987): 3–29.

Stacey, C.P. *Canada and the British Army, 1846–1871: A Study in the Practice of Responsible Government.* Toronto: University of Toronto Press, 1963.

Stanley, G.F.G. "Act or Pact? Another Look at Confederation." In Ramsay Cook, Craig Brown, and Carl Berger, eds. *Confederation.* Toronto: University of Toronto Press, 1967, 94–118.

Sturgis, James L. "The Opposition to Confederation in Nova Scotia, 1864–1868." In Ged Martin, ed. *The Causes of Canadian Confederation.* Fredericton: Acadiensis Press, 1990, 114–129.

Waite, P.B. *The Life and Times of Confederation, 1864–1867: Politics, Newspapers, and the Union of British North America.* Toronto: University of Toronto Press, 1962.

Whitelaw, William Menzies. *The Maritimes and Canada Before Confederation.* Toronto: Oxford University Press, 1934.

Wilson, David A. *Thomas D'Arcy McGee, Vol. 1: Reason, Passion, Politics.* Montreal and Kingston: McGill-Queen's University Press, 2008.

Winks, Robin W. *Canada and the United States: The Civil War Years.* Baltimore: The Johns Hopkins Press, 1960.

Young, Brian. *George-Etienne Cartier: Montreal Bourgeois.* Montreal and Kingston: McGill-Queen's University Press, 1981.

Notes

[1] George Brown to Anne, 13 September 1864, "George Brown Describes the Charlottetown Conference, 1864" Library and Archives Canada, online at http://www.collectionscanada.ca/confederation/023001-271-e.html; part of the passage is quoted in Donald Creighton, *The Road to Confederation. The Emergence of Canada: 1863–1867* (Toronto: Macmillan, 1964), 116.

[2] James Young, *Public Men and Public Life in Canada* (Toronto: William Briggs, 1912), vol. 1, 201.

[3] NAC, Dufferin Papers, A 408, Kimberley to Dufferin, private, 20 November 1873.

[4] For an in-depth discussion of the alcohol issue, see Ged Martin, "John A. Macdonald and the Bottle," *Journal of Canadian Studies* 40 (Fall 2006): 162–185.

[5] Brian Young, *George-Etienne Cartier: Montreal Bourgeois* (Montreal and Kingston: McGill-Queen's University Press, 1981), xiii, xi, 80.

[6] As quoted by Ged Martin, "John A. Macdonald: Provincial Premier," *British Journal of Canadian Studies* 20: 1 (2007), 110–111.

[7] Head to E. Bulwer-Lytton, despatch. 102, 9 August 1858, Enclosure, Toronto *Daily Atlas*, 6 August 1858, Colonial Office Correspondence, CO 42/614, B 230, Library and Archives Canada.

8   Ged Martin, "John A. Macdonald: Provincial Premier," 113.

9   L.F.S. Upton, "The Idea of Confederation: 1754–1858," in Morton, W.L., ed. *The Shield of Achilles: Aspects of Canada in the Victorian Age* (Toronto: McClelland & Stewart, 1968), 186, 195, 198, 200, 202.

10 Lady Monck to Henry, 21 March 1863, *Monck Letters and Journals 1863–868: Canada from Government House at Confederation.* W.L. Morton, ed. (Toronto: McClelland & Stewart, 1970), 14.

11 Frances Monck, *My Canadian Leaves: An Account of a Visit to Canada in 1864–1865* (Toronto: Canadian Library Service facsimile edition, 1963), 4 January 1865, 109. Available through Early Canadiana Online at http://www.canadiana.org/ECO/mtq?doc=10127.

12 Rusty Bittermann and Margaret McCallum, "Upholding the Land Legislation of a 'Communistic and Socialist Assembly': The Benefits of Confederation for Prince Edward Island" *Canadian Historical Review* 87 (March 2006): 1–28

13 Donald Creighton, *The Road to Confederation,* 14.

14 Ged Martin, *Britain and the Origins of Canadian Confederation, 1837–67* (London: Macmillan, 1995), 5.

15 As quoted by Donald Creighton, *The Road to Confederation: The Emergence of Canada, 1863–1867* (Toronto: Macmillan, 1964), 65.

16 As quoted in Robin B. Burn, "Thomas D'Arcy McGee," *Dictionary of Canadian Biography,* http://www.biographi.ca.

17 David Shanahan, "Young Ireland in a Young Canada: Thomas D'Arcy McGee and the New Nationality," *British Journal of Canadian Studies* 12 (1) 1997, 4.

18 *Halifax Citizen,* 13 August 1864, "The Canadian Visit," 2, http://www.collectionscanada.ca/confederation/023001-507-e.html.

19 As quoted by W.L. Morton, *The Critical Years: The Union of British North America, 1857–1873* (Toronto: McClelland & Stewart, 1964), 143.

20 As quoted by Alfred G. Bailey, "The Basis and Persistence of Opposition to Confederation in New Brunswick," in Ramsay Cook, ed. *Confederation* (Toronto: University of Toronto Press, 1967), 75.

21 Charlottetown Vindicator, Wednesday 7 September 1864, as quoted in P.B. Waite, ed. *Confederation, 1854–1867* (Toronto: Holt, Rinehart, and Winston, 1972), 80.

22 Will Ferguson, *Bastards and Boneheads: Canada's Glorious Leaders Past and Present* (Vancouver: Douglas and McIntyre, 1999), 82.

23 J.K. Hiller, "Sir Ambrose Shea," *Dictionary of Canadian Biography,* http://www.biographi.ca.

24 Frances Monck, journal excerpt, 16 October 1864, *Monck Letters and Journals,* 155; 14 October 1864, 153; 20 October 1864, 158; 26 November 1864, 177. Some of Feo Monck's juicier gossip was omitted from the published version.

25 Peter Burroughs, "Sir Richard Graves Macdonnell" *Dictionary of Canadian Biography,* http://www.biographi.ca.

26 As quoted by P.B. Waite, *The Life and Times of Confederation, 1864–1867* (Toronto: University of Toronto Press, 1962), 31, 33.

27 As quoted by Ged Martin, "Introduction to the 2006 Edition," in P.B. Waite, ed., *The Confederation Debates in the Province of Canada, 1865,* 2nd ed. (Montreal and Kingston: McGill-Queen's University Press, 2006), xxv.

28 As quoted by W.L. Morton, *The Critical Years,* 165.

29 Paul Romney, *Getting It Wrong: How Canadians Forgot Their Past and Imperilled Confederation* (Toronto: University of Toronto Press, 1999), 101.

30 Alexander Anderson, "Prince Edward Island Legislative Council, 1 April 1865," in Janet Ajzenstat, Paul Romney, Ian Gentles, and William D. Gairdner, eds. *Canada's Founding Debates* (Toronto: University of Toronto Press, 1999), 62.

31 Andrew Smith, "Toryism, Classical Liberalism, and Capitalism: The Politics of Taxation and the Struggle for Canadian Confederation," *Canadian Historical Review* 89 (March 2008), 7, 7n.

32 Ibid., 10.

33 As quoted by David Shanahan, "Young Ireland in a Young Canada," 3–4.

[34] A.A. Dorion, in P.B. Waite, ed. *The Confederation Debates in the Province of Canada, 1865,* 2nd ed. (Montreal and Kingston: McGill-Queen's University Press, 2006), 62; as quoted in Ged Martin, "The Case against Canadian Confederation," in Ged Martin, ed., *The Causes of Canadian Confederation* (Fredericton: Acadiensis Press, 1990), 36.

[35] As quoted by Ged Martin, "The Case against Canadian Confederation," 38, 40.

[36] Ibid, 40.

[37] Stratford Beacon, 17 March 1865, as quoted in P.B. Waite, The Life and Times of Confederation, 156.

[38] "Botheration Scheme," *Morning Chronicle,* 11 January 1865, http://www.collectionscanada.gc.ca/confederation/023001-520-e.html.

[39] As quoted by Andrew Smith, "Toryism, Classical Liberalism, and Capitalism," 13.

[40] Phillip A. Buckner, "The Maritimes and Confederation: A Reassessment," in Ged Martin, ed., *The Causes of Canadian Confederation* (Fredericton: Acadiensis Press, 1990).

[41] E.R. Forbes and D. A. Muise. *The Atlantic Provinces in Confederation* (Toronto: University of Toronto Press, 1993).

[42] Andrew Smith, "Toryism, Classical Liberalism, and Capitalism," 15–16.

[43] Cardwell to Monck, private, 26 November 1864, Monck Papers, microfilm A 755, Library and Archives Canada.

[44] Andrew Smith, "The Reaction of the City of London to the Quebec Resolutions, 1864–1866," *Journal of the Canadian Historical Association* 17 (2007), 4.

[45] *The Times* [of London] 12 April 1865, as quoted in P.B. Waite, "Edward Cardwell and Confederation," in Ramsay Cook, Craig Brown, and Carl Berger, eds., *Confederation* (Toronto: University of Toronto Press, 1967), 37; The Times, 1 March 1867, as quoted in C.P. Stacey, "Britain's Withdrawal from North America, 1864–1871" in Ramsay Cook, Craig Brown and Carl Berger, eds., *Confederation* (Toronto: University of Toronto Press, 1967), 14.

[46] As quoted in P.B. Waite, *The Life and Times of Confederation,* 271.

[47] Janet Ajzenstat, Paul Romney, Ian Gentles, and William D. Gairdner, eds. *Canada's Founding Debates* (Toronto: University of Toronto Press, 2003), 1.

[48] Peter J. Smith, "The Ideological Origins of Canadian Confederation," *Canadian Journal of Political Science* 20 (March 1987): 3–29.

[49] The idea of the "Tory touch" is explained in G. Horowitz, "Conservatism, Liberalism, and Socialism in Canada: An Interpretation," *Canadian Journal of Economics and Political Science* 32 (May 1966): 143–171. Janet Ajzenstat, *The Canadian Founding: John Locke and Parliament* (Montreal and Kingston: McGill-Queen's University Press, 2007), xvi, xii, xv.

[50] Andrew Smith, "Toryism, Classical Liberalism, and Capitalism," 5, 25.

[51] Lord Stanley to Frederick Bruce, 23 March 1867, as quoted in C.P. Stacey, "Britain's Withdrawal from North America, 1864–1871," in Ramsay Cook, Craig Brown and Carl Berger, eds., *Confederation* (Toronto: University of Toronto Press, 1967), 15.

[52] See Ged Martin, "John A. Macdonald and the Bottle," 171.

[53] As quoted by Ged Martin, *Britain and the Origins of Canadian Confederation,* 288, 290.

Index

1745: Britain is preoccupied by the Jacobite threat.

1746: A French bid to retake Louisbourg and Acadia goes awry.

1747: Canadian militia defeat New England force at Grand Pré.

1748: The Treaty of Aix-la-Chapelle restores Louisbourg to the French.

1749: The British establish a fortress at Halifax.

1750–1751: The British establish Fort Lawrence and the French build Fort Beauséjour.

1749: The Ohio Company aims to expand English settlement west.

1750: French and British diplomats attempt to settle disputes.

1754: The French construct Fort Duquesne in disputed territory in the Ohio Valley.

1754: French forces triumph over George Washington's Virginia militia in the Ohio Valley.

1754: Albany Conference contemplates a union of the "American" colonies.

1755: British launch a four-pronged attack on French positions.

1755: Braddock's British forces are soundly defeated by a combined French and Native force at Fort Duquesne.

1755: Construction of the British Fort William Henry and French Fort Carillon marks conflicting claims in the area south of Lake Champlain.

1755: The British capture of Fort Beauséjour is a threat to continued Acadian neutrality.

1755–1758: Some 10 000 Acadians are banished from their homes.

May 1756: The British and French are now openly at war.

1756: Montcalm arrives in North America to command the French forces.

1756: The French win an important victory at Fort Oswego.

1756: The appointment of a ministry dominated by William Pitt marks a new British commitment to war in the empire.

1757: British plan for an attack on Louisbourg fails to come to fruition.

1757: The slaughter of the sick and wounded after the British defeat at Fort William Henry sparks outrage.

1757: Despite a string of French victories, the French commander Montcalm grows increasingly pessimistic.

1758: The British capture the strategically important fortress at Louisbourg.

1758: A British defeat at Fort Carillon (Ticonderoga) staves off an immediate assault on Quebec.

1758: The French surrender Fort Frontenac (Cataraqui).

1758: The French abandon Fort Duquesne.

As the 1759 season begins, France's commitment to North America's defence is minimal.

Spring 1759: Despite a budgetary crisis and fears of imminent invasion, Britain makes a strong commitment to the North American campaign.

Summer 1759: The French are forced to abandon both Fort Carillon and Fort Saint-Frédéric.

July 1759: The British and their Iroquois allies take Fort Niagara.

June 1759: British forces under Wolfe land within view of the fortified city of Quebec.

July 1759: The French repel an abortive British raid on Beauport.

Late summer 1759: British forces carry out a punitive campaign of destruction against Canadian farms and villages.

September 13, 1759: The famous Battle of the Plains of Abraham is fought for Quebec.

1759: The Battle of Quebec claims the lives of both Wolfe and Montcalm.

April 1760: The French win a victory in the Battle of Ste. Foy, but the cost in lives is high.

November 1759: A British naval victory at Quiberon Bay destroys any home of relief for the French in North America.

September 1760: The French surrender Montreal.

September 1762: In the Battle of Signal Hill, the British recapture St. John's from the French.

1763: Territories are traded in the Treaty of Paris ending the war.

1763: The end of the Seven Years War leaves the British treasury mired in debt.

1763: Throughout the summer, Native warriors seize British posts in the North American interior.

1763: British officials deliberately spread smallpox in a bid to break Aboriginal resistance.

1763: The Royal Proclamation sets out a pattern for treaty negotiation.

1763: The Royal Proclamation proposes to govern Quebec like Britain's other North American colonies.

1763: British Governor James Murray avoids implementing British-style political institutions in Quebec.

1766: James Murray is recalled and Sir Guy Carleton is appointed governor of Quebec.

1773: François Baby petitions the British government for the rights of Canadiens.

1774: With the Quebec Act, British authorities retreat from the original goal of assimilating French Canadians.

1764–1765: Britain's Parliament imposes new taxation measures on the American colonies.

1773: The Boston Tea Party was an open act of colonial defiance against British taxation.

1774: The "Intolerable Acts" spark a continental congress of American colonies.

April 19, 1775: American colonial minutemen clash when British soldiers at Lexington Green, Massachusetts.

November 3, 1775: The Congressionalist army takes Montreal.

1776: Benjamin Franklin comes to Montreal in April in a vain attempt to convince French Canadians to join the Patriot cause.

June 15, 1776: The Americans evacuate Montreal.

July 4, 1776: The 13 rebellious American colonies declare their independence.

November 2, 1776: Jonathan Eddy leads an attack on Fort Cumberland.

June 1777: John Allan organizes an abortive uprising at the mouth of the Saint John River.

1776: Henry Alline launches the "New Light" movement in Nova Scotia.

1776: Mohawk chief Joseph Brant makes a pledge of mutual support with the British.

October 1777: British forces suffer a defeat at Saratoga.

1781: The French aid the American cause at Chesapeake Bay and Yorktown.

September 3, 1783: Treaty of Paris recognizes American Independence.

June 18, 1784: Nova Scotia is divided and the Loyalist province of New Brunswick is created.

1784: Workers in Nova Scotia seek to drive out black competitors in a July 26 riot.

1792: Black Loyalists depart Nova Scotia for Sierra Leone.

1784: The Mississauga cede 1.2 million hectares of land to make way for Loyalist settlement.

1784: Joseph Brant and Six Nations Loyalists take up a land grant along the Grand River.

1791: Judicial reform in Newfoundland introduces civilian magistrates and a supreme court.

1792: The appointment of Sir John Wentworth as Nova Scotia's governor symbolizes Loyalist ascendancy.

1795–1799: New Brunswick's executive and legislature are frequently at odds.

1788: King's College established in Nova Scotia.

1783–1812: 17 000 Highland Scots immigrate to Cape Breton.

1791: The colony of Quebec is divided into Upper and Lower Canada.

1791: British parliamentarians fight a famous debate over the Constitutional Act.

1793: John Graves Simcoe selects York as the capital of Upper Canada.

1792: Governor Simcoe grants free land in Upper Canada to Americans willing to swear an oath of allegiance.

1793: An Act to Prevent the Further Introduction of Slaves is passed in Upper Canada.

1794: The Americans are victorious over Natives allied with the British at the Battle of Fallen Timbers.

1793: Britain and France are at war, and Simcoe organizes a militia for Upper Canada.

1794: Jay's Treaty seeks to resolve Anglo-American tensions in the interior.

1803: Thomas Talbot begins settlement schemes that will ultimately grow to encompass 200 000 hectares (500 000 acres) of land in Upper Canada.

1804: The Quebec Mercury is established as a voice for British Tories in Lower Canada.

1804: The reform-oriented Parti Canadien emerges in Lower Canada.

1806: The newspaper Le Canadien emerges as the voice of French-Canadian reform.

1809: Lower Canadian Governor Sir James Craig is thwarted in his attempt to secure a conservative-dominated assembly.

1811: The pragmatic and personable Sir George Prevost succeeds Craig as governor-in-chief.

1806: British North America's timber industry undergoes rapid development with the closing of the Baltic to British trade.

1770–1772: Samuel Hearne explores north and west to reach the Arctic Coast.

1774: The Hudson's Bay Company expands inland by establishing Cumberland House.

1779: Montreal traders join together to form the North West Company.

1789: Alexander Mackenzie is disappointed to learn that the Mackenzie River flows to the Arctic, and not the Pacific, Ocean.

1793: Alexander Mackenzie becomes the first European to reach the Pacific coast by land.

1790: The Nootka Convention averts war between Spain and Britain over the Pacific Northwest.

1792–1794: Captain George Vancouver maps North America's Pacific coast.

1805: American explorers Lewis and Clark reach the Pacific coast overland.

1808: Simon Fraser arrives at the mouth of the Fraser River.

1811: Nor'Wester David Thompson reaches the mouth of the Columbia River.

1812: Lord Selkirk launches a settlement at Red River.

1814: Red River Governor Miles Macdonell's "Pemmican Proclamation" threatens to disrupt Métis trade.

1807: The Chesapeake-Leopard affair heightens Anglo–American tensions.

1807: Commerce flourishes in the Maritime colonies following the passage of the American Embargo Act.

1808: British officials at Amherstburg encourage Aboriginal readiness for war against the Americans.

1811: American forces destroy Tecumseh's village of Tippecanoe.

1812: The United States declares war on Britain on June 18.

1812: The British win a surprise victory at Detroit on August 16, 1812.

October 13, 1812: The victorious Major General Isaac Brock is killed by an American sharpshooter at the Battle of Queenston Heights.

April 1813: American forces capture and loot York, the capital of Upper Canada.

May 27, 1813: The Americans capture Fort George.

June 5–6, 1813: The British win a victory at Stoney Creek.

June 24, 1813: Advance warnings foil an American offensive at Beaver Dams.

September 10, 1813: Americans win a naval victory in the Battle of Lake Erie (or "Put-in-Bay").

October 5, 1813: Tecumseh is killed at Moraviantown.

October 26, 1813: French-Canadian militia and Mohawk warriors repulse American invasion of Lower Canada at Châteauquay.

November 11, 1813: American invaders suffer defeat at John Crysler's farm in Upper Canada.

Spring 1914: Anglo–American peace negotiations break down.

July 25, 1814: The Americans are repelled in the bloodiest battle fought on Canadian soil at Lundy's Lane.

December 24, 1814: The Treaty of Ghent officially ends the War of 1812.

1818: An Anglo–American convention sets the border at the 49th parallel.

1816: Fur trade rivalry culminates in the Battle of Seven Oaks.

1821: The long-warring Hudson's Bay and North West Companies are merged.

1817: The newly arrived Scottish immigrant Robert Gourlay takes up the cause of land rights for Americans.

1819: Reform agitator Robert Gourlay exiled from Upper Canada.

1821: The election of Barnabas Bidwell sparked political conflict over the "alien question" in Upper Canada.

1824: Only a fraction of land grants in Upper Canada have been brought under cultivation.

1826: Free land grants in Upper Canada eliminated.

1817: Francis Pickmore appointed as Newfoundland's first year-round governor.

1817–1818: Newfoundland endures a difficult winter when fire destroys homes and supplies.

1820s: Freer trade policies open new opportunities for Nova Scotia mariners.

1817: The Bank of Montreal and later the Bank of Upper Canada (1821) serve the needs of Canadian merchants.

1825: The Miramichi Fire killed hundreds and destroyed thousands of square kilometres of New Brunswick timber.

1850: Logging employs 10 000 in the Ottawa Valley.

1815–1850: A million British immigrate to British North America.

1830: The Orange Order comes to Upper Canada.

1823–1825: Upper Canadian Peter Robinson organizes assisted emigration schemes in Ireland.

1834: The New Brunswick Company acquires 238 000 hectares (589 000 acres).

1836: Dozens of impoverished child immigrants are sent to New Brunswick.

1827: A typhus epidemic kills 800 in Halifax.

1832 and 1834: An estimated 20 000 died in cholera epidemics in the Canadas.

1825: Lachine Canal completed.

1832: Rideau Canal completed.

1829: The Welland Canal is constructed to meet the commercial challenge of the American Erie Canal.

1820s: The Parti Canadien use the assembly's control over financial legislation to attempt to force constitutional concessions.

1828: Lower Canadian reform petitioners appear before a British Commons committee.

1826: The Parti Canadien becomes more radical and is renamed the Parti Patriote.

1828: The Vindicator is founded as a voice for Irish radical reformers.

1828: William Lyon Mackenzie enters politics in Upper Canada.

1834: Lower Canada eliminates votes for women.

1830: France's "July Revolution" inspires radical reformers in Canada.

1832: Britain's Great Reform Act has a fundamentally conservative goal.

1831: William Lyon Mackenzie expelled from the legislative assembly.

1833: Inadequate harvests threaten hunger in many parishes of Lower Canada.

1832: Montreal's cholera epidemic serves to avert an immediate political crisis.

1834: The Saint Jean-Baptiste Society emerges as a symbol of French Canadian nationalism.

1834: Lower Canada's 92 Resolutions are sent to Britain's Parliament.

1834: Tories in Lower Canada form a "Constitutional Association" to oppose political radicals.

1835: Upper Canada produces the Seventh Report on Grievances.

1835: Aylmer is recalled as governor.

1836: Upper Canada's lieutenant governor, Sir John Colborne, is recalled.

1836: Sir Francis Bond Head manipulates a Tory victory in Upper Canada's election.

1836: Joseph Howe enters Nova Scotia politics.

1837: Nova Scotia produces the "Twelve Resolutions."

1837: Colonial Office makes modest concessions to reform in New Brunswick.

1837: Russell's Resolutions reject colonial demands for reform.

1837: Economic and social disturbances add to the political disquiet.

1837: Governor Gosford outlaws radical political demonstrations.

November 1837: Mackenzie calls for open revolt.

November 23, 1837: Rebel forces win a victory at the Battle of Saint-Denis.

November 25, 1837: The rebels suffer defeat at the Battle of Saint-Charles.

December 14, 1837: The Battle of Sainte-Eustache deals a definitive blow to the rebel cause.

December 7, 1837: Upper Canadian rebels are ill-prepared at the Battle of Montgomery's Tavern.

December 13, 1837: Dr. Charles Duncombe leads an uprising near Brantford.

December 29, 1837: The Caroline affair sparks intense reaction in the United States.

March 1, 1838: A cross-border raid on Lower Canada is thwarted.

1838: Black militia units help to defend the border against American-based rebels.

1838: The Hunters' Lodge and Frères Chasseurs emerge as new threats to security.

May 27, 1838: Durham arrives in Canada.

1838: Six Nations warriors capture rebel raiders in Upper Canada.

July 1838: Durham compromises by exiling captured rebels.

July 29, 1838: 15 rebel prisoners escape in Upper Canada.

1838: First police force is instituted in Lower Canada.

October 1838: Durham resigns and lashes out at his home government.

November 3, 1838: A fresh rebellion erupts at Napierville.

November 9, 1838: The rebel forces suffer a defeat at Odelltown.

November 17, 1838: Nils von Schoultz's rebel force is defeated at the Battle of the Windmill near Prescott, Upper Canada.

December 4, 1838: At Windsor, Upper Canada, five rebel invaders are executed without trial.

February 11, 1839: Durham's Report is laid before Britain's Parliament.

February 10, 1841: The Act of Union is proclaimed, uniting Upper and Lower Canada.

August 25, 1840: La Fontaine addresses the electors of Terrebonne, inaugurating a new spirit in Canadian politics.

September 23, 1841: La Fontaine is elected in a Toronto constituency.

1843: In the "Metcalfe Crisis" late that year, almost all of the governor's council resigns.

1846: Lord Cathcart is commissioned as governor.

1839: New Brunswick and Maine lumbermen confront one another in the "Aroostook War."

1842: Ashburton–Webster Treaty sets boundary between New Brunswick and Maine.

1827: Hudson's Bay Company establishes Fort Langley on the Fraser River.

1830s: HBC establishes more northerly west-coast trading posts.

1843: Hudson's Bay Company extends operations to Vancouver Island with the establishment of Fort Victoria.

1846: The Oregon Treaty sets the border at the 49th parallel in the Pacific Northwest.

1845: Sir John Franklin's Arctic expedition vanishes.

1833: Britain abolishes slavery.

1846: Repeal of the sugar duties damages Nova Scotia shipping interests.

1846: Britain's repeal of the Corn Laws ends protective tariffs for the colonies on wheat.

1845 and 1846: Failures in the Irish potato crop lead to widespread famine.

1847: 90 000 immigrants arrive in British North America.

1847: 1195 die at New Brunswick's Partridge Island.

1845 and 1846: Two American Drawback Acts challenge the St. Lawrence commercial trade route.

November 1846: Colonial Secretary Earl Grey issues instructions concerning responsible government.

1848: The first responsible cabinet in a British colony is sworn into office in Nova Scotia.

1847: Elgin arrives in Canada as governor.

1848: The formation of the "Great Ministry" of La Fontaine and Baldwin signals the advent of responsible government in Canada.

1848 is a year of revolutions throughout Europe.

1849: Parliament is officially bilingual.

1849: Amnesty is extended to exiled rebels of 1837–1838.

1849: La Fontaine introduces the controversial Rebellion Losses Bill.

1849: Elgin's assent to the Rebellion Losses Bill triggers the "Tory Rebellion of 1849."

1849: Economic grievances heighten violence among canal labourers.

1849: Orange and Green forces clash in riots in Saint John.

1849: Montreal Annexation Association publishes manifesto.

1841: Fugitive slave Josiah Henson establishes Dawn Settlement in Canada West.

1850: The Underground Railroad becomes especially important after the passage of the Fugitive Slave Act in the United States.

1851: St. Catharines in Canada West becomes an important base for Harriet Tubman, "conductor" on the Underground Railroad.

1844: Egerton Ryerson is appointed superintendent of schools in Canada West and begins ambitious reforms.

1853: New regulations are introduced for grammar schools (high schools).

1850: The University of Toronto becomes a non-denominational university.

1851: Canada West's population exceeds that of Canada East.

1851: Globe editor George Brown enters politics as a voice for Canada West's Clear Grit reformers.

1853: The Gavazzi riots were sparked by an ex-priest's anti-Catholic speaking tour.

1854: A new Liberal–Conservative coalition emerges after the collapse of the old Baldwin–La Fontaine reform alliance.

1854: Canada East's seigneurial system ends; in Canada West, the clergy reserves are secularized.

1856: Canada implements an elected upper house.

1857: The long-lived Macdonald–Cartier political partnership begins.

1854: Reciprocity Treaty establishes free trade in natural products between the United States and British North America.

1852: New Brunswick is the first of the British North American colonies to convert from pounds to dollars.

1840: Nova Scotian Samuel Cunard begins a transatlantic steamer service for the British Royal Mail.

Mid-1850s: The shift from wooden sailing ships to iron-hulled steamers signals the end of an era in the Maritimes.

1846: Canada enters the age of the telegraph.

1852: The world's first submerged telegraph cable is laid between New Brunswick and Prince Edward Island.

1836: Canada's first railway is built.

1860: Montreal's Victoria Bridge is heralded as the eighth wonder of the modern world.

September 1, 1860: The Prince of Wales lays the cornerstone of Ottawa's new Parliament buildings.

1844: Grey nuns arrive to join Roman Catholic missionaries already working in Red River.

1849: The Sayer trial marks the effective end to the HBC trade monopoly in Rupert's Land.

1851: A clash between the Métis and Saulteaux allies and the Sioux consolidates Métis dominance of the plains.

1857: Britain's House of Commons launches a committee to plan the future of Rupert's Land.

1857: Geological expeditions led by Palliser and Hind reveal the agricultural potential of the western interior.

1849: The HBC begins coal-mining operations on Vancouver Island.

1850: HBC Governor Richard Blanshard launches a retaliatory raid against the Newitty.

1852: The Hudson's Bay Company begins coal-mining operations at Nanaimo.

1855: Esquimalt is established as a Royal Navy base on Vancouver Island.

1830: Responsibility for Native affairs moves from military authorities to civilian ones.

1829: The Beothuk vanish.

1836: Governor Bond Head proposes to relocate all Upper Canadian Natives to Manitoulin.

1842: The Bagot Commission recommends systematic schooling of Natives.

1844: New Brunswick's Indian Act provides for sale of reserve land.

1846: Chief Shinguakouse confronts Great Lakes mining party.